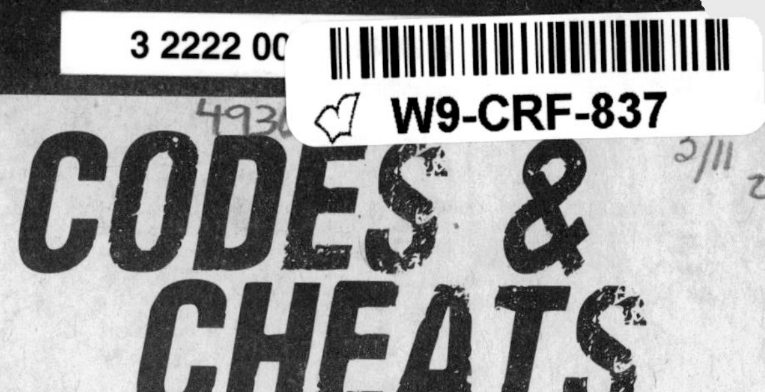

CODES & CHEATS

VOL. 2011

Prima Games
An Imprint of Random House, Inc.
3000 Lava Ridge Court, Suite 100
Roseville, CA 95661
www.primagames.com

Code Compiler: Nasson Boroumand
Product Manager: Todd Manning
Manufacturing: Suzanne Goodwin

Important:
Prima Games has made every effort to determine that the information contained in this book is accurate. However, the publisher makes no warranty, either expressed or implied, as to the accuracy, effectiveness, or completeness of the material in this book; nor does the publisher assume liability for damages, either incidental or consequential, that may result from using the information in this book. The publisher cannot provide any additional information or support regarding gameplay, hints and strategies, or problems with hardware or software. Such questions should be directed to the support numbers provided by the game and/or device manufacturers as set forth in their documentation. Some game tricks require precise timing and may require repeated attempts before the desired result is achieved.

ISBN: 978-0-3078-8998-0
Printed in the United States of America

11 12 13 14 HH 10 9 8 7 6 5 4 3 2 1

NEW CODES!...

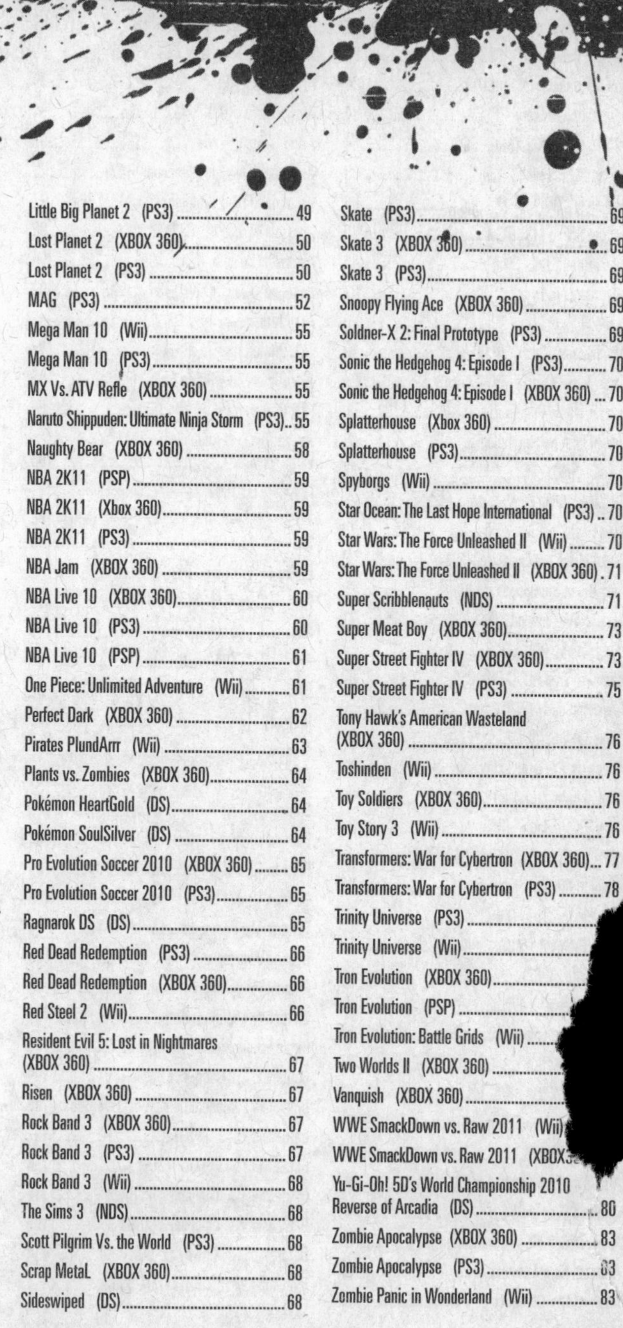

ALL CODES...

CONTENTS

CONTENTS

NEW!

NEW! A B C D E F G H I J K L M N O P Q R S T U V W X Y Z

AFTER BURNER CLIMAX (PS3)

UNLOCKABLE

UNLOCKABLE	HOW TO UNLOCK
Clouds of Twilight	Finish stage 9A or 9B with at least 4 stars.
Golden Valley	Finish stage 5 with at least 4 stars.
After Burner Helmet	Complete your Medal Collection.
After Burner Logo T-Shirt (females)	Unlock all Ex Options.
After Burner Logo T-Shirt (males)	Unlock all Ex Options.

EX OPTIONS

Meet the following conditions during Arcade Mode to unlock these special settings in EX Options. They can only be used in Arcade Mode.

UNLOCKABLE	HOW TO UNLOCK
Aircraft Count: 1	Play a Secret Stage five times.
Aircraft Count: 5	Play a Secret Stage one time.
Aircraft Count: 9	Play a Secret Stage three times.
Aircraft Speed: Fast	Play three different branched stages (A/B).
Aircraft Speed: Slow	Play all eight branched stages (A/B).
Armor: 1%	Get a down rate of over 70% 20 times.
Armor: Half Damage	Get a down rate of over 70% 10 times.
Armor: No Damage	Get a down rate of over 70% 50 times.
Auto-Missiles: On	Reach ending A.
Climax Gauge Recovery: Fast	Activate Climax Mode 50 times.
Climax Gauge Recovery: Free	Activate Climax Mode 200 times.
Climax Gauge Recovery: Slow	Activate Climax Mode 100 times.
Combo Window: Free	Get a combo totaling 3,000.
Combo Window: Long	Get a combo totaling 1,000.
Credits: 5	Get a Game Over one time.
Credits: 7	Get a Game Over three times.
Credits: 9	Get a Game Over five times.
Credits: Free	Get a Game Over 10 times.
Display: No Info	Get a score of over 2,000,000 points in one game.
Display: No Smoke (All)	Get a score of over 1,000,000 points in one game.
Display: No Smoke (Explosions)	Get a score of over 800,000 points in one game.
Display: No Smoke (Missiles)	Get a score of over 600,000 points in one game.
Enemy Attack: 1 Level Down	Shoot down 1,000 enemies.
Enemy Attack: 2 Levels Down	Shoot down 3,000 enemies.
Enemy Attack: 3 Levels Down	Shoot down 5,000 enemies.
Enemy Attack: No Attack	Shoot down 10,000 enemies.
Gun Power: Down	Shoot down 200 enemies with the gun.
Gun Power: Up	Shoot down 50 enemies with the gun.
Lock-On: Auto	Reaching the ending 10 times.
Lock-On: Large Cursor	Reaching the ending one time.
Lock-On: No Cursor	Reaching the ending five times.

UNLOCKABLE	HOW TO UNLOCK
Missile Recovery: Free	Fire 5,000 missiles.
Missile Recovery: Off	Fire 2,000 missiles.
Secret Mission: Always	Play Emergency Orders 20 times.

AFTER BURNER CLIMAX (XBOX 360)

EX OPTIONS

Meet the following conditions during Arcade Mode to unlock these special settings in EX Options. They can only be used in Arcade Mode.

UNLOCKABLE	HOW TO UNLOCK
Aircraft Count: 1	Play a Secret Stage five times.
Aircraft Count: 5	Play a Secret Stage one time.
Aircraft Count: 9	Play a Secret Stage three times.
Aircraft Speed: Fast	Play four different branched stages (A/B).
Aircraft Speed: Slow	Play all eight branched stages (A/B).
Armor: 1%	Get a down rate of over 70% 20 times.
Armor: Half Damage	Get a down rate of over 70% 10 times.
Armor: No Damage	Get a down rate of over 70% 50 times.
Auto-Missiles: On	Reach ending A.
Climax Gauge Recovery: Fast	Activate Climax Mode 50 times.
Climax Gauge Recovery: Free	Activate Climax Mode 200 times.
Climax Gauge Recovery: Slow	Activate Climax Mode 100 times.
Combo Window: Free	Get a combo totaling 3,000.
Combo Window: Long	Get a combo totaling 1,000.
Credits: 5	Get a Game Over one time.
Credits: 7	Get a Game Over three times.
Credits: 9	Get a Game Over five times.
Credits: Free	Get a Game Over 10 times.
Display: No Info	Get a score of over 2,000,000 points in one game.
Display: No Smoke (All)	Get a score of over 1,000,000 points in one game.
Display: No Smoke (Explosions)	Get a score of over 800,000 points in one game.
Display: No Smoke (Missiles)	Get a score of over 600,000 points in one game.
Enemy Attack: 1 Level Down	Shoot down 1,000 enemies.
Enemy Attack: 2 Levels Down	Shoot down 3,000 enemies.
Enemy Attack: 3 Levels Down	Shoot down 5,000 enemies.
Enemy Attack: No Attack	Shoot down 10,000 enemies.
Gun Power: Down	Shoot down 200 enemies with the gun.
Gun Power: Up	Shoot down 50 enemies with the gun.
Lock-On: Auto	Reaching the ending 10 time.
Lock-On: Large Cursor	Reaching the ending one time.
Lock-On: No Cursor	Reaching the ending five times.
Missile Recovery: Free	Fire 5,000 missiles.
Missile Recovery: Off	Fire 2,000 missiles.
Secret Mission: Always	Play Emergency Orders 20 times.

ALAN WAKE (XBOX 360)

UNLOCKABLES

UNLOCKABLE	HOW TO UNLOCK
Jacket and Scarf (female)	Play the Limited Collector's Edition Bonus Disc.
Jacket and Scarf (male)	Play the Limited Collector's Edition Bonus Disc.

Nightmare Mode	Successfully complete the game.

ALICE IN WONDERLAND (DS)

DGAMER HONORS + DGAMER AVATAR UNLOCKABLES

Before you begin the game, set up a DGamer profile and create an avatar in off-line mode. Go back to the game once you're done creating your avatar. As you play through the game, you'll unlock "Honors" and gain Alice-themed costumes and gear for your DGamer avatar by completing certain tasks during the game.

UNLOCKABLE	HOW TO UNLOCK
Alice Dress/Alice Armor	Gain all pieces of the Magic Armor.
Caterpillar Outfit	Have Absolem join your team.
Cheshire Outfit	Have the Cheshire Cat join your team.
Dormouse Coat	Enter "3676" at Password screen.
Hatter Outfit	Have the Hatter Join your team.
Living Oraculum	Unlock every chapter.
Puzzle Master	Find every map piece/explore all map locations.
Red Guard Outfit	Defeat one of the tougher, armed Red Guards for the first time.
Rushed Rabbit	Defeat 50 enemies using McTwisp's Slow Down Ability.
Savior of Underland	Beat the Jabberwocky!
Stayne Eyepatch	Defeat Stayne Twice.
Stayne Mantle	Defeat Stayne Once.
Vorpal Sword	Find the Vorpal Sword.
Weird, Wise, Malicious	Gain the remaining three characters in your party.
White Rabbit Jacket	Complete Chapter One.

ALIEN VS. PREDATOR (XBOX 360)

SKINS

Reach the indicated rank to unlock each skin.

UNLOCKABLE	HOW TO UNLOCK
Claw (Predator)	Obtain Rank 03.
Connor (Marine)	Obtain Rank 05.
Gibson (Marine)	Obtain Rank 02.
Hunter (Predator)	Obtain Rank 16.
Johnson (Marine)	Obtain Rank 22.
Moss (Marine)	Obtain Rank 13.
Nethead (Alien)	Obtain Rank 34.
Praetorian (Alien)	Obtain Rank 19.
Ridged (Alien)	Obtain Rank 10.
Rookie (Marine)	Obtain Rank 28.
Spartan (Predator)	Obtain Rank 31.
Stalker (Predator)	Obtain Rank 07.
Warrior Dome (Alien)	Obtain Rank 04.
Wolf (Predator)	Obtain Rank 25.

ALIEN VS. PREDATOR (PS3)

SKINS

Reach the indicated rank to unlock each skin.

UNLOCKABLE	HOW TO UNLOCK
Claw (Predator)	Obtain Rank 03.
Connor (Marine)	Obtain Rank 05.
Gibson (Marine)	Obtain Rank 02.

UNLOCKABLE	HOW TO UNLOCK
Hunter (Predator)	Obtain Rank 16.
Johnson (Marine)	Obtain Rank 22.
Moss (Marine)	Obtain Rank 13.
Nethead (Alien)	Obtain Rank 34.
Praetorian (Alien)	Obtain Rank 19.
Ridged (Alien)	Obtain Rank 10.
Rookie (Marine)	Obtain Rank 28.
Spartan (Predator)	Obtain Rank 31.
Stalker (Predator)	Obtain Rank 07.
Warrior Dome (Alien)	Obtain Rank 04.
Wolf (Predator)	Obtain Rank 25.

AIRACE (NDS)

CLASS AND AIRCRAFT UNLOCKABLES

Compete in the Championship mode of the game to unlock the following classes and aircraft.

UNLOCKABLE	HOW TO UNLOCK
Class II—Delta 21 (Vought F4U Corsair)	Complete Class I, Race V
Class II—Fatboy (Brewster F2A Buffalo)	Complete Class I, Race V
Class II—Sky Warrior (Supermarine Spitfire)	Complete Class I, Race V
Class III—Guardian (Mikoyan-Gurevich MiG-17 Fresco)	Complete Class II, Race VI
Class III—Interceptor (Messerschmitt Me-262)	Complete Class II, Race VI
Class III—Razor (Yakovlev Yak-17 Feather)	Complete Class II, Race VI

COURSES

UNLOCKABLE	HOW TO UNLOCK
Amazon River (Backward)	Complete Class I, Race III
City Streets	Complete Class I, Race I
City Streets (Backward)	Complete Class III, Race I
Great Canyon	Complete Class II, Race I
Great Canyon (Backward)	Complete Class II, Race VI
Hangars	Complete Class I, Race V
Hangars (Backward)	Complete Class III, Race II
Land of the Ice	Complete Class I, Race II
Land of the Ice (Backward)	Complete Class II, Race II
Storm Drains (Backward)	Complete Class I, Race IV

ALPHA PROTOCOL (XBOX 360)

UNLOCKABLES

UNLOCKABLE	HOW TO UNLOCK
Veteran Class	Complete the game on Recruit.

ALVIN AND THE CHIPMUNKS: THE SQUEAKQUEL (DS)

UNLOCKABLES

UNLOCKABLE	HOW TO UNLOCK
Expert Mode	Complete Normal Mode.

ASSASSIN'S CREED: BROTHERHOOD (XBOX 360)

CAPES

UNLOCKABLE	HOW TO UNLOCK
Auditore Cape	Rebuild Rome
Borgia Cape	Collect all Borgia Flags

Medici Cape	You need to get to Level 30 on the "Assassin's Creed: Project Legacy" Facebook game
Venetian Cape	You need to get to Level 30 on the "Assassin's Creed: Project Legacy" Facebook game

COSTUMES

UNLOCKABLE	HOW TO UNLOCK
Raiden's Costume	Complete all of the tasks in the Animus 2.0 training mode

MEMORY EXTRAS

When you complete a memory sequence, you will be awarded with a cheat that you can activate when you are replaying a completed memory.

UNLOCKABLE	HOW TO UNLOCK
Buns of Steel	100% sync on Sequence 2
Desmond Everywhere	100% sync on Sequence 8
Killing Spree	100% sync on Sequence 3
Ride the Unicorn	100% sync on Sequence 1
Sisterhood	100% sync on Sequence 4
Ultimate Guild	100% sync on Sequence 5
Unlimited Assassin Signals	100% sync on Sequence 6

GUILD REWARDS

By leveling up with the guilds, you can obtain certain items for Ezio to use. They will appear in Ezio's hideout.

UNLOCKABLE	HOW TO UNLOCK
Assassin's Guild Crest	Complete all Assassins Guild challenges.
Bartolomeo's Axe	Get each guild to Level 3
Courtesans Guild Crest	Get each guild to Level 2
La Volpe's Bite	Get each guild to Level 3
Maria's Dagger	Get each guild to Level 3
Mercenaries Guild Crest	Get each guild to Level 2
Sword of Altair	Complete all Assassins Guild challenges
Thieves Guild Crest	Get each guild to Level 2

UPLAY UNLOCKABLES

UNLOCKABLE	HOW TO UNLOCK
Altair armor skin for Ezio	Obtain 20 Uplay points and use them via Uplay account
Altair skin	Obtain 20 Uplay points and use them via Uplay account
Assassin's Creed Brotherhood Theme	Gain 10 Uplay points and spend them
Florentine Noble in-game skin	Gain 20 Uplay points and spend them
Hellequin (multiplayer character)	Obtain 40 Uplay points
Upgrade hidden pistol ammo capacity	Gain 30 Uplay points and spend them

ASSASSIN'S CREED: BROTHERHOOD (PS3)

CAPES

UNLOCKABLE	HOW TO UNLOCK
Auditore Cape	Rebuild Rome
Borgia Cape	Collect all Borgia Flags
Medici Cape	You need to get to level 30 on the "Assassin's Creed: Project Legacy" Facebook game
Venetian Cape	You need to get to level 30 on the "Assassin's Creed: Project Legacy" Facebook game

COSTUMES

UNLOCKABLE	HOW TO UNLOCK
Raiden's Costume	Complete all of the tasks in the Animus 2.0 training mode

MEMORY EXTRAS

When you complete a memory sequence, you will be awarded with a cheat that you can activate when you are replaying a completed memory.

UNLOCKABLE	HOW TO UNLOCK
Buns of Steel	100% sync on Sequence 2
Desmond Everywhere	100% sync on Sequence 8
Killing Spree	100% sync on Sequence 3
Ride the Unicorn	100% sync on Sequence 1
Sisterhood	100% sync on Sequence 4
Ultimate Guild	100% sync on Sequence 5
Unlimited Assassin Signals	100% sync on Sequence 6

REWARDS

When you complete a memory sequence, you will be awarded with a cheat that you can activate when you are replaying a completed memory.

UNLOCKABLE	HOW TO UNLOCK
Courtesans poison guards	Attain Rank 5 in Courtesans guild challenges
Faction discount	Attain Rank 10 in the corresponding guild challenges
Parachute	Destroy all of Leonardo da Vinci's War Machines
Sword of Altair and assassins crest	Complete all assassins guild challenges
Thieves pickpocket guards	Attain Rank 5 in Thieves guild challenges
War horse spawned at stables	Renovate all stables in Rome

BATMAN: THE BRAVE AND THE BOLD (Wii)

CODES

Enter the following code(s) at the Batcomputer to unlock in-game content.

EFFECT	CODE
Batman Costume: Medieval Batsuit	5644863

BIOSHOCK 2 (XBOX 360)

MULTIPLAYER UNLOCKABLES

Unlock by reaching the corresponding level.

UNLOCKABLE	HOW TO UNLOCK
Mask: Eagle/Tragic Comedy	Rank 10
Mask: Moon/Indigo Feather	Rank 20
Mask: Octopus/Demon	Rank 40
Mask: Peacock Feather/Sun God	Rank 30
Mask: Rabbit/Goat/Pink Feather	Rank 01
Melee: Crowbar/Flashlight	Rank 30
Melee: Hatchet	Rank 40
Melee: Machete/Rolling Pin	Rank 10
Melee: Mallet/Barbed Wire	Rank 20
Melee: Wrench/Candle Stick/Pipe	Rank 01
Plasmid: Air Dash	Rank 04
Plasmid: Electro Bol/Winter Blast/Incinerate	Rank 01

UNLOCKABLE	HOW TO UNLOCK
Plasmid: Geyser Trap	Rank 08
Plasmid: Houdini	Rank 16
Plasmid: Insect Swarm	Rank 20
Plasmid: Telekinesis	Rank 12
Tonic: Back Stabber	Rank 11
Tonic: Big Game Hunter	Rank 36
Tonic: Deadly Machine	Rank 32
Tonic: Death Trap	Rank 38
Tonic: Expert Researcher/Security Evasion	Rank 03
Tonic: Fast Feet	Rank 30
Tonic: Headhunter	Rank 34
Tonic: Leg Up	Rank 28
Tonic: Metabolic Eve	Rank 15
Tonic: Repairman	Rank 22
Tonic: Resurrection	Rank 40
Tonic: Sabotage	Rank 19
Tonic: Slugger	Rank 26
Tonic: Speedy Recovery/Eve Saver	Rank 07
Upgrade: Crossbow Damage Increase	Rank 21
Upgrade: Crossbow Rate of Fire	Rank 35
Upgrade: Elephant Gun Damage Increase	Rank 39
Upgrade: Elephant Gun Sniper Scope	Rank 25
Upgrade: Grenade Launcher Homing Grenades	Rank 17
Upgrade: Grenade Launcher Velocity Boost	Rank 33
Upgrade: Machine Gun Kickback Reduction	Rank 31
Upgrade: Machine Gun Magazine Size	Rank 13
Upgrade: Nail Gun Damage Increase	Rank 37
Upgrade: Nail Gun Magazine Size	Rank 23
Upgrade: Pistol Automatic Firing	Rank 05
Upgrade: Pistol Damage Upgrade	Rank 27
Upgrade: Shotgun Automatic Reload	Rank 29
Upgrade: Shotgun Rate of Fire	Rank 09
Upgrade: Speedy Hacker	Rank 24
Weapon: Crossbow	Rank 10
Weapon: Elephant Gun	Rank 18
Weapon: Grenade Launcher	Rank 06
Weapon: Machine Gun	Rank 02
Weapon: Nail Gun	Rank 14
Weapon: Pistol/Shotgun	Rank 01

BLAZBLUE: CONTINUUM SHIFT (XBOX 360)

UNLOCKABLES

UNLOCKABLE	HOW TO UNLOCK
Mu-12	Achieve every character's Clear ending in Story Mode and complete the True Ending. This also unlocks her stage and theme song for use in various game modes.
True Ending	Beat Ragna's Story, Jin's Story, Noel's Story, Rachel's Story, Tsubaki's Story, Hakumen's Story, and Hazama's story to unlock the True Ending.

UNLOCKABLE	HOW TO UNLOCK
Unlimited Characters	To unlock the Unlimited version of a character you must clear Score Attack Mode with that character.

BLAZBLUE: CONTINUUM SHIFT (PS3)

UNLOCKABLES

UNLOCKABLE	HOW TO UNLOCK
Mu-12	Achieve every character's Clear ending in Story Mode, and complete the True Ending. This also unlocks her stage and theme song for use in various game modes.
True Ending	Beat Ragna's Story, Jin's Story, Noel's Story, Rachel's Story, Tsubaki's Story, Hakumen's Story, and Hazama's story to unlock the True Ending.
Unlimited Characters	To unlock the Unlimited version of a character you must clear Score Attack Mode with that character.

CALL OF DUTY: BLACK OPS (Wii)

CODES

You have to use the classic controller for this to work. At the Main menu, look down at your hands and press "ZL" and "ZR" a couple of times to break free from the chair. Walk around behind the chair you were in, and you will see a computer. Press and hold the button it says to access the computer. Now you can use the computer like the other systems, but the codes don't work the same way.

EFFECT	CODE
A text-based game that you can plug a USB keyboard into your Wii to play	ZORK
Get a list of commands; it works like an old UNIX or DOS system	HELP
Unlock all the missions in the Mission Select screen in Campaign mode (no Zombie maps)	3ARC UNLOCK
Unlocks all the intel in the game	3ARC INTEL

TERMINAL CODES

Access the Central Intelligence Agency Data System and type the case-sensitive command "login." When you are prompted to log in with an account, enter the following usernames and passwords. Access their documents with the "dir" command or e-mail with the "mail" command.

EFFECT	CODE
Adrienne Smith	Username: asmith; password: roxy
Bruce Harris	Username: bharris; password: goskins
D. King	Username: dking; password: mfk
Frank Woods	Username: fwoods; password: philly
Grigori "Greg" Weaver	Username: gweaver; password: gedeon
J. Turner	Username: Jturner; password: condor75
Jason Hudson	Username: jhudson; password: bryant1950
John F. Kennedy	Username: jfkennedy; password: lancer
John McCone	Username: jmccone; password: berkley22
Vannevar Bush	Username: vbush; password: manhattan

CALL OF DUTY: BLACK OPS (PS3)

CIA DATA SYSTEM ACCOUNTS

When using the computer to access the CIA Data system, you can use the following login IDs and passwords. After logging into an account, you may then browse each user's unique files using the DIR command or read messages with the MAIL command.

EFFECT	CODE
The user account of Alex Mason, already logged in when you first use the terminal	Username: amason; password: PASSWORD
The user account of Bruce Harris	Username: bharris; password: GOSKINS
The user account of D. King	Username: dking; password: MFK
The user account of Dr. Adrienne Smith	Username: asmith; password: ROXY
The user account of Dr. Vannevar Bush	Username: vbush; password: MANHATTAN
The user account of Frank Woods	Username: fwoods; password: PHILLY
The user account of Grigori "Greg" Weaver	Username: gweaver; password: GEDEON
The user account of J. Turner	Username: jturner; password: CONDOR75
The user account of Jason Hudson	Username: jhudson; password: BRYANT1950
The user account of John McCone, director of Central Intelligence, 1961–1965	Username: jmccone; password: BERKLEY22
The user account of Joseph Bowman	Username: jbowman; password: UWD
The user account of President John Fitzgerald Kennedy	Username: jfkennedy; password: LANCER
The user account of President Lyndon Baines Johnson	Username: lbjohnson; password: LADYBIRD
The user account of President Richard Nixon	Username: rnixon; password CHECKERS
The user account of Richard Helms, director of the CIA from 1966 to 1973	Username: rhelms; password: LEROSEY
The user account of Richard Kain	Username: rkain; password: SUNWU
The user account of Ryan Jackson	Username: rjackson; password: SAINTBRIDGET
The user account of T. Walker	Username: twalker; password: RADI0 (zero, not "O")
The user account of Terrance Brooks	Username: tbrooks; password: LAUREN
The user account of William Raborn, director of Central Intelligence from 1965–1966	Username: wraborn; password: BROMLOW

TERMINAL CODES

On the Main menu, and press the L2 and R2 buttons repeatedly. After about five times for each button, you'll break free of your interrogation chair. When you get up, walk around behind you to a computer. When you access it, enter the following using the onscreen keyboard.

EFFECT	CODE
Activates Dead Ops Arcade	DOA
Displays a list of system commands in the terminal and Pentagon user e-mail access	HELP
FI FIE FOE	FOOBAR
Get to root of directory and see all codes	cd .. [Enter] cd .. [Enter] cd bin [Enter] ls [Enter]
Gives a list of audio files and pictures that you can open with the CAT command (e.g., CAT NoteX.txt)	DIR
Gives a list of login names for use with the RLOGIN function (but they require a password)	WHO
It will list all of your audio files and pictures	CAT
To List a directory (same as DIR but for LINUX)	LS
To view a file in a directory using the TYPE command "NAMEOFFILE.EXTENSION"	TYPE

EFFECT	CODE
Unlocks all Intel in the game for viewing	3ARC INTEL
Unlocks Dead Ops Arcade and Presidential Zombie Mode	3ARC UNLOCK
Unlocks Zork I: The Great Underground Adventure (a text adventure game from 1980) for play in Black Ops	ZORK
Virtual Therapist Software	ALICIA

EASTER EGGS

Nuketown Mannequin Secret

On the multiplayer map Nuketown, if you blow the heads off of all the mannequins in a short amount of time, the song "Sympathy for the Devil" by the Rolling Stones will play in the background.

Play the song "Don't Back Down" by Eminem in Five zombie maps

There are three red phones throughout the pentagon that ring and flash. The first is located where you first start after opening a set of doors in the corner. The second is on the catwalk circling the room after leaving the first elevator. The third is in one of the rooms after leaving the second elevator on the floor the power is on. Just listen for a cell phone ring and follow it to the red rotary phone. Look at them and hold X till the ringing stops and you hear a busy signal. Once you get the third phone, the music starts.

CALL OF DUTY: BLACK OPS (XBOX 360)

CIA DATA SYSTEM ACCOUNTS

When using the computer to access the CIA Data system, you can use the following login IDs and passwords. After logging into an account, you may then browse each user's unique files using the DIR command or read messages with the MAIL command.

EFFECT	CODE
The user account of Alex Mason, already logged in when you first use the terminal	Username: amason; password: PASSWORD
The user account of Bruce Harris	Username: bharris; password: GOSKINS
The user account of D. King	Username: dking; password: MFK
The user account of Dr. Adrienne Smith	Username: asmith; password: ROXY
The user account of Dr. Vannevar Bush	Username: vbush; password: MANHATTAN
The user account of Frank Woods	Username: fwoods; password: PHILLY
The user account of Grigori "Greg" Weaver	Username: gweaver; password: GEDEON
The user account of J. Turner	Username: jturner; password: CONDOR75
The user account of Jason Hudson	Username: jhudson; password: BRYANT1950
The user account of John McCone, director of Central Intelligence, 1961–1965	Username: jmccone; password: BERKLEY22
The user account of Joseph Bowman	Username: jbowman; password: UWD
The user account of President John Fitzgerald Kennedy	Username: jfkennedy; password: LANCER
The user account of President Lyndon Baines Johnson	Username: lbjohnson; password: LADYBIRD
The user account of President Richard Nixon	Username: rnixon; password: CHECKERS
The user account of Richard Helms, director of the CIA from 1966 to 1973	Username: rhelms; password: LEROSEY
The user account of Richard Kain	Username: rkain; password: SUNWU
The user account of Ryan Jackson	Username: rjackson; password: SAINTBRIDGET
The user account of T. Walker	Username: twalker; password: RADI0 (zero, not "O")

The user account of Terrance Brooks	Username: tbrooks; password: LAUREN
The user account of William Raborn, director of Central Intelligence from 1965–1966	Username: wraborn; password: BROMLOW

TERMINAL CODES

On the Main menu, and press the L2 and R2 buttons repeatedly. After about five times for each button, you'll break free of your interrogation chair. When you get up, walk around behind you to a computer. When you access it, enter the following using the onscreen keyboard.

EFFECT	CODE
Activates Dead Ops Arcade	DOA
Displays a list of system commands in the terminal and Pentagon user e-mail access	HELP
FI FIE FOE	FOOBAR
Get to root of directory and see all codes	cd .. [Enter] cd .. [Enter] cd bin [Enter] ls [Enter]
Gives a list of audio files and pictures that you can open with the CAT command (e.g., CAT NoteX.txt)	DIR
Gives a list of login names for use with the RLOGIN function (but they require a password)	WHO
It will list all of your audio files and pictures	CAT
To List a directory (same as DIR but for LINUX)	LS
To view a file in a directory using the TYPE command	Type "NAMEOFFILE. EXTENSION"
Unlocks all Intel in the game for viewing	3ARC INTEL
Unlocks Dead Ops Arcade and Presidential Zombie mode	3ARC UNLOCK
Unlocks Zork I: The Great Underground Adventure (a text adventure game from 1980) for play in Black Ops	ZORK
Virtual Therapist Software	ALICIA

EASTER EGGS

Nuketown Mannequin Secret

On the multiplayer map Nuketown, if you blow the heads off of all the mannequins in a short amount of time, the song "Sympathy for the Devil" by the Rolling Stones will play in the background.

Play the song "Don't Back Down" by Eminem in Five zombie maps

There are three red phones throughout the pentagon that ring and flash. The first is located where you first start after opening a set of doors in the corner. The second is on the catwalk circling the room after leaving the first elevator. The third is in one of the rooms after leaving the second elevator on the floor the power is on. Just listen for a cell phone ring and follow it to the red rotary phone. Look at it and hold X till the ringing stops and you hear a busy signal. Once you get the third phone, the music starts.

Activate Secret Song in Kino Der Toten

There is always a secret song in every Zombies map. For Kino Der Toten, you have to find the three meteor rocks. The first is on a pedestal in the main lobby, in a corner behind the soda. The second one is in the dressing room near some dummies; this one is also on a pedestal. The final one is the room upstairs near the alley. The rock is on a dresser sharing some space with black marquee letters. These rocks are easily distinguishable, as they have red veins. Hold the USE button on your controller on these rocks until your character says something or the veins glow red. The song is called "115" by Elena Siegman.

CASTLEVANIA: LORDS OF SHADOW (XBOX 360)

UNLOCKABLES

UNLOCKABLE	HOW TO UNLOCK
Solid Eye & Bandanna	Beat the game once
Vampire Wargame	Accept Laura's challenge and beat her at the Vampire Wargame during Chapter 6-3: Castle Hall. Check the "Extras" in the game menus for the unlocked game.

CASTLEVANIA: LORDS OF SHADOW (PS3)

UNLOCKABLES

UNLOCKABLE	HOW TO UNLOCK
Solid Eye & Bandanna	Beat the game once
Vampire Wargame	Accept Laura's challenge and beat her at the Vampire Wargame during Chapter 6-3: Castle Hall. Check the "Extras" in the game menus for the unlocked game.

COLOR CROSS (DS)

UNLOCKABLE THEMES

UNLOCKABLE	HOW TO UNLOCK
Baby	Finish any three puzzles.
Decoration	Finish any nine puzzles.
Fashion	Finish any 15 puzzles.
Horror	Finish any 12 puzzles.
Love	Finish any 21 puzzles.
Medieval	Finish any six puzzles.
Pirate	Finish any 24 puzzles.
Science-fiction	Finish any 18 puzzles.

UNLOCKABLE ICONS

UNLOCKABLE	HOW TO UNLOCK
Baby Icon	Complete all 15 "Baby"-themed puzzles.
Decorative Icon	Complete all 15 "Decoration"-themed puzzles.
Female Icon	Complete all 15 "Fashion"-themed puzzles.
Horror Icon	Complete all 15 "Horror"-themed puzzles.
Love-struck Icon	Complete all 15 "Love"-themed puzzles.
Medieval Icon	Complete all 15 "Medieval"-themed puzzles.
Pirate Icon	Complete all 15 "Pirate"-themed puzzles.
Science-fiction Icon	Complete all 15 "Science-fiction"-themed puzzles.

COMIC JUMPER: THE ADVENTURES OF CAPTAIN SMILEY (XBOX 360)

AVATAR AWARDS

UNLOCKABLE	HOW TO UNLOCK
Captain Smiley Giant Head (male or female)	Complete the whole game
Gerda T-Shirt (female only)	Complete Level 1
Star T-Shirt (male only)	Complete Level 1

CRACKDOWN 2 (XBOX 360)

GLITCH

Get on a mounted turret and start shooting, then have a friend punch or kick you off the turret. After you recover you will have infinite gun and grenade ammo.

AVATAR AWARDS

UNLOCKABLE	HOW TO UNLOCK
Freaky Slippers (Male and Female)	Complete the "First Hurdle" achievement.
Level 1 Agent Suit (Male and Female)	Complete the "Light Bringer" achievement.
Official Agency Hoodie (Male and Female)	Complete the "Jack of all Trades" achievement.
Orb Shirt (Male and Female)	"First Blood" achievement detected from Crackdown.
Ruffian Hat	Complete the "Hope Spring Savior" achievement.

CRESCENT PALE MIST (PS3)

UNLOCKABLES

UNLOCKABLE	HOW TO UNLOCK
Boss Only mode	Obtain the Mysterious Button from the enemy D'Artagnan on stage 5 (Normal mode and up only)
Fear difficulty	Obtain the terror medallion from one of the three black star enemies on stage 4 (Hard mode only); then beat the game on Hard mode
Music Room	Locate the music room key on stage 6 (Normal mode and up only)
Planeriel difficulty	Obtain the nightmare medallion from the nightmare of legend enemy on stage 3 (Fear mode only); then beat the game on Fear mode

DANCE PARADISE (XBOX 360)

AVATAR AWARDS

UNLOCKABLE	HOW TO UNLOCK
Ankle Boots	In Career mode, complete all Level 4 songs.
Cool Top	In Career mode, complete all Level 5 songs.
Dance T-Shirt	In Career mode, complete all Level 5 songs.
Hot Sunglasses	In Career mode, complete all Level 2 songs.
King of Dance Suit	In Career mode, complete all Level 6 songs.
Pink Stetson	In Career mode, complete all Level 3 songs.
Queen of Dance Suit	In Career mode, complete all Level 6 songs.
Shutter Shades	In Career mode, complete all Level 2 songs.
Silver Sneakers	In Career mode, complete all Level 4 songs.
Wool Cap	In Career mode, complete all Level 3 songs.

DANTE'S INFERNO (XBOX 360)

UNLOCKABLES

UNLOCKABLE	HOW TO UNLOCK
Making the Baby Feature	Beat the game on any difficulty.
Dante's Crusader Costume	Complete the game and start a new game (or Resurrection Mode game); you'll be prompted to choose the costume before the game begins.
Gates of Hell Survival Mode	Complete the game and it will be selectable from the Main menu.
New Game Plus (Resurrection Mode)	Complete the game.
Infernal Difficulty	Beat the game on any other difficulty.

DANTE'S INFERNO (PS3)

UNLOCKABLES

UNLOCKABLE	HOW TO UNLOCK
Making the Baby Feature	Beat the game on any difficulty.
Dante's Crusader Costume	Complete the game and start a new game (or Resurrection Mode game); you'll be prompted to choose the costume before the game begins.
Gates of Hell Survival Mode	Complete the game and it will be selectable from the Main menu.
New Game Plus (Resurrection Mode)	Complete the game.
Infernal Difficulty	Beat the game on any other difficulty.

DEADLIEST WARRIOR: THE GAME (XBOX 360)

AVATAR AWARDS

UNLOCKABLE	HOW TO UNLOCK
Samurai Armor	Complete Arcade Mode with any character on any difficulty.
Samurai Helmet	Complete Arcade Mode with every character on Deadliest difficulty.

UNLOCKABLES

UNLOCKABLE	HOW TO UNLOCK
Fight Lab Stage	Beat 10 opponents in Survival Mode.
Alternate Outfit	Defeat your warrior.
Long-range weapon	Beat Arcade Mode.
Mid-range weapon	Complete Slice.
Short-range weapon	Complete Target.
Challenge Mode	Successfully clear Arcade Mode with all characters on any difficulty setting.

DEAD RISING 2 (XBOX 360)

SUIT OF ARMOR

To get the suit of armor from Ghouls 'n Ghosts, you must gather all 4 pieces. When you wear all 4 pieces at once, your health is doubled, and just like in Ghouls 'n Ghosts, as you take damage, the armor chips away, leaving you in nothing but your underwear.

UNLOCKABLE	HOW TO UNLOCK
Full Beard	In the back of the store "Moe's Migitations" in Royal Flush Plaza.
Knight Armor	Complete the game with the "S" ending.
Knight Boots	Buy at the pawnshop in the Platinum Strip.
Knight Helmet	Eliminate Jack in Strip Poker in the "Ante Up" side mission.

CLOTHING

UNLOCKABLE	HOW TO UNLOCK
Champion's Jacket	Win a TIR episode (be the overall top player by the end).
Convicts	Kill 10 psychopaths.
Hockey Mask	Use every melee weapon on zombies.
Tattered Clothes	Kill 1,000 zombies using hand-to-hand combat.
TIR Helmet	Earn $1,000,000 in TIR Online.
TIR Outfit	Earn $5,000,000 in TIR Online.
Waitress outfit, bowling shirt, hunting jacket, and overalls	Start a game by importing a Case Zero file.
Willemette Mall Costume	Rescue 50 survivors.

GLITCH

After you first make it to the safe house, save your game, then go to "quit game" and restart the story. Do not press start to skip the cutscene. Now you will be able to redo the "Slicecycles" sequence again and can continue to earn $10,000 for coming in first place as many times as you like by doing this process.

DEAD RISING 2 (PS3)

SUIT OF ARMOR

To get the suit of armor from Ghouls 'n Ghosts, you must gather all 4 pieces. When you wear all 4 pieces at once, your health is doubled, and just like in Ghouls 'n Ghosts, as you take damage, the armor chips away, leaving you in nothing but your underwear.

UNLOCKABLE	HOW TO UNLOCK
Full Beard	In the back of the store "Moe's Migitations" in Royal Flush Plaza.
Knight Armor	Complete the game with the "S" ending.
Knight Boots	Buy at the pawnshop in the Platinum Strip.
Knight Helmet	Eliminate Jack in Strip Poker in the "Ante Up" side mission.

CLOTHING

UNLOCKABLE	HOW TO UNLOCK
Champion's Jacket	Win a TIR episode (be the overall top player by the end).
Convicts	Kill 10 psychopaths.
Hockey Mask	Use every melee weapon on zombies.
Tattered Clothes	Kill 1,000 zombies using hand-to-hand combat.
TIR Helmet	Earn $1,000,000 in TIR Online.
TIR Outfit	Earn $5,000,000 in TIR Online.
Willemette Mall Costume	Rescue 50 survivors.

DEAD RISING 2: CASE 0 (XBOX 360)

UNLOCKABLES

UNLOCKABLE	HOW TO UNLOCK
Easy $1,500	In the casino, there is a slot machine with a cow on it. Put in $100 to gamble and you will always win the first 5 times.
Ending A	Save all survivors, give Katey Zombrex, collect all bike parts, and leave.
Ending B	Collect all bike parts, give Katey Zombrex, then leave.
Ending C	Get caught by the military, away from Katey.
Ending D	Get caught by military on your bike.
Ending E	Forget to give Katey Zombrex.
Ending F (alt)	Forget to give Katey zombrex while near her.

DEATHSPANK (XBOX 360)

AVATAR AWARDS

UNLOCKABLE	HOW TO UNLOCK
Dragon Hatchling	Complete Ms. Heybenstance's quest to save her dragon hatchlings.
Unicorn Poop T-shirt	Kill the twin dragons guarding the artifact.

DEATHSPANK: THONGS OF VIRTUE (XBOX 360)

AVATAR AWARDS

UNLOCKABLE	HOW TO UNLOCK
DeathSpank Libre Tee	Complete the first quest in the game.
John Rumball Avatar Pet	Defeat the ultimate cookie warrior in the Jungle.

DECA SPORTS FREEDOM (XBOX 360)

AVATAR AWARDS

UNLOCKABLE	HOW TO UNLOCK
DSF/SIF Special Wear	Get a 20-hit rally in tennis
DSF/SIF T-Shirt	Enter sudden death in any sport
Hashisuke T-Shirt	Shout "HUDSON!" while in the locker room

DESPICABLE ME (PSP)

CODES

Input the codes in the Bonus menu while in Gru's Lab.

EFFECT	CODE
Unlocks the Minionettes Costume Set	●,●,■,▲,×
Unlocks the Taffy Web Gun	✣✣×,●,■,×,▲
Unlocks the Village Folk Costume Set	▲,×,×,●,×

DESPICABLE ME: MINION MAYHEM (NDS)

CODES

At the Mode Select screen, press Select to bring up the code entry window and enter the following:

EFFECT	CODE
Unlock Despicable Gru Level	B, A, Down, Down, Y
Unlock Minion Mania	L, A, B, B, Y, Up
Unlock Minion Mania EX	L, A, B, B, Y, Down
Unlock the Girls' Room level	B, L, A, B, B, Y
World Level Unlock	B, Up, Down, Down, Y

DISNEY EPIC MICKEY (Wii)

UNLOCKABLES

UNLOCKABLE	HOW TO UNLOCK
New Game +	Complete the game
Mickey Mouse "The Mad Doctor"	Collect 20 film reels
Oswald the Lucky Rabbit "Oh What a Knight"	Collect 30 film reels

GLITCH

When you first arrive at Mean Street, talk to Gilda (the cow lady in front of the fire station) more than once to receive a quest to retrieve her ax, which she lost on Mickeyjunk Mountain. If you recover the ax in the "Slopes" area during your ascent up the mountain, when you reach Oswald's lair, thin out the giant Oswald face in the middle of the floor to reach a hidden room. When you reach the end of the corridor, you'll find some large, metal bars you can't thin. Gus will offer you the opportunity to use Gilda's ax here to explore this area further; don't do this. Instead, return it to Gilda upon returning to OsTown. When you return to Mickeyjunk Mountain later in the game, thin out the Oswald face again and go back to the bars. Gus will still think you have the ax, and you'll be able to use it to pry your way in and explore! You'll now be able to reap the rewards of both the "hero" and "scrapper" outcomes of this quest, while it will be officially recorded in your quest log as having gone the "hero" route.

DJ MAX PORTABLE 3 (PSP)

MX SONG UNLOCKABLES

UNLOCKABLE	HOW TO UNLOCK
Beautiful Girl MX	Mission reward
Break! MX	Level 60+ random reward
Cosmic Fantastic Love Song MX	Mission reward

Desperado (Nu Skool Breakz Mix) MX	Mission reward
Dream of Winds MX	Level 90+ random reward
Dream of Winds MX	Level 90+ random reward
Enemy Storm (Dark Jungle Mix) MX	Level 90+ random reward
Everything MX	Level 50+ random reward
Funky People MX	Mission reward
Get Out (Hip Noodle Mix) MX	Mission reward
Gone Astray	Level 90+ random reward
Hanz Up ! MX	Level 70+ random reward
Keys to the World MX	Special Mission reward
La campanella: Nu Rave MX	Level 80+ random reward
Leave Me Along MX	Level 80+ random reward
Luv flow (Funky House Mix) MX	Special Mission reward
Masai (Electro House Mix) MX	Mission reward
Mellow D MX	Mission reward
NB Ranger: NonStop Remix MX	Mission reward
Out Law—Reborn MX	Level 80+ random reward
Put Em Up MX	Mission reward
Rain Maker MX	Level 60+ random reward
Raise Me Up MX	Mission reward
Season (Warm Mix) MX	Mission reward
SuperSonic (Mr. Funky Remix) MX	Level 70+ random reward
Trip MX	Level 70+ random reward
Whiteblue MX	Level 80+ random reward
Xslasher MX	Level 90+ random reward
Zet (Mr. Funky Remix) MX	Mission reward

LEVEL UP SONG UNLOCKABLES

UNLOCKABLE	HOW TO UNLOCK
Break!	Level 40+ random reward
Dream of Winds	Level 70+ random reward
Drum Town	Level 30+ random reward
Enemy Storm (Dark Jungle Mix)	Level 80+ random reward
Gone Astray	Level 70+ random reward
Hanz Up!	Level 50+ random reward
La Campanella: Nu Rave	Level 50+ random reward
Leave Me Alone	Level 60+ random reward
Rage of Demon	Level 80+ random reward
Rain Maker	Level 40+ random reward

DRAGON QUEST IX: SENTINELS OF THE STARRY SKIES (PS3)

ITEM DUPLICATION THROUGH AD-HOC

First, connect your DQIX to someone else. Give them any items you can, then shut your game off WITHOUT leaving their world. Since you never saved after leaving their world, you'll still have the items you traded, and so will they!

MINI MEDAL REWARDS

While playing the game, you will find numerous items called Mini Medals. In the town of Dourbridge, you can give these to a pirate king who lives there, and he will give you rare items in exchange. After you've given him 80 Mini Medals, he will sell you rare items. But you must use Mini Medals to buy them instead of Gold. Three Medals: Prayer Ring; 5 Medals: Elfin Elixir; 8 Medals: Saint's Ashes; 10 Medals: Reset Stone; 15 Medals: Orihalcum; 20 Medals: Pixie Boots.

UNLOCKABLE	HOW TO UNLOCK
Bunny Suit	Reward for giving 13 Mini Medals to Cap'n Max Meddlin
Dragon Robe	Reward for giving 80 Mini Medals to Cap'n Max Meddlin
Jolly Roger Jumper	Reward for giving 18 Mini Medals to Cap'n Max Meddlin
Mercury Bandanna	Reward for giving 8 Mini Medals to Cap'n Max Meddlin
Meteorite Bracer	Reward for giving 50 Mini Medals to Cap'n Max Meddlin
Miracle Sword	Reward for giving 32 Mini Medals to Cap'n Max Meddlin
Rusty Helmet	Reward for giving 62 Mini Medals to Cap'n Max Meddlin
Sacred Armor	Reward for giving 40 Mini Medals to Cap'n Max Meddlin
Thief's Key	Reward for giving 4 Mini Medals to Cap'n Max Meddlin
Transparent Tights	Reward for giving 25 Mini Medals to Cap'n Max Meddlin

SECRET SHOP IN DOURBRIDGE

If you go around to the back of the village shop in Dourbridge, there is a hidden door. Enter it (requires the Ultimate Key), and then you see a flight of stairs. Go down the stairs, and you can get into a secret shop with rare items.

DYNASTY WARRIORS: STRIKEFORCE (PS3)

UNLOCKABLES

UNLOCKABLE	HOW TO UNLOCK
Fourth Costume	Clear a minimum of 50 quests with the character.
Third Costume	Obtain Level 10 with the character.
Diao Chan	Clear "Battle of Hu Lao Gate" 5-Star Version.
Dong Zhuo	Clear "Battle of Luo Yang" and "Battle of Mei Castle" 5-Star Versions.
Lu Bu	Clear Chapter 6 of any Story Mode.
Meng Huo	Clear "Unification of Nan Zhong" (unlocked by clearing the previous two Nanman Quests given by the "Second Gatekeeper" in Chapter 3).
Yuan Shao	Clear "Zenith Tower" Request Mission.
Zhang Jiao	Clear "Yellow Turban Rebellion" 5-Star Version.

DYNASTY WARRIORS: STRIKEFORCE (XBOX 360)

UNLOCKABLES

UNLOCKABLE	HOW TO UNLOCK
Fourth Costume	Clear a minimum of 50 quests with the character.
Third Costume	Obtain Level 10 with the character.
Diao Chan	Clear "Battle of Hu Lao Gate" 5-Star Version.
Dong Zhuo	Clear "Battle of Luo Yang" and "Battle of Mei Castle" 5-Star Versions.
Lu Bu	Clear Chapter 6 of any Story Mode.
Meng Huo	Clear "Unification of Nan Zhong" (unlocked by clearing the previous two Nanman Quests given by the "Second Gatekeeper" in Chapter 3).
Yuan Shao	Clear "Zenith Tower" Request Mission.
Zhang Jiao	Clear "Yellow Turban Rebellion" 5-Star Version.

EA SPORTS NBA JAM (XBOX 360)

UNLOCKABLES

UNLOCKABLE	HOW TO UNLOCK
Team Adidas	When entering initials, enter ADI for player 1 and DAS for player 2. This unlocks Team Adidas, which includes Dwight Howard, Derick Rose, and Josh Smith.
Team Jordan	When entering initials, enter JOR for player 1 and DAN for player 2. This unlocks Team Jordan, which includes Dwayne Wade, Chris Paul, and Carmelo Anthony.

Team Sprite	When entering initials, enter SPR for player 1 and ITE for player 2. This unlocks Team Sprite, which includes Yellow and Green Lebron James.
J. Cole and 9th Wonder	Enter the following codes at the Start screen. A sound will confirm correct code entry. Select "Play Now" mode, then press Start at the Team Selection screen to have the corresponding character appear. Press Up, Left, Down, Right, Up, Left, Down, Right, A, B.
Beastie Boys	Enter the following codes at the Start screen. A sound will confirm correct code entry. Select "Play Now" mode, then press Start at the Team Selection screen to have the corresponding character appear. Press Up(2), Down(2), Left, Right, Left, Right, B, A.
Democrats	Enter the following codes at the Start screen. A sound will confirm correct code entry. Select "Play Now" mode, then press Start at the Team Selection screen to have the corresponding character appear. Press Left(13), A.
Michelle Beadle and Colin Cowherd from Sportsnation	In EA Sports NBA Jam for the Wii, you can unlock Colin Cowherd and Michelle Beadle. On the Enter Initials screen, type ESP for player 1 and NSN for player 2. Go to the Select Team screen and you should hear a noise confirming you've unlocked them, and you'll see them in the teams list.
NBA Mascots	On the Enter Initials screen, type MAS for player 1 and COT for player 2. Go to the Select Team screen; you should hear a noise confirming you've unlocked them, and you'll see them in the teams list.
Republicans	Enter the following codes at the Start screen. A sound will confirm correct code entry. Select "Play Now" mode, then press Start at the Team Selection screen to have the corresponding character appear. Press Right(13), A.
Tim Kitzrow (announcer) and Mark Turmell (developer)	On the Enter Initials screen, type MJT for player 1. Go to the Select Team screen and you should hear a noise confirming you've unlocked them, and you'll see them in the teams list.

FABLE III (XBOX 360)

AVATAR AWARDS

UNLOCKABLE	HOW TO UNLOCK
Crown	Become the ruler of Albion
Royal Boots	Win the support of the Dwellers
Royal Shirt	Win the support of the Bowerstone
Royal Trousers	Win the support of the Swift Brigade

DUPLICATION (PRE-PATCH)

This glitch allows you to duplicate gold or anything else. With a second controller, join your game. Then use player 1 to "gift" player 2 whatever you want to duplicate, then have player 2 leave player 1's sanctuary. Have player 2 go into his sanctuary and find the gift. Now have him reject the gift to send it back to player 1. Immediately have player 2 leave his sanctuary, then immediately drop him from the game. Now player 1 has a rejected gift in his sanctuary and player 2 will not be saved, meaning when you reload him, he will also have a gift the game didn't save as being rejected. You can dupe up to 100,000 gold at a time using this.

LIONHEAD STUDIO EASTER EGG

Swim out into the ocean in the Driftwood area. Once you hit the border, tilt your camera to look down into the water. There should be a Lionhead Studios logo on the sea floor.

PORTAL EASTER EGG

When going to capture Nigel Ferret (during the Hideout mission of bowerstone) you will come across a room with a silver key. At the far end of the room there is a path around the boxes to the other jail cell. The cell contains a hobbe worshiping the companion cube from Portal and there is of course some cake.

FALLOUT: NEW VEGAS (XBOX 360)

INFINITE XP GLITCH

With a Speech skill at 50 or higher, you can persuade Old Ben to offer his escort services to the local bar and gain 61 XP if you succeed in the speech challenge. Then follow him back to the bar and wait until he sits down, speak to him again, and redo the speech challenge for as much XP as you like! Old Ben is usually sitting by a fire close to the King's headquarters in Freeside.

INFINITE CAPS GLITCH

First, you must go to the town of Primm. Complete the "My Kind of Town" quest for them by getting a sheriff for the town. After you get them a sheriff, or the NCR's troops, you have to wait 3 to 7 in-game days, and the Vikki and Vance Casino will open again in Primm. Go there, and exchange some caps for some of the casino's chips. Then, turn in the casino's chips for caps. You will notice that when you turn the chips in, you don't have them removed from your inventory; however, you get the payout. You can exploit this for as long as you want.

VATS GLITCH

Obtain the Anti-Material Rifle and equip it with incendiary rounds. With the rifle equipped, target someone in VATS and then close VATS. They should catch fire and lose health. You can also select more than one person in VATS before closing it to burn more people. You will not lose karma or reputation.

MORE XP GLITCH

You need Speech of 30 or the perk Confirmed Bachelor. You must also be on the good side of NCR. Go to HELIOS One and the lady should automatically talk to you. Once she allows you access to HELIOS One, you should be able to start the mission "That Lucky Old Sun." Follow the mission and talk to Fantastic and Ignacio Rivas. While talking to Rivas, make sure you get him to reveal that he's a Follower of the Apocalypse by using Speech or Confirmed Bachelor and agree with his ideals about peace or just say you're neutral. Do the mission regularly until you get to the point where you activate the Mainframe Terminal. Configure the Power Grid to Full Region (Emergency Output Level). Finish the mission by hitting the Reflector Control Panel outside on top of the tower. Go back to Ignacio Rivas and choose the option "I overloaded the plant. No one . . ." The glitch is that the option never disappears, so you can choose to keep pressing it. You get 350 XP, 3 Stimpacks, and 2 Doctor's Bags.

INFINITE XP

This glitch can be found when arriving at the strip for the first time and you are invited into the Lucky 38 casino. Talk with Mr. House and ask about his lifespan (This requires a medicine check of 35). This will award 35 XP. Asking about his age again and reselecting the option "you appear to be more computer than man" will present the medicine check again, granting 35 XP each time (this glitch works in the current patched version of the game).

FALLOUT: NEW VEGAS (PS3)

INFINITE XP IN VAULT 11

Reach the sacrificial chamber and eliminate the robots, then go to the computer terminal through the previously closed wall and enter it. The last option can be pressed repeatedly to gain 500 XP each time. If any of the other options are chosen or if the terminal is exited, then you cannot use this exploit.

INFINITE CAPS

Once Primm obtains a new sheriff, The Vikki and Vance Casino will become available. If you save before each hand in blackjack, you can reload the game if you lose. You can trade in your chips for caps at the register. The NPC will give you the equivalent chips in caps, but will not take any away. This is repeatable.

EASY KILL

Obtain and equip the Anti-Material Rifle and then equip .50MG Incendiary rounds. Target some one in VATS and then close VATS, they should catch fire and lose health. You can also select more then one person in VATS before closing it, burning more people using the right analog. You will not aggro enemies or friendlies. Also you will not lose karma or Reputation with each kill.

INFINITE EXPERIENCE GLITCH

If you have a speech skill of 50 or higher, you can persuade Old Ben to offer his escort services to the local bar. If you succeed in the Speech Challenge, you'll gain 61 XP. If you follow him back to the bar afterwards, waiting until he sits down, you can speak to him again and redo the same Speech Challenge repeatedly for infinite XP! You can find Old Ben sitting by a fire close to The King's headquarters in Freeside.

INFINITE XP

Obtain "Speech" 30 or the perk "Confirmed Bachelor." You must also be friendly with NCR. Go to "HELIOS One" and the lady should automatically talk to you. Once she allows you to access HELIOS One, you will now be able to start the mission "That Lucky Old Sun." Follow the mission and talk to Fantastic and Ignacio Rivas. While speaking with Rivas, make sure you get him to reveal that he's a Follower of the Apocalypse by. This is accomplished by using Speech or Confirmed Bachelor while agreeing with his ideals about peace...or just say you're neutral. Once you get to the point where you activate the Mainframe Terminal, configure the Power Grid to "5 Full Region (Emergency Output Level). Complete the mission by hitting the Reflector Control Panel outside on top of the tower. Go back to Ignacio Rivas and select "I overloaded the plant. No one....." The glitch is that the option never disappears, so you can choose to keep pressing it. You get 350XP, 3 Stimpacks, and 2 Doctor's Bag.

FIFA WORLD CUP SOUTH AFRICA - 2010 (XBOX 360)

CELEBRATIONS

In the Main menu, go to EA Extras and then enter the codes below.

EFFECT	CODE
Flying Dive	ZTSMBDRGJLQBUMSA
African Dance	QCZCGTXKWYWBNPJK
Baby Cradle	VXYJZLXTRPBZUXXJ
Side Slide	BNDIPYYTCDZVJCCN
River Dance	NLGAHWCHCCUCTNUH
Prancing Bird	YMEOCBDOIWYUEVQN
Ice Skating	TLHDMYMCUITLAYJL

FIFA WORLD CUP SOUTH AFRICA - 2010 (Wii)

UNLOCKABLES

UNLOCKABLE	HOW TO UNLOCK
Play the World Classic XI Team	Get at least a bronze medal against every team in Zakumi's Dream Team Mode.
Use the World Classic XI Team	Beat the World Classic XI Team (Hit the Pitch Mode only).

CELEBRATION PACKS

UNLOCKABLE	HOW TO UNLOCK
Goal Celebration Pack #1	Win the Adidas Golden Boot Award by winning the FIFA World Cup and having one of the members on your team be the top scorer of the World Cup.
Goal Celebration Pack #2	Take the lead by scoring within the first 5 minutes of any match.
Goal Celebration Pack #3	Score within 5 minutes following a goal you just made.
Goal Celebration Pack #4	Score 100 goals.
Goal Celebration Pack #5	Perform a Hat Trick or score three goals with the same player in a single match.

FINAL FANTASY XIII (XBOX 360)

GAMER PICS

UNLOCKABLE	HOW TO UNLOCK
Fang	Obtain the Treasure Hunter (Gold) trophy.
Hope	Obtain the Instrument of Change (Gold) trophy.
Lightning	Obtain the Superstar (Gold)" trophy.
Sazh	Obtain the Lore Master (Gold) trophy.
Serah	Obtain the Ultimate Hero (Platinum) trophy.
Snow	Obtain the L'Cie Paragon (Gold) trophy.
Vanille	Obtain the Instrument of Faith (Silver) trophy.

FINAL FANTASY XIII (PS3)

GAMER PICS

UNLOCKABLE	HOW TO UNLOCK
Fang	Obtain the Treasure Hunter (Gold) trophy.
Hope	Obtain the Instrument of Change (Gold) trophy.
Lightning	Obtain the Superstar (Gold) trophy.
Sazh	Obtain the Lore Master (Gold) trophy.
Serah	Obtain the Ultimate Hero (Platinum) trophy.
Snow	Obtain the L'Cie Paragon (Gold) trophy.
Vanille	Obtain the Instrument of Faith (Silver) trophy.

FINAL FIGHT: DOUBLE IMPACT (PS3)

STREET FIGHTER CARTOON

Earn 570,000 points in the Uptown stage and you will be able to view the episode of the "Street Fighter Cartoon" in which the Final Fight Characters have cameo roles.

FINAL FIGHT: DOUBLE IMPACT (XBOX 360)

STREET FIGHTER CARTOON

Earn 570,000 points in the Uptown stage and you will be able to view the episode of the "Street Fighter Cartoon" in which the Final Fight Characters have cameo roles.

GOD OF WAR III (PS3)

BONUS PLAY ITEMS

There are several bonus play items that can be collected throughout the game. Once they have been obtained, they can be used during bonus play (after you have beaten the game once). Note: enabling any bonus play items will disable Trophies.

UNLOCKABLE	HOW TO UNLOCK
Hades' Helm —Max health, magic, item meters	After killing Hades and jumping into the River Styx, swim down and to the right (against the current) and and locate the helm at the bottom of the river.
Helios' Shield —Triples combo meter	Located to the right of where you kill Helios.
Hera's Chalice —Slowly drains health meter	Located to the left of where Hera falls in the garden.
Hercules' Shoulder Guard —Decrease damage taken by a third.	After finding Hercules floating in the water, swim beneath him to find his Shoulder Guard.
Hermes' Coin—10x red orbs	Located behind the rubble while chasing Hermes.
Poseidon's Conch Shell —Infinite Magic	Located in the chamber where you rescue the Poseidon Princess.
Zeus' Eagle —Infinite Rage of Sparta	Climb the wall to the right of the Heart of Gaia; item is located on the ground in plain view.

UNLOCKABLES

UNLOCKABLE	HOW TO UNLOCK
Challenges of Olympus	Beat the game.
Combat arena	Beat all challenges.
Chaos Difficulty	Complete any difficulty.
Fear Kratos Costume	Complete any difficulty.

GOD OF WAR: GHOST OF SPARTA (PSP)

THE TEMPLE OF ZEUS

The Optional Bonus Temple that allows you to get the Grave Digger's Shovel relic.

UNLOCKABLE	HOW TO UNLOCK
The Temple of Zeus	Complete the game on any difficulty

COSTUMES

UNLOCKABLE	HOW TO UNLOCK
Deimos	Beat the game on Spartan mode (Hard)
Ghost of Sparta	Beat the game on God mode (Very Hard)
God Armor	Beat the game on Spartan mode (Hard)
Grave Digger	Beat Temple of Zeus
Robotos	Purchase for 250,000 in Temple of Zeus

MODES

UNLOCKABLE	HOW TO UNLOCK
Combat Arena	Beat the game
God (Very Hard)	Beat the game

SPECIAL ITEMS

These items can be used after finding them and completing the game.

UNLOCKABLE	HOW TO UNLOCK
Aphrodite's Ambrosia: Gain the Might of Sparta attack	Complete the sex minigame in Sparta 3 times.
Athena's Owl: Helps find treasures	After Kratos destroys the Athena statue in a cutscene, search the right side in a pile of debris.
Bonds of Ares: Infinite Magic	After you enter the Domain of Death through the Death Gate in Atlantis, look in the south section of the screen.
Callisto's Armlet: Automatically win context-sensitive minigames.	Right after you beat Callisto, search the ground by the battle.
Grave Digger's Shovel: Play as Zeus in Arena Combat	Unlock everything in the Temple of Zeus and follow the path created.
King's Ring: Collects 10 times the amount of red orbs	After King Midas turns the lava into gold, drop down by the area where he touched it.

GRAN TURISMO 5 (PS3)

LICENSE TESTS

UNLOCKABLE	HOW TO UNLOCK
A License Tests	Reach Level 3 and complete the B license tests
B License Tests	Buy your first car
International A License Tests	Reach Level 12 and complete the International B license tests
International B License Tests	Reach Level 9 and complete the International C license tests
International C License Tests	Reach Level 6 and complete the A license tests
S License Tests	Reach Level 15 and complete the International A license tests

GUITAR HERO: WARRIORS OF ROCK (XBOX 360)

CODES

Input at the "Input Cheat" menu.

EFFECT	CODE
Absolutely nothinge	Press Green, Green, Green, Green, Green, Green, Green, Green
Air instruments	Press Yellow, Red, Red, Blue, Yellow, Green, Green, Green
Placebo	Press Green, Green, Green, Blue, Blue, Green, Green, Green
All taps	Press Blue, Green, Green, Red, Red, Yellow, Blue, Yellow
Color shuffle	Press Blue, Green, Blue, Red, Yellow, Green, Red, Yellow
Focus mode	Press Green, Yellow, Green, Red, Green, Yellow, Blue, Green
HUD Free mode	Press Green, Green, Red, Green, Green, Yellow, Green, Green
Invisible rocker	Press Green, Green, Red, Yellow, Yellow, Yellow, Blue, Blue
Note shuffle	Press Blue, Blue, Red, Blue, Green, Green, Red, Green
Performance mode	Press Red, Yellow, Yellow, Blue, Red, Blue, Green, Red
Unlock all characters	Press Blue, Green, Green, Red, Green, Red, Yellow, Blue
Unlock all venues	Press Red, Blue, Blue, Red, Red, Blue, Blue, Red

GUITAR HERO: WARRIORS OF ROCK (PS3)

CODES

Input at the "Input Cheat" menu.

EFFECT	CODE
Absolutely nothinge	Press Green, Green, Green, Green, Green, Green, Green, Green
Air instruments	Press Yellow, Red, Red, Blue, Yellow, Green, Green, Green
Placebo	Press Green, Green, Green, Blue, Blue, Green, Green, Green
All taps	Press Blue, Green, Green, Red, Red, Yellow, Blue, Yellow
Color shuffle	Press Blue, Green, Blue, Red, Yellow, Green, Red, Yellow
Focus mode	Press Green, Yellow, Green, Red, Green, Yellow, Blue, Green
HUD Free mode	Press Green, Green, Red, Green, Green, Yellow, Green, Green
Invisible rocker	Press Green, Green, Red, Yellow, Yellow, Yellow, Blue, Blue
Note shuffle	Press Blue, Blue, Red, Blue, Green, Green, Red, Green
Performance mode	Press Red, Yellow, Yellow, Blue, Red, Blue, Green, Red
Unlock all characters	Press Blue, Green, Green, Red, Green, Red, Yellow, Blue
Unlock all venues	Press Red, Blue, Blue, Red, Red, Blue, Blue, Red

GUITAR HERO: WARRIORS OF ROCK (Wii)

CODES

Input at the "Input Cheat" menu.

EFFECT	CODE
Unlock all characters	Press Blue, Green, Green, Red, Green, Red, Yellow, Blue
Unlock all venues	Press Red, Blue, Blue, Red, Red, Blue, Blue, Red

HALO: REACH (XBOX 360)

AVATAR AWARDS

UNLOCKABLE	HOW TO UNLOCK
Carter's Helmet	Clear a Campaign mission on Legendary without dying.
Emile's Helmet	Earned a Bulltrue medal in either multiplayer or Firefight Matchmaking.
Jorge's Helmet	Earn a Killtacular in multiplayer Matchmaking.
Jun's Helmet	Kill 100 enemies in a row without dying in either the Campaign or Firefight.
Kat's Helmet	Avenged a teammate's death in multiplayer Matchmaking.

MULTIPLAYER NAMEPLATES

UNLOCKABLE	HOW TO UNLOCK
Assault Rifle	Played the Halo Reach Beta in May 2010.
Halo 2 logo	Played Halo 2 on Xbox Live before April 15, 2010.
Halo 3 logo	Play any Campaign level in Halo 3 while connected to Xbox Live.
Marathon Durandal symbol	Have Marathon Durandal in your recently played games list and log in at Bungie.net.
MJOLNIR Mk VI helmet logo	Unlock any 4 of the Halo PC, Halo 2, Halo 3, Halo 3: ODST, or Halo Reach Beta nameplates.
ODST logo	Play Halo 3:ODST while connected to Xbox Live.
Original Halo logo	Register your Halo PC product code at Bungie.net.
The Septagon (7th Column symbol)	Join Bungie.net and log in with your Gamertag's e-mail address.

HARMS WAY (XBOX 360)

GAMER PICTURE

UNLOCKABLE	HOW TO UNLOCK
Harms Way Turret	Unlock the First Win Achievement

HARRY POTTER AND THE DEATLY HALLOWS, PART 1 (XBOX 360)

CODES

EFFECT	CODE
Elite Challenges	Y, Up, X, LT, RT, A
Protego Totalum	Y, B, Up, Left, RT, Right
Superstrength potions	X, Left, Right, A, RT, RB

HOOPWORLD (DS)

UNLOCKABLES

UNLOCKABLE	HOW TO UNLOCK
Crazy Difficulty	Beat Tournament Mode on Hard.
Team Kalans	Beat Tournament Mode on Normal.
Team Nalaks	Complete a Tournament on Crazy Mode.
Team ShadowSkulls	Beat Tournament Mode on Hard.
Team SlimeSkulls	Clear Tournament Mode under the Hard difficulty with all standard teams.
Magma Rumble Court	Beat Tournament Mode on Normal.
Olympus O.D Court	Beat Tournament Mode on Easy.

INFINITE SPACE (DS)

UNLOCKABLE

Infinite Space has two unlockable modes. New Game+ is Story Mode with additional blue prints that are not available in the first play-through. Extra Mode is a challenging mode in which the player is given limited resources to hunt down and conquer 13 systems, each with 3 out of 5 unique opponents per system.

UNLOCKABLE	HOW TO UNLOCK
Extra Mode	Complete Story Mode once.
New Game+	Complete Story Mode once.

JUST CAUSE 2 (XBOX 360)

UNLOCKABLES

UNLOCKABLE	HOW TO UNLOCK
Bubble Blaster	South-Southwest of the Communication Outpost Gurun Lautan Lama Gamma in the Lautan Lama Desert Territory, there is a wide-open field full of trees with white leaves. In the northern part of this field there is a lone bell tower. If you climb to the top of this bell tower you will find a small table with a purple gun on it. You can equip this gun. It is the called the Bubble Blaster.
Lost Easter Egg	If you go to the top-left corner of the map you see an island shaped like a square. If you fly a plane over the island your plane will explode, causing you to parachute down to the beach (if over it). You will see a search sign on the beach with an arrow pointing to the jungle. Go into the jungle and you'll find the hatch from "Lost." It is even said by people that you actually can hear the smoke monster in the background.

KINECT ADVENTURES! (XBOX 360)

AVATAR AWARDS

UNLOCKABLE	HOW TO UNLOCK
Adventures Gloves	Participate in the reward ceremony for the Treasure Grab adventure
Adventures Sunglasses	Participate in the reward ceremony for the Chasing the Sun adventure
Adventures Sweatband	Participate in the reward ceremony for the Gearing Up adventure
Adventures Watch and Band	Participate in the reward ceremony for the Winning Time adventure
Expert Adventures Outfit	Participate in the reward ceremony for the Ultimate Treasure adventure

KINECT JOY RIDE (XBOX 360)

AVATAR AWARDS

UNLOCKABLE	HOW TO UNLOCK
Aviator Ranch Goggles	Play each activity once in solo play
Boss Hoodie	Play on all tracks
Marathon Racer Suit	Get behind the wheel for 10 hours
Raven Leather Jacket	Drive every vehicle style
Smashing Helmet	Play each activity 10 times in offline play

KINECT SPORTS (XBOX 360)

AVATAR AWARDS

UNLOCKABLE	HOW TO UNLOCK
Classic Kinect Sports Cap	Earn the Amateur Sports Badge
Classic Kinect Sports Tee	Earn the Professional Sports Badge
I Heart Kinect Sports Tee	Earn the Champion Sports Badge
Kinect Sports Champ Trophy	Earn the Legendary Sports Badge
Kinect Sports Star Tee	Earn the Master Sports Badge

KINECTIMALS (XBOX 360)

AVATAR AWARDS

UNLOCKABLE	HOW TO UNLOCK
African Leopard T-Shirt	Visit the Cherry Blossom Grove
African Lion T-Shirt	Visit the Fiddler's Beach
Cheetah T-Shirt	Visit the La Selva
Panther T-Shirt	Visit the Suri Mountain

Royal Bengal Tiger T-Shirt	Visit the Glade

KINGDOM HEARTS: BIRTH BY SLEEP (PS3)

UNLOCKABLES

UNLOCKABLE	HOW TO UNLOCK
Final Chapter	Acquire all Xehanort Reports
Lingering Spirit Vanitas boss	Clear Final Story
Mysterious Figure boss	Beat Lingering spirit Vanitas at Keyblade Graveyard
UNLOCKABLE	**HOW TO UNLOCK**
Trinity Archives	Complete the story with any character

SECRET MOVIE

To unlock the secret movie, you must do the following:

UNLOCKABLE	HOW TO UNLOCK
On Critical mode	Complete the final episode
On Proud mode	Complete the final episode
On Standard mode	Complete 100% of the Reports Section % and complete the final episode

LEGO HARRY POTTER: YEARS 1-4 (XBOX 360)

GOLD BRICK CODES

Enter the codes upstairs in Wiseacres Wizarding Supplies.

EFFECT	CODE
Gold Brick 01	QE4VC7
Gold Brick 02	FY8H97
Gold Brick 03	3MQT4P
Gold Brick 04	PQPM7Z
Gold Brick 05	ZY2CPA
Gold Brick 06	3GMTP6
Gold Brick 07	XY6VYZ
Gold Brick 08	TUNC4W
Gold Brick 09	EJ42Q6
Gold Brick 10	GFJCV9
Gold Brick 11	DZCY6G

MISCELLANEOUS CODES

Enter the codes upstairs in Wiseacres Wizarding Supplies.

EFFECT	CODE
Carrot Wands	AUC8EH
Character Studs	H27KGC
Character Token Detector	HA79V8
Christmas	T7PVVN
Disguise	4DMK2R
Extra Hearts	J9U6Z9
Fall Rescue	ZEX7MV
Fast Dig	Z9BFAD
Fast Magic	FA3GQA
Gold Brick Detector	84QNQN
Hogwarts Crest Detector	TTMC6D
Ice Rink	F88VUW
Invincibility	QQWC6B
Red Brick Detector	7AD7HE
Regenerate Hearts	89ML2W

EFFECT	CODE
Score x2	74YKR7
Score x4	J3WHNK
Score x6	XK9ANE
Score x8	HUFV2H
Score x10	H8X69Y
Silhouettes	HZBVX7
Singing Mandrake	BMEU6X
Stud Magnet	67FKWZ

SPELL CODES

Enter the codes upstairs in Wiseacres Wizarding Supplies.

EFFECT	CODE
Accio	VE9VV7
Anteoculatia	QFB6NR
Calvorio	6DNR6L
Colovaria	9GJ442
Engorgio Skullus	CD4JLX
Entomorphis	MYN3NB
Flipendo	ND2L7W
Glacius	ERA9DR
Herbifors	H8FTHL
Incarcerous	YEB9Q9
Locomotor Mortis	2M2XJ6
Multicorfors	JK6QRM
Redactum Skullus	UW8LRH
Rictusempra	2UCA3M
Slugulus Eructo	U6EE8X
Stupefy	UWDJ4Y
Tarentallegra	KWWQ44
Trip Jinx	YZNRF6

LEGO HARRY POTTER: YEARS 1-4 (PS3)

GOLD BRICK CODES

Enter the codes upstairs in Wiseacres Wizarding Supplies.

EFFECT	CODE
Gold Brick 01	QE4VC7
Gold Brick 02	FY8H97
Gold Brick 03	3MQT4P
Gold Brick 04	PQPM7Z
Gold Brick 05	ZY2CPA
Gold Brick 06	3GMTP6
Gold Brick 07	XY6VYZ
Gold Brick 08	TUNC4W
Gold Brick 09	EJ42Q6
Gold Brick 10	GFJCV9
Gold Brick 11	DZCY6G

MISCELLANEOUS CODES

Enter the codes upstairs in Wiseacres Wizarding Supplies.

EFFECT	CODE
Carrot Wands	AUC8EH
Character Studs	H27KGC
Character Token Detector	HA79V8
Christmas	T7PVVN
Disguise	4DMK2R
Extra Hearts	J9U6Z9
Fall Rescue	ZEX7MV
Fast Dig	Z9BFAD
Fast Magic	FA3GQA
Gold Brick Detector	84QNQN
Hogwarts Crest Detector	TTMC6D
Ice Rink	F88VUW
Invincibility	QQWC6B
Red Brick Detector	7AD7HE
Regenerate Hearts	89ML2W
Score x2	74YKR7
Score x4	J3WHNK
Score x6	XK9ANE
Score x8	HUFV2H
Score x10	H8X69Y
Silhouettes	HZBVX7
Singing Mandrake	BMEU6X
Stud Magnet	67FKWZ

SPELL CODES

Enter the codes upstairs in Wiseacres Wizarding Supplies.

EFFECT	CODE
Accio	VE9VV7
Anteoculatia	QFB6NR
Calvorio	6DNR6L
Colovaria	9GJ442
Engorgio Skullus	CD4JLX
Entomorphis	MYN3NB
Flipendo	ND2L7W
Glacius	ERA9DR
Herbifors	H8FTHL
Incarcerous	YEB9Q9
Locomotor Mortis	2M2XJ6
Multicorfors	JK6QRM
Redactum Skullus	UW8LRH
Rictusempra	2UCA3M
Slugulus Eructo	U6EE8X
Stupefy	UWDJ4Y
Tarentallegra	KWWQ44
Trip Jinx	YZNRF6

LEGO HARRY POTTER: YEARS 1-4 (Wii)

GOLD BRICK CODES

Enter the codes upstairs in Wiseacres Wizarding Supplies.

EFFECT	CODE
Gold Brick 01	QE4VC7
Gold Brick 02	FY8H97
Gold Brick 03	3MQT4P
Gold Brick 04	PQPM7Z
Gold Brick 05	ZY2CPA
Gold Brick 06	3GMTP6
Gold Brick 07	XY6VYZ
Gold Brick 08	TUNC4W
Gold Brick 09	EJ42Q6
Gold Brick 10	GFJCV9
Gold Brick 11	DZCY6G

MISCELLANEOUS CODES

Enter the codes upstairs in Wiseacres Wizarding Supplies.

EFFECT	CODE
Carrot Wands	AUC8EH
Character Studs	H27KGC
Character Token Detector	HA79V8
Christmas	T7PVVN
Disguise	4DMK2R
Extra Hearts	J9U6Z9
Fall Rescue	ZEX7MV
Fast Dig	Z9BFAD
Fast Magic	FA3GQA
Gold Brick Detector	84QNQN
Hogwarts Crest Detector	TTMC6D
Ice Rink	F88VUW
Invincibility	QQWC6B
Red Brick Detector	7AD7HE
Regenerate Hearts	89ML2W
Score x2	74YKR7
Score x4	J3WHNK
Score x6	XK9ANE
Score x8	HUFV2H
Score x10	H8X69Y
Silhouettes	HZBVX7
Singing Mandrake	BMEU6X
Stud Magnet	67FKWZ

SPELL CODES

Enter the codes upstairs in Wiseacres Wizarding Supplies.

EFFECT	CODE
Accio	VE9VV7
Anteoculatia	QFB6NR
Calvorio	6DNR6L
Colovaria	9GJ442
Engorgio Skullus	CD4JLX

EFFECT	CODE
Entomorphis	MYN3NB
Flipendo	ND2L7W
Glacius	ERA9DR
Herbifors	H8FTHL
Incarcerous	YEB9Q9
Locomotor Mortis	2M2XJ6
Multicorfors	JK6QRM
Redactum Skullus	UW8LRH
Rictusempra	2UCA3M
Slugulus Eructo	U6EE8X
Stupefy	UWDJ4Y
Tarentallegra	KWWQ44
Trip Jinx	YZNRF6

LEGO HARRY POTTER: YEARS 1-4 (DS)

GOLD BRICK CODES

Enter the codes upstairs in Wiseacres Wizarding Supplies.

EFFECT	CODE
Gold Brick 01	QE4VC7
Gold Brick 02	FY8H97
Gold Brick 03	3MQT4P
Gold Brick 04	PQPM7Z
Gold Brick 05	ZY2CPA
Gold Brick 06	3GMTP6
Gold Brick 07	XY6VYZ
Gold Brick 08	TUNC4W
Gold Brick 09	EJ42Q6
Gold Brick 10	GFJCV9
Gold Brick 11	DZCY6G

LIMBO (XBOX 360)

AVATAR AWARDS

UNLOCKABLE	HOW TO UNLOCK
LIMBO Pet	Beat the game.
LIMBO T-shirt	Get your first LIMBO achievement.

LITTLE BIG PLANET 2 (PS3)

SECRET PINS

These special pins do not appear normally in the pin list (and do not count toward your pin total).

UNLOCKABLE	HOW TO UNLOCK
Amy's Birthday Pressie	Play on Amy's Birthday (July 29)
Festive Spirit	Wear a Christmas costume on Christmas Day
Halloween Hauntings	Wear the Pumpkin Head costume on Halloween
Mm Picked!	Have one of your levels feature in Mm Picks
Mm's Birthday	Play LBP2 on Media Molecule's birthday (January 4)
Royalty	You are awarded a Crown (LBP1 or LBP2)
Thanksgiving Turkey	Wear the Turkey Head costume on Thanksgiving
Who's Who	Watch the credits all the way through

LOST PLANET 2 (XBOX 360)

UNLOCKABLES

UNLOCKABLE	HOW TO UNLOCK
Albert Wesker	Have a save from Resident Evil 5.
Devil May Cry Noms de Guerre	Have a Devil May Cry 4 save.
Frank West	Have a save from Dead Rising.
Marcus Phoenix and Dom Santiago	Finish Campaign.
Street Fighter Noms de Guerre	Have a save of Street Fighter IV.

WEAPONS

UNLOCKABLE	HOW TO UNLOCK
Akrid Launcher	Reach level 50 with Snow Pirate Elites.
Energy Gun SP	Reach level 70 with Femme Fatale.
Fire Cracker	Reach level 30 with Femme Fatale.
Gun Sword SP	Reach level 70 with the Rounders.
Hand Cannon SP	Reach level 50 with the Rounders.
Machine Gun SP	Have a saved game file from the Lost Planet 2 demo.
Plasma Gun SP	Get NEVEC Black Ops to level 30.
Shotgun SP	Reach level 50 with Femme Fatale.
Shuriken	Reach level 30 with the Rounders.
V-Device SP	Achieve career level 70 with NEVEC.

UNLOCKABLES

UNLOCKABLE	HOW TO UNLOCK
AI Enemy Battle	Beat all the training levels and modes for both Basic and Advanced training.
Extreme Difficulty	Beat Hard Difficulty.

CODES

From any character customization screen, press Y to bring up the slot machine, then enter the password.

EFFECT	CODE
4Gamer.net Shirt	25060016
Black shirt	63152256
Blue shirt	56428338
Famitsu Weekly Magazine T-Shirt	73154986
Famitsu.com Shirt	88020223
Green shirt with WCP baseball cap T-shirt	18213092
Midnight Live 360 shirt	69088873
Monthly GAMEJAPAN shirt	52352345
Pink JP Playboy shirt	34297758
Purple + tan	65162980
Purple shirt with "D" logo and Japanese characters T-shirt	71556463
Street Jack	12887439
White shirt with blue sleeves with face T-shirt	26797358
White shirt with person holding Gatling gun T-shirt	31354816
Xbox 360 shirt (male and female)	94372143
Yellow shirt	96725729

LOST PLANET 2 (PS3)

SKINS

UNLOCKABLE	HOW TO UNLOCK
Albert Wesker	Have save data of Resident Evil 5 or Resident Evil 5 Gold Edition.

Frank West	Have a saved game file from the original Lost Planet.

TITLES

UNLOCKABLE	HOW TO UNLOCK
BSAA	Have a saved game file from Resident Evil 5.
Decorated Soldier	Have Lost Planet save data on your hard drive.
Devil May Cry	Have a saved game file from Devil May Cry 4.
I Played the Demo	Have Lost Planet 2 Multiplayer Demo save data on your hard drive.
Legendary Warrior	Have Lost Planet save data on your hard drive.
Street Fighter	Have a saved game file from Street Fighter 4.

WEAPONS

UNLOCKABLE	HOW TO UNLOCK
Akrid Launcher	Reach level 50 with Snow Pirate Elites.
Energy Gun SP	Reach level 70 with Femme Fatale.
Fire Cracker	Reach level 30 with Femme Fatale.
Gun Sword SP	Reach level 70 with the Rounders.
Hand Cannon SP	Reach level 50 with the Rounders.
Machine Gun SP	Have a saved game file from the Lost Planet 2 demo.
Plasma Gun SP	Get NEVEC Black Ops to level 30.
Shotgun SP	Reach level 50 with Femme Fatale.
Shuriken	Reach level 30 with the Rounders.
V-Device SP	Achieve career level 70 with NEVEC.

UNLOCKABLES

UNLOCKABLE	HOW TO UNLOCK
AI Enemy Battle	Beat all the training levels and modes for both Basic and Advanced training.
Extreme Difficulty	Beat Hard difficulty.

CODES

From any character customization screen, press Y to bring up the slot machine, then enter the password.

EFFECT	CODE
4Gamer.net Shirt	25060016
Black shirt	63152256
Blue shirt	56428338
Famitsu Weekly Magazine T-Shirt	73154986
Famitsu.com Shirt	88020223
Green shirt with WCP baseball cap t-shirt	18213092
Midnight Live 360 shirt	69088873
Monthly GAMEJAPAN shirt	52352345
Pink JP Playboy shirt	34297758
Purple + Tan	65162980
Purple shirt with "D" logo and Japanese characters T-shirt	71556463
Street Jack	12887439
White shirt with blue sleeves with face T-shirt	26797358
White shirt with person holding Gatling gun T-shirt	31354816
Xbox 360 shirt (male and female)	94372143
Yellow shirt	96725729
Man in Uniform	I LOVE A MAN IN UNIFORM

EFFECT	CODE
Play as Jack	OH MY SON, MY BLESSED SON
Sharp Dressed Man	DON'T YOU LOOK FINE AND DANDY
Spawn a horse-drawn coach.	NOW WHO PUT THAT THERE?
Spawn a horse	BEASTS AND MAN TOGETHER
Unlock all areas	YOU GOT YOURSELF A FINE PAIR OF EYES
Unlock all gang outfits	YOU THINK YOU TOUGH, MISTER?

MAG (PS3)

UNLOCKABLE MEDALS

UNLOCKABLE	HOW TO UNLOCK
AAA Demolition Medal	Awarded for destroying 200 anti-aircraft batteries in your career.
AAA Support Medal	Awarded for repairing 200 anti-aircraft batteries in your career.
Armchair General Medal	Awarded for killing 1,000 enemies with a bunker turret gun in your career.
Assault Master Specialist Medal	Awarded for killing 1,000 enemies with an assault rifle in your career.
Athena's Shield Medal	Awarded for winning 100 battles in your career as a defender.
Bad Commute Medal	Awarded for destroying 200 motor pools in your career.
Bomb Squad Medal	Awarded for disarming 250 explosive charges in your career.
Bronze Field Engineer Medal	Awarded for repairing 200 roadblocks in your career.
Bronze MVP Medal	Awarded for winning the 3rd place MVP award 25 times in your career.
Bunker Buster Medal	Awarded for destroying 200 bunkers in your career.
Butterfingers Medal	Awarded for killing yourself 100 times in your career. Good work, slick.
Combat Mechanic Medal	Awarded for repairing 100 vehicles in your career.
Elite Trooper Medal	Awarded for winning 100 major victories in your career.
Gate Keeper Medal	Awarded for repairing 200 gates in your career.
Gold Command Medal	Awarded for winning 100 battles as a Squad Leader in your career.
Gold Field Engineer Medal	Awarded for repairing 200 bunkers in your career.
Gold MVP Medal	Awarded for winning the 1st place MVP award 25 times in your career.
Golden Cross Medal	Awarded for reviving 500 teammates in your career.
Golden Gallipoli Medal	Awarded for losing 100 battles in your career as an attacker.
Grim Reaper Medal	Awarded for killing 2,000 enemies in your career.
Grizzled Veteran Medal	Awarded for completing 100 battles in your career.
Launcher Master Specialist Medal	Awarded for killing 250 enemies with a rocket launcher in your career.
Leader of Men Medal	Awarded for earning 1,000 leadership points in your career.
Longshot Medal	Awarded for killing 50 enemies at over 120 m in your career.
Machine Gun Master your Specialist Medal	Awarded for killing 1,000 enemies with a machine gun in career.

Marauder Medal	Awarded for planting 500 explosive charges in your career.
Master Engineer Medal	Awarded for repairing 10,000 things in your career.
Master Fragger Medal	Awarded for killing 500 enemies with a grenade in your career.
Melee Master Specialist Medal	Awarded for killing 1,000 enemies with a knife in your career.
Miner's Medal	Awarded for placing 1,000 mines in your career.
Mortar Demolition Medal	Awarded for destroying 200 mortar batteries in your career.
Mortar Support Medal	Awarded for repairing 200 mortar batteries in your career.
Mr. Badwrench Medal	Awarded for destroying 500 vehicles in your career.
Network Support Medal	Awarded for repairing 200 sensor arrays in your career.
Party Crasher Medal	Awarded for destroying 200 gates in your career.
Purple Heart Medal	Awarded for dying 1,000 times in your career.
Purple Sidekick Medal	Awarded for earning 2,000 kill assists in your career.
Road Rage Medal	Awarded for running over 250 enemies with a vehicle in your career.
Rocket Man Medal	Awarded for killing 1,000 enemies with a bunker turret rocket in your career.
Screaming Eagle Medal	Awarded for parachuting into battle 500 times in your career.
Shotgun Master Specialist Medal	Awarded for killing 1,000 enemies with a shotgun in your career.
Sidearm Master Specialist Medal	Awarded for killing 1,000 enemies with a sidearm in your career.
Silver Bullet Medal	Awarded for killing 1000 enemies with a headshot in your career.
Silver Cross Medal	Awarded for healing 10,000 units of damage in your career.
Silver Field Engineer Medal	Awarded for repairing 100 bridges in your career.
Silver MVP Medal	Awarded for winning the 2nd place MVP award 25 times in your career.
Skeet Practice Medal	Awarded for killing 100 enemy paratroopers in your career.
SMG Master Specialist Medal	Awarded for killing 1,000 enemies with a submachine gun in your career.
Sniper Master Specialist Medal	Awarded for killing 1,000 enemies with a sniper rifle in your career.
Streaker Medal	Awarded for earning a minimum of 15 uninterrupted kills in one battle in your career.
The Alamo Medal	Awarded for losing 100 battles in your career as a defender.
The Comeback Kid Medal	Awarded for spawning 1,000 times in your career.
Thor's Hammer Medal	Awarded for winning 100 battles in your career as an attacker.
Top Squad Medal	Awarded for winning the top squad award 25 times in your career.
Total Blackout Medal	Awarded for destroying 200 sensor arrays in your career.
Vanguard Medal	Awarded for completing 100 primary objectives in your career.
Vehicle Support Medal	Awarded for repairing 200 motor pools in your career.
Wrecking Crew Medal	Awarded for destroying 200 roadblocks in your career.

UNLOCKABLE RIBBONS

UNLOCKABLE	HOW TO UNLOCK
AAA Demolition	Destroy three AA batteries.
AAA Support	Repair three AA batteries.
Armchair General	Kill 30 enemies with the bunker turret.
Bomb Squad	Disarm five explosives.
Bronze Field Engineer	Repair three roadblocks.
Butterfingers	Kill yourself five times.
Combat Assault	Kill 30 enemies with an assault rifle.
Combat Fragger	Kill 10 enemies with grenades.
Combat Launcher	Kill five enemies with a Rocket Launcher.
Combat Mechanic	Repair five vehicles.
Combat Melee	Kill 15 enemies with the knife.
Combat Shotgun	Kill 30 enemies with a shotgun.
Combat Sidearm	Kill 30 enemies with a sidearm.
Combat SMG	Kill 30 enemies with a SMG.
Combat Sniper	Kill 30 enemies with a sniper rifle.
Gate Keeper	Repair three gates.
Gold Field Engineer	Repair three bunkers.
Golden Cross	Resuscitate 15 teammates.
Grim Reaper	35 kills
Longshot	Kill three enemies from at least 120 m distance.
Marauder	Plant 10 explosives.
Master Engineer	Repair 250 units.
Miners	Place 30 mines.
Mortar Demolition	Destroy three mortar batteries.
Mortar Support	Repair three mortar batteries.
Mr. Badwrench	Destroy five vehicles.
Network Support	Repair three sensor arrays.
Party Crasher	Destroy three gates.
Purple Heart	30 deaths.
Purple Sidekick	15 assisted kills.
Road Rage	Run over five enemies.
Rocket Man	Kill five enemies with the turret rocket.
Screaming Eagle	Parachute 15 times.
Silver Bullet	Kill 10 enemies via headshot.
Silver Cross	Heal 250 units.
Silver Field Engineer	Repair three bridges.
Total Blackout	Destroy three sensor arrays.
Wrecking Crew	Destroy three roadblocks.

UNLOCKABLES

UNLOCKABLE	HOW TO UNLOCK
258 player domination match	Reach level 8
Change Faction option	Reach level 60.
Squad Leader option	Reach level 15.

MAG: INTERDICTION (DLC) TROPHIES

UNLOCKABLE	HOW TO UNLOCK
King of the Hills (Bronze)	Earn the Roadside Assistance medal while playing Interdiction.

Red Ball Express (Silver)	Earn the Designated Driver medal while playing Interdiction.
Road Runner (Gold)	Capture three Interdiction control points in a single round.

MEGA MAN 10 (Wii)

CHALLENGES

There are two challenge types. Type 1 are like mini-stages or boss battles and are accessed from the Challenge menu. Type 2 are like Xbox's Achievements and don't need to be unlocked to do them. Type 1 boss and miniboss challenges generally require reaching the corresponding boss on the corresponding difficulty mode (the challenge is unlocked when you reach the boss, not when you kill it).

UNLOCKABLE	HOW TO UNLOCK
Easy boss challenges	Reach the boss on Easy difficulty.
Easy miniboss challenges	Reach the miniboss on Easy or Normal difficulty.
Hard boss challenges	Reach the boss on Hard difficulty.
Hard miniboss challenges	Reach the miniboss on Hard difficulty.
Normal boss challenges	Reach the boss on Normal difficulty.
Normal minboss challenges	Reach the miniboss on Normal difficulty.

MEGA MAN 10 (PS3)

PLAYSTATION HOME T-SHIRTS

Play through the game to unlock T-shirts for Playstation Home

UNLOCKABLE	HOW TO UNLOCK
Black Mega Man + Proto Man shirt	Achieve Rank B in Challenge Mode (at least 75% completed).
Mega Man and Roll Shirt	Achieve Rank A and complete 90% of the challenges.
Mega Man Shirt	Beat the game with Megaman.
Proto Man Shirt	Beat the game with Protoman.

MX VS. ATV REFLE (XBOX 360)

CODES

Enter codes in Cheat Code screen.

EFFECT	CODE
Unlocks KTM's and Justin Brayton	READYTORACE
Unlocks all AI guys	allai
Unlocks all ATVs	couches
Unlocks all boots	kicks
Unlocks all gear	gearedup
Unlocks all goggles	windows
Unlocks all helmets	skullcap
Unlocks all locations	whereto

NARUTO SHIPPUDEN: ULTIMATE NINJA STORM (PS3)

UNLOCKABLE

UNLOCKABLE	HOW TO UNLOCK
Hokage Naruto	Pray at the Shrine inside the House at Mount Myoboku

SP UNLOCKABLES

A list of what gets unlocked when you get a certain amount of SP. Title is the name you can set to your Ninja Info Card, which stands above your GT (default is Shinobi) Ninja Info Card is the picture you can have on your Ninja Info Card Support means that you can use all types of support (Attack, Defense, Balanced) with that character.

UNLOCKABLE	HOW TO UNLOCK
Chiyo	140,000 SP
Deidara	100,000 SP
Hidan	260,000 SP
Itachi	400,000 SP
Jiraiya	440,000 SP
Jugo	360,000 SP
Kabuto	220,000 SP
Kakuzu	280,000 SP
Karin	340,000 SP
Killer Bee	540,000 SP
Kisame	120,000 SP
Konan	480,000 SP
Lars	600,000 SP
Minato (Fourth Hokage)	580,000 SP
Naruto (Rasen Shuriken)	300,000 SP
Naruto (Sage Mode)	520,000 SP
Ninja Info Card 003	610,000 SP
Ninja Info Card 026	630,000 SP
Ninja Info Card 028	650,000 SP
Ninja Info Card 056	670,000 SP
Ninja Info Card 057	700,000 SP
Ninja Info Card 073	730,000 SP
Ninja Info Card 077	760,000 SP
Ninja Info Card 098	790,000 SP
Ninja Info Card 105	820,000 SP
Ninja Info Card 107	850,000 SP
Ninja Info Card 124	880,000 SP
Ninja Info Card 135	910,000 SP
Ninja Info Card 159	940,000 SP
Ninja Info Card 177	960,000 SP
Ninja Info Card 178	980,000 SP
Ninja Info Card 199	999,999 SP
Orochimaru	240,000 SP
Pain	500,000 SP
Sai	200,000 SP
Sasori	160,000 SP
Sasuke ("Taka")	560,000 SP
Sasuke (Kirin)	380,000 SP
Suigetsu	320,000 SP
Support: Asuma	660,000 SP
Support: Chiyo	680,000 SP
Support: Deidara	810,000 SP
Support: Hidan	840,000 SP
Support: Itachi	780,000 SP
Support: Jiraiya	690,000 SP
Support: Jugo	770,000 SP
Support: Kabuto	720,000 SP

Support: Kakuzu	860,000 SP
Support: Karin	750,000 SP
Support: Killer Bee	950,000 SP
Support: Kisame	800,000 SP
Support: Konan	890,000 SP
Support: Lars	990,000 SP
Support: Minato	970,000 SP
Support: Naruto (Rasengan, Rasen Shuriken)	620,000 SP
Support: Naruto (Sage Mode)	920,000 SP
Support: Orochimaru	710,000 SP
Support: Pain	900,000 SP
Support: Sasori	830,000 SP
Support: Sasuke ("Taka")	930,000 SP
Support: Sasuke (Chidori, Kirin)	640,000 SP
Support: Suigetsu	740,000 SP
Support: Tobi	870,000 SP
Title: Adolescent	675,000 SP
Title: Akatsuki's	855,000 SP
Title: Apprentice	230,000 SP
Title: Artistic	765,000 SP
Title: Bargaining	130,000 SP
Title: Bipolar	725,000 SP
Title: Bonds	310,000 SP
Title: Bounty	350,000 SP
Title: Bounty Hunter	330,000 SP
Title: Buddy	190,000 SP
Title: Bushy Brows	510,000 SP
Title: Crying	90,000 SP
Title: Desert	625,000 SP
Title: Friend	290,000 SP
Title: Frog	695,000 SP
Title: Glasses-wearing	705,000 SP
Title: Gutsy	470,000 SP
Title: Hebi's	865,000 SP
Title: Immortal	785,000 SP
Title: Joyful	60,000 SP
Title: Large Bounty	370,000 SP
Title: Mangekyo Sharingan	745,000 SP
Title: Master	270,000 SP
Title: Modeler	775,000 SP
Title: Ninja	10,000 SP
Title: No1 Knucklehead	390,000 SP
Title: Odd Beast	755,000 SP
Title: Outrageous	70,000 SP
Title: Passive	170,000 SP
Title: Popular	210,000 SP
Title: Prodigy	715,000 SP
Title: Pupil	250,000 SP

UNLOCKABLE	HOW TO UNLOCK
Title: Rinnegan	825,000 SP
Title: Rouge Ninja	50,000 SP
Title: Sad	80,000 SP
Title: Scared	665,000 SP
Title: Sharingan	655,000 SP
Title: Smiling	110,000 SP
Title: Space Cadet	685,000 SP
Title: Supporter	150,000 SP
Title: The Angel	815,000 SP
Title: The Chubby	570,000 SP
Title: The Cloud Village's	965,000 SP
Title: The Flower Shop's	590,000 SP
Title: The Genius	550,000 SP
Title: The Good Kid	805,000 SP
Title: The Hot Water Village's	995,000 SP
Title: The Idiot	410,000 SP
Title: The Land of Earth's	895,000 SP
Title: The Land of Fire's	875,000 SP
Title: The Land of Lightning's	905,000 SP
Title: The Land of Water's	915,000 SP
Title: The Land of Wind's	885,000 SP
Title: The Leaf Village's	925,000 SP
Title: The Main Branch's	615,000 SP
Title: The Masked	795,000 SP
Title: The Mist Village's	945,000 SP
Title: The Monster-strong	430,000 SP
Title: The Puppet Master	635,000 SP
Title: The Rapper	835,000 SP
Title: The Rock Village's	955,000 SP
Title: The Sand Village's	935,000 SP
Title: The Savage Beast	450,000 SP
Title: The Side Branch's	605,000 SP
Title: The Sound Village's	975,000 SP
Title: The Waterfall Village's	985,000 SP
Title: The Yellow Flash	845,000 SP
Title: Uber Brows	530,000 SP
Title: Uneasy	645,000 SP
Title: Unscathed	735,000 SP
Title: Utterly Gutsy	490,000 SP
Tobi	420,000 SP
Tsunade	460,000 SP
Yamato	180,000 SP

NAUGHTY BEAR (XBOX 360)

UNLOCKABLES

UNLOCKABLE	HOW TO UNLOCK
Cop Naughty (hat)	Get Gold on Episode 1.
Epic Naughty (hat)	Get Gold on all Top Hat Challenges.

Naughticorn	Get a Total Score of 100,000,000.
Naughty the Party Animal (hat)	Complete Chapter 1.

NBA 2K11 (PSP)

CODES

Accessed in the cheat menu under "features."

EFFECT	CODE
2K Development Team	nba2k
2K Sports China Team	2kchina
2K Sports team	2ksports
ABA Ball	payrespect
Bobcats Nascar Racing Uniform	agsntrccai
Cavs Cavfanatic Uniform	aifnaatccv
Hardwood Classics Uniforms (7 teams only)	wasshcicsl
Hornets Mardi Gras Uniform	asrdirmga
Secondary Road Uniforms (Grizzlies, Hawks, Mavs, and Rockets)	eydonscar
St Patrick's Day Uniforms (Bulls, Celtics, Knicks, and Raptors)	riiasgerh
Trail Blazers Rip City Uniform	ycprtii
Visual Concepts Team	vcteam

NBA 2K11 (XBOX 360)

CODES

Accessed in the cheat menu under "features."

EFFECT	CODE
2k Sports team	2Ksports
2k China team	2kchina
ABA Ball	payrespect
MJ: Creating a Legend	icanbe23
NBA2k Development Team	nba2k
Visual Concepts Team	vcteam

NBA 2K11 (PS3)

CODES

Accessed in the cheat menu under "features."

EFFECT	CODE
2k Sports team	2Ksports
2k China team	2kchina
ABA Ball	payrespect
MJ: Creating a Legend	icanbe23
NBA2k Development Team	nba2k
Visual Concepts Team	vcteam

NBA JAM (XBOX 360)

CHARACTERS

UNLOCKABLE	HOW TO UNLOCK
Allen Iverson	Elusive // Perform 10 successful shove counters.
Beastie Boys Team	3 The Hard Way // Defeat the Beastie Boys team in Remix Tour.
Bill Laimbeer, Isiah Thomas	Central Division Represent // Beat the Central Division Legend Team in Classic Campaign.
Brad Daugherty	Double Up // Beat the CPU in a 2V2 game by doubling their score or better.

UNLOCKABLE	HOW TO UNLOCK
Bryant Reeves	100 Club // Win 100 games.
Chris Mullin, Tim Hardaway	Pacific Division Represent // Beat the Pacific Division Legend Team in Classic Campaign.
Chuck Person	Fired Up // Get on Fire 4 times in a single game.
Clyde Drexler	NBA Domination // Beat Classic Campaign with a team from each division in the NBA.
Dan Majerle	Century Scorer // Score 100 points in one game.
Danny Manning	Grand Scorer // Score 1,000 points.
Patrick Ewing and John Starks	Beat Atlantic Legend Team in Classic Campaign

NBA LIVE 10 (XBOX 360)

CODES

Go to Main menu, My NBA Live 10, EA Sports Extras, NBA Codes, then type the code.

EFFECT	CODE
Unlock the Blazers, Cavaliers, Jazz, Magic, Raptors, Timberwolves, and Warriors Hardwood Retro Jerseys.	hdogdrawhoticns
Unlock the Rockets, Mavericks, Hawks, and Grizzlies alternate jerseys	ndnba1rooaesdc0
Nike Air Max LeBron VII's 1	ere1nbvlaoeknii
Nike Air Max LeBron VII's 2	2ovnaebnkrielei
Nike Air Max LeBron VII's 3	3rioabeneikenvl
Nike Huarache Legion	aoieuchrahelgn
Nike KD 2	kk2tesaosepinrd
Nike Zoom Flip'n	epfnozaeminolki
Nike Zoom Kobe V's 1	ovze1bimenkoko0
Nike Zoom Kobe V's 2	m0kveokoiebozn2
Nike Zoom Kobe V's 3	eev0nbimokk3ozo
Nike Zoom Kobe V's 4	bmo4inozeeo0kvk

NBA LIVE 10 (PS3)

CODES

Go to Main menu, My NBA Live 10, EA Sports Extras, NBA Codes, then type the code.

EFFECT	CODE
Second set of secondary jerseys for Cleveland, Golden State, Minnesota, Orlando, Philadelphia, Portland, Toronto, Utah, and Washington	hdogdrawhoticns
Bobcats NASCAR Race Day Jersey	ceobdabacarstcy
Mavericks, Rockets, Grizzlies, Hawks secondary road jerseys	Ndnba1rooaesdc0
Hornets Mardi Gras Jersey	nishrag1rosmad0
Jordan CP3 III	iaporcdian3ejis
Jordan Melo M6	emlarmeoo6ajdsn
Jordan Sixty Plus	aondsuilyjrspxt
Nike Air Max LeBron VII	ivl5brieekaeonn
Nike Air Max LeBron VII	n6ieirvalkeeobn
Nike Air Max LeBron VII	ri4boenanekilve
Nike Air Max LeBron VII	3rioabeneikenvl
Nike Air Max LeBron VII	2ovnaebnkrielei

Nike Air Max LeBron VII	ere1nbvlaoeknii
Nike Huarache Legion	aoieuchrahelgn
Nike KD 2	kk2tesaosepinrd
Nike Zoom Flip	epfnozaeminolki
Nike Zoom Kobe V	m0kveokoiebozn2
Nike Zoom Kobe V	eev0nbimokk3ozo
Nike Zoom Kobe V	bmo4inozeeo0kvk
Nike Zoom Kobe V	ovze1bimenkoko0

NBA LIVE 10 (PSP)

CODES

Go to My NBA Live, go to Options, and select Codes. Now type the codes.

EFFECT	CODE
Unlock additional Hardwood Classics Nights for the Cleveland Cavaliers, Golden State Warriors, Minnesota Timberwolves, Orlando Magic, Philadelphia 76e	hdogdrawhoticns
Unlock the Adidas Equations.	adaodqauieints1
Unlock the Adidas TS Creators with ankle braces.	atciadsstsdhecf
Unlock the Charlotte Bobcats' 2009/2010 Race Day alternate jerseys.	ceobdabacarstcy
Unlock the Jordan CP3 IIIs.	iaporcdian3ejis
Unlock the Jordan Melo M6s.	emlarmeoo6ajdsn
Unlock the Jordan Sixty Pluses.	aondsuilyjrspxt
Unlock the new alternate jerseys for the Atlanta Hawks, Dallas Mavericks, Houston Rockets and Memphis Grizzlies.	ndnba1rooaesdc0
Unlock the New Orleans Hornets' 2009/2010 Mardi Gras alternate jerseys.	nishrag1rosmad0
Unlock the Nike Huarache Legions.	aoieuchrahelgn
Unlock the Nike KD 2s.	kk2tesaosepinrd
Unlock the Nike Zoom Flip'Ns.	epfnozaeminolki
Unlock the TS Supernatural Commanders.	andsicdsmatdnsr
Unlock TS Supernatural Creators.	ard8siscdnatstr

ONE PIECE: UNLIMITED ADVENTURE (Wii)

UNLOCKABLE CHARACTERS

UNLOCKABLE	HOW TO UNLOCK
Aokiji	Beat him in the Dimension Zone.
Arlong	Beat him in Story Mode at the Cave area.
Bon Clay	Defeat him at the Seaside Zone area.
Calgara	Beat him at Jungle Zone near a fishing spot.
Crocodile	Beat him at the Cave area. He is the second boss; to reach him hit the wall with a character not a pick axe.
Don Krieg	Defeat him in the Jungle Zone.
Eneru	Beat him in Story Mode at the Ruins Zone area.
Kaku	Defeat him in the Jungle area.
Lucci	Defeat him in the Dimension Zone
Mihawk	Beat him in story Mode at the Fossil Beach area.
Paulie	Beat him at Cave Zone.
Portgas D. Ace	Defeat him in the Mountain Zone.
Rampaging Chopper	Beat him in Mountain Zone; you need a Revive Medicine to get to his arena.
Rob Lucci	Beat him in the Dimension Zone; he's the first boss.

UNLOCKABLE	HOW TO UNLOCK
Shanks	Defeat him in the Mountain Zone.
Smoker	Beat him right before you enter Fossil Beach.
Spandam	Beat him at the Ruins zone he is the first boss.
Vivi	Beat her at Ruins Zone.
Whitebeard	Beat him in the Dimension Zone. Golden Whale is required to get to the arena.

UNLOCK SURVIVAL MODE

Unlock the following characters in Vs. Mode to unlock Survival Mode. Locations are of the first encounter with the enemy.

UNLOCKABLE	HOW TO UNLOCK
Bazooka Marine	Defeat one in the Seaside Zone.
Blue Demon General	Defeat one in the Cave Zone.
Cluster Demon Soldier	Defeat one in the Cave Zone.
Crimson Demon General	Defeat one in the Cave Zone.
Knuckle Pirate	Defeat one in the Ruins Zone.
Marine Corps Chief	Defeat one in the Jungle Zone.
Normal Marine	Defeat one in the Seaside Zone.
Pistol Pirate	Defeat one in the Jungle Zone.
Sabre Pirate	Defeat one in the Jungle Zone.
Sword Demon Soldier	Defeat one in the Cave Zone.
World Government Agent	Defeat one in the Ruins Zone.

PERFECT DARK (XBOX 360)

UNLOCKABLES

UNLOCKABLE	HOW TO UNLOCK
Elvis Plushie	Complete a special mission unlocked by beating the game on any difficulty.
Perfect Dark Shirt	Headshot someone in any game mode.
Maian SOS mission	Beat single-player on Special Agent or Perfect Agent.
Mr. Blondes Revenge mission	Beat single-player on any difficulty.
The Duel mission	Get bronze or higher with every gun in the firing range.
War! Mission	Beat single-player on Perfect Agent.
Gamer Pic 1	Get all four multiplayer medals in one match (highest accuracy, most headshots, most kills, fewest deaths).
Skedar Theme	Complete the three specialist achievements
All Guns in Solo Mode	Perfect Dark Zero save game on your profile.
Cloaking Device in Solo Mode	Perfect Dark Zero save game on your profile.
Hurricane Fists in Solo Mode	Perfect Dark Zero save game on your profile.
Weapons Stash Locator in Solo Mode	Perfect Dark Zero save game on your profile.

SPEED RUN CHEATS

There are a number of cheats that you can unlock in the solo missions. These are called "speed run" cheats because many of them consist of beating a level on a certain difficulty in a certain amount of time, similar to the cheats in Goldeneye. They can be accessed under the Cheats section inside the Carrington Institute in the Start menu.

UNLOCKABLE	HOW TO UNLOCK
Alien (Co-op Buddy)	Beat Attack Ship: Covert Assault on Special Agent in under 5:17.
All Guns in Solo	Beat Skedar Ruins: Battle Shrine on Perfect Agent in under 5:31.

Classic Sight	Beat dataDyne Central: Defection on Agent.
Cloaking Device	Beat G5 Building: Reconnaissance on Agent in under 1:30.
DK Mode (everyone has big arms and heads)	Beat Chicago: Stealth on Agent.
Enemy Rockets	Beat Pelagic II: Exploration on Agent.
Enemy Shields	Beat Carrington Institute: Defense on Agent.
Farsight XR-20	Beat Deep Sea: Nullify Threat on Perfect Agent in under 7:27.
Hit and Run (Co-op Buddy)	Beat Carrington Villa: Hostage One on Special Agent in under 2:30.
Hotshot (Co-op Buddy)	Beat Area 51: Infiltration on Special Agent in under 5:00.
Hurricane Fists	Beat dataDyne Central: Extraction on Agent in under 2:03.
Invincible	Beat Area 51: Escape on Agent in under 3:50.
Jo Shield	Beat Deep Sea: Nullify Threat on Agent.
Laptop Gun	Beat Air Force One: Anti-Terrorism on Agent.
Marquis of Queensbury Rules (Enemies Don't Have Guns)	Beat dataDyne Central: Defection on Special Agent in under 1:30.
Perfect Darkness	Beat Crash Site: Confrontation on Agent.
Phoenix	Beat Attack Ship: Covert Assault on Agent.
Play As Elvis	Beat Area 51: Rescue on Perfect Agent in under 7:59.
Psychosis Gun (makes enemies attack other enemies)	Beat Chicago: Stealth on Perfect Agent in under 2:00.
Pugilist (Co-op Buddy)	Beat dataDyne Research: Investigation on Perfect Agent in under 6:30.
R-Tracker/Weapon Cache Locations	Beat Skedar Ruins: Battle Shrine on Agent.
Rocket Launcher	Beat dataDyne Central: Extraction on Agent.
Slo-mo Single Player	Beat dataDyne Research: Investigation on Agent.
Small Characters	Beat Area 51: Infiltration on Agent.
Small Jo	Beat G5 Building: Reconnaissance on Agent.
Sniper Rifle	Beat Carrington Villa: Hostage One on Agent.
Super Dragon	Beat Area 51: Escape on Agent.
Super Shield	Beat Carrington Institute: Defense on Agent in under 1:45.
Team Heads Only	Beat Air Base: Espionage on Agent.
Trent's Magnum	Beat Crash Site: Confrontation on Agent in under 2:50.
Unlimited Ammo	Beat Pelagic II: Exploration on Special Agent in under 7:07.
Unlimited Ammo: Laptop Sentry Gun	Beat Air Force One: Anti-Terrorism on Perfect Agent in under 3:55.
Unlimited Ammo: No Reloads	Beat Air Base: Espionage on Special Agent in under 3:11.
Velvet Dark (Co-op Buddy)	Unlocked from the start.
X-Ray Scanner	Beat Area 51: Rescue on Agent.

PIRATES PLUNDARRR (Wii)

UNLOCKABLE CHARACTERS

UNLOCKABLE	HOW TO UNLOCK
Amazon	Defeat Tecciztecatl, Witch Doctor.
Spectral	Defeat Nanauatl, Hero of the Sun.

PLANTS VS. ZOMBIES (XBOX 360)

CODES

To enter a cheat code, press LB, RB, LT, RT in game; some codes require a tall enough tree of wisdom.u.

EFFECT	CODE
A shower of candy when a zombie dies	pinata
Alternate lawn mower appearance	trickedout
Gives zombies futuristic shades	future
Mustaches for zombie	mustache
Once zombies are killed, they leave small daisies behind	daisies
Toggles the zombie's call for brains sound	sukhbir
Zombies dance	dance

POKÉMON HEARTGOLD (DS)

UNLOCKABLES

UNLOCKABLE	HOW TO UNLOCK
National Dex	Beat the Elite Four once and go to the S.S Aqua ship in Olivine City to get the National Dex.
Beautiful Beach	Obtain 200 Watts.
Beyond the Sea	Obtain a foreign Pokémon via use of the GTS.
Big Forest	Obtain 40,000 Watts and own the National Dex.
Blue Lake	Obtain 2,000 Watts.
Dim Cave	Obtain 1,000 Watts.
UNLOCKABLE	HOW TO UNLOCK
Hoenn Field	Obtain 5,000 Watts and own the National Dex.
Icy Mountain Rd.	Obtain 30,000 Watts and own the National Dex.
Night Sky's Edge	Trade a fateful-encounter Jirachi onto your HG or SS.
Noisy Forest	Available from the start.
Quiet Cave	Obtain 100,000 Watts and own the National Dex.
Refreshing Field	Available from the start.
Resort	Obtain 80,000 Watts and own the National Dex.
Rugged Road	Obtain 50 Watts.
Scary Cave	Obtain 20,000 Watts and own the National Dex.
Sinnoh Field	Obtain 25,000 Watts and own the National Dex.
Stormy Beach	Obtain 65,000 Watts and own the National Dex.
Suburban Area	Obtain 500 Watts.
Town Outskirts	Obtain 3,000 Watts.
Tree House	Obtain 15,000 Watts and own the National Dex.
Volcano Path	Obtain 10,000 Watts and own the National Dex.
Warm Beach	Obtain 7,500 Watts and own the National Dex.
White Lake	Obtain 50,000 Watts and own the National Dex.

POKÉMON SOULSILVER (DS)

UNLOCKABLES

UNLOCKABLE	HOW TO UNLOCK
National Dex	Beat the Elite Four once and go to the S.S. Aqua ship in Olivine City to get the National Dex.
Amity Meadow	Unreleased to all versions.
Beautiful Beach	Collect 200 Watts.
Beyond the Sea	Trade for an International Pokémon in the GTS in Goldenrod City.

Big Forest	Collect 40,000 Watts + National Dex.
Blue Lake	Collect 2,000 Watts.
Dim Cave	Collect 1,000 Watts.
Hoenn Field	Collect 5,000 Watts + National Dex.
Icy Mountain Road	Collect 30,000 Watts + National Dex.
Night Sky's Edge	Obtain the PokéDex Data for Jirachi.
Quiet Cave	Collect 100,000 Watts + National Dex.
Rally	Unreleased to U.S. versions.
Rugged Road	Collect 50 Watts.
Scary Cave	Collect 20,000 Watts + National Dex.
Sightseeing	Unreleased to U.S. versions.
Sinnoh Field	Collect 25,000 Watts + National Dex.
Stormy Beach	Collect 65,000 Watts + National Dex.
Suburban Area	Collect 500 Watts.
The Resort	Collect 80,000 Watts + National Dex.
Town Outskirts	Collect 3,000 Watts.
Treehouse	Collect 15,000 Watts + National Dex.
Volcano Path	Collect 10,000 Watts + National Dex.
Warm Beach	Collect 7,500 Watts + National Dex.
White Lake	Collect 50,000 Watts + National Dex.

PRO EVOLUTION SOCCER 2010 (XBOX 360)

UNLOCKABLES

Unlock by winning the International Cup with the respective team

UNLOCKABLE	HOW TO UNLOCK
Classic Argentina	Win International Cup with Argentina.
Classic Brazil	Win International Cup with Brazil.
Classic England	Win International Cup with England.
Classic France	Win International Cup with France.
Classic Germany	Win International Cup with Germany.
Classic Italy	Win International Cup with Italy.

PRO EVOLUTION SOCCER 2010 (PS3)

UNLOCKABLES

Unlock by winning the International Cup with the respective team.

UNLOCKABLE	HOW TO UNLOCK
Classic Argentina	Win International Cup with Argentina.
Classic Brazil	Win International Cup with Brazil.
Classic England	Win International Cup with England.
Classic France	Win International Cup with France.
Classic Germany	Win International Cup with Germany.
Classic Italy	Win International Cup with Italy.

RAGNAROK DS (DS)

MIRAGE TOWER

Mirage Tower consists of 50 floors with random monsters. This dungeon allows you to play online with other Ragnarok Online DS players. This dungeon is found at the lower-right portal of the North Sograt Desert

UNLOCKABLE	HOW TO UNLOCK
Mirage Tower	Complete the main quest till quest 25.

RED DEAD REDEMPTION (PS3)

CODES

Enabling a code will permanently prevent the game from being saved and trophies from being earned.

EFFECT	CODE
Become a nobody	HUMILITY BEFORE THE LORD
Decrease Bounty	THEY SELL SOULS CHEAP HERE
Diplomatic Immunity	I WISH I WORKED FOR UNCLE SAM
Enable the Sepia filter	THE OLD WAYS IS THE BEST WAYS
Fame	I AM ONE OF THEM FAMOUS FELLAS
Get $500	THE ROOT OF ALL EVIL, WE THANK YOU!
Good Guy	IT AINT PRIDE. IT'S HONOR
Gun Set 1	IT'S MY CONSTITUTIONAL RIGHT
Gun Set 2	I'M AN AMERICAN. I NEED GUNS
Infinite ammo	ABUNDANCE IS EVERYWHERE
Infinite Dead Eye	I DON'T UNDERSTAND IMNFINITY
Infinite Horse Stamina	MAKE HAY WHILE THE SUN SHINES
Invincibility	HE GIVES STRENGTH TO THE WEAK
Man in Uniform	I LOVE A MAN IN UNIFORM
Play as Jack	OH MY SON, MY BLESSED SON
Sharp Dressed Man	DON'T YOU LOOK FINE AND DANDY
Spawn a horse-drawn coach	NOW WHO PUT THAT THERE?
Spawn a horse	BEASTS AND MAN TOGETHER
Unlock all areas	YOU GOT YOURSELF A FINE PAIR OF EYES
Unlock all gang outfits	YOU THINK YOU TOUGH, MISTER?

RED DEAD REDEMPTION (XBOX 360)

CODES

Enabling a code will permanently prevent the game from being saved and achievements from being earned.

EFFECT	CODE
Become a nobody	HUMILITY BEFORE THE LORD
Decrease Bounty	THEY SELL SOULS CHEAP HERE
Diplomatic Immunity	I WISH I WORKED FOR UNCLE SAM
Enable the Sepia filter	THE OLD WAYS IS THE BEST WAYS
Fame	I AM ONE OF THEM FAMOUS FELLAS
Get $500	THE ROOT OF ALL EVIL, WE THANK YOU!
Good Guy	IT AINT PRIDE. IT'S HONOR
Gun Set 1	IT'S MY CONSTITUTIONAL RIGHT
Gun Set 2	I'M AN AMERICAN. I NEED GUNS
Infinite ammo	ABUNDANCE IS EVERYWHERE
Infinite Dead Eye	I DON'T UNDERSTAND IMNFINITY
Infinite Horse Stamina	MAKE HAY WHILE THE SUN SHINES
Invincibility	HE GIVES STRENGTH TO THE WEAK

RED STEEL 2 (Wii)

CODES

Go to the Extras menu then to "Preorder" and enter the codes.

EFFECT	CODE
Barracuda	3582880

EFFECT	CODE
Nihonto Hana Sword (alternate code)	58855558
Sora Katana of the Katakara Clan	360152
Tataro Magnum	357370402
The Lost Blade of the Kusagari Clan	360378

RESIDENT EVIL 5: LOST IN NIGHTMARES (XBOX 360)

UNLOCKABLES

UNLOCKABLE	HOW TO UNLOCK
Jill Valentine playable character	Complete Lost in Nightmares
Figures	Beat the game to unlock figurines. Viewable in the Bonus Gallery.
Old-School Resident Evil Camera Mode:	When the chapter starts, turn around and try to open the front door. Do this three times and a "?" will appear. Click to activate classic camera!

RISEN (XBOX 360)

GLITCH

Seek out Rhobart in the Bandit Camp and then go and collect the 10 reeds of Brugleweed he asks for. When you return to him with the reeds, he will give you 70 gold and 50 XP. Attack him until he is unconscious but do not kill him. Loot his body and retrieve the Brugleweed you just gave him. When he gets up, give him the pilfered Brugleweed for additional gold and XP. Repeat as often as you like (will go faster with higher amounts of Brugleweed).

ROCK BAND 3 (XBOX 360)

CODES

Enter the following codes at the Main menu of the game.

EFFECT	CODE
Ovation D-2010 Guitar	Orange, Blue, Orange, Orange, Blue, Blue, Orange, Blue
Stop! Guitar unlocked	Orange, Orange, Blue, Blue, Orange, Blue, Blue, Orange
Unlocks Guild X-79 Guitar in Customization Options	Blue, Orange, Orange, Blue, Orange, Orange, Blue, Blue

SECRET INSTRUMENTS

UNLOCKABLE	HOW TO UNLOCK
Baroque Stage Kit	Expert Hall of Fame induction in Pro Drums: Expert Song Progress
Clear Microphone Song	Expert Hall of Fame induction in Vocal Harmony: Expert Progress
Cthulhu's Revenge	Expert Hall of Fame induction in Pro Guitar: Expert Song Progress
DKS-5910 Pro-Tech High Performance Kit	Expert Hall of Fame Induction in Drums: Expert Song Progress
Gold Microphone	Expert Hall of Fame induction in Vocals: Expert Song Progress
Gretsch Bo-Diddley	Expert Hall of Fame induction in Guitar: Expert Song Progress
Gretsch White Falcon	Expert Hall of Fame induction in Bass: Expert Song Progress
The Goat Head	Expert Hall of Fame induction in Pro Bass: Expert Song Progress
The Green Day Guitar	Welcome to Paradise in Guitar: Green Day: Rock Band
VOX Continental	Expert Hall of Fame induction in Keys: Expert Song Progress
Yamaha CS-50	Expert Hall of Fame induction in Pro Keys: Expert Song Progress

ROCK BAND 3 (PS3)

CODES

Enter the following codes at the Main menu of the game.

EFFECT	CODE
Ovation D-2010 Guitar	Orange, Blue, Orange, Orange, Blue, Blue, Orange, Blue
Unlocks Guild X-79 Guitar n Customization Options	Blue, Orange, Orange, Blue, Orange, Orange, Blue, Blue

UNLOCKABLE

UNLOCKABLE	HOW TO UNLOCK
Play Keys on Guitar	Achieve the Guitar Immortal goal 5* 50 Medium Rock Band 3 Songs (or 3* on a higher difficulty)

ROCK BAND 3 (Wii)

CODES

Enter the following codes at the Main menu of the game.

EFFECT	CODE
Ovation D-2010 Guitar	Orange, Blue, Orange, Orange, Blue, Blue, Orange, Blue
Unlocks Guild X-79 Guitar in Customization Options	Blue, Orange, Orange, Blue, Orange, Orange, Blue, Blue

THE SIMS 3 (NDS)

KARMA POWERS

Karma Powers can be unlocked after you have accumulated enough Lifetime Happiness for each one. To trigger Karma Powers, go to the locations that follow and click on the object described.

UNLOCKABLE	HOW TO UNLOCK
Bless This Mess	Garden Gnome outside Landgraab house
Casanova	Dance Club, near the restrooms
Cosmic Curse	Graveyard at night only
Epic Fail	Statue at Goth's house
Giant Jackpot	Bench near the Lighthouse
Muse	Painting in the Art Museum
Super Satisfy	Wrought Iron Trellis off path near Lighthouse
The Riddler	Jet statue near Military Base
Winter Wonderland	Alcove near the Stadium
Wormhole	Potted flower outside Poet's Abode

SCOTT PILGRIM VS. THE WORLD (PS3)

UNLOCKABLES

UNLOCKABLE	HOW TO UNLOCK
Nega-Scott	Beat the game using Kim, Stills, Ramona, and Scott.

SCRAP METAL (XBOX 360)

UNLOCKABLES

UNLOCKABLE	HOW TO UNLOCK
Scrap Metal RC car	Complete all missions in the single-player game.
Scrap Metal T-Shirt	Complete first race.

SIDESWIPED (DS)

UNLOCKABLES

UNLOCKABLE	HOW TO UNLOCK
Extra Missions	Pass all missions to unlock extra missions.
Nerai Bonus Game	Pass all missions and criteria.
Big Bang (Bus)	Complete all Mission Mode criteria.

SKATE (PS3)

CODES

Activate the codes by pressing Start, Options, then Extras and then entering them.

EFFECT	CODE
Enables Mini-Skater Mode	miniskaters
Enables Zombie Mode Pedestrians chase you; screen goes yellowish	zombie
Hoverboard Mode Trucks and wheels disappear from your deck mcfly	zombie
Resets all objects in every area back to their original positions	streetsweeper
Unlocks Isaac from Dead Space as a playable skater	deadspacetoo

SKATE 3 (XBOX 360)

CODES

Activate the codes by pressing Start, Options, then Extras, and then entering them.

EFFECT	CODE
Enables Mini-Skater Mode	miniskaters
Enables Zombie Mode Pedestrians chase you; screen goes yellowish	zombie
Hoverboard Mode Trucks and wheels disappear from your deck	mcfly
Resets all objects in every area back to their original positions	streetsweeper
Unlocks Isaac from Dead Space as a playable skater	deadspacetoo

SKATE 3 (PS3)

CODES

Pause the game, go to Options, Extras, and then enter the following codes.

EFFECT	CODE
Enables Mini-Skater Mode	miniskaters
Enables Zombie Mode	zombie
Hoverboard Mode	mcfly
Resets all objects in every area back to their original positions	streetsweeper
Unlocks Isaac from Dead Space as a playable skater	deadspacetoo

SNOOPY FLYING ACE (XBOX 360)

UNLOCKABLES

Use the Avatar Costumes/Shirts by downloading them from the "Download Avatar Awards" option in the Help & Options menu after completing the requirements below.

UNLOCKABLE	HOW TO UNLOCK
Snoopy Gamer Pic	Obtain 5,000 Online Points.
Woodstock Gamer Pic	Reach level 20.
Red Baron Avatar Costume	Reach the rank of Flying Ace.
Snoopy Avatar Shirt	Receive at least one medal on all missions.

SOLDNER-X 2: FINAL PROTOTYPE (PS3)

UNLOCKABLES

UNLOCKABLE	HOW TO UNLOCK
Stage 5	Collect at least 4 keys from any stage
Stage 6	Collect at least 4 keys from any 3 stages
Stage 7	Collect at least 4 keys from stages 1–6
Final Ship	Complete the Challenge "Assassin"

UNLOCKABLE	HOW TO UNLOCK
Extra Hard difficulty	Complete the game on Hard difficulty
Hard difficulty	Complete the game on Normal difficulty

SONIC THE HEDGEHOG 4: EPISODE I (PS3)

SUPER SONIC

Complete all 7 special stages by collecting the Chaos Emerald at the end. Then enter any level, collect 50 rings, and press the Square button or Triangle button to transform into Super Sonic.

SONIC THE HEDGEHOG 4: EPISODE I (XBOX 360)

AVATAR AWARDS

UNLOCKABLE	HOW TO UNLOCK
Sonic Costume (Body)	After collecting the 7 Chaos Emeralds, defeat the final boss one more time.
Sonic Costume (Head)	Collect all rings during the ending of the final stage.

SPLATTERHOUSE (Xbox 360)

UNLOCKABLE CLASSIC SPLATTERHOUSE GAMES

UNLOCKABLE	HOW TO UNLOCK
Splatterhouse	Finish Phase 2: "The Doll That Bled"
Splatterhouse 2	Finish Phase 4: "The Meat Factory"
Splatterhouse 3	Finish Phase 8: "Reflections in Blood"

SPLATTERHOUSE (PS3)

UNLOCKABLES

UNLOCKABLE	HOW TO UNLOCK
Splatterhouse	Finish Phase 2: "The Doll That Bled"
Splatterhouse 2	Finish Phase 4: "The Meat Factory"
Splatterhouse 3	Finish Phase 8: "Reflections in Blood"
Unlock PS3 Exclusive Mask	Complete the Splatterhouse Story mode

SPYBORGS (Wii)

UNLOCKABLES

UNLOCKABLE	HOW TO UNLOCK
Infinite Arena	Complete the game on any difficulty level.

STAR OCEAN: THE LAST HOPE INTERNATIONAL (PS3)

UNLOCKABLES

UNLOCKABLE	HOW TO UNLOCK
Chaos difficulty	Beat the game on Universe Mode.
Universe difficulty	Beat the game on Galaxy Mode.
Additional Battle Voices, Set 1	Obtain 30% of the character's Battle Trophies.
Additional Battle Voices, Set 2	Obtain 75% of the character's Battle Trophies.
Level cap increase	Obtain 50% of the character's Battle Trophies.
More CP	Obtain 100% of the character's Battle Trophies.

STAR WARS: THE FORCE UNLEASHED II (Wii)

CODES

Enter Story mode and go to the corresponding menu for the code you intend to input. Hold Z until you hear a sound, then press buttons on your Wii Remote:

EFFECT	CODE
Unlocks all costumes (Costume menu)	Hold down Z (until you hear a sound) then press LEFT, RIGHT, C, LEFT, RIGHT, C, UP, DOWN

UNLOCKABLE

UNLOCKABLE	HOW TO UNLOCK
Unlimited Force Energy	Upgrade all force powers to max level
Unlimited Health	Find all of the holocrons

STAR WARS: THE FORCE UNLEASHED II (XBOX 360)

CODES

In the "Options" selection of the Pause Game menu, select the "Cheat Codes" option, then enter the following codes.

EFFECT	CODE
Dark Green Lightsaber Crystal (healing)	LIBO
Experimental Jedi Armor	NOMI
Jedi Mind Trick	YARAEL
Jumptrooper Costume	AJP400
Lightsaber Throw	TRAYA
Play as a Neimoidian	GUNRAY
Play as Boba Fett	Mandalore
Stormtrooper character skin	TK421
Force Repulse	MAREK
Dark Apprentice costume	VENTRESS
Saber guard outfit	MORGUKAI
Sith acolyte costume	HAAZEN
General Kota costume	RAHM
Rebel trooper costume	REBELSCUM
Terror trooper costume	SHADOW
Wisdom Lightsaber crystals	SOLARI

UNLOCKABLE

UNLOCKABLE	HOW TO UNLOCK
General Kota costume	Achieve Silver medal in "Deadly Path Trial" Challenge
Saber guard costume	Achieve Silver medal in "Cloning Spire Trial" Challenge
Terror trooper costume	Achieve Silver Medal in "Terror Trial" Challenge
Ceremonial Jedi robes	Have a Force Unleashed save file with the Light Side ending unlocked
Sith stalker armor	Have a Force Unleashed save file with the Dark Side ending unlocked
Sith training gear	Have a Force Unleashed save file in your hard drive
Guybrush Threepkiller Costume	On the second level after the casino type rooms, you'll come to a room with a Jabba the Hutt hologram and some golden Guybrush Threepwood statues. Unlock the costume by destroying the three machines in the room.

SUPER SCRIBBLENAUTS (NDS)

MERITS

UNLOCKABLE	HOW TO UNLOCK
Astronomer	Decorate the sky with every planet in the solar system.
Avatar Maniac	Purchase all avatars.
Behind the Scenes	Create three 5th Cell developers.
Brand New Pencil	Use 10 unique adjectives.
Break Time	Use the arcade machine.
Broken Pencil	Use 300 unique adjectives.
Clever Creation	Attach any three objects together.

UNLOCKABLE	HOW TO UNLOCK
Coloring Book	Create 10 objects with altered colors.
Colossal Contraption	Attach any 10 objects together.
Connect the Dots	Complete any constellation.
Cracked Pencil	Use 200 unique adjectives.
Creative Concoction	Attach any six objects together.
Cthulhu Fhtagn	Create a mythos monster.
Daily Horoscope	Decorate the sky with the 12 zodiac symbols.
Dedicated Collector	Purchase 25 avatars.
Easter Egg	Create 5 hidden historical figures.
English Eagle	Create 10 unique objects.
Fantasy Fulfillment	Create 5 fantasy objects or use 5 fantasy adjectives.
Fatality!	Destroy the world.
Forbidden Fruit	Use Maxwell's notebook.
Full Replay	Complete all advanced mode levels.
Ginormous	Create the largest possible object.
Grammar General	Create 200 unique objects.
History Lesson	Use the time machine.
Home Grown	Complete a custom level.
Hypnotized	Hypnotize another character.
It's Alive!	Grant life to an inanimate object.
Kiss Me	Transform a creature into a frog.
Language Lion	Create 100 unique objects.
Letter Lieutenant	Create 25 unique objects.
Lion Tamer	Ride a creature that's normally hostile.
Looking Ahead	Create 5 science-fiction objects or use 5 science-fiction adjectives.
Master Morpher	Apply 5 adjectives to an object.
Maxwell in Disguise	Play as a different avatar.
Mega Mutator	Apply 8 adjectives to an object.
Micronized	Create the smallest possible object.
Money Vault	Hold $10,000 in your bank.
Nice Wallet	Hold $5,000 in your bank.
Over Budget	Completely fill the budget meter.
Piggy Bank	Hold $1,000 in your bank.
Rad Recombiner	Apply 3 adjectives to an object.
Really Big Lizards	Create 5 dinosaurs.
Replay	Complete a level in Advanced mode.
Russian Doll	Put an object inside an object inside an object.
Sharpened Pencil	Use 25 unique adjectives.
Skin of Your Teeth	Catch a Starite while Maxwell is being defeated.
Starite Apprentice	Catch 10 Starites.
Starite King	Catch 121 Starites.
Starite Master	Catch 60 Starites.
Suit Up	Fully equip Maxwell.
Syllable Savant	Create 50 unique objects.
Teleported	Use the teleporter.
Texture Artist	Create 5 objects made out of altered materials.
The Fourth Wall	Apply the secret Super Scribblenauts adjective.

Welcome Mat	Set a custom level as your playground.
Well Used Pencil	Use 50 unique adjectives.
Window Shopper	Purchase 10 avatars.
Word Warrior	Create 300 unique objects.
Worn Down Pencil	Use 100 unique adjectives.
You Can Fly	Equip any flying gear or mount.

121ST STARITE

To find the missing 121st star, create a time machine and use it repeatedly until you are taken to a stage with another Maxwell and a Starite in a tree. This Starite is the last one you need to complete the game.

SUPER MEAT BOY (XBOX 360)

AVATAR AWARDS

UNLOCKABLE	HOW TO UNLOCK
Super Meat Boy (Male/Female)	Beat the Light World
Super Meat Boy T-Shirt (Male/Female)	Play the game for a few minutes

UNLOCKABLES

UNLOCKABLE	HOW TO UNLOCK
Teh Internets Chapter	Collect 20 bandages
Brownie Gamerpic	Beat Brownie in a race
Glitch Level	Reach Bandage Girl when her model is glitched in any level after defeating the chapter boss

CHARACTERS

UNLOCKABLE	HOW TO UNLOCK
4 Color Meat Boy	Collect 80 bandages
4Bit Meat Boy	Collect 60 bandages
8Bit Meat Boy	Collect 40 bandages
Alien Hominid	Collect 30 bandages
Commander Video (Bit Trip)	Warp Zone in World 1
Flywrench	Complete the Fly Guy! Warp zones 4–18
Gish	Collect 10 bandages
Jill (Mighty Jill Off)	Warp Zone in World 2
Meat Ninja	Achieve 100% completion
Ninja (N+)	Collect 100 bandages
Ogmo (Jumper)	Complete The Jump Man! Warp zones 3–16
Pink Knight (Castle Crashers)	Collect 90 bandages
Spelunky	Collect 70 bandages
The Kid (I Wanna Be the Guy)	Complete The Guy! Warp zone 5
Tim (Braid)	Collect 50 bandages

SUPER STREET FIGHTER IV (XBOX 360)

CHARACTER ICONS AND TITLES

There are a number of character specific icons and titles that are unlocked by clearing Arcade Mode and through each character's unique set of trials.

UNLOCKABLE	HOW TO UNLOCK
Blue Character Title	Clear Arcade with the character on any difficulty.
Character Icon #1	Complete any trial with the character.
Character Icon #2	Complete eight different trials with the character.
Character Icon #3	Complete 16 different trials with the character.
Character Icon #4	Complete all trials with the character.
Gold Character Title #1	Complete 12 different trials with the character.

UNLOCKABLE	HOW TO UNLOCK
Gold Character Title #2	Complete 14 different trials with the character.
Gold Character Title #3	Complete 18 different trials with the character.
Gold Character Title #4	Complete 20 different trials with the character.
Gold Character Title #5	Complete 22 different trials with the character.
Red Character Title	Clear Arcade with the character on the hardest difficulty.
Silver Character Title #1	Complete two different trials with the character.
Silver Character Title #2	Complete three different trials with the character.
Silver Character Title #3	Complete four different trials with the character.
Silver Character Title #4	Complete six different trials with the character.
Silver Character Title #5	Complete 10 different trials with the character.

ADDITIONAL COLORS AND TAUNTS (PERSONAL ACTIONS)

For each match you use a character on, you will unlock a new color and Personal Action or Taunt.

UNLOCKABLE	HOW TO UNLOCK
Color #10	Play 16 matches with the character.
Color #11	Start a game with a Street Fighter IV save file.
Color #12	Start a game with a Street Fighter IV save file.
Color #3	Play two matches with the character.
Color #4	Play four matches with the character.
Color #5	Play six matches with the character.
Color #6	Play eight matches with the character.
Color #7	Play 10 matches with the character.
Color #8	Play 12 matches with the character.
Color #9	Play 14 matches with the character.
Taunt #10	Play 16 matches with the character.
Taunt #2	Play one match with the character.
Taunt #3	Play three matches with the character.
Taunt #4	Play five matches with the character.
Taunt #5	Play seven matches with the character.
Taunt #6	Play nine matches with the character.
Taunt #7	Play 11 matches with the character.
Taunt #8	Play 13 matches with the character.
Taunt #9	Play 15 matches with the character.

UNLOCKABLES

UNLOCKABLE	HOW TO UNLOCK
Barrel Buster Bonus Stage	Beat Arcade Mode in any difficulty.
Car Crusher Bonus Stage	Beat Arcade Mode in any difficulty.
Color 11	Have saved data from Street Fighter IV.
Color 12	Have saved data carry over from the original Street Fighter IV.
Japanese Voices	Beat Arcade Mode in any difficulty.
Remixed Character BGM for Use in Battles	Earn "It Begins" achievement.

FIGHT GOUKEN IN ARCADE MODE

The following requirements must be met while playing Arcade Mode to fight Gouken, who will appear after the battle with Seth (in default settings, i.e., three rounds):

* Do not lose a single round.

* Perform five Super or Ultra Combo Finishes.

* Score two Perfect Rounds (not get hit a single time during a round)

* Connect 10 "First Hits" (when you're the first to connect a strike during a round).

SUPER STREET FIGHTER IV (PS3)

CHARACTER ICONS AND TITLES

There are a number of character specific icons and titles which are unlocked by clearing Arcade Mode and through each character's unique set of trials.

UNLOCKABLE	HOW TO UNLOCK
Blue Character Title	Clear Arcade with the character on any difficulty.
Character Icon #1	Complete any trial with the character.
Character Icon #2	Complete eight different trials with the character.
Character Icon #3	Complete 16 different trials with the character.
Character Icon #4	Complete all trials with the character.
Gold Character Title #1	Complete 12 different trials with the character.
Gold Character Title #2	Complete 14 different trials with the character.
Gold Character Title #3	Complete 18 different trials with the character.
Gold Character Title #4	Complete 20 different trials with the character.
Gold Character Title #5	Complete 22 different trials with the character.
Red Character Title	Clear Arcade with the character on the hardest difficulty.
Silver Character Title #1	Complete two different trials with the character.
Silver Character Title #2	Complete three different trials with the character.
Silver Character Title #3	Complete four different trials with the character.
Silver Character Title #4	Complete six different trials with the character.
Silver Character Title #5	Complete 10 different trials with the character.

ADDITIONAL COLORS AND TAUNTS (PERSONAL ACTIONS)

For each match you use a character on, you will unlock a new color and Personal Action or Taunt.

UNLOCKABLE	HOW TO UNLOCK
Color #10	Play 16 matches with the character.
Color #11	Start a game with a Street Fighter IV save file.
Color #12	Start a game with a Street Fighter IV save file.
Color #3	Play two matches with the character.
Color #4	Play four matches with the character.
Color #5	Play six matches with the character.
Color #6	Play eight matches with the character.
Color #7	Play 10 matches with the character.
Color #8	Play 12 matches with the character.
Color #9	Play 14 matches with the character.
Taunt #10	Play 16 matches with the character.
Taunt #2	Play one match with the character.
Taunt #3	Play three matches with the character.
Taunt #4	Play five matches with the character.
Taunt #5	Play seven matches with the character.
Taunt #6	Play nine matches with the character.
Taunt #7	Play 11 matches with the character.
Taunt #8	Play 13 matches with the character.
Taunt #9	Play 15 matches with the character.

UNLOCKABLES

UNLOCKABLE	HOW TO UNLOCK
Barrel Buster Bonus Stage	Beat Arcade Mode in any difficulty.
Car Crusher Bonus Stage	Beat Arcade Mode in any difficulty.
Color 11	Have saved data from Street Fighter IV.
Color 12	Have saved data carry over from the original Street Fighter IV.
Japanese Voices	Beat Arcade Mode in any difficulty.
Remixed Character BGM for Use in Battles	Earn "It Begins" achievement.

FIGHT GOUKEN IN ARCADE MODE

The following requirements must be met while playing Arcade Mode to fight Gouken, who will appear after the battle with Seth (in default settings, i.e., three rounds):

* Do not lose a single round.
* Perform five Super or Ultra Combo Finishes.
* Score two Perfect Rounds (not get hit a single time during a round).
* Connect 10 "First Hits" (when you're the first to connect a strike during a round).

TONY HAWK'S AMERICAN WASTELAND (XBOX 360)

CODES

Enter codes in the Options menu under "codes."

EFFECT	CODE
Helps you keep balance when grinding	grindXpert
Hitch a ride on the back of cars	h!tchar!de
Lil John	hip2DHop
Moon Gravity	2them00n
Perfect manuals	2wheels!
Play as Jason Ellis	sirius-DJ
Play as Mindy	help1nghand
Unlock legendary skater Matt Hoffman	the_condor

TOSHINDEN (Wii)

UNLOCKABLE CHARACTERS

UNLOCKABLE	HOW TO UNLOCK
Dan	Beat Story Mode on hard difficulty
Lilith	Beat Story Mode on any difficulty.
Moritz	Beat Story Mode on any difficulty.
Shouki	Beat Story Mode on hard difficulty.

TOY SOLDIERS (XBOX 360)

UNLOCKABLES

UNLOCKABLE	HOW TO UNLOCK
Gas Mask (Avatar Item)	Buy the game and play the first level on campaign.
Allied Toy Soldier Gamerpic	Play the first level after buying the game.
Central Toy Soldier Gamerpic	Destroy all 24 golden cubes.

TOY STORY 3 (Wii)

GOLD STARS

UNLOCKABLE	HOW TO UNLOCK
Amateur Bug Collector	Rescue three Caterpillars.
Amateur Ghost Sucker	Capture three ghosts with the Lightning Rod.
Amateur Haunter	Possess three townspeople.

Amateur Kicker	Drop-kick five townspeople.
Avid Customer	Collect all customizations for Haunted House, Enchanted Glen, and Zurg's Spaceport.
Big Spender	Spend 30,000.
Breaking Boards	Smash 25 crates and barrels.
Enchanted Sheriff	Complete all Enchanted Glen Missions.
Gone Wanderin'	Travel a long distance on foot.
Haunted Explorer	Find all prize capsules in Haunted House.
Having a Ball	Hit 30 things with a ball.
Jr Monster Slayer	Destroy five gargoyles.
Jr Pixie Torcher	Torch five pixies with the dragon.
Jr Re-animator	Create three zombie townspeople.
Jumpin' Jackrabbits!	Jumped a long distance with Bullseye.
Knock It Off	Clobber 10 mission givers.
Long Haul	Explore in a vehicle.
Master Grower	Make 10 things bigger.
Master Monster Slayer	Destroy 10 gargoyles.
Master Pixie Slayer	Defeat 10 pixies.
Master Re-animator	Create 10 zombie townspeople.
Master Shrinker	Make 10 things smaller.
Miner 49er	Mine 15 gold veins.
Mission Master	Complete 50 missions.
On A Mission	Complete 10 missions.
Parachute King	Hit 15 paratrooper targets.
Power Shopper	Buy 10 things from the catalog.
Prize Capsule Collector	Collect 15 prize capsules.
Prize Capsule Enthusiast	Collect 25 prize capsules.
Pro Kicker	Drop-kick 10 townspeople.
Ridin' the Range	Travel a long distance on Bullseye.
Riding the Rails	Slide a long distance on the rails.
Rolly Polly	Do 40 barrel rolls in a vehicle.
Saddle the Dragon	Travel a long distance on the dragon.
Saving Up	Earn more than 30,000 gold.
Sheriff of the Future	Complete all Zurg's Spaceport missions.
Space Explorer	Find all prize capsules in the Spaceport.
Spooky Sheriff	Find all prize capsules in the Haunted House.
Strongman	Carry a heavy object for a long distance.
Swimming Lessons	Throw five townspeople into the water.
Triple Flusher	Flush outhouse three times.
Under the Sea	Jump in the water 10 times.
Wand Waver	Give wings to 10 things.
Winner's Circle	Attempt 20 Bullseye races.
Woodland Explorer	Found all prize capsules by the rainbows
Zurg Bot Destroyer	Destroy 10 Zurg bots.
Zurg Bot Smasher	Destroy three Zurg bots.

TRANSFORMERS: WAR FOR CYBERTRON (XBOX 360)

UNLOCKABLES

Unlockable characters are available for Escalation Mode and Multiplayer.

UNLOCKABLE	HOW TO UNLOCK
Arcee	Complete the Autobot campaign to unlock this character.
Slipstream	Complete the Decepticon campaign to unlock this character.

GLITCH

Finish a level on Easy or Normal, then reload the final checkpoint of the mission and go to the Select screen, change the difficulty to Hard, finish the level again and the game credits you with finishing the whole level on Hard.

TRANSFORMERS: WAR FOR CYBERTRON (PS3)

UNLOCKABLES

Unlockable characters are available for Escalation Mode and Multi-player.

UNLOCKABLE	HOW TO UNLOCK
Arcee	Complete the Autobot campaign to unlock this character.
Slipstream	Complete the Decepticon campaign to unlock this character.

TRINITY UNIVERSE (PS3)

UNLOCKABLES

UNLOCKABLE	HOW TO UNLOCK
New Game+	Successfully complete the game to unlock New Game+. It lets you play the game again with all the items (including abilities, equipment, Managraphics, meteorites, recipes), money, and Universe Rank from your previous games. Unfortunately, all the unlocked characters and the level of all characters will be gone.

TRINITY UNIVERSE (Wii)

UNLOCKABLES

UNLOCKABLE	HOW TO UNLOCK
Unlock EX form of characters	Get 10 or more wins in Survival mode in Single Battle. To use a character's EX form, press left or right on the Character Select screen.
Unlock images from Gallery mode	Beat Story mode using two characters from the same franchise to unlock the first three rows of images. To obtain the other images, beat Story mode using the same method but in their EX form.
Unlockable narrators (system voices)	Beat All Battle mode with any character to unlock their voice in the System Voice option in the Sound Settings.

TRON EVOLUTION (XBOX 360)

UNLOCKABLES

UNLOCKABLE	HOW TO UNLOCK
Insane mode	Beat the story mode on Hard without changing the difficulty

TRON EVOLUTION (PSP)

CODES

Enter the codes on the Code menu. These codes are case sensitive.

EFFECT	CODE
Unlock Rectifier Disc Battle Arena for Quickplay	Endofline

TRON EVOLUTION: BATTLE GRIDS (Wii)

CODES

These are typed in the Cheat Code menu.

EFFECT	CODE
Makes your lightcycle trails taller	lctalltrails
Sharp sliding turns for light cycle arena	lcsupersharpslide

TWO WORLDS II (XBOX 360)

CODES

Pause the game and enter the code at "Enter Bonus Code."

EFFECT	CODE
Anathros Sword	6770-8976-1634-9490
Axe	1775-3623-3298-1928
Dragon Armor	4149-3083-9823-6545
Elexorie	3542-3274-8350-6064
Hammer	6231-1890-4345-5988
Lucienda Sword	9122-5287-3591-0927
Scroll	6972-5760-7685-8477

VANQUISH (XBOX 360)

UNLOCKABLES

UNLOCKABLE	HOW TO UNLOCK
Unlock God Hard Difficulty	Rotate right analog stick clockwise 20 times at the title screen.

WWE SMACKDOWN VS. RAW 2011 (Wii)

CODES

You can access the cheat code menu by going to "My WWE," then "Options," then "Cheat Codes."

EFFECT	CODE
John Cena Street Fight gear and Avatar T-Shirt	SLURPEE
Randy Orton Alternate Attire	apexpredator
"Tribute to the Troops" arena	8thannualtribute

WWE SMACKDOWN VS. RAW 2011 (XBOX360)

CODES

You can access the cheat code menu by going to "My WWE," then "Options," then "Cheat Codes."

EFFECT	CODE
John Cena Street Fight gear and Avatar T-Shirt	SLURPEE
Randy Orton Alternate Attire	apexpredator
"Tribute to the Troops" arena	8thannualtribute

UNLOCKABLES

UNLOCKABLE	HOW TO UNLOCK
ECW Create Modes Content	Hold 10 matches in Exhibition Mode
Edge/Christian custom entrance (as seen in Christian's RTWM)	In Christian's RTWM, between Weeks 10 and 12, cash in the money in the bank against Edge and win
Backlash	Win once at Backlash with any superstar (WWE Universe, select match, not custom)
Bragging Rights	Win once at Bragging Rights with any superstar (WWE Universe, select match, not custom)
Breaking Point	Win once at Breaking Point with any superstar (WWE Universe, select match, not custom)
Druid Arena	Complete all 5 RTWMs
ECW	Win once at SummerSlam with any superstar (WWE Universe, select match, not custom)
Extreme Rules	Win once at Extreme Rules with any superstar (WWE Universe, select match, not custom)
Hell In A Cell	Win once at Hell In A Cell with any superstar (WWE Universe, select match, not custom)

UNLOCKABLE	HOW TO UNLOCK
Judgment Day	Win once at Royal Rumble with any superstar (WWE Universe, select match, not custom)
Night of Champions	Win once at Night of Champions with any superstar (WWE Universe, select match, not custom)
Survivor Series	Win once at Survivor Series with any superstar (WWE Universe, select match, not custom)
The Bash	Win once at the Bash with any superstar (WWE Universe, select match, not custom)
TLC	Win once at TLC with any superstar (WWE Universe, select match, not custom)
Tribute to the Troops	Win once at WrestleMania XXVI with any superstar (WWE Universe, select match, not custom)
Batista (Civilian)	In Jericho's RTWM, win against Kofi, Henry, and Batista in Week 8
Edge (Civilian)	In Christian's RTWM, defeat Big Show in a locker room area during Elimination Chamber
Jake the Snake Roberts	In week 9 of the vs Undertaker RTWM, win your match with minimal damage taken
Masked Kane Attire	In week 11 of the vs Undertaker RTWM, win your match
Mickie James	When Vince McMahon says you have to wrestle Mickie James after you've won a match, defeat Mickie James and she'll be unlocked for play.
MVP (Civilian)	In Cena's RTWM, win both Week 5 and Week 7 Tag Team Challenge Match against R-Truth and Mike Knox.
Paul Bearer	In week 12 of the vs Undertaker RTWM, knock him out backstage in less than 90 seconds.
Play as Finlay	When Vince McMahon says you have to wrestle Finlay after you've won a match, defeat Finlay and he'll be unlocked for play.
Play as Vladimir Kozlov	When Vince McMahon says you have to wrestle Kozlov after you've won a match, defeat Kozlov and he'll be unlocked for play.
Ricky "The Dragon" Steambot	In week 12 of Jericho's RTWM, defeat him in a singles match.
Rob Van Dam	Complete Rey Mysterio's RTWM
Superfly Jimmy Snuka	In week 10 of the vs Undertaker RTWM, win your match in less than 3 minutes.
Ted DiBiase (T-Shirt)	In Cena's RTWM, defeat Ted DiBiase to win the Week 11 Tag Team Challenge against Ted DiBiase and Cody Rhodes.
Terry Funk	Defeat him at Wrestlemania in Rey Mysterio's RTWM.
The Rock	In week 12 of the vs Undertaker RTWM, you can find the Rock in the food room, and you have to win the match against him to get him.
Todo Americano attire for Jack Swagger	Perform your finisher against him in Rey Mysterio's RTWM
Triple H (Civilian)	In Jericho's RTWM, during Week 6, escape to the parking lot without losing to Triple H.
Zack Ryder	Win a Falls Count Anywhere Match in WWE Universe.

YU-GI-OH! 5D'S WORLD CHAMPIONSHIP 2010 REVERSE OF ARCADIA (DS)

CLOTHES AND DUEL DISKS

UNLOCKABLE	HOW TO UNLOCK
Academia Disk (Blue)	Buy for five star chips from Chihiro.
Academia Disk (Red)	Buy for five star chips from Chihiro.
Academia Disk (Yellow)	Buy for five star chips from Chihiro.

Black Bird Disk	Beat Crow 10 times in Turbo Duels.
Black Chain Disk	Defeat each level of the single tournament once.
Black Jail Disk	Win all levels of Tournament Mode.
Career Suit	Box item found in the southwest room of the Securities building.
Dark magician outfit	Defeat the duel runner owners 10 times.
Dark Singer	Buy for 15 star chips from Chihiro after beating the main story.
Dark Singer Disk	Buy for 10 star chips from Chihiro after beating the main story.
Denim Jacket	Buy for five Star Chips from Chihiro if male.
K.C. Mass Production Disk	Buy for five star chips from Chihiro.
King Replica Model	Beat Jack 10 times in both duels and Turbo Duels.
Leo's Custom Disk	Beat Leo and Luna in 10 Tag Duels.
Luna's Custom Disk	End three duels in a draw.
One-piece	Buy for five star chips from Chihiro if female.
Race Queen	Buy for five star chips from Chihiro if female.
Rock N' Roller	Box item found inside the third duel gang's hideout if male.
Rose Disk	Box item found in the southwest room of the Securities building.
Rough Style	Box item found in the basement of the first duel gang's hideout.
Sailor Uniform	Box item found inside Zeman's castle if female.
Security Disk	Securities' building, northeast room
Security Helmet	60% card completion
Security Uniform	Given to you by Crow during Chapter 2.
Stuffed Collar Uniform	Box item found inside Zeman's castle if male.
Tag Force Set	100% card completion
The Enforcers	Unlocked automatically at the start of Chapter 2.
Wheel of Fortune (Disk)	Beat Jack 10 times in both duels and Turbo Duels.
Wild Style	Buy for five Star Chips from Chihiro if male.
Witch's dress	Defeat Akiza 10 times in a Turbo Duel.
Worn-out Clothes	Box item found inside the third duel gang's hideout if female.
Yusei Jacket	Beat Yusei 10 times in Turbo Duels.
Yusei's Hybrid Disk	Beat Yusei 10 times.

CPU OPPONENTS

Fulfill the following conditions to unlock CPU opponents for World Championship Mode. Teams not listed are either unlocked from the start, or unlocked by progressing through Story Mode.

UNLOCKABLE	HOW TO UNLOCK
Ancient Gear Gadjiltron Dragon	Summon Ancient Gear Gadjiltron Dragon.
Archlord Kristya	Beat "Green Baboon, Defender of the Forest" three times.
Blackwing-Vayu the Emblem of Honor	Summon Blackwing-Silverwind the Ascendant.
Blue-Eyes White Dragon	Beat "Darklord Desire" three times.
Chaos Sorcerer	Beat "Solar Flare Dragon" three times.
Crusader of Endymion	Activate Mega Ton Magical Cannon.
Cyber Eltanin	Beat "B.E.S. Big Core MK-2" three times.

UNLOCKABLE	HOW TO UNLOCK
Dark Simorgh	Beat "Great Shogun Shien" three times.
Darkness Neosphere	Play for 100 hours.
Destiny End Dragoon	Beat "Underground Arachnid" three times.
Dragunity Knight-Gadearg	Beat "Ancient Fairy Dragon" three times.
Earthbound Immortal Wiraqocha Rasca	Win with by using the effect of Final Countdown.
Elemental Hero Absolute Zero	Beat "Fabled Leviathan" three times.
Elemental Hero Neos	Beat "Ancient Sacred Wyvern" three times.
Explosive Magician	Beat "Ally of Justice Decisive Armor" three times.
Fabled Ragin	Beat "Evil Hero Dark Gaia" three times.
Fossil Dyna Pachycephalo	Have 666 or more Summons.
Garlandolf, King of Destruction	Play for 50 hours.
Gigaplant	Summon Perfectly Ultimate Great Moth.
Gladiator Beast Gyzarus	Summon Gladiator Beast Heraklinos.
Gravekeeper's Visionary	Beat "Jurrac Meteor" three times.
Green Gadget	Beat "Power Tool Dragon" three times.
Harpie Queen	Win by using the effect of Vennominaga the Deity of Poisonous Snakes.
Hundred Eyes Dragon	Beat "Ojama Yellow" three times.
Judgment Dragon	Summon Judgment Dragon.
Locomotion R-Genex	Summon Flying Fortress Sky Fire.
Lonefire Blossom	Beat "Gungnir, Dragon of the Ice Barrier" three times.
Majestic Red Dragon	Summon Majestic Red Dragon.
Naturia Beast	Beat "Reptilianne Vaskii" three times.
Raiza the Storm Monarch	Beat "Lava Golem" three times.
Stardust Dragon /Assault Mode	Unlock 50% or more Duel Bonuses.
Supersonic Skull Flame	Beat "Mist Valley Apex Avian" three times.
Swap Frog	Beat "The Dark Creator" three times.
The Immortal Bushi	Beat "Naturia Landoise" three times
Worm Zero	Highest damage is 10,000 or more.
XX-Saber Hyunlei	Win 10 duels in a row.

TAG TEAMS

Fulfill the following conditions to unlock CPU Teams for Tag Duel in World Championship Mode. Teams not listed are either unlocked from the start, or unlocked automatically as you progress through Story Mode.

UNLOCKABLE	HOW TO UNLOCK
Child of Chaos	Beat Team "Water & Fire" three times.
Cyber Regeneration	Beat Team "Angels & The Fallen" three times.
Dragon & Dragon	Summon Five-Headed Dragon.
Dual Duel	Beat Team "Removal Guys" three times.
Duel Ritual	Complete 300 Single Duels.
E & D Impact	Beat Team "Darkness + Fiends" three times.
Earthbound Crystal	Summon Rainbow Dragon.
Fish-the-World	Have 200 Spells and Traps activated.
Gadget Emperor	Complete 150 Tag Duels.
Grinder Summoning	Beat Team "Explosive Tag" three times.

Legend's Anniversary	Beat Team "Love Reptiles " three times.
Lo and Behold	Beat Team "Protect & Burn" three times.
Mausoleum's Legend	Beat Team "Order in Chaos" three times.
Simochi Study	Beat Team "Cyber Dragunity" three times.
Storm of Darkness	Beat Team "Fusion & Synchro" three times.
To the Graveyard	Complete 75 Turbo Duels.
Trago Genex	Summon VWXYZ-Dragon Catapult Cannon.
Zombie Path	Win by attacking with Skull Servant.

DUEL RUNNERS

UNLOCKABLE	HOW TO UNLOCK
Blackbird (crow's d-wheel)	Unlock every other frame.
Chariot Frame	Beat the headless ghost in a duel (speak to Trudge after completing Story Mode).
Giganto L (Kalins duel runner)	Buy for 40 star chips from Chihiro after beating the main story.
Wheel of Fortune D-Wheel Frame	Clear all Duel Runner Race battles courses with S Rank.
Yusei D-Wheel Frame	Clear all Duel Runner Race Time courses with S Rank.

ZOMBIE APOCALYPSE (XBOX 360)

UNLOCKABLE

UNLOCKABLE	HOW TO UNLOCK
Chainsaw Only Mode	Complete a day with only a chainsaw.
Hardcore Mode	Survive for seven consecutive days.
Turbo Mode	Achieve a multiplier over 100.

ZOMBIE APOCALYPSE (PlayStation 3)

UNLOCKABLE

UNLOCKABLE	HOW TO UNLOCK
Chainsaw Only Mode	Complete a day with only a chainsaw.
Hardcore Mode	Survive for seven consecutive days.
Turbo Mode	Achieve a multiplier over 100.

ZOMBIE PANIC IN WONDERLAND (Wii)

UNLOCKABLE

UNLOCKABLE	HOW TO UNLOCK
Alice	Beat Story Mode twice
Bunny Girl Snow White	Beat Story Mode three times.
Dorothy	Reach Stage 2-1 in Story Mode.
Little Red Riding Hood	Beat Story Mode four times.
Snow White	Reach Stage 3-2 in Story Mode.
Survival Stage in Arcade Mode (Pirate Ship)	Beat Story Mode once.

.HACK//PART 2: MUTATION (PlayStation 2)

UNLOCKABLE	CODE
DVD EASTER EGG	On the companion DVD, from the Title Menu—select Data, highlight Gallery, press ➔, then enter/confirm your selection.

.HACK//PART 4: QUARANTINE (PlayStation 2)

UNLOCKABLE	OBJECTIVE
Parody Mode	Complete the game once.

18 WHEELER AMERICAN PRO TRUCKER (PlayStation 2)

UNLOCKABLE	CODE
Extra Truck	At the Start screen, hold any button and press START.

1942: JOINT STRIKE (XBOX 360)

SECRET PLANE

Beat the game on Wing King Difficulty setting, then select Shinden in the Plane Selection screen by pressing "Y." This enables you to use a black and red version of the Shinden with maxed out power.

300: MARCH TO GLORY (PSP)

Enter this code while the game is paused.

UNLOCKABLE	CODE
25,000 Kleos	⇩, ⇦, ⇩, ⇦, ⇧, ⇦

50 CENT: BLOOD ON THE SAND (PlayStation 3)

UNLOCKABLES

Accessed through the Unlockables menu.

UNLOCKABLE	HOW TO UNLOCK
Infinite Ammo	Earn 52 medals/badges in Story mode.
Infinite Grenades	Earn 56 medals/badges in Story mode.

50 CENT BULLETPROOF (XBOX)

To enter these passwords, pause the game. Go into Options, then enter the Cheat menu.

UNLOCKABLE	PASSWORD
Action 26	orangejuice
All Music Tracks	GrabAllThat50
All Music Videos	HookMeUp50
All Weapons	GotThemRachets
Bloodhound Counterkill	gunrunner
Bulletproof aka Invincible	ny'sfinestyo
Empty n' Clips Counterkill	workout
"G'd Up" Counterkill	GoodDieYoung
"Guillotine" Counterkill	GettingDropped
Infinite Ammo	GrizzSpecial
Mike Mode	the hub is broken
My Buddy video	sayhellotomylittlefriend

So Seductive video	yayoshome Tony Yayo
"Wanksta" Counter-Kill	AintGotNothin

50 CENT BULLETPROOF (PlayStation 2)

To enter these passwords, pause the game. Go into Options, then enter the Cheat menu.

UNLOCKABLE	PASSWORD
Action 26	orangejuice
All Music Tracks	GrabAllThat50
All Music Videos	HookMeUp50
All Weapons	GotThemRachets
Bloodhound Counterkill	gunrunner
Bulletproof aka Invincible	ny'sfinestyo
Empty n' Clips Counterkill	workout
"G'd Up" Counterkill	GoodDieYoung
"Guillotine" Counterkill	GettingDropped
Infinite Ammo	GrizzSpecial
Mike Mode	the hub is broken
My Buddy video	sayhellotomylittlefriend
So Seductive video	yayoshome Tony Yayo
"Wanksta" Counter-Kill	AintGotNothin

A BOY AND HIS BLOB (Wii)

UNLOCKABLES

UNLOCKABLE	HOW TO UNLOCK
Bonus Content	Complete a Challenge Level to unlock bonus content that is accessible from the hideout.
Challenge Levels	Find all three treasure chests in a regular level to unlock a Challenge Level that is accessible from the hideout.

ACTRAISER (Wii)

HIDDEN EXTRA LIVES

Do the following to find four hidden extra lives in the game's towns.

TOWN	ACTION
Fillmore	When you get the Compass, use it here.
Bloodpool	Make it rain over the big lake.
Kasandora	Cause an earthquake after uncovering the pyramid.
Northwall	Strike the town's shrine with a lightning bolt.

PROFESSIONAL MODE

UNLOCKABLE	HOW TO UNLOCK
Professional Mode	First, beat the game. Then on the title screen, highlight "New Game" and press ✚ or SELECT.

ADVENT RISING (XBOX)

Enter this code while the game is paused.

UNLOCKABLE	CODE
Cheat menu	Up, Up, Down, Down, Left, Right, Left, Right, WHT, BLK, X

To enter this code, select a spot for a 'new game'. After you do that, enter this code.

UNLOCKABLE	CODE
Unlock all levels and cutscenes	BLK, WHT, BLK, WHT, X

ADVENTURE ISLAND (Wii)

PASSWORDS

PASSWORD	EFFECT
3WSURYXZY763TE	Advanced items/abilities
RMAYTJEOPHALUP	Disable sounds
NODEGOSOOOOOOO	Start the game as Hu man
3YHURYW7Y7LL8C	Start the game as Hawk man
3YHURYW7Y7LRBW	Start the game as Lizard man
3YHURYW7Y7LN84	Start the game as Piranha man
3YHURYW7Y7LK88	Start the game as Tiger man

ADVENTURES OF LOLO (Wii)

LEVEL PASSWORDS

PASSWORD	EFFECT
BCBT	Level 1-2
BDBR	Level 1-3
BGBQ	Level 1-4
BHBP	Level 1-5
BJBM	Level 2-1
BKBL	Level 2-2
BLBK	Level 2-3
BMBJ	Level 2-4
BPBH	Level 2-5
BQBG	Level 3-1
BRBD	Level 3-2
BTBC	Level 3-3
BVBB	Level 3-4
BYZZ	Level 3-5
BZZY	Level 4-1
CBZV	Level 4-2
CCZT	Level 4-3
CDZR	Level 4-4
CGZQ	Level 4-5
CHZP	Level 5-1
CJZM	Level 5-2
CKZL	Level 5-3
CLZK	Level 5-4
CMZJ	Level 5-5
CPZH	Level 6-1
CQZG	Level 6-2
CRZD	Level 6-3
CTZC	Level 6-4
CVZB	Level 6-5
CYYZ	Level 7-1
CZYY	Level 7-2
DBYV	Level 7-3
DCYT	Level 7-4
DDYR	Level 7-5
DGYQ	Level 8-1
DHYP	Level 8-2
DJYM	Level 8-3
DKYL	Level 8-4

DLYK	Level 8-5
DMYJ	Level 9-1
DPYH	Level 9-2
DQYG	Level 9-3
DRYD	Level 9-4
DTYC	Level 9-5
DVYB	Level 10-1
DYVZ	Level 10-2
DZVY	Level 10-3
GBVV	Level 10-4
GCVT	Level 10-5

LEVEL SKIP

UNLOCKABLE	HOW TO UNLOCK
Level Skip	This only works if you have a password that starts with A, B, C, or D and if the second letter in the password appears earlier in the alphabet than the fourth letter. If so, switch the second and fourth letters in the password. Use the new password to start at a level one higher than the original.

ADVENTURES OF LOLO 2 (Wii)

NEW DIFFICULTY LEVELS

PASSWORD	EFFECT
PPHP	Floor 01, Room 1
PHPK	Floor 01, Room 2
PQPD	Floor 01, Room 3
PVPT	Floor 01, Room 4
PRPJ	Floor 01, Room 5
PZPC	Floor 02, Room 1
PGPG	Floor 02, Room 2
PCPZ	Floor 02, Room 3
PLPY	Floor 02, Room 4
PBPM	Floor 02, Room 5
PYPL	Floor 03, Room 1
PMPB	Floor 03, Room 2
PJPR	Floor 03, Room 3
PTPV	Floor 03, Room 4
PDPQ	Floor 03, Room 5
PKPH	Floor 04, Room 1
HPPP	Floor 04, Room 2
HHKK	Floor 04, Room 3
HQKD	Floor 04, Room 4
HVKT	Floor 04, Room 5
HRKJ	Floor 05, Room 1
HBKM	Floor 05, Room 2
HLKY	Floor 05, Room 3
HCKZ	Floor 05, Room 4
HGKG	Floor 05, Room 5
HZKC	Floor 06, Room 1
HYKL	Floor 06, Room 2
HMKB	Floor 06, Room 3

HJKR	Floor 06, Room 4
HTKV	Floor 06, Room 5
HDKQ	Floor 07, Room 1
HKKH	Floor 07, Room 2
QPKP	Floor 07, Room 3
QHDK	Floor 07, Room 4
QQDD	Floor 07, Room 5
QVDT	Floor 08, Room 1
QRDJ	Floor 08, Room 2
QBDM	Floor 08, Room 3
QLDY	Floor 08, Room 4
QCDZ	Floor 08, Room 5
QGDG	Floor 09, Room 1
QZDC	Floor 09, Room 2
QYDL	Floor 09, Room 3
QMDB	Floor 09, Room 4
QJDR	Floor 09, Room 5
QTDV	Floor 10, Room 1
QDDQ	Floor 10, Room 2
QKDH	Floor 10, Room 3
VPDP	Floor 10, Room 4
VHTK	Floor 10, Room 5
VQTD	Last Level

AGASSI TENNIS GENERATION (PlayStation 2)

UNLOCKABLE	CODE
All Players	In the Main menu, press R2, L2, L3, ●, ×, ●.

AGE OF EMPIRES: MYTHOLOGIES (DS)

UNLOCKABLES

UNLOCKABLE	HOW TO UNLOCK
Ladon the Lamia	Beat the Greek campaign.
Setekh	Beat the Egyptian campaign.

AIR ZONK (Wii)

CODES

UNLOCKABLE	HOW TO UNLOCK
Expert Mode	On the Configuration screen, hold ✚ and press SELECT
Sound Test	Hold ① and ② and SELECT as you turn on the game

ALEX KIDD IN THE ENCHANTED CASTLE (Wii)

SKIP BOSS SEQUENCES

UNLOCKABLE	HOW TO UNLOCK
Skip Boss Sequences	Wait until the conversation with the boss has ended. After that, Press START to get to the Options screen, then press START again and you should skip the sequence.

ALEX RIDER: STORMBREAKER (DS)

Enter the password screen from the main menu and input the following.

PASSWORD	EFFECT
JESSICA PARKER	Allows you to purchase black belt
6943059	Allows you to purchase disk 6 after completing game

VICTORIA PARR	Allows you to purchase M16 badge
RENATO CELANI	Allows you to purchase the fugu
SARYL HIRSCH	Allows you to purchase the sunglasses
9785711	Allows you to select level HARD
4298359	Everything at shop is at half price!
9603717	Gallery is added to Secret mode
5204025	Get 10,000 spy points
6894098	Outfit change is added to Secret mode

ALIAS (XBOX)

LEVEL SELECT

Successfully complete the game, then enter the code below

CODE	EFFECT
Hold (L3)+(RB)+(BLK)+(WHT)	Level select

ALIEN CRUSH (Wii)

BONUS

UNLOCKABLE	HOW TO UNLOCK
1 Million Points + Bonus Ball	Get to the bonus round with skulls and green aliens. Kill everything except for one skull. Keep going until a pterodactyl appears. Hit the pterodactyl with the ball to get a million points and a bonus ball once the stage is cleared.

ALIEN HOMINID (PlayStation 2)

Use the following passwords to unlock additional hats. Sound confirms correct entry.

HAT DESCRIPTION	CODE
Flowers Hat	Grrl
Abe Lincoln Hat	Abe
Hunting Hat	Cletus
Blonde Wig Hat	April
Afro Hat	Superfly
Slick Hair Hat	Goodman
Crazy Hair Hat	Tomfulp
Tiara Hat	Princess

ALIEN HOMINID HD (XBOX 360)

UNLOCKABLE HATS

To unlock each hat do the following. Note: you must finish the level for it to unlock. Just doing the task isn't enough.

UNLOCKABLE	HOW TO UNLOCK
Area 51 Agent Hat	Beat 3-2
Black Afro	Beat 1-5
Blond Wig/Pearls	Beat 1-2
Brown Hair	On Hard, jump off the spaceship before the screen fades after beating the final boss
Brown Hat	In 2-5, kill 7 birds
UNLOCKABLE	**HOW TO UNLOCK**
Brown Wig/Pearls	Beat 1-3
Chef Hat	Beat 1-3
Conical Purple Hat	In 1-3, destroy "Castle of Crap" building
Crown of Flowers	1-1 with gore off
Daisy-petal	Beat 2-3
Jester's Cap	Beat 3-4 on Hard

Jheri Curl	In 1-4 destroy "fish are like plants" building
KGB Agent Hat	Beat 2-1
Nurse Cap	In 3-5, get to final boss (don't have to win)
Pirate Hat	1-1 destroy "Hairy Mommy Daycare"
Private Eye hat	Beat 3-2 on Hard
Red Bandana	Beat 1-4
Rooster Hat	In 1-4 destroy the Behemoth-logo building (must be out of tank)
Stove Pipe Hat	1-1 with gore off
Tiara	2-2 on Hard
Yellow Shark Fin	In 2-4 dig/suffocate before riding snowmobile

ALIEN SOLDIER (Wii)

LEVEL PASSWORDS

PASSWORD	EFFECT
1985	Level 1
3698	Level 2
0257	Level 3
3745	Level 4
7551	Level 5
8790	Level 6
5196	Level 7
4569	Level 8
8091	Level 9
8316	Level 10
6402	Level 11
9874	Level 12
1930	Level 13
2623	Level 14
6385	Level 15
7749	Level 16
3278	Level 17
1039	Level 18
9002	Level 19
2878	Level 20
3894	Level 21
4913	Level 22
2825	Level 23
7406	Level 24
5289	Level 25

ALIEN SYNDROME (Wii)

UNLOCK EXTRA DIFFICULTIES

UNLOCKABLE	HOW TO UNLOCK
Unlock Expert Difficulty	Beat the game on Hard difficulty
Unlock Hard Difficulty	Beat the game on Normal difficulty

ALIENS VS. PREDATOR: EXTINCTION (XBOX)

UNLOCKABLE	CODE
Cheats	Pause the game and press RT, RT, LT, RT, LT, LT, RT, LT, RT, RT, LT, RT, LT, LT, RT, LT. The cheats are now available via the Options menu.

ALONE IN THE DARK (XBOX 360)

ACHIEVEMENTS

UNLOCKABLE	HOW TO UNLOCK
A Day in Central Park	Complete the game.
Basic Combination	A bottle with tape.
Blackout	Finish Episode 1 without skipping any sequence.
Blazing Roots	Burn all roots of evil.
Bloody Mary	Heal 5 bleeding wounds.
Burning Root	Burn a root of evil.
Car Thievery	Break into a locker car by shattering the window.
Cockpit Addict	Complete the 59th Street run with Episode 2 in cockpit view.
Cocoon	Burn a monster cocoon.
Countdown to Death	Stop your bleeding wound.
Demolition Expert	Build the most destructive weapon.
Eradication	Kill 100 Humanz.
Fight Back and Loss	Finish Episode 4 without skipping any sequence.
Fire Bullets	Make Fire Bullet by combining fuel with your pistol.
Fisherman's Foe	Shoot a goldfish in one of the Central Park ponds.
Fissure	Burn one of the snaking fissures.
Flaming Roots	Burn half of the roots of evil.
Free Gasoline	Pierce a car gas tank with a knife or screwdriver and fill a bottle with fuel.
Goal!	Give 10 kicks to Bugz.
Handyman Carnby	Make all possible combinations in the inventory.
Hidden Cave	Discover what's under the blockhouse in Episode 8.
Massage	Save Sarah from a cocoon.
Meet Again	Meet Theo in Room 943 in the museum.
Never Leave a Key Here	Find car keys in the sun visor.
Not Alone Anymore	Finish Episode 5 without skipping any sequence.
Nuke	Kill 3 Humanz with a single attack.
Painful Answers	Finish Episode 3 without skipping any sequence.
Purification by Fire	Destroy a Vampirz Nest.
Questions	Finish Episode 2 without skipping any sequence.
Stuntman	Jump across the gap in front of the museum using the tow truck.
The 10 Miles Race	Drive at least 10 miles in a vehicle.
The Air Bomb	Shoot a bottle filled with flammable content out of the air.
The Biggest of All	Defeat the monster at the end of the Episode 5.
The Blind Man	Finish the "Wake up" sequence in the beginning of the game without closing your eyes.
UNLOCKABLE	HOW TO UNLOCK
The Cocktail Molotov	Combine a bottle with flammable content with handkerchief.
The Glowstick Bomb	Tape a glowstick to a fuel-filled bottle.
The Light Bringer	Finish Episode 8 without skipping any sequence.
The Path of Darkness	Kill Sarah.
The Path of Light	Don't kill Sarah.
The Path of Light	Finish Episode 7 without skipping any sequence.

The Sharp Shooter	Finish a monster by shooting its fissures with fire bullets.
The Smart Fighter	Kill a monster with spray + lighter combination.
The Sticky Bomb	Combine a bottle filled with flammable content with tape and use it against an enemy.
The Truth	Finish Episode 6 without skipping any sequence.
Toasted Eggs	Burn a Bugz nest.
Unlimited Offer	Call all contacts in your phone's address book.
Useless!	Combine an empty taped bottle, a wick, and an emergency flare.
Vampirz	Burn a Vampirz.
Wired	Hotwire a car.

ALONE IN THE DARK: INFERNO (PlayStation 3)

CODES

Enter the following code (combination of Action Buttons and D-Pad) in the game, when in third-person view and without anything in the hands. Entering the same code again will disable the Infinite Ammo Cheat.

EFFECT	CODE
Infinite Ammo Enabled	▲,●,⇩,■,↑,→,↓,←,▲,■,×,●,↑,←,↓,→

ALTER ECHO (PlayStation 2)

Enter the following codes during gameplay.

UNLOCKABLE	CODE
Restore Health	↑,↑,↓,↓,←,→,←,→,L3 +→
Restore Time Dilation	↑,↑,↓,↓,←,→,←,→,L3 +↑

ALTERED BEAST (Wii)

CODES

Enter these on the title screen.

UNLOCKABLE	HOW TO UNLOCK
Beast Select	Hold Ⓐ+Ⓑ+Ⓒ+✚ and then press START
Character Kicks Credits	When the credits are being displayed on the screen after you have beaten the game, you can control your character to kick away the credited names
Continue from Last Stage Played	Hold Ⓐ and press SELECT after a Game Over
Level Select	Press Ⓑ and START
Sound Test	Hold Ⓐ+Ⓒ+✚ and then press START

AMPED 2 (XBOX)

Go to Options and enter the following codes in the Cheats menu.

UNLOCKABLE	CODE
All Courses Are Icy	AllIce
All Secret Boarders	AllMyPeeps
Cheats Are Deactivated	NoCheats
Low Gravity	LowGravity
Max Out Rider Stats	MaxSkills
No Collisions with Other Riders	NoCollisions
Open All Levels	AllLevels
Rider Moves Faster	FastMove
Rider Never Crashes	DontCrash
Spin Faster	SuperSpin
Unlock a Pink Bunny	Bunny

AMPED 3 (XBOX 360)

At the Main menu, go into Options, then into the Cheats menu to enter this code.

UNLOCKABLE	CODE
All Sleds	(RT), (X), (LT), D-pad ↓, D-pad →, (LB), (LT), (RT), (Y), (X)

ANIMANIACS: LIGHTS, CAMERA, ACTION! (DS)

To activate a cheat, pause the game and enter the code, then un-pause the game.

CHEAT CODES

CODE	EFFECT
(L), (R), ←, ←, ↑, ↑	Disable Time
→, →, →, ←, ←, ←, (R), (L)	Kingsize Pickups
(L), (L), (R), (R), ↓, ↓	Skip Level
Wakko, Wakko, Wakko, Wakko, Wakko	Level 1
Dot, Yakko, Brain, Wakko, Pinky	Level 2
Yakko, Dot, Wakko, Wakko, Brain	Level 3
Pinky, Yakko, Yakko, Dot, Brain	Level 4
Pinky, Pinky, Yakko, Wakko, Wakko	Level 5
Brain, Dot, Brain, Pinky, Yakko	Level 6
Brain, Pinky, Wakko, Pinky, Brain	Level 7
Brain Pinky, Pinky, Wakko, Wakko	Level 8
Dot, Dot, Yakko, Pinky, Wakko	Level 9
Brain, Dot, Brain, Yakko, Wakko	Level 10
Akko, Yakko, Pinky, Dot, Dot	Level 11
Pinky, Pinky, Brain, Dot, Wakko	Level 12
Yakko, Wakko, Pinky, Wakko, Brain	Level 13
Pinky, Wakko, Brain, Wakko, Yakko	Level 14
Dot, Pinky, Wakko, Wakko, Yakko	Level 15

APEX (XBOX)

Enter all codes as brand names in Dream mode.

UNLOCKABLE	CODE
All Concept Cars in Arcade Mode	Dreamy
All Production Cars in Arcade Mode	Reality
All Tracks in Arcade Mode	World

ARMED AND DANGEROUS (XBOX)

Enter the following codes at the Cheats screen in the Options menu.

UNLOCKABLE	CODE
Big Boots	(RT), (WHT), (Y), (A), (LT), (B), (WHT), (X)
Big Hands	(RT), (WHT), (X), (LT), (WHT), (RT), (RT), (Y)
Big Heads	(LT), (BLK), (B), (WHT), (WHT), (B), (BLK), (LT)

Enter the following codes at the Cheats screen in the Options menu.

UNLOCKABLE	CODE
Fill Ammo	(BLK), (B), (A), (RT), (RT), (A), (LT), (BLK)

UNLOCKABLE	CODE
Fill Health Bar	(X), (RT), (A), (Y), (BLK), (B), (A), (RT)
Invincible	(X), (X), (X), (RT), (A), (LT), (LT), (Y)
Topsy Turvy	(X), (A), (B), (B), (A), (B), (WHT), (WHT)

ARMORED CORE 3 (PlayStation 2)

UNLOCKABLE	CODE
Add Defeated AC Emblems	Press SELECT+START when viewing a defeated AC at the Victory screen to add the defeated AC's emblem to the list. A sound confirms correct code entry.
Drop Parts	Hold L1+L2+R1+R2+▲ to drop your R arm weapon, Back Unit, and Inside parts. Hold L1+L2+R1+R2+L3 to drop Extension parts. Hold L1+L2+R1+R2+● to drop L arm weapons.
First-Person View	Insert a memory card with saved game files from Armored Core 2 or Armored Core 2: Another Age. After saving and resuming in Armored Core 3 from that memory card, pause gameplay, then press L1+R2+✕+■+Dir for a first-person view of the current screen. The screen returns to normal when you resume the game.

ARMORED CORE 4 (PlayStation 3)

HARD DIFFICULTY

UNLOCKABLE	HOW TO UNLOCK
Hard Difficulty	Successfully complete any chapter on normal difficulty. Press ■ to toggle between difficulties.

ARMORED CORE: FORMULA FRONT (PSP)

MANUAL CONTROLLED TRICKS

Use during a manually controlled battle.

CODE	EFFECT
✣ and ✣ Simultaneously	Drop Extensions
✣ and ● Simultaneously	Drop Left Arm Weapon
✣ and ■ Simultaneously	Drop Right Arm Weapon
Boost Forward on the ground and press ●	Fire Energy Wave

UNLOCKABLE FEATURES

For *Armored Core: Formula Front International* version only.

UNLOCKABLE	HOW TO UNLOCK
50 Exhibition Matches	Beat Formula Regular League
Ending Credits (movie attachment)	Beat all 50 Exhibition Matches

ARMORED CORE: SILENT LINE (PlayStation 2)

UNLOCKABLE	CODE
Get Bonus Parts	Get an A or S on any mission.
Get Defeated AC Emblems	Press START and SELECT when the victory slogan appears.

ARMY OF TWO (XBOX 360)

ACHIEVEMENTS

UNLOCKABLE	HOW TO UNLOCK
Alright, Who Wants Some? (20)	Kill 250 enemies using SMGs.
Beast with Two Fronts (20)	Kill 50 enemies in Back-to-Back.
Big Boom! Big Bada Boom! (20)	Kill 25 enemies using RPGs.
Boots on the Ground (10)	Finish playing a versus ranked match.
Dead Man's Hand (20)	Kill 150 enemies using handguns.
Elite PMC (50)	Complete all missions as a Professional.
Fear Is the Mind Killer (45)	Spend one minute straight at full Aggro.
Field Medic (30)	Drag and heal your partner 25 times.
Fission Mailed (20)	Kill 25 Martyrs by shooting the Bomb Packs on their chests.

Flip You. Flip You For Real. (20)	Kill 50 enemies using the Melee Attack.
If I Were a Rich Man (40)	Earn one million dollars over the course of Campaign mode.
If It Bleeds, We Can Kill It (30)	Kill 25 Heavy Armor enemies.
L'Abattoir (30)	Kill 100 enemies while in the power mode of Overkill.
Man of Many Masks (50)	Purchase every mask variant.
Mission 1 Complete (30)	Completed Mission 1 as Contractor or higher.
Mission 2 Complete (30)	Completed Mission 2 as Contractor or higher.
Mission 3 Complete (15)	Completed Mission 3 as Contractor or higher.
Mission 4 Complete (15)	Completed Mission 4 as Contractor or higher.
Mission 5 Complete (15)	Completed Mission 5 as Contractor or higher.
Mission 6 Complete (15)	Completed Mission 6 as Contractor or higher.
My Kind of Case! (40)	Collect all of the information cases in the entire game.
My Virtual Friend (35)	Complete all missions with the Partner AI.
One Gun Is Enough (35)	Win a ranked match without purchasing any additional weapons.
One Shot. One Kill. (20)	Kill 100 enemies using Sniper Rifles.
Out of Debt (15)	Heal your partner for the first time. Training does not count.
Retirement Savings Plan (40)	Earn one billion dollars in ranked matches.
Running Man (30)	Kill 75 enemies while in the stealth mode of Overkill.
Say Hello to My Little Friends (45)	Purchase the MP7, M134, DAO-X Protecta, MGL MK-X, and the M107 Light Fifty.
Seven-six-two Millimeter (20)	Kill 250 enemies using Assault Rifles.
Spray and Pray (20)	Kill 250 enemies using Machine Guns.
Starting a Riot (30)	Kill 50 enemies in Co-op Riot Shield.
Stonewall (30)	Kill 30 enemies using the Riot Shield melee attack.
Surviving the Game (25)	Complete a ranked match without ever needing to be revived.
The Devil's in the Details (20)	Complete 20 minor objectives in a ranked match.
This Is My Boom Stick! (20)	Kill 250 enemies total using Shotguns.
Two Eyes Are Better Than One (35)	Kill five enemies total using Co-op Snipe.
Weapon Specialist (15)	Purchase three weapons.

ARMY OF TWO (PlayStation 3)

CODES

During gameplay press the following:

EFFECT	CODE
Unlimited Life and Ammo	▲,▲,×,×,L2,R2,R1,R2,●,■

ARMY OF TWO: 40TH DAY (XBOX 360)

UNLOCKABLES

UNLOCKABLE	HOW TO UNLOCK
Big Heads	Complete the campaign on Casual difficulty.
Infinite Ammo	Complete the campaign on Casual difficulty.

COSTUMES

Upon completing the game for the first time on any difficulty, several outfits will be made available. You can change your current outfit at the character selection screen.

UNLOCKABLE	HOW TO UNLOCK
Beat-up (end game armor)	Complete the game once.
Civilian clothes (no armor)	Complete the game once.

Light armor	Complete the game once.
Mall clothes (bare armor)	Complete the game once.
Medium armor	Complete the game once.
Old-school armor (original Army of Two **armor)**	Complete the game once.

GLITCH

When you first start the game you are given money to upgrade your weapons. Upgrade your weapons or buy new ones, then continue with the game until the cutscene with the moral choice plays. Once you make your decision, go back to the Main menu during the cutscene with the explosions and select "Campaign" then select the one you just did. Select "New." You will have all the weapons, upgrades, and money from the previous mission, and can upgrade your weapons once more. Repeat until all beginning weapons are upgraded or purchased.

ARMY OF TWO: 40TH DAY (PlayStation 3)

UNLOCKABLES

UNLOCKABLE	HOW TO UNLOCK
Big Heads	Complete the campaign on Casual difficulty
Infinite Ammo	Complete the campaign on Casual difficulty.

COSTUMES

Upon completing the game for the first time on any difficulty, several outfits will be made available. You can change your current outfit at the character selection screen.

UNLOCKABLE	HOW TO UNLOCK
Beat-up (end game armor)	Complete the game once.
Civilian clothes (no armor)	Complete the game once.
Light armor	Complete the game once.
Mall clothes (bare armor)	Complete the game once.
Medium armor	Complete the game once.
Old-school armor (original Army of Two **armor)**	Complete the game once.

EXTRA WEAPONS

To unlock the AS-KR1 and the SB-Z Grand Pinger, you need to have a save file from the original Army of Two game. The weapons will then appear in the customization menu. The AS-KR1 costs $300,000 and the SB-Z costs $450,000. They are not customizable.

UNLOCKABLE	HOW TO UNLOCK
AS-KR1	Have an original Army of Two save file present.
SB-Z Grand Pinger	Have an original Army of Two save file present.

ARMY OF TWO: 40TH DAY (PSP)

UNLOCKABLES

UNLOCKABLE	HOW TO UNLOCK
Dante	Finish the game by always making morally bad choices .
Isaac Clarke	Finish the game by always making morally good choices.
Jonah	Finish the game once on any mode.
Smiley	Finish the game once on any mode.
Spreadgun	Finish the game once.
Tesla Cannon	Finish the game once.

ART OF FIGHTING (Wii)

CHARACTER UNLOCKABLES

UNLOCKABLE	HOW TO UNLOCK
Mr. Big	Get to Mr. Big in 1-player mode and lose the match. Restart the game and Mr. Big will now be unlocked in 2-player mode.
Mr. Karate	Get to Mr. Karate in 1-player mode and lose the match. Restart the game and Mr. Karate will now be unlocked in 2-player mode.

ASSASSIN'S CREED (XBOX 360)

ACHIEVEMENTS

Complete each achievement to get the allotted gamerscore.

UNLOCKABLE	HOW TO UNLOCK
Absolute Symbiosis (45)	Have a complete Synchronization bar.
Blade in the Crowd (30)	Kill one of your main targets like a true assassin.
Conversationalist (20)	Go through every dialog with Lucy.
Defender of the People: Acre (20)	Complete every free mission in Acre.
Defender of the People: Damascus (20)	Complete every free mission in Damascus.
Defender of the People: Jerusalem (20)	Complete every free mission in Jerusalem.
Disciple of the Creed (30)	Assassinate all your targets with a full DNA bar.
Eagle's Challenge (20)	Defeat 25 guards in a single fight.
Eagle's Dance (10)	Perform 50 leaps of faith.
Eagle's Dive (20)	Perform 50 combo kills in fights.
Eagle's Eye (15)	Kill 75 guards by throwing knives.
Eagle's Flight (20)	Last 10 minutes in open conflict.
Eagle's Prey (20)	Assassinate 100 guards.
Eagle's Swiftness (20)	Perform 100 counter kills in fights.
Eagle's Talon (15)	Perform 50 stealth assassinations.
Eagle's Will (20)	Defeat 100 opponents without dying.
Enemy of the Poor (5)	Grab and throw 25 harassers.
Fearless (25)	Complete all reach high points.
Gifted Escapist (5)	Jump through 20 merchant stands.
Hero of Masyaf (20)	You've protected Masyaf from the Templar invasion.
Hungerer of Knowledge (20)	See 85% of all the memory glitches.
Keeper of the 8 Virtues (10)	Find all Hospitalier flags in Acre.
Keeper of the Black Cross (10)	Find all Teutonic flags in Acre.
Keeper of the Creed (10)	Find all flags in Masyaf.
Keeper of the Crescent (20)	Find all flags in Damascus.
Keeper of the Four Gospels (20)	Find all flags in Jerusalem.
Keeper of the Lions Passant (25)	Find all of Richard's flags in the kingdom.
Keeper of the Order (10)	Find all Templar flags in Acre.
March of the Pious (5)	Use scholar blending 20 times.
Personal Vendetta (40)	Kill every Templar.
The Blood of a Corrupt Merchant (25)	You've slain Tamir, Black Market Merchant in Damascus.
The Blood of a Doctor (25)	You've slain Garnier de Naplouse, Hospitalier Leader in Acre.

The Blood of a Liege-Lord(25)	You've slain William of Montferrat, Liege-Lord of Acre.
The Blood of a Nemesis(25)	You've slain Robert de Sable, but there is one more.
The Blood of a Regent (25)	You've slain Majd Addin, Regent of Jerusalem.
The Blood of a Scribe(25)	You've slain Jubair, the Scribe of Damascus.
The Blood of a Slave Trader (25)	You've slain Tatal, Slave Trader of Jerusalem.
The Blood of a Teutonic Leader(25)	You've slain Sibrand, the Teutonic Leader of Acre.
The Blood of the Merchant King (25)	You've slain Abul Nuqoud, Merchant King of Damascus.
The Eagle and the Apple —1191 (100)	Complete *Assassin's Creed.*
The Hands of a Thief (15)	Pickpocket 200 throwing knives.
The Punishment for Treason (20)	You have found the traitor and have brought him before Al Mualim.
Visions of the Future (50)	After the credits roll, walk back into Desmond's bedroom and activate Eagle Vision by pressing Ⓨ and look at the wall above the bed.
Welcome to the Animus (20)	You've successfully completed the Animus tutorial.

ASSASSINS CREED II (XBOX 360)

FEATHERS

Collect feathers within the game to unlock the following items.

UNLOCKABLE	HOW TO UNLOCK
Auditore Cape	Collect 100 feathers.
Condottiero War Hammer	Collect 50 feathers.

EASTER EGG

In the assassin's tomb Santa Maria Delle Visitazione, there is a large room filled with water and an obstacle course. Before attempting the course, activate the lever, stand on the edge of the floor, and stare into the water. After about a minute, something swims across the water and stares at you with its yellow eye. Once the lever resets, activate it again and take up your previous position. In a moment, a giant squid tentacle will shoot out of the water! Ezio will dodge it at the last minute.

ASSASSIN'S CREED II (PlayStation 3)

ASSASSIN'S CREED: BLOODLINES UNLOCKABLE WEAPONS

Players may unlock bonus weapons by syncing save data from the Assassin's Creed: Bloodlines PSP game with Assassin's Creed II on the PS3. Connect the PSP to the PS3 via a USB cable with BOTH games running. Then, select "Connectivity" from the Assassin's Creed II Options menu, and "Connect to PS3" from Assassin's Creed: Bloodlines. The games will evaluate each others' save data and unlock in-game weapons and bonuses based on the player's progress. A complete Story Mode playthrough of Assassin's Creed: Bloodlines will unlock six weapons that will be stored at the villa.

UNLOCKABLE	HOW TO UNLOCK
Bouchart's Blade	Defeat Armand Bouchart in Assassin's Creed: Bloodlines.
Dark Oracle's Bone Dagger	Defeat the Dark Oracle in Assassin's Creed: Bloodlines.
Fredrick's Hammer	Defeat Fredrick the Red in Assassin's Creed: Bloodlines.
Mace of the Bull	Defeat the Bull in Assassin's Creed: Bloodlines.
Maria Thorpe's Longsword	Defeat Maria Thorpe in Assassin's Creed: Bloodlines.
Twins' Blade	Defeat the Twins in Assassin's Creed: Bloodlines.

FEATHERS

Collect feathers within the game to unlock the following items.

UNLOCKABLE	HOW TO UNLOCK
Auditore Cape	Collect 100 feathers.
Condottiero War Hammer	Collect 50 feathers.

EASTER EGG

In the assassin's tomb Santa Maria Delle Visitazione, there is a large room filled with water and an obstacle course. Before attempting the course, activate the lever, stand on the edge of the floor, and stare into the water. After about a minute, something swims across the water and stares at you with its yellow eye. Once the lever resets, activate it again and take up your previous position. In a moment, a giant squid tentacle will shoot out of the water! Ezio will dodge it at the last minute.

ATV OFFROAD FURY (PlayStation 2)

To access the following unlockables, select Pro-Career mode and enter code. You will then return to the Main menu and begin gameplay.

UNLOCKABLE	CODE
2 ATVs	CHACHING
All Tracks	WHATEXIT
Tougher A.I.	ALLOUTAI

ATV OFFROAD FURY 2 (PlayStation 2)

Go to Profile Editor, Unlock Items, Cheats, and enter the following:

UNLOCKABLE	CODE
1,000 Profile Points	GIMMEPTS
Aggressive AI	EATDIRT—Re-enter the code to deactivate it.
All ATVs	SHOWROOM
All Mini-Games	GAMEON
All Equipment	THREADS
All Tracks	TRLBLAZR
All Championship Events	GOLDCUPS
Disable Wrecks	FLYPAPER—Re-enter the code to deactivate it.
San Jacinto Isles	GABRIEL
Unlock Everything	IGIVEUP
Widescreen Mode	WIDESCRN

ATV OFFROAD FURY 3 (PlayStation 2)

At the Main menu, go to Options. Select Player Profile, then select Enter Cheat.

UNLOCKABLE	CODE
Everything Except Fury Bike	!SLACKER!

ATV OFFROAD FURY BLAZIN TRAILS (PSP)

To enter these passwords go to the Options menu, select the Player Profile menu, and then enter the Cheat menu.

UNLOCKABLE	CODE
1,500 Credits	$MONEYBAGS$
All Music Videos	BILLBOARDS
All Rider Gear	DUDS
Unlock Everything (except the Fury Bike)	ALL ACCESS
Unlock Rims	DUBS

AVATAR: THE LAST AIRBENDER (Wii)

PASSWORDS

PASSWORD	EFFECT
37437	All treasure maps
97831	Character concept gallery
34743	Double damage
54641	One hit dishonor
24463	Unlimited chi
23637	Unlimited copper
94677	Unlimited health
53467	Unlimited stealth

UNLOCKABLE GALLERIES

UNLOCKABLE	HOW TO UNLOCK
Character Story Board Gallery	Collect all Set Items through level 6
Level Art Gallery	Collect all Set Items through level 3
Story Board Gallery	Collect all Set Items through level 5

AVATAR: THE LAST AIRBENDER—THE BURNING EARTH (XBOX 360)

CODES

In the Password screen in the main menu, click the left arrow, and then go to "cheat entry."

UNLOCKABLE	HOW TO UNLOCK
All Bonus Games	99801
All Gallery Items	85061
Double Damage	90210
Infinite Life	65049
Infinite Special Attacks	66206
Max Level	89121
One-Hit Dishonor	28260

ACHIEVEMENTS

UNLOCKABLE	HOW TO UNLOCK
One with Combat (300)	Achieve a Hit Counter of 50.
The Art of Combat (200)	Achieve a Hit Counter of 40.
The Flow of Combat I (150)	Achieve a Hit Counter of 10.
The Flow of Combat II (150)	Achieve a Hit Counter of 20.
The Flow of Combat III (200)	Achieve a Hit Counter of 30.

AVATAR: THE LAST AIRBENDER—THE BURNING EARTH (Wii)

CODES

In the Password screen in the main menu, click the left arrow and then go to Cheat Entry.

UNLOCKABLE	HOW TO UNLOCK
All Bonus Games	99801
All Gallery Items	85061
Double Damage	90210
Infinite Life	65049
Infinite Special Attacks	66206
Max Level	89121
One-Hit Dishonor	28260

B

BACKYARD WRESTLING (XBOX)

Enter this code at the Main menu.

UNLOCKABLE	CODE
All Wrestlers and Stages	Hold LT, then press A,X,Y,B,A,X,Y,B.

BALDUR'S GATE: DARK ALLIANCE (PlayStation 2)

Enter the following codes during gameplay, then press START.

UNLOCKABLE	CODE
Invulnerability and Level Warp	L1+R2+▲+←
Level 20 Character	L1+R2+←

BALDUR'S GATE: DARK ALLIANCE II (PlayStation 2)

UNLOCKABLE	CODE
Invulnerability and Level Warp	During gameplay, hold L1+R1+▲+■+●+× and press START.
Level 10	During gameplay, hold L1+R1+▲+■+●+× and press L2.
Level Warp and Infinite Health	During game play press and hold L1 + R1 + ▲ + ■ + ● + × then, while still holding these buttons, press START. A menu should appear.

BAND HERO (XBOX 360)

CODES

Select "Input Cheats" under the Options menu. G = Green, R = Red, Y = Yellow, B = Blue.

EFFECT	CODE
Air Instruments	B,Y,B,R,R,Y,G,Y
All HO/POs	R,G,B,G,B,G,R,G
Always Slide	Y,G,Y,Y,Y,R,B,R
Auto Kick	Y,G,Y,B,B,R,B,R
Electrika Steel Unlocked	B,B,R,Y,R,Y,B,B
Focus Mode	Y,Y,G,G,R,R,B,B
HUD-Free Mode	G,R,G,R,Y,B,G,R
Invisible Characters	G,R,Y,G,Y,B,Y,G
Most Characters Unlocked	B,Y,G,Y,R,G,R,Y
Performance Mode	Y,Y,B,G,B,R,R,R

BONUS CHARACTERS

Complete the mission on Tour to unlock the listed characters.

UNLOCKABLE	HOW TO UNLOCK
Adam Levine	Successfully complete the Maroon 5 "She Will Be Loved" gig.
Adrian Young	Successfully complete the No Doubt "Don't Speak" gig.
Frankenrocker	Successfully complete the Diamond Bonus Challenge for the Fall Out Boy "Sugar, We're Goin' Down" gig.
Gwen Stefani	Successfully complete the No Doubt "Don't Speak" gig.
Shadow Character	Successfully complete the Gold Bonus Challenge for the David Bowie "Let's Dance" gig.
UNLOCKABLE	HOW TO UNLOCK

Taylor Swift	Successfully complete the Taylor Swift "Love Story" gig.
Tom Dumont	Successfully complete the No Doubt "Don't Speak" gig.
Tony Kanal	Successfully complete the No Doubt "Don't Speak" gig.

BANJO-KAZOOIE: NUTS & BOLTS (XBOX 360)

UNLOCKABLES

After beating the game, L.O.G. will give you a Banjo Head Vehicle. The Banjo Head Vehicle can be loaded from the L.O.G's choice option.

THE BARD'S TALE (XBOX)

While playing, hold (LT)+(RT), then enter the following codes.

UNLOCKABLE	CODE
Damage x100	↑,↓,↑,↓,←,→,←,→
Full Mana and Health	←,←,→,→,↑,↓,↑,↓
Intangible	←,→,←,→,↑,↓,↑,↓
Invincible	→,←,→,←,↑,↓,↑,↓
Silver and Adderstones	↑,↑,↓,↓,←,→,←,→

THE BARD'S TALE (PlayStation 2)

During gameplay, hold [L1]+[R1] and press the following buttons:

UNLOCKABLE	CODE
Can't Be Hurt	→,←,→,←,↑,↓,↑,↓
Can't Be Struck	←,→,←,→,↑,↓,↑,↓
Damage X100	↑,↓,↑,↓,←,→,←,→
Everything On	↑,↑,↓,↓,←,→,←,→
Full Health and Mana	←,←,→,→,↑,↓,↑,↓

BARNYARD (Wii)

GAMEPLAY CHEAT CODES

During gameplay hold (C)+[Z] and enter codes.

UNLOCKABLE	HOW TO UNLOCK
9,999 Gopher Bucks	↓, ↓, ←, ←, ←, ←, ↑, ←
All Flower Pack and Knapsack Items	↓, ↓, ↑, →, ←, ←, →, ↑

MAIN MENU CHEAT CODES

While on the main menu screen, hold (C)+[Z] and enter codes.

UNLOCKABLE	HOW TO UNLOCK
Unlock All Antics	↑, ←, ↓, →, →, ↓, ←, ↑
Unlock All Bonus Items	↑, →, ↓,←, ←, ↓, →, ↑

BAROQUE (Wii)

BAROQUES

Successfully complete the indicated task to unlock the corresponding Baroque.

UNLOCKABLE	HOW TO UNLOCK
Appraiser	Identify over 50 items.
Arrow of Eros	Successfully complete the Neuron Tower while in Lust mode.
Bomber	Purify over 50 Meta-beings using the explosion brand.
Box bOx boX BOX	Successfully complete the Neuro Tower or die while holding over 15 types of boxes.
Broken Doll	Watch "Consciousness Simulation End VV."
Bug Nurturer	Raise over 10 larva until they grow into another parasite.
Careless Death	Die outside the Neuro Tower when your level is over 2.
Cat Fan	Use the Cat Torturer three times on one floor.
Cat Lover	Use the Cat Torturer six times on one floor.

Close to God	Die at the lowest level.
Collector	Get items from Urim, The Mind Reader, The Worker Angel, and Doctor Angelicus.
Confused World	Successfully complete the Neuro Tower while confused.
Cursebringer	Combine items over 30 times using a Curse Bringer angel on a single floor.
Deadly Meta-Beings	Purify Manas, Perisomats, Malecificia, and Tabula Smaragdina.
Defenseless Champ	Conquer the Defenseless dungeon.
Disk Collector	Successfully complete the Neuro Tower or die while holding over 15 types of disks.
Distant Wanderer	You have not qualified for any other Baroques.
Executioner	Successfully complete the Neuro Tower after purifying over 100 Meta-beings with torturers.
Explosive End	Die by consuming a boom bone.
Fashion Plate	Successfully complete the Neuro Tower or die while holding over 15 types of coats.
Fasting Penance	Successfully complete the Neuro Tower without eating hearts, flesh, or bones.
Fragile Splendor	Successfully complete the Neuro Tower while wearing Glass Sword, Glass Coat, and Glass Wings.
Fragments of Truth	Hear over 200 messages about the Baroques from the Baroque Monger.
Friendly Fire	Purify all the Koriel Members by using the Angelic Rifle.
Frugal Champ	Conquer the Frugal dungeon.
Hell Champ	Conquer the Hell dungeon.
Hunger Champ	Conquer the Hunger dungeon.
Hunger Strike	Die by losing HP from 0 Vitality (only if Vitality is over 499).
Hurting Dervish	Successfully complete the Neuro Tower after purifying over 100 Meta-beings by throwing items.
I am the World	Fuse with the absolute God when blind and deaf.
Icarus's Student	Successfully complete the Neuro Tower or die while holding over 15 types of wings.
Irony	Die while invincible.
Liberator	Once buried, purify Longneck, Horned Girl, and The Bagged One.
March On	Switch floors over 10 times while a Meta-being is in the room.
Masochist	Successfully complete the Neuro Tower or die while holding over 15 types of brands.
Medical Partner	Successfully complete the Neuro Tower or die while holding over 15 types of fluids.
Mugged	Let Gliro steal an item over 20 times.
Orb Seeker	Successfully complete the Neuro Tower after using every Consciousness Orb.
Parasite Museum	Successfully complete the Neuro Tower or die while holding over 15 types of parasites.
Power House	Successfully complete the Neuro Tower without a weapon and an attack above 50.
Promise of Peace	Successfully complete the Neuro Tower without purifying any Meta-beings.
Reverse Disk Champ	Conquer the Reverse Disk dungeon.
Rotten Champ	Conquer the Rotten dungeon.
Screaming Tower	Enter the Neuro Tower over 100 times.
Self Reliant	Reach the lowest level without using any consciousness orbs.
Serial Thrower	Throw over 100 items.

Shadow Boxer	Swing your sword over 100 times without hitting anything.
Skeleton Man	Successfully complete the Neuro Tower or die while holding over 15 types of bones.
Special Hunter	Successfully complete the Neuro Tower after purifying over 300 Meta-beings by sword.
Sword's Miracle	Land five consecutive critical hits with the sword.
The World's Tears	Find all the idea Sephirah that are in the item list.
Torture Master	Successfully complete the Neuro Tower or die while holding over 15 types of torturers.
Trap Champ	Conquer the Trap dungeon.
Unforgettable	Have a conversation with a specific phantom brother.
Unfortunate Death	Die from a Meta-being stepping on a disk.
Unrewarded Effort	Successfully complete the Neuro Tower without opening a Trials Box for over 2,000 cu.
Unstoppable	Successfully complete the Neuro Tower after taking over 5,000 damage.
Useless	Die without doing anything in the outer world.
Vacant Coffin	Conquer all training dungeons.
Warrior's Spirit	Successfully complete the Neuro Tower or die while holding over 15 types of swords.
Wasted Core	Successfully complete the Neuro Tower or die while holding over 15 types of crystals.
Wasted Effort	Lose either a coat or a sword with over 30.

BASES LOADED (Wii)

PASSWORDS

PASSWORD	EFFECT
LFBDJHE	Boston, one game away from the World Series
PFACNHK	DC, one game away from the World Series
CHXAACC	Game 162
LNADJPD	Hawaii, one game away from the World Series
CBIDNEP	Jersey, last game of the World Series
LFADNHH	Jersey, one game away from the World Series
PNCBNHD	Kansas, one game away from the World Series
PFBCNPD	LA, one game away from the World Series
PFCANHK	Miami, one game away from the World Series
PFDAJHH	New York, one game away from the World Series
LNDAJPD	Omaha, one game away from the World Series
JAELECO	Password for Pennant, must have selected "Pennant" option from menu
LFDBJHE	Philly, one game away from the World Series
Select Pennant Mode and Enter JALECO as Password	Skip to the last team
LNCBJPD	Texas, one game away from the World Series
LNBCJPD	Utah, one game away from the World Series

OTHER ACTIONS

ACTION	HOW TO ENACT
Don't Get Ejected During a Fight	Continually press ⊕ during the fight
Hitter Charges the Mound and Gets Ejected	After the 3rd inning, bean the 3rd or 4th hitter in the lineup

	...et two kills with a landing craft.
	...ill four enemies with air raids.
	Defend five flags.
	Kill four enemies with grenades or explosives.
	Get four kills with a heavy machine gun.
	Get four kills with a car.
	Kill four players with melee weapons.
	Kill at least 20 enemies.
	Kill four enemies with a pistol.
	Get five kills with a fighter plane.
	Kill four enemies with a semi-automatic rifle.
...ency	Kill four enemies with rifle grenades.
	Kill four enemies with a submachine gun.
	Kill four enemies with a scoped rifle.
...ce	Each squad member gets any one stamp and kills 10 enemies.
...y	Get four kills with a tank.
	Get 10 squad assists.
...ist Efficiency	Get five vehicle assist kills.
...iciency	Destroy six vehicles in any fashion.

...FIELD 2: MODERN COMBAT (XBOX 360)

...K ALL WEAPONS (CAMPAIGN)

	EFFECT
...he LB and RB and ... Right, Right, Down, Up, Left, Left on the d-pad	Unlock all Weapons

...LTIPLAYER RANKS

...advance in rank in multiplayer you must get the right number of ...edals, Points, and PPH (points per hour).

...NLOCKABLE	HOW TO UNLOCK
Brigadier General	12 Medals, 19,390 Points, 85 PPH
Captain	8 Medals, 8,430 Points, 65 PPH
Chief Warrant Officer	5 Medals, 3,700 Points, 50 PPH
Colonel	11 Medals, 16,070 Points, 80 PPH
Commanding Sergeant Major	3 Medals, 1,820 Points, 40 PPH
Corporal	0 Medals, 70 Points, 15 PPH
First Lieutenant	7 Medals, 6,560 Points, 60 PPH
Five Star General	15 Medals, 32,000 Points, 100 PH
Lieutenant Colonel	10 Medals, 13,150 Points, 75 PPH
Lieutenant General	14 Medals, 27,330 Points, 95 PH
Major	9 Medals, 10,620 Points, 70 PPH
Major General	13 Medals, 23,150 Points, 90 PPH
Master Sergeant	1 Medal(s), 720 Points, 30 PPH
Private	0 Medals, 0 Points, 0 PPH
Private First Class	0 Medals, 20 Points, 10 PPH
Second Lieutenant	6 Medals, 4,900 Points, 55 PPH
Sergeant	0 Medals, 190 Points, 20 PPH
Sergeant First Class	0 Medals, 390 Points, 25 PPH
Sergeant Major	2 Medals, 1,180 Points, 35 PPH
Warrant Officer	4 Medals, 2,650 Points, 45 PPH

BATMAN: ARKHAM ASYLUM (XBOX 360)

UNLOCKABLES

UNLOCKABLE	HOW TO UNLOCK
Armored-suit Batman	Complete the game.

BATMAN: ARKHAM ASYLUM (PlayStation 3)

UNLOCKABLES

UNLOCKABLE	HOW TO UNLOCK
Armored-suit Batman	Complete the game. Can only be used in Challenge Mode.

BATMAN: RISE OF SIN TZU (Xbox)

At the Mode Select screen, hold LT+RT, then enter the codes.

UNLOCKABLE	CODE
All Rewards	Left, Down, Left, Right, Left, Left, Down, Right
All Upgrades	Down, Up, Down, Left, Down, Right, Up, Down
Dark Knight Mode	Right, Up, Up, Right, Left, Down, Right, Up
Infinite Health	Up, Right, Up, Left, Down, Left, Down, Right
Unlimited Combo Meter	Left, Right, Down, Up, Up, Down, Right, Left

BATMAN: RISE OF SIN TZU (PlayStation 2)

At the "Press Start" screen, hold L1+L2+R1+R2 and enter the following codes.

UNLOCKABLE	CODE
All Characters at 100%	↑, ↑, ←, ←, →, →, ↓, ↓
All Rewards	↓, ↑, ↓, ↑, ←, →, ←, →
All Upgrades	↑, ↑, ←, ←, →, →, →, ↓, ↓
Everything	↓, ↑, ↓, ↑, ←, →, ←, →
Infinite Combo Bar	←, →, ↑, ↓, →, ←, ↓, ↑
Infinite Health	↑, →, ↓, ←, ↑, ←, ↓, →

BATMAN VENGEANCE (Xbox)

Input the following codes at the Main menu. Many of them will make a sound to confirm correct code entry.

UNLOCKABLE	CODE
Bonus Characters	Press Left, Right, Down, WHT, LT + RT, then press START
Master Code	Press LT, RT, LT, RT, X, X, Y, Y
Unlimited Batarangs	Press LT, RT, WHT, Y
Unlimited Electric Batarangs	Press LT, RT, B, WHT, LT

BATMAN VENGEANCE (PlayStation 2)

At the Main menu, enter the following codes.

UNLOCKABLE	CODE
All Cheats	L2, R2, L2, R2, ■, ■, ●, ●
Infinite Batcuffs	■, ●, ■, ●, L2, R2, R2, L2
Infinite Bat Launcher	●, ■, ●, ■, L1, R1, L2, R2
Infinite Electric Batarangs	L1, R1, L2, R2

BATTLE CITY (Wii)

STAGE SELECT

UNLOCKABLE	HOW TO UNLOCK
Stage Select	When you start the game and see the screen with "Stage 1," press Ⓐ and Ⓑ to choose any stage you want.

BATTLE ENGINE AQUILA (PlayStation 2)

Use these passwords as name profiles. You must have a memory card or it will not prompt you to enter a Profile. (Note: case sensitive).

UNLOCKABLE	PASSWORD
All Bonuses	105770Y2
God Mode	B4K42
Level Select	!EVAH!

BATTLEFIELD 1943 (XBOX 360)

POSTCARDS

UNLOCKABLE	HOW TO UNLOCK
Attacker	Capture thirty flags.
Best Squad	Be in the best squad three times on each map.
Bomb run	Launch an air raid killing at least one enemy.
Defender	Defend 20 flags.
Fighter Ace	Get 50 kills using fighter planes.
Infantryman	Kill 50 enemies with a submachine gun.
Lifer	Reach top rank.
Master Blaster	Kill 50 enemies with grenades, rifle grenades, or explosives.
Master of your Domain	Get 17 kills playing as each class.
Melee Man	Get 20 melee kills.
Milkrun	Fly a plane for 20 minutes.
Motorman	Get 25 kills with car, tank, and plane.
Pacific Campaign	Win twice on every map as any team.
Parachutist	Use the parachute four times.
Rifleman	Kill 50 enemies with a semi-automatic rifle.
Sniper!	Kill 50 enemies with a scoped rifle.
Squad Assister	Get 100 squad assists.
Squad Avenger	Avenge 100 squad members.
The Best	Get the highest score in a match.
Tour of Duty I	Play 50 matches.
Tour of Duty II	Play 130 matches.
Truly Elite	Get 10,000 Kills.
Veteran	Cap 50 enemy flags.
Wheelman	Get 50 kills using car, tank, or boat.

STAMPS

UNLOCKABLE	HOW TO UNLOCK
Air Defense Efficiency	Kill two planes with an anti-aircraft gun.
Air Superiority	Shoot down three bombers.
AT Efficiency	Kill four vehicles with recoilless rifle.
Attacker Efficiency	Capture five enemy flags.
Best Squad	Be the best squad of the round.
Boat Efficiency	Get two kills with a landing craft.
Bombing Efficiency	Kill four enemies with air raids.
Defender Efficiency	Defend five flags.
Explosives Efficiency	Kill four enemies with grenades or explosives.
HMG Efficiency	Get four kills with a heavy machine gun.
Jeep Efficiency	Get four kills with a car.
Knife Efficiency	Kill four players with melee weapons.

Leatherneck	Kil
Pistol Efficiency	
Plane Efficiency	
Rifle Efficiency	
Rifle Grenade Efficiency	
SMG Efficiency	
Sniper Efficiency	Kil
Squad Excellence	Each 10 enem
Tank Efficiency	Get four ki
Teamplayer	Get 10 squad
Vehicle Assist Efficiency	Get five vehicle
Vehicle Efficiency	Destroy six vehicle

BATTLEFIELD 1943 (PlayStation 3)

POSTCARDS

UNLOCKABLE	HOW TO UNLOCK
Attacker	Capture thirty flags.
Best Squad	Be in the best squad three times
Bomb run	Launch an air raid killing at least o
Defender	Defend 20 flags.
Fighter Ace	Get 50 kills using fighter planes.
Infantryman	Kill 50 enemies with a submachine gun.
Lifer	Reach top rank.
Master Blaster	Kill 50 enemies with grenades, rifle grenade explosives.
Master of your Domain	Get 17 kills playing as each class.
Melee Man	Get 20 melee kill.
Milkrun	Fly a plane for 20 minutes.
Motorman	Get 25 kills with car, tank and plane.
Pacific Campaign	Win twice on every map as any team
Parachutist	Use the parachute four times.
Rifleman	Kill 50 enemies with a semi-automatic rifle.
Sniper	Kill 50 enemies with a scoped rifle.
Squad Assister	Get 100 squad assists.
Squad Avenger	Avenge 100 squad members.
The Best	Get the highest score in a match.
Tour of Duty I	Play 50 matches.
Tour of Duty II	Play 100 and thirty matches.
Truly Elite	Get 10,000 Kills.
Veteran	Cap 50enemy flags.
Wheelman	Get 50kills using car, tank, or boat.

STAMPS

UNLOCKABLE	HOW TO UNLOCK
Air Defense Efficiency	Kill two planes with an anti-aircraft gun.
Air Superiority	Shoot down three bombers.
AT Efficiency	Kill four vehicles with recoilless rifle.
Attacker Efficiency	Capture five enemy flags.
Best Squad	Be the best squad of the round.

BATTLEFIELD 2: MODERN COMBAT (XBOX)

UNLOCK ALL WEAPONS

Receive All Weapons Permanently
During gameplay, hold ⓦ+ⓑ and press ▶,▶,▼,▲,◀,◀

BATTLEFIELD: BAD COMPANY (XBOX 360)

FIND ALL FIVE WEAPONS

UNLOCKABLE	HOW TO UNLOCK
Assault Rifle	Register your old *Battlefield* games at *http://www.veteran.battlefield.com/*.
Light Machine Gun	Sign up for the newsletter at *http://www.findallfive.com/*.
Semi-Automatic Shotgun	After playing an Online game, login and check your stats at *http://www.findallfive.com/*.
Sniper Rifle	Pre-order the game from a participating retailer before June 23rd, 2008.
Uzi	Play the "Battlefield: Bad Company Demo" and get to rank 4. (2,300 EXP required to reach rank 4.)

TROPHIES

Trophies are unlockable in Multiplayer modes.

UNLOCKABLE	HOW TO UNLOCK
Assault Rifle Efficiency Trophy	In a round, 6 kills with Assault rifle.
Avenger Trophy	In a round, 3 avenger points.
Best Squad Trophy	Awarded at end of round.
Big Guns Trophy	In a round, 5 kills with artillery.
Carbine Efficiency Trophy	In a round, 6 kills with M16A2.
Clear Skies Trophy	In a round, 5 kills with stationary weapon.
Combat Aviator Trophy	In a round, 5 kills with air vehicle.
Combat Efficiency Trophy	In a round, 6 kill streak.
Combat Engineer Trophy	In a round, 20 vehicle repair points (2 repairs).
Compact Assault Rifle Efficiency Trophy	In a round, 6 kills with compact assault rifle.
Demo Pack Efficiency Trophy	In a round, 3 kills with C4.
Emplacement Trophy	In a round, 5 kills with stationary weapon.
Explosive Efficiency Trophy	In a round, 10 kills with explosives.
Firearm Efficiency Trophy	In a round, 3 kills with handgun.
Frag Out Efficiency Trophy	In a round, 3 kills with grenade while playing Demolitionists.
Grenade Launcher Efficiency	In a round, 6 kills with grenade launcher.
Grenadier Efficiency Trophy	In a round, 3 kills with grenade playing Assault.
High Card Trophy	In a round, get the best IAR Score.
Kill Assists Trophy	In a round, 5 kill assists.
Laser Designating Efficiency Trophy	In a round, 3 kills from laser designating.
Light Machine Gun Efficiency Trophy	In a round, 6 kills with a light machine gun.
Marksman Trophy	In a round, 5 kills with sniper rifle.
Medic Trophy	In a round, 10 points from med kit (2 heals)
Melee Combat Trophy	In a round, 5 melee kills.
Mine Placement Efficiency Trophy	In a round, 3 kills with AT mines.
Mortar Strike Efficiency Trophy	In a round, 3 kills with mortar strike.
Naval Surface Warfare Trophy	In a round, 5 kills with sea vehicle.
Objective Attack Trophy	In a round, destroy the last objective.
Objective Defender Trophy	In a round, 30 defend points.

UNLOCKABLE	HOW TO UNLOCK
Objective Destroyer Trophy	In a round, destroy 3 objectives.
Rocket Launcher Efficiency Trophy	In a round, 3 kills with rocket launcher.
Savior Trophy	In a round, 3 savior points.
Shotgun Efficiency Trophy	In a round, 5 kills with a shotgun.
Squad Medication Trophy	In a round, 40 squad member heal points.
Squad Member Trophy	In a round, assist or save 5 squad members.
SVU Efficiency Trophy	In a round, 5 kills with the SVU.
Tank Warfare Trophy	In a round, 5 kills with tanks.
Target Tagging Efficiency Trophy	In a round, 2 kill assists from dartgun tagging.
Transport Vehicle Trophy	In a round, 5 kills with transport vehicle.
UMP	In a round, 6 kills with UMP.
Wheels of Hazard Trophy	In a round, 2 road kills.
Winning Team Trophy	Awarded at end of round.

WILD CARDS

UNLOCKABLE	HOW TO UNLOCK
1 on 1 Air	In a round, destroy an air vehicle of the same kind without assistance.
1 on 1 Land	In a round, destroy one land vehicle of the same kind without assistance.
1 on 1 Sea	In a round, destroy 1 sea vehicle of the same kind without assistance.
2 Pair	In a round, get 2 of any 2 trophies.
Airtime	In a round, 2 seconds air time in a land vehicle.
Armor Buster	In a round, kill 5 armored vehicles.
Avenger Trophies	Global: 50x avenger trophies.
Beat the House	In a round, 15 grenade kills.
Cab Driver	In a round, 5 min as driver in a vehicle with passengers.
Chopper Chopper Kills	In a round, kill 5 air vehicles.
Dead Eye Headshots	Global: Get 100 headshots with any sniper rifle.
Destruction Site	In a round, destroy 50 objects.
Deuces Are Wild	In a round, kill 2 enemies of each kind.
Five of a Kind	In a round, destroy 5 vehicles of the same kind.
Full Deck	In a round, 52 total kills.
Full House	In a round, destroy 3+2 vehicles of the same kind.
Gunslinger	Global: 80 kills with handgun.
Headshots	In a round, 20 kills from headshots.
Parashooter	In a round, 4 road kills with any air vehicle.
Santa's Little Helper	In a round, 10 kill assist points.
Savior Trophies	Global: 50x savior trophies.
Snake Eyes	In a round, get 11 kills as two different classes.
Squad Avenger Card	Global: Get 100 avenger points avenging squad members.
Squad Wild Card	In a round, 1 squad member trophy per squad member.
Staying Dry	In a round, 2 seconds air time with a sea vehicle.
Straight Flush	In a round, destroy 1 vehicle of each kind.
Strike	In a round, kill 10 enemies at the same time.
Tank Buster	In a round, kill 5 tanks.
Three of a Kind	In a round, destroy 3 vehicles of the same kind.

ACHIEVEMENTS

UNLOCKABLE	HOW TO UNLOCK
Action, Not Words! (25)	Complete "Welcome To Bad Company" on Hard.
Always Get Paid in Gold Bars (15)	Complete "Welcome To Bad Company" on Normal.
Be the Best (20)	(Online) Place #1 in a ranked match.
Beans Bullets Bandages (30)	(Online) Get 10,002 kills.
Been There, Drove That! (20)	Drive all vehicle types (jeep, tank, heli, boat).
Capitalist Pigs, Very Nice (25)	Complete "Crash and Grab" on Hard.
Cart Wheels (25)	Complete "Par for the Course" on Hard.
Catch the "Bad" Moment (15)	(Online) Take 3 pictures using the image system.
Check My Grill (20)	Find half of the gold bars.
Clean Sweep (25)	Find all collectables.
Colonel (25)	(Online) Reach Rank 20.
Darwin's Parachute (10)	(Online) Glide in the parachute for 3 seconds.
Death from Above (20)	Kill 25 enemies in a helicopter.
Dog Owner! (20)	(Online) Collect 5 unique dog tags.
Drive By (25)	(Online) 100 kills using vehicle.
Forest Ranger (15)	(Online) Knock down 1,000 trees.
General of the Army (35)	(Online) Reach Rank 25.
Get Me Started (15)	(Online) Participate in one online match (Ranked).
Get the Dog! (20)	(Online) Collect 50 unique dog tags.
Gold Digger (30)	Find all gold bars.
Half Way Thru (20)	Find half of all collectables.
He Might Come in Handy (15)	Complete "Par for the Course" on Normal.
Here Is Your DD-214 (30)	Complete "Ghost Town" on Hard.
Hold On! (15)	Complete "Air Force One" on Normal.
Home Wrecker (15)	Destroy 200 walls.
I Am Bad Company! (25)	(Online) Achieve all the awards.
I Love Gold! (10)	Find one gold bar.
Killer on the Loose (25)	Kill 25 enemies.
Leatherneck (25)	(Online) Play 100 online matches.
Let's Take That Boat (15)	Complete "Crash and Grab" on Normal.
Manic Lumberjack (15)	Knock down a small forest.
Master Sergeant (15)	(Online) Reach Rank 8.
Never Used a Door (15)	(Online) Destroy 1,000 walls.
Not Even a Nugget! (15)	Complete "Acta Non Verba" on Normal.
On Top of the World (20)	Climb to the highest spot in the game.
One In a Million (20)	Hit hostile helicopter with laser designator.
Ooh Rah (20)	(Online) Achieve half of all awards.
Russia? (25)	Complete "Air Force One" on Hard.
Say Goodbye to the Gold! (25)	Complete "Crossing Over" on Hard.
Sir, Yes Sir! (30)	Complete "Ghost Town" on Normal.
Specialist (10)	(Online) Reach Rank 3.
Staying Alive (15)	Complete one mission without dying (any difficulty).
The Anti-Mechanic (20)	Destroy 50 vehicles (containing enemy AI).
The Hypochondriac (20)	Use auto injector 50 times.
There Is No I in Squad (15)	(Online) Have 20 squad members spawn on you without dying in a single round.

UNLOCKABLE	HOW TO UNLOCK
Vehikill (20)	(Online) Get at least one kill in every vehicle.
Where Are They Going So Fast? (25)	Complete "Acta Non Verba" on Hard.
With My Devil Dogs (15)	(Online) Use squad in the menu, find a friend, and play one round.
You and What Army? (15)	Complete "Crossing Over" on Normal.
You Found It You Keep It (15)	Find 5 unique collectables.

BATTLEFIELD: BAD COMPANY (PlayStation 3)

FIND ALL FIVE WEAPONS

UNLOCKABLE	HOW TO UNLOCK
Assault Rifle	Register your old Battlefield games at http://www.veteran.battlefield.com/.
Light Machine Gun	Sign up for the newsletter at http://www.findallfive.com/.
Semi-Automatic Shotgun	After playing an Online game, login and check your stats at http://www.findallfive.com/.
Sniper Rifle	Pre-order the game from a participating retailer before June 23rd, 2008.
Uzi	Play the "Battlefield: Bad Company Demo" and get to rank 4. (2,300 EXP required to reach rank 4.)

TROPHIES

Trophies are unlockable in Multiplayer modes.

UNLOCKABLE	HOW TO UNLOCK
Assault Rifle Efficiency Trophy	In a round, 6 kills with assault rifle.
Avenger Trophy	In a round, 3 avenger points.
Best Squad Trophy	Awarded in end of round.
Big Guns Trophy	In a round, 5 kills with artillery.
Carbine Efficiency Trophy	In a round, 6 kills with M16A2.
Clear Skies Trophy	In a round, 5 kills with stationary weapon.
Combat Aviator Trophy	In a round, 5 kills with air vehicle.
Combat Efficiency Trophy	In a round, 6 kill streak.
Combat Engineer Trophy	In a round, 20 vehicle repair points (2 repairs).
Compact Assault Rifle Efficiency Trophy	In a round, 6 kills with compact assault rifle.
Demo Pack Efficiency Trophy	In a round, 3 kills with C4.
Emplacement Trophy	In a round, 5 kills with stationary weapon.
Explosive Efficiency Trophy	In a round, 10 kills with explosives.
Firearm Efficiency Trophy	In a round, 3 kills with handgun.
Frag Out Efficiency Trophy	In a round, 3 kills with grenade while playing Demolitionists.
Grenade Launcher Efficiency	In a round, 6 kills with grenade launcher.
Grenadier Efficiency Trophy	In a round, 3 kills with grenade while playing Assault.
High Card Trophy	In a round, get the best IAR score.
Kill Assists Trophy	In a round, 5 kill assists.
Laser Designating Efficiency Trophy	In a round, 3 kills from laser designating.
Light Machine Gun Efficiency Trophy	In a round, 6 kills with a light machine gun.
Marksman Trophy	In a round, 5 kills with sniper rifle.
Medic Trophy	In a round, 10 points from med kit (2 heals).
Melee Combat Trophy	In a round, 5 melee kills.
Mine Placement Efficiency Trophy	In a round, 3 kills with AT mines.

Mortar Strike Efficiency Trophy	In a round, 3 kills with mortar strike.
Naval Surface Warfare Trophy	In a round, 5 kills with sea vehicle.
Objective Attack Trophy	In a round, destroy the last objective.
Objective Defender Trophy	In a round, 30 defend points.
Objective Destroyer Trophy	In a round, destroy 3 objectives.
Rocket Launcher Efficiency Trophy	In a round, 3 kills with rocket launcher.
Savior Trophy	In a round, 3 savior points.
Shotgun Efficiency Trophy	In a round, 5 kills with a shotgun.
Squad Medication Trophy	In a round, 40 squad member heal points.
Squad Member Trophy	In a round, assist or save 5 squad members.
SVU Efficiency Trophy	In a round, 5 kills with the SVU.
Tank Warfare Trophy	In a round, 5 kills with tanks.
Target Tagging Efficiency Trophy	In a round, 2 kill assists from dart gun tagging.
Transport Vehicle Trophy	In a round, 5 kills with transport vehicle.
UMP	In a round, 6 kills with UMP.
Wheels of Hazard Trophy	In a round, 2 road kills.
Winning Team Trophy	Awarded in end of round.

WILD CARDS

UNLOCKABLE	HOW TO UNLOCK
1 on 1 Air	In a round, destroy an air vehicle of the same kind without assistance.
1 on 1 Land	In a round, destroy one land vehicle of the same kind without assistance.
1 on 1 Sea	In a round, destroy 1 sea vehicle of the same kind without assistance.
2 Pair	In a round, get 2 of any 2 trophies.
Airtime	In a round, 2 seconds air time in a land vehicle.
Armor Buster	In a round, kill 5 armored vehicles.
Avenger Trophies	Global: 50x avenger trophies.
Beat the House	In a round, 15 grenade kills.
Cab Driver	In a round, 5 min as driver in a vehicle with passengers.
Chopper Chopper Kills	In a round, kill 5 air vehicles.
Dead Eye Headshots	Global: Get 100 headshots with any sniper rifle.
Destruction Site	In a round, destroy 50 objects.
Deuces Are Wild	In a round, kill 2 enemies of each kind.
Five of a Kind	In a round, destroy 5 vehicles of the same kind.
Full Deck	In a round, 52 total kills.
Full House	In a round, destroy 3+2 vehicles of the same kind.
Gunslinger	Global: 80 kills with handgun.
Headshots	In a round, 20 kills from headshots.
Parashooter	In a round, 4 road kills with any air vehicle.
Santa's Little Helper	In a round, 10 kill assist points.
Savior Trophies	Global: 50x savior trophies.
Snake Eyes	In a round, get 11 kills as two different classes.
Squad Avenger Card	Global: Get 100 avenger points avenging squad members.
Squad Wild Card	In a round, 1 squad member trophy per squad member.
Staying Dry	In a round, 2 seconds air time with a sea vehicle.
Straight Flush	In a round, destroy 1 vehicle of each kind.
Strike	In a round, kill 10 enemies at the same time.
Tank Buster	In a round, kill 5 tanks.

UNLOCKABLE	HOW TO UNLOCK
Three of a Kind	In a round, destroy 3 vehicles of the same kind.

BATTLESTATIONS: MIDWAY (XBOX 360)

Enter this code at the mission select screen.

UNLOCKABLE	CODE
Unlock All Levels	Hold (RB), ■, ↑, ↖ and push ↘

BATTLESTATIONS: PACIFIC (XBOX 360)

VEHICLES—JAPANESE CAMPAIGN

UNLOCKABLE	HOW TO UNLOCK
Akizuki Class Destroyer	Achieve at least a silver medal on "Saving the Shoho."
H8K Emily	Achieve at least a silver medal on "Destruction of Z Force."
I-400 Submarine	Achieve at least a silver medal on "Hunt for the USS Hornet."
J7W1 Shinden	Achieve at least a silver medal on "Invasion of Port Moresby."
G4N Betty w/Ohka	Achieve a gold medal on "Invasion of Hawaii."
Shimikazi Destroyer	Achieve at least a silver medal on "Solomon's Skirmish."
Tone Class Cruiser	Achieve at least a silver medal on "Battle of Java Sea."
Type B Submarine (Kaiten equipped)	Achieve at least a silver medal on "Attack on Sydney's Harbor."
Yamato Class Battleship	Achieve a gold medal on "Invasion of Midway."

VEHICLES—US CAMPAIGN

UNLOCKABLE	HOW TO UNLOCK
Allen M. Sumner Class Destroyer	Achieve at least a silver medal on"Battle of Santa Cruz."
ASW Fletcher Class Destroyer	Achieve at least a silver medal on "Battle of Cape Engano."
Atlanta Class Anti-Aircraft Cruiser	Achieve at least a silver medal on "Battle of Cape Esperance."
B-29 SuperFortress	Achieve at least a silver medal on "Air Raid Against Indochina."
Gato Class Submarine	Achieve at least a silver medal on "Defense of Henderson Airfield."
Iowa Class Battleship	Achieve a gold medal on "First Battle of Guadalcanal."
TBM-3 Avenger	Achieve a gold medal on "Battle of Okinawa."

BAYONETTA (XBOX 360)

EXTRA COSTUMES

To unlock the extra costumes, you have to beat all chapters on Normal first. Load your Clear Data, go to "Gates of Hell," and then go to "Rodin's Treasure" menu. You'll see a Super Mirror there, which costs 100,000 Halos. Purchase this, and you'll unlock the rest of the costumes (Couture Bullets). To change costumes, press R1 at the Chapter Start screen, go to "Costume Change," and then choose your costume there.

UNLOCKABLE	HOW TO UNLOCK
d'Arc (Jeanne-like costume)	Purchase "Couture Bullet (d'Arc)" at Gates of Hell for 100.000 Halos.
Nun	Purchase "Couture Bullet (Nun)" at Gates of Hell for 100,000 Halos.
Old	Purchase "Couture Bullet (Old) at Gates of Hell for 100,000 Halos.

P.E. Uniform: Types A, B & C are available	Purchase "Couture Bullet (P.E. Uniform)" at Gates of Hell for 100,000 Halos.
Queen	Purchase "Couture Bullet (Queen)" at Gates of Hell for 100,000 Halos.
Umbra	Purchase "Couture Bullet (Umbra)" at Gates of Hell for 100,000 Halos.
Umbran Komachi (Kimono): Type A, B & C are available	Purchase "Super Mirror" at Gates of Hell for 100,000 Halos.
Various: Type A (Bikini), B (Bikini) & C (Cheerleader) are available	Purchase "Couture Bullet (Various) at Gates of Hell for 100,000 Halos.

DIFFICULTIES

UNLOCKABLE	HOW TO UNLOCK
Hard	Beat all chapters on Normal.
Nonstop Infinite Climax	Beat all chapters on Hard.

ACCESSORIES

The following accessories will be available to purchase at the shop, after their specific requirement has been completed.

UNLOCKABLE	HOW TO UNLOCK
Bracelet of Time	Complete the game on Normal difficulty or higher, in under three hours.
Climax Bracelet	Obtain all 101 Umbran Tears of Blood.
Eternal Testimony	Obtain 50 Umbran Tears of Blood.
Immortal Marionette	Beat the game on Very Easy or Easy difficulty.

CHARACTERS

Complete the following conditions to unlock the hidden characters below. To use them, you must select "New Game" and then the character. All data will be reset for that character only and will not affect your main file.

UNLOCKABLE	HOW TO UNLOCK
Jeanne	Acquire Platinum Medals all Verses in Normal difficulty or higher.
Little Zero	Beat the "Lost Chapter."

WEAPONS

Complete the following conditions to receive the weapons listed below.

UNLOCKABLE	HOW TO UNLOCK
Bazillions	Beat the game on Hard difficulty.
Handguns	Beat the game on Normal difficulty.
Pillowtalk	Beat the game on Non-Stop Infinite Climax difficulty.
Rodin	Buy the "Platinum Ticket" and beat the boss that is summoned.
Sai-Fon	Complete 100 Chapters on Normal difficulty or higher.

BAYONETTA (PlayStation 3)

EXTRA COSTUMES

To unlock the extra costumes, you have to beat all chapters on Normal first. Load your Clear Data, go to "Gates of Hell," and then go to "Rodin's Treasure" menu. You'll see a Super Mirror there, which costs 100,000 Halos. Purchase this, and you'll unlock the rest of the costumes (Couture Bullets). To change costumes, press R1 at the Chapter Start screen, go to "Costume Change," and then choose your costume there.

UNLOCKABLE	HOW TO UNLOCK
d'Arc (Jeanne-like costume)	Purchase "Couture Bullet (d'Arc)" at Gates of Hell for 100,000 Halos.
Nun	Purchase "Couture Bullet (Nun)" at Gates of Hell for 100,000 Halos.
Old	Purchase "Couture Bullet (Old) at Gates of Hell for 100,000 Halos.

UNLOCKABLE	HOW TO UNLOCK
P.E. Uniform: Types B & C are available	Purchase "Couture Bullet (P.E. Uniform)" at Gates of Hell for 100,000 Halos.
Queen	Purchase "Couture Bullet (Queen)" at Gates of Hell for 100,000 Halos.
Umbra	Purchase "Couture Bullet (Umbra)" at Gates of Hell for 100,000 Halos.
Umbran Komachi (Kimono): Types A, B & C are available	Purchase "Super Mirror" at Gates of Hell for 100,000 Halos.
Various: Type A (Bikini), B (Bikini) & C (Cheerleader) are available	Purchase "Couture Bullet (Various) Gates of Hell for 100,000 Halos.

DIFFICULTIES

UNLOCKABLE	HOW TO UNLOCK
Hard	Beat all chapters on Normal.
Nonstop Infinite Climax	Beat all chapters on Hard.

ACCESSORIES

The following accessories are available to purchase at the shop after their specific requirement has been completed.

UNLOCKABLE	HOW TO UNLOCK
Bracelet of Time	Complete the game on Normal difficulty or higher, in under three hours.
Climax Bracelet	Obtain all 101 Umbran Tears of Blood.
Eternal Testimony	Obtain 50 Umbran Tears of Blood.
Immortal Marionette	Beat the game on Very Easy or Easy difficulty.

CHARACTERS

Complete the following conditions to unlock the hidden characters. To use them, you must select "New Game" and then the character. All data will be reset for that character only and will not affect your main file.

UNLOCKABLE	HOW TO UNLOCK
Jeanne	Acquire Platinum Medals all Verses in Normal difficulty or higher.
Little Zero	Beat the "Lost Chapter."

WEAPONS

Complete the following conditions to receive the weapons listed below.

UNLOCKABLE	HOW TO UNLOCK
Bazillions	Beat the game on Hard difficulty.
Handguns	Beat the game on Normal difficulty.
Pillowtalk	Beat the game on Non-Stop Infinite Climax difficulty.
Rodin	Buy the "Platinum Ticket" and beat the boss that is summoned.
Sai-Fon	Complete 100 chapters on Normal difficulty or higher.

BEAUTIFUL KATAMARI (XBOX 360)

FORMAL OUTFIT

UNLOCKABLE	HOW TO UNLOCK
Royal Outfit	Obtain 100 percent on item collection.

ETERNAL MODE

Get 100 points on any level to unlock Eternal mode for that specific level. After that you can roll about without a time limit or a goal.

ACHIEVEMENTS

UNLOCKABLE	HOW TO UNLOCK
1,000 Cookies (40)	Obtain 1,000 cookies.
10 Cousins (5)	Find 10 cousins.
10 Presents (5)	Collect 10 presents.

100 Cookies (5)	Obtain 100 cookies.
100 Hours Playtime (80G)	Played for 100 hours.
20 Cousins (10)	Find 20 cousins.
20 Presents (10)	Collect 20 presents.
30 Cousins (20)	Find 30 cousins.
30 Presents (20)	Collect 30 presents.
40 Cousins (40)	Find 40 cousins.
50 Hours Playtime (40G)	Played for 50 hours.
All Cousins (80)	Download stages and find all cousins.
All Presents (80)	Download stages and collect all presents.
All Requests (60)	Complete all requests.
Astronomic Katamari (90)	Download stages and make a katamari over 1,500,000 km.
Big Katamari (10)	Make a katamari that's 30m or more!
Collection 100% (80G)	Roll up 100% of the collection.
Collection 20% (5)	Roll up 20% of the collection.
Collection 40% (10)	Roll up 40% of the collection.
Collection 60% (20)	Roll up 60% of the collection.
Collection 80% (40)	Roll up 80% of the collection.
Colossal Katamari (60)	Make a katamari that's 10,000 km or more!
Frequent Online Roller (10)	Play online 10 times.
Jumbo Katamari (20)	Make a katamari that's 500 m or more!
Katamari Fan (40G)	Complete requests 100 times in Normal mode.
Katamari Lover (80)	Complete 200 requests.
Katamari Perfectionist (100)	Clear all stages, and then do each (of the possible ones) on time attack.
Manic Roller (20)	Hint: Running into walls will destroy your katamari.
Mini Katamari (5)	Make a katamari that's 30cm or more!
Non-stop Roller (30)	Hint: Roll through the course without stopping once.
Online Roller (5)	Play online.
Quick Turner (10)	Hint: Use Quick Turn to your advantage.
Request x 3 (5)	Complete three requests.
Request x 6 (5)	Complete six requests.
Request x 9 (20)	Complete nine requests.
Resident Online Roller (40)	Play online 50 times.
Responsible Roller (30)	Hint: Roll through the course without bumping into any objects.
Small Katamari (5)	Make a katamari that's 1m or more!
Sorta Big Katamari (5)	Make a katamari that's 5m or more!
Speedy Roller (10)	Hint: Zip through the course with Dash.

BEJEWELED 2 DELUXE (XBOX 360)

MODE UNLOCKABLES

UNLOCKABLE	HOW TO UNLOCK
Remove Background Grid	Hold LB LT RB RT then press B
Change Jewel Types	Hold LB LT RB RT then press A
Unlock Cognito Mode	Finish all the puzzles in Puzzle mode. It is okay to look at hints constantly to solve all the puzzles. Cognito mode is basically Puzzle mode with no hints.
Finity Mode	Complete 280 levels of Endless mode

UNLOCKABLE	HOW TO UNLOCK
Hyper Mode	Complete 8 levels of Action mode
Twilight Mode	Complete 17 levels of Classic mode
Original Mode	Go into Play Game when you first load up the game. Select the Classic, Action, Endless, and Puzzle mode buttons (in that order) at the menu screen repeatedly (so you're basically maneuvering the cursor across the screen clockwise). After several rounds, a window will come up saying "Please Wait," and Original mode will load up.

BEN 10: PROTECTOR OF EARTH (Wii)

CODES

Press Start at the Map screen to bring up the Option menu, then select the "Enter Secret Code" menu and enter the following codes to get the corresponding effects.

UNLOCKABLE	HOW TO UNLOCK
Dark Heroes	Cannonbolt, Cannonbolt, Fourarms, Heatblast
DNA Force	Wildvine, Fourarms, Heatblast, Cannonbolt
Invincibility	XLR8, Heatblast, Wildvine, Fourarms
Master Control	Cannonbolt, Heatblast, Wildvine, Fourarms
Unlock Alien Forms	Wildvine, Fourarms, Heatblast, Wildvine
Unlock ALL Combos	Cannonbolt, Heatblast, Fourarms, Heatblast
Unlock All Locations on Map	Heatblast, XLR8, XLR8, Cannonbolt

BEN 10: PROTECTOR OF EARTH (PSP)

CODES

Press Start at the Map screen to bring up the Option menu, select the "Enter Secret Code" menu, and enter the following codes to get the corresponding effects.

UNLOCKABLE	HOW TO UNLOCK
Dark Heroes	Cannonbolt, Cannonbolt, Fourarms, Heatblast
DNA Force	Wildvine, Fourarms, Heatblast, Cannonbolt
Invincibility	XLR8, Heatblast, Wildvine, Fourarms
Master Control	Cannonbolt, Heatblast, Wildvine, Fourarms
Unlock Alien Forms	Wildvine, Fourarms, Heatblast, Wildvine
Unlock ALL Combos	Cannonbolt, Heatblast, Fourarms, Heatblast
Unlock All Locations on Map	Heatblast, XLR8, XLR8, Cannonbolt

BIONICLE HEROES (Wii)

SECRET CHARACTER

UNLOCKABLE	HOW TO UNLOCK
Vezon	Complete the game once

BIOSHOCK (XBOX 360)

ACHIEVEMENTS

ACHIEVEMENT	HOW TO UNLOCK
Ammo Inventor (25)	Successfully invented all possible ammo types.
Avid Inventor (10)	Successfully invent at least 100 items.
Basic Inventor (5)	Successfully invent at least one item.
Became a Big Daddy (30)	The player has become a Big Daddy.
Bought One Slot (5)	Purchase one slot in any Plasmid or Tonic track.
Brass Balls (100)	Beat the game on Hard difficulty without using a Vita Chamber.

Broke Fontaine's Mind Control (30)	The player has broken Fontaine's mind control.
Completed Cohen's Masterpiece (30)	The player has completed Sander Cohen's great masterpiece.
Completed Welcome (10)	Successfully complete the Welcome To Rapture level.
Dealt with Every Little Sister (40)	Either harvest or rescue every Little Sister in the game.
Defeated Andrew Ryan (30)	The player has defeated Andrew Ryan.
Defeated Atlas (100)	The player has defeated Atlas.
Defeated Dr. Steinman (15)	The player has defeated the crazed Dr. Steinman.
Defeated Peach Wilkins (15)	The player has defeated Peach Wilkins.
Five Fully Upgraded Weapons (10)	Fully upgrade five weapons.
Found Cohen's Room (10)	The player has entered Sander Cohen's personal quarters.
Four Fully Upgraded Weapons (10)	Fully upgrade four weapons.
Fully Researched Bouncer (10)	Fully research the Bouncer.
Fully Researched Gun Splicer (10)	Fully research the Leadhead Splicer.
Fully Researched Houdini Splicer (10)	Fully research the Houdini Splicer.
Fully Researched Little Sister (10)	Fully research the Little Sister.
Fully Researched Nitro Splicer (10)	Fully research the Nitro Splicer.
Fully Researched Rosie (10)	Fully research the Rosie.
Fully Researched Spider Splicer (10)	Fully research the Spider Splicer.
Fully Researched Thug Splicer (10)	Fully research the Thuggish Splicer.
Hacked a Safe (10)	Successfully hack a safe.
Hacked a Security Bot (10)	Successfully hack a security bot.
Hacked a Security Camera (10)	Successfully hack a security camera.
Hacked a Turret (10)	Successfully hack a turret.
Hacked a Vending Machine (10)	Successfully hack a vending machine.
Historian (50)	Find every audio diary.
Irony (10)	The player has taken a picture of Sander Cohen's corpse.
Little Sister Savior (100)	Complete the game without harvesting any Little Sisters.
Lucky Winner (10)	Hit the jackpot at a slot machine.
Maxed All Tracks (50)	Purchased every slot in all four Plasmid and Tonic tracks.
Maxed One Track (20)	Purchased every slot in one of the Plasmid or Tonic tracks.
One Fully Upgraded Weapon (5)	Fully upgrade one weapon.
One Successful Hack (5)	Perform at least one successful hack.
Prolific Photographer (5)	Take at least one photo in every research group.
Quality Research Photo (20)	Take a Research Photo of the highest grade.
Research PhD (20)	Max out all possible research.
Researched a Splicer (5)	Take at least one Research Photo of a Splicer.
Restored the Forest (15)	The player has restored the forests of Arcadia.
Seriously Good At This (40)	Complete the game on the hardest difficulty setting.

ACHIEVEMENT	HOW TO UNLOCK
Skilled Hacker (40)	Successfully complete 50 hacks.
Three Fully Upgraded Weapons (10)	Fully upgrade three weapons.
Toaster in the Tub (10)	Shock an enemy in the water.
Tonic Collector (50)	Collect or Invent 53 Tonics in the Physical, Engineering, and Combat tracks.
Two Fully Upgraded Weapons (5)	Fully upgrade two weapons.
Upgraded a Weapon (5)	Acquire at least one weapon upgrade.
Weapon Specialist (20)	Acquire all upgrades for all weapons.
ALTERNATE ENDINGS	
Bad Ending	Harvest more than one Little Sister.
Good Ending	Harvest one Little Sister, but rescue the rest.

BLACK (XBOX)

Enter this password as a profile name. Once it is entered you will be asked to enter a real profile name.

UNLOCKABLE	PASSWORD
Start with the BFG	5SQQ-STHA-ZFFV-7XEV

BLACK STONE: MAGIC AND STEEL (XBOX)

UNLOCKABLE	CODE
New Character Class	From the Class selection screen, press (RT) as you highlight each of the following classes: Pirate, Thief, Warrior, Archer, Pirate, Warlock, Thief, Warlock, Thief.

BLASTWORKS: BUILD, TRADE, DESTROY (Wii)

UNLOCKABLES

UNLOCKABLE	HOW TO UNLOCK
Original TUMIKI Fighters	Beat all five campaigns on any difficulty.
Rootage	Complete the Arcade mode.
Black & White Cheat	Complete Campaign 2 in Arcade mode on Pilot difficulty.
Choose Ship Cheat	Complete Campaign 4 in Arcade mode on Pilot difficulty.
Extra Bullet Sounds	Complete Campaign 5 in Arcade mode on Pilot difficulty.
Extra Hit Sounds	Complete Campaign mode on Pilot difficulty.
Extra Skin Settings	Complete Campaign mode on Pilot difficulty.
Gunroar	Complete Campaign 4 in Campaign mode on Pilot difficulty.
Ninety Nine Cheat	Complete Campaign 2 in Campaign mode on Pilot difficulty.
Torus Trooper	Complete Campaign 3 in Campaign mode on Pilot difficulty.
TUMIKI Folder	Complete Campaign 5 in Campaign mode on Pilot difficulty.
Turtle Speed Cheat	Complete Campaign 1 in Campaign mode on Pilot difficulty.
Virtual Cheat	Complete Campaign 3 in Arcade mode on Pilot difficulty.
Wireframe Cheat	Complete Campaign 1 in Arcade mode on Pilot difficulty.
Flip Cheat	Complete Campaign 2 in Arcade mode on Ace difficulty.
Hyper Speed Cheat	Complete Campaign 1 in Arcade mode on Ace difficulty.

BLAZBLUE: CALAMITY TRIGGER (XBOX 360)

UNLOCKABLES

UNLOCKABLE	HOW TO UNLOCK
True Ending	Individually clear each character's Story Mode.
Unlimited Hakumen	Beat Hakumen's Arcade Mode.
Unlimited Rachel	Beat Rachel's Arcade Mode.
Unlimited Ragna	Beat Ragna's Arcade Mode.
Unlimited v-13	Beat v-13's Arcade Mode.

ASTRAL HEAT

Ragna starts with his Astral Heat (finisher), but every other character needs to unlock theirs. Beat their Arcade Mode and they'll get their own.

BLAZBLUE: CALAMITY TRIGGER (PlayStation 3)

UNLOCKABLES

UNLOCKABLE	HOW TO UNLOCK
True Ending	Individually clear each character's Story Mode.
Unlimited Hakumen	Beat Hakumen's Arcade Mode.
Unlimited Rachel	Beat Rachel's Arcade Mode.
Unlimited Ragna	Beat Ragna's Arcade Mode.
Unlimited v-13	Beat v-13's Arcade Mode.

ASTRAL HEAT

Ragna starts with his Astral Heat (finisher), but every other character needs to unlock theirs. Beat their Arcade Mode and they'll get their own.

BLAZING ANGELS 2: SECRET MISSIONS OF WWII (PlayStation 3)

CODES

Enter the code for unlocking the planes and missions in the main menu, and enter the other two codes while paused when on a mission.

EFFECT	CODE
Damage Increased/Normal	Hold L2 and press L1,L1,R1. Release L2, hold R2 and press R1,R1,L1.
God Mode Active/Inactive	Hold L2 and press ■,▲,▲,■. Release L2, hold R2 and press ▲,■,■,▲.
Unlock All Planes and Missions	Hold both R2,L2 then press ■,L1,R1,▲,▲,R1,L1,■.

BLAZING ANGELS: SQUADRONS OF WW (XBOX 360)

Enter these codes while the game is paused.

UNLOCKABLE	CODE
Firepower Increased	Hold LT, press L3, L3, RB, release LT, hold RT, and then press RB, RB, L3
God Mode	Hold LT, press X, Y, Y, X, release LT, hold RT, and then press Y, X, X, Y

Enter this code at the Main menu.

UNLOCKABLE	CODE
Unlock all campaign levels and planes	Hold LT+RT, then press X, L3, RB, Y, Y, RB, L3, X

BLAZING ANGELS: SQUADRONS OF WWII (PlayStation 3)

Enter these codes while the game is paused.

UNLOCKABLE	CODE
Increase Damage of Weapons	Hold L2 and quickly press L1, L1, R1; release L2, then hold R2 and quickly press R1, R1, L1

UNLOCKABLE	CODE
Invincibility	Hold L2 and press ■, ▲, ▲, ■; release L2, then hold R2 and quickly press ▲, ■, ■, ▲

Enter this code at the Title menu while holding L2+R2

UNLOCKABLE	CODE
All Campaign Missions and Planes	■, L1, R1, ▲, ▲, R1, L1, ■

BLAZING ANGELS: SQUADRONS OF WWII (Wii)

UNLOCKABLES

UNLOCKABLE	HOW TO UNLOCK
All Aircraft/Missions/Paint Jobs	At the menu immediately following choose pilot, hold ⊖ and ⊕, then press ✚, ✚, ①, ②, ②, ①
B-17 Flying Fortress and Spitfire IX	Complete Campaign Mission 18—Counter Attack with at least a Veteran Pilot Ranking
B-25 Mitchell and Hs-129	Complete the Bombing Mini Campaign
Beaufighter and P-40C Warhawk	Complete Campaign Mission 6—Desert Rats with at least a Veteran Pilot Ranking
Boulton-Paul Defiant and Ki-43 Hayabusa (Oscar)	Complete Campaign Mission 10—Midway: Turning Point with at least a Veteran Pilot Ranking
De Havilland (DH) Mosquito and N1K Shiden (George)	Complete Campaign Mission 13—Rabaul Raid with at least a Veteran Pilot Ranking
Devastator and D3A1 Val	Complete Campaign Mission 7—Day of Infamy with at least a Veteran Pilot Ranking
Dornier Do-335 Pfeil (Arrow)	Complete Campaign mode
F2A Buffalo and B5N2 Kate	Complete Campaign Mission 8—Surprise Attack with at least a Veteran Pilot Ranking
Fw-190A and Me-109G	Complete Campaign Mission 14—Preemptive Strike with at least a Veteran Pilot Ranking
Hurricane I and Me-110C	Complete Campaign Mission 1—Training Day with at least a Veteran Pilot Ranking
Hurricane II and Me-110E	Complete Campaign Mission 5—Desert Recon with at least a Veteran Pilot Ranking
Me-262 Schwalbe (Sparrow) and Me-163 Komet	Complete the Dogfight Mini Campaign
Meteor and Kikka	Complete Campaign Mission 20—Berlin 1945 with at least a Veteran Pilot Ranking
P-51D Mustang and Me-109K	Complete Campaign Mission 16—D-Day Normandy with at least a Veteran Pilot Ranking
P-51H Mustang and Fw-190D-9	Complete Campaign Mission 19—Flying Fortresses with at least a Veteran Pilot Ranking
P-82 Twin Mustang and J2M Raiden (Jack)	Complete Campaign Mission 12—The Battle of New Georgia with at least a Veteran Pilot Ranking
SB2C Helldiver and SB2A Buccaneer	Complete Campaign Mission 11—Holding Guadalcanal with at least a Veteran Pilot Ranking
SBD-3 Dauntless and A6M Zero	Complete Campaign Mission 9—Midway: Opening with at least a Veteran Pilot Ranking
Seafire and Ju-87 Stuka	Complete Campaign Mission 4—London 1940 with at least a Veteran Pilot Ranking
Spitfire I and Me-109E	Complete Campaign Mission 2—Skies of Dunkirk with at least a Veteran Pilot Ranking
Swordfish and Spitfire V	Complete Campaign Mission 3—Dunkirk Evacuation with at least a Veteran Pilot Ranking
Tempest and A-1 Skyraider	Complete Campaign Mission 17—Paris: La Liberation with at least a Veteran Pilot Ranking
Typhoon and Me-110G	Complete Campaign Mission 15—Top Secret with at least a Veteran Pilot Ranking

Upgraded Bombs, Rockets, and Torpedos for All Aircraft	Complete the Bombing Mini Campaign
Upgraded Cannons and Machine Guns for All Fighters	Complete the Dogfight Mini Campaign

BLAZING ANGELS: SQUADRONS OF WWII (XBOX)

Enter this code at the Main menu.

UNLOCKABLE	CODE
All Planes and Missions	Hold (LT) + (RT) and press (X), (WHT), (BLK), (Y), (Y), (BLK), (WHT), (X)

Enter these codes while the game is paused.

UNLOCKABLE	CODE
Extra Damage	Hold (LT) and press (WHT), (WHT), (BLK), then release (LT). Then hold (RT) and press (BLK), (BLK), (WHT), then release (RT)
God Mode	Hold (LT) and press (X), (Y), (Y), (X), then release (LT). Then hold (RT) and press (Y), (X), (X), (Y), then release (RT)

BLEACH: HEAT THE SOUL 6 (PSP)

SOUL CODES

Play Soul Championship Mode to unlock Soul Codes, then use them instead of Soul Customize.

UNLOCKABLE	HOW TO UNLOCK
13Squads	Complete the 8th Game in Rank B.
5th Sword	Complete the 7th Game in Rank A.
8th Sword	Complete the 10th Game in Rank A.
Aizen's Man	Complete the 1st Game in Rank SS.
Annihilator	Complete Arcade Mode with new Record.
BLEACHMania	Complete Story Mode 100%.
Boar Rider	Complete the 6th Game in Rank C.
BoobFetish	Complete the 12th Game in Rank S.
Bostov	Complete the 12th Game in Rank C.
BtmSoul Mod	Complete the 12th Game in Rank B.
Burning Man	Complete the 12th Game in Rank A.
Central 46	Complete all games in Ranks D, C, B, A, and S.
Dark Dweller	Complete the 2nd Game in Rank A.
DynamiteBdy	Complete the 11th Game in Rank B.
Evil Beast	Complete the 9th Game in Rank B.
Evil Student	Complete the 7th Game in Rank S.
Ex-3rdBlade	Complete the 3rd Game in Rank S.
ExSquad3Cpt	Complete the 9th Game in Rank S.
ExSquad5Cpt	Complete the 10th Game in Rank S.
Fast Talker	Complete the 2nd Game in Rank B.
FemReaper	Complete the 4th Game in Rank S.
First Sword	Complete the 11th Game in Rank S.
Flash Master	Complete the 6th Game in Rank S.
Fmr Squad9Lt	Complete the 2nd Game in Rank S.
Hero	Complete the 1st game in Rank D.
HuecoPnthr	Complete the 11th Game in Rank A.
InfiniteEvo	Complete the 9th Game in Rank A.
InfiniteFol	Complete the 4th Game in Rank B.
KarakuraPnk	Complete the 12th Game in Rank D.
KarakuraRed	Complete the 10th Game in Rank D.
KUROSAKIFre	Complete the 2nd Game in Rank D.

UNLOCKABLE	HOW TO UNLOCK
Lucky !!	Complete the 1st Game in Rank A.
MaleReaper	Complete the 6th Game in Rank A.
MAYUTIsOpus	Complete the 9th Game in Rank C.
MdScientist	Complete the 5th Game in Rank B.
MedCollect	Collect 60 Soul Codes.
Mr.Popular	Complete the 3rd Game in Rank C.
Narcissist	Complete the 10th Game in Rank B.
NelBrothers	Complete the 5th Game in Rank A.
Newbie	Collect 30 Soul Codes.
OtherICHIGO	Complete the 8th game in Rank C.
P@rn Maniac	Complete the 2nd Game in Rank C.
Prankster	Complete the 8th Game in Rank S.
Preacher	Complete the 3rd Game in Rank A.
PunishLdr	Clear Arcade within 3 minutes.
Quip Demon	Complete the 7th Game in Rank D.
ReaperProf	Clear Tutorial fully.
RecoveryMed	Complete the 10th Game in Rank C.
SpecsClerk	Complete the 1st Game in Rank S.
Spirit King	Complete the 1st Game in Rank SSS.
Sqaud 11 Ltn	Complete the 5th Game in Rank D.
Squad 1 Ltn	Complete the 3rd Game in Rank D.
Squad 12 Cpt	Complete the 8th Game in Rank A.
Squad 12 Ltn	Complete the 4th Game in Rank D.
Squad 3 Ltn	Complete the 4th Game in Rank C.
Squad 4 # 7	Complete the 6th Game in Rank B.
Squad 4 Ltn	Complete the 8th Game in Rank D.
Squad 5 Ltn	Complete the 1st Game in Rank B.
Squad 6 Ltn	Complete the 9th Game in Rank D.
Squad 7 Ltn	Complete the 1st Game in Rank C.
Squad 9 Ltn	Complete the 7th Game in Rank C.
Squad11 Cpt	Complete the 5th Game in Rank C.
Squad11pos3	Complete the 11th Game in Rank D.
Squad13 Cpt	Complete the 4th Game in Rank A.
SummonedDev	Complete the 3rd Game in Rank B.
Talking Man	Complete the 5th Game in Rank S.
Thief Nel	Complete the 11th Game in Rank C.
Treasoners	Complete the 2nd Game in Rank SS.
UraharaMngr	Complete the 6th Game in Rank D.
YORUICHI Fan	Complete the 7th Game in Rank B.

UNLOCKABLE CHARACTERS

UNLOCKABLE	HOW TO UNLOCK
Dark Rukia	Complete Mission 60.
Tia Halibel	Complete Mission 49.

BLEACH: SHATTERED BLADE (Wii)

CHARACTERS

UNLOCKABLE	HOW TO UNLOCK
Aizen Sousuke	Clear Arcade mode with Ulquiorra.
Arturo Plateado	Clear Episode mode with Arturo Plateado.
Grimmjow Jaggerjack	Clear Arcade mode with Aizen Sousuke.
Hinamori Momo	Clear Hitsugaya Toushiro's story.

Hisagi Shuuhei	Clear Episode mode with Yamada Hanatarou.
Ichimaru Gin	Clear Arcade mode with Matsumoto Rangiku and Kira Izuru.
Kuchiki Rukia	Beat Story mode with Abarai Renji.
Kurotsuchi Mayuri	Clear Arcade mode with Ishida Uryuu.
Kusajishi Yachiru	Clear Arcade mode with Yumichika Ayasegawa and Zaraki Kenpachi.
Kyouraku Shunsui	Clear Arcade mode with Sado Yasutora.
Madarame Ikkaku	Clear Episode mode with Zaraki Kenpachi.
Shihouin Yoruichi	Clear Training mode.
Soi Fon	Clear Episode mode with Shihouin Yoruichi.
Tousen Kaname	Clear Arcade mode with Hisagi Shuuhei and Komamura Sajin.
Ukitake Juushiro	Clear Arcade mode with Kyouraku Shunsui.
Ulquiorra	Clear Arcade mode with Tousen Kaname and Ichimaru Gin.
Urahara Kisuke	Clear Arcade mode with Kurotsuchi Mayuri.
Yamada Hanatarou	Beat Story mode with Youshiro Hitsugaya.
Yamamoto Genryuusai Shigekuni	Clear Arcade mode with Ukitake Juushiro.
Yumichika Ayasegawa	Clear Arcade mode with Madarame Ikkaku.

COSTUMES

UNLOCKABLE	HOW TO UNLOCK
Hitsugaya School Costume	Win 15 matches with Toushiro Hitsugaya.
Ikkaku School Costume	Win 10 matches with Madarame Ikkaku.
Masked Komamura Costume	Win 15 matches with Komamura Sajin.
Matsumoto School Costume	AFTER unlocking Inoue Orihime's costume, win 15 matches with Matsumoto Rangiku.
Orihime School Costume	Win 15 matches with Inoue Orihime.
Renji School Costume	Win 15 matches with Abarai Renji.
Rukia School Costume	Win 15 matches with Kuchiki Rukia.
Shihouin Yoruichi Shunpo Costume	After completing practice mode, win 15 matches with Yoruichi.
Urahara Kisuke Shinigami Costume	Unlock everything, and it becomes available for free in Urahara's Shop.
Yumichika School Costume	Win 10 matches with Ayasegawa Yumichika.

STAGES

UNLOCKABLE	HOW TO UNLOCK
Arturo Battle Stage	Defeat Arturo Plateado on the final stage of Episode mode.
Ice Haven	Complete Hitsugaya's Episode mode.

BLITZ: OVERTIME (PSP)

PASSWORD

In the main menu in the "extras" option, input these codes to unlock the following.

PASSWORD	EFFECT
ONFIRE	Ball trails always on. Only affects Quick Play mode.
BOUNCY	Beach Ball. Only affects Quick Play mode.
PIPPED	Double unleash icons. Only affects Quick Play mode.
CHAMPS	In Campaign mode, highlight a team but do not select it. Stay on the menu and press ■,■,▲, Triangle to instantly win against the selected team.
NOTTIRED	Stamina disabled. Only affects Quick Play mode.

PASSWORD	EFFECT
CLASHY	Super Clash mode. Only affects Quick Play mode.
BIGDOGS	Super Unleash Clash mode. Only affects Quick Play mode.
CHUWAY	Two player co-op mode.

BLITZ: THE LEAGUE (XBOX 360)

Enter these passwords in the Code menu under Extras.

UNLOCKABLE	PASSWORD
Ball Trail Always On	ONFIRE
Beach Ball	BOUNCY
Double Unleash Icons	PIPPED
Stamina Off	NOTTIRED
Two Player Co-op	CHUWAY
Unlimited Clash Icons	CLASHY
Unlimited Unleash	BIGDOGS

BLITZ: THE LEAGUE (XBOX)

From the Main menu, go to "Extras," then "Codes" and enter the following passwords.

UNLOCKABLE	PASSWORD
Ball Trail Always On	ONFIRE
Beach Ball	BOUNCY
Double Unleash Icons	PIPPED
Stamina Off	NOTTIRED
Super Clash	CLASHY
Super Unleash Clash	BIGDOGS
Two Player Co-op	CHUWAY

BLITZ: THE LEAGUE (PlayStation 2)

From the Main menu, go to "Extras," then "Codes" and enter the following passwords.

UNLOCKABLE	PASSWORD
Ball Trail Always On	ONFIRE
Beach Ball	BOUNCY
Double Unleash Icons	PIPPED
Stamina Off	NOTTIRED
Super Clash	CLASHY
Super Unleash Clash	BIGDOGS
Two Player Co-op	CHUWAY

BLOODY WOLF (Wii)

CODES

UNLOCKABLE	HOW TO UNLOCK
10 Flash Bombs	When your strength is at "1," climb a barricade and press ↑+→+RUN+②
10 Super Grenades	When your strength is at "1," climb a barricade and press ↓+←+RUN+②
50 Bazooka Rounds	When your strength is at "2," climb a fence and press ←+①+②
50 Flame Thrower Charges	Hold ↑+①+② and press RUN when parachuting at the start of level 2 or level 5
50 Shotgun Rounds	When your strength is at "2," climb a fence and press →+①+②
Fast Mode	At the title screen, press ↑, ↓, →, →, ①, ①, ② SELECT, RUN

Hover Mode (in game, press jump to hover)	At the title screen, press ↓, ↑, ←, ←, ②, ②, ①, SELECT, RUN
Sound Test	At the title screen, press ↑, then hold ①+②+SELECT

LEVEL SELECT CODES

Press ②, ①, ①, ②, ①, ②, ②, ① at the title screen. Then press the following for the appropriate level.

CODE	EFFECT
Up	Level 1
Up/Right	Level 2
Right	Level 3
Down/Right	Level 4
Down	Level 5
Down/Left	Level 6
Left	Level 7
Up/Left	Level 8

BOLT (PlayStation 3)

CODES

Enter the "Extras" menu, then select "Cheats." Enter one of the following codes to unlock the corresponding cheat option. To toggle a cheat on or off, pause gameplay and enter the "Cheats" menu.

EFFECT	CODE
Unlimited Invulnerability	↓,↓,↑,←
Unlimited Laser Eyes	←,←,↑,→
Unlimited Stealth Camo	←,↓,↓,↓
Unlimited Enhanced Vision	←,↑,↑,↓
Unlimited Gas Mines	→,←,←,↑,↓,→
Unlimited SuperBark	→,←,←,↑,↓,↑
Level Select	→,↑,←,→,↑,→
All Mini Games	→,↑,→,→
Unlimited Ground Pound	→,↑,→,↑,←,↓

BONK'S REVENGE (Wii)

CODES

CODE	EFFECT
Bonus Levels	Press ①+② during the title screen
Clear Pause Screen	Pause the game and hold ①+②+SELECT
Ending Sequence Preview	First activate the "practice bonus rounds" code and then highlight the Exit option and press ②+RUN
Practice Bonus Rounds	Hold ② and then press RUN on the Difficulty Selection menu
Remove Pause Text	Pause the game (by pressing RUN) and then press ①+②+SELECT
View Ending	Enable the Bonus Levels cheat, then Highlight "Exit" and press ②+RUN

BOOGIE (Wii)

UNLOCKABLE SONGS AND STAGES

UNLOCKABLE	HOW TO UNLOCK
Song: Boogie Oogie Oogie	Beat Bubba's story
Song: Dancing in the Street	Beat Julius' story
Song: Love Shack	Beat Lea's story
Song: SOS (Rescue Me)	Beat Jet's story
Song: Tu y Yo	Beat Kato's story

UNLOCKABLE	HOW TO UNLOCK
Stage: Big Dub Hustle Club	Beat all 5 stories

BORDERLANDS (XBOX 360)

UNLOCKABLES

UNLOCKABLE	HOW TO UNLOCK
New Game +	Complete the game one time to unlock New Game +. All the enemies are super powerful on this playthrough.

BORDERLANDS (PlayStation 3)

UNLOCKABLES

UNLOCKABLE	HOW TO UNLOCK
New Game +	Complete the game one time to unlock New Game +. All the enemies are super powerful on this playthrough.

BRATZ: THE MOVIE (Wii)

HIDDEN CLOTHING LINES

To unlock these clothing lines, go to the small laptop near the computers in the Bratz Office and type in the following codes.

CODE	CLOTHING LINE
PRETTY	Feelin' Pretty Clothing Line
SCHOOL	High School Clothing Line
ANGELZ	Passion 4 Fashion Clothing Line
SWEETZ	Sweetz Clothing Line

BRAVOMAN (Wii)

CODES

UNLOCKABLE	HOW TO UNLOCK
Bravo Kombat Minigame	Keep tapping ②, SELECT at the title screen
Continue Game	Press ②+RUN as Bravoman is dying
Unlimited Continues	Get 10,000 points, then lose and wait for the title screen to come up, then press ↑, →, ↓, ←, ②, SELECT, ②, SELECT

BREATH OF FIRE II (Wii)

UNLOCKABLE	HOW TO UNLOCK
Old Friends	At Giant Island, in the northern area above the town gate, you'll find Bo and Karn from the first *Breath of Fire* game. They don't do anything, but you can talk to them. You need the whale or the bird to get there.

BRIAN LARA INTERNATIONAL CRICKET 2005 (XBOX)

Enter these passwords in the Cheat menu.

UNLOCKABLE	PASSWORD
Unlock All Classic Matches	BOWLEDHIM
Unlock All Teams	GOODLENGTH
Unlock All the Classic Players	GONEFORADUCK
Unlock All Trophys	DOLLY
Unlock the Classic XI Challenge	STUMPED
Unlock the Picture Gallery	SLEDGING

BRIAN LARA INTERNATIONAL CRICKET 2005 (PlayStation 2)

Enter these passwords in the Cheat menu.

UNLOCKABLE	PASSWORD
Unlock All Classic Matches	BOWLEDHIM
Unlock All Teams	GOODLENGTH
Unlock All the Classic Players	GONEFORADUCK
Unlock All Trophys	DOLLY
Unlock the Classic XI Challenge	STUMPED
Unlock the Picture Gallery	SLEDGING

BROTHERS IN ARMS: HELL'S HIGHWAY (XBOX 360)

CODES

Select the "Enter Codes" option at the main menu, then enter the codes.

EFFECT	CODE
All Recon Points	0ZNDRBICRA
Kilroy Alert (Notifies you when you are close to a Kilroy)	SH2VYIVNZF
Kilroy Detector (Alerts you when a Kilroy is nearby)	4V35JZHQD6
Two Extra Skins	HI9WTPXSUK

BROTHERS IN ARMS: HELL'S HIGHWAY (PlayStation 3)

CODES

Select the "Enter Codes" option at the main menu, then enter the codes.

EFFECT	CODE
All Recon Points	0ZNDRBICRA
Kilroy Alert (Notifies you when you are close to a Kilroy)	SH2VYIVNZF
Kilroy Detector (Alerts you when a Kilroy is nearby)	4V35JZHQD6
Two Extra Skins	HI9WTPXSUK

BROTHERS IN ARMS: ROAD TO HILL 30 (XBOX)

UNLOCKABLE	CODE
Unlock All Levels and Difficulties	BAKERSDOZEN

BROTHERS IN ARMS: ROAD TO HILL 30 (PlayStation 2)

UNLOCKABLE	CODE
All levels and difficulties BAKERSDOZEN	Create a profile with the name

BRUTAL LEGEND (XBOX 360)

UNLOCKABLES

UNLOCKABLE	HOW TO UNLOCK
Increased Nitrous Power	Complete all Racing Missions
Spike-Quilled Axe	Complete all Hunter Missions

BRUTAL LEGEND (PlayStation 3)

UNLOCKABLES

UNLOCKABLE	HOW TO UNLOCK
Increased Nitrous Power	Complete all Racing Missions
Spike-Quilled Axe	Complete all Hunter Missions

BULLET WITCH (XBOX 360)

UNLOCKABLE	CODE
Hell Mode	Beat Chaos and Hard modes

BULLY: SCHOLARSHIP EDITION (XBOX 360)

CODES

The following cheats can be input only on the 360's second controller, not the primary controller. Input all the codes during gameplay.

UNLOCKABLE	HOW TO UNLOCK
All Weapons	LB, ↑, ↑, ↑, ↑
Full Health (not the extra from kissing)	LB, →, →, →
Infinite Ammo (enter again to turn off)	LB, ↑, ↓, ↑, ↓
Massive Money Gain	LB, Y, X, B, A

ACHIEVEMENTS

UNLOCKABLE	HOW TO UNLOCK
After Hours (20)	Spend five hours out after curfew.
Black & White & Read All Over (20)	Complete All Paper Route Missions.
Boy Genius (30)	Complete nine Classes.
Casanova (20)	Receive 25 kisses from the ladies.
Down for the Count (20)	Beat up 200 opponents.
Dual Nebula (20)	Achieve a high score on Consumo, Nut Shots, and Monkey Fling Arcade Games.
Eggsellent! (20)	Egg 25 cars.
Freshman (20)	Complete Chapter 1.
Glass Dismissed (25)	Break 300 bottles at the shooting gallery.
Graduate (40)	Complete Chapter 5.
Green Thumb (20)	Complete all Lawn Mowing Jobs.
Green Thumbs Up (20)	Pick 50 flowers.
Helping Hand (20)	Complete 10 Errand Missions.
It's All in the Wrists (20)	Complete all four of the Carnival Games once.
Junior (20)	Complete Chapter 3.
Keener (20)	Complete three Classes.
Kickin' the Balls (20)	Kick 100 soccer balls.
Little Angel (20)	Complete 20 Errand Missions.
Marathon (25)	Travel 100,000 meters on foot.
Mission Accomplished (75)	Complete all Missions.
Momma's Boy (25)	Complete 30 Errand Missions.
Over the Rainbow (20)	Receive 20 kisses from the gents.
Perfectionist (125)	100% completion.
Pole Position (20)	Complete all Go Kart Races.
Senior (20)	Complete Chapter 4.
Sharp Dressed Man (25)	Collect 250 clothing items.
Skate Pro (25)	Travel 50,000 meters on the skateboard.
Skidmark (25)	Give 50 wedgies.
Smart Mouth (25)	Say 100 taunts.
Smell Ya Later (25)	Hit people with stink bombs 50 times.
Soda-licious (20)	Buy 100 sodas.
Sophomore (20)	Complete Chapter 2.
Speed Freak (20)	Complete half of all Go Kart Races.
Teacher's Pet (20)	Complete six Classes.
The Champion (20)	Complete all Bike Races.
The Wheel Deal (25)	Perform 200 wheelies on the bike.

Tour De Bullworth (25)	Travel 100 km on the bike.
Watch Your Step (20)	Trip 25 people with marbles.

BULLY SCHOLARSHIP EDITION (Wii)

UNLOCKABLES

UNLOCKABLE	HOW TO UNLOCK
Black Ninja Suit	Take a picture of all the students of Bullworth.
BMX Helmet	Complete all bike races.
Crash Helmet	Win the first set of Go-Kart races.
Double Carnival Tickets	Collect all G & G cards.
Fireman's Hat	Pull the fire alarm 15 times to unlock the fireman's hat.
Mo-Ped	Buy from carnival for 75 tickets.
Pumpkin Head	Smash all pumpkins either on Halloween or in basement.
Robber Mask	Break into 15 people's lockers without getting caught.
Rubber Band Ball	Collect all rubber bands.

BURNOUT PARADISE (XBOX 360)

UNLOCKABLE CARS

Acquire an A level license, then insert these codes in the in-game cheats menu.

UNLOCKABLE	HOW TO UNLOCK
Best Buy Car	Type BESTBUY
Circuit City Car	Type CIRCUITCITY
Game Stop Car	Type GAMESTOP
Wal-Mart Car	Type WALMART

OTHER UNLOCKABLE CARS

Insert this code in the in-game cheats menu under the "sponsor codes" section.

UNLOCKABLE	HOW TO UNLOCK
Steel Wheels Car	Type: U84D 3Y8K FY8Y 58N6

LICENSES

To unlock licenses, win the corresponding number of events.

UNLOCKABLE	HOW TO UNLOCK
A	26 events
B	16 events
C	7 events
D	2 events
Burnout Paradise	45 events
Elite	110 events

BURNOUT PARADISE (PlayStation 3)

UNLOCKABLE CARS

Acquire an A level license, then insert these codes in the in-game Cheats menu.

UNLOCKABLE	HOW TO UNLOCK
Best Buy Car	Type BESTBUY
Circuit City Car	Type CIRCUITCITY
Game Stop Car	Type GAMESTOP
Wal-Mart Car	Type WALMART

OTHER UNLOCKABLE CARS

Insert this code in the in-game Cheats menu under the "sponsor codes" section.

UNLOCKABLE	HOW TO UNLOCK
Steel Wheels Car	Type: U84D 3Y8K FY8Y 58N6

LICENSES

To unlock licenses, win the corresponding number of events in the game.

UNLOCKABLE	HOW TO UNLOCK
A	26 events
B	16 events
C	7 events
D	2 events
Burnout Paradise	45 events
Elite	110 events

PAINT COLORS

UNLOCKABLE	HOW TO UNLOCK
Gold Paint	Earn the elite license
Platinum Paint	Earn the elite license and achieve 100 percent completion.

BURNOUT REVENGE (XBOX 360)

UNLOCK SPECIAL CARS OFFLINE

UNLOCKABLE	HOW TO UNLOCK
Black Elite Racer	Gain the "Elite" Ranking
Criterion GT Racer	Complete Central Route's Challenge Sheet
Custom Classic	Complete Sunshine Keys' Challenge Sheet
EA GT Racer	Complete White Mountain's Challenge Sheet
Etnies Racer	Complete Motor City's Challenge Sheet
Euro Classic LM	Complete Eternal City's Challenge Sheet
Hot Rod	Complete Lone Peak's Challenge Sheet
Logitech World Racer	Complete Rank 10 Ultimate Revenge Grand Prix
Low Rider	Complete Angel Valley's Challenge Sheet
Nixon Special	Complete Eastern Bay's Challenge Sheet
Revenge Racer	Gain "100% Complete" Status
Unlock the Madden Van	Open Options, then Special Features, and bring up the Madden 06 preview

BURNOUT: REVENGE (XBOX)

Have a Madden NFL 06 and Burnout 3: Takedown saved before starting a new game. You will unlock two special cars for Crash mode.

UNLOCKABLE	CODE
Dominator Assassin	Burnout 3 Save
Madden Challenge Bus	Madden 06 Save

BURNOUT: REVENGE (PlayStation 2)

Have a Madden NFL 06 and Burnout 3: Takedown saved before starting a new game. You will unlock two special cars for Crash mode.

UNLOCKABLE	CODE
Dominator Assassin	Burnout 3 Save
Madden Challenge Bus	Madden 06 Save

BUST A MOVE (DS)

Enter this code at the Main menu.

UNLOCKABLE	CODE
Sound Test	SELECT, Ⓐ, Ⓑ, ←, →, Ⓐ, SELECT, →

BUST-A-MOVE BASH! (Wii)

MORE STAGES

UNLOCKABLE	HOW TO UNLOCK
250 More Stages	After completing the first 250 stages in Puzzle mode, return to the Select screen and press Ⓐ with the cursor hovering over Stage Select. The area should be mostly orange now instead of blue, and only the first stage will be available. This is how you access stages 251-500.

C

CALL OF DUTY BIG RED ONE (XBOX)

To enter this code, go into the Chapter Selection menu.

UNLOCKABLE	CODE
Level Select	Hold LT+RT and press ↑, ↑, ↓, ↓, ←, ←, →, →, ⓧ, ←, ⓧ, ←, ⓧ

CALL OF DUTY: BIG RED ONE (PlayStation 2)

To enter this code, go into the Chapter Selection menu.

UNLOCKABLE	CODE
Level Select	Hold L1+R1 and press ↑, ↑, ↓, ↓, ←, ←, →, →, ■, →, ■, →, ■

CALL OF DUTY: FINEST HOUR (PlayStation 2)

UNLOCKABLE	CODE
All levels	Hold up on controller two at the level select and enter with Start, Select, Select, Square with controller one.

CALL OF DUTY: MODERN WARFARE 2 (XBOX 360)

EXTRA CUSTOM CLASS SLOT

UNLOCKABLE	HOW TO UNLOCK
Extra Custom Class Slot	Obtain level 70 in multiplayer and enter Prestige Mode to unlock a sixth custom class slot.

KILLSTREAK REWARDS

You can unlock the Killstreaks by receiving the amount designated before dying.

UNLOCKABLE	HOW TO UNLOCK
AC130 Gunship (be the gunner of the AC130)	11 Kills
Attack Helicopter	07 Kills
Care Package (drops ammo/Killstreaks)	04 Kills
Chopper Gunner (be the gunner of the Helicopter)	11 Kills
Counter UAV (jams enemy radars)	04 Kills
Emergency Airdrop (4 ammo/Killstreak drops)	08 Kills
EMP (disables electronics)	15 Kills
Harrier Strike (choose bomb location and defending Harrier)	07 Kills
Nuclear Strike (kills everyone on map)	25 Kills
Pave Low (Armored Helicopter)	09 Kills
Precision Airstrike (drop airstrike)	06 Kills
Predator (guided missiles)	05 Kills
Sentry Gun (deployable gun)	05 Kills
UAV (shows enemy location)	03 Kills

PROFESSIONAL PERKS

With each perk you unlock you can upgrade it by completing various requirements.

UNLOCKABLE	HOW TO UNLOCK
Bling Pro (two primary weapon attachments + two secondary weapon attachments)	Get 200 Kills with a weapon with two attachments.

Cold-Blooded Pro (undetectable by UAV, air support, sentries, and thermal imaging + no red crosshair or name when you are targeted)	Destroy 40 enemy Killstreak Rewards with Cold-Blooded Perk.
Commando Pro (increased Melee Distance + no falling damage)	Get 20 Melee Kills using Commando Perk.
Danger Close Pro (increased explosive weapon damage + extra air support damage)	Get 100 Kills with explosives while using Danger Close Perk.
Hardline Pro (Killstreak Rewards require 1 less Kill + Deathstreak Rewards require 1 less death)	Get 40 Killstreaks (two or more in a row without dying) with Hardline Perk.
Last Stand Pro (pull out your pistol before dying + use equipment in last stand)	Get 20 Kills while in last stand.
Lightweight Pro (move faster + quick aim after sprinting)	Run 30 miles with Lightweight Perk.
Marathon Pro (unlimited sprint + climb obstacles faster)	Run 26 miles with Marathon Perk.
Ninja Pro (invisible to heartbeat sensors + your footsteps are silent)	Get 50 close-range Kills using Ninja Perk.
One Man Army Pro (swap classes at any time + swap classes faster)	Get 120 Kills using One Man Army.
Scavenger Pro (resupply from dead enemies + extra mags)	Resupply 100 times with Scavenger Perk.
Scrambler Pro (jam enemy radar near you + delay enemy claymore explosions)	Get 50 close-range Kills using Scrambler Perk.
Sitrep Pro (detect enemy explosives and tactical insertions + louder enemy footsteps)	Destroy 120 detected explosives or tactical insertions with Sitrep Perk.
Sleight of Hand Pro (faster reloading + faster aiming)	Get 120 kills with Sleight of Hand Perk.
Steady Aim Pro (increased hip fire accuracy + longer hold breath duration)	Get 80 hip fire Kills using Steady Aim.
Stopping Power Pro (extra bullet damage + extra damage to enemy vehicles)	Get 300 Kills with Stopping Power Perk.

MODERN WARFARE 2 MUSEUM

The Museum can be selected from the Mission Select screen once you've completed the game.

UNLOCKABLE	HOW TO UNLOCK
An evening with Infinity Ward: Modern Warfare 2 Gallery Exhibit	Complete the campaign.

MULTIPLAYER WEAPONS AND EQUIPMENT

Reach the level indicated to unlock the weapon and/or piece of equipment.

UNLOCKABLE	HOW TO UNLOCK
.44 Magnum (Pistol)	Level 26
AA-12 (Shotgun)	Level 12
ACR (Assault Rifle)	Level 48
AK-47 (Assault Rifle)	Level 70
AT4-HS (Grenade Launcher)	Level 01
AUG HBAR (LMG)	Level 32
Barret .50 Cal (Sniper)	Level 04
Blast Shield	Level 19
C4	Level 43

UNLOCKABLE	HOW TO UNLOCK
Claymore	Level 31
Desert Eagle (Pistol)	Level 62
F2000 (Assault Rifle)	Level 60
FAL (Assault Rifle)	Level 28
FAMAS (Assault Rifle)	Level 01
Frag Grenade	Level 01
Glock 18 (Secondary)	Level 22
Intervention (Sniper Rifle)	Level 01
Javelin (Grenade Launcher)	Level 50
L86 LSW (LMG)	Level 01
M1014 (Shotgun)	Level 54
M16A4 (Assault Rifle)	Level 40
M21 EBR (Sniper Rifle)	Level 56
M240 (LMG)	Level 52
M4A1 (Rifle)	Level 04
M9 (Pistol)	Level 46
M93 Raffica (Secondary)	Level 38
MG4 (LMG)	Level 16
Mini Uzi (SMG)	Level 44
MP5K (SMG)	Level 04
P90 (SMG)	Level 24
PP-2000 (Secondary)	Level 01
Ranger (Shotgun)	Level 42
RPD (SMG)	Level 04
RPG-7 (Grenade Launcher)	Level 65
SCAR-H (Assault Rifle)	Level 08
Semtex Grenade	Level 01
SPAS-12 (Shotgun)	Level 01
Stinger (Grenade Launcher)	Level 30
Striker (Shotgun)	Level 34
Tactical Insertion	Level 11
TAR-21 (Assault Rifle)	Level 20
Throwing Knife	Level 07
Thumper (Grenade Launcher)	Level 14
TMP (Secondary)	Level 58
UMP .45 (SMG)	Level 01
USP .45 (Pistol)	Level 01
Vector (SMG)	Level 12
WA2000 (Sniper)	Level 36
Winchester 1887 (Shotgun)	Level 67

CALL OF DUTY: MODERN WARFARE 2 (PlayStation 3)

EXTRA CUSTOM CLASS SLOT

UNLOCKABLE	HOW TO UNLOCK
Extra Custom Class Slot	Obtain level 70 in multiplayer and enter Prestige mode to unlock a sixth custom class slot.

KILLSTREAK REWARDS

You can unlock the Killstreaks by receiving the amount designated before dying.

UNLOCKABLE	HOW TO UNLOCK
AC130 Gunship (be the gunner of the AC130)	11 Kills
Attack Helicopter	07 Kills
Care Package (drops ammo/Killstreaks)	04 Kills
Chopper Gunner (be the gunner of the Helicopter)	11 Kills
Counter UAV (jams enemy radar's)	04 Kills
Emergency Airdrop (4 ammo/Killstreak drops)	08 Kills
EMP (disables electronics)	15 Kills
Harrier Strike (choose bomb location and defending Harrier)	07 Kills
Nuclear Strike (kills everyone on map)	25 Kills
Pave Low (Armored Helicopter)	09 Kills
Precision Airstrike (drop airstrike)	06 Kills
Predator (guided missiles)	05 Kills
Sentry Gun (deployable gun)	05 Kills
UAV (shows enemy location)	03 Kills

PROFESSIONAL PERKS

With each perk you unlock you can upgrade it by completing various requirements.

UNLOCKABLE	HOW TO UNLOCK
Bling Pro (two primary weapon attachments + two secondary weapon attachments)	Get 200 Kills with a weapon with two attachments.
Cold-Blooded Pro (undetectable by UAV, air support, sentries, and thermal imaging + no red crosshair or name when you are targeted)	Destroy 40 enemy Killstreak Rewards with Cold-Blooded Perk.
Commando Pro (increased Melee Distance + no falling damage)	Get 20 Melee Kills using Commando Perk.
Danger Close Pro (increased explosive weapon damage + extra air support damage)	Get 100 Kills with explosives while using Danger Close Perk.
Hardline Pro (Killstreak Rewards require 1 less Kill + Deathstreak Rewards require 1 less death)	Get 40 Killstreaks (two or more in a row without dying) with Hardline Perk.
Last Stand Pro (pull out your pistol before dying + use equipment in last stand)	Get 20 Kills while in last stand.
Lightweight Pro (move faster + quick aim after sprinting)	Run 30 miles with Lightweight Perk.
Marathon Pro (unlimited sprint + climb obstacles faster)	Run 26 miles with Marathon Perk.
Ninja Pro (invisible to heartbeat sensors + your footsteps are silent)	Get 50 close-range Kills using Ninja Perk.
One Man Army Pro (swap classes at any time + swap classes faster)	Get 120 Kills using One Man Army.
Scavenger Pro (resupply from dead enemies + extra mags)	Resupply 100 times with Scavenger Perk.
Scrambler Pro (jam enemy radar near you + delay enemy claymore explosions)	Get 50 close-range Kills using Scrambler Perk.
Sitrep Pro (detect enemy explosives and tactical insertions + louder enemy footsteps)	Destroy 120 detected explosives or tactical insertions with Sitrep Perk.
Sleight of Hand Pro (faster reloading + faster aiming)	Get 120 kills with Sleight of Hand Perk.

UNLOCKABLE	HOW TO UNLOCK
Steady Aim Pro (increased hip fire accuracy + longer hold breath duration)	Get 80 hip fire Kills using Steady Aim.
Stopping Power Pro (extra bullet damage + extra damage to enemy vehicles)	Get 300 Kills with Stopping Power Perk.

MODERN WARFARE 2 MUSEUM

The Museum can be selected from the Mission Select screen once you've completed the game.

UNLOCKABLE	HOW TO UNLOCK
An evening with Infinity Ward: Modern Warfare 2 Gallery Exhibit	Complete the campaign.

MULTIPLAYER WEAPONS AND EQUIPMENT

Reach the Level indicated to unlock each Weapon and/or Equipment

UNLOCKABLE	HOW TO UNLOCK
.44 Magnum (Pistol)	Level 26
AA-12 (Shotgun)	Level 12
ACR (Assault Rifle)	Level 48
AK-47 (Assault Rifle)	Level 70
AT4-HS (Grenade Launcher)	Level 01
AUG HBAR (LMG)	Level 32
Barret .50 Cal (Sniper)	Level 04
Blast Shield	Level 19
C4	Level 43
Claymore	Level 31
Desert Eagle (Pistol)	Level 62
F2000 (Assault Rifle)	Level 60
FAL (Assault Rifle)	Level 28
FAMAS (Assault Rifle)	Level 01
Frag Grenade	Level 01
Glock 18 (Secondary)	Level 22
Intervention (Sniper Rifle)	Level 01
Javelin (Grenade Launcher)	Level 50
L86 LSW (LMG)	Level 01
M1014 (Shotgun)	Level 54
M16A4 (Assault Rifle)	Level 40
M21 EBR (Sniper Rifle)	Level 56
M240 (LMG)	Level 52
M4A1 (Rifle)	Level 04
M9 (Pistol)	Level 46
M93 Raffica (Secondary)	Level 38
MG4 (LMG)	Level 16
Mini Uzi (SMG)	Level 44
MP5K (SMG)	Level 04
P90 (SMG)	Level 24
PP-2000 (Secondary)	Level 01
Ranger (Shotgun)	Level 42
RPD (SMG)	Level 04
RPG-7 (Grenade Launcher)	Level 65
SCAR-H (Assault Rifle)	Level 08

Semtex Grenade	Level 01
SPAS-12 (Shotgun)	Level 01
Stinger (Grenade Launcher)	Level 30
Striker (Shotgun)	Level 34
Tactical Insertion	Level 11
TAR-21 (Assault Rifle)	Level 20
Throwing Knife	Level 07
Thumper (Grenade Launcher)	Level 14
TMP (Secondary)	Level 58
UMP .45 (SMG)	Level 01
USP .45 (Pistol)	Level 01
Vector (SMG)	Level 12
WA2000 (Sniper)	Level 36
Winchester 1887 (Shotgun)	Level 67

CALL OF DUTY: WORLD AT WAR (XBOX 360)

MODES

UNLOCKABLE	HOW TO UNLOCK
Veteran mode	Reach Level 32 to unlock Veteran mode.
Zombie mode	Successfully complete Campaign mode to unlock Zombie mode, which is a four-player co-op mode against endless waves of Nazi zombies.

MULTIPLAYER UNLOCKABLES

Reach a certain rank on online multiplayer to achieve each unlockable.

UNLOCKABLE	HOW TO UNLOCK
.357 Magnum	Reach Level 49
Arisaka	Reach Level 4
BAR	Reach Level 4
Browning M1919	Reach Level 61
Clan Tag	Reach Level 11
Colt M1911	Reach Level 3
Custom Class Slot 10	Reach Prestige Level 10
Custom Class Slot 6	Reach Prestige Level 1
Custom Class Slot 7	Reach Prestige Level 2
Custom Class Slot 8	Reach Prestige Level 4
Custom Class Slot 9	Reach Prestige Level 7
Double-Barreled Shotgun	Reach Level 29
DP-28	Reach Rank 13
FG-42	Reach Rank 45
Gewehr 47	Reach Rank 6
Kar98K	Reach Rank 41
M1 Garand	Reach Rank 17
M1A1 Carbine	Reach Rank 65
M2 Flamethrower	Reach Rank 65
MG-42	Reach Rank 33
Mosin-Nagant	Reach Rank 21
MP-40	Reach Rank 10
Nambu	Reach Rank 1
PPSh 41	Reach Rank 53
PTRS 41	Reach Rank 57

UNLOCKABLE	HOW TO UNLOCK
Springfield	Reach Rank 3
STG-44	Reach Rank 37
SVT-40	Reach Rank 1
Thompson	Reach Rank 1
Tokarev TT38	Reach Rank 21
Trench Gun	Reach Rank 2
Type-100	Reach Rank 25
Type-99	Reach Rank 1
Walther P38	Reach Rank 2

MULTIPLAYER PERK UNLOCKABLES

Reach a certain rank on online multiplayer to achieve each unlockable perk.

UNLOCKABLE	HOW TO UNLOCK
Bandolier	Reach Level 40
Bouncing Betty x 2	Reach Level 24
Camouflage	Reach Level 12
Coaxial Machine Gun (vehicle)	Reach Level 40
Dead Silence	Reach Level 52
Double Tap	Reach Level 36
Fireproof	Reach Level 48
Iron Lungs	Reach Level 60
Juggernaut	Reach Level 4
Leadfoot (vehicle)	Reach Level 28
M2 Flamethrower	Reach Level 65
Martydom	Reach Level 20
Ordinance Training (vehicle)	Reach Level 12
Overkill	Reach Level 56
Primary Grenades x 2	Reach Level 44
Reconnaissance	Reach Level 64
Second Chance	Reach Level 9
Shades	Reach Level 32
Sleight of Hand	Reach Level 28
Toss Back	Reach Level 6

CALL OF DUTY: WORLD AT WAR (PlayStation 3)

MODES

UNLOCKABLE	HOW TO UNLOCK
Veteran mode	Reach Level 32 to unlock Veteran mode.
Zombie mode	Successfully complete Campaign mode to unlock Zombie mode, which is a four-player Co-op mode against endless waves of Nazi zombies.

CLAN TAG CODES

Enter the following codes as your Clan Tag to get the following effects.

EFFECT	CODE
RAIN	Makes a rainbow scroll through your name.
....	Makes an "o" bounce from left to right in your Clan Tag.
MOVE	Makes your name bounce from left to right.

MULTIPLAYER UNLOCKABLES

Reach a certain rank on online multiplayer to achieve each unlockable.

UNLOCKABLE	HOW TO UNLOCK
.357 Magnum	Reach Level 49
Arisaka	Reach Level 4
BAR	Reach Level 4
Browning M1919	Reach Level 61
Clan Tag	Reach Level 11
Colt M1911	Reach Level 3
Custom Class Slot 10	Reach Prestige Level 10
Custom Class Slot 6	Reach Prestige Level 1
Custom Class Slot 7	Reach Prestige Level 2
Custom Class Slot 8	Reach Prestige Level 4
Custom Class Slot 9	Reach Prestige Level 7
Double-Barreled Shotgun	Reach Level 29
DP-28	Reach Rank 13
FG-42	Reach Rank 45
Gewehr 47	Reach Rank 6
Kar98K	Reach Rank 41
M1 Garand	Reach Rank 17
M1A1 Carbine	Reach Rank 65
M2 Flamethrower	Reach rank 65
MG-42	Reach Rank 33
Mosin-Nagant	Reach Rank 21
MP-40	Reach Rank 10
Nambu	Reach Rank 1
PPSh 41	Reach Rank 53
PTRS 41	Reach Rank 57
Springfield	Reach Rank 3
STG-44	Reach Rank 37
SVT-40	Reach Rank 1
Thompson	Reach Rank 1
Tokarev TT38	Reach Rank 21
Trench Gun	Reach Rank 2
Type 100	Reach Rank 25
Type-99	Reach Rank 1
Walther P38	Reach Rank 2

MULTIPLAYER PERK UNLOCKABLES

Reach a certain rank on online multiplayer to achieve each unlockable perk.

UNLOCKABLE	HOW TO UNLOCK
Bandolier	Reach Level 40
Bouncing Betty x 2	Reach Level 24
Camouflage	Reach Level 12
Coaxial machine gun (vehicle)	Reach Level 40
Dead Silence	Reach Level 52
Double Tap	Reach Level 36
Fireproof	Reach Level 48
Iron Lungs	Reach Level 60
Juggernaut	Reach Level 4
Leadfoot (vehicle)	Reach Level 28

UNLOCKABLE	HOW TO UNLOCK
M2 Flamethrower	Reach Level 65
Martydom	Reach Level 20
Ordnance Training (vehicle)	Reach Level 12
Overkill	Reach Level 56
Primary Grenades x 2	Reach Level 44
Reconnaissance	Reach Level 64
Second Chance	Reach Level 9
Shades	Reach Level 32
Sleight of Hand	Reach Level 28
Toss Back	Reach Level 6

CALL OF DUTY: WORLD AT WAR (Wii)

UNLOCKABLES

UNLOCKABLE	HOW TO UNLOCK
.357 Magnum	Reach Level 49
Arisaka	Reach Level 4
Bandolier	Reach Level 40
BAR	Reach Level 4
Bomb Squad	Reach Level 16
Bouncing Betty x 2	Reach level 24
Browning M1919	Reach Level 61
Camouflage	Reach level 12
Colt M1911	Reach Level 3
Custom Class Slot 10	Reach Prestige Level 10
Custom Class Slot 6	Reach Prestige level 1
Custom Class Slot 7	Reach Prestige Level 2
Custom Class Slot 8	Reach Prestige Level 4
Custom Class Slot 9	Reach Prestige Level 7
Dead Silence	Reach Level 52
Deep Impact	Reach Rank 1
Double Tap	Reach Rank 36
Double-Barreled Shotgun	Reach Level 29
DP-28	Reach Level 13
Extreme Conditioning	Reach Rank 1
FG-42	Reach Level 45
Fireproof	Reach Level 48
Fireworks	Reach Level 1
Flak Jacket	Reach Level 1
Gas Mask	Reach Level 2
Gewher 47	Reach Level 6
Juggernaut	Reach Level 4
Kar98k	Reach Level 41
M1 Garand	Reach Level 17
M1A1 Carbine	Reach Level 65
M2 Flamethrower	Reach Level 65
M9A1 Bazooka x 2	Reach Level 2
Martydom	Reach Level 20
MG-42	Reach Level 33
Mosin-Nagant	Reach Level 21

MP-40	Reach Level 10
Nambu	Reach Level 1
Overkill	Reach Level 56
PPSh 41	Reach Level 53
Prestige Mode	Reach Level 65
Primary Grenades x 2	Reach Level 44
PTRS 41	Reach Level 57
Satchel Charge x 2	Reach Level 1
Second Chance	Reach Level 9
Sleight of Hand	Reach Level 28
Special Grenades x 3	Reach Level 1
Springfield	Reach Level 3
Steady Aim	Reach Level 1
STG-44	Reach Level 37
Stopping Power	Reach Level 1
SVT-40	Reach Level 1
Thompson	Reach Level 1
Tokarev TT38	Reach Level 21
Toss Back	Reach Level 6
Trench Gun	Reach Level 2
Type 100	Reach Level 25
Type 99	Reach Level 1
Walther P38	Reach Level 2

CALL OF DUTY 2 (XBOX 360)

Enter this code on the Mission Select screen.

UNLOCKABLE	CODE
Unlock all levels	Hold both the left and right bumpers, then quickly input ←, ←, →, →, Ⓨ, Ⓨ

CALL OF DUTY 3 (XBOX 360)

Enter this code at the Chapter Select screen.

UNLOCKABLE	CODE
Unlock All Levels and Pictures	Hold BACK then press →, →, ←, ←, Ⓧ, Ⓧ

CALL OF DUTY 3 (Wii)

Enter this code in the Chapter Select screen.

UNLOCKABLE	CODE
Unlock All Levels	Hold ⊕ and press →, →, ←, ←, ②, ②
Unlock All Extras	At the Chapter Select screen, hold ⊕, and press →, →, ←, ←, ②, ②

CALL OF DUTY 3 (XBOX)

Enter this code in the Chapter Select screen.

UNLOCKABLE	CODE
Unlock All Levels	Hold BACK and press →, →, ←, ←, Ⓧ, Ⓧ

CALL OF DUTY 3 (PlayStation 2)

Enter this code in the Chapter Select screen.

UNLOCKABLE	CODE
Unlock All Levels	Hold SELECT and press →, →, ←, ←, ■, ■

CALL OF DUTY 4: MODERN WARFARE (XBOX 360)

ARCADE AND CHEAT OPTIONS

These unlock automatically for completing *Call of Duty 4: Modern Warfare* on any difficulty level. During gameplay, find the Cheat menu in the Options menu.

UNLOCKABLE	HOW TO UNLOCK
Arcade Mode	Complete game on any difficulty
Cheat Menu	Complete game on any difficulty

CHEATS

Unlock cheats by collecting enemy intel (intelligence), which look like laptop computers that are hidden throughout the campaign. Note: Using cheats disables Achievements.

UNLOCKABLE CHEATS

UNLOCKABLE	HOW TO UNLOCK
A Bad Year: When you kill enemies, they explode into tires!	Collect 15 pieces of enemy intel.
Cluster Bombs: After one of your frag grenades explodes, four more explode in a cross-shaped pattern.	Collect 10 pieces of enemy intel.
CoD Noir: Turns all gameplay into black and white.	Collect 2 pieces of enemy intel.
Infinite Ammo: Weapons have unlimited ammo. Doesn't work with Perk 1 abilities such as C4 and Claymores.	Collect 30 pieces of enemy intel.
Photo-Negative: Inverses all of the game's colors.	Collect 4 pieces of enemy intel.
Ragtime Warfare: Gameplay goes black and white, dust and scratches fill the screen, it plays at 2x speed, and the music becomes piano music.	Collect 8 pieces of enemy intel.
Slow-Mo Ability: Use the melee button to change the game to slow-mo and play at half-speed.	Collect 20 pieces of enemy intel.
Super Contrast: Dramatically increases the game's contrast, making the darks much darker and the lights much lighter.	Collect 6 pieces of enemy intel.

Golden weapons are a special camo (or skin) that you unlock when you fully complete all the challenges under the weapon subtype in the barracks (SMG, LMG, etc.). Access them by choosing the camo of the respective weapon. The effect is purely cosmetic and does not enhance the ability of the weapon in any way.

GOLDEN WEAPONS

UNLOCKABLE	HOW TO UNLOCK
Golden AK-47	Complete all Assault Rifle challenges.
Golden Desert Eagle	Get to Level 55.
Golden Dragunov	Complete all Sniper challenges.
Golden M1014	Complete all Shotgun challenges.
Golden M60	Complete all LMG challenges.
Golden Mini-Uzi	Complete all SMG challenges.

MULTIPLAYER UNLOCKABLES

UNLOCKABLE	UNLOCKED AT RANK:
AK-74U Submachine Gun	28
Bandolier Perk Class 1	32
Barret Sniper Rifle	49
Bomb Squad Perk Class 1	13
Boot Camp Challenges 1	08

UNLOCKABLE	UNLOCKED AT RANK:
Sniper Class Weapon Class	02
UAV Jammer Perk Class 2	10

CALL OF DUTY 4: MODERN WARFARE (PlayStation 3)

Enter this code in the Chapter Select screen.

UNLOCKABLE	CODE
Unlock All Levels	Hold SELECT and press ⇨, ⇨, ⇦, ⇦, ■, ■

Arcade and Cheat Options

These unlock automatically for completing *Call of Duty 4: Modern Warfare* on any difficulty level. During gameplay, find the Cheat menu in the Options menu.

Unlockable	How to Unlock
Arcade Mode	Complete game on any difficulty
Cheat Menu	Complete game on any difficulty

EASTER EGG (HIDDEN MISSION)

Beat the game on any difficulty and let the credits run all the way through. When they finish, you'll start another mission. This mission takes place on a plane that resembles Air Force One, wherein you must fight your way through a horde of baddies, save the V.I.P., and escape the plane in less than two minutes.

CHEATS

Unlock cheats by collecting enemy intel (intelligence), which look like laptop computers that are hidden throughout the campaign. Note: Using cheats disables Achievements.

UNLOCKABLE CHEATS

UNLOCKABLE	HOW TO UNLOCK
A Bad Year: When you kill enemies, they explode into tires!	Collect 15 pieces of enemy intel.
Cluster Bombs: After one of your frag grenades explodes, four more explode in a cross-shaped pattern.	Collect 10 pieces of enemy intel.
CoD Noir: Turns all gameplay into black and white.	Collect 2 pieces of enemy intel.
Infinite Ammo: Weapons have unlimited ammo. Doesn't work with Perk 1 abilities such as C4 and Claymores.	Collect 30 pieces of enemy intel.
Photo-Negative: Inverses all of the game's colors.	Collect 4 pieces of enemy intel.
Ragtime Warfare: Gameplay goes black andwhite, dust and scratches fill the screen, it plays at 2x speed, and the music becomes piano music.	Collect 8 pieces of enemy intel.
Slow-Mo Ability: Use the melee button to change the game to slow-mo and play at half-speed.	Collect 20 pieces of enemy intel.
Super Contrast: Dramatically increases the game's contrast, making the darks much darker and the lights much lighter.	Collect 6 pieces of enemy intel.

Golden weapons are a special camo (or skin) that you unlock when you fully complete all the challenges under the weapon subtype in the barracks (SMG, LMG, etc.). Access them by choosing the camo of the respective weapon. The effect is purely cosmetic and does not enhance the ability of the weapon in any way.

GOLDEN WEAPONS

UNLOCKABLE	HOW TO UNLOCK
Golden AK-47	Complete all Assault Rifle challenges.
Golden Desert Eagle	Get to Level 55.
Golden Dragunov	Complete all Sniper challenges.

Golden M1014	Complete all Shotgun challenges.
Golden M60	Complete all LMG challenges.
Golden Mini-Uzi	Complete all SMG challenges.

MULTIPLAYER UNLOCKABLES

UNLOCKABLE	UNLOCKED AT RANK
Assault Rifle (G3)	Rank 25
Assault Rifle (G36C)	Rank 37
Assault Rifle (M14)	Rank 46
Assault Rifle (M4)	Rank 10
Assault Rifle (MP44)	Rank 52
LMG (M60E4)	Rank 19
Pistol (Desert Eagle)	Rank 43
Pistol (Golden Desert Eagle)	Rank 55
Pistol (M1911)	Rank 16
Shotgun (M1014)	Rank 31
SMG (AK-74U)	Rank 28
SMG (Mini Uzi)	Rank 13
SMG (P90)	Rank 40
Sniper Rifle (Barret)	Rank 49
Sniper Rifle (Dragunov)	Rank 22
Sniper Rifle (M40)	Rank 04
Sniper Rifle (R700)	Rank 34

CALL OF JUAREZ: BOUND IN BLOOD (XBOX 360)

CODES

From the Main menu go into Exclusive content and enter code.

EFFECT	CODE
Bonus Cash to buy better weapons earlier in the game.	735S653J

CALL OF JUAREZ: BOUND IN BLOOD (PlayStation 3)

CODES

From the Main menu go into Exclusive content and enter code.

EFFECT	CODE
Bonus Cash to be able to buy better weapons earlier in the game.	735S653J

CALLING ALL CARS! (PlayStation 3)

UNLOCKABLE VEHICLES

Complete the appropriate tasks in the correct game mode and difficulty to unlock extra vehicles.

UNLOCKABLE	HOW TO UNLOCK
BLUE BOMBER	Win at the Trainyards on Captain difficulty, using only the helicopter to score in a single-level, 5-minute game
CHERRY PICKER	In a single-level, 5 minute-game on Chief difficulty, win at the Burbs with at least 20 points
DUMPER	On Sergeant difficulty, beat Tournament mode
FLEABAG	On Chief difficulty, beat Tournament mode
HIGHROLLER	Beat the Burbs on Captain difficulty without letting the opponent score in a single-level, 5-minute game
LITTER BOX	On Captain difficulty, beat Tournament mode
SHAMROCK	In a single-level, 5-minute game on Sergeant difficulty, beat any level without letting the opponent score

UNLOCKABLE VEHICLES

Complete the appropriate tasks in the correct game mode and difficulty to unlock extra vehicles.

UNLOCKABLE	HOW TO UNLOCK
BLUE BOMBER	Win at the Trainyards on Captain difficulty, using only the
SWEET CHEEKS	In a single-level, 2-minute game on Captain difficulty, win any level without letting the opponent score
YELLOW ROSE	On Rookie difficulty, beat Tournament mode
YELLOWJACKET	In a single-level, 5-minute game on Captain difficulty, win using only the 3-point ramp in the Alpine

CAPCOM CLASSIC COLLECTION (XBOX)

Enter this code at the Press Start screen.

UNLOCKABLE	CODE
Unlock Everything	LT, RT, ↑, ↓ on right analog stick, LT, RT, ↑, ↓ on left analog stick, LT, RT, ↑, ↓ on the D-Pad.

CAPCOM CLASSIC COLLECTION (PlayStation 2)

Enter this code at the title screen.

UNLOCKABLE	CODE
Unlock Everything	L1, R1, Up Right Analog, Down Right Analog, L1, R1, Up Left Analog, Down Left Analog, L1, R1, ↑, ↓

CAPCOM CLASSIC COLLECTION REMIXED (PSP)

Enter this code at the Press Start screen.

UNLOCKABLE	CODE
Arts, Tips, and Sound Tests for Every Game	Press ←, → on D-pad, ←, → on Analog stick, ■, ●, ↑, ↓

CAPCOM CLASSIC COLLECTION VOL. 2 (PlayStation 2)

Enter this code at the Press Start screen.

UNLOCKABLE	CODE
Cheats, Tips, Arts, and Sound Tests for Every Game	←, →, ↑, ↓, L1, R1, L1, R1

CARS (XBOX 360)

PASSWORDS

PASSWORD	EFFECT
CONC3PT	All art concept
WATCHIT	All movies
R4MONE	All paint jobs
IMSPEED	Super fast start
VROOOOM	Unlimited boost
YAYCARS	Unlock all cars
MATTL66	Unlock all races
IF900HP	Unlock everything in the game

CARS (Wii)

Input codes in the password section under the Options menu.

UNLOCKABLE	CODE
All Cars	YAYCARS
All Concept Art	CONC3PT
All Movies	WATCHIT
All Paint Jobs	R4MONE
All Races	MATTL66
All Tracks and Mini-games	IF900HP

Mater's Speedy Circuit and Mater's Countdown Clean Up	TRGTEXC
Super Fast Start	IMSPEED
Unlimited Boost	VROOOOM

CARS (XBOX)

To enter these passwords, select Options, then select Cheat Codes.

UNLOCKABLE	PASSWORD
All cars	YAYCARS
All character skins	R4MONE
All tracks and mini games	MATTL66
Fast start	IMSPEED
Infinite boost	VROOOOM
Unlock art	CONC3PT
Unlock Master's speedy circuit and Master's countdown cleanup	TRGTEXC
Unlock movie clips	WATCHIT

CARS (PlayStation 2)

To enter these passwords, select Options, then select Cheat Codes.

UNLOCKABLE	PASSWORD
All cars	YAYCARS
All character skins	R4MONE
All tracks and mini games	MATTL66
Fast start	IMSPEED
Infinite boost	VROOOOM
Unlock art	CONC3PT
Unlock Master's speedy circuit and Master's countdown cleanup	TRGTEXC
Unlocks movie clips	WATCHIT

CASTLEVANIA: ORDER OF ECCLESIA (DS)

UNLOCKABLES

UNLOCKABLE	HOW TO UNLOCK
Boss Medals	During a boss fight, do not get hit once. After the fight, a treasure chest will appear from the ground to present you with the medal.
New Game+	After finishing the game, go to your file and press right to access the clear sign and start a new game.
Albus Mode	Complete the game after saving all villagers.
Boss Rush Mode	Complete the game after saving all villagers.
Hard Difficulty	Beat the game once.
Hard Mode Level 255	Complete Hard Mode Level 1 OR connect to Castlevania: Judgment
Sound Mode	Complete the game after saving all villagers.

CASTLEVANIA: SYMPHONY OF THE NIGHT (XBOX 360)

PLAY AS OTHER CHARACTERS AND EXTRAS

You must complete the game as Alucard with 180% or more and have a "CLEAR" Save.

PASSWORD	EFFECT
Enter AXEARMOR as your name	Alucard with Axelord armor
Enter RICHTER as your name	Play as Richter Belmont
Enter X-X!V"Q as your name	Alucard with lower stats and MAX Luck

CASTLEVANIA: THE ADVENTURE REBIRTH (Wii)

LEVEL SELECT

At the title screen, select "Game Start" and hold right on the D-pad for a few seconds. You'll be able to select and play any levels you have previously reached on the same difficulty.

CEL DAMAGE (XBOX)

Enter these passwords as profile names.

UNLOCKABLE	PASSWORD
Unlock all Melee Weapons	MELEEDEATH
Unlock Everything	ENCHILADA!
Unlock Ranged Weapons	GUNSMOKE!

CHAMPIONS OF NORRATH (PlayStation 2)

Enter this code during gameplay.

UNLOCKABLE	CODE
Instant Level 20 Character	Start a new character, and as soon as you have control of him or her, press L1+R2+▲+R3.

CHAMPIONS OF NORRATH: REALMS OF EVERQUEST (PlayStation 2)

UNLOCKABLE	CODE
Level 20 Character	During gameplay, press and hold L1+R2+▲+R3. This allows your character to unlock 75,000 coins, 999 skill points, and Level 20.

CHASE HOLLYWOOD STUNT DRIVER (XBOX)

Enter these passwords as profile names.

UNLOCKABLE	PASSWORD
Unlock Everything	Dare Angel
All multiplayer levels	BAM4FUN

CHEW-MAN-FU (Wii)

CODES

UNLOCKABLE	HOW TO UNLOCK
Golden Balls	At the title screen, hold ①+SELECT and press ←+↑

PASSWORDS

PASSWORD	EFFECT
573300	Area 1, Round 1 (2nd Playthrough)
344710	Area 1, Round 1 (3rd Playthrough)
274510	Area 1, Round 1 (4th Playthrough)
321310	Area 1, Round 1 (5th Playthrough)
536300	Area 1, Round 1 (6th Playthrough)
301710	Area 1, Round 1 (7th Playthrough)
231510	Area 1, Round 1 (8th Playthrough)
256310	Area 1, Round 1 (9th Playthrough)
441300	Area 1, Round 1 (10th Playthrough)
677261	Area 5, Round 50
075653	Fight enemy opponents only

CHINA WARRIOR (Wii)

CODES

UNLOCKABLE	HOW TO UNLOCK
Enable Invincibility and Level Select	Press RUN+SELECT to reset the game, keep the buttons held, then release RUN and press ✚↑ when the title screen is displayed. Release Select and press ✚↑, ✚↑, ✚↑, ✚→, ✚→, ✚→, ✚→, ✚→, ✚→, ✚↓, ✚↓, ✚←, ✚↓.
Level Skip	Hold ✚↑ then SELECT+①+② to skip the first level. For the other levels, hold ✚↓ instead of ✚↑.
Continue (up to three times) from the Start of the Las Level Played	Hold ①+②+✚↓ and press RUN, RUN when the phrase "The End" appears after gameplay is over. Alternately, hold ①+2+✚↓ and press RUN at the title screen after game play is over.

THE CHRONICLES OF NARNIA: THE LION, THE WITCH, AND THE WARDROBE (DS)

Enter these codes at the Main menu.

UNLOCKABLE	CODE
Acquire Armor	Ⓐ, Ⓧ, Ⓨ, Ⓑ, ↑, ↑, ↑, ↓
All Blessings	←, ↑, Ⓐ, Ⓑ, →, ↓, Ⓧ, Ⓨ
All Skills at Maximum	Ⓐ, ←, →, Ⓑ, ↓, ↑, Ⓧ, Ⓧ
Extra Money	↑, Ⓧ, ↑, Ⓧ, ↓, Ⓑ, ↓, Ⓑ
Invincibility	Ⓐ, Ⓨ, Ⓧ, Ⓑ, ↑, ↑, ↓, ↓
Maximum Attributes	←, Ⓑ, ↑, Ⓨ, ↓, Ⓧ, →, Ⓐ
Restore Health	←, →, ↑, ↓, Ⓐ, Ⓐ, Ⓐ, Ⓐ
Stronger Attacks	Ⓐ, ↑, Ⓑ, ↓, Ⓧ, Ⓧ, Ⓨ, Ⓨ

CHRONO TRIGGER (DS)

UNLOCKABLE ENDINGS

UNLOCKABLE	HOW TO UNLOCK
Ending 1 "Beyond Time"	Defeat Lavos after reviving Crono at Death Peak.
Ending 10 "Dino Age"	Defeat Lavos after facing Magus, but before facing Azala.
Ending 11 "What the Prophet Seeks"	Defeat Lavos after facing Azala, but before Schala opens the sealed door.
Ending 12 "Memory lane"	Defeat Lavos after Schala opens the sealed door, but before restoring the light to the pendant.
Ending 13 "Dream's Epilogue"	Defeat the Dream Devourer beyond Time's Eclipse
Ending 2 "Reunion"	Defeat Lavos while Crono is dead.
Ending 3 "The Dream Project"	Defeat Lavos in the Ocean Palace or immediately upon starting a new game.
Ending 4 "The successor of Guardia"	Defeat Lavos after saving Leene and Marle, but before visiting the End of Time.
Ending 5 "Good Night"	Defeat Lavos after visiting the End of Time, but before returning to the Middle Ages.
Ending 6 "The Legendary Hero"	Defeat Lavos after arriving in the Middle Ages, but before obtaining the Hero's Badge.
Ending 7 "The Unknown Past"	Defeat Lavos after obtaining the Hero's Badge, but before the Gate key is stolen.
Ending 8 "People of the times"	Defeat Lavos after regaining the gate key, but before giving the Masamune to Frog.
Ending 9 "The Oath"	Defeat Lavos after giving the Masamune to Frog but before fighting Magus.

ITEM DUPLICATION

Once you reach the Arena of Ages, send your monster out to train until it returns back with an item. When it returns, you will see the monster's status window showing the item it brought back. Without closing this window, press the A button to select the option "Train Monster." Then press the A button a second time and you will now be on the Consumables item screen. Press the B button once to return back to the original screen. This will duplicate the item that the monster brought back (though you will not see any evidence of this until you look in your own inventory). You can continue to do this to get 99 of that item. This is a great way to stock up on magic, speed, or strength capsules.

CLONING CLYDE (XBOX 360)

UNLOCK MUTANT CLYDE

UNLOCKABLE	HOW TO UNLOCK
Mutant Clyde	Beat all levels under par time

THE CLUB (XBOX 360)

UNLOCKABLES

Complete all 8 Tournaments, then replay any of the Tournaments as your preferred character to unlock concept art of that character.

UNLOCKABLE	HOW TO UNLOCK
Adjo concept art	After finishing all 8 Tournaments, complete any Tournament as Adjo.
Dragov concept art	After finishing all 8 Tournaments, complete any Tournament as Dragov.
Finn concept art	After finishing all 8 Tournaments, complete any Tournament as Finn.
Killen concept art	After finishing all 8 Tournaments, complete any Tournament as Killen.
Kuro concept art	After finishing all 8 Tournaments, complete any Tournament as Kuro.
Nemo concept art	After finishing all 8 Tournaments, complete any Tournament as Nemo.
Renwick concept art	After finishing all 8 Tournaments, complete any Tournament as Renwick.
Seager concept art	After finishing all 8 Tournaments, complete any Tournament as Seager.
Adjo ending	After finishing all 8 Tournaments, complete any Tournament as Adjo.
Dragov ending	After finishing all 8 Tournaments, complete any Tournament as Dragov.
Finn ending	After finishing all 8 Tournaments, complete any Tournament as Finn.
Killen ending	After finishing all 8 Tournaments, complete any Tournament as Killen.
Kuro ending	After finishing all 8 Tournaments, complete any Tournament as Kuro.
Nemo ending	After finishing all 8 Tournaments, complete any Tournament as Nemo.
Renwick ending	After finishing all 8 Tournaments, complete any Tournament as Renwick.
Seager ending	After finishing all 8 Tournaments, complete any Tournament as Seager.
Bunker concept art	Shoot all Secret Skullshots in all 6 Bunker stages.
Manor House concept art	Shoot all Secret Skullshots in all 6 Manor House stages.
Ocean Liner concept art	Shoot all Secret Skullshots in all 6 Ocean Liner stages.

Prison Cells concept art	Shoot all Secret Skullshots in all 6 Prison Cells stages.
Steel Mill concept art	Shoot all Secret Skullshots in all 6 Steel Mill stages.
Venice concept art	Shoot all Secret Skullshots in all 7 Venice stages.
Warehouse concept Art	Shoot all Secret Skullshots in all 6 Warehouse stages.
Warzone concept art	Shoot all Secret Skullshots in all 6 Warzone stages.
Bunker	Complete Manor House Tournament.
Manor House	Complete Warehouse Tournament.
Ocean Liner	Complete Prison Cells Tournament.
Prison Cells	Complete Venice Tournament.
Venice	Complete Steel Mill Tournament.
Warehouse	Complete Ocean Liner Tournament.
Warzone	Complete Bunker Tournament.

COLD WAR (XBOX)

Enter these codes while the game is paused.

UNLOCKABLE	CODE
All items, gadgets, and tech points	X, WHT, Y, BLK, Y
Complete current level	X, WHT, Y, BLK, X
Invulnerability	X, WHT, Y, BLK, ←

COMIX ZONE (Wii)

UNLOCKABLES

UNLOCKABLE	HOW TO UNLOCK
Fart	In some areas, press ✜.
Sega Plug	At any time during the main game, press START to pause. After a few seconds, Sketch will yell, "Sega!"
Stage Select	Go to the Jukebox mode and place the red checker on the following numbers in order, pressing ✜ at each one: 14, 15, 18, 5, 13, 1, 3, 18, 15, 6. Now, highlight a number from 1 to 6 and press ✜ to warp to the corresponding stage.
Unlimited Health	Go to Jukebox in the Options menu and push ✜ on these numbers: 3, 12, 17, 2, 2, 10, 2, 7, 7, 11. You hear Sketch say "oh yeah."
View Credits	At the Options mode, press Ⓐ+Ⓑ+Ⓒ.
Paper Airplane	During gameplay press and hold the Punch button. After a second or so Sketch will tear a piece of paper from the background and make a paper airplane out of it. The plane will travel to the edge of the panel and circle back around. The plane does massive damage to all enemies, objects, and Sketch himself, so be careful. You lose a considerable amount of health when creating the plane.

COMMANDOS STRIKE FORCE (XBOX)

Enter this password as a profile name.

UNLOCKABLE	PASSWORD
All Missions	TRUCO

CONDEMNED 2: BLOODSHOT (XBOX 360)

ACHIEVEMENTS

UNLOCKABLE	HOW TO UNLOCK
A La Mode (25)	Five scoops of everything.
Anger Management (10)	Get emotional!
Beat Cop (10)	Beat your way through a mission.

UNLOCKABLE	HOW TO UNLOCK
Big Game Hunter (10)	Get up close and personal with the antler.
Bloodshot (25)	Unlock all Bloodshot Fight Clubs.
Brick Wall (10)	MP—Block it away!
Bum King (30)	No guns, no problem.
Can You Hear Me Now? (30)	Emitter Removal Service.
Chain Gang (30)	Use all chain attacks a few times.
Chief Investigator (50)	Complete all missions in Hard mode.
Collector (10)	Scan the MP goodies once, twice, thrice—and more!
Cut Throat (30)	Finish it!
Decisive Restraint (25)	Restraint is a virtue.
Defender (25)	MP Defense 10 times over on the evidence.
Detective (30)	Get through a mission in FPS.
Detective—First Grade (50)	Shoot your way through it all in FPS.
EPA (Environmental Pwnage Area) (25)	Grab your foes by the neck and do what's necessary.
Flambe (25)	Splash, Shock, and Fry.
Gold-Plated (50)	Go gold in all missions.
GOOOAAALLLL! (10)	Use the foosball table piece to your advantage.
Investigator (25)	You took on the hardest and beat them at their game.
Just the Facts (25)	MP Crime Scene Goodness.
Magellan (25)	Explore all maps more than once!
Master Investigator (30)	PERFECTION as a sleuth all the way through.
MP Overachiever (50)	Win a Deathmatch game with 15 kills without dying.
Punch Drunk (10)	MP—Duke of Queensbury rules only
Restraint...Not (30)	Win Crime Scene games as SCU without firing a shot.
Rush Champ (25)	Take SCU out with the trash five times.
Self Medicated (25)	Heal thyself, physician.
Serial Killer (50)	Go kill, kill, kill in MP.
Sidekick (10)	Assist in scanning evidence in Crime Scene mode.
SKX (50)	Kill the killers.
Sleuth (10)	Be the PERFECT sleuth.
Survivor King (30)	Bum Rush Survivor multiple times.
The Final Word (10)	You never forget your first time.
The Plumber (25)	Find a pipe and use it frequently.
Trooper (30)	Complete the single-player game.
Tune In Tokyo (30)	Tune in all those TVs.

CONDEMNED: CRIMINAL ORIGINS (XBOX 360)

ALL LEVELS AND CONTENT

CODE	EFFECT
Enter ShovelFighter as a case-sensitive profile name	Unlocks all levels and all additional content usually unlocked through earning achievements

ACHIEVEMENTS

ACHIEVEMENT	HOW TO ACHIEVE	REWARD
Bird Bath Xbox 360	Find hidden Xbox 360 with the Bird Bath TV in Chapter 7	Initial crawler grabbing animation video
Bronze Detective Badge	Find hidden Bronze Detective Badge TV in Chapter 1	Video of some early forensic tool testing

ACHIEVEMENT	HOW TO ACHIEVE	REWARD
Bronze Melee Master Award	Complete a single chapter with only melee weapons (no firearms)	Stick-fighting animation video with special performance by Detective Dickenson
Chapter 1 Bronze Bird Award	Find a dead bird in Chapter 1	Concept artwork of addicts
Chapter 1 Completion Award	Finish Chapter 1	Concept artwork for Weisman Office Building
Chapter 1 Silver Bird Award	Find all six birds in Chapter 1	Concept artwork of police officers
Chapter 2 Bronze Bird Award	Find a dead bird in Chapter 2	Concept artwork of the Glassman character (who was cut from the final game)
Chapter 2 Completion Award	Finish Chapter 2	Concept artwork for Central Metro Station
Chapter 2 Silver Bird Award	Find all six birds in Chapter 2	Concept artwork and character model of Detective Dickenson
Chapter 3 Bronze Bird Award	Find a dead bird in Chapter 3	Concept artwork of the Sandhog (burly enemy in fireman-style uniform)
Chapter 3 Completion Award	Finish Chapter 3	Concept artwork of the subway tunnels
Chapter 3 Silver Bird Award	Find all six birds in Chapter 3	Concept artwork and character model of Officer Becker
Chapter 4 Bronze Bird Award	Find a dead bird in Chapter 4	Concept artwork of vagrant characters (and others)
Chapter 4 Completion Award	Finish Chapter 4	Additional concept artwork for the subway tunnels
Chapter 4 Silver Bird Award	Find all six birds in Chapter 4	Concept artwork of Agent Ethan Thomas (you)
Chapter 5 Bronze Bird Award	Find a dead bird in Chapter 5	Concept artwork of mannequins
Chapter 5 Completion Award	Finish Chapter 5	Concept artwork for Bart's Department Store
Chapter 5 Silver Bird Award	Find all six birds in Chapter 5	Concept artwork of Vanhorn
Chapter 6 Bronze Bird Award	Find a dead bird in Chapter 6	Concept artwork and character models of the Rejects (the weakest crawlers)
Chapter 6 Completion Award	Finish Chapter 6	Concept artwork of the first crime scene
Chapter 6 Silver Bird Award	Find all six birds in Chapter 6	Concept artwork of Rosa
Chapter 7 Bronze Bird Award	Find a dead bird in Chapter 7	Concept artwork of the Trespassers
Chapter 7 Completion Award	Finish Chapter 7	Concept artwork for Metro City Library
Chapter 7 Silver Bird Award	Find all six birds in Chapter 7	Additional character concept artwork
Chapter 8 Bronze Bird Award	Find a dead bird in Chapter 8	Concept artwork and character models of the crawlers
Chapter 8 Completion Award	Finish Chapter 8	Concept artwork for St. Joseph's Secondary School
Chapter 8 Silver Bird Award	Find all six birds in Chapter 8	Character model images for Samuel Tibbits
Chapter 9 Bronze Bird Award	Find a dead bird in Chapter 9	Additional character concept artwork
Chapter 9 Completion Award	Finish Chapter 9	Concept artwork for the Apple Seed Orchard

ACHIEVEMENT	HOW TO ACHIEVE	REWARD
Chapter 9 Silver Bird Award	Find all six birds in Chapter 9 model of the Match Maker	Concept artwork and character
Chapter 10 Bronze Bird Award	Find a dead bird in Chapter 10 and character model	Lunch lady concept artwork
Chapter 10 Silver Bird Award	Find all six birds in Chapter 10 model, and screenshots of Serial Killer X	Concept artwork, character
Chief Investigator Award	Find every crime scene clue in the game	Concept artwork of Dark enemies
Compassion Award	Let Serial Killer X live	Final pull video
DUO Report	Discover 29 metal pieces Report & related evidence photos	Deep Undercover Operative
Firearm Freedom Award	Wield every type of firearm in the game	Concept artwork of Dark enemies
Gold Detective Badge	Find hidden Gold Detective Badge TV in Chapter 9	Filipino stick-fighting video
Gold Game Completion Award	Finish entire game different weapons in the game	Concept artwork for the
Gold Melee Master Award	Complete game without using any firearms	Second prototype trailer video
Golden Bird Award	Find all birds in the game	Condemned E3 Trailer Video
Internal Affairs Report	Discover 20 metal pieces current events/background	Report that sheds light on
Melee Mayhem Award	Wield every type of debris and entry tool weapon in the game finishing moves)	Video of metal reduction animations (and some
Propaganda Report #1	Discover 9 metal pieces translated findings	Initial propaganda report and
Propaganda Report #2	Discover 20 metal pieces and additional translations	Secondary propaganda report
Propaganda Report #3	Discover 29 metal pieces additional translations	Third propaganda report and
Propaganda Report #4	Discover 30 metal pieces and a clue to shed additional light on the mystery	Fourth propaganda report
Revenge Award	Kill Serial Killer X speech video	Serial Killer X wire-frame
Ripple Xbox 360	Find hidden Xbox 360 with the Ripple TV in Chapter 2	Video of further concept artwork
Silver Detective Badge	Find hidden Silver Detective Badge TV in Chapter 6	Video of further concept artwork
Silver Melee Master Award	Complete three chapters without using any firearms	Crawler animation video
Static Xbox 360	Find hidden Xbox 360 with the Static TV in Chapter 4	A headless Ethan Thomas video
Test Pattern Xbox 360	Find hidden Xbox 360 with the Test Pattern TV in Chapter 8	Condemned credits video
Propaganda Report #2	Discover 20 metal pieces and additional translations	Secondary propaganda report
Propaganda Report #3	Discover 29 metal pieces additional translations	Third propaganda report and
Propaganda Report #4	Discover 30 metal pieces and a clue to shed additional light on the mystery	Fourth propaganda report
Revenge Award	Kill Serial Killer X speech video	Serial Killer X wire-frame
Ripple Xbox 360	Find hidden Xbox 360 with the Ripple TV in Chapter 2	Video of further concept artwork

Silver Detective Badge	Find hidden Silver Detective Badge TV in Chapter 6	Video of further concept artwork
Silver Melee Master Award	Complete three chapters without using any firearms	Crawler animation video
Static Xbox 360	Find hidden Xbox 360 with the Static TV in Chapter 4	A headless Ethan Thomas video
Test Pattern Xbox 360	Find hidden Xbox 360 with the Test Pattern TV in Chapter 8	Condemned credits video

THE CONDUIT (Wii)

CODES

Enter the code from the cheats menu

EFFECT	CODE
Custom ASE unlocked	NewASE11
Secret Agent skin unlocked	SuitMP13
Unlock Drone for Single-player	Drone4SP

UNLOCKABLES

These cheats can be unlocked after gaining achievements. Enable the cheats in the Cheats Menu, under Extras.

UNLOCKABLE	HOW TO UNLOCK
Fiery Death: Enemies Die As If They Had Been Killed By A Charged Shot	Complete the "Secret Master" achievement.
Fully Stocked: Infinite Ammo	Complete the "Annihilator Award" achievement.
Stopping Power: One Shot Kill	Complete the "Campaign Award" achievement.

CONFLICT ZONE (PlayStation 2)

Pause gameplay, then enter the following codes.

UNLOCKABLE	CODE
100 Population	×,→,→,←,↑
Access to All Missions in Replay Mode	×,↑,↑,←,→,←
Faster Building	×,↓,↓,↑,←,→
Money Cheat	×,←,→,↑,←

CONSTANTINE (XBOX)

To enter these codes, press BACK to open your journal.

UNLOCKABLE	CODE
Big Headed Demons	BLK,←,→,←,←,→,←,BLK
Big Weapon Mode	←,X,X,X,Y,Y,Y
Explosive Holy Bomb	→,←,X,Y,X,Y,←,→
Rapid Fire Shotgun	WHT,←,BLK,←,Y,X,Y,X
Shoot Fireballs	Y,Y,Y,←,→,→,←,←,→

CONSTANTINE (PlayStation 2)

Press SELECT to open your journal and enter this code.

UNLOCKABLE	CODE
Big Headed Demons	R2, ←, →, ←, ←, →, ←, R2.

CONTRA (XBOX 360)

CODES

CODE	EFFECT
↑↑↓↓←→←→BA	Start game with 30 lives. Your score is not eligible for the High Score Leader Board.

CONTRA: REBIRTH (Wii)

UNLOCKABLES

UNLOCKABLE	HOW TO UNLOCK
Nightmare (new difficulty)	Beat the game on Hard difficulty.
Plissken (new character)	Beat the game on Normal difficulty.
Tsugu-Min (new character)	Beat the game on Easy difficulty.

CONTRA: SHATTERED SOLDIER (PlayStation 2)

UNLOCKABLE	OBJECTIVE
Contra vs. Puppy	Complete the game with an "S" rank.
Database Option	Complete the game with a "B" or "C" rank under the Normal difficulty setting.
Final Boss Battle in Training Mode	Defeat the final boss under Normal difficulty setting.
Gallery Option	Complete the game with an "A" rank under the Normal difficulty setting.
In-Game Reset	Hold L1+L2+R1+R2+START+SELECT during gameplay.
Level 5 in Training Mode	Complete Level 5 during the game under Normal difficulty setting.
Level 6	Complete Level 5 with an "A" rank.
Level 6 in Training Mode	Complete Level 6 under Normal difficulty setting.
Level 7	Complete Level 6 with an "A" rank.
Level 7 in Training Mode	Complete Level 7 under Normal difficulty setting.
Return	Complete Level 7 up to the credits with an "A" rank.
Satellite Weapon	Complete Level 5 with a "B" or "C" rank.
Theater Option	Complete the game under the Normal difficulty setting. Your rank determines how much of the theater unlocks.
Thirty Lives (Only affects your first credit)	Press ↑, ↑, ↓, ↓, L1, R1, L2, R2, L3, R3 on controller two at the title screen. A sound confirms correct code entry. See Note.
Triumphant Return	Complete Level 7, including after the credits, with an "A" rank.

CORALINE (PlayStation 2)

CODES

From the Main Menu go to Options then to Cheats and enter the following code.

EFFECT	CODE
Button Eye Coraline	Cheese

CORVETTE (XBOX)

In the Options menu, select "Change Name," then enter this code.

UNLOCKABLE	CODE
All Cars and All Tracks	XOPENSEZ

CORVETTE (PlayStation 2)

UNLOCKABLE	CODE
All Cars and Courses	Go to Options, then Game Options and select "Change Name." Enter XOPENSEZ.

CRASH BANDICOOT: THE WRATH OF CORTEX (XBOX)

UNLOCKABLE	CODE
Alternate Ending Sequence	Collect all 46 gems.

CRASH TAG TEAM RACING (XBOX)

At the title screen, press and hold LT+RT, then enter the code.

UNLOCKABLE	CODE
Chicken heads for characters	A, B, B, X
Disable HUD	A, X, Y, B
Japanese-version characters	X, B, X, B
One-hit knockouts	A, B, B, A
No top speed on cars	B, B, Y, Y
Toy block cars	B, B, Y, X

CRASH: MIND OVER MUTANT (XBOX 360)

CODES

While playing story mode, pause the game. Hold guard and press the following buttons on the D-pad very quickly! To deactivate a cheat, enter its code again.

EFFECT	CODE
Crash freeze any enemy he touches	Down, Down, Down, Up
Crash turns into a shadow	Left, Right, Left, Right
Enemies leave behind x4 damage (Boxing glove)	Up, Up, Up, Right
Enemies leave behind Wumpa fruit	Right, Right, Right, Up
Make different parts of Crash bigger	Left, Left, Left, Down

CRASH: MIND OVER MUTANT (Wii)

CODES

While playing Story Mode, pause the game. Hold guard and press the following buttons on the D-pad very quickly! To deactivate a cheat, enter its code again.

EFFECT	CODE
Crash freezes any enemy he touches	Down, Down, Down, Up
Crash turns into a shadow	Left, Right, Left, Right
Enemies leave behind x4 damage (Boxing glove)	Up, Up, Up, Right
Enemies leave behind Wumpa fruit	Right, Right, Right, Up
Make different parts of Crash bigger	Left, Left, Left, Down

CRATERMAZE (Wii)

PASSWORDS

PASSWORD	EFFECT
Unlock All Normal Levels	Press RUN on the title screen and select Password. Enter this password, then use ① and ② to select a level before pressing RUN. Blue/Left, Blue/Left, Blue/Right, Red/Front
Expert Level Select	Blue/Back, Blue/Back, Red/Right, Blue/Forward

CRAZY TAXI (PlayStation 2)

UNLOCKABLE	CODE
Another View	Begin a game. While the game is in progress, press and hold L1 and R1, then press ● to enter first-person driving mode. Press ▲ (while holding L1 and R1) to show things from a wider angle.
Expert Mode	Press and hold L1 and R1, then press START before you see the character selection screen. "Expert" appears onscreen if done properly.

UNLOCKABLE	CODE
Taxi Bike	At the character select screen, hit L+R three times quickly. You can also gain access to the bike after you beat all Crazy Box challenges. Press 8 at the select screen to get it.
Turn Off Arrow	Hold R and press s before you see the character selection screen. "No Arrows" appears on the screen if entered correctly.
Turn Off Destination Mark	Press and hold R1, then press START before you see the character selection screen. "No Destination" appears on screen if done correctly.
Unlock Another Day	Press and hold R1. Keep holding it until you choose a taxi driver. After you do, "Another Day" appears onscreen, indicating correct code entry.

CYBERNATOR (Wii)

CODES

UNLOCKABLE	HOW TO UNLOCK
Extra Continues	At the title screen, hold ✚+✚+✚and then press START.
Napalm Gun	Complete the first level without shooting anything except the boss, then complete level 2 without dying.
Secret Bad Ending	Go through the first level, and do not destroy the boss. Finish the rest of the game to see the failed ending.

DAKAR 2 (XBOX)

Enter these passwords in the Cheat menu under Extras.

UNLOCKABLE	PASSWORD
All Cars	SWEETAS
All Tracks	BONZER

DANCE DANCE REVOLUTION HOTTEST PARTY (Wii)

UNLOCKABLES

UNLOCKABLE	HOW TO UNLOCK
Super Samurai—jun	Play 3 songs on Expert and get a AA or higher on the third song
tokyo EVOLVED—Naoki UNDERGROUND	Unlock all songs, then play 3 songs on Expert and get an AA or higher on the third song
Harmony's Alternate Outfit	Beat Harmony at the song Little Steps at the Genesis Venue
Root's Alternate Outfit	Beat Root at Break Down with a B ranking at the Tectonic Venue

DANCE DANCE REVOLUTION ULTRAMIX (XBOX)

Hook a controller to port 4. At the Main menu, go into options and select credits. Enter a code and you'll hear a sound if it was input correctly.

UNLOCKABLE	CODE
All Music + Cleared Challenge Mode	↑, ↑, ↓, ↓, ←, →, ←, →, B, A

DARK SECTOR (XBOX 360)

UNLOCKABLE

UNLOCKABLE	HOW TO UNLOCK
Brutal Difficulty	Complete the game once.

ACHIEVEMENTS

UNLOCKABLE	HOW TO UNLOCK
Baggage Claim (10)	Complete Chapter 3.
Champion (30)	Finish Best Overall in a Ranked Epidemic match (Multiplayer).
Colossus (50)	Defeated the Colossus.
Comrade (30)	Score 500 points in Ranked Epidemic games (Multiplayer).
Dark Sector—Brutal Difficulty (110)	Complete the game on Brutal difficulty.
Double Decap Latte (15)	Get two decapitations in one shot.
Electrician (10)	Electrocute 30 enemies.
Exposure (10)	Complete Chapter 2.
Finesse (40)	Kill 30 enemies with Aftertouch.
Ghost (35)	Used Shifting to get a Finisher.
Glaive Master (10)	Complete a level using only the Glaive.
Glory (30)	Finish Best Overall in a Ranked Infection match (Multiplayer).
Greed (10)	Collect over 50,000 rubles.
Hardball (35)	Kill 30 enemies with Power-throw.

UNLOCKABLE	HOW TO UNLOCK
Headhunter (10)	Decapitate 30 enemies.
Hero (40)	Score 2,000 points in Ranked Infection games (Multiplayer).
Hero of the People (40)	Score 2,000 points in Ranked Epidemic games (Multiplayer).
Incinerator (10)	Incinerate 30 enemies.
Industrial Evolution (10)	Complete Chapter 7.
Jack Frost (10)	Kill 30 frozen enemies.
Jack the Jackal (35)	Took the Jackal for a ride.
Master Researcher (15)	Collect all the Weapon Upgrades.
Moths to the Flame (10)	Complete Chapter 4.
Nemesis (85)	Defeated the Nemesis.
Prologue (10)	Complete Chapter 1.
Rebound (15)	Kill an enemy with a reflected projectile.
Researcher (10)	Collect 10 Weapon Upgrades.
Sharpshooter (10)	Get 30 headshots.
Skeet Shooter (10)	Shoot 10 projectiles in mid-flight.
Stalker (65)	Defeated the Stalker.
The Bait (10)	Complete Chapter 6.
The Dark Sector (100)	Complete the game.
The Finisher (10)	Perform 30 Finishers.
The Shipment (10)	Complete Chapter 5.
Threshold Guardian (10)	Complete Chapter 9.
Veteran (30)	Score 500 points in Ranked Infection games (Multiplayer).
Weaponsmith (10)	Apply five upgrades in the Black Market.

DARK SECTOR (PlayStation 3)

UNLOCKABLE

UNLOCKABLE	HOW TO UNLOCK
Brutal Difficulty	Complete the game once.

ENTITLEMENTS

Complete each entitlement to get the Unlockable.

UNLOCKABLE	HOW TO UNLOCK
Baggage Claim	Complete Chapter 3.
Champion	Best overall in a ranked team game (Multiplayer).
Comrade	Scored 500 points in ranked team games (Multiplayer).
Dark Sector —Brutal Difficulty	Complete the game on Brutal difficulty.
Double Decap Latte	Two decapitations in one shot.
Electrician	Electrocuted 30 enemies.
Exposure	Complete Chapter 2.
Finesse	30 Aftertouch kills.
Ghost	Used cloaking to get a finisher.
Glaive Master	Completed a level using only the Glaive.
Glory	Finished best overall in a ranked match (Multiplayer).
Greed	Collected over 50,000 rubles.
Hardball	30 Power-throw kills.
Headhunter	Decapitated 30 enemies.
Hero	Scored 5,000 points (Multiplayer).
Hero of the People	Scored 5,000 points in ranked team games

(Multiplayer).

Incinerator	Incinerated 30 enemies.
Industrial Evolution	Complete Chapter 7.
Jack Frost	Killed 30 frozen enemies.
Jack the Jackal	Took the Jackal for a ride.
Master Researcher	Collected all the weapon upgrades.
Moths to the Flame	Complete Chapter 4.
Prologue	Complete Chapter 1.
Rebound	Killed an enemy with a reflected projectile.
Researcher	Collected 10 weapon upgrades.
Sharpshooter	30 Headshots.
Skeet Shooter	Shot 10 projectiles in mid-flight.
The Bait	Complete Chapter 6.
The Dark Sector	Complete Chapter 10.
The Finisher	Performed 30 finishers.
The Shipment	Complete Chapter 5.
Threshold Guardian	Complete Chapter 9.
Unnatural History	Complete Chapter 8.
Veteran	Scored 500 points (Multiplayer).
Weaponsmith	Applied five upgrades in the market.

DARK VOID (XBOX 360)

UNLOCKABLES

The Improved Radar Unlock upgrades the in-game radar display to show collectibles in-game, shown as blue icons on the HUD.

UNLOCKABLE	HOW TO UNLOCK
Upgraded Radar	Complete the game once and a message will pop up at the end saying you unlocked the radar. To use it, simply replay Episodes from the title screen.

DARK VOID (PlayStation 3)

UNLOCKABLES

The Improved Radar Unlock upgrades the in-game radar display to show collectibles in-game, shown as blue icons on the HUD.

UNLOCKABLE	HOW TO UNLOCK
Upgraded Radar	Complete the game once and a message will pop up at the end saying you unlocked the radar. To use it, simply replay Episodes from the title screen.

THE DARKNESS (XBOX 360)

SPECIAL DARKLINGS

At any in-game phone, enter the number and you will unlock a special Darkling

PASSWORD	EFFECT
555-GAME	Unlocks Special 2K Darkling
555-5664	Unlocks the European Retailer (Golfer) Special Darkling

THE DARKNESS (PlayStation 3)

PHONE NUMBERS

Go to any phone and enter the 18 phone numbers, in no specific order, to unlock Keeper of Secrets accomplishment. Find these phone numbers throughout the game on posters, graffiti, etc. Out of the 25, you only need 18 to unlock the accomplishment.

PHONE NUMBER	COUNT
555-6118	1/18
555-9723	2/18
555-1847	3/18
555-5289	4/18
555-6667	5/18
555-6205	6/18
555-4569	7/18
555-7658	8/18
555-9985	9/18
555-1233	10/18
555-1037	11/18
555-3947	12/18
555-1206	13/18
555-9562	14/18
555-9528	15/18
555-7934	16/18
555-3285	17/18
555-7892	18/18

DARKSIDERS (XBOX 360)

CODES

Enter the Pause Screen during gameplay and select "Options." Under Game Options select "Enter Code" from the menu.

EFFECT	CODE
"The Harvester" Scythe	The Hollow Lord

DARKSIDERS (PlayStation 3)

CODES

Enter the Pause Screen during gameplay and select "Options." Under Game Options select "Enter Code" from the menu.

EFFECT	CODE
"The Harvester" Scythe	The Hollow Lord

DEAD MOON (Wii)

UNLOCKABLE

UNLOCKABLE	HOW TO UNLOCK
Option Screen	Hold the following: ✚+①+② and press SELECT

DEAD OR ALIVE 2: HARDCORE (DOA2) (PlayStation 2)

UNLOCKABLE	OBJECTIVE
Bayman	Beat Story mode with every character on the Easy Difficulty setting. Bayman becomes unlocked in all modes except for Story mode.
Bonus Options	Pause the game. Press ▲+✕.
CG Gallery	Beat Team mode with five characters.
Longer Credits	Beat the Story mode with all the characters on Very Hard Difficulty.
More Bounce	Go into the Options menu. Change your age between 13 and 99. The higher you set your age, the more bounce you will see from the female characters.

DEAD RISING (XBOX 360)

ENDING REQUIREMENTS

These are the requirements needed in 72 hour mode to unlock different endings, with A the best and F the worst.

UNLOCKABLE	HOW TO UNLOCK
Ending A	Solve all cases, talk to Isabella at 10 am, and return to the heliport at 12 pm on the 22nd
Ending B	Don't solve all cases and be at the heliport on time
Ending C	Solve all cases but do not talk to Isabella at 10 am on the last day
Ending D	Be a prisoner of the special forces at 12 pm on the 22nd
Ending E	Don't be at the heliport and don't solve all cases
Ending F	Fail to collect all of Carlito's bombs on act 7-2

UNLOCK WEAPON: MOLOTOV COCKTAIL

UNLOCKABLE	HOW TO UNLOCK
Molotov Cocktail (infinite supply)	Use fire extinguisher to save Paul, then bring him to the security room.

UNLOCKABLES

A handful of the Achievements have Unlockable content that becomes available once they've been activated. These, rewards, which include special costumes and items, can be found inside Shopping Bags behind the air duct in the Security Room after you've finished the game.

UNLOCKABLE	HOW TO UNLOCK
Ammo Belt	Perfect Gunner
Arthur's Boxers	7 Day Survivor
Cop Hat	Saint
Hockey Mask	PP Collector
Laser Sword	5 Day Survivor
Mall Employee Uniform	Transmissionary
Mega Man Boots	Unbreakable
Mega Man Tights	Punisher
Prisoner Garb	Carjacker
Pro Wrestling Boots	Item Smasher
Pro Wrestling Briefs	Karate Champ
Real Mega Buster	Zombie Genocide
Special Forces Boots	Legendary Soldier
Special Forces Uniform	Hella Copter
White Hat	Census Taker

UNLOCKABLE MODES

UNLOCKABLE	HOW TO UNLOCK
Infinity Mode	Complete Overtime mode
Overtime Mode	Complete all missions in 72 mode, talk to Isabella at 10am, and return to the helipad by noon on the 22nd

DEAD RISING: CHOP TILL YOU DROP (Wii)

UNLOCKABLES

UNLOCKABLE	HOW TO UNLOCK
Bikini Outfit	Beat the game with an A rank.
Bionic Commando	Beat the game twice.
Chicago Typewriter	Beat the game with an A rank on Normal.
Megaman Boots	Beat all "2nd Amendment" minigames.
Megaman Tights	Beat all "2nd Amendment" minigames with an A rank.

UNLOCKABLE	HOW TO UNLOCK
Prisoner Garb (Costume)	Get S Rank On Prisoners Mission
Real Mega Buster	Beat all "2nd Amendment" minigames with an S rank.
Red 9	Complete the mission "Lovers" with an S rank.
Riot Gun	S rank on "Dressed for Action."
Semi-Auto Rifle	S rank on "Mark of the Sniper."

MINI GAMES

UNLOCKABLE	HOW TO UNLOCK
Odd Jobs	Beat the game.
Second Amendments	Beat the first four Odd Jobs missions.

DEAD SPACE (XBOX 360)

CODES

Press Start, then insert the following codes. You will hear a chime if you've done it correctly.

EFFECT	CODE
1,000 credits (one time only per playthrough)	Ⓧ,Ⓧ,Ⓧ,Ⓨ,Ⓧ
10,000 credits (one time only per playthrough)	Ⓧ,Ⓨ,Ⓨ,Ⓨ,Ⓧ,Ⓧ,Ⓨ
2 Nodes (one time only per playthrough)	Ⓨ,Ⓧ,Ⓧ,Ⓧ,Ⓨ
2,000 credits (one time only per playthrough)	Ⓧ,Ⓧ,Ⓧ,Ⓨ,Ⓨ
5 Nodes (one time only per playthrough)	Ⓨ,Ⓧ,Ⓨ,Ⓧ,Ⓧ,Ⓨ,Ⓧ,Ⓧ,Ⓨ,Ⓧ,Ⓧ,Ⓨ
5,000 credits (one time only per playthrough)	Ⓧ,Ⓧ,Ⓧ,Ⓨ,Ⓧ,Ⓨ
Refill Your Oxygen	Ⓧ,Ⓧ,Ⓨ,Ⓨ,Ⓨ
Refill Your Stasis and Kinesis Energy	Ⓧ,Ⓨ,Ⓨ,Ⓧ,Ⓨ

DEAD SPACE (PlayStation 3)

Codes

Press Start, then insert the following codes. You will hear a chime if you've done it correctly.

EFFECT	CODE
1,000 Credits (one time only)	■,■,■,▲,■
2,000 Credits (one time only)	■,■,■,▲,▲
5,000 Credits (one time only)	■,■,■,▲,■,▲
10,000 Credits (one time only)	■,▲,▲,▲,■,■,▲
Adds 2 Power Nodes (one time only)	▲,■,■,■,▲
Adds 5 Power Nodes (one time only) ▲,■,▲,■,■,▲,■,■,▲,■,■,▲	
Refill Your Oxygen	■,■,▲,▲,▲
Refill Your Stasis and Kinesis Energy	▲,■,▲,▲,■,▲

DEAD TO RIGHTS (XBOX)

Enter the code at the Main menu.

UNLOCKABLE	CODE
Chapter Select	↑,↓,↑,↓,←,→,→,Ⓨ,Ⓧ,Ⓧ

DEAD TO RIGHTS (PlayStation 2)

Enter the follwing codes at the New Game screen, just after "Press Start" appears. After entering the following codes listen for a message that confirms correct code entry.

UNLOCKABLE	CODE
10,000 Bullets Mode (unlimited ammo)	Hold L1+L2+R1+R2 and press ↑,←,↓,→,●.

Bang Bang Mode	Hold L1+L2+R1+R2 and press ●,▲,■,●,→.
Boomstick Mode (unlimited shotguns)	Hold L1+L2+R1+R2 and press →,●,●,●,■.
Chow Yun Jack Mode (You receive a pair of double guns at the beginning of the level, even if you would normally have none.)	Hold L1+L2+R1+R2 and press ▲,●,↑,↑,↑.
Double Melee Attack Damage	Hold L1+L2+R1+R2 and press ●,●,↑,↑,■.
Enemies Disarmed	Hold L1+L2+R1+R2 and press →,■,←,●,▲.
Enemies More Accurate	Hold L1+L2+R1+R2 and press ▲,■,←,←,●.
Hard-Boiled Mode (increases the challenge level significantly)	Hold L1+L2+R1+R2 and press ▲,■,←,←,●.
Invisible Character (Enemies can still see you, but you can only see your own shadow.)	Hold L1+L2+R1+R2 and press ▲,▲,↑,↑,▲.
Lazy Mode (all levels, minigames, and FMV sequences)	Hold L1+L2+R1+R2 and press ↓,←,↓,▲,↓.
One-Hit Wonder Mode	Hold L1+L2+R1+R2 and press ▲,●,●,●,←.
Powered-up Punches and Kicks	Hold L1+L2+R1+R2 and press ↓,●,←,←,←.
Precursor Mode (turns off all targeting cursors)	Hold L1+L2+R1+R2 and press ↑,↑,↓,↓,↑.
Sharpshooter Mode	Hold L1+L2+R1+R2 and press ■,■,■,↓,→.
Super Cop Mode (harder difficulty)	Hold L1+L2+R1+R2 and press ■,▲,←,↑,→.
Time to Pay Mode (all disarms)	Hold L1+L2+R1+R2 and press ■,■,●,●,→.
Unlimited Adrenaline	Hold L1+L2+R1+R2 and press ←,→,←,●,■.
Unlimited Armor	Hold L1+L2+R1+R2 and press ↑,↑,↑,■,↓.
Unlimited Dual Guncons	Hold L1+L2+R1+R2 and press ▲,●,↑,↑,↑.
Unlimited Human Shields	Hold L1+L2+R1+R2 and press ■,▲,●,▲,■.
Unlimited Shadow Stamina	Hold L1+L2+R1+R2 and press ●,■,▲,●,↓.
Wussy Mode (less accurate enemies)	Hold L1+L2+R1+R2 and press ■,←,▲,↑,↓.

DEATH JR. (PSP)

To enter these codes, pause the game and hold L+R.

UNLOCKABLE	CODE
All Weapons and Weapon Upgrades	⇧, ⇧, ⇩, ⇩, ⇦, ⇨, ⇦, ⇨, ×, ●
Ammo Refilled	▲, ▲, ×, ×, ■, ●, ■, ●, ⇩, ⇨
Assist Extender	⇧, ⇧, ⇩, ⇩, ▲, ▲, ×, ×, ▲, ▲
Attacks Have Different Names	⇧, ⇧, ⇩, ⇦, ▲, ▲, ■, ×, ●, ■
Big Heads	▲, ●, ×, ■, ▲, ⇧, ⇨, ⇩, ⇦, ⇧
Big Scythe	▲, ■, ×, ●, ▲, ⇧, ⇦, ⇩, ⇨, ⇧
Bullet Holes Become Pictures	⇧, ⇨, ⇩, ⇦, ⇧, ▲, ●, ×, ■, ▲
Eyedoors Don't Require Souls to Open	⇧, ⇦, ⇩, ⇨, ⇦, ▲, ■, ×, ●, ■

UNLOCKABLE	CODE
Fill Pandora's Assist Meter	⇧, ⇧, ⇩, ⇩, ⇧, ⇨, ⇩, ⇦, ×, ×
Free All Characters and Unlock All Levels	⇧, ⇧, ⇧, ⇧, ⇩, ⇩, ⇩, ⇩, ×, × (Must be entered in the stage and re-entered in the museum)
Free Seep	⇦, ⇦, ⇨, ⇨, ⇦, ⇨, ⇦, ⇨, ×, ×
Increased Health and Stamina	⇧, ⇧, ⇩, ⇩, ×, ●, ▲, ■, ×, ×
Invincibility	⇧, ⇧, ⇩, ⇩, ⇦, ⇦, ⇨, ⇨, ■, ▲
Monsters Are Different Colors and Scythe Has Trails	⇩, ×, ⇩, ×, ⇩, ×, ⇩, ×, ⇩, ×
Odd Monsters and Scythe Has Trails	▲, ⇧, ●, ⇨, ×, ⇩, ■, ⇦, ▲, ⇧
Unlimited Ammo	▲, ▲, ×, ×, ■, ●, ■, ●, ⇨, ⇩
Warp to Advanced Training Stage	⇩, ×, ⇩, ×, ⇩, ×, ⇩, ×, ⇩, ■
Warp to Basic Training Stage	⇧, ▲, ⇧, ×, ⇩, ×, ⇩, ×, ⇩, ×
Warp to Big Trouble in Little Downtown Stage	⇧, ▲, ⇩, ×, ⇩, ×, ⇩, ×, ⇩, ×
Warp to Bottom of the Bell Curve Stage	⇩, ×, ⇩, ×, ⇩, ×, ⇩, ×, ⇩, ▲
Warp to Burn it Down Stage	⇩, ×, ⇧, ▲, ⇩, ×, ⇩, ×, ⇩, ×
Warp to Final Battle Stage	⇩, ×, ⇩, ×, ⇩, ×, ⇩, ▲, ⇧, ×
Warp to Growth Spurt Stage	⇩, ×, ⇩, ×, ⇩, ×, ⇩, ×, ⇧, ×
Warp to Happy Trails Insanitarium Stage	⇩, ×, ⇩, ▲, ⇧, ×, ⇩, ×, ⇩, ×
Warp to Higher Learning Stage	⇩, ×, ⇩, ×, ⇩, ×, ⇩, ▲, ⇩, ×
Warp to How a Cow Becomes a Steak Stage	⇩, ×, ⇩, ×, ⇩, ▲, ⇩, ×, ⇩, ×
Warp to Inner Madness Stage	⇩, ×, ⇩, ×, ⇧, ▲, ⇩, ×, ⇩, ×
Warp to Into the Box Stage	⇩, ×, ⇩, ×, ⇩, ×, ⇧, ▲, ⇩, ×
Warp to Moving on Up Stage	⇩, ▲, ⇧, ×, ⇩, ×, ⇩, ×, ⇩, ×
Warp to My House Stage	⇩, ×, ⇩, ▲, ⇩, ×, ⇩, ×, ⇩, ×
Warp to Seep's Hood Stage	⇩, ▲, ⇩, ×, ⇩, ×, ⇩, ×, ⇩, ×
Warp to Shock Treatment Stage	⇩, ×, ⇩, ×, ⇩, ▲, ⇧, ×, ⇩, ×
Warp to The Basement Stage	⇩, ×, ⇩, ×, ⇩, ×, ⇩, ×, ⇧, ▲
Warp to The Burger Tram Stage	⇩, ×, ⇩, ×, ⇩, ×, ⇧, ×, ⇩, ×
Warp to The Corner Store Stage	⇩, ×, ⇧, ×, ⇩, ×, ⇩, ×, ⇩, ×
Warp to The Museum	⇧, ×, ⇩, ×, ⇩, ×, ⇩, ×, ⇩, ×
Warp to Udder Madness Stage	⇩, ×, ⇩, ×, ⇧, ×, ⇩, ×, ⇩, ×
Weapons Have Different Names	⇩, ⇩, ⇧, ⇧, ⇦, ⇨, ⇦, ⇨, ■, ▲
Widget	⇨, ⇧, ⇩, ⇧, ▲, ⇧, ⇦, ■, ▲, ⇨

DEATH JR. II: ROOT OF EVIL (PSP)

Enter these codes while the game is paused.

UNLOCKABLE	CODE
All Weapon Upgrades	Hold L2 and press ⇧, ⇧, ⇩, ⇩, ⇦, ⇨, ⇦, ⇨, ×, ●
Invincibility	Hold L2 and press ⇧, ⇧, ⇩, ⇩, ⇦, ⇦, ⇨, ⇨, ■, ▲
Refill Ammunition	Hold L2 and press ▲, ▲, ×, ×, ■, ●, ■, ●, ⇩, ⇨
Unlimited Ammunition	Hold L2 and press ▲, ▲, ×, ×, ■, ●, ■, ●, ⇨, ⇩

DEF JAM: FIGHT FOR NY (XBOX)

Enter these codes in the Cheat menu.

UNLOCKABLE	CODE
100 Reward Points	NEWJACK
Anything Goes by CNN	MILITAIN
Bust by Outkast	BIGBOI
Comp by Comp	CHOCOCITY
Dragon House by Chiang	AKIRA
Koto by Chiang	GHOSTSHELL
Man Up by Sticky Fingaz	KIRKJONES

Move by Public Enemy	RESPECT
Original Gangster by Ice T	POWER
Take a Look at my Life by Fat Joe	CARTAGENA
Walk with Me by Joe Budden	PUMP

DEF JAM: FIGHT FOR NY—THE TAKEOVER (PSP)

Enter these passwords in the Cheats menu under extras.

UNLOCKABLE	PASSWORD
After Hours by Nyne	LOYALTY
Anything Goes by C-N-N	MILITAIN
Blindside by Baxter	CHOPPER
Bust by Outkast	BIGBOI
Comp by Comp	CHOCOCITY
Dragon House by Masa Mix	AKIRA
Get It Now by Bless	PLATINUMB
Koto by Chiang's Mix	GHOSTSHELL
Lil Bro by Ric-A-Che	GONBETRUBL
Man Up by Sticky Fingaz	KIRKJONES
Move! by Public Enemy	RESPECT
Original Gangster by Ice-T	POWER
Poppa Large by Ultramagnetic MC's	ULTRAMAG
Seize the Day by Bless	SIEZE
Take a Look at my Life by Fat Joe	CARTAGENA
Walk with Me by Joe Budden	PUMP
Add 100 reward points	REALSTUFF
Add 100 reward points	GOUNDRGRND
Add 100 reward points	THEEMCEE
Add 100 reward points	BULLETPROOF
Add 100 reward points	DASTREETS
Add 200 reward points	REAL STYLE
Add 200 reward points	SUPER FREAK
Add 200 reward points	DRAGONHOUSE
Add 300 reward points	NEWYORKCIT

DEF JAM: ICON (XBOX 360)

Enter these codes at the Press Start screen.

UNLOCKABLE	CODE
"It's Going Down" Music Track	Ⓑ, ↑, →, ←, Ⓨ
"Make It Rain" Music Track	↓, Ⓑ, Ⓐ, →

DEF JAM: ICON (PlayStation 3)

At the Press Start screen, enter these codes.

UNLOCKABLE	CODE
It's Going Down music track	●, ⇧, ⇨, ⇦, ▲
Make It Rain music track	⇩, ●, ⇩, ⇨

THE FOLLOWING CODES ALSO YIELD THE "100 REWARD POINTS" UNLOCKABLE: THESOURCE, CROOKLYN, DUCKET, GETSTUFF.

DEF JAM: VENDETTA (PlayStation 2)

Enter the following codes on any non-Story mode character select screen.

UNLOCKABLE	CODE
Arii	Hold L2 + L2 + R1 + R2 and press ×, ■, ▲, ●, ■.
Briggs	Hold L2 + L2 + R1 + R2 and press ×, ▲, ●, ■, ●.
Briggs (alternate costume)	Hold L2 + L2 + R1 + R2 and press ×, ▲, ■, ×, ●.

UNLOCKABLE	CODE
Carla	Hold L2 + L2 + R1 + R2 and press ×, ■, ×, ×, ×.
Chukklez	Hold L2 + L2 + R1 + R2 and press ■, ■, ▲, ×, ●.
Cruz	Hold L2 + L2 + R1 + R2 and press ●, ▲, ×, ×, ●.
D-Mob	Hold L2 + L2 + R1 + R2 and press ■, ▲, ●, ×, ●.
D-Mob (alternate costume)	Hold L2 + L2 + R1 + R2 and press ■, ■, ▲, ■, ■.
Dan G	Hold L2 + L2 + R1 + R2 and press ×, ●, ×, ●, ■.
Deebo	Hold L2 + L2 + R1 + R2 and press ●, ●, ×, ×, ▲.
Deja	Hold L2 + L2 + R1 + R2 and press ●, ■, ●, ●, ×.
DMX	Hold L2 + L2 + R1 + R2 and press ●, ×, ●, ▲, ■.
Drake	Hold L2 + L2 + R1 + R2 and press ▲, ■, ●, ×, ×.
Drake (alternate costume)	Hold L2 + L2 + R1 + R2 and press ×, ▲, ▲, ●, ●.
Funkmaster Flex	Hold L2 + L2 + R1 + R2 and press ●, ▲, ●, ●, ■.
Headache	Hold L2 + L2 + R1 + R2 and press ▲, ▲, ▲, ■, ●.
House	Hold L2 + L2 + R1 + R2 and press ▲, ×, ▲, ●, ×.
Iceberg	Hold L2 + L2 + R1 + R2 and press ■, ▲, ●, ■, ●.
Ludacris	Hold L2 + L2 + R1 + R2 and press ●, ●, ●, ■, ▲.
Manny (alternate costume)	Hold L2 + L2 + R1 + R2 and press ●, ■, ●, ■, ●.
Masa	Hold L2 + L2 + R1 + R2 and press ×, ●, ▲, ■, ■.
Method Man	Hold L2 + L2 + R1 + R2 and press ■, ●, ×, ▲, ●.
Moses	Hold L2 + L2 + R1 + R2 and press ▲, ▲, ■, ■, ×.
N.O.R.E.	Hold L2 + L2 + R1 + R2 and press ●, ■, ▲, ×, ●.
Nyne	Hold L2 + L2 + R1 + R2 and press ■, ●, ×, ×, ▲.
Omar	Hold L2 + L2 + R1 + R2 and press ●, ●, ■, ▲, ▲.
Opal	Hold L2 + L2 + R1 + R2 and press ●, ●, ■, ■, ▲.
Peewee	Hold L2 + L2 + R1 + R2 and press ×, ×, ■, ▲, ■.
Peewee (alternate costume)	Hold L2 + L2 + R1 + R2 and press ×, ▲, ▲, ■, ●.
Penny	Hold L2 + L2 + R1 + R2 and press ×, ×, ×, ▲, ●.
Pockets	Hold L2 + L2 + R1 + R2 and press ▲, ■, ●, ■, ×.
Proof (alternate costume)	Hold L2 + L2 + R1 + R2 and press ×, ■, ▲, ■, ●.
Razor	Hold L2 + L2 + R1 + R2 and press ▲, ■, ▲, ●, ×.
Razor (alternate costume)	Hold L2 + L2 + R1 + R2 and press ■, ●, ×, ▲, ▲.
Redman	Hold L2 + L2 + R1 + R2 and press ●, ●, ▲, ■, ×.
Ruffneck	Hold L2 + L2 + R1 + R2 and press ×, ■, ×, ▲, ●.
Ruffneck (alternate costume)	Hold L2 + L2 + R1 + R2 and press ■, ●, ▲, ×, ■.
Scarface	Hold L2 + L2 + R1 + R2 and press ●, ■, ×, ▲, ■.
Sketch	Hold L2 + L2 + R1 + R2 and press ▲, ▲, ●, ■, ×.
Snowman	Hold L2 + L2 + R1 + R2 and press ▲, ▲, ×, ×, ●.
Spider (alternate costume)	Hold L2 + L2 + R1 + R2 and press ■, ▲, ×, ■, ●.
Steel	Hold L2 + L2 + R1 + R2 and press ×, ▲, ●, ●, ▲.
T'ai	Hold L2 + L2 + R1 + R2 and press ●, ●, ■, ×, ●.
Zaheer	Hold L2 + L2 + R1 + R2 and press ▲, ▲, ■, ×, ×.

DESTROY ALL HUMANS (XBOX)

To activate these codes, pause the game and hold LT, then enter the code and release LT.

UNLOCKABLE	CODE
Ammo-A-Plenty	←, Y, WHT, →, BLK, X
Aware Like a Fox	→, X, WHT, BLK, →, WHT
Bulletproof Crypto	X, Y, ←, ←, Y, X
Deep Thinker	BLK, WHT, Y, →, WHT, Y

Mmmm...Brains! (This code increases DNA.)	BLK, BLK, WHT, WHT, ←, →, ←, →, WHT, BLK (You must be on the Mothership.)
Nobody Loves You	WHT, →, WHT, BLK, X, →

DESTROY ALL HUMANS (PlayStation 2)

To activate these codes, pause the game and hold L1, then enter the code and release L1.

UNLOCKABLE	CODE
Ammo-A-Plenty	⇦, ●, R2, ⇨, R1, ■
Aware Like a Fox	⇨, ■, R2, R1, ⇨, R2
Bulletproof Crypto	■, ●, ⇦, ⇦, ⇦, ●, ■
Deep Thinker	R1, R2, ●, ⇨, R2, ●
Mmmm...Brains! increases	R1, R1, R2, R2, ⇦, ⇨, ⇦, ⇨, R2 This code DNA. (You must be on the Mothership.)
More Upgrades Mothership.)	■, ●, ⇦, ⇦, ●, ■ (You must be on the
Nobody Loves You	⇨, R2, R1, ■, ⇨

DESTROY ALL HUMANS 2 (XBOX)

Pause the game, go to archives, press and hold L3, and enter following cheats.

UNLOCKABLE	CODE
Salad Days with Pox and Crypto Video	A, X, Y, B, X, B, X, A, A

DEUS EX: CONSPIRACY THEORY (PlayStation 2)

Activate Cheats: Enter the Goals/Notes/Images screen. Press L2, R2, L1, R1, START (3) to display another tab on this screen with the following cheats that you can turn on and off: God, Full Health, Full Energy, Full Ammo, Full Mods, All Skills, Full Credits, and Tantalus.

DEVIL MAY CRY 2 (PlayStation 2)

UNLOCKABLE	OBJECTIVE
Alternate Dante Costume	Complete the game with Dante at Normal difficulty.
Alternate Devil May Cry 1 Costume for Dante	Complete the game in Dante Must Die mode.
Alternate Costumes for Lucia Hard	Complete the game with Lucia to unlock her alternate costume. Complete the game with Lucia under the difficulty setting to unlock another costume.
Bloody Palace Mode	Complete the game with Dante and Lucia.
Dante Must Die Mode	Complete the game with Dante and Lucia under the Hard difficulty setting.
Dante's Diesel Bonus Level and Costume	Play Dante's Mission 1, then save the game. Reset the PlayStation2, and wait for the "Press Start button" message to reappear. Press L3, R3, L1, R1, L2, R2, L3, R3. A sound confirms correct code entry. Press START to return to the Main menu. Choose the "Load game" option, press L3 or R3 to access the new costume, and then load a game to play the bonus level.
Dante's Diesel Costume	Press R1, R1, ▲, ■, R2, R2 during gameplay.
Hard Difficulty Setting	Complete the game with Dante and Lucia.
In-Game Reset	Press START+SELECT during gameplay to return to the title screen.
Level Select	Complete the game as either character under any difficulty setting.
Lucia's Arius bod	Complete the game in Lucia Must Die mode.
Lucia Must Die Mode	Complete the game with Lucia under the Hard difficulty setting.

UNLOCKABLE	OBJECTIVE
Lucia's Diesel Bonus Level and Costume	Play Lucia's Mission 1, then save the game. Reset the PlayStation2, and wait for the "Press Start button" message to reappear. Press L3, R3, L1, R1, L2, R2, L3, R3. A sound confirms correct code entry. Press START to return to the Main menu. Choose the "Load game" option, press L3 or R3 to access the new costume, and then load a game to play the bonus level.
Lucia's Diesel Costume	Press L1, L1, ▲, ■, L2, L2 during gameplay.
Play as Trish	Complete the game with Dante under the Hard difficulty setting. Trish has Dante's stats and items and starts with the Sparda.

Completion Bonuses: Use the following to unlock the completion bonuses by only playing Dante's game. Switch from Disc 1 to 2 anytime during Dante's game. Complete the game to unlock Level Select mode, Hard mode, Bloody Palace mode, and the credits. If you change from Disc 1 to 2 before completing the game in Hard mode, you unlock Trish and other bonuses.

DEVIL MAY CRY 3 (PlayStation 2)

Enter at the Main menu.

UNLOCKABLE	CODE
Unlock Everything	Hold down L1, L2, R1, R2 and rotate the left analog stick until you hear Devil May Cry.

DEVIL MAY CRY 4 (XBOX 360)

UNLOCKABLES

UNLOCKABLE	HOW TO UNLOCK
Bloody Palace Survival Mode	Complete the game on Devil Hunter difficulty or Human difficulty.
Bonus Art and Character Art	Complete the game on Devil Hunter difficulty or Human difficulty.
Gallery	Complete the game on Devil Hunter difficulty or Human difficulty.
History of Devil May Cry	Complete the game on Devil Hunter difficulty or Human difficulty.
Son of Sparda Difficulty	Complete the game on Devil Hunter difficulty.

DEVIL'S CRUSH (Wii)

UNLOCKABLE

UNLOCKABLE	HOW TO UNLOCK
Sound Mode	Press ↑, →, ↓ after pausing
Sound Test	Press RUN, SELECT during gameplay to display the High Score screen, then press ↑, ↓, ←, →, ①

PASSWORDS

PASSWORD	EFFECT
EFGHIJKLMB	924,000,000 points and 73 balls
AAAAAAAAAAAAAAAAAB	A 2-player game with unlimited balls
THECRUSHEL	Beat the game—launch the ball and once you hit something, the game ends
DAVIDWHITE	Beat the game—launch the ball and once you hit something, the game ends
FFFFFFFEEE	Beat the game—launch the ball and once you hit something, the game ends
NAXATSOFTI	Infinite balls, 206,633,300 points
AAAAAAHAAA	Infinite balls, 734,003,200 points

DEVILSATAN	Infinite balls, 955,719,100 points
THEDEVILSI	Over 145,000,000 points and 70 balls
ONECRUSHME	Over 594,000,000 points and 27 balls
AAAAAAAAAAAAAAABCE	2-player mode—gives player 1 unlimited balls and player 2 32 balls
PPPPPPPPPA	Unlimited balls
CKDEIPDBFM	25 balls and a score of 300,138,400
OJFJGDEJPD	34 balls and a score of 404,330,300
PNBIJOKJNF	38 balls and a score of 533,501,000
CGIAGPECGK	42 balls and a score of 610,523,600
OEHALCBGPF	45 balls and a score of 710,529,000
OLGGGEAPOF	52 balls and a score of 804,379,700
CBEOBLJGHA	62 balls and a score of 900,057,102
PFFMGHGOLK	65 balls and a score of 999,927,400
NLJBCFHGPO	65 balls and a score of 999,999,000
KGCMMCMLBN	65 balls and a score of 999,999,600
OMGANLOIJA	67 balls and a score of 976,769,800

DEWY'S ADVENTURE (Wii)

UNLOCKABLES

UNLOCKABLE	HOW TO UNLOCK
Character Gallery	Complete Groovy Grasslands
Hall of Records	Complete Groovy Grasslands
Music Gallery	Complete Groovy Grasslands
Photo Gallery	Complete Groovy Grasslands
Tips and Tricks	Complete Groovy Grasslands

DIRT 2 (XBOX 360)

UNLOCKABLES

Beat the races below to unlock the cars.

UNLOCKABLE	HOW TO UNLOCK
Colin McRae R4 (X-G Version)	1st in X-Games Europe
Dallenbach Special	1st in Trailblazer World Tour
Ford Escort MKII	1st in ALL X-Games Events
Ford RS200 Evolution	1st in Rally Cross World Tour
MG Metro 6R4	1st in ALL X-Games Events
Mitsubishi Lancer Evolution X (X-G Version)	1st in X-Games Asia
Mitsubishi Pajero Dakar	1st in Raid World Tour
Subaru Impreza WRX STi	1st in Colin McRae Challenge
Subaru Impreza WRX STi (X-G Version)	1st in X-Games America
Toyota Stadium Truck	1st in Landrush World Tour

DISGAEA 3: ABSENCE OF JUSTICE (PlayStation 3)

UNLOCKABLE CLASSES

UNLOCKABLE	HOW TO UNLOCK
Archer (Female)	Level 15 Female Fighter and Level 15 Female Healer
Archer (Male)	Level 15 Male Fighter and Level 15 Male Healer
Berserker	Heavy Knight and Monster Tamer Level 40
Cheerleader (Idol)	Geo Master and Healer Level 25
Geo Master	Fist Fighter and Healer Level 20
Gunner Female	Female Thief and Mage Level 15

UNLOCKABLE	HOW TO UNLOCK
Gunner Male	Thief and Male Mage Level 15
Heavy Knight	Male Fighter and Fist Fighter Level 15
Magic Knight	Fighter and Mage Level 25
Majin	Clear second play through tutorial
Masked Hero	Thief and Gunner Level 45
Monster Tamer	Female Fighter and Fist Fighter Level 15
Ninja (Female)	Level 30 Female Monk and Level 30 Female Magician
Ninja (Male)	Level 30 Male Monk and Level 30 Male Magician
Samurai (Female)	Level 35 Female Fighter and Level 35 Female Archer
Samurai (Male)	Level 35 Male Fighter and Level 35 Male Archer
Shaman	Geo Master and Mage Level 25

UNLOCKABLE CAMEO CHARACTERS

UNLOCKABLE	HOW TO UNLOCK
Asagi	Beat extra map 4
Axel	Beat extra map 6
Laharl, Etna, and Flonne	Beat extra map 7
Marona	Beat extra map 5
Master Big Star	Beat extra map 1
Prism Red	Beat extra map 3
Salvatore	Beat extra map 2

UNLOCKABLE ENDINGS

UNLOCKABLE	HOW TO UNLOCK
Almaz's Ending	Win stage 8-4 with Almaz alone and the battle after
Human World Ending	Kill more then 99 allies and clear two alt. stages by stage 7-6
Laharl's Ending	Go to homeroom and propose "Watch a New Ending" and clear the stage
Mao's Ambition Ending	Clear stage 1-9 on 2nd or higher cycle before stage 4-4
Normal Ending	Don't meet any other ending's requirement
Raspberyl's Ending 1	Lose against Raspberyl on stage 1-5
Raspberyl's Ending 2	Lose against Raspberyl on stage 2-1
Super Hero Ending	Use Mao at Level 500 or higher to defeat final boss

UNLOCKABLE DIFFICULTIES

UNLOCKABLE	HOW TO UNLOCK
Samurai Mode	Complete the game at least once.
Tourny Mode	Complete the game on Samurai Difficulty.

DISGAEA: AFTERNOON OF DARKNESS (PSP)

ETNA MODE

Disgaea contains a hidden mode called Etna mode. Normally you have to get this mode by going through the game and reading Etna's diary every chapter, but you can unlock it instantly by entering the following code during the title screen, with the pointer on "New Game." If you're successful, you'll hear Etna's voice.

EFFECT	CODE
Unlock Etna Mode (US)	▲, ■, ●, ▲, ■, ●, ×

EXTRA CLASSES

UNLOCKABLE	HOW TO UNLOCK
Angel	Female Cleric, Knight, and Archer all at level 100 or higher.
Archer	Level 3 or higher in Bow Weapon Mastery.

EDF Soldier	Level 30 or higher Gun Weapon Mastery.
Galaxy Mage	Level a Prism Mage to Level 50.
Galaxy Skull	Level a Prism Skull to Level 50.
Knight	Female Warrior and Female Mage each at level 10 or higher.
Majin	Male Warrior, Brawler, Ninja, Rogue, and Scout all at level 200 or higher.
Ninja	Male Fighter and Male Warrior with a total level of 10 or higher.
Prism Mage	Level a Star Mage to Level 35.
Prism Skull	Level a Star Skull to Level 35.
Rogue	Both Fighter and Warrior, Males or Females, each at level 5 or higher.
Ronin	Female Warrior and Female Fighter with a total level of 10 or higher.
Scout	Two Fighters/Warriors, Males or Females, each at level 5 or higher.
Star Mage	Get one Fire, Ice, and Wind Mage and level all three of them to level 5.
Star Skull	Get one Fire, Ice, and Wind Skull and level all three of them to level 5.

THE DISHWASHER: DEAD SAMURAI (XBOX 360)

UNLOCKABLE DIFFICULTIES

UNLOCKABLE	HOW TO UNLOCK
Samurai Mode	Complete the game at least once.
Tourny Mode	Complete the game on Samurai Difficulty.

DISNEY'S CHICKEN LITTLE: ACE IN ACTION (Wii)

Input the codes under Cheat option.

UNLOCKABLE	CODE
All Levels Available	→, ↑, ←, →, ↑
All Weapons Available	→, ↓, →, ←
Unlimited Shield Available	→, ↓, →, ↓, →

DISNEY'S EXTREME SKATE ADVENTURE (XBOX)

Enter these codes in the Cheats menu.

UNLOCKABLE	CODE
All Create-a-Skater Items	gethotgear
All Levels	frequentflyers
All Skaters	xtremebuddies
Lion King Video	savannah
Special Meter always full	happyfeet
Tarzan Video	nugget
Toy Story Video	marin

DISNEY'S EXTREME SKATE ADVENTURE (PlayStation 2)

Go to Options, select Cheat Codes, then enter the following codes.

UNLOCKABLE	CODE
All Create-a-Skaters	sweetthreads
All Skaters	friendsofbob
All Levels	extremepassport
Filled Special Meter	supercharger
Lion King Video	savannah
Tarzan Video	nugget
Toy Story Video	marin

DISNEY'S KIM POSSIBLE KIMMUNICATOR (DS)

Enter these codes while playing—do not pause. You must hold down L+R to enter these codes.

UNLOCKABLE	CODE
9,999 parts	Ⓨ, Ⓨ, Ⓧ, Ⓑ, Ⓐ, Ⓨ
99 lives	Ⓐ, Ⓐ, Ⓐ, Ⓨ, Ⓧ, Ⓨ, Ⓑ, Ⓐ
Don't lose lives	Ⓨ, Ⓨ, Ⓨ, Ⓧ
Extra Life	Ⓐ, Ⓐ, Ⓐ, Ⓨ, Ⓧ, Ⓨ
Full Health	Ⓐ, Ⓐ, Ⓐ, Ⓨ
Invincibility	Ⓨ, Ⓨ, Ⓨ, Ⓧ, Ⓐ, Ⓑ
Unlock all gadgets	Ⓨ, Ⓨ, Ⓧ, Ⓑ, Ⓐ, Ⓨ, Ⓨ, Ⓐ
Unlock all missions	Ⓧ, Ⓨ, Ⓧ, Ⓐ, Ⓧ, Ⓑ
Unlock all outfits	Ⓑ, Ⓐ, Ⓧ, Ⓨ, Ⓐ, Ⓑ

DOG'S LIFE (PlayStation 2)

UNLOCKABLE	CODE
Enable Cheat menu	■, ■, ■ hold ■ (till the dog growls), hold ■ (till the dog growls), hold ■ (till the dog growls), ←, →, ↓

DOKAPON KINGDOM (Wii)

UNLOCKABLES

Here's how to unlock specific jobs.

UNLOCKABLE	HOW TO UNLOCK
Acrobat	Get a Casino Ticket
Alchemist	Master Magician and Thief
Cleric	Master 1 of the Starter Jobs
Monk	Master Priest
Ninja	Master Warrior and Thief
Spellsword	Master Warrior and Magician

DOOM (XBOX 360)

GAMER PICS

UNLOCKABLE	HOW TO UNLOCK
Secret Gamer Pic of a Demon	Beat any level on Nightmare difficulty
Secret Gamer Pic of a Doom Marine	Get a 100% kill rating on any level with a "Hurt Me Plenty" or higher difficulty level

DOOM 3 (XBOX)

These codes must be entered very quickly while playing.

UNLOCKABLE	CODE
God Mode	Hold LT and press Ⓧ, Ⓨ, Ⓑ, Ⓐ
Level Skip	Hold LT and press Ⓑ, Ⓐ, Ⓧ, Ⓨ

DOUBLE DUNGEONS (Wii)

PASSWORDS

At the Password screen, carefully enter the following passwords.

PASSWORD	EFFECT
cHR0EScxgoAq or iky7ihOfeBGe	In front of the last boss door
2R3KD4RG0J9D3YT0664LJ	Beginning of Level 22
YNzYSMChriGlgLV-ihOdfCGe	End of Level 22
Enter either Player01 or Player 02 as a password, with the remaining spaces filled inwith either +'s or -'s	Get 65,535 HP

Enter any working password for player 1, then enter KKKKKKKKKKKKKKKKKKKKKKKK as a password for player 2	Player 2 invincibility

NEW!
A B C D E F G H I J K L M N O P Q R S T U V W X Y Z

DR. MUTO (XBOX)

In the Options menu, select "Cheats" to enter these codes.

UNLOCKABLE	CODE
All Gadgets	TINKERTOY
All Morphs	EUREKA
Death No Touch	NECROSCI
Go Anywhere	BEAMMEUP
Never Take Damage	CHEATERBOY
Secret Morphs	LOGGLOGG
See all Movies	HOTTICKET
Super Ending Unlocked	BUZZOFF

DR. MUTO (PlayStation 2)

Enter the following as codes.

UNLOCKABLE	CODE
All Gadgets	TINKERTOY
Invincibility (This has no effect when you fall from high places.)	NECROSCI
All Morphs	EUREKA
Go Anywhere	BEAMMEUP
Never Take Damage	CHEATERBOY
Secret Morphs	LOGGLOGG
Super Ending	BUZZOFF
View FMV Sequences	HOTTICKET

DR. ROBOTNIK'S MEAN BEAN MACHINE (Wii)

EASY MODE PASSWORDS

PASSWORD	EFFECT
RRRH	Stage 2: Frankly
CPCG	Stage 3: Humpty
RCHY	Stage 4: Coconuts
CBBP	Stage 5: Davy Sproket
CRCP	Stage 6: Sqweel
PYRB	Stage 7: Dynamight
YPHB	Stage 8: Grounder
YPHB	Stage 9: Spike
RYCH	Stage 10: Sir Fuzzy Logik
GPBC	Stage 11: Dragon Breath
RHHY	Stage 12: Scratch
YHBB	Stage 13: Dr. Robotnik

HARD MODE PASSWORDS

PASSWORD	EFFECT
RRRH GCYY	Stage 2: Frankly
CPCG YPCP	Stage 3: Humpty
RCHY BGCB	Stage 4: Coconuts

PASSWORD	EFFECT
RPGG	Stage 5: Davy Sproket
YYCG	Stage 6: Sqweel
PCBB	Stage 7: Dynamight
CYHY	Stage 8: Grounder
PBBG	Stage 9: Spike
CGRY	Stage 10: Sir Fuzzy Logik
BYYH	Stage 11: Dragon Breath
GCCB	Stage 12: Scratch
HCPH	Stage 13: Dr. Robotnik

HARDEST MODE PASSWORDS

PASSWORD	EFFECT
BBGY	Stage 2: Frankly
GYGC	Stage 3: Humpty
PASSWORD	EFFECT
PPRH	Stage 4: Coconuts
GRPB	Stage 5: Davy Sproket
PCGY	Stage 6: Sqweel
BPGH	Stage 7: Dynamight
CPHY	Stage 8: Grounder
PGHC	Stage 9: Spike
GBYH	Stage 10: Sir Fuzzy Logik
GPHR	Stage 11: Dragon Breath
RGHB	Stage 12: Scratch
RRCY	Stage 13: Dr. Robotnik

UNLOCKABLES

UNLOCKABLE	HOW TO UNLOCK
Jumping Bean Title Screen	At the title screen, press Ⓐ, Ⓑ, or ✣ on controller 1 to make the "e," "a," and "n" in "Mean" jump. Press Ⓐ, Ⓑ, or ✣ on controller 2 to make the "e", "a", and "n" in "Bean" jump.
Last Boss	On Easy mode, enter Yellow Bean, Has Bean, Blue Bean, Blue Bean as your password. On Normal mode, enter Purple Bean, Yellow Bean, Has Bean, Clear Bean.

SCENARIO MODE PASSWORDS—NORMAL DIFFICULTY

Enter these passwords after selecting "Continue" to skip ahead to the desired level.

PASSWORD	EFFECT
R = Red Bean	
Y = Yellow Bean	
G = Green Bean	
B = Blue Bean	
P = Purple Bean	
C = Clear (Garbage) Bean	
H = Has Bean (the little orange fellow)	
HCYY	Stage 2: Frankly
BCRY	Stage 3: Humpty
YBCP	Stage 4: Coconuts
HGBY	Stage 5: Davy Sprocket
GPPY	Stage 6: Sqweel
PBGH	Stage 7: Dynamight
GHCY	Stage 8: Grounder

BPHH	Stage 9: Spike
HRYC	Stage 10: Sir Fuzzy Logik
CRRB	Stage 11: Dragon Breath
GGCY	Stage 12: Scratch
PYHC	Stage 13: Dr. Robotnik

DRAGON AGE: ORIGINS (XBOX 360)

EARLY LEVELING EXPLOIT

In Ostargar, there is a mission called Tainted Blood. Collect the three Vials of Darkspawn Blood but do not collect the Grey Warden Treaties. Return to camp, talk to Duncan, and select the option, "We have the blood, but not the scrolls." You will get the experience for the mission. Then go back and repeat this process until you are the level you want, or have reached the Level 25 max.

DRAGON BALL Z: BUDOKAI TENKAICHI 2 (Wii)

"WHAT IF" SAGAS

These special sagas become available when you win an "impossible" battle. Without these, you cannot attain 100% completion in Story mode. They're best attempted after you've run through Story mode and leveled up your characters.

UNLOCKABLE	HOW TO UNLOCK
Beautiful Treachery	Defeat Dodoria with Gohan and Krillin in Mission 01 of the Frieza Saga "A Pursuer Who Calls Death"
Destined Rivals	Defeat Gohan with Goten in Mission 01 of the Majin Buu Saga "Training with Goten"
Fateful Brothers	Defeat Raditz with Piccolo in Mission 00 of the Saiyan Saga "Mysterious Alien Warrior" (first mission of the game)

FIGHT INTRUDERS IN ULTIMATE BATTLE Z

Some towers in the Ultimate Battle Z mode have hidden battles that require specific conditions to trigger. They are available only in difficulty level 3.

UNLOCKABLE	HOW TO UNLOCK
Fight Broly Legendary SSJ in Saiyan Blood	Defeat Bardock with an Ultimate Blast
Fight Goku SSJ2 and Vegeta (Second 2 Form) SSJ2 in Dragon Tag	Defeat any opponent with an Ultimate Blast
Fight Hercule in Unlimited	Defeat Gogeta SSJ4
Fight Omega Shenron in Ultimate Dragon	Defeat Syn Shenron with an Ultimate Blast
Fight SSJ3 Gotenks in Ultimate Children	Defeat Kid Goku with an Ultimate Blast
Fight Super Baby 2 in Normal-ism	Defeat Super 13 with an Ultimate Blast
Fight Tao Pai Pai in Assault Force!	Defeat any opponent with an Ultimate Blast
Fight Uub in Kakarot Road	Defeat Kid Buu with an Ultimate Blast

UNLOCKABLE CHARACTERS

UNLOCKABLE	HOW TO UNLOCK
100% Full Power Frieza	Super Transformation + Final Form Frieza
Android 13	Computer + Hatred
Android 13 Fusion	Android 13 + Parts of 14 and 15
Baby Vegeta	Baby + Vegeta (second form)
Bardock	Defeat Lord Slug Saga

UNLOCKABLE	HOW TO UNLOCK
Bojack	Unsealed + Galactic Warrior
Broly	Son of Paragus + Hatred of Goku
Burter	Defeat Burter and Jeice with Goku
Cell	Defeat Cell with Piccolo and Android 17
Cell (2nd Form)	Defeat Cell (2nd Form) with Trunks and Vegeta
Cell (3rd Form or Perfect Form)	Defeat Cell (Perfect Form) with Gohan
Cell (Perfect or Perfect Cell)	Self Destruction + Cell Perfect Form
Cell Jr.	Defeat Cell Jrs. (5) with Gohan
Cooler	Frieza's Brother + Hatred of Goku
Cooler Final Form	Super Transformation + Cooler
Cui	Vegeta's Rival + Frieza's Soldier
Demon King Dabura	Defeat Dabura with Adult Gohan
Doboria	Defeat Doboria in Dragon Adventure
Dr. Gero	Defeat Dr. Gero with Krillin
Evil Buu	Evil Human Cannonball + Majin Buu
Full Power Bojak	Ultimate Transformation + Bojack
Garlic Jr.	Makyo Star + Dead Zone
General Tao	Bros. of Crane Hermit + Memorial Campaign
Giant Lord Slug	Slug + Giant Form
Ginyu	Defeat Ginyu (with Goku's body) and Jeice with Krillin, Vegeta, and Gohan
Gohan Super Buu	Gohan Absorbed + Evil Buu
Gotenks	Defeat Buu (Pure Evil) with Majin Buu and Hercule
Gotenks Super Buu	Gotenks Absorbed + Evil Buu
Grandpa Gohan	Master Roshi's Pupil + Fox Mask
Great Ape Baby	Super Baby 2 + Artificial Blutz Wave
Great Ape Bardock	Power Ball + Bardock
Great Ape Nappa	Power Ball + Nappa
Great Ape Raditz	Power Ball + Raditz
Great Ape Turles	Power Ball + Turles
Great Ape Vegeta	Power Ball + Vegeta (Scouter)
Great Saiyaman (Gohan)	Defeat Zangya and Bojack with Teen Gohan
Great Saiyaman 2 (Videl)	Defeat Broly with Goten and Adult Gohan
Guldo	Defeat Guldo with Vegeta, Krillin, and Gohan
Hercule	Defeat Perfect Cell with Super Trunks
Hirudegarn Half	Hirudegarn's Top Half + Hirudegarn's Lower
Janemba	Saike Demon + People's Bad Energy
Jeice	Defeat Jeice and Ginyu (with Goku's body) with Krillin, Vegeta, and Gohan
Kibitoshin	Kibito + Supreme Kai
Kid Buu	Defeat Kid Buu with Goku and Vegeta
Kid Goku	Defeat Grandpa Gohan
Legendary Super Saiyan Broly	Super Saiyan Broly + Breakthrough the Limit
Lord Slug	Namekian + Mutation
Majin Buu (Pure evil)	Human Gunman's Gun + Majin Buu
Majin Vegeta	Defeat Buu with Adult Gohan + Supreme Kai
Majin Vegeta	Defeat Majin Buu with Supreme Kai and Gohan
Majuub	Defeat Super Baby 2 with Pan and Uub

Master Roshi	Defeat Raditz with Goku
Master Roshi Full Power	Master Roshi + Seriousness
Mecha Frieza	Reconstructive Surgery + 100% Full Power Frieza
Metal Cooler	Big Gete Star + Cooler
Nappa	Defeat him in Dragon Adventure
Omega Shenron	Syn Shenron + Ultimate Dragon Ball
Pan	Defeat Hirudegarn with Tapion and Kid Trunks
Pikkon	Defeat Pikkon with Goku
Recoome	Defeat Recoome with Goku and Vegeta
Salza	Coolers Soldier + Armored Cavalry
Super Android 17	HFIL Fighter 17 + Android 17
Super Baby 1	Baby Vegeta + Lower Class Saiyan
Super Baby 2	Super Baby 1 + Power from Lower Class
Super Buu	Defeat Super Buu with Ultimate Gohan
Super Buu Gohan Absorbed	Absorb Gohan + Super Buu
Super Buu Gotenks Absorbed	Absorb Gotenks + Super Buu
Super Garlic Jr.	Garlic Jr. + Giant Form
Super Gogeta	Defeat Super Janemba with Pikkon + Buu
Super Gotenks	Defeat Pure Evil Buu with Buu + Hercule
Super Janemba	In item fusion combine Janemba + Ultimate Transformation
Super Perfect Cell	Suicide Bomb + Perfect Cell
Super Saiyan 1 Teen Gohan	Defeat Perfect Cell with Super Trunks
Super Saiyan 2 Goku	Defeat Majin Buu with Supreme Kai and Adult Gohan (Buu Saga)
Super Saiyan 2 Teen Gohan	Defeat Cell Jr. (5) with Super Saiyan 1 Gohan
Super Saiyan 2 Vegeta	Defeat Buu (Gotenks absorbed) with Goku
Super Saiyan 3 Goku	Defeat Majin Buu with Majin Vegeta
Super Saiyan 3 Gotenks	Defeat Super Buu with Gotenks
Super Saiyan 4 Gogeta	Defeat Omega Shenron with Super Saiyan 4 Goku and Vegeta
Super Saiyan 4 Goku	Defeat Super Baby with Majuub
Super Saiyan 4 Vegeta	Defeat Omega Shenron with Super Saiyan 4 Goku
Super Saiyan Broly	Broly + Super Saiyan
Super Saiyan Goku	Defeat Frieza Final Form with Piccolo, Krillin, and Kid Gohan (Frieza Saga)
Super Saiyan Goten	Defeat General Tao with Videl and Great Saiyaman
Super Saiyan Kid Trunks	Defeat General Tao with Videl and Great Saiyaman
Super Saiyan Trunks	Defeat Second Form Cell with Tien
Super Saiyan Trunks (Sword)	Defeat Androids 17 and 18 with Gohan
Super Saiyan Vegeta (Second Form)	Defeat Vegeta with Super Saiyan Teen Trunks (Buu Saga)
Super Trunks	Defeat Perfect Cell with Super Vegeta
Super Vegeta	Defeat Cell Form 2
Super Vegetto	Defeat Super Buu (Gohan Absorbed) with Goku and Vegeta
Supreme Kai	Defeat Android 18 with Hercule
Syn Shenron	Evil Dragon + Negative Energy
Tapion	Defeat Tapion with Trunks and Goten
Trunks	Unlock History of Trunks Saga

UNLOCKABLE	HOW TO UNLOCK
Turles	Lower-Class Saiyan Soldier + Fruit of the Gods
Ultimate Gohan (Mystic)	Defeat Buu with Piccolo or Super Saiyan 3 Gotenks
Uub	Defeat Hirudegarn with Super Saiyan 3 Goku
Vegeta (2nd Form)	Defeat Vegeta with Super Saiyan Teen Trunks (Buu Saga)
Vegeta (Post Namek)	Defeat Metal Cooler with Super Saiyan Goku (Return of Cooler Saga)
Vegetto	Defeat Super Buu + Gohan with Goku and Vegeta
Videl	Defeat Android 18 with Hercule (Buu Saga)
Videl	Defeat Bojack and Zangya with Piccolo + Gohan
Yajirobe	Defeat Great Ape Gohan with Piccolo
Zangya	The Fowers of Evil + Galactic Warrior
Zarbon Post-Transformation	Unsealed + Zarbon

WII EXCLUSIVE CHARACTERS

In the European, Australian or Japanese versions of the game, you can unlock 6 extra secret characters by playing through Ultimate Battle Z mode.

UNLOCKABLE	HOW TO UNLOCK
Appule	Complete Course 4
Cyborg Tao	Complete Course 6
Demon King Piccolo	Complete Course 8
Frieza Soldier	Complete Course 2
Pilaf Machine	Complete Course 10
Pilaf Machine Combined	Complete Course 10

EASTER EGG

UNLOCKABLE	HOW TO UNLOCK
Bra in the Training Mode	Complete Basic Training

DRAGON BALL Z: BUDOKAI TENKAICHI 3 (Wii)

CHARACTERS

UNLOCKABLE	HOW TO UNLOCK
Android 8	Clear "Affectionate Android" in Dragon History's What If Saga.
Arale	Clear "Dream Match: Goku Vs. Arale" in Dragon History's What If Saga.
Babidi	Clear "Farewell to the Proud Warrior" in Dragon History's Majin Buu Saga.
Cyborg Tao	Obtain victory in Otherworld Tournament level 2.
Devilman	Clear "Unexpected Help" in Dragon History's What If Saga.
Dr. Wheelo	Clear "Strongest in the World" in Dragon History's Special Saga.
Fasha	Obtain victory in Yamcha Game level 3.
Future Gohan	Wish from Shenron.
General Blue	Clear "Penguin Village" in Dragon History's Dragon Ball Saga.
Goku GT	Clear "Immortal Monster" in Dragon History's Dragon Ball GT Saga.
Kid Chi-Chi	Wish from Red Shenron.
King Cold	Obtain victory in Cell Games level 3.
King Piccolo	Clear "Goku Strikes Back" in Dragon History's Dragon Ball Saga.
King Vegeta	Clear "Galaxy Battle" in Dragon History's What If Saga.
Nail	Clear "Super Saiyan?!" in Dragon History's Frieza Saga.
Nam	Clear "Ceiling Vs. Ground" in Dragon History's Dragon Ball Saga.
Nuova Shenron	Clear "Solar Warrior 6000 Degrees of Power!" in Dragon History's Dragon Ball GT Saga.

Pilaf Machine	Obtain victory in World Martial Arts Big Tournament level 2.
Spopovich	Obtain victory in World Tournament level 3.
Super Saiyan 4 Gogeta	Beat "Ultimate Super Gogeta" in Dragon Ball GT Saga.
Super Saiyan 4 Goku	Beat "Ultimate Android" in Dragon Ball GT Saga.
Super Saiyan 4 Vegeta	Beat "Ultimate Super Gogeta" in Dragon Ball GT Saga.
Tambourine	Clear "Goku Strikes Back" in Dragon History's Dragon Ball Saga.

DRAGON BALL Z: BURST LIMIT (XBOX 360)

UNLOCKABLE CHARACTERS

UNLOCKABLE	HOW TO UNLOCK
100% Final Form Frieza	Beat Chapter 16 on Frieza Saga.
1st Form Frieza	Beat Chapter 8 on Frieza Saga.
2nd Form Frieza	Beat Chapter 9 on Frieza Saga.
3rd Form Frieza	Beat Chapter 12 on Frieza Saga.
Android #17	Beat Chapter 3 on Cell Saga.
Android #18	Beat Chapter 2 on Cell Saga.
Bardock	Beat Chapter 1 on Bardock Storyline.
Broly	Beat Chapter 1 on Broly Storyline.
Captain Ginyu	Beat Chapter 4 on Frieza Saga.
Final Form Frieza	Beat Chapter 14 on Frieza Saga.
Imperfect Cell	Beat Chapter 4 on Cell Saga.
Kaioken Goku	Beat Chapter 7 on Saiyan Saga.
Nappa	Beat Chapter 5 on Saiyan Saga.
Perfect Cell	Beat Chapter 12 on Cell Saga.
Piccolo Fuse with Kami	Beat Chapter 4 on Cell Saga.
Piccolo Sync with Nail	Beat Chapter 11 on Frieza Saga.
Raditz	Beat Chapter 1 on Saiyan Saga.
Recoome	Beat Chapter 1 on Frieza Saga.
Saibamen	Beat Chapter 3 on Saiyan Saga.
Semi-Perfect Cell	Beat Chapter 6 on Cell Saga.
Super Perfect Cell	Beat Chapter 18 on Cell Saga.
Super Perfect Cell	Beat Chapter 19 on Cell Saga.
Super Saiyan 2 Teen Gohan	Beat Chapter 19 on Cell Saga.
Super Saiyan Goku	Beat Chapter 16 on Frieza Saga.
Super Saiyan Trunks	Beat Chapter 7 on Cell Saga.
Super Saiyan Vegeta	Beat Chapter 2 on Cell Saga.
Super Trunks	Beat Chapter 13 on Cell Saga.
Super Vegeta	Beat Chapter 10 on Cell Saga.
Teen Gohan	Beat Chapter 1 on Cell Saga.
Trunks	Beat Chapter 7 on Cell Saga.
Vegeta	Beat Chapter 8 on Saiyan Saga.

UNLOCKABLE DIFFICULTIES

UNLOCKABLE	HOW TO UNLOCK
Hard	Beat Z Chronicles on Normal.
Very Hard	Beat Z Chronicles on Normal.
Z	Beat Z Chronicles on Very Hard.

UNLOCKABLE MOVIES

UNLOCKABLE	HOW TO UNLOCK
Credits	Beat Broly's Storyline.
Movie 1	Beat Frieza Saga.
Movie 2	Beat Cell Saga.

ACHIEVEMENTS

UNLOCKABLE	HOW TO UNLOCK
A Beginner Awakens!	Clear Basic tutorials: 5 points.
Advanced Victory!	Clear Advanced tutorials: 15 points.
All Cell Fighters	Unlock all of the Cell Saga fighters: 5 points.
All Frieza Fighters	Unlock all of the Frieza Saga fighters: 5 points.
All Saiyan Fighters	Unlock all of the Saiyan Saga fighters: 5 points.
Battler (Custom)	Play the Survival Trial (Custom Drama): 5 points.
Battler (Default)	Play the Survival Trial (Default Drama): 5 points.
Bloodless Victory!	Win a battle without taking any damage. (Z Chronicles/ Versus only): 20 points.
Cell Saga Allies	Unlock all of the Cell Saga ally characters: 5 points.
Destructive Win!	Win a battle while changing or destroying the background. (Z Chronicles/Versus only): 5 points.
Family Bonds	Clear all chapters of the Cell Saga: 15 points.
Fierce Warrior	Clear all of the Saga chapters with the difficulty set to Very Hard: 40 points.
Frieza Saga Allies	Unlock all of the Frieza Saga ally characters: 5 points.
Frieza Z Award: 35g	Clear all Frieza Saga chapters with a Z rank on Normal difficulty.
Full Drama Unlock	Unlock all of the Drama Pieces for one character: 5 points.
Goku's Father	Unlock Bardock: 20 points.
Intermediate Fire!	Clear Intermediate tutorials: 5 points.
Legendary Saiyan	Unlock Broly: 20 points.
Legendary Warrior	Clear all chapters of the Frieza Saga: 15 points.
Master of History	Clear all chapters: 15 points.
Meeting a Rival	Clear all chapters of the Saiyan Saga: 5 points.
Powerful Allies	Unlock all ally characters: 15 points.
Saiyan Saga Allies	Unlock all of the Saiyan Saga ally characters: 5 points.
Saiyan Saga Drama	Unlock all of the Drama Pieces from the Saiyan Saga: 20 points.
Saiyan Z Award	Clear all Saiyan Saga chapters with a Z rank on Normal difficulty: 35 points.
Score Beyond Terror	Clear the Battle Point Trial (Course A) and get a result: 5 points.
Speed Beyond Power	Clear the Time Attack Trial (Course B) and get a result: 5 points.
Speed Beyond Terror	Clear the Time Attack Trial (Course A) and get a result: 5 points.
Sturdy Warrior	Unlock all fighters: 20 points.
Survivor (Custom)	Play the Survival Trial (Custom Drama) and defeat 50 opponents: 35 points.
The First Z Award	Clear a chapter with a Z rank on Normal difficulty: 20 points.
The Story Begins	Clear the first chapter of the Saiyan Saga: 5 points.
Ultimate Unlock	Unlock all of one character's Ultimate Attacks: 5 points.

Ultimate Warrior	Unlock all characters' Ultimate Attacks: 15 points.
Unleashed Ki Win!	Transform, use Aura Spark, and win with an Ultimate Attack. (Z Chronicles/Versus only): 5 points.
Worldwide Contender	Join 10 sessions over Xbox LIVE: 5 points.
Worldwide Warrior	Create 10 sessions over Xbox LIVE: 5 points.

DRAGON BALL Z: BURST LIMIT (PlayStation 3)

UNLOCKABLE CHARACTERS

UNLOCKABLE	HOW TO UNLOCK
100% Final Form Frieza	Beat Chapter 16 on Frieza Saga.
1st Form Frieza	Beat Chapter 8 on Frieza Saga.
2nd Form Frieza	Beat Chapter 9 on Frieza Saga.
3rd Form Frieza	Beat Chapter 12 on Frieza Saga.
Android #17	Beat Chapter 3 on Cell Saga.
Android #18	Beat Chapter 2 on Cell Saga.
Bardock	Beat Chapter 1 on Bardock Storyline.
Broly	Beat Chapter 1 on Broly Storyline.
Captain Ginyu	Beat Chapter 4 on Frieza Saga.
Final Form Frieza	Beat Chapter 14 on Frieza Saga.
Imperfect Cell	Beat Chapter 4 on Cell Saga.
Kaioken Goku	Beat Chapter 7 on Saiyan Saga.
Nappa	Beat Chapter 5 on Saiyan Saga.
Perfect Cell	Beat Chapter 12 on Cell Saga.
Piccolo Fuse with Kami	Beat Chapter 4 on Cell Saga.
Piccolo Sync with Nail	Beat Chapter 11 on Frieza Saga.
Raditz	Beat Chapter 1 on Saiyan Saga.
Recoome	Beat Chapter 1 on Frieza Saga.
Saibamen	Beat Chapter 3 on Saiyan Saga.
Semi-Perfect Cell	Beat Chapter 6 on Cell Saga.
Super Perfect Cell	Beat Chapter 18 on Cell Saga.
Super Perfect Cell	Beat Chapter 19 on Cell Saga.
Super Saiyan 2 Teen Gohan	Beat Chapter 19 on Cell Saga.
Super Saiyan Goku	Beat Chapter 16 on Frieza Saga.
Super Saiyan Trunks	Beat Chapter 7 on Cell Saga.
Super Saiyan Vegeta	Beat Chapter 2 on Cell Saga.
Super Trunks	Beat Chapter 13 on Cell Saga.
Super Vegeta	Beat Chapter 10 on Cell Saga.
Teen Gohan	Beat Chapter 1 on Cell Saga.
Trunks	Beat Chapter 7 on Cell Saga.
Vegeta	Beat Chapter 8 on Saiyan Saga.

UNLOCKABLE DIFFICULTIES

UNLOCKABLE	HOW TO UNLOCK
Hard	Beat Z Chronicles on Normal.
Very Hard	Beat Z Chronicles on Normal.
Z	Beat Z Chronicles on Very Hard.

UNLOCKABLE MOVIES

UNLOCKABLE	HOW TO UNLOCK
Credits	Beat Broly's Storyline.

UNLOCKABLE	HOW TO UNLOCK
Movie 1	Beat Frieza Saga.
Movie 2	Beat Cell Saga.

DRAGON BALL Z: SAGAS (PlayStation 2)

Pause the game and go into the Controller screen, then enter these codes.

UNLOCKABLE	CODE
All Upgrades	⇧, ⇦, ⇩, ⇨, SELECT, START, ■, ×, ●, ▲
Invincibility	⇩, ×, SELECT, START, ⇨, ■, ⇦, ●, ⇧, ▲

DRAGON BALL Z: SHIN BUDOKAI (PSP)

UNLOCKABLES

You must complete every fight quickly and with most of your health.

CARD SHEET	HOW TO UNLOCK
No. 10	Finish all fights in Chapter 5
No. 13	Z rank on all fights for Chapter 1
No. 14	Z rank on all fights for Chapter 2
No. 15	Z rank on all fights for Chapter 3
No. 16	Z rank on all fights for Chapter 4
No. 17	Z rank on all fights for Chapter 5
No. 24	Z rank on all fights for Dragon Road

UNLOCKABLE CHARACTERS

Defeat the specified characters in Dragon Road mode.

UNLOCKABLE	HOW TO UNLOCK
Adult Gohan—Mystic Form	Defeat Vegeta in Chapter 4-A-B 5
Adult Gohan—Super Saiyan 2 Form	Defeat Broly in Chapter 2-6
Adult Gohan—Super Saiyan Form	Defeat Frieza in Chapter 1-8
Broly—Legendary Super Saiyan Form	Defeat Frieza in Chapter 4-A-B 6
Cell—Super Perfect Form	Defeat Cell in Chapter 2-5
Cooler—Final Form	Defeat Pikkon in Chapter 4-B-A 5
Frieza—100% Full Power Form	Defeat Frieza in Chapter 3-2
Future Trunks—Super Saiyan Form	Defeat Gotenks in Chapter 4-2
Goku—Kaioken Form	Defeat Krillin in Chapter 1-2
Goku—Super Saiyan 2 Form	Defeat Fake Goku in Chapter 2-2
Goku—Super Saiyan 3 Form	Defeat Vegeta in Chapter 3-7
Goku—Super Saiyan Form	Defeat Janemba in Chapter 1-9
Goku SS3	Beat Majin Vegeta in Chapter 3
Gotenks	Defeat Gotenks in Chapter 1-4
Gotenks—Super Saiyan 3 Form	Defeat Cell in Chapter 3-A-4
Gotenks—Super Saiyan Form	Defeat Gotenks in Chapter 1-5
Janemba	Beat Story Mode
Krillin—Unlock Potential Form	Defeat Goku in Chapter 5-1
Piccolo—Fuse with Kami Form	Defeat Cell in Chapter 2-1
Pikkon	Defeat Janemba in Chapter 2- 9
Teen Gohan—Super Saiyan 2 Form	Defeat Teen Gohan in Chapter 3-9
Teen Gohan—Super Saiyan Form	Defeat Cell in Chapter 3-8
Vegeta—Majin Form	Defeat Vegeta in Chapter 4-7
Vegeta—Super Saiyan 2 Form	Defeat Janemba in Chapter 2-7
Vegeta—Super Saiyan Form	Defeat #18 in Chapter 2-3
Vegetto and Gogeta	Beat the last chapter choosing either path
Vegetto—Super Saiyan Form	Defeat Kid Buu in Chapter 5–B-9

DRAGON BALL: RAGING BLAST (XBOX 360)

CHARACTERS

Note: The Legendary Super Saiyan Reborn and the Strongest Super Saiyan 3 each require 20 stars to unlock.

UNLOCKABLE	HOW TO UNLOCK
Broly, Super Broly, LSSJ Broly	Beat Beat Freedom! (What-if stories)
SSJ3 Broly	Beat The Legendary Super Saiyan Reborn (Secret Battle 39: Legendary Super Saiyan Saga)
SSJ3 Vegeta	Beat The Strongest Super Saiyan 3 (Secret Battle 47: What-if stories)
Super Gogeta stories)	Beat Fusion & Potara Part 1: Super Gogeta (What-if
Vegito, Super Vegito	Beat Fusion & Potara Part 2: Super Vegito (What-if stories)
Videl	Beat The Student (What-if stories)

TITLES

These are titles you can earn by playing on XBOX Live.

UNLOCKABLE	HOW TO UNLOCK
Counter Monster	Execute five counters in a battle.
Death Chaser	Execute 20 Vanishing in a battle.
Dirty Fireworks	Take five Upwards Attacks in a battle.
Elite Warrior	Earn 10 victories.
Embarrassment to the Clan	Lose 10 Saiyan-against-Saiyan battles.
Fireworks Master	Execute five Upwards Attacks in a battle.
Flying Dragon	Execute two Air Combo in a battle.
Greenhorn	Earn 50 losses.
Incomplete Power	Achieve a rank of G.
Legendary Warrior	Earn 100 victories.
Martial Arts Warrior	Execute 30 HITS in a battle.
Nature Lover	Win a battle on the Wasteland stage without destroying anything.
Non-Combatant	Earn 10 perfect losses.
Nothing But A Bluff	Lose 20 battles despite transforming.
Preliminary Qualifier	Record 10 victories in the World Tournament Stage.
Prince of Cruelty	Execute five Knockdown Attacks in a battle.
Saiyan Killer	Defeat Saiyan characters 100 times.
Speedies in the Universe	Execute 30 Vanishing in a battle.
Super Elite Warrior	Earn 50 victories.
Total Amateur	In World Tournament mode, lose a total of 10 first-round battles.
Turtle Practitioner	Earn 10 victories with the Kamehameha.
Warrior of Light	Use Solar Flare 10 times in a battle.
Waste of Space	Earn 100 losses.
World Tournament Champion	Win a total of 10 World Tournament Finals.
World-Class Speed	Execute 10 Vanishing in a battle.

DRAGON BLADE: WRATH OF FIRE (Wii)

CODES

At the Stage Select screen, Hold Ⓩ and press ⊕ to start inputting the codes. To clear the codes, hold Ⓩ and press ⊖. You will hear a confirmation when you do the combination to enter the codes, when you enter the codes, and when you clear them.

UNLOCKABLE	HOW TO UNLOCK
Tail Power	Swing your Wii Remote Down, Up, Left, and Right
Double Fist Power	Swing your Nunchuk Right-> Swing your Wii Remote left-> Swing your Nunchuk right while swinging your Wii Remote left->Swing both Wii Remote and Nunchuk down

UNLOCKABLES

UNLOCKABLE	HOW TO UNLOCK
Long Sword	Beat the game once

DRAGON BOOSTER (DS)

At the Main menu, select Password to enter these cheats.

UNLOCKABLE	PASSWORD
999,999 Dracles	8, 9, 7, 10, 5, 13
Blue Energy Bolt Gear Obtained	9, 2, 13, 8, 1, 12
Draculim Bars are replaced by sushi in All City Race/Free Run	7, 8, 13, 12, 10, 10
Dragon Booster and Legendary Beau are unlocked	12, 6, 12, 10, 13, 3
Dragon-Human Duel vs. Reepyr	1, 9, 3, 6, 5, 2
Green Charging Gear Obtained	5, 12, 13, 5, 8, 11
Shadow Booster and Shadow Dragon are unlocked	2, 5, 4, 11, 6, 2
Skills Competition vs. Wulph	13, 9, 8, 12, 10, 1
Sprint Meter can't be recharged	1, 7, 5, 3, 2, 11
Take Super Damage from obstacles and opponents in All City Race/Free Run	11, 11, 11, 11, 11, 11
Unlimited sprint meter	9, 13, 6, 5, 5, 12

DRAGON QUEST MONSTERS: JOKER (DS)

MONSTERS

UNLOCKABLE	HOW TO UNLOCK
Empyrea	Obtain ALL monsters.
Grandpa Slime	Obtain 200 monsters.
Leopold	Obtain ALL skills.
Liquid Metal Slime	Obtain 100 monsters.
Metal Kaiser Slime	Obtain 150 skills.
Metal King Slime	Obtain 100 skills.
Robbin' Hood	Complete both monster and skill libraries.
Trode	Complete both monster and skill libraries and speak to the skill library NPC.

DRAGON QUEST V: HAND OF THE HEAVENLY BRIDE (DS)

UNLOCKABLES

Beat the game and load your save. Go to Mt. Zugzwang and then into the poison swamp to enter Estark's Lair. Beat Estark to unlock the Stark Raving T'n'T Board. Beat the board.

UNLOCKABLE	HOW TO UNLOCK
Rebjorn	Get Starkers and go to the Pothold to find Rebjorn.
Starkers	Prize for beating the Stark Raving T'n'T board.

DRAGON SPIRIT (Wii)

CODES

UNLOCKABLE	HOW TO UNLOCK
100 Continues	Press ↓, →, SELECT, ↓, ②, ↓, ①, ←, SELECT, ↑, ①, ②, ① at the title screen
Arcade Mode Screen	Hold Select and press RUN 57 times to reset the game for a narrow screen

Sound Test	←, →, ↓, ↑, SELECT, ← at the title screen
Two Continues	Hold ① and press ② at the title screen

DRAGON'S CURSE (Wii)

UNLOCKABLE

UNLOCKABLE	HOW TO UNLOCK
Full Life	After dying, use a potion while holding ②

PASSWORDS

PASSWORD	EFFECT
3YHURYW7Y7LL8C	Start game at beginning with Max. Gold (983,040)/All Equipment/Full Health (8 Hearts)/Max. Stones (99)/All Items/Hawk-Man Status
3YHURYW7Y7LPBS	Start game at beginning with Max. Gold (983,040)/All Equipment/Full Health (8 Hearts)/Max. Stones (99)/All Items/Hu-Man Status
3YHURYW7Y7LRBW	Start game at beginning with Max. Gold (983,040)/All Equipment/Full Health (8 Hearts)/Max. Stones (99)/All Items/Lizard-Man Status
3YHURYW7Y7LM80	Start game at beginning with Max. Gold (983,040)/All Equipment/Full Health (8 Hearts)/Max. Stones (99)/All Items/Mouse-Man Status
3YHURYW7Y7LN84	Start game at beginning with Max. Gold (983,040)/All Equipment/Full Health (8 Hearts)/Max. Stones (99)/All Items/Piranha-Man Status
3YHURYW7Y7LK88	Start game at beginning with Max. Gold (983,040)/All Equipment/Full Health (8 Hearts)/Max. Stones (99)/All Items/Tiger-Man Status
W0CV5ATVKYR1SV	Start with all the necessary transformations and items to enter the final dungeon
MODE FOR 0000 000	Be Hu Man at Start (JP ONLY)
PLAY THE ONGA KUN	Disable door noise (JP ONLY)
NODEGOS0000000	Start as Be Hu Man
3WSURYXZY763TE	Start with advanced abilities and items
RMAYTJEOPHALUP	Take away the noises from doors
3ZHURYNZY726VH	Start as Hu-Man with 8 hearts, all equipment, all transformations unlocked, and only the final dungeon to beat

DRIV3R (XBOX)

Enter the following codes at the Main menu.

UNLOCKABLE	CODE
All Missions	Ⓧ,Ⓧ,Ⓨ,Ⓨ,RT,RT,LT
All Weapons	LT,LT,Ⓧ,Ⓨ,Ⓨ,RT,RT
Immunity	Ⓧ,Ⓨ,RT,RT,LT,LT,Ⓨ
Invincibility	Ⓧ,Ⓨ,LT,RT,LT,RT,RT—(NOTE: Does not work in Story mode)
Unlimited Ammo	RT,RT,LT,LT,Ⓧ,Ⓨ,Ⓨ
Unlock All Vehicles	Ⓧ,Ⓧ,Ⓨ,Ⓨ,LT,RT,LT

DRIV3R (PlayStation 2)

In the Main menu, enter the following cheats. Go to the Options menu and select Cheats to enable or disable them.

UNLOCKABLE	CODE
All Missions	L1,R1,L1,L2,■,■,●
All Vehicles	L1,L1,■,●,L1,R1,●

All Weapons	R1, L2, ■, ●, R1, R2, L2
Immunity	●, ●, L1, L2, R1, R2, ■
Invincibility (Take a Ride)	■, ■, L1, R1, L2, R2, R2
Unlimited Ammo	R1, R2, R1, R2, ■, ●, ■

DRIVER: PARALLEL LINES (Wii)

PASSWORD

PASSWORD	EFFECT
steelman	Invincibility

COLLECTING STARS

Collect the scattered golden stars throughout the map to unlock the following rewards. Note: Everything resets once you get to the 2006 era, and collecting another 50 Stars will unlock the same attributes. (There are 100 total in the game.)

UNLOCKABLE	HOW TO UNLOCK
Double Ammunition Capacity	Collect 30 Stars
Double Car Durability	Collect 40 Stars
Free Vehicle Upgrades	Collect 50 Stars
Health Increase	Collect 10 Stars
Nitrous Increase	Collect 20 Stars

UNLOCKABLE CARS

UNLOCKABLE	HOW TO UNLOCK
Andec Racer	Win the Jersey Racetrack race in 1978 on Hard
Bonsai Racer	Win the La Guardia race in 1978 on Medium
Brooklyn Racer	Win the Jersey Racetrack race in 1978 on Medium
Hot Rod	Win the Driver GP Long Island Race in 2006
Raven Racer	Win the Driver GP Long Island Race in 1978
San Marino Racer	Win the Hunts Points race in 1978 on Hard

UNLOCKABLES

UNLOCKABLE	HOW TO UNLOCK
Far Out Mode	Reach 900 miles
Night Night Mode	Reach 700 miles
Play as a Pedestrian/Policeman	Reach 666 miles + melee attack the person you want to play as
Shortest Day Mode	Reach 800 miles

DRIVER PARALLEL LINES (XBOX)

Enter these passwords in the Cheat menu.

UNLOCKABLE	PASSWORD
All Vehicles	CARSHOW
All Weapons in Your Time Zone	GUNRANGE
Indestructible Cars	ROLLBAR
Infinite Ammunition	GUNBELT
Infinite Nitro	ZOOMZOOM
Invincibility	IRONMAN
Weaker Cops	KEYSTONE
Zero Cost	TOOLEDUP

DRIVER PARALLEL LINES (PlayStation 2)

Enter these passwords in the Cheat menu.

UNLOCKABLE	PASSWORD
All Vehicles	CARSHOW

All Weapons in Your Time Zone	GUNRANGE
Indestructible Cars	ROLLBAR
Infinite Ammunition	GUNBELT
Infinite Nitro	ZOOMZOOM
Invincibility	IRONMAN
Weaker Cops	KEYSTONE
Zero Cost	TOOLEDUP

DROP OFF (Wii)

UNLOCKABLES

UNLOCKABLE	HOW TO UNLOCK
Level Select	Press SELECT 16 times then press RUN
Sound Mode	Hold SELECT+①
Sound Test	Hold ② and press SELECT
Unlimited Continues	RUN+①, RUN+②

DUNGEON EXPLORER (Wii)

PASSWORDS

PASSWORD	EFFECT
CHECK NAMEA	Change names
ADGDP-CJLPG	Final Dungeon is open
DEBDE DEBDA then press RUN+①	Invincibility
JBBNJ HDCOG	Play as Princess Aki
IMGAJ MDPAI	Play as the Hermit
HOMING AAAA	Precision guided weapons (smart weapons)

LEVEL SELECT

Enable the "Invincibility" code. Enter one of the following 15 bushes in front of Axis castle to jump to the corresponding location. (Bush 1 is on the left end, bush 15 is on the right end.)

BUSH	LOCATION
1	Natas
2	Balamous Tower
3	Rotterroad (path to Judas)
4	Mistose Dungeon
5	Ratonix Dungeon
6	Reraport Maze
7	Rally Maze
8	Bullbeast
9	Melba Village
10	After Gutworm
11	Nostalgia Dungeon
12	Water Castle
13	Road to Cherry Tower
14	Stonefield
15	Karma Castle

UNLOCKABLES

UNLOCKABLE	HOW TO UNLOCK
Secret Ending	Input the Invincibility code so you can pass through objects. When you take the ORA stone back to the King and he leaves, pass through the blockade to his throne, which initiates the secret ending.
Use the Harmit (Hermit) the hard way	To use the Harmit (*sic*), level a Bard until you have at least 50 HP. (Go into the second house to the west of Axis Castle.

DYNAMITE HEADDY (Wii)

UNLOCKABLES

UNLOCKABLE	HOW TO UNLOCK
Head Animations	At the title screen select "Options" and press: Ⓒ, Ⓐ, ←, →, Ⓑ. You hear "nice" when you've entered the code correctly. Then press START to view the head animations.
Stage Select	When the title screen appears, press START once. Leaving the cursor at Start Game, enter the code: Ⓒ, Ⓐ, ←, →, Ⓑ. You hear a sound. Press START and you'll access the Stage Select. Choose your level and stage, then press START to play! (Note: This trick was done on an early version of the game. It may or may not work on later versions.)
Hard Mode (1-hit Death Mode)	At the title screen, press START once, then leave the cursor on "Start Game." Just like the Stage Select code, press Ⓒ, Ⓐ, ←, →, Ⓑ. You hear Headdy say "Nice" when you've entered the code correctly. Then press and hold START. Continue holding START until you see the "Opening Demo" scene appear. Now release START and continue as normal. Be warned: 1 hit is all it takes to kill you now.
Secret Final Scene	After the end credits have finished rolling, you are prompted to enter a 4-digit secret code on a keypad. The code is different eachtime the game is played. Complete the basketball minigame four times while going through the game to determine your game's secret code.

DYNASTY WARRIORS 3 (PlayStation 2)

After inputting the following codes, listen for the cheer that confirms correct code entry.

UNLOCKABLE	CODE
All FMV Sequences	Highlight the Free Mode icon at the main menu. Press ▲, L1, ▲, R1, ▲, ■, L2, ■, R2, ■.
All Generals	Highlight the Free Mode icon at the main menu. Press R2, R2, R2, L1, ▲, L2, L2, L2, R1, ■.
All Items	Go to the "Options" in the main menu and highlight "Open Screen." Press R1, ■, R1, ▲, R1, L1, ■, L1, ▲, L1.
All Shu Generals	Highlight the Free Mode icon at the main menu. Press L1, ■, ▲, R2, L1, L2, L2, R1, ■, L1.
All Wei Generals	Highlight the Free Mode icon at the main menu. Press ▲, ▲, L1, ■, R1, R2, L1, L2, L2, L2.
All Wu Generals	Highlight the Free Mode icon at the main menu. Press L2, L1, ■, ▲, L1, L2, R1, R2, L1, L2.

***TIP:* START THE GAME WITH A MEMORY CARD WITH A SAVED GAME FROM DYNASTY WARRIORS 2 AND SOME CHARACTERS UNLOCKED IN DYNASTY WARRIORS 2 ARE AVAILABLE IN YOUR NEW GAME!**

UNLOCKABLE	CODE
Bonus FMV Sequence	Highlight the "Replay" option at the Opening Edit screen, hold R1+L1+R2+L2, then press ✕. Alternately, hold R1+L1+R2+L2 and press START. You see all the people from the gray army dancing.
Control Loading Screen	Press ● to increase the wind as the level name flutters on the loading screen before a battle. Press ✕ to decrease the wind speed.
Free Mode Side Selection	Highlight the Free Mode icon at the main menu. Press R1, R2, L2, L1, ■, L1, L2, R2, R1, ▲.
In-game Reset	Press SELECT+START during gameplay.
Opening Edit Option	Highlight the Free Mode icon at the main menu. Press R1, ■, R1, ▲, R1, L1, ■, L1.

DYNASTY WARRIORS 5 EMPIRES (XBOX 360)

UNLOCKABLES

UNLOCKABLE	HOW TO UNLOCK
1,000 K.O Ribbon	Defeat 1,000 enemies in one battle. You also must win the battle.
All Created Officer Attire	Create an officer, then complete the Yellow Turban campaign.
Extra Models (Unique Characters only)	Reach the maximum number of Experience Points (60,000) with any unique character to unlock all of their models.
A Divided Land Scenario	Successfully complete the Dong Zhou in Luo Yang scenario to unlock the A Divided Land scenario.
Battle of Guan Du Scenario	Successfully complete the A Divided Land scenario to unlock the Battle of Guan Du scenario.
Dong Zhou in Luo Yang Scenario	Successfully complete The Yellow Turban Rebellion scenario to unlock the Dong Zhou in Luo Yang scenario.
Flames over Chi Bi scenario	Successfully complete the Battle of Guan Du scenario to unlock the Flames over Chi Bi scenario.
Level 4 weapons	Raise a weapon type to maximum, then get 500 kills with the person who you want to get the 4th weapon.
Executions/Old Age Death	Beat Empire mode once.
Isolate	Beat Empire mode once.
Unlimited Time	Beat Empire mode once.

UNLOCKABLE ENDING EVENTS

All endings must be unlocked on Empire mode using any difficulty and on any era.

UNLOCKABLE	HOW TO UNLOCK
Death	Fail to conquer all 25 territories when the campaign time limit runs out. Campaign time limit option must be on.
Unification (Evil Ruler)	Continuously use evil deeds such as Despotism and become Emperor. Then conquer all 25 territories without committing a good deed.
Unification (Good Ruler)	Continuously use good deeds such as Philanthropy and become Emperor. Then conquer all 25 territories without committing a evil deed.
Unification (Neutral)	Conquer all 25 territories without being extremely good or evil.

DYNASTY WARRIORS 6 (XBOX 360)

CHARACTERS

UNLOCKABLE	HOW TO UNLOCK
Cao Cao	Clear Musou mode with three Wei characters.
Cao Pi	Defeat Cao Pi within five minutes on Wu side of He Fei.
Cao Ren	Succeed in Battle Objective 2 on the Lu Bu side of Fan Castle.
Diao Chan	Clear Musou mode with one character from each Kingdom.
Dong Zhuo	Clear Musou mode with Lu Bu.
Gan Ning	Clear Musou mode with one Wu character.
Guan Ping	Succeed in two battle objectives on the Shu side of Fan Castle and finish battle with Guan Ping alive.
Huang Gai	Succeed in Battle Objective 3 on the Wu side of The Battle of Chi Bi.
Huang Zhong	Succeed in one battle objective on the Wei side of Ding Jun Mountain.
Ling Tong	Succeed in Battle Objective 1 on the Wei side of the Battle of Shi Ting.

UNLOCKABLE	HOW TO UNLOCK
Liu Bei	Clear Musou mode with three Shu characters.
Lu Bu	Clear Musou mode with Liu Bei, Cao Cao, and Sun Jian.
Lu Meng	Succeed in two battle objectives on the Wei side of He Fei.
Ma Chao	Succeed in two battle objectives on the Wei side of Han Zhong Attack Defense Battle.
Pang Tong	Succeed in three battle objectives at Cheng Du battle and finish battle with Pang Tong alive.
Sun Ce	Succeed in Battle Objective 1 on the Sun Jian side of the Battle of Xia Pi.
Sun Jian	Clear Musou mode with three Wu characters.
Sun Quan	Succeed in Battle Objective 1 on the Lu Bu side of the Battle of Chi Bi.
Taishi Ci	Defeat him in the Battle for Wu Territory.
Wei Yan	Succeed in two battle objectives on the Shu side of WuZhang Plains and finish battle with Wei Yan alive.
Xiahou Yuan	Succeed in one battle objective on the Shu side of Ding Jun Mountain.
Xiao Quio	Succeed in Battle Objective 3 on the Wu side of the Battle of Shi Ting.
Xu Chu	He Fei, Wu side, personally kill Cao Ren and Xu Chu.
Xu Huang	Succeed in two battle objectives on the Wei/Wu side of Fan Castle.
Yuan Shao	As Wei, complete all three targets and capture Wu Chao before completing the stage.
Yue Ying	Succeed in Battle Objective 1 on the Wei side of the Battle of Wu Zhang Plains.
Zhang Jiao	Beat stage while completing all three targets in the Yellow Turban Rebellion. Playable in only Free mode and Challenge mode.
Zhang Liao	Clear Musou mode with one Wei character.
Zhen Ji	Succeed in Battle Objective 1 on the Lu Bu side of the Xu Du Invasion.
Zheng He	Succeed in two battle objectives on the Shu side of Han Zhong Attack Defense Battle.
Zhou Tai	Succeed in three battle objectives on the Shu side of Yi Ling.
Zhuge Liang	Clear Musou mode with one Shu character.

DIFFICULTIES

UNLOCKABLE	HOW TO UNLOCK
Chaos Difficulty	Clear Musou mode with one character from Wu, Shu, Wei, and Other.
Hell Difficulty	Beat Wei, Wu, Shu, and Other Musou mode.
Master Difficulty	Beat any Musou mode on Easy or Normal.
Very Hard Difficulty	Clear Musou mode with any one character.

ACHIEVEMENTS

UNLOCKABLE	HOW TO UNLOCK
1st in RAMPAGE (10)	Rank first (personal best) in Rampage.
1st in GAUNTLET (10)	Rank first (personal best) in Gauntlet.
1st in HAVOC (10)	Rank first (personal best) in Havoc.
1st in SPEED RUN (10)	Rank first (personal best) in Speed Run.
1st in SUDDEN DEATH (10)	Rank first (personal best) in Sudden Death.
Musou Mode Master (50)	All Musou modes cleared.
Scenario Captain (40)	30 or more scenarios cleared.
Scenario Corporal (30)	20 or more scenarios cleared
Scenario General (50)	All scenarios cleared.
Scenario Private (20)	10 or more scenarios cleared.

Target Captain (50)	100 or more targets achieved.
Target Corporal (40)	70 or more targets achieved.
Target General (60)	All targets achieved.
Target Private (30)	50 or more targets achieved.
The Arm of Cao Cao (10)	Xiahou Yuan has been unlocked.
The Barbarian Lord (10)	Wei Yan has been unlocked.
The Beautiful Dancer (30)	Diao Chan has been unlocked.
The Courageous Lord (10)	Xu Huang has been unlocked.
The Ferocious Warrior (10)	Taishi Ci has been unlocked.
The Fledgling Phoenix (10)	Pang Tong has been unlocked.
The Forthright Lord (30)	Zhang Liao has been unlocked.
The General of Heaven (10)	Zhang Jiao has been unlocked.
The Little Conqueror (10)	Unlock Sun Ce.
The Lord of Beauty (10)	Zhang He has been unlocked.
The Loyal Warrior (10)	Zhou Tai has been unlocked.
The Master General (10)	Lu Meng has been unlocked.
The Patriarch of Yuan (10)	Yuan Shao has been unlocked.
The Reckless Pirate (30)	Gan Ning has been unlocked.
The Sleeping Dragon (30)	Zhuge Liang has been unlocked.
The Son of Guan Yu (10)	Guan Ping has been unlocked.
The Splendid One (10)	Ma Chao has been unlocked.
The Tiger General (10)	Huang Zhong has been unlocked.
The Tiger of Jiang Dong (10)	Unlock Sun Jian.
The Veteran General (10)	Huang Gai has been unlocked.
The Wise Lady (10)	Yue Ying has been unlocked.

DYNASTY WARRIORS 6 (PlayStation 3)

CHARACTERS

UNLOCKABLE	HOW TO UNLOCK
Cao Cao	Clear Musou mode with three Wei characters.
Cao Pi	Deafeat Cao Pi within five minutes on Wu side of He Fei.
Cao Ren	Succeed in Battle Objective 2 on the Lu Bu side of Fan Castle.
Diao Chan	Clear Musou mode with one character from each Kingdom.
Dong Zhuo	Clear Musou mode with Lu Bu.
Gan Ning	Clear Musou mode with one Wu character.
Guan Ping	Succeed in two battle objectives on the Shu side of Fan Castle and finish battle with Guan Ping alive.
Huang Gai	Succeed in Battle Objective 3 on the Wu side of The Battle of Chi Bi.
Huang Zhong	Succeed in one battle objective on the Wei side of Ding Jun Mountain.
Ling Tong	Succeed in Battle Objective 1 on the Wei side of the Battle of Shi Ting.
Liu Bei	Clear Musou mode with three Shu characters.
Lu Bu	Clear Musou mode with Liu Bei, Cao Cao, and Sun Jian.
Lu Meng	Succeed in two battle objectives on the Wei side of He Fei.
Ma Chao	Succeed in two battle objectives on the Wei side of Han Zhong Attack Defense Battle.
Pang Tong	Succeed in three battle objectives at Cheng Du battle and finish battle with Pang Tong alive.
Sun Ce	Succeed in Battle Objective 1 on the Sun Jian side of the Battle of Xia Pi.

Sun Jian	Clear Musou mode with three Wu characters.
Sun Quan	Succeed in Battle Objective 1 on the Lu Bu side of The Battle of Chi Bi.
Taishi Ci	Defeat him in the Battle for Wu Territory.
Wei Yan	Succeed in two battle objectives on the Shu side of Wu Zhang Plains and finish battle with Wei Yan alive.
Xiahou Yuan	Succeed in one battle objective on the Shu side of Ding Jun Mountain.
Xiao Quio	Succeed in Battle Objective 3 on the Wu side of the Battle of Shi Ting.
Xu Chu	He Fei, Wu side, personally kill Cao Ren and Xu Chu.
Xu Huang	Succeed in two battle objectives on the Wei/Wu side of Fan Castle.
Yuan Shao	As Wei, complete all three targets and capture Wu Chao before completing the stage.
Yue Ying	Succeed in Battle Objective 1 on the Wei side of the Battle of Wu Zhang Plains.
Zhang Jiao	Beat stage and complete all three targets in the Yellow Turban Rebellion. Playable in only Free mode and Challenge mode.
Zhang Liao	Clear Musou mode with 1 Wei character.
Zhen Ji	Succeed in Battle Objective 1 on the Lu Bu side of the Xu Du Invasion.
Zheng He	Succeed in two battle objectives on the Shu side of Han Zhong Attack Defense Battle.
Zhou Tai	Succeed in three battle objectives on the Shu side of Yi Ling.
Zhuge Liang	Clear Musou mode with one Shu character.

DIFFICULTIES

UNLOCKABLE	HOW TO UNLOCK
Chaos Difficulty	Clear Musou mode with one character from Wu, Shu, Wei, and other.
Hell Difficulty	Beat Wei, Wu, Shu, and Other Musou mode.
Master Difficulty	Beat any Musou mode on Easy or Normal.
Very Hard Difficulty	Clear Musou mode with any one character.

DYNASTY WARRIORS: GUNDAM (XBOX 360)

UNLOCKABLE CHARACTERS AND PILOTS

UNLOCKABLE	HOW TO UNLOCK
Char Aznable and Char's Char's Gelgoog	Complete Amuro Ray's Story mode on any difficulty in Official mode
Char's Zaku II	Complete Char Aznable's Story mode on any difficulty in Official mode
Elpe Ple and Qubeley Mk-II (Black)	Complete Both Judau Ashita and Domon Kasshu's Story modes on any difficulty
Emma Sheen	Complete Both Char Aznable and Rolan Cehack's Story modes on any difficulty
Haman Karn, Judau Ashita, Qubeley Gundam, and Gundam ZZ	Complete Judau Ashita's Story mode on any difficulty in Official mode
Hyaku Shiki	Complete Mission 4 of Char Aznable's Official mode on any difficulty
Jerid Messa and Gundam Mk-II (Black)	Complete Both Kamille Bidan and Heero Yuy's Story modes on any difficulty
Master Gundam /Master Asia	Beat Domon/Burning Gundam's Story mode on any difficulty
Milliardo Peacecraft and Gundam Epyon	Complete Heero Yuy's Story mode on any difficulty in Original mode

Musha Gundam	Complete Story mode for Amuro Ray, Kamille Bidan, Judau Ashita, Domon Kasshu, Heero Yuy, and Rolan Cehack on any difficulty
Paptimus Scirocco and The O	Complete Kamille Bidan's Story mode on any difficulty in Official mode
Ple Two	Complete Elpe Ple's Story mode on any difficulty i n Original mode
Qubeley Mk-II (Red)	Complete Both Elpe Ple and Rolan Cehack's Story modes on any difficulty
Roux Louka	Complete Both Judau Ashita and Haman Karn's Story modes on any difficulty

DYNASTY WARRIORS: GUNDAM (PlayStation 3)

EXTRA CHARACTERS AND MOBILE SUITS

UNLOCKABLE	HOW TO UNLOCK
Any Mobile Suit for a Pilot	Finish a pilot's Story mode at least once
Char's Gelgoog	Complete Amuro Ray's Official mode
Char's Zaku II	Complete Char Aznable's Official mode
Gundam Mk-II (Black)	Complete Kamille Bidan's Official mode and Heero Yuy's Original mode
Gundam ZZ	Complete Judau Ashita's Official mode
Hyaku Shiki (Gold Gundam)	Complete Char Aznable's Official mode Mission 4
Master Asia and Master Gundam	Finish Domon Kasshu's Original mode
Milliardo Peacecraft and Epyon	Finish Heero's story in Original mode
Musha Gundam	Beat Original mode with all 6 protagonists: Amuro, Kamille, Judau, Domon, Heero, and Loran
Official: Char Aznable	Complete Amuro Ray's Official mode
Official: Haman Karn	Complete Kamille Bidan's Official mode
Official: Paptimus Scirocco	Complete Judau Ashita's Official mode
Original: Amuro Ray	Complete Amuro Ray's Official mode
Original: Char Aznable	Complete Char Aznable's Official mode
Original: Elpe Puru	Complete Judau Ashita's Official mode and Domon Kasshu's Original mode
Original: Emma Sheen	Complete Char Aznable's Official mode and Rolan Cehack's Original mode
Original: Haman Karn	Complete Haman Karn's Official mode
Original: Jerid Messa	Complete Kamille Bidan's Official mode and Heero Yuy's Original mode
Original: Judau Ashita	Complete Judau Ashita's Official mode
Original: Kamille Bidan	Complete Kamille Bidan's Official mode
Original: Paptimus Scirocco	Complete Paptimus Scirocco's Official mode
Original: Puru Two	Complete Elpe Puru's Original mode
Original: Roux Louka	Complete Judau Ashita's Original mode and Haman Karn's Official mode
Qubeley	Complete Judau Ashita's Official mode
Qubeley Mk-II (Red)	Complete Elpe Puru's Original mode and Rolan Cehack's Original mode
Qubeley Mk-II (Black)	Complete Judau Ashita's Official mode and Domon Kasshu's Original mode
The O	Complete Kamille Bidan's Official mode

EA SPORTS BIO AWARDS (XBOX)

UNLOCKABLE	CODE
2002 All-American Team	Level 18
Butter Fingers Pennant	Level 4
Orange Bowl Pennant	Level 8
Rose Bowl Pennant	Level 2
Tostitos Bowl Pennant	Level 12

ECCO: THE TIDES OF TIME (Wii)

UNLOCKABLES

UNLOCKABLE	HOW TO UNLOCK
Debug Menu	Pause while Ecco is facing you. Once Ecco is facing you, press Ⓐ, Ⓑ, Ⓒ, Ⓑ, Ⓒ, Ⓐ, Ⓒ, Ⓐ, Ⓑ If you entered the code correctly, a menu will pop up with all sorts of options such as a sound test, level select, tempo, etc. This code can be entered as many times as you'd like, as long as the game is paused while Ecco is facing you.
Hard Mode	In the starting area, break the two shells above you, and then swim through the tunnel to start the game in Hard mode.

PASSWORDS

LEVEL	PASSWORD
Crystal Springs	UEPMCVEB
Fault Zone	OZUNSKZA
Two Tides	KDKINTYA
Skyway	SZXHCLDB
Sky Tides	OZWIDLDB
Tube of Medusa	QSJRYHZA
Skylands	MULXRXEB
Fin to Feather	YCPAWEXA
Eagle's Bay	YCJPDNDB
Asterite's Cave	AOJRDZWA
Four Islands	UOYURFDB
Sea of Darkness	UQZWIIAB
Vents of Medusa	MMVSOPBB
Gateway	KDCGTAHB
Big Water	QQCQRDRA
Deep Ridge	UXQWJIZD
Hungry Ones	WBQHMIUE
Secret Cave	CHGTEYZE
Gravitorbox	UIXBGWXE
Globe Holder	SBFPWWJE
Dark Sea	MXURVMLA
Vortex Queen	OKIMTBPA
Home Bay	CSNCMRUA
Epilogue	CEWSXKPA
Fish City	SGTDYSPA
City of Forever	WSSXZKVA

PASSWORDS FOR HARD MODE

* = New level found only in Hard mode

LEVEL	PASSWORD
Crystal Springs	WPHSAAFB
Fault Zone	CRNPTFZA
Two Tides	QUKGZZYA
Skyway	MCMBPJDB
Sky Tides	OZMRKIDB
Tube of Medusa	ODFADPYA
Aqua Tubeway*	KNHRKJYA
Skylands	WXRDJYEB
Fin to Feather	UQTFBRXA
Eagle's Bay	QSNVMMDB
Asterite's Cave	EGAQRVXA
Maze of Stone*	EUTQQQWA
Four Islands	CZVQNHCB
Sea of Darkness	WFMYIDAB
Vents of Medusa	SHWZZNBB
Gateway	QKLLFPHB
Moray Abyss	YCFSBRAB
The Eye	AGNEXBTE
Big Water	YCBXONIA
Deep Ridge	UPODMUQD
The Hungry Ones	YOHVUVLE
Secret Cave	SPKHKISE
Lunar Bay	WTHXKISE
Black Clouds	USKIKDOE
GraviatorBox	WNQWZMME
Globe Holder	MIPGDOME
New Machine*	GOSTCXJA
Vortex Queen	OOSFBXAA
Home Bay	QNSGAPGA
Epilogue	AXBGKHBA
Fish City	WKGETHCA
City of Forever	WQHFTZHA
"Secret" Password	AVQJTCBA

UNLOCKABLE

UNLOCKABLE	HOW TO UNLOCK
Unlimited Air and Health	Turn Ecco left or right and pause the game while Ecco is facing the screen. Press A, A, right, A, C, A, left, A, A, right, A and then unpause. You will now never die from lack of air or injuries.

THE ELDER SCROLLS III: MORROWIND (XBOX)

During Gameplay, go to the Statistics page to enter the following codes. You can only enter one code at a time.

UNLOCKABLE	CODE
Restore Fatigue	Highlight Fatigue and press BLK, BLK, WHT, WHT, BLK, then hold A to reach the desired level.
Restore Health	Highlight Health and press BLK, WHT, BLK, BLK, BLK, then hold A to reach the desired level.
Restore Magicka	Highlight Magicka and press BLK, WHT, WHT, BLK, WHT, then hold A to reach the desired level.

CODES & CHEATS

ELEBITS (Wii)

UNLOCKABLE	CODE
Alpha Wave Unit	Beat 15 Missions in Challenge mode
Aroma Unit	Earn the title "King of Surveillance" after beating the last boss
Berserk Elebits	Earn the title "King of Capture" after beating the last boss
Extreme Silence	Earn the title "King of Noise" after beating the last boss
High Power Mode	Beat the third boss, then watch the cutscene at the beginning of the next level
Limit Release (Strongest Level Capture Gun)	Beat 25 Challenge Missions
Main Unit Only	Beat 5 Challenge Missions
Permanent Homing Laser (Deactivates Vacuum Laser)	Beat 20 Challenge Missions
Permanent Vacuum Laser (Deactivates Homing Laser)	Get 25 S ranks in Normal Mission
Worn Capture Gun	Beat 10 Missions in Challenge mode

ELEMENTS OF DESTRUCTION (DS)

CODES

Pause the game and hold the following four buttons simultaneously.

UNLOCKABLE	HOW TO UNLOCK
Unlimited Energy	Ⓨ, L, ➡, SELECT
Unlimited Time	Ⓧ, R, ⬇, SELECT

ALL LEVELS

Hold down the following buttons during the first cutscene to unlock all levels for the current profile.

UNLOCKABLE	HOW TO UNLOCK
Unlock All Levels	Ⓑ, L, SELECT

ENCLAVE (XBOX)

UNLOCKABLE	CODE
God Mode and Complete Mission	Pause the game and enter Ⓧ,Ⓨ,Ⓧ,Ⓧ,Ⓨ,Ⓨ,Ⓧ,Ⓨ,Ⓧ,Ⓧ,Ⓨ,Ⓨ.

ENDGAME (PlayStation 2)

Enter these codes at the Main menu. The numbers represent how many times you shoot the screen. One shot is the letter "A," two shots are "B," and so forth. In between each letter you reload. For example: 3-15-4-5 ("code") means you shoot three times, reload, shoot 15 times, reload, shoot four times, reload, and then shoot five times.

UNLOCKABLE	CODE
All Mighty Joe Jupiter Mode	13-9-7-8-20-9-5-18 ("MIGHTIER")
All Specials	13-5-2-9-7-3-8-5-1-20 ("MEBIGCHEAT")
Arcade Mode	2-12-1-13 ("BLAM")
Country Challenges	1-2-18-15-1-4 ("ABROAD")
Unlock the Jukebox	12-5-20-19-2-15-15-7-9 ("LETSBOOGIE")

ERAGON (XBOX 360)

UNLIMITED FURY MODE

Pause the game while in a level.

UNLOCKABLE	HOW TO UNLOCK
Unlimited Fury Mode	Hold Ⓛ + LT + Ⓡ + RT and press Ⓧ Ⓑ Ⓑ Ⓑ (Note: This makes magic cooldown go much faster.)

ESCAPE FROM BUG ISLAND (Wii)

UNLOCKABLE

UNLOCKABLE	HOW TO UNLOCK
Samurai Sword and Death Scythe in Inventory	If you clear the game with either an "A" or "S" ranking, the next time you start the game, both the Samurai Sword and Death Scythe will be in your inventory.

ESPN NBA BASKETBALL (XBOX)

UNLOCKABLE	CODE
All 24/7 Items	Create a Player with the first name HUNT and the last name 4TREASURE.

ESPN NFL 2K5 (XBOX)

Get these unlockables by changing your VIP profile name to the following:

UNLOCKABLE	PROFILE NAME
1,000,000 Crib Credits	PhatBank
All Crib items	CribMax
All Milestones complete (full trophy room)	MadSkilz

ESPN NFL 2K5 (PlayStation 2)

Change VIP Profile name to the following and access the specified unlockable.

UNLOCKABLE	VIP PROFILE NAME
1,000,000 Crib Credits	"PhatBank"
All Crib items	"CribMax"
All Milestones complete (full trophy room)	"MadSkilz"

ESPN NHL 2K5 (PlayStation 2)

UNLOCKABLE	CODE
Everything in the Skybox	Create a profile with the name LuvLeafs.

ESPN NHL HOCKEY (PlayStation 2)

Enter this code at the Game Modes screen.

UNLOCKABLE	CODE
Unlock everything	R1, R1, L1, ←, ←, ↓, ●, R1, ●, L1, ↑, →, ●, ↓, ←, ←, ●, R1, ↓, ↑

ESWAT: CITY UNDER SIEGE (Wii)

UNLOCKABLES

UNLOCKABLE	HOW TO UNLOCK
Level Select	Start a game, and the Hero and Mission screen appears. Now hold down Ⓐ+Ⓑ+Ⓒ and press ←, →, ↑, ↓. Select the level by pressing ←/→. Then during the ending sequence, press and hold Ⓐ+Ⓐ+Ⓒ+↓+←. Keep holding these and press START until the Sound Test screen appears.

EVOLUTION SKATEBOARDING (PlayStation 2)

After entering the following codes, listen for the sound to confirm correct entry.

UNLOCKABLE	CODE
All Characters and Alt skins	↑, ↓, ←, →, ↑, ↓, ←, →, ↑, ↓, ←, →, ●
All Stages	L2, R2, ←, →, ←, →, ←, →, ↓, ↓, ↑, ↑, ↓, ↑

EXCITEBOTS: TRICK RACING (Wii)

NEW ITEMS FOR PURCHASE

UNLOCKABLE	HOW TO UNLOCK
Statue of bot available for purchase.	10 races completed with a bot.
Exclusive paint job available for purchase.	15 races completed with a bot.

NEW PLAYER ICONS FOR PURCHASE

UNLOCKABLE	HOW TO UNLOCK
Ace of Spades (1,000 stars)	Obtain an S rank on all Poker Races.
Alien (2,500 stars)	Obtain a B rank or higher on Nebula track.
Angry Face	Obtain an S rank on all minigames.
Baseball (500 stars)	Obtain an S rank on all minigames.
Basketball (1,000 stars)	Obtain an S rank on all minigames.
Bomb (25,000 stars)	Obtain at least a B ranking on all Mirror Excite cups.
Bowling (2,500 stars)	Obtain an S rank on all minigames.
Boxing Glove (2,500 stars)	Obtain an S rank on all minigames.
Cocky Face	Obtain an S rank on all minigames.
Crescent Moon (5,000 stars)	Obtain a B rank or higher on Nebula track.
Devil Face	Obtain an S rank on all minigames.
Die (1,000 stars)	Obtain an S rank on all Poker Races.
Earth (10,000 stars)	Obtain a B rank or higher on Nebula track.
Football (1,000 stars)	Obtain an S rank on all minigames.
Four-Leaf Clover (2,500 stars)	Obtain an S rank on all Poker Races.
Gold Coin (5,000 stars)	Obtain an S rank on all Poker Races.
Gold Horseshoe (5,000 stars)	Obtain an S rank on all Poker Races.
Magic 8 Ball (2,500 stars)	Obtain an S rank on all Poker Races.
Ping-Pong (500 stars)	Obtain an S rank on all minigames.
Pirate Face	Obtain an S rank on all minigames.
Radioactive (50,000 stars)	Obtain at least a B ranking on all Mirror Excite cups.
Rocket (5,000 stars)	Obtain a B rank or higher on Nebula track.
Saturn (10,000 stars)	Obtain a B rank or higher on Nebula track.
Skull and Crossbones (50,000 stars)	Obtain at least a B ranking on all Mirror Excite cups.
Snake (10,000 stars)	Obtain at least a B ranking on all Mirror Excite cups.
Spaceman (2,500 stars)	Obtain a B rank or higher on Nebula track.
Spider (10,000 stars)	Obtain at least a B ranking on all Mirror Excite cups.
Sunglasses Face	Obtain an S rank on all minigames.
Surprised Face	Obtain an S rank on all minigames.
Thunderbolt (25,000 stars)	Obtain at least a B ranking on all Mirror Excite cups.

UNLOCKABLE BOTS

UNLOCKABLE	HOW TO UNLOCK
Ant	Super Excite mode, reach lifetime rank requirement, pay 10,000 stars.

UNLOCKABLE	HOW TO UNLOCK
Centipede	Purchase for 5,000 stars.
Crab	Purchase for 10,000 stars.
Hornet	Super Excite mode, reach lifetime rank requirement, pay 10,000 stars.
Hummingbird	Purchase for 2,500 stars.
Lizard	Super Excite mode, reach lifetime rank requirement, pay 10,000 stars.

Lobster	Super Excite mode, reach lifetime rank requirement, pay 10,000 stars.
Mantis	Purchase for 2,500 stars.
Mouse	Purchase for 2,500 stars.
New unlockable bots.	Unlock Super Excite mode.
Roach	Super Excite mode, reach lifetime rank requirement, pay 10,000 stars.
Scorpion	Super Excite mode, reach lifetime rank requirement, pay 10,000 stars.
Spider	Purchase for 5,000 stars.
Squid	Super Excite mode, reach lifetime rank requirement, pay 10,000 stars.

UNLOCKABLE PAINT JOBS

UNLOCKABLE	HOW TO UNLOCK
Armor	Purchase for 250,000 stars or earn 25 S ranks as the beetle.
Army Ant	Purchase for 250,000 stars or earn 25 S ranks as the ant.
Ballerina	Purchase for 250,000 stars or earn 25 S ranks as the mouse.
Boxer	Purchase for 250,000 stars or earn 25 S ranks as the crab.
Chef	Purchase for 250,000 stars or earn 25 S ranks as the lobster.
Chicken	Purchase for 250,000 stars or earn 25 S ranks as the hornet.
Cow	Purchase for 250,000 stars or earn 25 S ranks as the grasshopper.
Cowboy	25 S wins with turtle or 250,000 stars.
Diver costume-Lizard	Achieve 25 S runs with lizard bot, or pay 250,000.
Dracula	25 S wins with bat or 250,000 stars.
Dragon	25 S ranks with centipede or 250,000 stars.
Extreme	Purchase for 250,000 stars or earn 25 S ranks as the Boulder.
Hearts	Purchase for 250,000 stars or earn 25 S ranks as the ladybug.
King	25 S wins with cockroach or 250,000 stars.
Magic Act	Purchase for 250,000 stars or earn 25 S ranks as the frog.
Magician	Pay 250,000 stars or gain 25 S ranks.
Pilot	25 S ranks with hummingbird or 250,000 stars.
Pirate	Purchase for 250,000 stars or earn 25 S ranks as the squid.
Punk Rock	25 S wins with spider or 250,000 stars.
Punk Rocker	Purchase for 250,000 stars or earn 25 S ranks as the spider.
Space Mantis	Purchase for 250,000 stars or earn 25 S ranks as the mantis.
Top hat and suit	25 S wins with frog or 250,000 stars.
Wizard	Purchase for 250,000 stars or earn 25 S ranks as the spider.

EXIT (PSP)

In order to use these codes, you must complete the first situation level.

UNLOCKABLE	CODE
Unlocks Situation 8	L, R, ←, →, ■, ●, ×, ▲
Unlocks Situation 9	▲, ↓, ●, ←, ×, ↑, ■, →
Unlocks Situation 10	→, ↓, ↑, ←, ●, ×, R, L

F

F.E.A.R. (XBOX 360)

To unlock all levels but disable achievements, enter F3ARDAY1 as a profile/gamertag.

F.E.A.R. 2: PROJECT ORIGIN (XBOX 360)

MAIN MENU BACKGROUND CHANGE

The menu's background changes upon completion of the game on any difficulty level.

UNLOCKABLE	HOW TO UNLOCK
Project Harbinger Main Menu Background	Complete the single-player mode on any difficulty.

FABLE II (XBOX 360)

EASTER EGG

In the side quest "Treasure Island of Doom," the Lionhead Studios Lion can be found when you get to the treasure island. Look at the island in the middle of the lake and you'll see it is in the shape of the Studio's Lionhead logo.

INFINITE EXPERIENCE

Once you have access to Bowerstone Market, walk to Town Square. There is a potion shopkeeper on the left side. Walk around the right side of the buildings there and down an alley to find a house known as Monster Manor. Sleep there to gain its benefit (+1 star of Physique) Once you gain this benefit, go to your abilities list, select physique, and hit Y to unlearn it. The bonus star from the house does not disappear, but the experience is given to you anyway. Repeat this process as many times as you like, the more stars you have in physique the more exp you get each time. This experience is general experience and can be applied to any skills.

INFINITE EXPERIENCE II

Wait until your character is at least somewhat leveled up. Plug in a second controller and begin a co-op game without using a second profile. Using the second controller, go to your henchman's abilities and discard all of them, returning the experience to the pool. Then quit out of the co-op game. You should find that all the "leftover" experience has been transferred to your hero. Repeat as often as you like. Note: Your co-op henchman will have the same abilities that you do, so the stronger the hero, the more abilities there are to sell off and thus more experience.

FALLOUT 3 (XBOX 360)

INFINITE XP

You can gain infinite XP if your Speech skill is high enough (approximately level 30). Go Big Town, north of Vault 101. Speak with a girl named Bittercup. She'll tell you about her dating exploits. After speaking with her, go into the house marked "Common House" and speak to a man named Pappy. There should be a speech skill dialogue option that says "You came here with Bittercup, right?" You get XP every time you click it. Continue to do this as long as you like to gain free XP.

EARLY DETECTION

When heading into seemingly hostile territory, try hitting the VATS button over and over again as you make your character turn around, searching all angles. Doing so will alert you to any enemies you may not yet see by zooming in on them in VATS mode. You won't be able to do damage to your foes from such a distance, but it's a good way to spot foes before they spot you so you know what you're getting yourself into.

SANDMAN GLITCH (PRE-PATCH)

This a glitch for getting infinite experience. Steps: Reach Level 10 with a sneak skill of 60 and get the Mr. Sandman perk. Go to Andale (south central part of the map). Wait until around 1 A.M. and go into the Smith house while they are sleeping. Go upstairs and into the kid's bedroom. Use sandman on him (crouch and select him and use the first option). Repeat the last steps. Increase difficulty for more XP.

FANTASTIC 4: RISE OF THE SILVER SURFER (PlayStation 3)

UNLOCKABLES

Collect the indicated number of Tokens to unlock the corresponding bonus.

UNLOCKABLE	HOW TO UNLOCK
1990's Fantastic Four	Collect 12 Tokens
2000's Fantastic Four	Collect 12 Tokens
Comic Covers #1	Collect 4 Tokens
Comic Covers #2	Collect 4 Tokens
Game Concept Art	Collect 4 Tokens
Ultimate Costumes	Collect 12 Tokens

FANTASTIC 4: RISE OF THE SILVER SURFER (Wii)

UNLOCKABLES

UNLOCKABLE	HOW TO UNLOCK
1990's Fantastic 4	12 Tokens
2000's Fantastic 4	12 Tokens
Comic Covers 1	4 Tokens
Comic Covers 2	4 Tokens
Concept Art	4 Tokens
Ultimate Costumes	12 Tokens

FANTASTIC FOUR (XBOX)

Enter these codes quickly at the Main menu. You will hear a sound to confirm a correct entry.

UNLOCKABLE	CODE
Barge Arena and Stan Lee Interview #1	Ⓧ,Ⓑ,Ⓧ,↓,↓,Ⓑ,↑
Bonus Level Hell	→, →, Ⓧ, Ⓑ, ←, ↑, ↓
Infinite Cosmic Powers	↑, Ⓧ, Ⓧ, Ⓧ, ←, →, Ⓑ

FANTASTIC FOUR (PlayStation 2)

Enter these codes quickly at the Main menu. You will hear a sound to confirm a correct entry.

UNLOCKABLE	CODE
Barge Arena Level and Stan Lee Interview #1	■,●,■,⇩,⇩,●,⇧
Bonus Level Hell	⇨,⇨,■,●,⇦,⇧,⇩
Infinite Cosmic Power	⇧,■,■,■,⇦,⇨,●

FAR CRY 2 (PlayStation 3)

CODES

In the menu, go to Additional Content, then Promotion Code, and input the code.

EFFECT	CODE
Unlock all missions.	6aPHuswe
Bonus Mission	tr99pUkA
Bonus Mission	THaCupR4
Bonus Mission	tar3QuzU
Bonus Mission	SpujeN7x
Bonus Mission	sa7eSUPR

EFFECT	CODE
Bonus Mission	JeM8SpaW
Bonus Mission	Cr34ufrE
Bonus Mission	96CesuHu
Bonus Mission	2Eprunef
Bonus Mission	zUmU6Rup

FAR CRY INSTINCTS (XBOX)

To enter these passwords, pause the game and select the Cheat menu. Note that these passwords are case sensitive.

UNLOCKABLE	PASSWORD
100 Health Points	GiveMeHealth
All Maps	TheWorldIsMine
Disables Auto-Aim	NotForSissies
Feral Attack Ability	PunchMeHard
Infinite Adrenaline	VitruviAnRush
Infinite Ammo	BulletsofHell

Enter this code after you select Map Maker.

UNLOCKABLE	CODE
Secret Message	LT, RT, Y, B, X, click and hold left D-pad, click and hold right D-pad, A

FAR CRY INSTINCTS PREDATOR (XBOX 360)

To enter these passwords, pause the game and select the Cheat menu. Note that these passwords are case sensitive.

UNLOCKABLE	PASSWORD
Enable Evolutions	FeralAttack
Evolution Game	GiveMeItAll
Heal Yourself	ImJackCarver
Infinite Adrenaline	Bloodlust
Infinite Ammo	UnleashHell
Unlock All Maps	GiveMeTheMaps

FAR CRY VENGEANCE (Wii)

PASSWORD

PASSWORD	EFFECT
GiveMeTheMaps	Unlock All Maps

FATAL FURY (Wii)

UNLOCKABLE

UNLOCKABLE	HOW TO UNLOCK
Good Ending	Beat the game on Normal or Hard without using a continue

FIFA 06 (XBOX 360)

BONUS TEAM, KITS, AND BALLS

UNLOCKABLE	HOW TO UNLOCK
Adidas Etrusco Ball	Win an 8 (or more) Team Custom Knockout Tournament
Adidas Tango Espana Ball	Win a 16 (or more) Team Custom Knockout Tournament
Adidas Tricoloure Ball	Win a 5 (or more) Team Custom League
Classic 11 Team	Qualify for the World Cup in Road to the World Cup Mode
England 1966 World Cup Kit	Win the International Masters Tournament with England in Road to the World Cup mode
England 1990 World Cup Kit	Win the International Open Tournament with England in Road to the World Cup mode

FIFA STREET (PlayStation 2)

UNLOCKABLE	CODES
Mini Players	Pause the game and hold L1+▲ and press ↑,←,↓,↓,→,↓,↑,←.
Normal Size Players	Pause the game and hold L1+▲ and press →,→,↑,↓,↓,←,→,←.
All Apparel	At the main menu hold L1+▲ and press →,→,←,↑,↑,↑,↓,←.

FIFA STREET 2 (XBOX)

Enter this code at the Main menu while holding LT + Y.

UNLOCKABLE	CODE
All stages unlocked	←,↑,↑,→,↓,↓,→,↓

FIFA STREET 2 (PlayStation 2)

Enter this code at the Main menu while holding L1 + ▲.

UNLOCKABLE	CODE
All stages unlocked	←, ↑, ↑, →, ↓, ↓, →, ↓

FIFA STREET 3 (XBOX 360)

BONUS TEAMS

Complete the following tasks to unlock the corresponding team.

UNLOCKABLE	HOW TO UNLOCK
Predator (Gerrard, Beckham, etc.)	Complete Adidas Challenge in FIFA Street Challenge.
The Blasters (Gerrard, Ballack, etc.)	Win 40 Games in FIFA Street Challenge.
The Champions (Baresi, Voller, etc.)	Complete Champion Challenge in FIFA Street Challenge.
The Classics (Cantona, Zico, etc.)	Complete Classic Challenge in FIFA Street Challenge.
World Stars (Ronaldinho, Eto'o, etc.)	Complete All Stars Challenge in FIFA Street Challenge.

ACHIEVEMENTS

UNLOCKABLE	HOW TO UNLOCK
Challenge Heavyweight (100)	With the lead *FIFA Street 3* profile, complete a match with World Stars.
Challenge Lightweight (35)	With the lead *FIFA Street 3* profile, complete a match with the Champions.
Challenge Middleweight (75)	With the lead *FIFA Street 3* profile, complete a match with F50.
Five-A-Side Match (15)	Complete a Five-A-Side match with the lead *FIFA Street 3* profile.
Gamebreaker (25)	Score a Gamebreaker goal with the lead *FIFA Street 3* profile in any game mode except Practice.
Gamebreaker Match (15)	Complete a Gamebreaker Goal match with the lead *FIFA Street 3* profile.
Gamebreaker Possession (25)	With the lead *FS3* profile, fill your Gamebreaker bar in one possession in any mode except Practice.
Gamebreaker Spoiler (50)	Score with the lead *FIFA Street 3* profile while your opponent is on Gamebreaker.
Get Online (25)	Complete a ranked or unranked match with the lead *FIFA Street 3* profile on Xbox LIVE.
Golden Gamebreaker (75)	Score a golden goal with the lead *FIFA Street 3* profile in a timed match while on Gamebreaker.

UNLOCKABLE	HOW TO UNLOCK
Guest Picks (25)	Win a completed Xbox LIVE Playground Picks match hosted by another player with the lead *FS3* profile.
Hat Trick Hero (50)	With the lead *FIFA Street 3* profile, score a hat trick with CROUCH in any game mode except Practice.
Head to Head Breaker (25)	With the lead *FS3* profile, complete the last Gamebreaker Goals match to three goals in a best of seven.
Head to Head Headache (50)	With the lead *FS3* profile, complete the last Headers and Volleys match to seven goals in a best of five.
Head to Head Series (25)	With the lead *FS3* profile, complete the last Head to Head match in a best of three of any type.
Headers and Volleys Match (15)	Complete a Headers and Volleys match with the lead *FIFA Street 3* profile.
Host Picks (25)	Win a completed match as the host of an Xbox LIVE Playground Picks match with the lead *FS3* profile.
Ranked Champ (100)	Complete and win 25 ranked matches on Xbox LIVE with the lead *FIFA Street 3* profile.
Ranked Goals (50)	Score 50 goals in completed ranked matches on Xbox LIVE with the lead *FIFA Street 3* profile.
Score Difference Match (15)	Complete a Score Difference match with the lead *FIFA Street 3* profile.
Score Match (15)	Complete a Score match with the lead *FIFA Street 3* profile.
Shooting Gallery (10)	Take 50 shots on goal in any game mode except Practice with the lead *FIFA Street 3* profile.
Street Fever (45)	Complete an Xbox LIVE match against another player who has Street Fever with the lead *FS3* profile.
Timed Match (15)	Complete a Timed match with the lead *FIFA Street 3* profile.
Tourist (10)	Score a goal in every environment in any game mode except Practice with the lead *FS3* profile.
Triple Gamebreaker (50)	Score three Gamebreakers with the lead *FS3* profile on the same Gamebreaker in any mode except Practice.
Wally (35)	Run on the walls 50 times in any game mode except Practice with the lead *FIFA Street 3* profile.

FIFA STREET 3 (PlayStation 3)

BONUS TEAMS

Complete the following tasks to unlock the corresponding team.

UNLOCKABLE	HOW TO UNLOCK
Predator (Gerrard, Beckham, etc.)	Complete Adidas Challenge in FIFA Street Challenge.
The Blasters (Gerrard, Ballack, etc.)	Win 40 Games in FIFA Street Challenge.
The Champions (Baresi, Voller, etc.)	Complete Champion Challenge in FIFA Street Challenge.
The Classics (Cantona, Zico, etc.)	Complete Classic Challenge in FIFA Street Challenge.
World Stars (Ronaldinho, Eto'o, etc.)	Complete All Stars Challenge in FIFA Street Challenge.

FIFA WORLD CUP - 2006 (XBOX 360)

UNLOCKABLE	CODE
Beat the Host Nation	Beat the host nation Germany in a full match
Complete a Scenario	Complete any Challenge in Global Challenge

Complete all Scenarios	Complete all the Challenges in Global Challenge
Qualify for the World Cup	Qualify for the World Cup in 2006 FIFA World Cup mode
Win the World Cup	Win the World Cup in 2006 FIFA World Cup mode

FIGHT CLUB (PlayStation 2)

UNLOCKABLE	CODE
Play as a skeleton	Create a fighter and name him Skeleton

FIGHT NIGHT 2004 (XBOX)

UNLOCKABLE	CODE
All Venues	At the Main menu, highlight My Corner and press ←,←,←,→,→,→,←,→,→.
Big Tigger	In the Record Book menu, go to most wins and press ↑,↑.
Miniature Fighters	At the Main menu, hightlight Play Now and press ←,←,←,→,→,→,←,Ⓐ.

FIGHT NIGHT ROUND 2 (XBOX)

UNLOCKABLE	CODE
All Venus	At the game mode select screen hold ← until you hear a bell.
Mini Fighters	At the choose Venue screen hold ↑ until you hear a bell ring.
Unlock Fabulous	Create a character with the first name GETFAB then cancel out and Fabulous will be available for Play Now and Career mode.

FIGHT NIGHT ROUND 2 (PlayStation 2)

UNLOCKABLE	CODE
Mini Fighters	At the choose Venue screen hold ↑ until you hear a bell ring.
Unlock Fabulous	Create a character with the first name GETFAB then cancel out and Fabulous will be available for Play Now and Career mode.
All Venues Unlocked	At the game mode selection screen hold ← until you hear a bell.

FIGHT NIGHT ROUND 3 (XBOX 360)

Create a new boxer with this first name.

UNLOCKABLE	CODE
All Venues	newview

UNLOCKABLES

UNLOCKABLE	HOW TO UNLOCK
ESPN Classic Fight	Clear the Under Armor Bout in Career mode to unlock the fight of Big E vs. Goliath.
Judge Jab	Defeat Joe Frazier with Ali.
Ko Rey Mo	In the light heavy division, defeat him in Career mode.
Lethal Uppercuts	Win a classic fight with Roberto Duran.
Madison Square Garden Venue	Win a match at Madison Square Garden.
Sinister Cross	Win a classic fight with Roy Jones Jr.
Smooth Style	Defeat Muhammad Ali in a challenge event.
Textbook	Win a classic fight with Oscar De La Hoya.
Staples Center Venue	Win at the Staple's Center in Career mode.
Rey Mo and Burger King Trainer—Light Heavyweight	Create a boxer with the last name YAXKUKMO and complete, or have previously completed the Burger King sponsored bout in Career mode to unlock.

ACHIEVEMENTS

UNLOCKABLE	HOW TO UNLOCK
Burger King Achievement: 100 points	Win The BK Invitational Fight.
Dodge Achievement: 100 points	Win the Dodge sponsored fight.

UNLOCKABLE	HOW TO UNLOCK
EA SPORTS Achievement: 150 points	Win any EA SPORTS sponsored fight.
ESPN FNF Achievement: 150 points	Win any ESPN Friday Night Fight event.
ESPN PPV Achievement: 150 points	Win any ESPN Pay Per View fight event.
ESPN WNF Achievement: 150 points	Win any ESPN Wednesday Night Fight event.
Everlast Achievement: 100 points	Win the Everlast sponsored fight.
Under Armor Achievement: 100 points	Win the Under Armor sponsored fight.

FIGHT NIGHT ROUND 3 (PlayStation 3)

CODES

UNLOCKABLE	CODE
All Venues	newview

UNLOCKABLES

UNLOCKABLE	HOW TO UNLOCK
Madison Square Garden	Win a match there in Career mode.
The Staples Center	Win a match there in Career mode.
"Hard Straights" Style	Win that style match in ESPN Classic Fights mode or Career mode.
"Hook Master" Style	Win that style match in ESPN Classic Fights mode or Career mode.
"Judge Jab" Style	Win that style match in ESPN Classic Fights mode or Career mode.
"Lethal Uppercuts" Style	Win that style match in ESPN Classic Fights mode or Career mode.
"Philly Shell" Style	Win that style match in ESPN Classic Fights mode or Career mode.
"Sinister Cross" Style	Win that style match in ESPN Classic Fights mode or Career mode.
"Slickster" Style	Win that style match in ESPN Classic Fights mode or Career mode.
"Smooth" Style	Win that style match in ESPN Classic Fights mode or Career mode.
"Textbook" Style	Win that style match in ESPN Classic Fights mode or Career mode.
"Uptight" Style	Win that style match in ESPN Classic Fights mode or Career mode.
Ko Rey Mo	Defeat him in the Lightweight Career mode.
The Burger King select	Finish the Burger King event in Career mode and **(Trainer)** him as a trainer.

FIGHT NIGHT ROUND 4 (XBOX 360)

UNLOCKABLES

UNLOCKABLE	HOW TO UNLOCK
Unlock Extra Offline Accessories	In Legacy Mode, become a champion in two weight divisions then reach "G.O.A.T" status.
Unlock Extra Online Accessories	Win the Lightweight, Middleweight, and Heavyweight Online belts.

FINAL FANTASY CRYSTAL CHRONICLES: THE CRYSTAL BEARERS (Wii)

UNLOCKABLES

UNLOCKABLE	HOW TO UNLOCK
Layle Moogle in Alfitaria Entrance	Start a New Game +
New Game +	Defeat the final boss, then save at the end.

FINAL FANTASY FABLES: CHOCOBO'S DUNGEON (Wii)

ADDITIONAL DUNGEONS

UNLOCKABLE	HOW TO UNLOCK
Chocobo's Memories (Standard Dungeon)	Accessed through the Chocobo statue in the park
Croma's Future (Special Dungeon)	Accessed through Croma in Stella's House

JOBS

Jobs are like classes. You begin with the "Natural" job and can unlock nine others during the game.

UNLOCKABLE	HOW TO UNLOCK
Black Mage	Make it to 10F in Guardian of the Flame.
Dancer	Enter "Pirouette" (capital P at the beginning, the rest lowercase, AND a musical note at the end) as a Romantic Phrase.
Dark Knight	Defeat Croma Shade in 30F in Guardian of the Light.
Dragoon	Complete Meja's Memories.
Knight	Complete Freja's Memories.
Ninja	Complete Volg's Memories.
Scholar	Defeat the four elements in 20F Guardian of the Water.
Thief	Steal the item behind Merchant Hero X in any of his dungeon shops.
White Mage	Complete Pastor Roche's Memories.

FINAL FANTASY XII (PlayStation 2)

SKY PIRATE DEN FIGURINES

UNLOCKABLE	HOW TO UNLOCK
Ashe	Have the average party level over 50.
Ba'Gamnan	Complete the hunt catalog.
Balthier	Attack 300 times.
Basch	Kill 500 foes.
Belias	Obtain every esper.
Carrot	Defeat the monster, Carrot.
Chocobo	Walk 50,000 steps.
Crystal	Obtain every character's magics.
Dalan	Complete every map.
DeathGaze	Defeat the monster, Death Gaze.
Fafnir	Defeat the monster, Fafnir.
Fran	Use magic 200 times.
Gabranth	Initiate every fusion technique.
Gilgamesh	Defeat the monster, Gilgamesh.
Gurdy	Use/spend 1,000,000 gil.
Hell Wyrm	Defeat the monster, Devil Dragon.
King Behemoth	Defeat the monster, King Behemoth.
Migelo	Sell 1,000 loot.
Mimic?	Unlock and buy all Monographs and Canopic Jar; also create and buy several Bazaar items to unlock.
Montblanc	Attain (monster) chain Level 50.
Penelo	Get 100,000 gil.
Rasler	Master all characters' license board.
Reks	Earn 500,000 clan points.
Trickster	Defeat the monster, Trickster.
Ultima	Defeat the esper, Ultima.
Vaan	Steal 50 times from enemies.

UNLOCKABLE	HOW TO UNLOCK
Vayne	Use techniques 100 times.
Vossler	Obtain every character's techniques.
Yazmat	Defeat the monster, Yazmat.
Zodiac	Defeat the esper, Zodiac.

FISHING SPOTS

The Fishing minigame only lets you fish in the Lower Reaches fishing spot initially; however, you can unlock more fishing spots when you fulfill certain requirements.

UNLOCKABLE	HOW TO UNLOCK
Master Den	Fish up Cactoid Crest in the Secret Reaches.
Middle Reaches	Get five perfect fishing in the Lower Reaches.
Secret Reaches	Fish up Cactoid Bond in the Upper Reaches with Matamune.
Taikou Chest (treasure)	Get nine perfect fishing in the Master Den.
Upper Reaches	Get five perfect fishing in the Middle Reaches.

ZODIAC SPEAR

The Zodiac Spear is the most powerful weapon in the game, but it will not appear if you have the urge to open up every treasure chest. There are four areas with treasure chests that must not be opened for the Zodiac Spear to appear:

1) Treasure chest in Lowtown, outside of Old Dalan's place.

2) When sneaking into the palace (before getting the Goddess Tear), there are several chests in the Cellar. Do not open the two chests in the southeast corner.

3) All treasure chests in the Confiscatory (the place where you get your weapons and armor back after being captured).

4) In the Phon Coast; later in the game, there is an island with 16 chests all near each other. The fourth chest that must not be opened is among these, so it is best to leave them all alone. They only contain Gil anyway.

If you've left the previous treasure chests alone, you'll find the Zodiac Spear in the Necrohol of Nabudis. It will give you a +150 attack and +8 Evasion.

FINAL FIGHT (Wii)

UNLOCKABLE

UNLOCKABLE	HOW TO UNLOCK
Secret Option Menu	Hold ←, press START (on title screen)

FINAL SOLDIER (Wii)

LEVEL SELECT

UNLOCKABLE	HOW TO UNLOCK
Level Select	Before the demo starts, press ←, ←, ①, →, →, ②, ↑, ↓, ↑, ↓

FINDING NEMO (XBOX)

Enter all the codes at the Main menu and the word Cheat will show up if done correctly.

UNLOCKABLE	CODE
Credits	Y, X, B, Y, Y, X, B, Y, X, B, Y, X, X, B, Y, X, B, Y, X, B, B, X, Y
Invincibility	Y, X, X, B, B, B, Y, Y, X, X, X, B, B, B, B, X, Y, B, B, B, X, B, Y, B, B, X, B, B, Y, B, X, B, B, B, Y
Level Select	Y, Y, Y, X, X, B, X, Y, B, X, Y, X, Y, X, Y, B, Y, Y
Secret Level	Y, X, B, B, X, Y, Y, X, B, B, X, Y, Y, B, X, Y, X, B, B, X, Y

FINDING NEMO (PlayStation 2)

UNLOCKABLE	CODE
Credits	▲,■,●,▲,▲,■,●,▲,■,●,▲,■,■,●,▲,■,●,▲,■,●,●,▲,■,●
Invincibility	▲,■,■,●,●,●,▲,▲,■,■,■,●,●,●,●,■,▲,●,●,●,■,●,▲,●,●,■,●,●,▲,●,■,●,●,●,▲
Level Select	▲,▲,▲,■,■,●,■,▲,●,■,▲,■,▲,■,▲,●,▲,▲
Secret Level	▲,■,●,●,■,▲,▲,■,●,●,■,▲,▲,●,■,▲,■,●,●,■,▲

FLAPPY (Wii)

PASSWORDS

Press Select on the title screen and then enter one of the following passwords. Note: each password allows you to chose your starting side (that's how levels are called in this game) from five corresponding levels. Just press ✜ or ✜ after you input a password.

PASSWORD	EFFECT
4NADA	Side 001-005
MATUI	Side 006-010
0MORI	Side 011-015
OK8MA	Side 016-020
YO4DA	Side 021-025
MA2N0	Side 026-030
MORII	Side 031-035
KA582	Side 036-040
H8SHI	Side 041-045
MEGU3	Side 046-050
EAMRA	Side 051-055
KITA9	Side 056-060
SAPP6	Side 061-065
CHUO9	Side 066-070
KITA1	Side 071-075
ZAXES	Side 076-080
VOLGD	Side 081-085
08ATA	Side 086-090
OIKA8	Side 091-095
MRSRM	Side 096-100
7GB17	Side 101-105
NZ100	Side 106-110
HINAM	Side 111-115
K0D00	Side 116-120
ATTAK	Side 121-125
NO130	Side 126-130
PAPAT	Side 131-135
MAMAA	Side 136-140
110NN	Side 141-145
LUCKY	Side 146-150
B5BAY	Side 151-155
EBIRA	Side 156-160
YA3ZW	Side 161-165
YA379	Side 166-170
WOMAN	Side 171-175
00ZAR	Side 176-180
B0KUD	Side 181-185

PASSWORD	EFFECT
X3Y48	Side 186-190
LAST1	Side 191-195
04MA5	Side 196-200

FLATOUT (XBOX)

Create a profile using these passwords.

UNLOCKABLE	PASSWORDS
Lots of Cash	GIVECASH
Unlock Everything	GIVEALL
Use the Shift Up Button to Launch the Driver	Ragdoll

FLATOUT (PlayStation 2)

Create a profile using these passwords.

UNLOCKABLE	CODE
Lots of Cash	GIVECASH
Unlocks Everything	GIVEALL
Use the Shift Up Button to Launch the Driver	Ragdoll

FLATOUT 2 (XBOX)

Enter these passwords in the Cheats menu under extras.

UNLOCKABLE	PASSWORD
All Cars and 1 Million Credits	GIEVEPIX
All Tracks	GIVEALL
Big Rig	ELPUEBLO
Flatmobile Car	WOTKINS
Lots of Money	GIVECASH
Mob Car	BIGTRUCK
Pimpster Car	RUTTO
Rocket Car	KALJAKOPPA
School Bus	GIEVCARPLZ

FLATOUT 2 (PlayStation 2)

Enter these passwords in the Cheats menu under extras.

UNLOCKABLE	PASSWORD
All Cars and 1 Million Credits	GIEVEPIX
All Tracks	GIVEALL
Big Rig	ELPUEBLO
Flatmobile Car	WOTKINS
Lots of Money	GIVECASH
Mob Car	BIGTRUCK
Pimpster Car	RUTTO
Rocket Car	KALJAKOPPA
School Bus	GIEVCARPLZ

FLATOUT: HEAD ON (PSP)

CODES

At main screen, go to Extras, then to Enter Code.

EFFECT	CODE
All Cars and 1 Million Credits	GIEVEPIX
All Tracks	GIVEALL
Big Rig	ELPUEBLO
Big Rig Truck	RAIDERS
Flatmobile Car	WOTKINS
Mob Car	BIGTRUCK

Pimpster Car	RUTTO
Rocket Car	KALJAKOPPA
School Bus	GIEVCARPLZ

FLATOUT: ULTIMATE CARNAGE (XBOX 360)

UNLOCK VEHICLES

Perform well enough to get a Bronze medal or better in each stage of three/four races to unlock the following cars. Please note that to unlock the cars, you don't need to complete the other objectives such as Time Trial, only races count. Also note that one or two of each class are unlocked in the Carnage mode. You'll have to earn gold to unlock them.

UNLOCKABLE	HOW TO UNLOCK
Bonecracker (Derby)	Get Gold in the Bonecracker Demolition Derby
Bullet, Lentus, and Ventura (Race)	Complete the Race Class Stage 2
Canyon (Street)	Get Gold in the Canyon, beat the Bomb Race
Crusader (Street)	Get Gold in the Crusader Deathmatch Derby
Flatmobile (Special)	Get Gold in the Flatmobile, beat the Bomb Race
Grinder (Derby)	Get Gold in the Grinder Demolition Derby
Insetta (Race)	Get Gold in the Insetta Carnage Race
Lancea, Daytana, and Fortune (Race)	Complete the Race Class Stage 1
Mob Car (Special)	Get Gold in the Mob Car Carnage Race
Road King (Street)	Get Gold in the Road King, beat the Bomb Race
Shaker, Blaster XL, and Banger (Derby)	Complete the Derby Class Stage 1
Sparrowhawk, CTR Sport, and Vexter XS (Street)	Complete the Street Class Stage 1
Speedshifter, Terrator, Speeddevil, Bullet GT, and Sunray (Street)	Complete the Street Class Stage 2
Splitter, Switchblade, and Venom (Derby)	Complete the Derby Class Stage 2
Truck (Special)	Get Gold in the Truck Deathmatch Derby

FLOCK (XBOX 360)

UNLOCKABLES

UNLOCKABLE	HOW TO UNLOCK
Blanka Ball	Get a perfect abduction on all single-player levels.
Chicken Trophy	Get at least a Bronze Medal on all single-player levels.
Cow Trophy	Get Gold Medals on all single-player levels.
Infinite Boost	Get Gold Medals on all single-player levels.
Pig Trophy	Get at least a Silver Medal on all single-player levels.
Sheep Trophy	Get a perfect abduction on all single-player levels.

FLOCK (PlayStation 3)

UNLOCKABLES

UNLOCKABLE	HOW TO UNLOCK
Blanka Ball	Get a perfect abduction on all single-player levels.
Chicken Trophy	Get at least a Bronze Medal on all single-player levels.
Cow Trophy	Get Gold Medals on all single-player levels.
Infinite Boost	Get Gold Medals on all single-player levels.
Pig Trophy	Get at least a Silver Medal on all single-player levels.

UNLOCKABLE	HOW TO UNLOCK
Sheep Trophy	Get a perfect abduction on all single-player levels.

FOLKLORE (PlayStation 3)

SPECIAL FOLKS

UNLOCKABLE	HOW TO UNLOCK
Ellen—Collbrande	Score 150,000 Campaign Points in Dungeon Trial mode.
Ellen—Duergar	Score 30,000 Campaign Points in Dungeon Trial mode.
Ellen—Kaladbolg	Upload a 4,500-point dungeon.
Keats—Alphard	Upload a 4,500-point dungeon.
Keats—Collbrande	Score 150,000 Campaign Points in Dungeon Trial mode.
Keats—Duergar	Score 30,000 Campaign Points in Dungeon Trial mode.
Keats—Valiant	Score 100,000 Campaign Points in Dungeon Trial mode.

FORZA MOTORSPORT (XBOX)

Start a new profile with this name. Note: the code is case sensitive.

UNLOCKABLE	CODE
Start Career with 900,000,000 Credits	tEAm4za

FORZA MOTORSPORT 2 (XBOX 360)

AMATEUR RACE SERIES

Get first place in all the races in the series.

UNLOCKABLE	HOW TO UNLOCK
#22 3R-Racing Viper Competition Coupe	Complete 5X5 V10 Super Sprint
1973 Porsche 911 Carrera RS	Complete Sports Car Classic
1992 Toyota Do-Luck Supra	Complete Boosted Shootout
2000 Acura VIS Racing Integra Type-R	Complete Inline 4 Showcase
2002 Chevrolet Lingenfelter 427 Corvette	Complete Big Block Shootout
2002 Nissan Tommy Kaira Skyline GT-R R34	Complete 6-Cylinder Showoff
Corvette Goldstrand Edition	Complete American Iron Runoff
ME Four-Twelve Concept	Complete Extreme Performance Shoot-Out
Mugen S2000	Complete Free-Breathing Challenge
VeilSide Supra Fortune 99	Complete 20th Century Supercar Invitational

ASIA LEVEL REWARD CARS

Reach these levels in Asia to unlock the cars.

UNLOCKABLE	HOW TO UNLOCK
1969 Nissan Fairlady Z 432R	Reach Level 5
2004 Mitsubishi Lancer Evolution VIII MR	Reach Level 10
1998 Subaru Impreza 22B STi	Reach Level 15
2002 Nissan Skyline GT-R V-Spec II Nur	Reach Level 20
2002 Mazda RX-7 Spirit R Type-A	Reach Level 25
2005 Honda NSX-R GT	Reach Level 30
2003 Subaru #77 CUSCO SUBARU ADVAN IMPREZA	Reach Level 35
2006 Toyota #25 ECLIPSE ADVAN SUPRA	Reach Level 40
1998 Nissan #32 NISSAN R390 GTI	Reach Level 45
1999 Toyota #3 Toyota Motorsports GT-ONE TS020	Reach Level 50

EUROPE LEVEL REWARD CARS

Reach these levels in Europe to unlock the cars.

UNLOCKABLE	HOW TO UNLOCK
1961 Jaguar E-type S1	Reach Level 5
1974 Lancia Stratos HF Stradale	Reach Level 10
1982 Porsche 911 Turbo 3.3	Reach Level 15
1989 Lotus Carlton	Reach Level 20
1987 Porsche 959	Reach Level 25
1998 Ferrari F355 Challenge	Reach Level 30
2005 Porsche #3 Lechner Racing School Team 1 911 GT3 Cup	Reach Level 35
2005 BMW Motorsport #2 BMW Motorsport M3-GTR	Reach Level 40
McLaren #41 Team McLaren F1 GTR	Reach Level 45
Audi #1 Infineon Audi R8	Reach Level 50

MANUFACTURER CLUB RACES

Get first place in all the races in the series.

UNLOCKABLE	HOW TO UNLOCK
1967 Ferrari 330 P4	Complete Club Ferrari
1995 Toyota VIS Racing MR2 Turbo T-bar	Complete MR2 Cup
1999 Lamborghini Diablo GTR	Complete Running of the Bulls
2000 Audi AWE S4 Tuning Silver Bullet S4	Complete Audi Cup
2000 Dodge Hennessey Viper 800TT	Complete Viper Performance Cup
2000 Nissan Top Secret D1-Spec S15	Complete Nissan Racing Club
2002 Honda Mugen Integra Type-R	Complete Integra Cup
2003 Volkswagen Golf R32	Complete Volkswagen Driver's Club
2005 Chevrolet #99 Tiger Racing Corvette Z06	Complete Corvette Touring Cup
2006 Porsche #82 Red Bull 911 GT3 Cup	Complete Porsche Sports Car Club

NORTH AMERICA LEVEL REWARD CARS

Reach these levels in North America to unlock the cars.

UNLOCKABLE	HOW TO UNLOCK
1968 Shelby Mustang GT-500KR	Reach Level 5
1969 Dodge Charger R/T-SE	Reach Level 10
1970 Chevrolet Chevelle SS-454	Reach Level 15
2000 Ford Mustang Cobra R	Reach Level 20
1996 Chevrolet Corvette Grand Sport	Reach Level 25
1999 Dodge Viper GTS ACR	Reach Level 30
2005 Chevrolet #31 Whelen Engineering Corvette Z06	Reach Level 35
2005 Panoz #51 JML Team Panoz Esperante GTLM	Reach Level 40
2002 Saleen #11 Graham Nash Motorsport S7R	Reach Level 45
2002 Cadillac #6 Team Cadillac NorthStar LMP-02	Reach Level 50

PROVING GROUNDS UNLOCKABLE CARS

Get first place in all the races in the series.

UNLOCKABLE	HOW TO UNLOCK
1969 Chevrolet Camaro Z28	Complete North American Open
1970 Porsche 914/6	Complete European Open
1985 Toyota AE86 Sprinter Trueno	Complete Asian Open
1992 Lancia Delta Integrale EVO	Complete RWD Shootout

UNLOCKABLE	HOW TO UNLOCK
1994 Honda Do-Luck NSX	Complete Flyweight Invitational
1995 Toyota Border MR2 Turbo T-bar	Complete Mid-Engine Challenge
2001 Mazda Mazdaspeed Roadster	Complete FWD Shootout
2003 Renault Sport Clio V6 RS	Complete Hot Hatch Runoff
2004 Honda Wings West Civic Si	Complete AWD Shootout
2007 Shelby GT500	Complete Heavyweight Open

SEMI-PRO RACES

Get first place in all the races in the series.

UNLOCKABLE	HOW TO UNLOCK
1995 Mazda AB Flug RX-7	Complete Kumho 250HP
1998 Nissan R390	Complete Nissan 350HP
1998 Subaru Tommy Kaira Impreza M20b	Complete Goodyear 150HP
2003 Dodge #23 Viper Comp Coupe	Complete Stoptech 400HP
2003 Mitsubishi Sparco Lancer Evo VIII	Complete Sparco 200HP
2004 Volvo #24 At-Speed S60-R	Complete Toyo 450HP
2005 Maserati #35 Risi Comp MC12	Complete Risi Comp 600HP
2006 Audi #2 FSI Champion Racing R8	Complete K&N 700HP
2006 Panoz #81 Team LNT Esperante GTLM	Complete Panoz 500HP
2007 Peugeot 207 Super 2000	Complete Castrol 300HP

FRACTURE (XBOX 360)

CODES

In Campaign mode, press Start. While in the Start menu, press the following code.

EFFECT	CODE
Unlocks New Skin	↑,→,←,↓,↑,←,→,↓

FREEDOM FIGHTERS (XBOX)

Enter these codes during gameplay.

UNLOCKABLE	CODE
Change Spawn Point	Ⓨ,Ⓐ,Ⓧ,Ⓑ,Ⓐ,↑
Fast Motion	Ⓨ,Ⓐ,Ⓧ,Ⓑ,Ⓑ,↓
Heavy Machine Gun	Ⓨ,Ⓐ,Ⓧ,Ⓑ,Ⓨ,↓
Infinite Ammo	Ⓨ,Ⓐ,Ⓧ,Ⓑ,Ⓐ,→
Invisibility	Ⓨ,Ⓐ,Ⓧ,Ⓑ,Ⓑ,←
Max Charisma	Ⓨ,Ⓐ,Ⓧ,Ⓑ,Ⓐ,↓
Nail Gun	Ⓨ,Ⓐ,Ⓧ,Ⓑ,Ⓐ,←
Ragdolls	Ⓨ,Ⓐ,Ⓧ,Ⓑ,Ⓧ,↑
Rocket Launcher	Ⓨ,Ⓐ,Ⓧ,Ⓑ,Ⓨ,←
Shotgun	Ⓨ,Ⓐ,Ⓧ,Ⓑ,Ⓑ,↑
Slow Motion	Ⓨ,Ⓐ,Ⓧ,Ⓑ,Ⓑ,→
Sniper Rifle	Ⓨ,Ⓐ,Ⓧ,Ⓑ,Ⓨ,→
Sub Machine Gun	Ⓨ,Ⓐ,Ⓧ,Ⓑ,Ⓨ,↑

FREEDOM FIGHTERS (PlayStation 2)

Enter these codes during gameplay.

UNLOCKABLE	CODE
Blind AI	▲,×,■,●,●,←
Nail Gun	▲,×,■,●,×,←

Slow Motion	▲,×,■,●,●,→
Unlimited Ammo	▲,×,■,●,×,→

FROGGER (XBOX 360)

MAKE FROGGER BIGGER

UNLOCKABLE	HOW TO UNLOCK
Make Frogger Bigger	At the screen where you are selecting to choose One or Two players, enter ↑ ↑ ↓ ↓ ← → ← → Ⓑ Ⓐ

FRONTLINES: FUEL OF WAR (XBOX 360)

MORE LEVELS

To unlock two extra single-player levels in the game, insert the following passwords into the in-game passwords menu.

UNLOCKABLE	HOW TO UNLOCK
Urban Level	sp-street
Village Level	sp-village

ACHIEVEMENTS

UNLOCKABLE	HOW TO UNLOCK
Anvil (15)	Complete the third mission on Normal difficulty or higher.
Anvil—Ironman (20)	Complete the third mission in a single session without dying.
Anvil—Stopwatch (25)	Complete the third mission in under 25 minutes.
Bull's-eye (90)	Complete the first or second half of a mission with an accuracy higher than 50%.
Bulletproof (90)	Kill 100 hostiles without dying in the first or second half of a single-player mission.
Captains of Industry (15)	Complete the second mission on Normal difficulty or higher.
Captains of Industry —Ironman (20)	Complete the second mission in a single session without dying.
Captains of Industry —Stopwatch (25)	Complete the second mission in under 25 minutes.
Darkness Falls (15)	Complete the first mission on Normal difficulty or higher.
Darkness Falls —Ironman (20)	Complete the first mission in a single session without dying.
Darkness Falls —Stopwatch (25)	Complete the first mission in under 15 minutes.
Flawless (50)	Win a ranked match without dying.
Graveyard (15)	Complete the fourth mission on Normal difficulty or higher.
Graveyard —Ironman (20)	Complete the fourth mission in a single session without dying.
Graveyard	Complete the fourth mission in under 50 minutes.
History Repeats (15)	Complete the final mission on Normal difficulty or higher.
History Repeats —Ironman (20)	Complete the final mission in a single session without dying.
History Repeats —Stopwatch (25)	Complete the final mission in under 40 minutes.
Killing Spree (50)	Score five kills in a row without dying in multiplayer.
Living Quarter (15)	Complete the sixth mission on Normal difficulty or higher.
Living Quarter —Ironman (20)	Complete the sixth mission in a single session without dying.
Living Quarter) —Stopwatch (25	Complete the sixth mission in under 25 minutes.
Marksman (75)	Finish a ranked match with an accuracy level higher than 40%.

UNLOCKABLE	HOW TO UNLOCK
Noob (0)	Suicide 10 times in a Multiplayer match.
Rampage (75)	Score 10 kills in a row without dying in multiplayer.
The Mountain King (15)	Complete the fifth mission on Normal difficulty or higher.
The Mountain King—Ironman (20)	Complete the fifth mission in a single session without dying.
The Mountain King—Stopwatch (25)	Complete the fifth mission in under 30 minutes.
Top Scorer (50)	Be the player with the highest score on the winning team of a ranked match.

FRONTLINES: FUEL OF WAR (PlayStation 3)

MORE LEVELS

To unlock two extra single-player levels, insert the following passwords at the in-game Passwords menu.

UNLOCKABLE	HOW TO UNLOCK
Urban Level	sp-street
Village Level	sp-village

FULL AUTO (XBOX 360)

To unlock everything, you must make a new profile from the Xbox 360 dashboard.

UNLOCKABLE	PASSWORD
Unlock everything	magicman

FULL AUTO 2: BATTLELINES (PlayStation 3)

In the Option menu, select the Cheats option to enter these codes.

UNLOCKABLE	CODE
Unlock Sceptre and Mini-Rockets	10E6CUSTOMER
Unlock Vulcan and Flamethrower	5FINGERDISCOUNT

FULL AUTO 2: BATTLELINES (PSP)

Enter these codes in the codes section under features.

UNLOCKABLE	CODE
All Cars	⇧, ⇧, ⇧, ⇧, ⇦, ⇩, ⇧, ⇨, ⇩, ⇩, ⇩, ⇩
All Events	START, ⇦, SELECT, ⇨, ⇨, ▲, ×, ■, START, R, ⇩, SELECT

FUZION FRENZY (XBOX)

Enter the following codes after pressing START to pause gameplay. Repeat each code to disable its effect.

UNLOCKABLE	CODE
Enable "Real Controls"	Hold LT and press Y, Y, Y, B.
First-Person Mode	Hold LT and press Y, B, Y, B.
Mutant Mode	Hold LT and press Y, B, X, X. To get Mutant mode two, repeat the code. To return to Mutant mode, repeat the code again. To disable the code, repeat it one more time.
Squeaky Voices	Hold LT and press Y, X, Y, Y.
Turbo Mode (during a mini-game)	Hold LT and press Y, B, X, X.
Welsh Mode	Hold LT and press Y, Y, Y, Y.

G-FORCE (PlayStation 2)

SECRET AGENT MODE

UNLOCKABLE	HOW TO UNLOCK
Secret Agent Mode	Beat the game once on any difficulty.

G.I. JOE: THE RISE OF COBRA (XBOX 360)

CODES

Enter the following codes with the D-pad at the Main menu. A sound effect will play if you entered the code correctly.

EFFECT	CODE
Shana "Scarlett" O'Hara Costume	→,↑,↓,↓,Ⓨ
Duke Costume	←,↑,Ⓧ,↑,→,Ⓨ

GAIN GROUN (Wii)

LEVEL SELECT

UNLOCKABLE	HOW TO UNLOCK
Level Select	On the Options screen press Ⓐ, Ⓒ, Ⓑ, Ⓒ

GALAGA '90 (Wii)

UNLOCKABLES

UNLOCKABLE	HOW TO UNLOCK
Galactic Bonus	Just stand still (don't move) and don't shoot in the bonus stage.
Red Capsule	Hold ↑ and press RUN at the title screen. The capsule on the ship will turn red instead of blue to confirm code entry. Shoot the last target on the first level to capture the red capsule and power-up to a triple ship.

GATE OF THUNDER (Wii)

UNLOCKABLES

UNLOCKABLE	HOW TO UNLOCK
Hidden Bomberman Game	Press ↑, →, ↓, ←, ②. You'll hear a sound and in a moment you'll be at the Bomberman title screen.
Stage Select	At the title screen press: ①, ②, ②, ①, SELECT, ①, ②, ①, ②, SELECT, SELECT, RUN.

GAUNTLET (XBOX 360)

WALLS BECOME EXITS

UNLOCKABLE	HOW TO UNLOCK
Walls Become Exits	On any level, all players must stand still for 200 seconds. After 200 seconds, all the walls in the level will become exit doors. If players wish to, they can shoot enemies, and change the direction of their shooting, just as long as they do not move. This works on single and multiplayer.

GAUNTLET: DARK LEGACY (XBOX)

Enter the following codes as names to access these unlockables.

UNLOCKABLE	NAME
10,000 Gold per Level	10000K
Always Have Nine Potions and Keys	ALLFUL

UNLOCKABLE	NAME
Dwarf in S&M Costume	NUD069
Dwarf Is a Large Jester	ICE600
Invincibility	INVULN
Jester Is a Stick Figure with Baseball Cap Head	KJH105
Jester Is a Stick Figure with Mohawk Head	PNK666
Jester Is a Stick Figure with Smiley Face	STX222
Knight Is a Bald Man in Street Clothes (Sean Gugler)	STG333
Knight Is a Ninja (Sword and Claws)	TAK118
Knight Is a Quarterback	RIZ721
Knight Is a Roman Centurion	BAT900
Knight Is an Orange-Skirted Waitress	KA0292
Knight Wears Black Karate Outfit with Twin Scythes	SJB964
Knight Wears Black Outfit and Cape	DARTHC
Knight Wears Street Clothes	ARV984
Knight Wears Street Clothes (Chris Sutton)	CSS222
Knight Wears Street Clothes and Baseball Cap	DIB626
Permanent Anti-Death	1ANGEL
Permanent Full Turbo	PURPLE
Permanent Invisibility	000000
Permanent Pojo the Chicken	EGG911
Permanent Reflect Shot	REFLEX
Permanent Shrink Enemy and Growth	DELTA1

GAUNTLET: DARK LEGACY (PlayStation 2)

Enter the codes in the spot where you name new characters. You can only utilize one special character or game mode at a time. Choose the character type (i.e. Dwarf, Valkyrie, etc.), as well as naming that character according to the code. Use special game modes (i.e., Unlimited Supershot, Unlimited Invulnerability) with any character type.

UNLOCKABLE	CODE
$10,000 Gold per level	10000K
9 Keys and 9 Potions Per Level	ALLFUL
Battle General (Knight)	BAT900
Castle General (Warrior)	CAS400
Chainsaw Jester	KJH105
Cheerleader (Valkyrie)	CEL721
Created By Don (Knight)	ARV984
Desert General (Wizard)	DES700
Dwarf General	ICE600
Employee Stig (Knight)	STG333
Ex-Employee Chris (Knight)	CSS222
Football Dude (Knight)	RIZ721
Happy Face Jester	STX222
Karate Steve (Knight)	SJB964
Manager Mike (Knight)	DIB626
Mountain General (Warrior)	MTN200
Ninja (Knight)	TAK118
Punkrock Jester	PNK666
Rat Knight (Warrior)	RAT333
Regular Garm (Wizard)	GARM99
S & M Dwarf	NUD069
School Girl (Valkyrie)	AYA555

Sickly Garm (Wizard)	GARM00
Sky General (Wizard)	SKY100
Sumner (Wizard)	SUM224
Town General (Valkyrie)	TWN300
Unlimited 3 Way Shot	MENAGE
Unlimited Extra Speed	XSPEED
Unlimited Full Turbo	Purple
Unlimited Halo and Levitate	1ANGLI
Unlimited Invisibility	000000
Unlimited Invulnerability	INVULN
Unlimited Play As Pojo	EGG911
Unlimited Rapid Fire	QCKSHT
Unlimited Reflective Shot	REFLEX
Unlimited Shrink Enemy and Growth	DELTA1
Unlimited Supershot	SSHOTS
Unlimited X-Ray Glasses	PEEKIN
Waitress (Knight)	KA0292

GEARS OF WAR (XBOX 360)

UNLOCKABLE	HOW TO UNLOCK
Insane Difficulty	Complete the game on either Casual or Hardcore difficulty.
Secret Gamer Pic	Complete the game on Insane difficulty to unlock a secret gamer picture.
Secret Gamer Pic #2	Unlock the "Seriously..." achievement by getting 10,000 kills in ranked multiplayer matches to get that respective GamerPic.

GEARS OF WAR 2 (XBOX 360)

SKINS

Successfully complete the following tasks to unlock the corresponding skin in multiplayer mode.

UNLOCKABLE	HOW TO UNLOCK
Anthony Carmine	Successfully complete Act 1 in the original Gears Of War.
Dizzy Wallin	Successfully complete Act 1 in single-player mode.
Flame Grenadier	Successfully complete Act 4 in single-player mode.
Kantus	Successfully complete Act 2 in single-player mode.
Lt. Minh Young Kim	Find 10 COG tags in the original Gears Of War.
RAAM	Defeat RAAM in the original Gears of War on Hardcore difficulty.
Skorge	Successfully complete Act 5 in single-player mode.
Tai Kaliso	Successfully complete Act 3 in single-player mode.

GENPEI TOUMADEN (Wii)

UNLOCKABLE

UNLOCKABLE	HOW TO UNLOCK
Options Menu	At the title screen, press ↑, →, ↓, ←, ①, ②

THE GETAWAY (PlayStation 2)

During the opening movie, press the following buttons to access these cheats:

UNLOCKABLE	CODE
Armored Car Weapon	↑,↓,←,→,■,▲,●

UNLOCKABLE	CODE
Double Health	↑,↑,←,←,→,→,●,●,↓
Free Roam Mode and Credits	▲,▲,▲,←,■,▲,▲,▲,←,●
Unlimited Ammo	↑,↓,←,→,▲,↑,↓,←,→,■

GHOSTBUSTERS THE VIDEOGAME (XBOX 360)

NES GHOSTBUSTERS ENDING SCREEN

In the Ghostbusters headquarters, one of the monitors on the upstairs desk has the ending screen from the original Ghostbusters game on the NES. The monitor comes complete with all the spelling and punctuation errors.

GHOSTBUSTERS THE VIDEOGAME (PlayStation 3)

NES GHOSTBUSTERS ENDING SCREEN

In the Ghostbusters headquarters, one of the monitors on the upstairs desks has the ending screen from the original Ghostbusters game on the NES. The monitor comes complete with all the spelling and punctuation errors.

GHOSTBUSTERS THE VIDEOGAME (Wii)

UNLOCKABLES

Complete the tasks to unlock the following active mods.

UNLOCKABLE	HOW TO UNLOCK
Equipment Strength Upgrade	Collect all of the Art.
Faster Health Recovery	Collect 50% of the Art.
Gozerian Rookie Outfit (Immune to Sliming)	Beat the game on Gozerian (Hard) difficulty.
Increased Scanning Speed	Scan 50% of ghosts and/or scannable objects in the game.
Invulnerability	Collect all of the Art and scan data and beat the game.
No Equipment Overheat	Collect all scan data.

GHOSTBUSTERS THE VIDEOGAME (PlayStation 2)

UNLOCKABLES

Complete the tasks to unlock the following active mods

UNLOCKABLE	HOW TO UNLOCK
Equipment Strength Upgrade	Get all 103 illustrations (100%) for Tobin's Spirit Guide.
Faster Health Regeneration	Get over 50% of illustrations for Tobin's Spirit Guide.
Gozerian Rookie Outfit	Get 100% Completion on Gozerian difficulty.
Increased Scanning Speed	Get over 50% of scans for Tobin's Spirit Guide.
Invulnerability	Get 100% Completion on any difficulty.
No Equipment Overheat	Get all 103 scans (100%) for Tobin's Spirit Guide.

GHOSTHUNTER (PlayStation 2)

DESCRIPTION	CODE
Increase damage	Hold right on d-pad while pressing L3 for 5 seconds, then press ●
Laz never dies	Hold right on d-pad while pressing L3 for 5 seconds, then press ▲

GHOULS 'N GHOSTS (Wii)

UNLOCKABLES

UNLOCKABLE	HOW TO UNLOCK
Japanese Mode	Enter the Options menu. Choose "26" for the music and "56" for sound selections, then hold ✥+ Ⓐ+Ⓑ+Ⓒ+START.

Slow-Mo	At the title screen, press ↑, Ⓐ, ↓, Ⓐ, ←, Ⓐ, →, Ⓐ. Begin the game, press START to pause, and hold Ⓑ and unpause.

LEVEL SELECT

Press ↑, ↓, ←, → repeatedly at the title screen. You'll hear a harp if you did it right. Enter one of the following controller actions to select the corresponding level.

EFFECT	CODE
The Execution Place	Press START
The Floating Island	Press Ⓐ, START
The Village of Decay	Press ↑, START
Town of Fire	Press ↑+Ⓐ, START
Baron Rankle's Tower	Press ↓, START
Horrible Faced Mountain	Press ↓+Ⓐ, START
The Crystal Forest	Press ←, START
The Ice Slopes	Press ←+Ⓐ, START
Beginning of Castle	Press →, START
Middle of Castle	Press →+Ⓐ, START
Loki	Press ↘, START

DEBUG MODE

While "Press Start Button" is flashing at the title screen, input Ⓐ, Ⓐ, Ⓐ, Ⓐ, ↑, ↓, ←, → and you hear a chime. Start the game and you are in debug mode. Three functions can be accessed from the Pause menu now.

CODE	EFFECT
Tap ↓ During Pause	Frame Advance
Pause, Ⓐ, Pause	Invincibility Toggle (falling is still fatal)
Hold Ⓑ During Pause	Slow Motion

GLADIUS (XBOX)

Enter these codes while paused in different locations.

UNLOCKABLE	CODE
1,000 Dinars every time you input this code	Paused in the school →, ↓, ←, ↑, ←, ←, ←, ←, Ⓨ, ←
1,000 exp. points every time you input this code	Paused in the school →, ↓, ←, ↑, ←, ←, ←, ←, Ⓨ, →
Control camera	Pause during combat ↑, ←, ↓, →, →, →, →, →, ↑, ↑, ↑, ↑
Higher level enemies	Pause at a league office →, →, →, ↑, ↑, ←, ←, ←, ←, →, ↑, ↑, ↑, ↑, ↓
Lower Level Enemies & Recruits	Pause at a league office →, →, →, ↑, ↑, ←, ←, ←, ←, →, ↓, ↓, ↓, ↓, ↑

GLADIUS (PlayStation 2)

At school, pause the game and enter the following codes.

UNLOCKABLE	CODE
Equip Anything	→, ↓, ←, ↑, ←, ←, ←, ←, ▲, ▲, ▲
More Experience	→, ↓, ←, ↑, ←, ←, ←, ←, ▲, →
More Money	→, ↓, ←, ↑, ←, ←, ←, ←, ▲, ←

THE GODFATHER (XBOX 360)

CHEAT CODES

CODE	EFFECT
Ⓨ ← Ⓨ → Ⓧ →	Full Ammo
← Ⓧ → Ⓨ → LB	Full Health
Ⓨ Ⓧ Ⓨ Ⓧ Ⓨ LB **(click)**	Film Clips

INFINITE AMMO

UNLOCKABLE	HOW TO UNLOCK
Infinite Ammo	Become Don of NYC

THE GODFATHER (XBOX)

UNLOCKABLE	CODE
$5,000	Ⓧ, Ⓨ, Ⓧ, Ⓧ, Ⓨ, Ⓛ
Full Ammo	Ⓨ, ◀, Ⓨ, ▶, ▼, Ⓡ
Full Health	◀, Ⓧ, ▶, Ⓨ, ▶, Ⓛ

Enter this code on the Join Family menu.

UNLOCKABLE	CODE
Unlock All Movies	Ⓨ, Ⓧ, Ⓨ, Ⓧ, Ⓧ, Ⓛ

THE GODFATHER (PlayStation 2)

These codes can be entered on the pause screen.

UNLOCKABLE	CODE
$5,000	■, ●, ■, ■, ●, L3
Full Ammo	●, ⇦, ●, ⇨, ■, L3
Full Health	⇦, ■, ⇨, ●, ⇨, L3

Enter this code on the Join Family menu.

UNLOCKABLE	CODE
Unlock All Movies	●, ■, ●, ■, ■, L3

THE GODFATHER: BLACKHAND EDITION (Wii)

Enter these codes while the game is paused. For the film clips, enter that clip in the Film Archives screen.

UNLOCKABLE	CODE
$5,000	⊖, ②, ⊖, ⊖, ②, ✚ (Up)
Full Ammo	②, ✚ (Left), ②, ✚ (Right), ⊖, ✚ (Down)
Full Health	✚ (Left), ⊖, ✚ (Right), ②, ✚ (Right), ✚ (Up)
Unlock Film Clips	②, ⊖, ②, ⊖, ⊖, ✚ (Up)

THESE CODES MAY ONLY BE ENTERED ROUGHLY EVERY FIVE MINUTES. IF YOU REALLY NEED THE HEALTH OR AMMO BEFORE FIVE MINUTES, PAUSE AND WAIT A FEW MINUTES, THEN ENTER THE GAME.

THE GODFATHER: THE DON'S EDITION (PlayStation 3)

Enter these codes while the game is paused.

UNLOCKABLE	CODE
$5,000	■, ▲, ■, ■, ▲, L2
Full Ammo	▲, ⇦, ▲, ⇨, ■, R1
Full Health	⇦, ■, ⇨, ▲, ⇨, L2

GODZILLA: UNLEASHED (Wii)

CODES

At the main menu, press Ⓐ and ✚ (Up) at the same time.

CODE	EFFECT
31406	Add 90,000 store points.
0829XX	Set day (where the "xx" equals the actual day you wish to set to).
411411	Show monster moves.
787321	Toggle version number.
204935	Unlock everything.

MONSTERS

After you complete the following tasks, you unlock the corresponding monster.

UNLOCKABLE	HOW TO UNLOCK
Baragon	Free Baragon from the crystals in "A Friend in Need" at Monster Island as an Alien. Defeat him in the "Baragon" stage and buy him for 15,000 points.
Biollante	Be an Earth Defender and play "Rumble in the Surf" at Tokyo. Destroy the building with vines, defeat Biollante later on, and buy her for 30,000 pts.
Krystalak	Play "Terran Mind-Control" at New York as an Alien. Destroy large crystal in crater and nine days later defeat Krystalak and buy him for 20,000 pts.
Mecha-King Ghidorah	Play "Invasion" as an Earth Defender at San Francisco and defeat Ghidorah. Play "M.K.G" and defeat Mecha Ghidorah and buy him for 50,000 points.
Megagurius	Be an ED and play "Enter General Gyozen" at London. Destroy three teal crystals. Return near the end and defeat Megaguirus. Buy her for 20,000 pts.
Obsidius	Play a mech from GDF and play "Big Trouble" at Seattle. Destroy three cone crystals. Defeat Obsidius later and buy him for 20,000 pts.
SpaceGodzilla	Play as a Mutant, obtain four Power Surges, and beat "Tyrant" at the end of the game. SpaceGodzilla gets added to the shop and costs 100,000.
Titanosaurus	Use a mech from GDF and play "Soloist" at Sydney. Destroy three circular ice structures. Return later and defeat the dinosaur. Buy him for 25,000 pts.
Varan	Play as an Alien and destroy the crystals on the Mothership in "On the Mothership." Return to the level and defeat Varan and buy him for 30,000 pts.
Godzilla 90s	Buy a monster from each faction or beat the game with a monster from each faction. Then buy him for 20,000 points.
Godzilla 1954	Unlock every monster for purchase or play a set number of hours. Then buy him for 100,000 points.

GOLDEN AXE (Wii)

UNLOCKABLES

UNLOCKABLE	HOW TO UNLOCK
9 Continues	Hold ✚+Ⓐ+Ⓒ. Release and press START.
Level Select	Select Arcade mode. Hold ✚+Ⓑ and press START at the Character Selection screen. A number that corresponds to the starting level appears in the screen's upper left. Use the D-pad to change it to the level you want.

GOLDEN AXE 2 (Wii)

UNLOCKABLES

UNLOCKABLE	HOW TO UNLOCK
Level Select	While the opening screen scrolls, simultaneously hold down Ⓐ+Ⓑ+Ⓒ+START. Still holding Ⓐ, release Ⓑ+Ⓒ and press them again. This brings you to the Options screen. Still holding Ⓐ, let go of the other two, pick "exit," and press Ⓑ+Ⓒ once more. You'll be back at the main menu. Still holding Ⓐ, release Ⓑ+Ⓒ and hit them again to choose the number of players. Keep all the buttons down and press START. Release only START, select your character, then still holding down Ⓐ+Ⓑ+Ⓒ, press ✚ and hit START. You can now select the level you want to play.
Level Select and 8 Credits (ultimate procedure)	With the cursor go to "Options" sign. Now press and hold Ⓐ+Ⓑ+Ⓒ. In the Options screen, release only Ⓑ+Ⓒ. Now configure the game if you want. Use Ⓑ to confirm successive selections, until the warrior selection. For the 8 credits, the cheat is identical, but release only Ⓐ and use START to confirm successive selections.

NEW! A B C D E F G H I J K L M N O P Q R S T U V W X Y Z

GOLDEN AXE: BEAST RIDER (XBOX 360)

COSTUMES

UNLOCKABLE	HOW TO UNLOCK
The Classic Look	Finish Death=Adder
Diyar Tracker	Finish Firstborn
Fiend's Battle Path Armor	Finish the Last Titan
Undead Scout	Finish Queen of the Dead
Wastelands Scout	Finish Secondborn

GOLDEN EYE: ROGUE AGENT (XBOX)

In the Extras menu, enter the following:

UNLOCKABLE	CODE
Paintball Mode	→, ←, →, ←, ↓, ↓, ↑, ↑
Unlock All Skins in Multiplayer	↓, ←, ↑, ←, →, ↓, ←, ↑

GOLDEN EYE: ROGUE AGENT (PlayStation 2)

Enter these codes while the games is paused.

UNLOCKABLE	CODE
All Eye Powers	L1, L1, R2, R2, R1, R2, L1, L2
Full Health and Armor	R1, R1, R2, L2, R2, R1, L1, R2
Fully Charge Eye power	L1, R1, L1, L2, L2, R2, R1, L2

Enter these codes at the Extras Screen.

UNLOCKABLE	CODE
No Eye powers in multiplayer mode	↑, ↑, ↓, ←, →, →, ←, ↓
One-Life mode	←, ↓, ↑, →, ↑, →, ←, ↓
Unlock all levels	↓, →, ↓, →, ↑, ↓, ↑, ←

GOTTLIEB PINBALL CLASSICS (Wii)

PASSWORDS

PASSWORD	EFFECT
NYC	Unlock Central Park Table
LIS	Unlock Free Play in Black Hole table
PHF	Unlock Free Play in Goin' Nuts table
HOT	Unlock Free Play in Love Meter
HEF	Unlock Free Play in Playboy table
PBA	Unlock Free Play in Strikes 'N Spares table
PGA	Unlock Free Play in Tee'd Off table
BIG	Unlock Free Play in Xoltan

UNLOCKABLES

UNLOCKABLE	HOW TO UNLOCK
Goin Nuts: Free Play Mode	Complete the table goal for El Dorado
Teed Off: Free Play Mode	Complete the table goal for Big Shot

GRABBED BY THE GHOULIES (XBOX)

UNLOCKABLE	CODE
20 Challenges	Collect 100 Rare Bonus Books
21st Challenge	Get Gold on all 20 Challenges

GRADIUS (Wii)

UNLOCKABLES

UNLOCKABLE	HOW TO UNLOCK
10,000 Bonus Points	Get 6 power-ups so that the ? box is selected, then, when the thousands digit of your score is a 5, get a 7th power-up
Continue	At the Game Over Screen, press ↓, ↑, Ⓑ, Ⓐ, Ⓑ, Ⓐ, Ⓑ, Ⓐ, START (once per game)
Full Option Command	Press START during the game, then press ↑, ↑, ↓, ↓, ←, →, ←, →, Ⓑ, Ⓐ, START.
Warp to Level 3 (after defeating Core Fighter)	In level 1, when the thousands digit of your score is even, destroy 4 hatches
Warp to Level 4	Destroy Xaerous Core at end of level 2 within 2 seconds of its core turning blue
Warp to Level 5 (after beating level)	Destroy 10 stone heads in level 3

GRADIUS 2 (Wii)

UNLOCKABLES

UNLOCKABLE	HOW TO UNLOCK
30 Lives	At the title screen, press ↑,↑, ↓, ↓, ←, →, ←, →, Ⓑ, Ⓐ
Max Out Abilities	During game, press ↑, ↑, ↓, ↓, ←, →, ←, →, Ⓑ, Ⓐ (once per level)
Sound Test Menu	Hold Ⓐ+Ⓑ and turn on. When the screen comes up, press START, hold Ⓐ+Ⓑ until title screen, then press START again.

GRADIUS 3 (Wii)

UNLOCKABLES

UNLOCKABLE	HOW TO UNLOCK
30 Extra Ships	At the title screen, hold ←Ⓒ and press ⓧ, ⓧ, ⓧ, START
Arcade Mode	In the Options menu, highlight the Game Level, and rapidly tap Ⓐ until the level turns into ARCADE
Extra Credits	At the title screen, press ↓ as many times as you can and then press START before the screen fades out
Easy Final Boss attack	The final boss, Bacterion, will die whether or not you him. Just dodge his blasts, and in 15 or so seconds, he will spontaneously die. Even cheaper, park your ship in the screen's bottom center, and you can't be hit!
Extended Demo Mode	Continue to hold Ⓐ through the initial demo, and you'll see the entire first stage including the boss.
Full Power-Up	Pause the game and press ↑Ⓒ,↑Ⓒ,↓Ⓒ,↓Ⓒ,←Ⓒ,Ⓒ→,←Ⓒ,Ⓒ→,Ⓨ,ⓧ
Full Power-Up (without using the code)	Choose "speed down" for the "!" option in the Weapon highlight Select screen. If you can get enough power-ups to the last weapon, which will not be visible, and use it without powering up on speed up, you get all four options, missiles, and the shield. But if you have the laser already, it will be taken away.
Random Weapon Select	At the Weapon Select screen, press Ⓒ→ to enter Edit mode, then press ↓, ↑Ⓒ, ↓, ↓, ↑Ⓒ, ↑Ⓒ, ↓, ↑Ⓒ
Spread the Options	Activate the R-Option and collect enough power-ups that the option selection is highlighted. Now press and hold Ⓐ.
Suicide	Pause the game and press ↑Ⓒ, ↑Ⓒ, ↓Ⓒ, ↓Ⓒ, ←Ⓒ, Ⓒ→, ←Ⓒ, Ⓒ→, Ⓨ, Ⓐ, START

BONUS STAGES

When you clear a bonus stage, you end up in the next level. That's right, you don't have to fight the boss of the level you were in previously. However, if you get killed in the bonus stage, you go back to the regular level, and cannot reenter the bonus stage.

STAGE	HOW TO UNLOCK
Stage 2	When you see a hole in the wall at the bottom of the screen, fly down there. Prerequisite: None.
Stage 3	When you reach the lower level, a platform in the ceiling drops down. Fly just below the part where the platform was. Prerequisite: Destroy all of the ground targets in the stage up to that point.
Stage 4	In the last set of Moai heads (they look like Easter Island heads), one that's lying down lifts up. Fly behind it. Prerequisite: Nothing must be highlighted on your power-up bar.
Stage 5	Fly just below the ceiling before the narrow corridor. Prerequisite: The hundreds digit of your score reads 5, 7, or 3.
Stage 7	Just after the long downward slope in the second half of the level, stay close to the ground and fly into the wall formation shaped like this: ..../ ....\ _____*/ (Key: dots are empty space, lines are walls, the asterisk is where your ship should be.) Prerequisite: Unknown.

GRADIUS COLLECTION (PSP)

CODES

Unlockable	How to Unlock
All Power-ups and Weapons	Pause the game and then insert the famous "Konami Code": ↑,↑,↓,↓,←,→,←,→,←,→

GRAN TURISMO 5 PROLOGUE (PlayStation 3)

UNLOCKABLES

UNLOCKABLE	HOW TO UNLOCK
BMW Concept 1 Series tii '07	Beat all Class B Races.
Daihatsu OFC-1	Beat all Class C Races.
Nissan GT-R Proto '05	Beat all Class S Races.
Nissan Skyline Coupe Concept '07	Beat all Class A Races.
S Class Events	Complete all main A, B, and C Classes with at least Bronze Medal or better.

GRAND THEFT AUTO 3 (XBOX)

UNLOCKABLE	CODE
All Weapons	BLK, BLK, LT, BLK, ←,↓,→,↑,←,↓,→,↑
Full Health	BLK, BLK, LT, RT, ←,↓,→,↑,←,↓,→,↑
Full Armor	BLK, BLK, LT, WHT, ←,↓,→,↑,←,↓,→,↑

GRAND THEFT AUTO 3 (XBOX)

UNLOCKABLE	CODE
All Weapons	BLK, BLK, LT, BLK, ←,↓,→,↑,←,↓,→,↑
Full Health	BLK, BLK, LT, RT, ←,↓,→,↑,←,↓,→,↑
Full Armor	BLK, BLK, LT, WHT, ←,↓,→,↑,←,↓,→,↑

GRAND THEFT AUTO 4 (XBOX 360)

CODES

During gameplay, pull out Niko's phone and dial these numbers for the corresponding effect. Cheats will affect missions and Achievements.

EFFECT	CODE
Change weather	468-555-0100
Get the Ak-47, knife, Molotov Cocktails, pistol, RPG, sniper rifle and Uzi, and "Cleaned the Mean Streets" Achievement blocked	486-555-0150
Get the baseball bat, grenades, M4, MP5, pistol, RPG, and sniper rifle, and "Cleaned the Mean Streets" Achievement blocked	486-555-0100
Raise wanted level	267-555-0150
Remove wanted level; "One Man Army" and "Walk Free" Achievements blocked	267-555-0100
Restore armor; "Cleaned the Mean Streets," "Finish Him," "One Man Army," and "Walk Free" Achievements blocked	362-555-0100
Restore health; "Cleaned the Mean Streets" Achievement blocked	482-555-0100
Spawn a Cognoscenti	227-555-0142
Spawn a Comet	227-555-0175
Spawn a Jetmax	938-555-0100
Spawn a Sanchez	625-555-0150
Spawn a SuperGT	227-555-0168
Spawn a Turismo	227-555-0147
Spawn an Annihilator; "One Man Army" and "Walk Free" Achievements blocked	359-555-0100
Spawn an FIB Buffalo	227-555-0100
Spawn an NRG-900	625-555-0100

MAP LOCATIONS

Enter the password into any of the in-game computers.

EFFECT	CODE
Weapon, health, armor, vehicle, pigeon, ramp/stunt, and entertainment locations	www.whattheydonotwantyoutoknow.com

ACHIEVEMENTS

UNLOCKABLE	HOW TO UNLOCK
Assassin's Greed	Complete all 9 assassin missions: 20 points
Auf Wiedersehen, Petrovic	Win all ranked multiplayer variations, all races, and Cops 'n' Crooks, as both sides: 30 points
Chain Reaction	Blow up 10 vehicles in 10 seconds: 20 points
Cleaned the Mean Streets	Capture 20 criminals through the police computer: 20 points
Courier Service	Complete all 10 package delivery jobs: 10 points
Cut Your Teeth	Earn a personal rank promotion in multiplayer: 5 points
Dare Devil	Complete 100% of the unique stunt jumps: 30 points
Dial B for Bomb	Unlock the special ability of phoning for a bomb to be placed: 10 points
Driving Mr. Bellic	Unlock the special ability of taxi: 10 points
Endangered Species	Collect every hidden package: 50 points
Fed the Fish	Complete the mission "Uncle Vlad": 5 points
Finish Him	Complete 10 melee counters in 4 minutes: 15 points
Fly the Coop	Beat Rockstars time in ranked versions of Deal Breaker, Hangman's NOOSE, and Bomb da Base II: 15 points
Full Exploration	Unlock all the islands
Genetically Superior	Come first in 20 single-player street races: 25 points

UNLOCKABLE	HOW TO UNLOCK
Gobble Gobble	Score 3 strikes in a row, a turkey, in 10-pin bowling: 10 points
Gracefully Taken	Complete mission "I'll Take Her": 10 points
Half Million	Reach a balance of $500,000: 55 points
Impossible Trinity	Complete mission "Museum Piece": 10 points
It'll Cost Ya	Complete a taxi ride without skipping from one island to another: 5 points
Join the Midnight Club	Win a ranked multiplayer race without damaging your vehicle too much and have damage enabled: 10 points
Key to the City	Achieve 100% in "Game progress" statistic: 100 points
King of QUB3D	Beat the High Score in QUB3D: 15 points
Let Sleeping Rockstars Lie	Kill a Rockstar developer in a ranked multiplayer match: 10 points
Liberty City (5)	After you meet all friends, the ones left alive like you above 90%: 20 points
Liberty City Minute	Complete the story missions in less than 30 hours: 30 points
Lowest Point	Complete mission "Roman's Sorrow": 5 points
Manhunt	Complete the most wanted side missions from police computer: 15 points
No More Strangers	Meet all random characters: 5 points
Off the Boat	Complete the first mission: 5 points
One Hundred and Eighty	In a game of darts, score 180 with only 3 darts: 10 points
One Man Army	Survive 5 minutes on 6-star wanted level: 40 points
Order Fulfilled	Complete all 10 Exotic Export orders: 10 points
Pool Shark	Beat a friend at pool: 10 points
Retail Therapy	Unlock the ability to buy guns from a friend: 10 points
Rolled Over	Do 5 car rolls in a row from one crash: 30 points
Sightseer	Fly on all helicopter tours of Liberty City: 5 points
Taking It for the Team	Be on the winning team in all ranked multiplayer games: 10 points
Teamplayer	Kill five players who are not in your team, in any ranked multiplayer team game: 10 points
That Special Someone	Complete the mission "That Special Someone": 10 points
That's How We Roll!	Unlock the special ability of helicopter: 10 points
Top of the Food Chain	Kill 20 players with a pistol in a ranked multiplayer deathmatch : 10 points
Top the Midnight Club	Come first in 20 different ranked standard multiplayer races: 20 points Wanted
Under the Radar	Fly underneath the main bridges in the game that cross water with a helicopter : 40 points
Walk Free	Lose a 4-star wanted level by outrunning the cops: 50 points
Wanted	Achieve the highest personal rank in multiplayer: 20 points
Warm Coffee	Successfully date a girl to be invited into her house: 5 points
Wheelie Rider	Do a wheelie lasting at least 500 feet on a motorbike: 30 points
You Got the Message	Deliver all 30 cars ordered through text messages: 20 points
You Won!	Complete the final mission: 60 points

UNLOCKABLES

UNLOCKABLE	HOW TO UNLOCK
Annihilator Helicopter	Kill all 200 Flying Rats (Pigeons)

EASTER EGGS

UNLOCKABLE	HOW TO UNLOCK
The Heart of Liberty City	Gain access to Happiness Island. Once you're able to go there legally, find the Helicopter Tours (which is directly east of Happiness Island) and steal a helicopter. Fly over the Statue of Liberty and jump out at the statue's feet. Land on the topmost tier of the statue, which is basically a square platform with a door in the center of each side. Look for a door with a plaque on either side of it that reads, "No Hidden Content Here." Don't try to open the door; just walk through it. Inside, you'll find an empty room with a tall ladder. Climb it, and when you reach the top, look up; there is a gigantic beating heart, held in place by chains.

CODES

During gameplay, pull out Niko's phone and dial these numbers for the corresponding effect. Cheats will affect missions and achievements.

EFFECT	CODE
Banshee	265-555-2423
Feltzer	662-555-0147
Presidente	265-555-2423
Song Information	948-555-0100

FRIENDSHIP BONUSES

Gain the following bonuses by gaining the corresponding amount of friendship.

UNLOCKABLE	HOW TO UNLOCK
Boom? (Call Packie for him to make you a car bomb)	Gain 75% friendship with Packie.
Chopper Ride (He will pick you up in his helicopter)	Gain 70% friendship with Brucie.
Discount Guns (Buy weapons at a cheaper price from Little Jacob)	Gain 60% friendship with Little Jacob.
Extra Help (A car of gang members will be sent to help you out)	Gain 60% friendship with Dwayne.
Free Ride (Call for a taxi)	Gain 60% friendship with Roman.

UNLOCKABLES

UNLOCKABLE	HOW TO UNLOCK
Rastah Color Huntley SUV	Complete 10 Package Delivery missions.
Remove Ammo Limit	Get 100% completion.

GRAND THEFT AUTO 4 (PlayStation 3)

CODES

During gameplay, pull out Niko's phone and dial these numbers for the corresponding effect. Cheats will affect missions and achievements.

EFFECT	CODE
Change weather	468-555-0100
Get the Ak-47, knife, Molotov Cocktails, pistol, RPG, sniper rifle and Uzi	486-555-0150
Get the baseball bat, grenades, M4, MP5, pistol, RPG, and sniper rifle	486-555-0100
Raise wanted level	267-555-0150
Remove wanted level	267-555-0100
Restore armor	362-555-0100
Restore health	482-555-0100
Spawn a Cognoscenti	227-555-0142

EFFECT	CODE
Spawn a Comet	227-555-0175
Spawn a Jetmax	938-555-0100
Spawn a Sanchez	625-555-0150
Spawn a SuperGT	227-555-0168
Spawn a Turismo	227-555-0147
Spawn an Annihilator	359-555-0100
Spawn an FIB Buffalo	227-555-0100
Spawn an NRG-900	625-555-0100

MAP LOCATIONS

Enter the password into any of the in-game computers.

EFFECT	CODE
Weapon, health, armor, vehicle, pigeon, ramp/stunt, and entertainment locations	www.whattheydonotwantyoutoknow.com

UNLOCKABLES

UNLOCKABLE	HOW TO UNLOCK
Annihilator Helicopter	Kill all 200 Flying Rats (Pigeons)

EASTER EGGS

UNLOCKABLE	HOW TO UNLOCK
The Heart of Liberty City	Gain access to Happiness Island. Once you're able to go there legally, find the Helicopter Tours (which is directly east of Happiness Island) and steal a helicopter. Fly over the Statue of Liberty and jump out at the statue's feet. Land on the topmost tier of the statue, which is basically a square platform with a door in the center of each side. Look for a door with a plaque on either side of it that reads, "No Hidden Content Here." Don't try to open the door; just walk through it. Inside, you'll find an empty room with a tall ladder. Climb it, and when you reach the top, look up;there is a gigantic beating heart, held in place by chains.

FRIENDSHIP BONUSES

Gain the following bonuses by gaining the corresponding amount of friendship.

UNLOCKABLE	HOW TO UNLOCK
Boom? (Call Packie for him to make you a car bomb)	Gain 75% friendship with Packie.
Chopper Ride (He will pick you up in his helicopter)	Gain 70% friendship with Brucie.
Discount Guns (Buy weapons at a cheaper price from Little Jacob)	Gain 60% friendship with Little Jacob.
Extra Help (A car of gang members will be sent to help you out)	Gain 60% friendship with Dwayne.
Free Ride (Call for a taxi)	Gain 60% friendship with Roman.
50% Off for All Clothing Stores	Gain 80% Relationship Status with Alex.
Health Boost (Call Carmen and select "Health Boost")	Gain 80% Relationship Status with Carmen.
Remove Up to 3 Wanted Stars (Call Kiki and select "Remove Wanted")	Gain 80% Relationship Status with Kiki.

UNLOCKABLES

UNLOCKABLE	HOW TO UNLOCK
Rastah Color Huntley SUV	Complete 10 Package Delivery missions.
Remove Ammo Limit	Get 100% completion.

GRAND THEFT AUTO 4: THE BALLAD OF GAY TONY (XBOX 360)

CODES

EFFECT	CODE
Akuma (Bike)	625-555-0200
APC(Tank)	272-555-8265
Buzzard(Helicopter)	359-555-2899
Change Weather	468-555-0100
Floater(Boat)	938-555-0150
Health & Armor	362-555-0100
Health, Armor and Advanced Weapons	482-555-0100
Parachute	359-555-7272
Raise Wanted Level	267-555-0150
Remove Wanted Level	267-555-0100
Sniper rifle bullets explode	486-555-2526
Spawn Annihilator	359-555-0100
Spawn Bullet GT	227-555-9666
Spawn Cognoscenti	227-555-0142
Spawn Comet	227-555-0175
Spawn Jetmax	938-555-0100
Spawn NRG-900	625-555-0100
Spawn Sanchez	625-555-0150
Spawn Super GT	227-555-0168
Spawn Turismo	227-555-0147
Spawns a FIB Buffalo	227-555-0100
Super Punch (exploding punches)	276-555-2666
Vader(Bike)	625-555-3273
Weapons (Advanced) (New Weapons)	486-555-0100
Weapons (Poor)	486-555-0150

UNLOCKABLES

UNLOCKABLE	HOW TO UNLOCK
.44 in Safehouse	Complete 10 gang wars.
Advanced MG in Safehouse	Complete 20 gang wars.
Explosive Shotgun in Safehouse	Complete 30 gang wars.
Gold SMG in Safehouse	Complete 50 gang wars.
NOOSE APC at construction site	Kill all 50 seagulls.
Parachute in Safehouse	Complete all 20 base jumps.
Remove ammo cap	Achieve 100% completion.
Sticky Bombs in Safehouse	Complete 40 gang wars.
Yellow Super Drop Diamond outside Yusef's Apartment	Beat the game.

GRAND THEFT AUTO: CHINATOWN WARS (DS)

CODES

Enter these during gameplay without pausing

EFFECT	CODE
Armor	L, L, R, B, B, A, A, R
cloud	Up, Down, Left, Right, X, Y, L, R
Explosive Pistol Round	L, R, X, Y, A, B, Up, Down
health	L, L, R, A, A, B, B, R
Hurricane	Up, Down, Left, Right, B, Y, R, L

EFFECT	CODE
lots of rain	Up, Down, Left, Right, A, X, R, L
rain	Up, Down, Left, Right, Y, A, L, R
sunny	Up, Down, Left, Right, A, B, L, R
wanted level down	R, X, X, Y, Y, R, L, L
wanted level up	L, L, R, Y, Y, X, X, R
weapons 1 (grenade, nightstick, pistol, minigun, assault, micro SMG, stubby shotgun)	R, Up, B, Down, Left, R, B, Right
weapons 2 (molotov, taser, dual pistols, flamethrower, carbine, SMG, dual-barrel)	R, Up, A, Down, Left, R, A, Right
weapons 3 (mine, chainsaw, revolver, flamethrower, carbine, SMG, dual-barrel)	R, Up, Y, Down, Left, R, Y, Right
weapons 4 (flashbang, bat, pistol, RPG, carbine, micro SMG, stubby shotgun)	R, Up, X, Down, Left, R, X, Right

UNLOCKABLES

UNLOCKABLE	HOW TO UNLOCK
Discount on the Ammu-nation store	Score gold medals on all weapons at the Gun-Club.
Gold medal	Attain a score of 10,000 or more for a weapon.
Immunity to Fire	Get a Gold in the Fire Truck minigame.
Increased body armor strength	Complete all 5 waves of vigilante missions with 100% kill rate.
Infinite Sprint	Complete 5 Paramedic Missions.
Regenerating health	Beat both noodle delivery missions (to gold ranking).
Upgraded delivery bag	Beat both mail courier missions (to gold ranking).

UNLOCKABLE CARS

UNLOCKABLE	HOW TO UNLOCK
500 XLR8	Get a bronze medal in all Algonquin races
Banshee	Complete the mission "Weapons of Mass Destruction."
Bulldozer	Complete the mission "Counterfeit Gangster."
Cityscape	Get a bronze medal in all time trials.
Cognoscetti	Complete the mission "Grave Situation."
Comet	Complete the mission "Jackin' Chan".
Coquette	Complete the mission "Raw Deal."
Formula R	Get a bronze medal in all street races.
Go-Kart	Get a bronze medal in all Go-Kart time trials.
Hearse	Complete the mission "Wheelman."
Hellenbach	Complete the mission "Bomb Disposal."
Infernus	Complete the mission "Cash & Burn."
Limo	Complete all of Guy's missions.
MK GT9	Get a bronze medal in all Broker and Dukes races.
NRG 900	Complete the mission "Wheelman."
Patriot	Complete the mission "Wheelman."
Resolution X	Complete the mission "Pimp His Ride."
Rhino	Complete all story missions.
Sabre GT	Complete the mission "Operation Northwood."
Style SR	Get a bronze medal in all Bohan races.

GRAND THEFT AUTO: CHINATOWN WARS (PSP)

BONUS MISSION REWARDS

UNLOCKABLE	HOW TO UNLOCK
Ammunition Discount	Score gold medals on all weapons at the Gun-Club.
Bullet Proof Taxis	Complete 15 Taxi Fares in a row (in the same taxi).
Immune to Fire	Complete five waves of Fire Brigade Missions.
increased Body Armor	Complete five waves of Vigilante Missions with a 100% kill rate.
infinite Sprint	Complete five Paramedic Missions.
Regenerating Health	Beat both Noodle Delivery Missions (with a Gold ranking).
Upgraded Delivery Bag	Beat both Mail Courier Missions (with a Gold ranking).

TROPHIES

You can unlock Trophies for the Trophy Shelf in your apartment by performing the following actions.

UNLOCKABLE	HOW TO UNLOCK
Diamond Pillbox	Deal 30+ Downers
Gold Medal	Attain a score of 10,000 or more for a weapon.
Golden Binoculars	Find 40 Drug Dealers.
Jeweled Bong	Deal 30+ in Weed.
Jeweled Key to the City	Own all 21 Safe Houses.
Platinum Syringe	Purchase 5+ Heroin.
Silver Safe	Make a $2,000 profit on drugs.
Silver Safe	Make a $2,000 profit.
Titanium Briefcase	Find all 80 dealers.
Wooden Spoon	Eat a loss of $500.

VEHICLES FOR THE BOABO AUTO SHOP

UNLOCKABLE	HOW TO UNLOCK
500 XLR8	Win a Bronze Medal in all Algonquin races.
Banshee	Beat "Weapons of Mass Destruction."
Bulldozer	Beat "Counterfeit Gangster."
Bulletproof Patriot	GameStop pre-order bonus.
Cityscape	Win a Bronze Medal in all time trials.
Cognoscetti	Beat "Grave Situation."
Comet	Beat "Jackin' Chan."
Coquette	Beat "Raw Deal."
Formula R (F1)	Win a Bronze Medal in all street races.
Go-Kart	Win a Bronze Medal in all Go-Kart time trials.
Hearse	Beat "Wheelman."
Hellenbach	Beat "Bomb Disposal."
Infernus	Beat "Cash & Burn."
Limo	Complete all of Guy's missions.
MK GT9	Win a Bronze Medal in all Broker and Dukes races.
NRG 900	Beat "Wheelman."
Patriot	Beat "Wheelman."
Resolution X	Beat "Pimp His Ride."
Rhino	Complete all Story missions.
Sabre GT	Beat "Operation Northwood."
Style SR	Win a Bronze Medal in all Bohan races.

GRAND THEFT AUTO: LIBERTY CITY STORIES (PSP)

Enter these codes during gameplay. Do not pause the game.

UNLOCKABLE	CODE
$250,000	L, R, ▲, L, R, ●, L, R
Aggressive Drivers	■, ■, R, ×, ×, L, ●, ●
All Green Lights	▲, ▲, R, ■, ■, L, ×, ×
All Vehicles Chrome Plated	▲, R, L, ↓, ↓, R, R, ▲
Black Cars	●, ●, R, ▲, ▲, L, ■, ■
Bobble Head World	↓, ↓, ↓, ●, ●, ×, L, R
Cars Drive On Water	●, ×, ↓, ●, ×, ↑, L, L
Change Bike Tire Size	●, →, ×, ↑, →, ×, L, ■
Clear Weather	↑, ↓, ●, ↑, ↓, ■, L, R
Commit Suicide	L, ↓, ←, R, ×, ●, ↑, ▲
Destroy All Cars	L, L, ←, L, L, →, ×, ■
Display Game Credits	L, R, L, R, ↑, ↓, L, R
Faster Clock	L, L, ←, L, L, →, ●, ×
Faster Gameplay	R, R, L, R, R, L, ↓, ×
Foggy Weather	↑, ↓, ▲, ↑, ↓, ×, L, R
Full Armor	L, R, ●, L, R, ×, L, R
Full Health	L, R, ×, L, R, ■, L, R
Have Girls Follow You	↓, ↓, ↓, ▲, ▲, ●, L, R
Never Wanted	L, L, ▲, R, R, ×, ■, ●
Overcast Weather	↑, ↓, ×, ↑, ↓, ▲, L, R
Pedestrians Attack You	L, L, R, L, L, R, ↑, ▲
Pedestrians Have Weapons	R, R, L, R, R, L, →, ●
Pedestrians Riot	L, L, R, L, L, R, ←, ■
Perfect Traction	L, ↑, ←, R, ▲, ●, ↓, ×
Rainy Weather	↑, ↓, ■, ↑, ↓, ●, L, R
Raise Media Attention	L, ↑, →, R, ▲, ■, ↓, ×
Raise Wanted Level	L, R, ■, L, R, ▲, L, R
Random Pedestrian Outfit	L, L, ←, L, L, →, ■, ▲
Slower Gameplay	R, ▲, ×, R, ■, ●, ←, →
Spawn Rhino	L, L, ←, L, L, →, ▲, ●
Spawn Trashmaster	▲, ●, ↓, ▲, ●, ↑, L, L
Sunny Weather	L, L, ●, R, R, ■, ▲, ×
Upside Down Gameplay	↓, ↓, ↓, ×, ×, ■, R, L
Upside Up	▲, ▲, ▲, ↑, ↑, →, L, R
Weapon Set 1	↑, ■, ■, ↓, ←, ■, ■, →
Weapon Set 2	↑, ●, ●, ↓, ←, ●, ●, →
Weapon Set 3	↑, ×, ×, ↓, ←, ×, ×, →
White Cars	×, ×, R, ●, ●, L, ▲, ▲

GRAND THEFT AUTO: LIBERTY CITY STORIES (PlayStation 2)

Enter these codes during game play—do not pause.

UNLOCKABLE	CODE
$250,000	L1, R1, ▲, L1, R1, ●, L1, R1
Aggressive Drivers	■, ■, R1, ×, ×, L1, ●, ●
All Green Lights	▲, ▲, R1, ■, ■, L1, ×, ×
All Vehicles Chrome Plated	▲, R1, L1, ↓, ↓, R1, R1, ▲
Black Cars	●, ●, R1, ▲, ▲, L1, ■, ■
Big Heads	↓, ↓, ↓, ●, ●, ×, L1, R1
Cars Drive On Water	●, ×, ↓, ●, ×, ↑, L1, L1
Change Bike Tire Size	●, →, ×, ↑, →, ×, L1, ■

UNLOCKABLE	CODE
Clear Weather	↑, ↓, ●, ↑, ↓, ■, L1, R1
Commit Suicide	L1, ↓, ←, R1, ✕, ●, ↑, ▲
Destroy All Cars	L1, L1, ←, L1, L1, →, ✕, ■
Display Game Credits	L1, R1, L1, R1, ↑, ↓, L1, R1
Faster Clock	L1, L1, ←, L1, L1, →, ●, ✕
Faster Gameplay	R1, R1, L1, R1, R1, L1, ↓, ✕
Foggy Weather	↑, ↓, ▲, ↑, ↓, ✕, L1, R1
Full Armor	L1, R1, ●, L1, R1, ✕, L1, R1
Full Health	L1, R1, ✕, L1, R1, ■, L1, R1
Never Wanted	L1, L1, ▲, R1, R1, ✕, ■, ●
Overcast Weather	↑, ↓, ✕, ↑, ↓, ▲, L1, R1
Peds Attack You	L1, L1, R1, L1, L1, R1, ↑, ▲
Peds Have Weapons	R1, R1, L1, R1, R1, L1, →, ●
Peds Riot	L1, L1, R1, L1, L1, R1, ←, ■
People Follow You	↓, ↓, ↓, ▲, ▲, ●, L1, R1
Perfect Traction	L1, ↑, ←, R1, ▲, ●, ↓, ✕
Rainy Weather	↑, ↓, ■, ↑, ↓, ●, L1, R1
Raise Media Attention	L1, ↑, →, R1, ▲, ■, ↓, ✕
Raise Wanted Level	L1, R1, ■, L1, R1, ▲, L1, R1
Slower Gameplay	R1, ▲, ✕, R1, ■, ●, ←, →
Spawn a Rhino	L1, L1, ←, L1, L1, →, ▲, ●
Spawn a Trashmaster	▲, ●, ↓, ▲, ●, ↑, L1, L1
Sunny Weather	L1, L1, ●, R1, R1, ■, ▲, ✕
Upside Down Gameplay	↓, ↓, ↓, ✕, ✕, ■, R1, L1
Upside Down Gameplay2	✕, ✕, ✕, ↓, ↓, →, L1, R1
Upside Up	▲, ▲, ▲, ↑, ↑, →, L1, R1
Weapon Set 1	↑, ■, ■, ↓, ←, ■, ■, →
Weapon Set 2	↑, ●, ●, ↓, ←, ●, ●, →
Weapon Set 3	↑, ✕, ✕, ↓, ←, ✕, ✕, →
White Cars	✕, ✕, R1, ●, ●, L1, ▲, ▲

GRAND THEFT AUTO: SAN ANDREAS (XBOX)

Enter these codes during gameplay; do not pause the game.

UNLOCKABLE	CODE
$250,000 Plus Full Health and Armor	RT, BLK, LT, A, ←, ↓, →, ↑, ←, ↓, →, ↑
Adrenaline Mode	A, A, X, RT, LT, A, ↓, ←, A
Aggressive Drivers	←, BLK, ↑, ↑, BLK, B, X, BLK, LT, ←, ↓, LT
Aggressive Traffic	BLK, B, RT, WHT, ←, RT, LT, BLK, WHT
Aiming while Driving	↑, ↑, X, WHT, →, A, RT, ↓, BLK, B
All Cars Are Pink	B, LT, ↓, WHT, ←, A, RT, LT, →, B
All Cars Fly Away When Hit	X, BLK, ↓, ↓, ←, ↓, ←, ←, WHT, A
All Cars Have Nitrous	←, Y, RT, LT, ↑, X, Y, ↓, B, WHT, LT, LT
All Cars Have Tank Properties	LT, WHT, WHT, ↑, ↓, ↓, ↑, RT, BLK, BLK
All Cars You Drive Can Drive on Water	→, BLK, B, RT, WHT, X, RT, BLK
All Cars You Drive Can Fly	X, ↓, WHT, ↑, LT, B, ↑, A, ←
All Vehicles Are Black	B, WHT, ↑, RT, ←, A, RT, LT, ←, B
All Vehicles Are Farm Vehicles and Everyone Is Dressed Like Farmers	LT, LT, RT, RT, WHT, LT, BLK, ↓, ←, ↑
All Vehicles Are Invisible (except motorcycles)	Y, LT, Y, BLK, X, LT, LT

UNLOCKABLE	CODE
All Vehicles Are Junk Cars	WHT, →, LT, ↑, A, LT, WHT, BLK, RT, LT, LT, LT
Always Midnight	X, LT, RT, →, A, ↑, LT, ←, ←
Beach Mode	↑, ↑, ↓, ↓, X, B, LT, RT, Y, ↓
Better Car Suspension	X, X, BLK, ←, ↑, X, BLK, A, A, A
Chaos Mode	WHT, →, LT, Y, →, →, RT, LT, →, LT, LT, LT
Cloudy	WHT, ↓, ↓, ←, X, ←, BLK, X, A, RT, LT, LT
Clown Mode	Y, Y, LT, X, X, B, X, ↓, B
Destroy All Cars	BLK, WHT, RT, LT, WHT, BLK, X, Y, B, Y, WHT, LT
Faster Cars	→, RT, ↑, WHT, WHT, ←, RT, LT, RT, RT
Faster Clock	B, B, LT, X, LT, X, X, X, LT, Y, B, Y
Faster Gameplay	Y, ↑, →, ↓, WHT, LT, X
Flying Boats	BLK, B, ↑, LT, →, RT, →, ↑, X, Y
Foggy Weather	BLK, A, LT, LT, WHT, WHT, WHT, A
Full Wanted Level	B, →, B, →, ←, X, A ↓
Hitman Rank (all weapons)	↓, X, A, ←, RT, BLK, ←, ↓, ↓, LT, LT, LT
Increase Car Speed	↑, LT, RT, ↑, →, ↑, A, WHT, A, LT
Infinite Air	↓, ←, LT, ↓, ↓, BLK, ↓, WHT, ↓
Infinite Ammo	LT, RT, X, RT, ←, BLK, RT, ←, X, ↓, LT, LT
Infinite Health	↓, A, →, ←, →, RT, →, ↓, ↑, Y
Jetpack	←, →, LT, WHT, RT, BLK, ↑, ↓, ←, →
Lower Wanted Level	RT, RT, B, BLK, ↑, ↓, ↑, ↓, ↑, ↓
Max Fat	Y, ↑, ↑, ←, →, X, B, ↓
Max Muscle	Y, ↑, ↑, ←, →, X, B, →
Max Respect	LT, RT, Y, ↓, BLK, A, LT, ↑, WHT, WHT, LT, LT
Max Sex Appeal	B, Y, Y, ↑, B, RT, WHT, ↑, Y, LT, LT, LT
Max Stamina	↑, A, Y, A, Y, A, X, BLK, →
Max Vehicle Stats	X, WHT, A, RT, WHT, WHT, →, RT, →, LT, LT, LT
Morning	BLK, A, LT, LT, WHT, WHT, WHT, X
Never Hungry	X, WHT, RT, Y, ↑, X, WHT, ↑, A
No Muscle and No Fat	Y, ↑, ↑, ←, →, X, B, →
No Pedestrians and Low Traffic	A, ↓, ↑, BLK, ↓, Y, LT, Y, ←
Noon	BLK, A, LT, LT, WHT, WHT, WHT, ↓
Orange Sky	←, ←, WHT, RT, →, X, X, LT, WHT, A
Overcast	BLK, A, LT, LT, WHT, WHT, WHT, X
Parachute	←, →, LT, WHT, RT, BLK, BLK, ↑, ↓, →, LT
Pedestrian Attack (This code cannot be turned off.)	↓, ↑, ↑, ↑, A, BLK, RT, WHT, WHT
Pedestrian Riot Mode (This code cannot be turned off.)	↓, ←, ↑, ←, A, BLK, RT, WHT, LT
Pedestrians Dress Like Elvis	LT, B, Y, LT, LT, X, WHT, ↑, ↓, ←
Pedestrians Have Guns	A, LT, ↑, X, ↓, A, WHT, Y, ↓, RT, LT, LT
Pedestrians Have Weapons	BLK, RT, A, Y, A, Y, ↑, ↓
Perfect Handling in Vehicles	Y, RT, RT, ←, RT, LT, BLK, LT
Pimp Mode	X, →, X, X, WHT, A, Y, A, Y
Prostitutes Pay You	→, WHT, WHT, ↓, WHT, ↑, ↑, WHT, BLK
Recruit Anyone (9mm)	↓, X, ↑, BLK, BLK, ↑, →, →, ↑
Recruit Anyone (rockets)	BLK, BLK, BLK, A, WHT, LT, BLK, LT, ↓, A
Sand Storm	↑, ↓, LT, LT, WHT, WHT, LT, WHT, RT, BLK
Skinny	Y, ↑, ↑, ←, →, X, B, →
Slow Down Gameplay	Y, ↑, →, ↓, X, BLK, RT
Spawn Bloodring Banger	↓, RT, B, WHT, WHT, A, RT, LT, ←, ←

Spawn Caddy	B, LT, Up, RT, WHT, A, RT, LT, B, A
Spawn Dozer	BLK, LT, LT, Right, Right, Up, Up, A, LT, Left
Spawn Hotring Racer #1	RT, B, BLK, Right, LT, WHT, A, A, X, RT
Spawn Hotring Racer #2	BLK, LT, B, Right, LT, RT, Right, Up, B, BLK
Spawn Hunter	B, A, LT, B, B, LT, B, RT, BLK, WHT, LT, LT
Spawn Hydra	Y, Y, X, B, A, LT, LT, Down, Up
Spawn Monster	Right, Up, RT, RT, RT, Down, Y, Y, A, B, LT, LT
Spawn Quadbike	Left, Left, Down, Down, Up, Up, X, B, Y, RT, BLK
Spawn Rancher	Up, Right, Right, LT, Right, Up, X, WHT
Spawn Rhino	B, B, LT, B, B, B, LT, WHT, RT, Y, B, Y
Spawn Stretch	BLK, Up, WHT, Left, Left, RT, LT, B, Right
Spawn Stunt Plane	B, Up, LT, WHT, Down, RT, LT, LT, Left, Left, A, Y
Spawn Tanker	RT, Up, Left, Right, BLK, Up, Right, X, Right, WHT, LT, LT
Spawn Vortex	Y, Y, X, B, A, LT, WHT, Down, Down
Stormy	BLK, A, LT, LT, WHT, WHT, WHT, B
Super Bike Jumps	Y, X, B, B, X, B, B, LT, WHT, WHT, RT, BLK
Super Jumps	Up, Up, Y, Y, Up, Up, Left, Right, X, BLK, BLK,
Super Punches	Up, Left, A, Y, RT, B, B, B, WHT
Traffic Lights Stay Green	Right, RT, Up, WHT, WHT, Left, RT, LT, RT, RT
Unlock Romero	Down, BLK, Down, RT, WHT, Left, RT, LT, Left, Right
Unlock Trashmaster	B, RT, B, RT, Left, Left, RT, LT, B, Right
Weapon Set 1	RT, BLK, LT, BLK, Left, Down, Right, Up, Left, Down, Right, Up
Weapon Set 2	RT, BLK, LT, BLK, Left, Down, Right, Up, Left, Down, Down, Left
Weapon Set 3	RT, BLK, LT, BLK, Left, Down, Right, Up, Left, Down, Down, Down
Yakuza Mode	A, A, Down, BLK, WHT, B, RT, B, X

GRAND THEFT AUTO: SAN ANDREAS (PlayStation 2)

DESCRIPTION	CODE
250,000 & full health and armor	R1, R2, L1, ×, ←, ↓, →, ↑, ←, ↓, →, ↑
4 star wanted level	R1, R1, ●, L1, ↑, ↓, ↑, ↓, ↑, ↓
Aggressive Traffic	R2, ●, R1, L2, ← R1, L1, R2, L2
All Traffic Lights Stay Green	→, R1, ↑, L2, L2, ←, R1, L1, R1, R1
All Vehicles Invisible (Except Motorcycles)	▲, L1, ▲, R2, ■, L1, L1
Attain 2 star wanted level	R1, R1, ●, ←, →, ←, →
Black Traffic	●, L2, ↑, R1, ←, ×, R1, L1, ←, ●
Cars on Water	→, R2, ●, R1, L2, ■, R1, R2
Commit Suicide	→, L2, ↓, R1, ←, ←, R1, L1, L2, L1
Destroy Cars	R2, L2, R1, L1, L2, R2, ■, ▲, ●, ▲, L2, L1
Faster Cars	→, R1, ↑, L2, L2, ←, R1, L1, R1, R1
Faster Clock	●, ●, L1, ■, L1, ■, ■, ■, L1, ▲, ●, ▲
Faster Gameplay	▲, ↑, →, ↓, L2, L1, ■
Flying Boats	R2, ●, ↑, L1, →, R1, →, ↑, ■, ▲
Fog	R2, ×, L1, L1, L2, L2, L2, ×
Get a Bounty on your head	↓, ↑, ↑, ↑, ×, R2, R1, L2, L2
Lower Wanted Level	R1, R1, ●, R2, ↑, ↓, ↑, ↓, ↑, ↓
Morning	R2, ×, L1, L1, L2, L2, L2, ■
Night	R2, ×, L1, L1, L2, L2, L2, ▲
Overcast	R2, ×, L1, L1, L2, L2, L2, ■

DESCRIPTION	CODE
Pedestrian Attack (can't be turned off)	↓, ↑, ↑, ↑, ×, R2, R1, L2, L2
Pedestrian Riot (can't be turned off)	↓, ←, ↑, ←, ×, R2, R1, L2, L1
Pedestrians have weapons	R2, R1, ×, ▲, ×, ▲, ↑, ↓
Perfect Handling	▲, R1, R1, ←, R1, L1, R2, L1
Pink Traffic	●, L1, ↓, L2, ←, ×, R1, L1, →, ●
Play as Wuzi	L2, R2, R2, L2, L2, L2, L1, L1, L1, L1, ▲, ▲, ●, ●, ■, L2, L2, L2, L2, L2, L2
Raise Wanted Level	R1, R1, ●, R2, →, ←, →, ←, →, ←
Romero	↓, R2, ↓, R1, L2, ←, R1, L1, ←, →
Slower Gameplay	▲, ↑, →, ↓, ■, R2, R1
Spawn a Ranger	↑, →, →, L1, →, ↑, ■, L2
Spawn A Rhino	●, ●, L1, ●, ●, ●, L1, L2, R1, ▲, ●, ▲
Spawn a Stretch	R2, ↑, L2, ←, ←, R1, L1, ●, →
Spawn Bloodring Banger	↓, R1, ●, L2, L2, ×, R1, L1, ←, ←
Spawn Caddy	●, L1, ↑, R1, L2, ×, R1, L1, ●, ×
Spawn Hotring Racer #1	R1, ●, R2, →, L1, L2, ×, ×, ■, R1
Spawn Hotring Racer #2	R2, L1, ●, →, L1, R1, →, ↑, ●, R2
Spawn Rancher	↑, →, →, L1, →, ↑, ■, L2
Spawns jetpack	L1, L2, R1, R2, ↑, ↓, ←, →, L1, L2, R1, R2, ↑, ↓, ←, →
Storm	R2, ×, L1, L1, L2, L2, L2, ●
Trashmaster	●, R1, ●, R1, ←, ←, R1, L1, ●, →
Weapons 1	R1, R2, L1, R2, ←, ↓, →, ↑, ←, ↓, →, ↑
Weapons 2	R1, R2, L1, R2, ←, ↓, →, ↑, ←, ↓, ↓, ←
Weapons 3	R1, R2, L1, R2, ←, ↓, →, ↑, ←, ↓, ↓, ↓

GRAND THEFT AUTO: VICE CITY (XBOX)

Enter these codes while playing; do not pause.

UNLOCKABLE	CODE
Aggressive Drivers	BLK, B, RT, WHT, ←, RT, LT, BLK, WHT
Bikini Girls with Guns	→, LT, B, WHT, ←, A, RT, LT, LT, A
Black Cars	B, WHT, ↑, RT, ←, A, RT, LT, ←, B
Blow Up Cars	BLK, WHT, RT, LT, WHT, BLK, X, Y, B, Y, WHT, LT
Cars Can Drive on Water	→, BLK, B, RT, WHT, X, RT, BLK
Change Clothes	→, →, ←, ↑, LT, WHT, ←, ↑, ↓, →
Change Vehicle Wheel Size (Repeat to change again)	RT, A, Y, →, BLK, X, ↑, ↓, X
Cloudy Weather	BLK, B, LT, LT, WHT, WHT, WHT, Y
Dodo Cheat	→, BLK, B, RT, WHT, ↓, LT, RT (Press the analog stick back to fly)
Foggy Weather	BLK, A, LT, LT, WHT, WHT, WHT, A
Higher Top Speed for Your Vehicle	→, RT, ↑, WHT, WHT, ←, RT, LT, RT, RT
Ladies Man (Certain women follow you)	B, A, LT, LT, BLK, A, A, B, Y
Pedestrians Hate You (code cannot be undone)	↓, ↑, ↑, ↑, A, BLK, RT, WHT, WHT
Pedestrians Have Weapons (code cannot be undone)	BLK, RT, A, Y, A, Y, ↑, ↓

Pedestrians Riot (code cannot be undone)	Down, Left, Up, Left, A, Black, R, White, L
Perfect Handling	Y, R, R, Left, R, L, Black, L
Pink Cars	B, L, Down, White, Left, A, R, L, Right, A
Play As Candy Suxxx	B, Black, Down, R, Left, Right, R, L, A, White
Play As Hilary King	R, B, Black, L, Right, R, L, A, Black
Play As Ken Rosenberg	Right, L, Up, White, L, Right, R, L, A, R
Play As Lance Vance	B, White, Left, A, R, L, A, L
Play As Love Fist Guy #1	Down, L, Down, White, Left, A, R, L, A, A
Play As Love Fist Guy #2	R, White, Black, L, Right, Black, Left, A, X, L
Play As Mercedes	Black, L, Up, L, Right, R, Right, Up, B, Y
Play As Phil Cassady	Right, R, Up, Black, L, Right, R, L, Right, B
Play As Ricardo Diaz	L, White, R, Black, Down, L, Black, White
Play As Sonny Forelli	B, L, B, White, Left, A, R, L, A, A
Police Return from Dead	B, L, Down, White, Left, A, R, L, Right, A
Raise Wanted Level	R, R, B, Black, Left, Right, Left, Right, Left, Right
Repair Vehicle Tires	Black, White, L, B, Left, Down, Right, Up, Left, Down, Right, Up
Slow Down Time	Y, Up, Right, Down, X, Black, R
Spawn A Bloodring Banger	Up, Right, Right, L, Right, Up, X, White
Spawn A Bloodring Racer	Down, R, B, White, White, A, R, L, Left, Left
Spawn A Caddie	B, L, Up, R, White, A, R, L, B, A
Spawn A Hotring Racer #1	R, B, Black, Right, L, White, A, A, X, R
Spawn A Hotring Racer #2	Black, L, B, Right, L, R, Right, Up, B, Black
Spawn A Love Fist	Black, Up, White, Left, Left, R, L, B, Right
Spawn A Rhino Tank	B, B, L, B, B, B, L, White, R, Y, B, Y
Spawn A Romero's Hearse	Down, Black, Down, R, White, Left, R, L, Left, Right
Spawn A Sabre Turbo	Right, White, Down, White, White, A, R, L, B, Left
Spawn A Trashmaster	B, R, B, R, Left, Left, R, L, B, Right
Speed Up Time	B, B, L, X, L, X, X, X, L, Y, B, Y
Stormy Weather	Black, A, L, L, White, White, White, B
Suicide	Right, White, Down, R, Left, Left, R, L, White, L
Sunny Weather	Black, A, L, L, White, White, White, Down
Very Cloudy Weather	Black, A, L, L, White, White, White, X
Weapons #1	R, Black, L, Black, Left, Down, Right, Up, Left, Down, Right, Up
Weapons #2	R, Black, L, Black, Left, Down, Right, Up, Left, Down, Down, Left
Weapons #3	R, Black, L, Black, Left, Down, Right, Up, Left, Down, Down, Down

GRAND THEFT AUTO: VICE CITY (PlayStation 2)

Enter all of the following codes during gameplay. After doing so, wait for the message to confirm correct code entry.

DESCRIPTION	CODE
Aggressive Traffic	Press R2, ●, R1, L2, ←, R1, L1, R2, L2
Armor	Press R1, R2, L1, ×, ←, ↓, →, ↑, ←, ↓, →, ↑
Better Driving Skills	Press ▲, R1, R1, ←, R1, L1, R2, L1. Press L3 or R3 to jump while driving.
Bikini Women with Guns (The women drop guns when they die.)	Press →, L1, ●, L2, ←, ×, R1, L1, L1, ×
Black Traffic	Press ●, L2, ↑, R1, ←, ×, R1, L1, ←, ●
Bloodring Banger (Style 1)	Press ↑, →, →, L1, →, ↑, ■, L2.
Bloodring Banger (Style 2)	Press ↓, R1, ●, L2, L2, ×, R1, L1, ←, ←

NEW! A B C D E F G H I J K L M N O P Q R S T U V W X Y Z

DESCRIPTION	CODE
Caddy	Press ●, L1, ↑, R1, L2, ×, R1, L1, ●, ×
Candy Suxxx Costume	Press ●, R2, ↓, R1, ←, →, R1, L1, ×, L2.
Car Floats on Water	Press →, R2, ●, R1, L2, ■, R1, R2. See Note.
Change Wheel Size (The wheels of some vehicles become larger, while others become smaller.)	Press R1, ×, ▲, →, R2, ■, ↑, ↓, ■. Repeat this code to increase its effect.
Destroy Cars	Press R2, L2, R1, L1, L2, R2, ■, ▲, ●, ▲, L2, L1
Dodo Car (Flying)	Press →, R2, ●, R1, L2, ↓, L1, R1. Accelerate and press the analog stick back to glide.
Extended Wanted Level Status	Press R2, ●, ↑, L1, →, R1, →, ↑, ■, ▲. A box will appear under your felony stars showing how long you have had a felony and how close the cops are.
Faster Game Clock	Press ●, ●, L1, ■, L1, ■, ■, ■, L1, ▲, ●, ▲
Faster Gameplay	Press ▲, ↑, →, ↓, L2, L1, ■
Foggy Weather	Press R2, ×, L1, L1, L2, L2, L2, ×
Health	Press R1, R2, L1, ●, ←, ↓, →, ↑, ←, ↓, →, ↑
Hilary King Costume	Press R1, ●, R2, L1, →, R1, L1, ×, R2
Hotring Racer (Style 1)	Press R1, ●, R2, →, L1, L2, ×, ×, ■, R1
Hotring Racer (Style 2)	Press R2, L1, ●, →, L1, R1, →, ↑, ●, R2
Increase Your Vehicle's Top Speed	Press →, R1, ↑, L2, L2, ←, R1, L1, R1, R1
Ken Rosenberg Costume	Press →, L1, ↑, L2, L1, →, R1, L1, ×, R1
Lance Vance Costume	Press ●, L2, ←, ×, R1, L1, ×, L1
Love Fist Limousine	Press R2, ↑, L2, ←, ←, R1, L1, ●, →
Love Fist Musician 1 Costume	Press ↓, L1, ↓, L2, ←, ×, R1, L1, ×, ×
Love Fist Musician 2 Costume	Press R1, L2, R2, L1, →, R2, ←, ×, ■, L1
Lower Wanted Level	Press R1, R1, ●, R2, ↑, ↓, ↑, ↓, ↑, ↓
Mercedes Costume	Press R2, L1, ↑, L1, →, R1, →, ↑, ●, ▲
Normal Weather	Press R2, ×, L1, L1, L2, L2, L2, ↓
Overcast Skies	Press R2, ×, L1, L1, L2, L2, L2, ■
Pedestrian Costume	Press →, →, ←, ↑, L1, L2, ←, ↑, ↓, → Repeat this code to cycle through the various pedestrian costumes.
Pedestrians Attack You	Press ↓, ↑, ↑, ↑, ×, R2, R1, L2, L2 You cannot disable this code.
Pedestrians from "Thriller"	Press ■, L1, ▲, R2, ■, L1, L1 No confirmation message appears.
Pedestrians Have Weapons	Press R2, R1, ×, ▲, ×, ▲, ↑, ↓ You cannot disable this code.
Pedestrians Riot	Press ↓, ←, ↑, ←, ×, R2, R1, L2, L1 You cannot disable this code.
Phil Cassady Costume	Press →, R1, ↑, R2, L1, →, R1, L1, →, ●.
Pink Traffic	Press ●, L1, ↓, L2, ←, ×, R1, L1, →, ● or ×.
Police Return from Dead	Press ●, L1, ↓, L2, ←, ×, R1, L1, →, ×.
Rainy Weather	Press R2, ×, L1, L1, L2, L2, L2, ●.
Raise Wanted Level	Press R1, R1, ●, R2, ←, →, ←, →, ←, →.
Rhino Tank	Press ●, ●, L1, ●, ●, ●, L1, L2, R1, ▲, ●, ▲.
Ricardo Diaz Costume	Press L1, L2, R1, R2, ↓, L1, R2, L2.
Romero's Hearse	Press ↓, R2, ↓, R1, L2, ←, R1, L1, ←, →.
Sabre Turbo	Press →, L2, ↓, L2, L2, ×, R1, L1, ●, ←.
Slower Gameplay	Press ▲, ↑, →, ↓, ■, R2, R1.
Sonny Forelli Costume	Press ●, L1, ●, L2, ←, ×, R1, L1, ×, ×.
Suicide	Press →, L2, ↓, R1, ←, ←, R1, L1, L2, L1.
Sunny Weather	Press R2, ×, L1, L1, L2, L2, L2, ▲.
Tommy Groupies	Press ●, ×, L1, L1, R2, ×, ×, ●, ▲.

Trashmaster	Press ●, [R1], ●, [R1], ←, ←, [R1], [L1], ●, →.
Weapons (Tier 1)	Press [R1], [R2], [L1], [R2], ←, ↓, →, ↑, ←, ↓, →, ↑ The least powerful weapons in each category are unlocked.
Weapons (Tier 2)	Press [R1], [R2], [L1], [R2], ←, ↓, →, ↑, ←, ↓, ↓, ←.
Weapons (Tier 3)	Press [R1], [R2], [L1], [R2], ←, ↓, →, ↑, ←, ↓, ↓, ↓.

AFTER ENABLING THIS CODE WHILE DRIVING ON THE WATER, REPEAT THE CODE TO DEACTIVATE IT. THE CAR YOU DRIVE GOES DIRECTLY TO THE BOTTOM OF THE WATER AND KEEPS GOING WITHOUT LOSING ANY HEALTH. YOU SOON HIT A PIECE OF LAND AND EITHER END UP STUCK IN THE GROUND OR CAN DRIVE AGAIN. YOU DO NOT LOSE ANY HEALTH DURING THE ENTIRE TIME.

GRAND THEFT AUTO: VICE CITY STORIES (PSP)

Enter any of these codes while playing.

UNLOCKABLE	CODE
25% of MP Content	⇧, ⇧, ⇧, ■, ■, ▲, [R], [L]
50% of MP Content	⇧, ⇧, ⇧, ●, ●, ×, [L], [R]
75% of MP Content	⇧, ⇧, ⇧, ⇧, ×, ×, ■, [R], [L]
100% of MP Content	⇧, ⇧, ▲, ▲, ●, [L], [R]
All Cars Are Black	[L], [R], [L], [R], ⇦, ●, ⇧, ×
Armor	⇧, ⇩, ⇦, ⇨, ■, ■, [L], [R]
Cars Avoid You	⇧, ⇧, ⇨, ⇦, ▲, ●, ●, ■
Chrome Cars	⇨, ⇧, ⇦, ⇩, ▲, ▲, [L], [R]
Clear Weather	⇦, ⇩, [R], [L], ⇨, ⇧, ⇦, ×
Commit Suicide	⇨, ⇨, ●, ●, [L], [R], ⇩, ×
Destroy All Cars	[L], [R], [R], ⇦, ⇨, ■, ⇩, [R]
Faster Clock	[R], [L], [L], ⇩, ⇧, ×, ⇩, [L]
Faster Gameplay	⇦, ⇦, [R], [R], ⇧, ▲, ⇩, ×
Foggy Weather	⇦, ⇩, ▲, ×, ⇨, ⇧, ⇦, [L]
$250,000	⇧, ⇩, ⇦, ⇨, ×, ×, [L], [R]
Guys Follow You	⇨, [L], ⇩, [L], ●, ⇧, [L], ■
Health	⇧, ⇩, ⇦, ⇨, ●, ●, [L], [R]
Lower Wanted Level	⇧, ⇨, ▲, ▲, ⇩, ⇦, ×, ×
Nearest Ped Gets in Your Vehicle (Must Be in a Car)	⇩, ⇧, ⇨, [L], [L], ■, ⇧, [L]
Overcast Weather	⇦, ⇩, [L], [R], ⇨, ⇧, ⇦, ■
Peds Attack You	⇩, ▲, ⇧, ×, [L], [R], [L], [R]
Peds Have Weapons	⇧, [L], ⇩, [R], ⇦, ●, ⇨, ▲
Peds Riot	[R], [L], [L], ⇩, ⇦, ●, ⇩, [L]
Perfect Traction	⇩, ⇦, ⇧, [L], [R], ▲, ●, ×
Rainy Weather	⇦, ⇩, [L], [R], ⇨, ⇧, ⇦, ▲
Raise Wanted Level	⇧, ⇨, ■, ■, ⇩, ⇦, ●, ●
Slower Gameplay	⇦, ⇦, ●, ●, ⇩, ⇧, ▲, ×
Spawn Rhino	⇧, [L], ⇩, [R], ⇦, [L], ⇨, [R]
Spawn Trashmaster	⇩, ⇧, ⇨, ▲, [L], ▲, [L], ▲
Sunny Weather	⇦, ⇩, [R], [L], ⇨, ⇧, ⇦, ●
Upside Down Mode 1	■, ■, ■, [L], [L], [R], ⇦, ⇨
Upside Down Mode 2	⇦, ⇦, ⇦, [R], [R], [L], ⇨, ⇦
Weapon Set 1	⇦, ⇨, ×, ⇧, ⇩, ■, ⇦, ⇨
Weapon Set 2	⇦, ⇨, ■, ⇧, ⇩, ▲, ⇦, ⇨
Weapon Set 3	⇦, ⇨, ▲, ⇧, ⇩, ●, ⇦, ⇨

GRAND THEFT AUTO: VICE CITY STORIES (PlayStation 2)

Enter these codes while playing.

UNLOCKABLE	CODE
Acquire Weapon Set 1	⇦, ⇨, ×, ⇧, ⇩, ■, ⇦, ⇨
Acquire Weapon Set 2	⇦, ⇨, ■, ⇧, ⇩, ▲, ⇦, ⇨
Acquire Weapon Set 3	⇦, ⇨, ▲, ⇧, ⇩, ●, ⇦, ⇨
All Green Lights	⇧, ⇩, ▲, ×, L1, R1, ⇦, ●
Cars Avoid You	⇧, ⇧, ⇨, ⇦, ▲, ●, ●, ■
Clear Weather	⇦, ⇩, R1, L1, ⇨, ⇧, ⇦, ×
Destroy Cars Near You	L1, R1, R1, ⇦, ⇨, ■, ⇩, R1
Foggy Weather	⇦, ⇩, ▲, ×, ⇨, ⇧, ⇦, L1
Full Armor	⇧, ⇩, ⇦, ⇨, ■, ■, L1, R1
Full Health	⇧, ⇩, ⇦, ⇨, ●, ●, L1, R1
$250,000	⇧, ⇩, ⇦, ⇨, ×, ×, L1, R1
Guy Magnet	⇨, L1, ⇩, L1, ●, ⇧, L1, ■
Never Wanted (turns off after rampages)	⇧, ⇨, ▲, ▲, ⇩, ⇦, ×, ×
No Traction	⇩, ⇦, ⇧, L1, R1, ▲, ●, ×
Overcast Weather	⇦, ⇩, L1, R1, ⇨, ⇧, ⇦, ■
Pedestrians Attack You	⇩, ▲, ⇧, ×, L1, R1, L1, R1
Pedestrians Have Weapons	⇧, L1, ⇩, R1, ⇦, ●, ⇨, ▲
Pedestrians Riot	R1, L1, L1, ⇩, ⇦, ●, ⇩, L1
Rainy Weather	⇦, ⇩, L1, R1, ⇨, ⇧, ⇦, ▲
Raise Wanted Level	⇧, ⇨, ■, ■, ⇩, ⇦, ●, ●
Slow Down Game	⇦, ⇦, ●, ●, ⇩, ⇧, ▲, ×
Spawn Rhino Tank	⇧, L1, ⇩, R1, ⇦, L1, ⇨, R1
Spawn Trashmaster Truck	⇩, ⇧, ⇨, ▲, L1, ▲, L1, ▲
Speed Up Clock	R1, L1, L1, ⇩, ⇧, ×, ⇩, L1
Speed Up Game	⇦, ⇦, R1, R1, ⇧, ▲, ⇩, ×
Sunny Weather	⇦, ⇩, R1, L1, ⇨, ⇧, ⇦, ●
Color Changed to Black (Except for Cop Cars)	L1, R1, L1, R1, ⇦, ●, ⇧, ×
Vehicles Color Changed to Chrome	⇨, ⇧, ⇦, ⇩, ▲, ▲, L1, R1
Wasted! (Commit Suicide)	⇨, ⇨, ●, ●, L1, R1, ⇩, ×

GREAT ESCAPE (PlayStation 2)

Press the following button combinations at the Main menu.

UNLOCKABLE	CODE
All Movies	L2, L2, ■, ●, ●, R2, R1, ■, ■, ●, L2, R1
Level Select	■, L2, ■, R1, ●, R2, ●, L2, L2, R2, ●, ■
Unlimited Ammo	■, ●, L2, R1, R2, L2, ●, ■, L2, R1, L2, R1

GRETZKY NHL (PSP)

At the Gretzky Challenge Unlockables screen, press START to bring up the cheat entry.

UNLOCKABLE	PASSWORD
Get One Gretzky Point	CANADIAN DOLLAR
RoboEnforcer Model-44	ROBO CHECKS
Unlock 1910 Montreal Canadians Uniform	THE HABS
Unlock 1924 Montreal Canadians Uniform	LE HABITANT
Unlock 1927 Detroit Red Wings Uniform	BEEP BEEP
Unlock 1928 Boston Bruins Uniform	WICKED HAAAAAHD

Unlock 1929 Ottawa Senators Uniform	THE SENANATOR
Unlock 1930 Toronto Maple Leafs Uniform	NORTH OF THE BORDER
Unlock 1967 Pittsburgh Penguins Away Uniform	POPPIN TALK
Unlock 1970 Minnesota North Stars Uniform	TWIN STARS
Unlock 1975 Kansas City Scouts Uniform	YOU LITTLE DEVIL
Unlock 1976 New York Rangers Away Uniform	NEW YORK NEW YORK
Unlock 1977 Calgary Flames Away Uniform	FLAME ON
Unlock 1977 Colorado Rockies Uniform	DEVIL MADE ME DO IT
Unlock 1977 Vancouver Canucks Home Uniform	GREAT WHITE NORTH
Unlock 1977 Washington Capitals Away Uniform	CONGRESSIONAL WISDOM
Unlock 1978 New York Islanders Away Uniform	ORDWAY MADE ME DO IT
Unlock 1979 Edmonton Oilers Away Uniform	A SCARY SIGHT TO THE HOME CROWD
Unlock 1979 Edmonton Oilers Home Uniform	THREADS OF CHAMPS
Unlock 1979 St. Louis Blues Away Uniform	A BLUE NOTE
Unlock 1979 St. Louis Blues Home Uniform	MARDI GRAS
Unlock 1980 Quebec Nordiques Uniform	FRENCH FOR CANADIAN
Unlock 1983 Edmonton Oilers Away Uniform	ALL HAIL WAYNE
Unlock 1988 Pittsburgh Penguins Away Uniform	STEEL TOWN
Unlock 1989 Los Angeles Kings Away Uniform	KING GRETZKY
Unlock 1989 Los Angeles Kings Home Uniform	KING WAYNE
Unlock 1990 Winnipeg Jets Away Uniform	PORTAGE AND MAIN
Unlock 1990 Winnipeg Jets Home Uniform	MIDDLE OF CANADA
Unlock 1993 San Jose Sharks Away Uniform	SHARK BAIT
Unlock 1995 St. Louis Blues Away Uniform	VINTAGE BLUES
Unlock 1999 New York Rangers Home Uniform	UPPER WEST SIDE
Unlock Alternate Anaheim Mighty Ducks Uniform	FLYING VEE
Unlock Alternate Atlanta Thrashers Uniform	THRASHED TO THE MAX
Unlock Alternate Boston Bruins Uniform	NOMAR STILL RULES
Unlock Alternate Buffalo Sabers Uniform	IN THE SNOW BELT
Unlock Alternate Calgary Flames Uniform	THREE ALARM BLAZE
Unlock Alternate Chicago Blackhawks Uniform	WINDY CITY
Unlock Alternate Colorado Avalanche Uniform	SNOW DRIFTS
Unlock Alternate Columbus Blue Jackets Uniform	BLUE SHOES
Unlock Alternate Dallas Stars Uniform	HOCKEY IN TEXAS
Unlock Alternate Edmonton Oilers Uniform	PUMPIN OIL
Unlock Alternate Florida Panthers Uniform	SOUTH BEACH
Unlock Alternate Los Angeles Kings Uniform	IT IS GOOD TO BE THE KING
Unlock Alternate Minnesota Wild Uniform	COLD AS HECK
Unlock Alternate Nashville Predators Uniform	ALIEN VS NASHVILLE
Unlock Alternate New York Islanders Uniform	LAWNG ISLAND
Unlock Alternate New York Rangers Uniform	GREAT WHITE WAY
Unlock Alternate Ottawa Senators Uniform	MAJORITY RULE
Unlock Alternate Philadelphia Flyers Uniform	FANATICAL
Unlock Alternate San Jose Sharks Uniform	GET A BIGGER BOAT
Unlock Alternate Toronto Maple Leafs Uniform	HEY TERRANCE
Unlock Alternate Vancouver Canucks Uniform	WEST COAST EH
Unlock Big Boards Checking Option	ALL ABOARD
Unlock Everything	SHOENLOC
Unlock No Skate Fatigue Option	CAFFEINATED
Unlock Perfect Aim Option	THREAD THE NEEDLE
Unlock Perfect Slap Shots Option	SLAP THAT PUCK
Wayne Gretzky 1979	UNSTOPPABLE GREATNESS

UNLOCKABLE	PASSWORD
Wayne Gretzky 1987	GLORY DAZE
Wayne Gretzky 1994	WEST COAST WAYNE
Wayne Gretzky 1999	A LEGEND ON ICE

GRETZKY NHL 06 (PSP)

At the Main menu, select Features. Next, select "Gretzky Challenge" and unlockables. At the unlockables screen, press START to bring up the Password Entry menu.

UNLOCKABLE	PASSWORD
Earn one Gretzky point	CULKY NETC
Unlock all alternate uniforms	NNIADOUAMFM
Unlock all vintage uniforms	DLEONG ARE
Unlock all Wayne Gretzkys	TEH ESATGRTE NOES
Unlock big boards checking	LAL ABRAOD
Unlock bigger players	ARGLE NI RAGECH
Unlock everything	CONHEOSL
Unlock no skater fatigue	EFDTAFEACIN
Unlock perfect aim mode	TADHRE TEH EDNELE
Unlock perfect slap shots	SAPL TATH CUKP
Unlock RoboEnforcer Model-44	OBOR SKHECC
Unlock smaller players	IGHTMY UOSEM
Unlock Stanley Cup Championship video	VINIOS FO LYRGO

THE GRIM ADVENTURES OF BILLY AND MANDY (Wii)

VIEW CONCEPT ART SKETCH Enter this code at the main menu screen.

UNLOCKABLES

UNLOCKABLE	HOW TO UNLOCK
Concept Art Sketch	Hold ①, press ↑, ↑, ↓, ↓, ←, →, ←, ↓, and release ①
Extra Costume	Choose the character that you wish to have the extra costume and use him/her to clear Story mode
Unlock Boogey	In Mission mode, finish Mission 9 in Tier 4
Unlock Chicken	Finish Story mode with all characters on any difficulty with 10 hours of gameplay
Unlock Clown	Beat Story mode once with every character and fight a total of 100 Vs. mode matches
Unlock Dracula	In Mission mode finish Mission 5 in Tier 3
Unlock Eris	Finish Story mode once with either Billy, Mandy, Grim, or Irwin
Unlock Fred Fredburger	Finish Story mode once with either Billy, Mandy, Grim, or Irwin
Unlock General Skarr	In Mission mode finish Mission 6 in Tier 4
Unlock Hoss Delgado	Finish Mission 9 in Tier 1 in Mission mode
Unlock Jack O'Lantern	In Mission mode finish Mission 9 in Tier 2
Unlock Lord Pain	Finish Mission 9 in Tier 5
Unlock Mogar	Finish Story mode once with either Billy, Mandy, Grim, or Irwin
Unlock Nergal	Finish Story mode once with either Billy, Mandy, Grim, or Irwin
Unlock Nergal Jr.	In Mission mode finish Mission 9 in Tier 3
Unlock Nerglings	Finish Story mode with all characters on any difficulty
Unlock Pumpkin	Beat Story mode once with every character and accumulate a total of 100,000 damage in Vs. mode
Unlock Vikings	Finish Story mode with all characters and destroy every letter in the credits sequence

GT PRO SERIES (Wii)

UNLOCKABLES

UNLOCKABLE	HOW TO UNLOCK
Brake Street	Win Championship Race (Beginner)
Filter Grade-A	Win Enjoy Cup (Beginner)
Headlight Blue	Win 3 Door Cup (Beginner)
Highspeed Class	Win all cups in Intermediate Class
Intermediate Class	Win all cups in Beginner's Class
Mazda RX-7 Tune (FD3S)	Get at least a Great!, 20+ for max combo in Heights Mountain
Mazda RX-8	Win Championship Race (Beginner)
Nissan 180SX S13	Win Enjoy Cup (Beginner)
Nissan Silvia S14 Tune	Complete the first race in drift mode
Nissan Silvia Tune (S15)	Get at least a Good!, 15+ for max combo in Downtown Street
Professional Class	Win all cups in Highspeed Class
Toyota Celica LB TA27	Win 3 Door Cup (Beginner)

GUILTY GEAR XX ACCENT CORE PLUS (Wii)

UNLOCKABLES

Unlock these characters by completing their story mode.

UNLOCKABLE	HOW TO UNLOCK
Justice	Beat her Story Mode.
Kliff	Beat his Story Mode.
Ex Characters	Play their Story Mode (all paths) or defeat them in Survival Mode
Unlock GG mode	Beat all 30 Missions in Mission Mode

GUITAR HERO (PlayStation 2)

Enter these codes on Game Mode selection screen.

UNLOCKABLE	CODE
Crowd has Monkey Heads	Blue, Orange, Yellow, Yellow, Yellow, Blue, Orange
Crowd has Skull Heads	Orange, Yellow, Blue, Blue, Orange, Yellow, Blue, Blue
Character uses Air Guitar	Orange, Orange, Blue, Yellow, Orange
Rock meter will always stay green	Yellow, Blue, Orange, Orange, Blue, Blue, Yellow, Orange
Unlock Everything	Yellow, Orange, Blue, Blue, Orange, Yellow, Yellow
Unlocks Hero Guitar	Blue, Orange, Yellow, Blue, Blue
Venue Disappears	Blue, Yellow, Orange, Blue, Yellow, Orange

GUITAR HERO 2 (XBOX 360)

CODES

Enter code at the main menu screen where it shows "Career" and "Quick Play."

UNLOCKABLE	HOW TO UNLOCK
Air Guitar	Y, B, Y, O, Y, B
UNLOCKABLE	HOW TO UNLOCK
Enables Hyperspeed	B, O, Y, O, B, O, Y, Y
Eyeball Head Crowd	Y, O, B, B, B, O, Y
Flaming Heads	O, Y, Y, O, Y, Y, O, Y, Y, B, Y, Y, B, Y, Y
Monkey Head Crowd	O, Y, B, B, Y, O, B, B
Performance Mode	B, B, Y, B, B, O, B, B
Unlock All Songs	B, Y, O, R, Y, O, B, Y, B, Y, B, Y, B, Y, B, Y

UNLOCKABLE GUITARS

UNLOCKABLE	HOW TO UNLOCK
"The Log" Guitar	5 Star every song on Expert mode
Axe Guitar	Beat Expert mode
Casket Guitar	Beat Medium mode
Eyeball Guitar	5 Star every song on Hard mode
Fish Guitar	Beat Easy mode
Snaketapus Guitar	Beat Hard mode
USA Guitar	5 Star every song on Easy mode
Viking Guitar	5 Star every song on Medium mode

EXTRA BASS GUITARS UNLOCKABLE IN CO-OP

"EXTRA" SONGS DO NOT COUNT TOWARD THESE UNLOCKABLES.

Cream SG	Get 5 stars on 20 Co-Op song
Gibson Grabber	Beat 20 Co-Op songs
Gibson SG Bass	Beat 10 Co-Op songs
Gibson Thunderbird	Beat 30 Co-Op songs
Hofner Bass	Beat all Co-Op songs
Lava Pearl Musicman Stingray	Get 5 stars on 10 Co-Op songs
Natural Maple Gibson Grabber Bass	Get 4 stars on all Co-Op songs
Natural Sunburst Gibson Thunderbird Bass	Get 5 stars on all Co-Op Songs

GUITAR HERO 2 (PlayStation 2)

Enter codes at the main menu.

UNLOCKABLE	CODE
Air Guitar	Yellow, Yellow, Blue, Orange, Yellow, Blue
Crowd Has Eyeball Heads	Blue, Orange, Yellow, Orange, Yellow, Orange, Blue
Crowd Has Monkey Heads	Orange, Blue, Yellow, Yellow, Orange, Blue, Yellow, Yellow
Flaming Head	Orange, Yellow, Orange, Orange, Yellow, Orange, Yellow, Yellow
Horse Head	Blue, Orange, Orange, Blue, Orange, Orange, Blue, Orange, Orange, Blue
Hyper Speed	Orange, Blue, Orange, Yellow, Orange, Blue, Orange, Yellow
Performance mode	Yellow, Yellow, Blue, Yellow, Yellow, Orange, Yellow, Yellow

GUITAR HERO 3: LEGENDS OF ROCK (XBOX 360)

Enter the following in the Cheats menu under Options. You must strum every note/chord. The letters correspond to colored frets G=Green, R=Red, Y=Yellow, B=Blue, O=Orange

CODE	EFFECT
(BY) (GY) (GY) (RB) (RB) (RY) (RY) (BY) (GY) (GY) (RB) (RB) (RY) (RY) (GY) (GY) (RY) (RY)	Air guitar
(GR) (GR) (GR) (GB) (GB) (GB) (RB) R R R (RB) R R R (RB) R R R	Bret Michaels singer
(GR) (GY) (YB) (RB) (BO) (YO) (RY) (RB)	Easy Expert
O, B, O, Y, O, B, O, Y	Hyperspeed
(GR) (B) (GR) (GY) (B) (GY) (RY) (O) (RY) (GY) (Y) (GY) (GR)	No fail (does not work in Career mode)
RY, RB, RO, RB, RY, GB, RY RB	Performance mode
GR, GR, GR, RY, RY, RB, RB, YB, YO, YO, GR, GR, GR, RY, RY, RB, RB, YB, YO, YO	Precision mode
YO, RB, RO, GB, RY, YO, RY, RB, GY, GY, YB, YB, YO, YO, YB, Y, R, RY, R, Y, O	Unlock all songs
(GR_BO) (GRYB_) (GRY_O) (G_BYO) (GRYB_) (_RYBO) (GRYB_) (G_YBO) (GRYB_) (GRY_O) (GRY_O) (GRYB_) (GRY_O)	Unlock everything (no sound plays when you enter these chords)

UNLOCKABLE	HOW TO UNLOCK
Lou	Defeat this boss and you can buy him for $15,000
Slash	Defeat this boss and you can buy him for $10,000
Tom Morello	Defeat this boss and you can buy him for $10,000

After unlocking these guitars, you can buy them in the shop.

UNLOCKABLE GUITARS

UNLOCKABLE	HOW TO UNLOCK
Assassin Bass	5-star Co-op Expert mode.
Bat Guitar	5-star all songs in Easy mode.
Beach Life Bass	Complete Co-Op Career Hard mode.
El Jefe Guitar	5-star all songs in Expert mode.
Jolly Roger Guitar	5-star all songs in Medium mode.
Moon Guitar	Complete Easy mode.
Pendulaxe Blade Bass	Complete Co-op Expert mode.
Risk Assessment Guitar	Complete Expert mode.
Rojimbo! Guitar	Complete Hard mode.
Saint George Guitar	Complete Medium mode.
Tiki Face Guitar	5-star all songs in Hard mode.
Tiki Fortune 4 Bass	Complete Co-op Easy mode.

GUITAR HERO 5 (XBOX 360)

CODES

Enter these codes to activate the following cheats. (G = Green; R = Red; Y =Yellow; B = Blue)

EFFECT	CODE
Air Instruments	R R B Y G G G Y
All HOPOs	G G B G G G Y G
Always Slide	G G R R Y B Y B
AutoKick	Y G R B B B B R
Contest Winner 1	G G R R Y R Y B
Focus Mode	Y G R G Y B G G
HUD-Free Mode	G R G G Y G G G
Invisible Characters	G R Y Y Y B B G
Performance Mode	Y Y B R B G R R
Unlock All Characters	B B G G R G R Y

UNLOCKABLES

UNLOCKABLE	HOW TO UNLOCK
Character: Carlos Santana	Complete the song "No One to Depend On (Live)" on any difficulty, any instrument.
Character: Johnny Cash	Complete the song "Ring of Fire" on any difficulty, any instrument.
Character: Kurt Cobain	Complete the song "Smells Like Teen Spirit" on any difficulty, any instrument.
Character: Matt Bellamy	Complete the song "Plug In Baby" on any instrument on any difficulty.
Character: Shirley Manson	Complete the song "I'm Only Happy When It Rains" on any difficulty, any instrument.
Cheat: All HOPOs (Changes almost every note possible into a HOPO or Hammer-On/ Pull-Off note)	As guitarist, whammy sustain notes on the song "Hurts So Good" for 25 seconds total or more (in Club Boson venue).
Cheat: All Slider Gems (All single notes are changed into slider/tap notes)	As guitarist, hit 230 tap notes on the song "Du Hast" (in Neon Oasis venue).

UNLOCKABLE	HOW TO UNLOCK
Cheat: Auto-kick (all kick bass notes are autoplayed)	As drummer, hit 200 non-cymbal notes on "Mirror People" (in Angel's Crypt venue, fills don't count).
Extra: Air Instruments (Instruments will be almost completely invisible, guitar strings will still be visible)	As Guitarist, strum 340 chords or more on the song "Sultans of Swing" (in O'Connel's Corner venue).
Extra: Focus Mode (blacks out background)	As a drummer, hit 265 tom notes on "Brianstorm" (in the Golden Gate venue).
Extra: HUD-Free Mode (removes rock meter, star power gauge, score display)	as a vocalist, get Excellent on 75 consecutive phrases in the rap song "Bring The Noise 20XX" (in Neon Oasis venue).
Extra: Performance Mode (removes track and HUD)	With two players, get a band multiplier for 42 seconds on "Bleed American" (in the Aqueduct venue).
Quickplay Venue "Wormhole" (required for The Grand Tour)	As guitarist, 4X multiplier for 50 seconds on "Play That Funky Music" (in Sideshow venue).

UNLOCKABLES

UNLOCKABLE	HOW TO UNLOCK
Character: Carlos Santana	Complete the song "No One to Depend On (Live)" on any difficulty, any instrument.
Character: Johnny Cash	Complete the song "Ring of Fire" on any difficulty, any instrument.
Character: Kurt Cobain	Complete the song "Smells Like Teen Spirit" on any difficulty, any instrument.
Character: Matt Bellamy	Complete the song "Plug In Baby" on any instrument on any difficulty.
Character: Shirley Manson	Complete the song "I'm Only Happy When It Rains" on any difficulty, any instrument.

GUITAR HERO 5 (PlayStation 3)

CODES

Enter these codes to activate the following cheats. (G = Green; R = Red; Y =Yellow; B = Blue)

EFFECT	CODE
Air Instruments	R R B Y G G G Y
All HOPOs	G G B G G G Y G
Always Slide	G G R R Y B Y B
AutoKick	Y G R B B B B R
Contest Winner 1	G G R R Y R Y B
Focus Mode	Y G R G Y B G G
HUD-Free Mode	G R G G Y G G G
Invisible Characters	G R Y Y Y B B G
Performance Mode	Y Y B R B G R R
Unlock All Characters	B B G G R G R Y

UNLOCKABLES

UNLOCKABLE	HOW TO UNLOCK
Character: Carlos Santana	Complete the song "No One to Depend On (Live)" on any difficulty, any instrument.
Character: Johnny Cash	Complete the song "Ring of Fire" on any difficulty, any instrument.
Character: Kurt Cobain	Complete the song "Smells Like Teen Spirit" on any difficulty, any instrument.
Character: Matt Bellamy	Complete the song "Plug In Baby" on any instrument on any difficulty.

Character: Shirley Manson	Complete the song "I'm Only Happy When It Rains" on any difficulty, any instrument.
Cheat: All HOPOs (Changes almost every note possible into a HOPO, or Hammer-On/ Pull-Off note)	As guitarist, whammy sustain notes on the song "Hurts So Good" for 25 seconds total or more (in Club Boson venue).
Cheat: All Slider Gems (All single notes are changed into slider/tap notes)	As guitarist, hit 230 tap notes on the song "Du Hast" (in Neon Oasis venue).
Cheat: Auto-kick (all kick bass notes are autoplayed)	As drummer, hit 200 non-cymbal notes on "Mirror People" (in Angel's Crypt venue, fills don't count).
Extra: Air Instruments (Instruments will be almost completely invisible, guitar strings will still be visible)	As Guitarist, strum 340 chords or more on the song "Sultans of Swing" (in O'Connel's Corner venue).
Extra: Focus Mode (blacks out background)	As a drummer, hit 265 tom notes on "Brianstorm" (in The Golden Gate venue).
Extra: HUD-Free Mode (removes rock meter, star, power gauge score display)	As a vocalist, get Excellent on 75 consecutive phrases in the rap song "Bring The Noise 20XX" (in Neon Oasis venue).
Extra: Performance Mode (removes track and HUD)	With two players, get a band multiplier for 42 seconds on "Bleed American" (in the Aqueduct venue).
Quickplay Venue "Wormhole" (required for The Grand Tour)	As guitarist, 4X multiplier for 50 seconds on "Play That Funky Music" (in Sideshow venue).

GUITAR HERO 5 (Wii)

CODES

Enter these codes to activate the following cheats. (G = Green; R = Red; Y =Yellow; B = Blue)

EFFECT	CODE
Air Instruments	R R B Y G G G Y
All HOPOs	G G B G G G Y G
Always Slide	G G R R Y B Y B
AutoKick	Y G R B B B B R
Contest Winner 1	G G R R Y R Y B
Focus Mode	Y G R G Y B G G
HUD-Free Mode	G R G G Y G G G
Invisible Characters	G R Y Y Y B B G
Performance Mode	Y Y B R B G R R
Unlock All Characters	B B G G R G R Y

UNLOCKABLES

UNLOCKABLE	HOW TO UNLOCK
Character: Carlos Santana	Complete the song "No One to Depend On (Live)" on any difficulty, any instrument.
Character: Johnny Cash	Complete the song "Ring of Fire" on any difficulty, any instrument.
Character: Kurt Cobain	Complete the song "Smells Like Teen Spirit" on any difficulty, any instrument.
Character: Matt Bellamy	Complete the song "Plug in Baby" on any instrument on any difficulty.
Character: Shirley Manson	Complete the song "I'm Only Happy When It Rains" on any difficulty, any instrument.

GUITAR HERO: AEROSMITH (XBOX 360)

CHEAT CHORDS

Strum the following chords in the "Cheats" menu. A message should appear if you strummed them correctly. You can then turn them on or off in from the menu.

EFFECT	CODE
Air Guitar (Guitarist plays without a guitar in the game)	(RY) (GR) (RY) (RY) (RB) (RB) (RB) (RB) (RB) (YB) (YB) (YO)
Hyperspeed (Faster Gameplay)	(YO) (YO) (YO) (YO) (YO) (RY) (RY) (RY) (RY) (RB) (RB) (RB) (RB) (RB) (YB) (YO) (YO)
No Fail (Makes it impossible to fail a song, doesn't work in Career mode, and disables online scores)	(GR) (B) (GR) (GY) (B) (GY) (RY) (O) (RY) (GY) (Y) (GY) (GR)
Performance Mode (No notes, just the song playing)	(GR) (GR) (RO) (RB) (GR) (GR) (RO) (RB)
Precision Mode (Makes it harder to miss notes)	(RY) (RB) (RB) (RY) (RY) (YB) (YB) (YB) (RB) (RY) (RB) (RB) (RY) (RY) (YB) (YB) (YB) (RB)
Unlock All Songs (except for "Pandora's Box" by Aerosmith)	(RY) (GR) (GR) (RY) (RY) (GR) (RY) (RY) (GR) GR) (RY) (RY) (GR) (RY) (RB)

CHARACTERS

Once unlocked, the following characters will be available for purchase in Career mode.

UNLOCKABLE	HOW TO UNLOCK
DMC	Beat "King of Rock" by Run DMC.
Joe Perry	Defeat Joe Perry in a Guitar Battle in Career mode.

SONGS

Once unlocked, the following songs can be accessed by pushing the blue fret button on the main setlist.

UNLOCKABLE	HOW TO UNLOCK
Aerosmith: "Kings and Queens"	Complete the Career Tour.
Joe Perry: "Joe Perry Guitar Battle"	Defeat Joe Perry in a Guitar Battle in Career mode.

GUITAR HERO: AEROSMITH (PlayStation 3)

CHEAT CHORDS

Strum the following chords in the "Cheats" menu. A message should appear if you strummed them correctly. You can then turn them on or off in from the menu.

EFFECT	CODE
Air Guitar (Guitarist plays without a guitar in the game)	(RY) (GR) (RY) (RY) (RB) (RB) (RB) (RB) (RB) (YB) (YB) (YO)
Hyperspeed (Faster Gameplay)	(YO) (YO) (YO) (YO) (YO) (RY) (RY) (RY) (RY) (RB) (RB) (RB) (RB) (RB) (YB) (YO) (YO)
No Fail (Makes it impossible to fail a song, doesn't work in Career mode, and disables online scores)	(GR) (B) (GR) (GY) (B) (GY) (RY) (O) (RY) (GY) (Y) (GY) (GR)
Performance Mode (No notes, just the song playing)	(GR) (GR) (RO) (RB) (GR) (GR) (RO) (RB)
Precision Mode (Makes it harder to miss notes)	(RY) (RB) (RB) (RY) (RY) (YB) (YB) (YB) (RB) (RY) (RB) (RB) (RY) (RY) (YB) (YB) (YB) (RB)
Unlock All Songs (except for "Pandora's Box" by Aerosmith)	(RY) (GR) (GR) (RY) (RY) (GR) (RY) (RY) (GR) GR) (RY) (RY) (GR) (RY) (RB)

UNLOCKABLES

UNLOCKABLE	HOW TO UNLOCK
Character: DMC	Complete all of the songs in the fourth tier list to unlock him for purchase for $15,000.
Guitar: Doubleneck	Get a "5 Star" rank on all songs, except the bonus song, under the Expert difficulty.
Guitar: Get a Grip	Complete Career mode under the Hard difficulty.
Guitar: Nine Lives (Daredevil)	Complete Career mode under the Easy difficulty.
Guitar: Permanent Vacation	Complete the game under the Medium difficulty.
Guitar: Rock in a Hard Place (Zeitgeist)	Get a "5 Star" rank on all songs, except the bonus song, under the Medium difficulty.
Guitar: Toys in the Attic (Rocking Horse)	Get a "5 Star" rank on all songs, except the bonus song, under the Easy difficulty.
Guitar: Walk This Way	Complete Career mode under the Expert difficulty.
Song: "Joe Perry Guitar Battle" by Joe Perry	Complete "Guitar Battle vs. Joe Perry" after the sixth tier warm-up acts.
Song: "Kings and Queens" by Aerosmtih	Complete Career mode.

GUITAR HERO: METALLICA (XBOX 360)

CODES

At the main menu select "Settings," "Cheats," and then "Enter New Cheat." Input the cheats below using the Green, Red, Yellow, and Blue colored fret buttons. You will receive a special message if you entered the codes correctly.

EFFECT	CODE
Air Instruments	RRBYGGGY
Always Drum Fill	RRRBBGGY
Always Slide	GGRRYRYB
Auto Kick	YGRBBBBR
Black Highway	YRGRGRRB
Extra Line 6 Tones	GRYBRYBG
Flame Color	GRGBRRYB
Gem Color	BRRGRGRY
Hyperspeed Mode	GBRYYRGG
Invisible Characters	GRYYYBBG
Metallica Costumes	GRYBBYRG
Performance Mode	YYBRBGRR
Star Color	RRYRBRRB
Vocal Fireball	RGGYBGYG

UNLOCKABLES

UNLOCKABLE	HOW TO UNLOCK
James Hetfield	Earn 100 stars in vocalist career.
James Hetfield Classic	Earn 150 stars in vocalist career.
James Hetfield Zombie	Earn 200 stars in vocalist career.
King Diamond	Beat the song "Evil" in any instrument career.
Kirk Hammett	Earn 100 stars in guitar career.
Kirk Hammett Classic	Earn 150 stars in guitar career.
Kirk Hammett Zombie	Earn 200 stars in guitar career.
Lars Ulrich	Earn 100 stars in drum career.
Lars Ulrich Classic	Earn 150 stars in drum career.
Lars Ulrich Zombie	Earn 200 stars in drum career.

UNLOCKABLE	HOW TO UNLOCK
Lemmy	Beat the song "Ace of Spades" in any instrument career mode.
Robert Trujillo	Earn 100 stars in bass career.
Robert Trujillo Classic	Earn 150 stars in bass career.
Robert Trujillo Zombie	Earn 200 stars in bass career.

GUITAR HERO: METALLICA (PlayStation 3)

CODES

At the main menu select "Settings," "Cheats," and then "Enter New Cheat." Input the cheats below using the Green, Red, Yellow, and Blue colored fret buttons. You will receive a special message if you enter the codes correctly.

EFFECT	CODE
Air Instruments	RRBYGGGY
Always Drum Fill	RRRBBGGY
Always Slide	GGRRYRYB
Auto Kick	YGRBBBBR
Black Highway	YRGRGRRB
Extra Line 6 Tones	GRYBRYBG
Flame Color	GRGBRRYB
Gem Color	BRRGRGRY
Hyperspeed Mode	GBRYYRGG
Invisible Characters	GRYYYBBG
Metallica Costumes	GRYBBYRG
Performance Mode	YYBRBGRR
Star Color	RRYRBRRB
Vocal Fireball	RGGYBGYG

UNLOCKABLES

UNLOCKABLE	HOW TO UNLOCK
James Hetfield	Earn 100 stars in vocalist career.
James Hetfield Classic	Earn 150 stars in vocalist career.
James Hetfield Zombie	Earn 200 stars in vocalist career.
King Diamond	Beat the song "Evil" in any instrument career.
Kirk Hammett	Earn 100 stars in guitar career.
Kirk Hammett Classic	Earn 150 stars in guitar career.
Kirk Hammett Zombie	Earn 200 stars in guitar career.
Lars Ulrich	Earn 100 stars in drum career.
Lars Ulrich Classic	Earn 150 stars in drum career.
Lars Ulrich Zombie	Earn 200 stars in drum career.
Lemmy	Beat the song "Ace of Spades" in any instrument Career mode.
Robert Trujillo	Earn 100 stars in bass career.
Robert Trujillo Classic	Earn 150 stars in bass career.
Robert Trujillo Zombie	Earn 200 stars in bass career.

GUITAR HERO: METALLICA (Wii)

CODES

At the main menu select "Settings," "Cheats," and then "Enter New Cheat." Input the cheats below using the Green, Red, Yellow, and Blue colored fret buttons. You will receive a special message if you entered the codes correctly.

EFFECT	CODE
Air Instruments	RRBYGGGY
Always Drum Fill	RRRBBGGY
Always Slide	GGRRYRYB
Auto Kick	YGRBBBBR
Black Highway	YRGRGRRB
Extra Line 6 Tones	GRYBRYBG
Flame Color	GRGBRRYB
Gem Color	BRRGRGRY
Hyperspeed Mode	GBRYYRGG
Invisible Characters	GRYYYBBG
Metallica Costumes	GRYBBYRG
Performance Mode	YYBRBGRR
Star Color	RRYRBRRB
Vocal Fireball	RGGYBGYG

GUITAR HERO: SMASH HITS (PlayStation 2)

CODES

Enter these in the Enter Cheat option in the Cheats menu under Options.

EFFECT	CODE
Air Instruments (Cannot be combined with Invisible Rocker)	YRBGYRRR
Always Drum Fill	GGRRBBYY
Always Slide	BYRGBGGY
Flame Color	YBRGYRGB
Gem Color	RRRBBBYG
Hyperspeed (Broken into HyperGuitar, HyperBass, and HyperDrum, and goes from Off to 5)	RGBYGYRR
Invisible Rocker (Cannot be combined with Air Instruments)	BRRRRYBG
Star Color	GRGYGBYR
Vocal Fireball	GBRRYYBB

GUITAR HERO: VAN HALEN (XBOX 360)

CODES

From the Main menu go to "Settings," then "Cheats," then "Enter New Cheat."

EFFECT	CODE
Air instruments	R,R,B,Y,G,G,G,Y
Always Drum Fill	R,R,R,B,B,G,G,Y
Always Slide	G,G,R,R,Y,R,Y,B
Auto Kick	Y,G,R,B,B,B,B,R
Black Highway	Y,R,G,R,G,R,R,B
Extra Line 6 Tones	G,R,Y,B,R,Y,B,G
Flame Color	G,R,G,B,R,R,Y,B
Gem Color	B,R,R,G,R,G,R,Y
Invisible Rocker	G,R,Y,Y,Y,B,B,G
Performance Mode	Y,Y,B,R,B,G,R,R
Star Color	R,R,Y,R,B,R,R,B
Vocal Fireball	R,G,G,Y,B,G,Y,G

GUITAR HERO ENCORE: ROCKS THE 80S (PlayStation 2)

At the main menu, enter a code to get the desired effect.

G: Press the Green fret button.

R: Press the Red fret button.

Y: Press the Yellow fret button.

B: Press the Blue fret button.

O: Press the Orange fret button.

CODE	CODE EFFECT
Y,B,Y,O,B,B	Air Guitar
Y,B,O,O,O,B,Y	Crowd Has Eyeball Heads
B,B,O,Y,B,B,O,Y	Crowd Has Monkey Heads
Y,O,Y,O,Y,O,B,O	Flame Head
B,O,O,B,Y,B,O,O,B,Y	Horse Head
Y,B,O,O,B,Y,Y,O	Hyperspeed Activate/De-Activate
B,B,O,Y,Y,B,O,B	Performance Mode
B,O,Y,R,O,Y,B,Y,R,Y,B,Y,R,Y,B,Y	Unlock Everything

UNLOCKABLE GUITARS

Complete the following to be able to buy the guitar in the shop.

Axe Guitar	Beat Expert Career
Casket Guitar	Beat Medium Career
Eyeball Guitar	Five star every song on Hard Career
Fish Guitar	Beat Easy Career
Snaketapus Guitar	Beat Hard Career
The LOG Guitar	Five star every song on Expert Career
USA Guitar	Five star every song on Easy Career
Viking Guitar	Five star every song on Medium Career

GUNSTAR HEROES (Wii)

UNLOCKABLES

UNLOCKABLE	HOW TO UNLOCK
Hidden Special Move	With either Gunstar Red or Gunstar Blue motion: ↓, →↓, →, →←, ←+shot button to execute a powerful standing slide.
Make the Logo Rotate	Hold ↓ on controller 1 before the Gunstar Heroes logo appears on the screen in order to rotate it.

Timeron's Secret

During the second Timeron encounter (which is in the Space Battle stage) a timer begins ticking from 00'00"00. As the timer keeps going, the Timeron's attacks change, and every 20 minutes or so, a circular drone appears, accompanied by Smash Daisaku's laughter. Avoid this drone for about 2 minutes until it self-destructs, because a single hit will reduce your health to zero. At about 50'00"00 or so, large blue balls appear. These rebound once against the screen, and do 11 points of damage instead of the normal 10 points from the smaller ones. Once the timer gets up to 99'50"00 or so, don't destroy the Timeron yet. Instead, wait out the remaining 10 seconds while avoiding the Timeron's attacks, but don't stay too close to the Timeron, or you'll get killed by the drone. Once the timer reaches 00'00"00 again, you'll hear that nasty laughter again, but this time, "GIVE UP!!" appears in the middle of the screen, and the Timeron self-destructs, accompanied by the message, "YOU OPENED THE - SATORI MIND -." A bit more of that nasty laughter accompanies the next message, "REPROGRAMMED BY NAMI - 1993." Now, instead of getting a Timer Bonus as you usually would, a Soul Bonus of exactly 930,410 points is added to your score.

HALF-LIFE (PlayStation 2)

Go to Options, then Cheat Codes, and enter the following:

UNLOCKABLE	CODE
Alien Mode	↑,▲,↑,▲,↑,▲,↑,▲
Infinite Ammo	↓,×,←,●,↓,×,←,●
Invincibility	←,■,↑,▲,→,●,↓,×
Invisibility	←,■,→,●,←,■,→,●
Slow Motion	→,■,↑,▲,→,■,↑,▲
Xen Gravity	↑,▲,↓,×,↑,▲,↓,×

HALF-LIFE 2 (XBOX)

Enter these codes while playing; do not pause the game.

UNLOCKABLE	CODE
Restores 25 points of health (per use)	↑, ↑, ↓, ↓, ←, →, ←, →, B, A
Restores ammo for current weapon	Y, B, A, X, WHT, Y, X, A, B, WHT
Unlocks all chapters	←, ←, ←, ←, BLK, →, →, →, →, WHT

HALF-LIFE 2: THE ORANGE BOX (XBOX 360)

HALF-LIFE 2 *CODES*

Enter the code while playing *Half Life 2*. No specific requirements other than the game. Can be entered at any time on any level. Using cheats does not disable Achievements.

CODE	EFFECT
LB,↑,RB,↑,LB,LB,↑,RB,RB,↑	Invincibility
↑,↑,↓,↓,←,→,←,→,B,A	Restores health by 25 points
Y,B,A,X,RB,Y,X,A,B,RB	Restores ammo for current weapon
←,←,←,←,P,→,→,→,→,RB	Unlocks all levels, which can then be accessed from the new game window

PORTAL CODES

Enter these codes anytime during gameplay.

CODE	EFFECT
↓,B,A,B,Y,↓,B,A,B,Y	Create box
LB,↓,RB,↓,LB,LB,↑,RB,RB,↑	Enables invincibility
↑,Y,Y,X,X,A,A,B,B,↑	Fire energy ball
Y,A,B,A,B,Y,Y,A,←,→	Portal placement anywhere
X,B,LB,RB,←,→,LB,RB,LT,RT	Upgrade Portalgun

HALF-LIFE 2: THE ORANGE BOX (PlayStation 3)

HALF-LIFE 2 CODES

Enter the code while playing. Codes can be entered at any time on any level.

EFFECT	CODE
Restore Ammo (for current weapon)	R1,▲,●,×,■,R1,▲,■,×,●,R1
Restore Health by 25 Points	↑,↑,↓,↓,←,→,←,→,●,×
Unlock All Levels	←,←,←,←,L1,→,→,→,→,R1

PORTAL CODES

Enter these codes any time during gameplay.

EFFECT	CODE
Create a Cube	↓,●,×,●,▲,↓,●,×,●,▲
Fire Energy Ball	↑,▲,▲,■,■,×,×,●,●,↑
Unlock All Levels	←,←,←,←,L1,→,→,→,→,R1

HALO 3 (XBOX 360)

CODES

The following cheats can be performed during a local match or replay only. Press and hold the corresponding buttons for 3 SECONDS to toggle the effect on / off.

EFFECT	CODE
Toggle Hide Weapon	LB,RB,L3,A,↓
Toggle Pan-Cam / Normal while Show Coordinates is enabled.	Hold L3 and R3 and press ←
Toggle Show Coordinates / Camera Mode	LB,+,L3,A,↑

ARMOR PERMUTATIONS UNLOCKABLES

Body Pieces: Spartan marked with (S) and Elite marked with (E).

UNLOCKABLE	HOW TO UNLOCK
(E) Ascetic Body	Unlock "Up Close and Personal" Achievement
(E) Ascetic Head	Unlock "Steppin' Razor" Achievement
(E) Ascetic Shoulders	Unlock "Overkill" Achievement
(E) Commando Body	Unlock "Triple Kill" Achievement
(E) Commando Head	Unlock "Overkill" Achievement
(E) Commando Shoulders	Unlock "Killing Frenzy" Achievement
(E) Flight Body	Complete Tsavo Highway on Heroic or Legendary
(E) Flight Head	Complete Campaign mode on Heroic
(E) Flight Shoulders	Complete The Ark on Heroic difficulty or higher
(S) EOD Body	Complete Tsavo Highway on Legendary
(S) EOD Head	Complete Campaign mode on Legendary
(S) EOD Shoulders	Complete The Ark on Legendary
(S) EVA Body	Complete Tsavo Highway on Normal or higher
(S) EVA Head	Complete Campaign mode on Normal
(S) EVA Shoulders	Complete The Ark on Normal difficulty or higher
(S) Hayabusa Chest	Collect 5 hidden skulls
(S) Hayabusa Helmet	Collect 13 hidden skulls
(S) Hayabusa Shoulders	Collect 9 hidden skulls
(S) Mark V Head	Unlock "UNSC Spartan" Achievement
(S) ODST Head	Unlock "Spartan Graduate" Achievement
(S) Rogue Head	Unlock "Spartan Officer" Achievement
(S) Scout Body	Unlock "Too Close to the Sun" Achievement
(S) Scout Head	Unlock "Used Car Salesman" Achievement
(S) Scout Shoulders	Unlock "Mongoose Mowdown" Achievement
(S) Security Head	Earn 1,000 Gamerscore points
(S) Security Shoulders	Earn 850 Gamerscore points
Katana	Complete all Achievements (1,000/1,000)

BLACK-EYE SKULL

Effect: Melee hits instantly recharge your shield.

Level: Crow's Nest

NEW!
A B C D E F G H I J K L M N O P Q R S T U V W X Y Z

Location: As soon as you start the level, head straight up to the higher level. Head toward the door with the red light, then turn around. Jump onto the racks, onto the red metal light holders, then onto the ventilation tube. The skull spawns at the end.

BLIND SKULL

Effect: "Shoot from the hip."

Level: First Stage

Location: When you get to the area where you see the Phantom overhead (one of the marines points it out) jump over the rocks and keep following the path on the right. When you get to the cliff, there's a rock over on the side. The skull is on the end of the rock. Note: This skull has to be activated before you start a Campaign map.

CATCH SKULL

Effect: all enemies have 2 grenades, throw more grenades.

Level: The Storm

Location: From the start, go through until you go outside again. Outside, look straight across to a small round building. The skull is on top. To get up there, either use a warthog as a platform or grenade-jump. DO NOT destroy the wraith near the door or the skull will disappear.

COWBELL SKULL

Effect: Explosive force increased (sputnik from H2).

Level: The Ark

Location: First pick up a grav lift from the small building near where you fight the scarab. Now proceed through the level until you reach the second sloping hallway (stairway). You should see some partitioned risers (platforms) halfway down. The skull is on the top level. Toss the grav-lift on the right side of the hall so it lands on the fourth little green dot from the door. Then run, jump, and use the grav-lift to propel you to the top. You reach a checkpoint just as you enter the room, so if you miss, just try again.

FAMINE SKULL

Effect: "Trust us. Bring a magazine." Dropped weapons have very little ammo compared to normal.

Level: The Ark

Location: When you first go into the valley to the right after the wrecked phantom, look left to see a huge boulder. Use a ghost and get to the side of the boulder closest to the bridge overhead. It is easy to pilot the ghost up the side of the wall using the thrust. To get the skull, pilot 2 ghosts up the wall to the top of the bridge and stack them one on top of another next to the beam where the skull is placed. Simply jump from the top of the ghosts toward the skull and land on the beam.

FOG SKULL

Effect: "You'll miss those eyes in the back of your head." Your motion sensor disappears.

Level: Floodgate

Location: As you are walking down from the anti-air gun you destroyed in the previous mission, you encounter a ramp (next to a missile launcher). Around this ramp, you hit a checkpoint. At this point, you should also hear a marine yelling, "There! Over There!" Look up and to the right, directly at the roof of the building next to the missile launcher. A single flood form (not to be mistaken for the two other flood forms jumping in front of you) holds the skull. Kill him before he jumps, and he drops the skull down to the ground where you can retrieve it. If you shoot too early, and the skull gets stuck on the roof.

GRUNT BIRTHDAY PARTY SKULL

Effect: Headshots on grunts cause heads to explode with confetti.

Level: Crow's Nest

Location: Right after the first objective, while en route to the barracks, you fall onto a pipe. At the end of this pipe, look over the edge to see a small space a few feet below you. Drop over and as quickly as you can, pull back to land under the floor you were just on. The skull is at the end.

IRON SKULL

Effect: When either player dies in Co-Op on any difficulty both players restart at last checkpoint. In single player, you restart the level if you die.

Level: Sierra 117

Location: In the area where you rescue Sarge, behind the prison cell is a large ledge. Go to the far right side and jump on the boxes, then onto the pipes to get up on the ledge. Go to the far end of the ledge, turn two corners, and the skull is at the far end.

IWHBYD SKULL

Effect: "But the dog beat me over the fence." Unlocks bonus dialogue throughout the game. For most, this is the last skull, so this gives you the Hayabusa Helmet as well.

Level: The Covenant

Location: To get this, get to the room where you "fight" the Prophet of Truth. Let the Arbiter kill him, turn around, and kill all the flood here as well. This makes it a lot easier. Then jump through the Halo holograms in this order: 4 6 5 4 5 3 4. When you jump through the final hologram, they all light up in a sequential pattern. The skull is at the end, right before the energy bridge leading to Truth's corpse.

MYTHIC SKULL

Effect: Every enemy on the field now has double the normal amount of health.

Level: Halo

Location: As soon as the mission starts, walk up the hill in front of you and into the cave. Hug the right side of the cave, and after a large boulder you see a path on your right. Take the short path and find it at the end.

THUNDERSTORM SKULL

Effect: "Field promotions for everyone!" Upgrades enemies to their stronger versions.

Level: The Covenant

Location: After you shut down tower 1 and get access to the hornet, fly to tower 2 (the one the Arbiter shut down). While walking up the stairs, go to the middle part that connects both. A stair leads up to a platform where the skull is.

TILT SKULL

Effect: "What was once resistance is now immunity." Enemies have different body parts that may be resistant to certain bullet types.

Level: Cortana

Location: When in the circular type room with all the flood, look for a small structure piece next to two archways. Jump on top of it and up on the rocks to the top left, turn left and jump up again, then do a 180 and jump to the rocks across from you. Follow the rock sticking out and leading up on top of the original circular room. The skull is in a pile of blood.

TOUGH LUCK SKULL

Effect: Enemies do saving throws.

Level: Tsavo Highway

Location: On Tsavo Highway, about halfway through the mission (right after you are forced to walk through a large blue barrier), you will come out of a tunnel on the highway, and see a large pipeline on your left. Drop down in between the two, and run to the wall in front of you. Follow the wall all the way to where it connects with the cliff on your right, and turn to the left. There should be a few ledges—simply crouch-jump from ledge to ledge, and the last one should have the "Tough Luck" skull on it.

THE SEVEN TERMINALS

The Ark:

1. Start the mission and once you enter the first building, take a left into another door and emerge in a curved corridor. On the inside is a Terminal.

2. After activating the bridge to let your comrades across the gap, do a 180 and you should see it. (It does not open until you activate the bridge.)

3. In the third building after defeating the scarab, kill the group of sleeping covenant, then follow the corridor downward. Once you reach a door in front that is locked, immediately on the left there's an open door. Go through and walk straight, then do a 180 to find a secret room. It is in there.

The Covenant:

1. When in the first tower standing on the lift, face the access panel and turn left. Jump over and it's right there.
2. Land your hornet on the second tower, walk toward the entrance, but when you see the locked door, do a 180.
3. When in the third tower standing on the lift, face the access panel and turn right. Jump over.

Halo:

1. After reaching the end of the first cave, hug the right wall and you see a building. Jump up onto the walkway and hang a left once inside.

HALO 3: ODST (XBOX 360)

FIREFIGHT MISSIONS

Complete certain campaign missions to unlock new maps for the Firefight game mode.

UNLOCKABLE	HOW TO UNLOCK
Alpha Site	Complete the ONI Alpha Site campaign mission on any difficulty.
Chasm Ten	Complete the Date Hive campaign mission on any difficulty.
Last Exit	Complete the Coastal Highway campaign mission on any difficulty.
Lost Platoon	Complete the Uplift Reserve campaign mission on any difficulty.

FIREFIGHT UNLOCKABLE CHARACTERS

Perform the task to unlock characters for use in Firefight mode.

UNLOCKABLE	HOW TO UNLOCK
Buck Firefight Character	Complete "Tayari Plaza" on Normal or higher.
Dare Firefight Character	Complete the campaign on Legendary difficulty.
Dutch Firefight Character	Complete "Uplift Reserve" on Normal or higher.
Mickey Firefight Character	Complete "Kizingo Boulevard" on Normal or higher.
Romeo Character	Complete "NMPD HQ" on Normal or higher.

HALO WARS (XBOX 360)

BLACK BOXES

Black boxes in each level unlock new Halo History entries.

UNLOCKABLE	HOW TO UNLOCK
All Others	Win on each Skirmish map and win Skirmish with each leader.
Black Box 01—Alpha Base	Under the last bridge before entering Alpha Base.
Black Box 02—Relic Approach	Top left of the map, behind a Covenant shield.
Black Box 03—Relic Interior	On the small ramp on the left side, right at the start, before going inside the Relic.
Black Box 04—Arcadia City	Just north of the starting point, right next to the skyscraper where you can save Adam.
Black Box 05—Arcadia Outskirts	Go down the first ramp as you are fleeing from the Covenant; it's behind a downed Pelican.
Black Box 06—Dome of Light	Far left of the map, to the left of where you transport the third Rhino tank.
Black Box 07—Scarab	Far right side of the map, in a small alcove with supply crates.
Black Box 08—Anders' Signal	Near the big brute fire line at the start, on a ridge to the right.
Black Box 09—The Flood	Straight out from the base ramp on the other side of the map.
Black Box 10—Shield World	Alongside Bravo platoon, which is the middle platoon you pick up.
Black Box 11—Cleansing	Left rear of the ship, on wings that slant down; you'll need a flying unit.

Black Box 12—Repairs	Left edge of Spirit of Fire, not far from the Power Core building, on the left side.
Black Box 13—Beachhead	On a ledge near the second set of teleporters, near the Covenant base.
Black Box 14—Reactor	Up and left at the top of the first ramp, on the edge of the ramp.
Black Box 15—Escape	Directly opposite the starting point on the north edge of the map, between the Flood and the Covenant base.

SKULLS LOCATIONS/REQUIREMENTS

In each mission, you must meet the requirement before heading to the skull's location.

UNLOCKABLE	HOW TO UNLOCK
Skull Name: Boomstick (Mission 12: Repairs)	Kill 12 Spirit Transports—take a Hawk to the Lower 2 Airlocks and it's right up the little ramp in the air.
Skull Name: Bountiful Harvest (Mission 14: Reactor)	Kill 20 Vampires—head to the second Covenant base and it's in the far corner at the bottom of the next ramp.
Skull Name: Catch (Mission 10: Shield World)	Kill 350 Swarms—get at least 2 Hornets and fly east of you base past the First Tower to a Plateau covered with Flood Eggs; it is in the center.
Skull Name: Cowbell (Mission 3: Relic Interior) up	Kill 45 Hunters—take a Grizzly, Anders, Forge and your Marines back to where they were held on the central pad.
Skull Name: Emperor (Mission 15: Escape)	Kill 3 Scarabs—Head to the very north of the map and it's dead center in the flood.
Skull Name: Fog (Mission 5: Arcadia Outskirts)	Kill 5 Wraiths—get a Warthog and rush back up the tracks to the left of your main base and just keep going straight past the split in the tracks.
Skull Name: Grunt Birthday Party (Mission 2: Relic Approach)	Kill 20 Jackals—head back to Alpha base with a Warthog; it's in the south end of the base.
Skull Name: Look Daddy! (Mission 1: Alpha Base)	Kill 100 Grunts—get a Warthog and rush back to the front gate of Alpha base; the skull is where the Marines were held up.
Skull Name: Pain Train (Mission 13: Beachhead)	Kill 10 Bomber Forms—head back to the beginning of the map by the first teleporter and head down the path to a flood nest; it's right next to it.
Skull Name: Rebel Leader (Mission 9: The Flood)	Kill 20 Flood Stalks—just to the northeast of your main base is a downed Pelican. Just take a Warthog to claim it fast and easy.
Skull Name: Rebel Supporter (Mission 8: Anders' Signal)	Kill 750 Infection Forms—head to north side of the map where you got the Elephant, head east toward a cliff. But you'll see a ridge. Go into ridge.
Skull Name: Rebel Sympathizer (Mission 7: Scarab)	Kill 10 Locusts—get a Warthog and take it to the top-left of the map, where there were 2 Locusts and a Power Nod; it's right there.
Skull Name: Sickness (Mission 6: Dome of Light)	Kill 50 Banshees—take a squad of Marines to the hanger behind your base; it's right there.
Skull Name: Sugar Cookies (Mission 11: Cleansing)	Kill 100 Sentinels—take a Hornet to the front end of the Spirit of Fire and it is right on the nose of the ship.
Skull Name: Wuv Woo (Mission 4: Arcadia City)	Kill 50 Elites—where you set up base 2 in the streets there are some stairs next to it leading to a bronze statue. It's next to the statue.

HAPPY FEET (Wii)

UNLOCKABLES

UNLOCKABLE	HOW TO UNLOCK
"All Together Now"	33 Gold Medals
"Amigo Racing"	15 Gold Medals
"Boogie Wonderland"	21 Gold Medals
"Driving Gloria Away"	26 Gold Medals
"Mumble the Outsider"	06 Gold Medals
"Out of the Egg"	01 Gold Medal
"Somebody to Love"	12 Gold Medals
"The Zoo"	31 Gold Medals

HARRY POTTER AND THE GOBLET OF FIRE (PSP)

UNLOCKABLE LEVELS

UNLOCKABLE	HOW TO UNLOCK
Defense Against the Dark Arts (Lesson 1)	Finish the opening level
Moody's Challenges	Complete the "Forbidden Forest" level

UNLOCKABLE MINIGAMES

UNLOCKABLE	HOW TO UNLOCK
Dugbog Bulb Raid	Get 5 Tri-wizard Shields
Exploding Snap	Get 2 Tri-wizard Shields
Niffler Time Challenge	Get 8 Tri-wizard Shields
Wizard Pairs	Beat the first level of the game

HARRY POTTER AND THE HALF BLOOD PRINCE (XBOX 360)

UNLOCKABLES

Collect the following number of crests to unlock the corresponding bonuses.

UNLOCKABLE	HOW TO UNLOCK
Two-Player Dueling Pack 4: Paved Courtyard Dueling Arena	113 Hogwarts Crests
More mini-crests with each cast	129 Hogwarts Crests
Two-Player Dueling Pack 2: Training Ground Dueling Arena	14 Hogwarts Crests
Dungbombs in prank boxes around Hogwarts	21 Hogwarts Crests
Two-Player Dueling Pack 2: Crabbe & Goyle	29 Hogwarts Crests
Two-Player Dueling Pack 1: Draco & Luna	3 Hogwarts Crests
Score boost in flying events	38 Hogwarts Crests
Exploding Cauldrons in prank boxes around Hogwarts	48 Hogwarts Crests
Two-Player Dueling Pack 4: The Transfiguration Dueling Arena	59 Hogwarts Crests
Even More health in duels	71 Hogwarts Crests
More health in duels	8 Hogwarts Crests
Two-Player Dueling Pack 5: Ginny & Hermione	84 Hogwarts Crests
Love Potion in Potions Club	98 Hogwarts Crests

HARRY POTTER AND THE HALF BLOOD PRINCE (PlayStation 2)

CODES

Enter code at the rewards menu.

EFFECT	CODE
Unlocks Castle Gates two-player Dueling Arena	⇨,⇨,⇩,⇩,⇦,⇨,⇦,⇨,⇦,⇨,⬀

HARRY POTTER AND THE ORDER OF THE PHOENIX (XBOX 360)

ROOM OF REWARDS TROPHIES

UNLOCKABLE	HOW TO UNLOCK
Characters Cup	Meet all 58 characters in Hogwarts
Defense Against the Dark Arts Cup	Cast all defensive spells in six duels
House Ghost Cup	Find all four House Ghosts
Nature Trail Cup	Find all animal footprints

HARRY POTTER AND THE ORDER OF THE PHOENIX (PlayStation 3)

ROOM OF REWARDS TROPHIES

Successfully complete the indicated task to unlock the corresponding trophy.

UNLOCKABLE	HOW TO UNLOCK
Characters Cup	Meet all 58 characters in Hogwarts
Defense Against the Dark Arts Cup	Cast all defensive spells in 6 duels
House Ghost Cup	Find all 4 House Ghosts
Nature Trail Cup	Find all animal footprints

HAUNTED MANSION (XBOX)

To access the following unlockables, hold (RT) on the D-Pad, then enter code.

UNLOCKABLE	CODE
Level Select	(B),(B),(X),(Y),(Y),(X),(B),(A)
God Mode	(X),(B),(B),(B),(X),(B),(Y),(A)

HAUNTED MANSION (PlayStation 2)

While playing hold right on the d-pad and enter these codes.

UNLOCKABLE	CODE
God Mode	■, ●, ●, ●, ■, ●, ▲, ×
Level Select	●, ●, ■, ▲, ▲, ■, ●, ×
Upgrade Weapon	■, ■, ▲, ▲, ●, ●, ●, ×

HEADHUNTER (PlayStation 2)

DESCRIPTION	CODE
Activate Cheat Mode	Hold (R1) + ■ and press (START) during gameplay.

HEATSEEKER (Wii)

UNLOCKABLES

UNLOCKABLE	HOW TO UNLOCK
The Big One (SR-71 Blackbird's fourth Weapon Pack)	Successfully complete the Ace bonus objective
Top Secret plane (SR-71 Blackbird)	Successfully complete the Pilot bonus objective

HEAVENLY SWORD (PlayStation 3)

DIFFICULTIES

To unlock Hell mode, beat the game on Normal mode.

MAKING OF HEAVENLY SWORD

Unlock "Making of" videos by collecting the specified number of glyphs.

UNLOCKABLE	HOW TO UNLOCK
Bringing Design to Life	Obtain 37 glyphs.
Capturing Performance	Obtain 42 glyphs.
Creating the Music	Obtain 86 glyphs.
Introduction	Obtain 3 glyphs.
The Sound of Combat	Obtain 77 glyphs.

ART GALLERY

Unlock 107 pieces of concept and pre-production art by obtaining the following number of glyphs.

UNLOCKABLE	HOW TO UNLOCK
Andy Serkis as Bohan	Obtain 26 glyphs.
Andy Serkis as Bohan (2nd)	Obtain 40 glyphs.
Andy Serkis as Bohan (3rd)	Obtain 96 glyphs.
Andy Serkis Facial Sketch	Obtain 119 glyphs.
Anime Character Concept Art	Obtain 88 glyphs.
Arena Balcony Concept Art	Obtain 69 glyphs.
Arena Concept Art	Obtain 67 glyphs.
Assassin Concept Art	Obtain 85 glyphs.
Assassin Weapon Concept Art	Obtain 84 glyphs.
Axeman Concept Art	Obtain 35 glyphs.
Back of Snowy Fort	Obtain 2 glyphs.
Back of Snowy Fort (2nd)	Obtain 102 glyphs.
Bazooka Concept Art	Obtain 52 glyphs.
Bohan and Raven Concept Art	Obtain 90 glyphs.
Bohan Armor Concept Art	Obtain 17 glyphs.
Bohan Armor Concept Art (2nd)	Obtain 105 glyphs.
Bohan Early Concept Art	Obtain 33 glyphs.
Bohan Early Concept Art (2nd)	Obtain 44 glyphs.
Bohan Early Concept Art (3rd)	Obtain 123 glyphs.
Bohan Promo Screenshot	Obtain 39 glyphs.
Bohan Promo Screenshot (2nd)	Obtain 49 glyphs.
Bohan Weapon Concept Art	Obtain 21 glyphs.
Central Hall Early Concept Art	Obtain 53 glyphs.
Ch. 5 Port Concept Art	Obtain 19 glyphs.
Chainman Concept Art	Obtain 66 glyphs.
Clansmen Concept Art	Obtain 63 glyphs.
Commander Concept Art	Obtain 94 glyphs.
Cover Art—Bazooka	Obtain 71 glyphs.
Cover Art—Bohan	Obtain 97 glyphs.
Cover Art—Nariko	Obtain 73 glyphs.
Cover Art—Power Stance	Obtain 110 glyphs.
Cover Art—Ranged Attack	Obtain 70 glyphs.
Crossbowman Concept Art	Obtain 104 glyphs.
Decrepit Temple Concept Art	Obtain 89 glyphs.
Desert Battleground Concept Art	Obtain 81 glyphs.
Desert Buildings Concept Art	Obtain 99 glyphs.
Desert Fort Concept Art	Obtain 93 glyphs.
Desert Level Concept Art	Obtain 116 glyphs.
Early Bohan Weapon Concept Art	Obtain 106 glyphs.
Early Packaging Concept Art	Obtain 72 glyphs.
Early Pond Concept Art	Obtain 111 glyphs.
Encampment Concept Art	Obtain 103 glyphs.
Encampment Concept Art (2nd)	Obtain 114 glyphs.
Environment Early Concept Art	Obtain 55 glyphs.

Environment Early Concept Art (2nd)	Obtain 59 glyphs.
Environment Early Concept Art (3rd)	Obtain 115 glyphs.
Flying Fox Costume Concept Art	Obtain 25 glyphs.
Flying Fox Facial Concept Art	Obtain 30 glyphs.
Forest Patch Concept Art	Obtain 57 glyphs.
Funeral Boat Concept Art	Obtain 124 glyphs.
Funeral Landscape Concept Art	Obtain 125 glyphs.
Funeral Landscape Painting	Obtain 126 glyphs.
Heaven and Hell Concept Art	Obtain 118 glyphs.
Heavenly Sword Concept Art	Obtain 60 glyphs.
Kai Concept Art	Obtain 6 glyphs.
Kai Early Concept Art	Obtain 8 glyphs.
Kai Early Concept Art (2nd)	Obtain 34 glyphs.
Kai Promo Screenshot	Obtain 46 glyphs.
Kai Promo Screenshot (2nd)	Obtain 127 glyphs.
Kai with Bow Concept Art	Obtain 29 glyphs.
Nariko Approaching Cage	Obtain 101 glyphs.
Nariko Color Sketch	Obtain 9 glyphs.
Nariko Costume Concept Art	Obtain 23 glyphs.
Nariko Early Concept Art	Obtain 80 glyphs.
Nariko Early Concept Art (2nd)	Obtain 87 glyphs.
Nariko Early Concept Art (3rd)	Obtain 109 glyphs.
Nariko Early Cover	Obtain 13 glyphs.
Nariko Imprisoned Concept Art	Obtain 64 glyphs.
Nariko Pencil Sketch	Obtain 12 glyphs.
Nariko Promo Screenshot	Obtain 20 glyphs.
Nariko Promo Screenshot (2nd)	Obtain 31 glyphs.
Nariko Promo Screenshot (2nd)	Obtain 129 glyphs.
Nariko with Heavenly Sword	Obtain 27 glyphs.
Natural Bridge Concept Art	Obtain 62 glyphs.
Oraguman Concept Art	Obtain 78 glyphs.
Oraguman Sketch	Obtain 79 glyphs.
Packaging Artwork	Obtain 98 glyphs.
Prison Approach Concept Art	Obtain 56 glyphs.
Prison Exterior Concept Art	Obtain 112 glyphs.
Prison Interior Concept Art	Obtain 113 glyphs.
Rain Battle Concept Art	Obtain 100 glyphs.
Raven Concept Art	Obtain 117 glyphs.
Raven God Concept Art	Obtain 121 glyphs.
Raven God Early Concept Art	Obtain 122 glyphs.
Raven God Facial Sketch	Obtain 120 glyphs.
Roach Concept Art	Obtain 41 glyphs.
Roach Weapon Concept Art	Obtain 83 glyphs.
Shen Concept Art	Obtain 4 glyphs.
Shen Promo Screenshot	Obtain 128 glyphs.
Shen with Staff	Obtain 5 glyphs.
Snowy Fort Concept Art	Obtain 1 glyph.
Swordsman Concept Art	Obtain 11 glyphs.

UNLOCKABLE	HOW TO UNLOCK
Swordsman Concept Art (2nd)	Obtain 51 glyphs.
The Sword Early Concept Art	Obtain 50 glyphs.
The Sword Landscape Concept Art	Obtain 107 glyphs.
The Sword Landscape Painting	Obtain 108 glyphs.
Throne Room Concept Art	Obtain 43 glyphs.
Tower Interior Concept Art	Obtain 92 glyphs.
Water Lift Concept Art	Obtain 91 glyphs.
Water Temple Interior	Obtain 95 glyphs.
Whiptail Costume Art	Obtain 75 glyphs.
Whiptail Early Concept Art	Obtain 38 glyphs.
Whiptail Early Concept Art (2nd)	Obtain 45 glyphs.
Whiptail Eel Concept Art	Obtain 36 glyphs.
Whiptail Promo Screenshot	Obtain 76 glyphs.
Young Kai Concept Art	Obtain 15 glyphs.
Young Nariko Sketch	Obtain 82 glyphs.

HEROES OF THE PACIFIC (XBOX)

Enter these codes at the Main menu.

UNLOCKABLE	CODE
Cheat Menu	Y, LT, D-pad ←, RT, D-pad →, WHT
Unlock All Planes and Missions	Right thumbstick ↑, Right thumbstick ↓, WHT, BLK, Right thumbstick ←, Right thumbstick →
Unlock Japanese Planes	WHT, BLK, LT, RT, Right thumbstick ↑, Right thumbstick ←
Upgrade Planes	LT, Right thumbstick ←, RT, Right thumbstick →, WHT, Y

HEROES OF THE PACIFIC (PlayStation 2)

Enter these codes at the Main menu. Note that you will disable game-saving when these codes are entered.

UNLOCKABLE	CODE
Cheat Menu	L1, R2, L2, R3, R1, L3
Unlock all planes and missions	Right Analog stick up, Right Analog stick down, Right Analog stick left, R2, L1, Right Analog stick right
Unlock Japanese Planes	●, R2, L1, L2, ←, ↑
Upgrade planes	L1, Right Analog stick left, R2, Right Analog stick right, →, ↓

HEROES OVER EUROPE (XBOX 360)

UNLOCKABLE PLANES

On Rookie difficulty, you only need to complete the mission to unlock the plane. On Pilot and Ace difficulties, you also need to complete the Bonus Objective to unlock the plane.

UNLOCKABLE	HOW TO UNLOCK
Beaufighter TF Mk X	Complete Operation Cerberus on Pilot difficulty.
Bf-109 E4	Complete London Burning on Rookie difficulty.
Bf-109 E4 Ace	Complete Heart of the Empire on Ace difficulty.
Bf-109 G10	Complete Heart of the Empire on Pilot difficulty.
Bf-109 G6	Complete London Burning on Pilot difficulty.
Bf-110 C-4	Complete Firestorm on Rookie difficulty.
Bf-110 G-4	Complete Firestorm on Pilot difficulty.
Fw190 A8	Complete Operation Jericho on Rookie difficulty.
Fw190 F8	Complete Operation Jericho on Pilot difficulty.

UNLOCKABLE PLANES

UNLOCKABLE	HOW TO UNLOCK
Fw190 F8 Ace	Complete The Butcher's Birds on Ace difficulty.
G41 Meteor Mk III	Complete Eye of the Storm on Ace difficulty.
He 219A-7/RI Owl	Complete Firestorm on Ace difficulty.
Hurricane Mk I I-c	Complete Phoney War on Pilot difficulty.
Hurricane Mk I I-d	Complete Defense of the Realm on Pilot difficulty.
Ju-87-B Stuka	Complete Fighter Superiority on Rookie difficulty.
Macchi.202 Folgore	Complete Defense of the Realm on Ace difficulty.
Me-262 A-2	Complete Operation Jericho on Ace difficulty.
Me-262 Ace	Complete The Black Heart on Ace difficulty.
Mosquito FB Mk V Series 3	Complete Party Crashers on Pilot difficulty.
Mosquito NF Mk V Series 2	Complete Operation Cerberus on Rookie difficulty.
P-38J Lightning	Complete Eagle Day on Ace difficulty.
P-40-B Tomahawk	Complete Phoney War on Rookie difficulty.
P-47B Thunderbolt	Complete Party Crashers on Rookie difficulty.
P-47D-23 Thunderbolt	Complete The Butcher's Birds on Pilot difficulty.
P-51A Mustang	Complete Eagle Day on Rookie difficulty.
P-51D (NA-124) Mustang	Complete Battle of the Bulge on Pilot difficulty.
P-51D Mustang	Complete Battle of the Bulge on Rookie difficulty.
P-51H (NA-126) Mustang	Complete The Black Heart on Pilot difficulty.
P-61 Black Widow	Complete The Black Heart on Rookie difficulty.
P-80 Shooting Star	Complete Battle of the Bulge on Ace difficulty.
Spitfire Mk I-a	Complete Defense of the Realm on Rookie difficulty.
Spitfire Mk IX-c	Complete Fighter Superiority on Ace difficulty.
Spitfire Mk V-b	Complete Fighter Superiority on Pilot difficulty.
Spitfire XVI-e	Complete Party Crashers on Ace difficulty.
Swordfish	Complete Heart of the Empire on Rookie difficulty.
Tempest FB Mk II	Complete Eye of the Storm on Pilot difficulty.
Tempest Mk V-II	Complete Eye of the Storm on Rookie difficulty.
Typhoon Mk I-b	Complete The Butcher's Birds on Rookie difficulty.
Whirlwind Mk II	Complete Eagle Day on Pilot difficulty.
Yak-9U	Complete Phoney War on Ace difficulty.

HITMAN: BLOOD MONEY (PlayStation 2)

On the Opera House mission, in the basement at the back part of the stage, there is a room that leads to staircases to bathrooms on the first floor. After heading down the stairs, enter a room, kill the three rats on the ground, and check the bench at the end of the room. There is a keycard for the rat club. Head to the second level where you collect the lightroom keycard. There is a door that cannot be opened. Use the rat club keycard and in there are rats boxing and gambling.

HITMAN: CONTRACTS (XBOX)

Enter the following codes at the Main menu.

UNLOCKABLE	CODE
Level Select	Ⓧ,Ⓨ,Ⓑ,◀✚,▲✚,✚▶,LT,RT
Level Skip and Silent Assasin Rating	RT,LT,▲✚,▼✚,Ⓧ,Ⓐ,LT,Ⓑ,Ⓐ,Ⓑ,Ⓐ

HITMAN: CONTRACTS (PlayStation 2)

UNLOCKABLE	CODE
Complete Level	During gameplay, press R2,L2,↑,↓,×,L3,●,×,●,×
Level Select	In the Main menu, press ■,▲,●,←,↑,→,L2,R2

NEW!
A B C D E F G H I J K L M N O P Q R S T U V W X Y Z

HITMAN 2: SILENT ASSASSIN (XBOX)

UNLOCKABLE	CODE
All Weapons	Press RT, LT, ↑, ↓, A, ↑, X, A during gameplay.
Bomb Mode	Press RT, LT, ↑, ↓, A, ↑, WHT during gameplay.
Full Heal	Press RT, LT, ↑, ↓, A, ↑, ↓ during gameplay.
God Mode	Press RT, LT, ↑, ↓, A, RT, LT, BLK, WHT during gameplay.
Hitman AI	During gameplay press RT, LT, ↑, ↓, A, ↑, ↑.
Lethal Charge	Press LT, RT, ↑, ↓, A, BLK, BLK during gameplay.
Level Select	Press RT, LT, ↑, ↓, Y, B at the main menu.
Level Skip	Press RT, LT, ↑, ↓, A, X, click L, and press B, A, B, A during gameplay. Enable this code immediately after starting a level to complete it with a Silent Assassin rank.
Megaforce Mode	Press RT, LT, ↑, ↓, A, RT, RT during gameplay. Restart the level to remove its effect.
Nailgun Mode (Weapons pin people to walls when you activate this code.)	Press RT, LT, ↑, ↓, A, WHT, WHT during gameplay.
Punch Mode	Press RT, LT, ↑, ↓, A, ↑, ↑ during gameplay.
Slow Motion	Press RT, LT, ↑, ↓, A, ↑, LT during gameplay.
SMG and 9mm Pistol SD	Press LT, RT, ↑, ↓, A, ↑, RT, RT during gameplay.
Toggle Gravity	Press RT, LT, ↑, ↓, A, LT, LT during gameplay.

HITMAN 2: SILENT ASSASSIN (PlayStation 2)

Enter the following codes during gameplay.

DESCRIPTION	CODE
All Weapons	R2, L2, ↑, ↓, ×, ↑, ■, ×
Bomb Mode	R2, L2, ↑, ↓, ×, ↑, L1
Full Heal	R2, L2, ↑, ↓, ×, ↑, ↓
God Mode	R2, L2, ↑, ↓, ×, R2, L2, R1, L1
Lethal Charge	R2, L2, ↑, ↓, ×, R1, R1
Level Skip	R2, L2, ↑, ↓, ×, L3, ●, ×, ●, × Enable this code immediately after starting a level to complete it with a Silent Assassin rank.
Megaforce Mode	R2, L2, ↑, ↓, ×, R2, R2 Restart the level to remove its effect.
Nailgun Mode (Weapons pin people to walls.)	R2, L2, ↑, ↓, ×, L1, L1
Punch Mode	R2, L2, ↑, ↓, ×, ↑, ↑
Slow Motion	R2, L2, ↑, ↓, ×, ↑, L2
SMG and 9mm Pistol SD	L2, R2, ↑, ↓, ×, ↑, R2, R2
Toggle Gravity	R2, L2, ↑, ↓, ×, L2, L2
Level Select	R2, L2, ↑, ↓, ■, ▲, ●

HOT SHOTS GOLF 3 (PlayStation 2)

DESCRIPTION	CODE
In-Game Reset	Press L1 + R1 + L2 + R2 + START + SELECT during gameplay.
Left-Handed Golfer	Press START when selecting a golfer.

HOT SHOTS GOLF FORE! (PlayStation 2)

In the Options menu, go into the Password screen to enter these passwords.

UNLOCKABLE	PASSWORD
Capsule 1	WXAFSJ
Capsule 2	OEINLK
Capsule 3	WFKVTG
Capsule 4	FCAVDO

Capsule 5	YYPOKK
Capsule 6	GDQDOF
Capsule 7	HHXKPV
Capsule 8	UOKXPS
Capsule 9	LMIRYD
Capsule 10	MJLJEQ
Capsule 11	MHNCQI
Price Reduction	MKJEFQ
Tourney Rank Down	XKWGFZ
Unlock 100t Hammer Club	NFSNHR
Unlock All Golfers	REZTWS
Unlock Aloha Beach Resort	XSREHD
Unlock Bagpipe Classic	CRCNHZ
Unlock Beginner's Ball	YFQJJI
Unlock Big Air Club	DLJMFZ
Unlock Bir Air Ball	CRCGKR
Unlock Blue Lagoon C.C.	WVRJQS
Unlock Caddie Clank	XCQGWJ
Unlock Caddie Daxter	WSIKIN
Unlock Caddie Kayla	MZIMEL
Unlock Caddie Kaz	LNNZJV
Unlock Caddie Simon	WRHZNB
Unlock Caddie Sophie	UTWIVQ
Unlock Dream G.C.	OQUTNA
Unlock Everybody's CD - Voice Version	UITUGF
Unlock Extra Pose Cam	UEROOK
Unlock Extra Swing Cam	RJIFQS
Unlock Extra Video	DPYHIU
Unlock Heckletts	DIXWFE
Unlock HSG Rules	FKDHDS
Unlock Infinity Ball	DJXBRG
Unlock Infinity Club	RZTQGV
Unlock Landing Grid	MQTIMV
Unlock Menu Character Brad	ZKJSIO
Unlock Menu Character Phoebe	LWVLCB
Unlock Menu Character Renee	AVIQXS
Unlock Mike Costume	YKCFEZ
Unlock Mini-Golf 2 G.C.	RVMIRU
Unlock Nanako Costume	BBLSKQ
Unlock Phoebe Costume	GJBCHY
Unlock Pin Hole Ball	VZLSGP
Unlock Replay Cam A	PVJEMF
Unlock Replay Cam B	EKENCR
Unlock Replay Cam C	ZUHHAC
Unlock Sidespin Ball	JAYQRK
Unlock Silkroad Classic	ZKOGJM
Unlock Suzuki Costume	ARFLCR
Unlock Turbo Spin Ball	XNETOK

UNLOCKABLE	PASSWORD
Unlock United Forest G.C.	UIWHLZ
Unlock Wallpaper Set 2	RODDHQ
Unlock Western Valley C.C.	LIBTFL
Unlock Wild Green C.C.	YZLOXE
Upgrade 100t Hammer Club to mid-level	BVLHSI
Upgrade Big Air Club from mid-level to top level	JIDTQI
Upgrade Big Air Club to mid-level	TOSXUJ
Upgrade Infinity Club from mid-level to top level	EIPCUL
Upgrade Infinity Club to mid-level	WTGFOR
Upgrade Pin Hole Club from mid-level to top level	RBXVEL
Upgrade Pin Hole Club to mid-level	TTIMHT
Upgrade Turbo Spin Club from mid-level to top level	DTIZAB
Upgrade Turbo Spin Club to mid-level	NIWKWP

HOT SHOTS GOLF: OPEN TEE

UNLOCKABLE	CODE
Easy Loyalty	To gain loyalty much quicker than playing an entire round of golf, start a match play game under challenge mode. Give up on the first three holes by pressing Select then Start to forfeit. After the match you will still gain loyalty for your character.

HOT SHOTS GOLF: OUT OF BOUNDS (PlayStation 3)

CAPSULES

Capsules contain items that are added to the course. They have no effect on the gameplay, they are just there for show.

UNLOCKABLE	HOW TO UNLOCK
Armored Zombie	Play 20 rounds at Euro Classic G.C. (Regular Tee).
Bear	Play 20 rounds at Highland C.C. (Long Tee).
Blue Whale	Play 20 rounds at The Crown Links (Long Tee).
Child Witch	Play 20 rounds at Euro Classic G.C. (Long Tee).
Glider	Play 20 rounds at The Crown Links (Regular Tee).
Gnome	Play 20 rounds at Silver Peaks G.C. (Regular Tee).
Helicopter	Play 20 rounds at Highland C.C. (Regular Tee).
Jet Formation	Play 20 rounds at Okinawa Golf Resort (Regular Tee).
Lion	Play 20 rounds at Great Safari C.C. (Long Tee).
Manta	Play 20 rounds at Okinawa Golf Resort (Long Tee).
Rhino	Play 20 rounds at Great Safari C.C. (Regular Tee).
Unicorn	Play 20 rounds at Silver Peaks G.C. (Long Tee).

HOT WHEELS VELOCITY X (PlayStation 2)

UNLOCKABLE	CODE
All Cars and Tracks	In the Main menu, hold L1+R1 and press ●,■,■,▲,×

THE HOUSE OF THE DEAD: OVERKILL (Wii)

UNLOCKABLES

UNLOCKABLE	HOW TO UNLOCK
Director's Cut mode	Complete Story mode to unlock Director's Cut mode.
Dual Wield mode	Clear Director's Cut.
Handcannon Weapon	Complete Story mode to unlock the handcannon.
Mini-Gun Weapon	Complete all levels in Director's Cut.

I-NINJA (XBOX)

CODES

UNLOCKABLE	HOW TO UNLOCK
Big Head Mode	Press [START] to pause gameplay, then hold (RB) and press. (Y), (Y), (Y), (Y) Release (RB), then hold (L3) and press (Y), (Y). Hold (RB)+(L3), then press (Y), (B), (Y).
Level Skip	Press start to pause game, hold (RT) then press (X), (X), (X), (B). Release (RT) then hold (LT) and press (Y), (Y). Release (LT) then hold (RT), (X), (X).

UNLOCKABLES

UNLOCKABLE	HOW TO UNLOCK
Battle Arena	Collect all 64 Grades to unlock Battle Arena in Robot Beach

I-NINJA (PlayStation 2)

To enter the following codes, pause the game and enter code.

UNLOCKABLE	CODE
Big Head	Hold R1 and press ▲,▲,▲,▲. Release R1, hold L1, and press ▲,▲. Hold R1+L1, and press ▲,●,▲.
Level Skip	Hold R1 and press ■,■,■,●. Release R1, hold L1, and press ▲,▲. Release L1, hold R1, and press ■,■.
Sword Upgrade	Hold L1+R1 and press ●,■,●,▲,▲,■,●,■.

ICE AGE 2 (PlayStation 2)

Pause the game to enter these codes.

UNLOCKABLE	CODE
Unlimited Energy	↓, ←, →, ↓, ↓, →, ←, ↓
Unlimited Health	↑, →, ↓, ↑, ←, ↓, →, ←
Unlimited Pebbles	↓, ↓, ←, ↑, ↑, →, ↑, ↓

ICE AGE 2: THE MELTDOWN (Wii)

CODES

Pause the game and press the following codes.

UNLOCKABLE	HOW TO UNLOCK
Unlimited Health	↑, →, ↓, ↑, ←, ↓, →, ←

ICE AGE 2: THE MELTDOWN (XBOX)

CODES

UNLOCKABLE	HOW TO UNLOCK
Unlimited Energy	↓, ←, →, ↓, ↓, →, ←, ↓
Unlimited Health	↑, →, ↓, ↑, ←, ↓, →, ←
Unlimited Pebbles	↓, ↓, ←, ↑, ↑, →, ↑, ↓

IMAGE FIGHT (Wii)

UNLOCKABLES

UNLOCKABLE	HOW TO UNLOCK
Arcade Mode	Do a reset (START+SELECT), then immediately hold ①
Mr. Heli mode	Highlight song C in Sound Test mode and press ↑, SELECT, ②+①, then press ① on Mr. Heli and then press RUN
Sound Test	Press SELECT on the title screen

THE INCREDIBLES: RISE OF THE UNDERMINER (PlayStation 2)

To enter these codes, pause the game. Press ● to open the menu, then select Secrets to enter a password.

UNLOCKABLE	PASSWORD
All of Frozone's moves upgraded	FROZMASTER
All of Mr. Incredible's moves upgraded	MRIMASTER
Frozone's Super Move	FROZBOOM
Give Frozone 1,000 Experience Points	FROZPROF
Give Mr. Incredible 1,000 Experience Points	MRIPROF
Mr. Incredible's Super Move	MRIBOOM

INDIANA JONES AND THE EMPEROR'S TOMB (XBOX)

Enter this code at the Main menu.

UNLOCKABLE	CODE
God Mode	Hold LT+RT and press ↑, ↑, ↓, ↑, Ⓐ, Ⓧ, Ⓐ, Ⓑ, ↑, ↓, Ⓨ, START

INDIANA JONES AND THE STAFF OF KINGS (Wii)

CODES

EFFECT	CODE
Unlock Fate of Atlantis game	In the main menu, while holding down Ⓩ press: Ⓐ, ↑, ↑Ⓑ, ↓, ↓, ←, →, ←, Ⓑ

UNLOCKABLE SKINS

UNLOCKABLE	HOW TO UNLOCK
Big Heads	6 Artifacts
Han Solo	36 Artifacts
Henry Jones	34 Artifacts
Tuxedo Indy	16 Artifacts

UNLOCKABLE CONCEPT ART

UNLOCKABLE	HOW TO UNLOCK
Allies	12 Artifacts
Co-op Levels(Wii Only)	8 Artifacts
Cutting Room Floor	36 Artifacts
Enemies	22 Artifacts
Extras	20 Artifacts
Istanbul	28 Artifacts
Nepal	26 Artifacts
Odin and Seabed	32 Artifacts
Panama	18 Artifacts
San Francisco	14 Artifacts
Sudan	2 Artifacts

UNLOCKABLE TRAILERS

UNLOCKABLE	HOW TO UNLOCK
"Raiders of the Lost Ark" movie trailer	3 Artifacts
"Temple of Doom" movie trailer	10 Artifacts
"The Last Crusade movie trailer"	24 Artifacts
"The Kingdom of the Crystal Skull" movie trailer	30 Artifacts

IRON MAN (XBOX 360)

UNLOCKABLES

UNLOCKABLE	HOW TO UNLOCK
Classic	Beat the "One Man Army vs. Mercs" challenge.

Classic Mark I	Beat the "One Man Army vs. AIM" challenge.
Extremis	Beat the "One Man Army vs. Maggia" challenge.
Hulkbuster	Beat the "One Man Army vs. AIM-X" challenge.
Mark II	Beat the "One Man Army vs. Ten Rings" challenge.
Mark III	Unlocked by default.
Silver Centurion (Xbox 360 Exclusive)	Beat the Mission "Showdown" (or beat the game, since "Showdown" is the last mission).

ACHIEVEMENTS

UNLOCKABLE	HOW TO UNLOCK
AIM Obsoleted (25)	Complete the One Man Army vs. AIM challenge without an armor breach.
AIM-X Obsoleted (25)	Complete the One Man Army vs. AIM-X challenge without an armor breach.
Air Superiority (15)	Destroy all dropships before the Stark Gunship is stolen in the First Flight mission.
An Object in Motion (15)	Destroy any target using a ramming attack.
City Protector (25)	Destroy drones without civilian damage in the First Flight mission.
Classic Confrontation (15)	Defeat Titanium Man using the Classic armor.
Collateral Damage (15)	Destroy a Prometheus missile by destroying a fuel truck in the Maggia Compound mission.
Decommissioner (25)	Destroy all Prometheus missiles in the Maggia Compound mission.
Disarmed (25)	Destroy stockpiled Stark weapons in the Escape mission.
Eject! (25)	Spare the US fighter pilots in the Stark Weapons mission.
Escape Velocity (25)	Sever the tether before the satellite overloads in the Space Tether mission.
Excelsior! (70)	Complete Hero Objectives for all missions.
Ground Pound (15)	Defeat an opponent using the ground pound in the Extremis armor.
Grounded (15)	Successfully grapple and throw a plane.
Guardian (25)	Protect warehouse workers in the Maggia Factories mission.
Hero (75)	Complete all missions on Normal difficulty (or harder).
Hulk Smash! (15)	Successfully grapple an opponent in the Hulkbuster armor.
Impenetrable (15)	Complete a mission (other than Escape or First Flight) without an armor breach.
In the Drink (25)	Avoid civilian casualties in the Flying Fortress mission.
Launch Aborted (15)	Destroy all Prometheus missiles within 10 minutes in the Maggia Compound mission.
Long Shot (15)	Damage or destroy another enemy while grappling a howitzer.
Maggia Obsoleted (25)	Complete the One Man Army vs. Maggia challenge without an armor breach.
Mercs Obsoleted (25)	Complete the One Man Army vs. Mercs challenge without an armor breach.
Not a Scratch (25)	Avoid harming the destroyer and its crew in the Lost Destroyer mission.
Old School (15)	Defeat Iron Monger using the Silver Centurion armor.
Overkill (15)	Defeat a soldier using the Unibeam.
Personnel Vendetta (15)	Defeat 20 soldiers in the Arctic Battle mission.
Power Saver (25)	Avoid disrupting the city's power supply in the On Defense mission.
Proton Shut Out (25)	Prevent cannon attacks on civilian targets in the Island Meltdown mission.

UNLOCKABLE	HOW TO UNLOCK
Pugilist (15) using	Complete any mission (other than Escape) without weapons systems.
Road King (15) the	Destroy all convoy vehicles in less than 2 minutes in Stark Weapons mission.
Shocking! (25)	Protect outlying occupied buildings in the Save Pepper mission.
Sidekick (75)	Complete all missions on Easy difficulty (or harder).
Smack Down (15)	Defeat Titanium Man before his second recharge in the On Defense mission.
Super Hero (75)	Complete all missions on Formidable difficulty.
Tatyana, Interrupted (25)	Protect the nuclear facility in the Arctic Battle mission.
Ten Rings Obsoleted (25)	Complete the One Man Army vs. Ten Rings challenge without an armor breach.
You're Fired! (25)	Destroy power regulators in the Iron Monger mission.
Your Own Medicine (15)	Damage or destroy another enemy while grappling a SAM launcher.

J.J. AND JEFF (Wii)

UNLOCKABLES

UNLOCKABLE	HOW TO UNLOCK
Continue	When the Game Over screen appears, hold ①+②, then press RUN
Extra Lives	Stand at least five blocks away from a lamppost, then jump while kicking and hit the post perfectly.
Hidden Level Warps	Locate the brick bridge on level 1-4B. Kick the right corner of the bridge and underneath. This allows gameplay to continue in fields 2, 3, or 4. Locate the area halfway through level 3-3B where two rats begin to follow your character. Jump on top of them to reach the two bricks, then jump up. Gameplay resumes at 6-4.

JAMES BOND: QUANTUM OF SOLACE (PlayStation 2)

UNLOCKABLES

UNLOCKABLE	HOW TO UNLOCK
Level Select	Beat the game once.

JEREMY MCGRATH SUPERCROSS WORLD (PlayStation 2)

Enter the following codes at the Main menu.

UNLOCKABLE	CODE
Unlimited Turbo Boost	R2, L1, ■, ●, ●, ●
Weird Gravity	⇧, ⇧, ⇧, ⇧, R2, ■, ●

JUICED (XBOX)

Enter this passwords in the Password menu.

UNLOCKABLE	PASSWORD
All Cars in Arcade Mode	PINT

JUICED (PlayStation 2)

Enter this password in the Password menu.

UNLOCKABLE	PASSWORD
All Cars in Arcade Mode	PINT

JUICED 2: HOT IMPORT NIGHTS (XBOX 360)

DRIVER DNA CAR UNLOCKABLES

Enter the passwords in the DNA lab to unlock the special challenges. If you win the challenges, you unlock a custom version of the following cars.

UNLOCKABLE	HOW TO UNLOCK
Audi TT 1.8L Quattro	YTHZ
BMW Z4 Roadster	GVDL
Frito-Lay Infiniti G35	MNCH
Holden Monaro	RBSG
Hyundai Coupe 2.7L V6	BSLU
Infiniti G35	MRHC
Koenigsegg CCX	KDTR
Mitsubishi Prototype X	DOPX

UNLOCKABLE	HOW TO UNLOCK
Nissan 350Z	PRGN
Nissan Skyline R34 GT-R	JWRS
Saleen S7	WIKF
Seat Leon Cupra R	FAMQ

ACHIEVEMENTS

UNLOCKABLE	HOW TO UNLOCK
Billionaire! (25)	One billion dollars!
Daredevil! (15)	Entered 25 pink slip races!
Dealer! (10)	Traded five cars online.
DNA Collector! (10)	Downloaded somebody's DNA.
Drift Marathon! (100)	20,000,000 point drift.
Elite (5)	Promoted to Elite.
Elite Legend (10)	Completed all Elite goals.
Feelin' Lucky! (5)	Entered a pink slip race.
Flawless Drift! (50)	5,000,000 point drift.
HIN Champion (45)	Completed all HIN crew challenges.
Juiced! (25)	Maxed out 10 cars!
League 1 (5)	Promoted to League 1.
League 1 Legend (10)	Completed all League 1 goals.
League 2 (5)	Promoted to League 2.
League 2 Legend (10)	Completed all League 2 goals.
League 3 (5)	Promoted to League 3.
League 3 Legend (10)	Completed all League 3 goals.
League 4 (5)	Promoted to League 4.
League 4 Legend (10)	Completed all League 4 goals.
League 5 (5)	Promoted to League 5.
League 5 Legend (10)	Completed all League 5 goals.
League 6 (5)	Promoted to League 6.
League 6 Legend (10)	Completed all League 6 goals.
League 7 (5)	Promoted to League 7.
League 7 Legend (10)	Completed all League 7 goals.
Loaded! (20)	One hundred million dollars!
Lookin' Smooth! (10)	Traded five decal presets online.
Millionaire! (15)	One million dollars!
Nailed! (100)	100% completion.
Nice Bodywork! (5)	Traded a decal preset online.
Online Elite (5)	Promoted to Elite online.
Online Elite Legend (10)	Completed all online Elite goals.
Online League 1 (5)	Promoted to League 1 online.
Online League 1 Legend (10)	Completed all online League 1 goals.
Online League 2 (5)	Promoted to League 2 online.
Online League 2 Legend (10)	Completed all online League 2 goals.
Online League 3 (5)	Promoted to League 3 online.
Online League 3 Legend (10)	Completed all online League 3 goals.
Online League 4 (5)	Promoted to League 4 online.
Online League 4 Legend (10)	Completed all online League 4 goals.
Online League 5 (5)	Promoted to League 5 online.

Online League 5 Legend (10)	Completed all online League 5 goals.
Online League 6 (5)	Promoted to League 6 online.
Online League 6 Legend (10)	Completed all online League 6 goals.
Online League 7 (5)	Promoted to League 7 online.
Online League 7 Legend (10)	Completed all online League 7 goals.
Online Rookie Legend (10)	Completed all online Rookie goals.
Online World Class (5)	Promoted to World Class online.
Online World Class Legend (10)	Completed all online World Class goals.
Prestige (45)	Completed all celebrity challenges.
Revved! (20)	Maxed out five cars!
Risk Taker! (10)	Entered 10 pink slip races.
Rookie Legend (10)	Completed all Rookie goals.
Style King! (15)	Traded 10 decal presets online!
Trader! (5)	Bought or sold a car online.
Tuned! (15)	Maxed out a car!
Tycoon! (10)	Traded 10 cars online!
Unstoppable Drift! (150)	50,000,000 point drift!
World Class (5)	Promoted to World Class.
World Class Legend (10)	Completed all World Class goals.

JURASSIC: THE HUNTED (XBOX 360)

UNLOCKABLE

UNLOCKABLE	HOW TO UNLOCK
Laser Rifle	Beat the game on normal to unlock the Laser Rifle for Hard mode.

JUSTICE LEAGUE HEROES (XBOX)

CODES

CODE	EFFECT
All Cinematics	↓, →, ↓, ←
Get 20 Shields	↑, ↑, ↓, ↓
Gives 35 Random Boosts	←, →, ←, →
Infinite Energy	↓, ↓, →, →, ↑, ↑, ←, ←
Invincibility	←, ↓, →, ↑, ←, ↓, →, ↑
Maxes Out Abilities	→, ↓, →, ↓
One Hit Kills	↑, ↑, ↓, ←, ↑, ↑, ↓, ↓
Purchase All Heroes	→, ↓, ←, ↑
Take Less Damage	←, ↑, →, ↓
Unlock all Costumes	↓, ←, ↑, →

JUSTICE LEAGUE HEROES (PlayStation 2)

To enter these codes, pause the game and hold L1, L2, R1, R2

UNLOCKABLE	CODE
Gives 20 points to shields	↑, ↑, ↓, ↓
Gives 25 Random Boosts	←, →, ←, →
Invincibility	←, ↓, →, ↑, ←, ↓, →, ↑
Maxes out abilities	→, ↓, →, ↓
Unlimited Energy	↓, ↓, →, →, ↑, ↑, ←, ←
Unlock everything	↓, ←, ↑, →

KAMEO: ELEMENTS OF POWER (XBOX360)

THORN'S CASTLE — UNLOCKABLE

REQUIRED	DESCRIPTION	PTS.
Audio—The Troll Song	You have to hear it to believe it.	1,000,000
Cheats #1	Big Troll heads, Big Kameo head	2,500,000
Classic Kameo Skin	Have Kameo don her original purple outfit!	100,000
Video—Cutscene Style Test	A test clip of an early cutscene.	2,000,000
Video—Making Backgrounds	Shows how the background were made.	500,000
REQUIRED	DESCRIPTION	PTS.
Video—Trailer Concept	An insight into the development process of the trailer.	1,500,000

FORGOTTEN FOREST— UNLOCKABLE

REQUIRED	DESCRIPTION	PTS.
Cheats #2	Warrior Vision, Screen FX	2,000,000
FMV Player	The Story Begins, Kameo Meets Thorn, Pummel Weed Evolves, Rubble Evolves, Major Ruin Evolves, Deep Blue Evolves, Flex Evolves, 40 Below Evolves, Thermite Evolves, Shadow Troll Vision, Halis Vision, Lenya Vision, Yeros Vision, Airship, Warp, Death, The End…, Credits.	1,600,000
Pummel Weed Skin	Enable a new skin for Pummel Weed!	400,000
Rubble Skin	Enable a new skin for Rubble!	1,200,000
Video—Animation Creation	The magic of animation.	200,000
Video—The Wotnot Book	Learn more about the ancient tome.	800,000

WATER TEMPLE — UNLOCKABLE

REQUIRED	DESCRIPTION	PTS.
Ash Skin	Enable a new skin for Ash!	1,000,000
Boss Battles	Old Mawood, Corallis, Queen Thyra, Lord Cheats #3	3,000,000
Drok, Thorn	Retro FX, Hard Trolls (disables Battle Points)	2,500,000
Cutscene Extras	Bonus bits for cutscene aficionados.	1,500,000
Gothic Kameo Skin	Kameo goes goth.	500,000
Major Ruin Skin	Enable a new skin for Major Ruin!	2,000,000

SNOW TEMPLE — UNLOCKABLE

REQUIRED	DESCRIPTION	PTS.
Bonus Music Player	Bonus Tune #1—Umchacka, Bonus Tune #2—Alternative Theme	1,500,000

Cheats #4	Fire Proof (disables Battle Points), Troll Traitors—flip-kick a Troll to turn it against the others! (disables Battle Points), Scaredy-Trolls (disables Battle Points)	3,000,000
Chilla Skin	Enable a new skin for Chilla!	2,000,000
Deep Blue Skin	Enable a new skin for Deep Blue!	1,000,000
Group Shot Movie Player	An evolution of the group; Group Shot—2003, Group Shot—2004 #1, Group Shot—2004 #2	500,000
Video—Model Gallery	Check out the different character models.	2,500,000

THORN'S PASS— UNLOCKABLE

REQUIRED	DESCRIPTION	PTS.
Animatic Player #1	Kameo Meets Thorn, Pummel Weed Evolves, Flex Evolves, 40 Below Evolves, Thermite Evolves, Transform Animatic	4,500,000
Cheats #5	Max Health (disables Battle Points), Elemental Override: fire (disables Battle Points), Elemental Override: ice (disables Battle Points)	5,000,000
Coyote Kameo Skin	Kameo blends in with the animals.	2,500,000
Flex Skin	Enable a new skin for Flex!	4,000,000
Old Evolve Sequences Player	Video—Evolving Rubble, Video—Evolving 40 Below, Video—Evolving Pummel Weed, Video—Evolving Deep Blue	3,500,000
Video—Old Chars. & Moves	View some old character and moves.	3,000,000

THORN'S AIRSHIP— UNLOCKABLE

REQUIRED	DESCRIPTION	PTS.
40 Below Skin	Enable a new skin for 40 Below!	1,500,000
Video —Airship Concept	Working on Thorn's Airship.	2,000,000
Cheats #6	Easy Trolls (disables Battle Points), One-Hit Kills (disables Battle Points), Invulnerable (disables Battle Points), Upgrade All Warriors (disables Battle Points)	3,000,000
Other Deleted Scenes Player	Video—Kalus Attacks!, Video—Evolving Cloud Monster, Video—Kameo Rare Logo, Video—Vortex Capture	1,000,000
Video —Early Years	Check out footage of a very early version of Kameo.	500,000
Video —Ending Concept	An early idea for the ending sequence.	2,500,000

OVERALL SCORE— UNLOCKABLE

REQUIRED	DESCRIPTION	PTS.
Animatic Player #2	The Release of Thorn, Cailem Goes to the Citadel, Cailem Leads the Trolls, Tree Monster Evolves, Cloud Monster Evolves, Whirly Bird Evolves, Death Animatic	18,000,000
Concept Art Gallery #1	Concept art straight from the designers.	9,000,000
Concept Art Gallery #2	More awesome concept art.	12,000,000

REQUIRED	DESCRIPTION	PTS.
Snare Skin	Enable a new skin for Snare!	15,000,000
Video—Deleted Cutscenes	See what didn't make the cut.	21,000,000
Thermite Skin	Enable a new skin for Thermite!	24,000,000

KANE & LYNCH: DEAD MEN (XBOX360)

ACHIEVEMENTS

UNLOCKABLE	HOW TO UNLOCK
50 to Won (25)	Win 50 rounds of Fragile Alliance.
A Lot (15)	Escape with $1,500,000 from a Fragile Alliance heist.
Behemoth (10)	Stop the roaring beast.
Berserkopath (30)	Make the most of Lynch's condition.
Boomstick (20)	Shotgun messiah.
Bulletproof (10)	Avoid using adrenaline on a level.
Bullseye (20)	Lynch reacts fast at the Exchange.
By the Grace of... (10)	Lynch puts them out of their misery.
Cash Addict (25)	Help to get all the money out in a Fragile Alliance round.
Celebrity (0)	Play as Lynch in Fragile Alliance.
Crime Buster (10)	Kill 10 traitors in Fragile Alliance.
Crowd Control (30)	Surgical precision in the nightclub.
Damned If You Do (20)	Let them burn.
Damned If You Don't (30)	No rest for the wicked.
Double Trouble (25)	Kill two traitors in a Fragile Alliance round.
End of the Road (50)	Complete the game in co-op.
Family Member (5)	Complete a Fragile Alliance session.
Frag Out (20)	Five with one fragmentation grenade.
Fragile Alliance (10)	Complete the first level in co-op.
Have Gun, Will Travel Part I (20)	Travel into the Rising Sun.
Have Gun, Will Travel Part II (20)	Counter-revolution.
Have Gun, Will Travel Part III (20)	The Beginning of the End.
Headmaster (10)	47 headshots.
Hindsight (10)	Get that bird out of the sky.
Impact (20)	Escape from death row.
Iron Flower (50)	Complete the game on hard.
Mercenary (15)	Complete one session in each Fragile Alliance scenario.
Most Wanted (50)	Escape with $150,000,000 from Fragile Alliance heists.
Mr. Play-It-Straight (50)	Win 50 rounds of Fragile Alliance as a merc.
Mr. Popularity (35)	Kill 100 traitors in Fragile Alliance.
Never Give Up (30)	Get three personal revenge kills in a Fragile Alliance session.
No Going Back Now (30)	Go to the point of no return in co-op.
Perfect Split (25)	All players split the money equally from a Fragile Alliance heist.
Pushblade Symphony (20)	Points for getting up close and personal.
Return to Sender (10)	Throw back enemy grenades.
Revenge Part I (20)	Silencing the silent one.
Revenge Part II & III (20)	Who's the old timer now?

Revenge Part IV (20)	Shouldn't have gotten personal.
Revenge Part V (30)	Glad it got personal.
Rush Hour (15)	Escape in all rounds of a Fragile Alliance session.
Some (5)	Escape with $50,000 from a Fragile Alliance heist.
Sun Tzu (20)	Let your crew do the dirty work.
Sweet Revenge (5)	Get personal revenge in Fragile Alliance.
Teflon (20)	Avoid damage on a level.
The Cleaner (30)	Get 30 personal revenge kills in Fragile Alliance.
True Elite (0)	Play as Kane in Fragile Alliance.
Veteran (35)	Complete 200 Fragile Alliance sessions.

KARAOKE REVOLUTION (XBOX360)

UNLOCKABLES

Meet the following conditions to unlock these items for use in Edit Venue Mode.

UNLOCKABLE	HOW TO UNLOCK
Angel Heart Venue Item	Complete 30 gigs in Career Mode.
Area 51 Venue Item	Complete 55 gigs in Career Mode.
Cityscapes Venue Backdrops	Complete three gigs in Career Mode.
Flaming Biker Venue Item	Complete 90 gigs in Career Mode.
Giant Gorilla Venue Item	Complete 80 gigs in Career Mode.
Glowing Stairway and Fire Valley Backdrops	Complete 25 gigs in Career Mode.
Hearts Venue Item	Complete 60 gigs in Career Mode.
Hong Kong Venue Item	Complete seven gigs in Career Mode.
Leaping Tiger Venue Item	Complete 35 gigs in Career Mode.
Liberty Venue Item	Complete 45 gigs in Career Mode.
Music Genres Venue Item	Complete five gigs in Career Mode.
Nature Venue Backdrops	Complete 70 gigs in Career Mode.
Pirate Ship Venue Item	Complete 65 gigs in Career Mode.
Pods Venue Item	Complete 50 gigs in Career Mode.
Space Cruiser Venue Set	Complete 20 gigs in Career Mode.
Stone Heads Venue Item	Complete 15 gigs in Career Mode.
Urban Venue Backdrops	Complete 10 gigs in Career Mode.
Zombie Venue Item	Complete 40 gigs in Career Mode.

KARAOKE REVOLUTION (PlayStation 3)

UNLOCKABLES

Meet the following conditions to unlock these items for use in Edit Venue mode.

UNLOCKABLE	HOW TO UNLOCK
Angel Heart Venue Item	Complete 30 gigs in Career Mode.
Area 51 Venue Item	Complete 55 gigs in Career Mode.
Cityscapes Venue Backdrops	Complete 3 gigs in Career Mode.
Flaming Biker Venue Item	Complete 90 gigs in Career Mode.
Giant Gorilla Venue Item	Complete 80 gigs in Career Mode.
Glowing Stairway and Fire Valley Backdrops	Complete 25 gigs in Career Mode.
Hearts Venue Item	Complete 60 gigs in Career Mode.
Hong Kong Venue Item	Complete 7 gigs in Career Mode.

NEW! A B C D E F G H I J K L M N O P Q R S T U V W X Y Z

UNLOCKABLE	HOW TO UNLOCK
Leaping Tiger Venue Item	Complete 35 gigs in Career Mode.
Liberty Venue Items	Complete 45 gigs in Career Mode.
Music Genres Venue Item	Complete 5 gigs in Career Mode.
Nature Venue Backdrops	Complete 70 gigs in Career Mode.
Pirate Ship Venue Item	Complete 65 gigs in Career Mode.
Pods Venue Item	Complete 50 gigs in Career Mode.
Space Cruiser Venue Set	Complete 20 gigs in Career Mode.
Stone Heads Venue Item	Complete 15 gigs in Career Mode.
Urban Venue Backdrops	Complete 10 gigs in Career Mode.
Zombie Venue Item	Complete 40 gigs in Career Mode.

KARAOKE REVOLUTION VOLUME 2 (PlayStation 2)

Enter the following codes at the main title screen.

UNLOCKABLE	CODE
GMR (Aneeka)	→,←,R3,←,↑,↑,L3,↓,●,■
Harmonix (Ishani)	L3,●,↑,●,■,L3,↓,↓,R3
Konami (Dwyane)	→,R3,→,R3,■,→,●,■,↓,←

KID CHAMELEON (Wii)

UNLOCKABLES

UNLOCKABLE	HOW TO UNLOCK
5,000 Bonus Points	Complete any level without collecting any special items, or complete a stage without being hurt by an enemy
10,000 Bonus Points	Complete Blue Lake Woods in less than 20 seconds
Last Boss Warp	At the end of Blue Lake Woods there is a series of blocks just above the flag. Jump to the last one and then press down and right, jump and special together. You get warped to Plethora, the last level.

KILL.SWITCH (XBOX)

UNLOCKABLE	CODE
Infinite Ammo	After completing the game, pause the game and press LT,RT,X,X

KILLZONE (PlayStation 2)

Enter these codes at the Main menu.

UNLOCKABLE	CODE
Big Head Enemies	Hold L1 and press ●, ■, ×, ●, ●
More Powerful Weapons	Hold L1 and press ●, ▲, ●, ▲, ×
Unlock All Levels and Characters	Enter Shooterman as a profile name
Unlocks All Movies	Hold L1 and press ●, ■, ▲, ●, ■

KILLZONE 2 (PlayStation 3)

MEDALS

Complete the following tasks to unlock medals and rewards:

UNLOCKABLE	HOW TO UNLOCK
Aerial Supportive	8x Air Support Specialist (Unlocks Combine Tactician 2nd Ability)
Army Superior Unit Award	50x Clan Matches Won with Clan (Unlocks 100,000 Valor)
Assassins League	5x Assassination Kill Specialist (Unlocks Increased Points/Assassination Kills)
Black Belt	5x Close Combat Specialist (Unlocks Increased Points/Melee Kill)

Bodyguard Alliance	5x Assassination Defend Specialist (Unlocks Increased Points per Survival)
Bomb Squad	5x Search and Destroy Specialist (Unlocks Increased Points/Returns/Disarms)
Corpse Counters	5x Body Count Specialist (Unlocks Increased Points/ Defensive Kills)
Defense Initiative	5x Capture and Hold Defend Specialist (Unlocks Increased Points/Defensive Kills)
Defensive Specialist	8x Turret Specialist (Unlocks 2nd Engineer Ability)
Example Soldier	8x Good Conduct (Unlocks Increased Start Ammo Amount)
Explosives Expert	8x C4 Specialist (Unlocks Combine Saboteur 2nd Ability)
Field Mechanic	8x Repair Specialist (Unlocks Combine Engineer 2nd Ability)
Field Medic	8x Healing Specialist (Unlocks Combine Medic 2nd Ability)
Forward Observer	8x Spot and Mark Specialist (Unlocks Combine Scout 2nd Ability)
Front Runner	8x Boost Specialist (Unlocks Combine Assault 2nd Ability)
Hawk's Eye	5x Sniper Specialist (Unlocks Second Sniper Zoom)
Head Fetish	5x Headshot Specialist (Unlocks Increased Points/ Headshot)
Master of Disguise	8x Disguise Specialist (Unlocks Saboteur Ability)
Meritorious Unit Award	10x Clan Matches Won with Clan (Unlocks 1000 Valor)
Meritorious Unit Award	25x Clan Matches Won with Clan (Unlocks 10,000 Valor)
Natural Born Killer	8x Kill Count (Unlocks Increased Grenade Amount)
Quick Draw	5x Sidearm Specialist (Unlocks M4 Revolver 2nd Weapon)
Retrieval Corps	5x Search and Retrieve Specialist (Unlocks Increased Points/Return)
Shadow Marshall	8x Cloak Specialist (Unlocks 2nd Scout Ability)
Spawn Authority	8x Spawn Point Specialist (Unlocks 2nd Tactician Ability)
Trauma Surgeon	8x Revival Specialist (Unlocks 2nd Medic Ability)

RANKS

Unlock higher ranks by earning more points and a higher "Difference" score.

UNLOCKABLE	HOW TO UNLOCK
Captain	1100 points, 300 difference: unlocks VC9 missile launcher.
Colonel	2300 points, 450 difference: unlocks saboteur badge.
Corporal	30 points, 30 difference: can create squad option.
General	2800 points, 500 difference: unlocks scout badge.
Lieutenant	880 points, 250 difference: unlocks engineer badge.
Lieutenant-Colonel	1850 points, 400 difference: unlocks grenade launcher.
Major	1450 points, 350 difference: unlocks tactician badge.
Master Sergeant	350 points, 150 difference: unlocks the medic badge
Sergeant	100 point, 70 difference: can create clan option.
Sergeant 1st Class	200 points, 100 difference: unlocks Shotgun and SMG.
Sergeant Major	550 points, 250 difference: unlocks HGH and ISA LMG.

RIBBONS

Complete the following tasks to unlock the corresponding ribbons.

UNLOCKABLE	HOW TO UNLOCK
Air Support Specialist	5 kills by Air Support called.

UNLOCKABLE	HOW TO UNLOCK
Assassination Defend Specialist	Stayed alive as Target.
Assassination Kill Specialist	1 Assassination Target killed.
Body Count Specialist	10 kills made during a mission.
Boost Specialist	Perform 5 Boosts.
C4 Specialist	5 kills by placed C4 Explosives.
Capture and Hold Defend Specialist	10 mission points earned Capturing a Point.
Cloak Specialist	Kill 5 enemies while Cloaked.
Close Combat Specialist	10 kills by Close-Combat Melee.
Disguise Specialist	Kill 5 enemies while Disguised.
Good Conduct	0 Team-Kills/Suicides are made by the player and they have scored at least 20 points.
Headshot Specialist	10 kills by Headshots.
Healing Specialist	Heal 5 players.
Repair Specialist	Repair 5 Objects.
Revival Specialist	Successfully Revive 5 players.
Search and Destroy Specialist	2 Objectives placed/disarmed.
Search and Retrieve Specialist	2 Objectives returned.
Sidearm Specialist	10 kills by Pistols.
Sniper Specialist	10 kills by Sniper Rifle.
Spawn Point Specialist	5 players Spawn on Placed Area.
Spot and Mark Specialist	Spot and Mark 5 players.
Turret Specialist	5 kills by Sentry Turret Placed.

KINGDOM UNDER FIRE: CIRCLE OF DOOM (XBOX360)

UNLOCKABLES

UNLOCKABLE	HOW TO UNLOCK
Curian	Clear Celine's campaign on Normal difficulty or higher.
Extreme Mode	Beat the game on Normal and Hard difficulty.
Stone Golem	Use Petrifying Breath on the Wood Golem enemy to produce a Stone Golem enemy.

KLONOA 2 (PlayStation 2)

DESCRIPTION	OBJECTIVE
Hidden Levels	In each stage are six stars. If you collect all six, you gain a doll that appears on the R1 screen. Collect eight dolls to unlock the first hidden level, and all sixteen for the second.
Music Box	Complete both hidden levels to unlock the Music Box sound test. The first hidden level gives you the first 27 tracks, while the second one gives you the remaining songs.
Pictures in Image Gallery	Each stage has 150 little gems scattered about. If you collect all 150, you'll open up more images in the special image gallery.

KNIGHTS IN THE NIGHTMARE (DS)

UNLOCKABLES

UNLOCKABLE	HOW TO UNLOCK
Hard Mode	Beat the game on Normal mode.
Play as Astart	Beat the game.
Nightmare mode	Beat the game on Hard mode.

KUNG FU PANDA (XBOX360)

ACHIEVEMENTS

UNLOCKABLE	HOW TO UNLOCK
Awesomely Awesome (30)	Defeat 250 enemies.
Fastest Warrior (20)	Obtain a Hit Chain of 10 or higher using only Fast Attacks.
Fearless (20)	Make it through an entire level without blocking an attack.
Game Completed: Master (20)	Complete the entire game on the Master Difficulty setting.
Invincible (50)	Make it through the entire game without dying.
Kung Fu Warrior (20)	Obtain a Hit Chain of 15 or higher using any combination of attacks.
Level 1 100% Completion! (20)	Complete level "Po's Dream" 100%.
Level 2 100% Completion! (20)	Complete level "Tournament of the Dragon Warrior" 100%.
Level 3 100% Completion! (20)	Complete level "Level Zero" 100%.
Level 4 100% Completion! (20)	Complete level "Protect the Palace" 100%.
Level 5 100% Completion! (20)	Complete level "Lake of Tears" 100%.
Level 6 100% Completion! (20)	Complete level "Wudang Temple" 100%.
Level 7 100% Completion! (20)	Complete level "Treacherous Waters" 100%.
Level 8 100% Completion! (20)	Complete level "Wudang Rescue" 100%.
Level 9 100% Completion! (20)	Complete level "Howling Moon" 100%.
Level 10 100% Completion! (20)	Complete level "Secret of the Sands" 100%.
Level 11 100% Completion! (20)	Complete level "The Palace" 100%.
Level 12 100% Completion! (20)	Complete level "The Warrior's Destiny" 100%.
Level 13 100% Completion! (20)	Complete level "The Final Battle" 100%.
Master of All (30)	Unlock Everything.
Panda Stumble Extreme (20)	Panda Stumble for 60 seconds. Forced Stumble doesn't count.
Panda Stumble Warrior (20)	Obtain a Hit Chain of 5 or higher using only Panda Stumble.
Strongest Warrior (20)	Obtain a Hit Chain of 5 or higher using only Strong Attacks.
Ultimate Dragon Warrior (30)	Purchase all upgrades.
Untouchable (20)	Make it through an entire level without getting hit.

CODES

From the main menu, select Extras and then select Cheats.

EFFECT	CODE
All Multiplayer Characters	←,↓,←,→,↓
Big Head Mode (Story Mode)	↓,↑,←,→,→
Infinite Chi	↓,→,←,↑,↓
Invulnerability	↓,↓,→,↑,←
Dragon Warrior Outfit (Multiplayer Mode)	←,↓,→,←,↑
4x Damage Multiplier	↑,↓,↑,→,←

KUNG FU PANDA (PlayStation 3)

CODES

From the main menu, select Extras and then select Cheats.

EFFECT	CODE
All Multiplayer Characters	←,↓,←,→,↓

EFFECT	CODE
Big Head Mode (Story Mode)	↓,↑,←,→,→
Infinite Chi	↓,→,←,↑,↓
EFFECT	CODE
Invulnerability	↓,↓,→,↑,←
Dragon Warrior Outfit (Multiplayer Mode)	←,↓,→,←,↑
4x Damage Multiplier	↑,↓,↑,→,←

KUNG FU PANDA (Wii)

CODES

From the main menu, select Extras and then select Cheats.

EFFECT	CODE
All Multiplayer Characters	Left, Down, Left, Right, Down
Big Head Mode (Story Mode)	Down, Up, Left, Right, Right
Infinite Chi	Down, Right, Left, Up, Down
Invulnerability	Down, Down, Right, Up, Left
Dragon Warrior Outfit (Multiplayer Mode)	Left, Down, Right, Left, Up
4x Damage Multiplier	Up, Down, Up, Right, Left

KUNG FU PANDA (PlayStation 2)

CODES

From the main menu, select extras, and then select cheats.

EFFECT	CODE
All Multiplayer Characters	←,↓,←,→,↓
Big Head Mode (Story Mode)	↓,↑,←,→,→
Dragon Warrior Outfit (Multiplayer Mode)	←,↓,→,←,↑
Infinite Chi	↓,→,←,↑,↓
Invulnerability	↓,↓,→,↑,←
4x Damage Multiplier	↑,↓,↑,→,←

L.A. RUSH (PlayStation 2)

Enter codes while playing. Do not pause.

UNLOCKABLE	CODE
$5,000	⇧, ⇩, ⇦, ⇨, ●, ⇦, R2, ⇧
Disable Police	⇩, ⇦, ⇨, R2, ■, ⇨, R1, ⇦
Fast Traffic	⇧, ⇩, ⇦, ⇨, ■, ⇨, ●, ⇦
No Catching Up on Races	Enter C-VHARD as a profile name.
Unlimited N20	⇧, ⇩, ⇦, ⇨, ■, ⇧, ⇩, ●, ⇧

LAIR (PlayStation 3)

PASSWORDS

Enter into the game's Cheat menu:

PASSWORD	EFFECT
chicken	Chicken Curry video
686F7420636F66666565	Hot Coffee video
koelsch	Unlocks Stable option for all levels on the Mission Select screen

LAND OF THE DEAD: ROAD TO FIDDLER'S GREEN (XBOX)

Enter these codes during gameplay.

UNLOCKABLE	CODE
All Weapons	↑, ↓, ←, →, Ⓐ, Ⓑ
God Mode	↑, ↓, ←, →, ↑, ↓, ←, →
Kill All Spawned Enemies	Ⓐ, Ⓑ, Ⓨ, Ⓧ, Ⓐ, Ⓑ, Ⓨ, Ⓧ
Kungfu Fists	→, ↓, ←, Ⓐ
Minigun	↑, ↑, ↓, ↓, Ⓐ, Ⓑ, Ⓐ, Ⓑ
No Knockdown	↑, Ⓐ, ↑, Ⓑ, ↑, Ⓨ, ↑, Ⓧ

LE MANS 24 HOURS (PlayStation 2)

Enter the following codes as your name at the Championship mode name screen.

UNLOCKABLE	CODE
All Cars	ACO
All Championships	NUMBAT
All Tracks	SPEEDY
Le Mans	WOMBAT
See the Credits	HEINEY

LEFT 4 DEAD (XBOX360)

UNLOCKABLE	HOW TO UNLOCK
Rocket Launcher	Complete the game on any difficulty.

LEGACY OF KAIN: DEFIANCE (XBOX)

To access the following, pause the game any time and enter code.

UNLOCKABLE	CODE
All Bonuses	BLK, ↓, WHT, RT, ←, WHT, ↓, LT, Ⓨ
Infinite Reaver Charge	↓, ↓, ↑, ←, RT, BLK, ↓, Ⓨ, Ⓑ

UNLOCKABLE	CODE
Card Board Tube Reaver	↑,↓,←,→,BLK,WHT,Y,↓,B
God Mode	↑,↓,→,↓,RT,BLK,↓,Y,LT

LEGACY OF KAIN: DEFIANCE (PlayStation 2)

Pause gameplay to enter the following codes.

UNLOCKABLE	CODE
All Bonuses	R2,↓,L2,R1,←,L2,↓,L1,▲
All Combo Moves	→,↓,↑,↓,↓,R1,▲,●,↓
All Dark Chronicles	R1,↓,R2,L1,→,R2,▲,↓,L1
All Power Ups	←,←,↑,↑,L1,R2,●,↓,▲
Cartoon Version	↑,↓,↑,↓,R1,R2,↓,●,▲
Full Health and Reaver Charge	←,→,←,→,R1,L1,●,▲,↓
No Textures	L1,↓,R2,→,R2,↑,▲,L1,↓
Tube Reaver	↑,↓,←,→,R2,L2,▲,↓,●
Unlimited Reaver Charge and Balance Emblem	↓,↓,↑,←,R1,R2,↓,▲,●
Wireframe	L1,↓,L1,↑,R1,L2,L1,↓,▲

LEGEND OF KAGE (Wii)

UNLOCKABLES

UNLOCKABLE	HOW TO UNLOCK
1-Up	If you stay in the water of the moat and kill seven ninjas with your sword, a blue creature flies across the screen. Catch him for a 1-Up. This works in all of the moat scenes.

THE LEGEND OF SPYRO: A NEW BEGINNING (PlayStation 2)

Enter these codes while the game is paused.

UNLOCKABLE	CODE
Infinite Breath	↑, ↑, ↓, ↓, ←, →, ←, →, L1, R1, L1, R1
Infinite Health	↑, ↑, ↓, ↓, ←, →, ←, →, L1, L1, R1, R1

LEGENDS OF WRESTLING (XBOX)

UNLOCKABLE	CODE
All Wrestlers	At the Main menu, press ↑,↑,↓,↓,←,→,←,→,Y,Y,X. The save prompt appears to let you know 266the code worked.

LEGO BATMAN (XBOX360)

CODES

Enter the codes on the second level of the Batcave at the computer above the outfit changer.

EFFECT	CODE
Alfred	ZAQ637
Bat-Tank	KNTT4B
Batgirl	JKR331
Bruce Wayne	BDJ327
Bruce Wayne's Private Jet	LEA664
Catwoman (Classic)	M1AAWW
Catwoman's Motorcycle	HPL826
Clown Goon	HJK327
Commissioner Gordon	DDP967
Fishmonger	HGY748
Freeze Girl	XVK541

Garbage Truck	DUS483
Glideslam	BBD7BY
Goon Helicopter	GCH328
Harbor Helicopter	CHP735
Harley Quinn's Hammer Truck	RDT637
Joker Goon	UTF782
Joker Henchman	YUN924
Mad Hatter	JCA283
Mad Hatter's Glider	HS000W
Mad Hatter's Steamboat	M4DM4N
Man-Bat	NYU942
Military Policeman	MKL382
Mr. Freeze's Iceberg	ICYICE
Mr. Freeze's Kart	BCT229
Nightwing	MVY759
Penguin Goon	NKA238
Penguin Goon Submarine	BTN248
Penguin Henchman	BJH782
Penguin Minion	KJP748
Poison Ivy Goon	GTB899
Police Bike	LJP234
Police Boat	PLC999
Police Car	KJL832
Police Helicopter	CWR732
Police Marksman	HKG984
Police Officer	JRY983
Police Van	MAC788
Police Watercraft	VJD328
Riddler Goon	CRY928
Riddler Henchman	XEU824
Riddler's Jet	HAHAHA
Robin's Submarine	TTF453
S.W.A.T.	HTF114
Sailor	NAV592
Scientist	JFL786
Security Guard	PLB946
The Joker (Tropical)	CCB199
The Joker's Van	JUK657
Two-Face's Armored Truck	EFE933
Yeti	NJL412
Zoo Sweeper	DWR243

EXTRA CODES

EFFECT	CODE
Always Score Multiply	9LRGNB
Area Effect	TL3EKT
Armor Plating	N8JZEK
Bats	XFP4E2
Beep Beep	RAFTU8

EFFECT	CODE
Character Studs	DY13BD
Decoy	TQ09K3
Disguise	GEC3MD
Extra Toggle	EWAW7W
Extra Hearts	ML3KHP
Fast Batarangs	JRBDCB
Fast Build	GHJ2DY
Fast Grapple	RM4PR8
Fast Walk	ZOLM6N
Faster Pieces	EVG26J
Flaming Batarangs (Used with heat batman)	D8NYWH
Freeze Batarang	XPN4NG
Ice Rink	KLKL4G
Immune to Freeze	JXUDY6
Invincible	WYD5CP
Minikit Detector	ZXGH9J
More Batarang Targets	XWP645
More Detonators	TNTN6B
Piece Detector	KHJ544
Power Brick Detector	MMN786
Regenerate Hearts	HJH7HJ
Score x2	N4NR3E
Score x4	CX9MAT
Score x6	MLVNF2
Score x8	WCCDB9
Score x10	18HW07
Silhouettes	YK4TPH
Slam	BBD7BY
Sonic Pain	THTL4X
Stud Magnet	LK2DY4

LEGO BATMAN (PlayStation 3)

CODES

Enter the codes on the second level of the Batcave at the computer above the outfit changer.

EFFECT	CODE
Alfred	ZAQ637
Bat-Tank	KNTT4B
Batgirl	JKR331
Bruce Wayne	BDJ327
Bruce Wayne's Private Jet	LEA664
Catwoman (Classic)	M1AAWW
Catwoman's Motorcycle	HPL826
Clown Goon	HJK327
Commissioner Gordon	DDP967
Fishmonger	HGY748
Freeze Girl	XVK541
Garbage Truck	DUS483

Glideslam	BBD7BY
Goon Helicopter	GCH328
Harbor Helicopter	CHP735
Harley Quinn's Hammer Truck	RDT637
Joker Goon	UTF782
Joker Henchman	YUN924
Mad Hatter	JCA283
Mad Hatter's Glider	HS000W
Mad Hatter's Steamboat	M4DM4N
Man-Bat	NYU942
Military Policeman	MKL382
Mr. Freeze's Iceberg	ICYICE
Mr. Freeze's Kart	BCT229
Nightwing	MVY759
Penguin Goon	NKA238
Penguin Goon Submarine	BTN248
Penguin Henchman	BJH782
Penguin Minion	KJP748
Poison Ivy Goon	GTB899
Police Bike	LJP234
Police Boat	PLC999
Police Car	KJL832
Police Helicopter	CWR732
Police Marksman	HKG984
Police Officer	JRY983
Police Van	MAC788
Police Watercraft	VJD328
Riddler Goon	CRY928
Riddler Henchman	XEU824
Riddler's Jet	HAHAHA
Robin's Submarine	TTF453
S.W.A.T.	HTF114
Sailor	NAV592
Scientist	JFL786
Security Guard	PLB946
The Joker (Tropical)	CCB199
The Joker's Van	JUK657
Two-Face's Armored Truck	EFE933
Yeti	NJL412
Zoo Sweeper	DWR243

EXTRA CODES

EFFECT	CODE
Always Score Multiply	9LRGNB
Area Effect	TL3EKT
Armor Plating	N8JZEK
Bats	XFP4E2
Beep Beep	RAFTU8
Character Studs	DY13BD

NEW! A B C D E F G H I J K **L** M N O P Q R S T U V W X Y Z

EFFECT	CODE
Decoy	TQ09K3
Disguise	GEC3MD
Extra Toggle	EWAW7W
Extra Hearts	ML3KHP
Fast Batarangs	JRBDCB
Fast Build	GHJ2DY
Fast Grapple	RM4PR8
Fast Walk	ZOLM6N
Faster Pieces	EVG26J
Flaming Batarangs (Used with heat batman)	D8NYWH
Freeze Batarang	XPN4NG
Ice Rink	KLKL4G
Immune to Freeze	JXUDY6
Invincible	WYD5CP
Minikit Detector	ZXGH9J
More Batarang Targets	XWP645
More Detonators	TNTN6B
Piece Detector	KHJ544
Power Brick Detector	MMN786
Regenerate Hearts	HJH7HJ
Score x2	N4NR3E
Score x4	CX9MAT
Score x6	MLVNF2
Score x8	WCCDB9
Score x10	18HW07
Silhouettes	YK4TPH
Slam	BBD7BY
Sonic Pain	THTL4X
Stud Magnet	LK2DY4

LEGO BATMAN (Wii)

CODES

Enter the codes on the second level of the Batcave at the computer above the outfit changer.

EFFECT	CODE
Bruce Wayne	BDJ327
Commissioner Gordon	DDP967
More Batarang Targets	XWP645
Nightwing	MVY759
Penguin Minion	KJP748
Police Van	MAC788
The Joker (Tropical)	CCB199
Yeti	NJL412

FREE PLAY CODES

EFFECT	CODE
Unlocks Alfred in Free Play	ZAQ637
Unlocks Commissioner Gordon in Free Play	DPP967
Unlocks Free Girl in Free Play	XVK541

Unlocks Harley Quinn's Hammer Truck	RDT637
Unlocks More Batarang Targets	XWP645
Unlocks Penguin Henchman in Free Play	BJH782
Unlocks Yeti in Free Play	NJL412

LEGO BATMAN (DS)

CODES

Enter the following codes at the main menu. If you enter them correctly you will hear a sound.

EFFECT	CODE
Add 1 Million Studs	X, Y, B, B, Y, X, L, L, R, R, Up, Down, Left, Right, START, SELECT
All Characters	X, Up, B, Down, Y, Left, START, Right, R, R, L, R, R, Down, Down, Up, Y, Y, Y, START, SELECT
All Episodes and Free Play mode	Right, Up, R, L, X, Y, Right, Left, B, L, R, L, Down, Down, Up, Y, Y, X, X, B, B, Up, Up, L, R, START, SELECT
All Extras	Up, Down, L, R, L, R, Left, Right, X, X, Y, Y, B, B, L, Up, Down, L, R, L, R, Up, Up, Down, START, SELECT

LEGO BATMAN (PSP)

CODES

Enter the codes on the second level of the Batcave at the computer above the outfit changer.

EFFECT	CODE
Alfred	ZAQ637
Bat-Tank	KNTT4B
Batgirl	JKR331
Bruce Wayne	BDJ327
Bruce Wayne's Private Jet	LEA664
Catwoman (Classic)	M1AAWW
Catwoman's Motorcycle	HPL826
Clown Goon	HJK327
Commissioner Gordon	DDP967
Fishmonger	HGY748
Freeze Girl	XVK541
Garbage Truck	DUS483
Glideslam	BBD7BY
Goon Helicopter	GCH328
Harbor Helicopter	CHP735
Harley Quinn's Hammer Truck	RDT637
Joker Goon	UTF782
Joker Henchman	YUN924
Mad Hatter	JCA283
Mad Hatter's Glider	HS000W
Mad Hatter's Steamboat	M4DM4N
Man-Bat	NYU942
Military Policeman	MKL382
Mr. Freeze's Iceberg	ICYICE
Mr. Freeze's Kart	BCT229
Nightwing	MVY759
Penguin Goon	NKA238
Penguin Goon Submarine	BTN248
Penguin Henchman	BJH782
Penguin Minion	KJP748

Poison Ivy Goon	GTB899
Police Bike	LJP234
Police Boat	PLC999
Police Car	KJL832
Police Helicopter	CWR732
Police Marksman	HKG984
Police Officer	JRY983
Police Van	MAC788
Police Watercraft	VJD328
Riddler Goon	CRY928
Riddler Henchman	XEU824
Riddler's Jet	HAHAHA
Robin's Submarine	TTF453
S.W.A.T.	HTF114
Sailor	NAV592
Scientist	JFL786
Security Guard	PLB946
The Joker (Tropical)	CCB199
The Joker's Van	JUK657
Two-Face's Armored Truck	EFE933
Yeti	NJL412
Zoo Sweeper	DWR243

EXTRA CODES

EFFECT	CODE
Always Score Multiply	9LRGNB
Area Effect	TL3EKT
Armor Plating	N8JZEK
Bats	XFP4E2
Beep Beep	RAFTU8
Character Studs	DY13BD
Decoy	TQ09K3
Disguise	GEC3MD
Extra Toggle	EWAW7W
Extra Hearts	ML3KHP
Fast Batarangs	JRBDCB
Fast Build	GHJ2DY
Fast Grapple	RM4PR8
Fast Walk	ZOLM6N
Faster Pieces	EVG26J
Flaming Batarangs (Used with heat batman)	D8NYWH
Freeze Batarang	XPN4NG
Ice Rink	KLKL4G
Immune to Freeze	JXUDY6
Invincible	WYD5CP
Minikit Detector	ZXGH9J
More Batarang Targets	XWP645
More Detonators	TNTN6B
Piece Detector	KHJ544
Power Brick Detector	MMN786
Regenerate Hearts	HJH7HJ

Score x2	N4NR3E
Score x4	CX9MAT
Score x6	MLVNF2
Score x8	WCCDB9
Score x10	18HW07
Silhouettes	YK4TPH
Slam	BBD7BY
Sonic Pain	THTL4X
Stud Magnet	LK2DY4

LEGO BATMAN (PlayStation 2)

CODES

Enter the codes on the second level of the Batcave at the computer above the outfit changer.

EFFECT	CODE
Alfred	ZAQ637
Bat-Tank	KNTT4B
Batgirl	JKR331
Bruce Wayne	BDJ327
Bruce Wayne's Private Jet	LEA664
Catwoman (Classic)	M1AAWW
Catwoman's Motorcycle	HPL826
Clown Goon	HJK327
Commissioner Gordon	DDP967
Fishmonger	HGY748
Freeze Girl	XVK541
Garbage Truck	DUS483
Glideslam	BBD7BY
Goon Helicopter	GCH328
Harbor Helicopter	CHP735
Harley Quinn's Hammer Truck	RDT637
Joker Goon	UTF782
Joker Henchman	YUN924
Mad Hatter	JCA283
Mad Hatter's Glider	HS000W
Mad Hatter's Steamboat	M4DM4N
Man-Bat	NYU942
Military Policeman	MKL382
Mr. Freeze's Iceberg	ICYICE
Mr. Freeze's Kart	BCT229
Nightwing	MVY759
Penguin Goon	NKA238
Penguin Goon Submarine	BTN248
Penguin Henchman	BJH782
Penguin Minion	KJP748
Poison Ivy Goon	GTB899
Police Bike	LJP234
Police Boat	PLC999
Police Car	KJL832
Police Helicopter	CWR732
Police Marksman	HKG984
Police Officer	JRY983

EFFECT	CODE
Police Van	MAC788
Police Watercraft	VJD328
Riddler Goon	CRY928
Riddler Henchman	XEU824
Riddler's Jet	HAHAHA
Robin's Submarine	TTF453
S.W.A.T.	HTF114
Sailor	NAV592
Scientist	JFL786
Security Guard	PLB946
The Joker (Tropical)	CCB199
The Joker's Van	JUK657
Two-Face's Armored Truck	EFE933
Yeti	NJL412
Zoo Sweeper	DWR243

EXTRA CODES

EFFECT	CODE
Always Score Multiply	9LRGNB
EFFECT	CODE
Area Effect	TL3EKT
Armor Plating	N8JZEK
Bats	XFP4E2
Beep Beep	RAFTU8
Character Studs	DY13BD
Decoy	TQ09K3
Disguise	GEC3MD
Extra Toggle	EWAW7W
Extra Hearts	ML3KHP
Fast Batarangs	JRBDCB
Fast Build	GHJ2DY
Fast Grapple	RM4PR8
Fast Walk	ZOLM6N
Faster Pieces	EVG26J
Flaming Batarangs (Used with heat batman)	D8NYWH
Freeze Batarang	XPN4NG
Ice Rink	KLKL4G
Immune to Freeze	JXUDY6
Invincible	WYD5CP
Minikit Detector	ZXGH9J
More Batarang Targets	XWP645
More Detonators	TNTN6B
Piece Detector	KHJ544
Power Brick Detector	MMN786
Regenerate Hearts	HJH7HJ
Score x2	N4NR3E
Score x4	CX9MAT
Score x6	MLVNF2
Score x8	WCCDB9
Score x10	18HW07
Silhouettes	YK4TPH

Slam	BBD7BY
Sonic Pain	THTL4X
Stud Magnet	LK2DY4

LEGO BATTLES (DS)

CODES

Go to the "LEGO store" then select "Cheat Codes" and then input the codes.

EFFECT	CODE
Double LEGO bricks	BGQOYRT
Fast Building	QMSLPOE
Fast Harvesting	PQZLJOB
Fast Magic	JRTPASX
Fast Mining	KVBPQRJ
Full Unit Cap	UMSXIRQ
Invincible Hero	HJCRAWK
Long Range Magic	ZPWJFUQ
One Hit Kill (Hero Only)	AVMPWHK
Regenerating Health	ABABLRX
Reveal Map	SKQMXPL
Show Enemies	IBGOFWX
Show LEGO Studs (Blue)	CPLYREK
Show Minikit	LJYQRAC
Show Red Bricks	RTGYPKC
Super Explosions	THNBGRE
Super Magic	DWFTBNS
Unlock Islander	UGDRSQP
Unlock Ninja Master	SHWSDGU
Unlock Space Criminal Leader	ZVDNJSU
Unlock Troll King	XRCTVYB
Upgraded Towers	EDRFTGY

UNLOCKABLES

UNLOCKABLE	HOW TO UNLOCK
Queen	Complete King story mode.
Santa	Set DS system date to December 25th (12/25).
Sorceress	Complete Wizard story mode.
Wizard	Complete King Act 1.

LEGO INDIANA JONES: THE ORIGINAL ADVENTURES (XBOX360)

CHARACTER CODES

Enter the codes on the blackboard in the math classroom of Barnett College (the 2nd door on the left in the main hallway).

EFFECT	CODE
Bandit	12N68W
Bandit Swordsman	1MK4RT
Barranca	04EM94
Bazooka Trooper (Crusade)	MK83R7
Bazooka Trooper (Raiders)	S93Y5R
Belloq	CHN3YU
Belloq (Jungle)	TDR197
Belloq (Robes)	VEO29L

EFFECT	CODE
British Officer	VJ5TI9
British Troop Commander	B73EUA
British Troop Soldier	DJ5I2W
Captain Katanga	VJ3TT3
Chatter Lal	ENW936
Chatter Lal (Thuggee)	CNH4RY
Chen	3NK48T
Colonel Dietrich	2K9RKS
Colonel Vogel	8EAL4H
Dancing Girl	C7EJ21
Donovan	3NFTU8
Elsa (Desert)	JSNRT9
Elsa (Officer)	VMJ5US
Enemy Boxer	8246RB
Enemy Butler	VJ48W3
Enemy Guard	VJ7R51
Enemy Guard (Mountains)	YR47WM
Enemy Officer (Desert)	2MK450
Enemy Officer	572 E61
Enemy Pilot	B84ELP
Enemy Radio Operator	1MF94R
Enemy Soldier (Desert)	4NSU7Q
Fedora	V75YSP
First Mate	0GIN24
Grail Knight	NE6THI
Hovitos Tribesman	H0V1SS
Indiana Jones (Desert Disguise)	4J8S4M
Indiana Jones (Officer)	VJ85OS
Jungle Guide	24PF34
Kao Kan	WM046L
Kazim	NRH23J
Kazim (Desert)	3M29TJ
Lao Che	2NK479
Maharaja	NFK5N2
Major Toht	13NS01
Masked Bandit	N48SF0
Mola Ram	FJUR31
Monkey Man	3RF6YJ
Pankot Assassin	2NKT72
Pankot Guard	VN28RH
Sherpa Brawler	VJ37WJ
Sherpa Gunner	ND762W
Slave Child	0E3ENW
Thuggee	VM683E
Thuggee Acolyte	T2R3F9
Thuggee Slavedriver	VBS7GW
Village Dignitary	KD48TN

Village Elder	4682 E1
Willie (Dinner Suit)	VK93R7
Willie (Pajamas)	MEN4IP
Wu Han	3NSLT8

ITEM CODES

Enter the codes on the blackboard in the math classroom of Barnett College (the 2nd door on the left in the main hallway).

EFFECT	CODE
Artifact Detector	VIKED7
Beep Beep	VNF59Q
Character Treasure	VIES2R
Disarm Enemies	VKRNS9
Disguises	4ID1N6
Fast Build	V83SLO
Fast Dig	378RS6
Fast Fix	FJ59WS
Fertilizer	B1GW1F
Ice Rink	33GM7J
Parcel Detector	VUT673
Poo Treasure	WWQ1SA
Regenerate Hearts	MDLP69
Secret Characters	3X44AA
Silhouettes	3HE85H
Super Scream	VN3R7S
Super Slap	0P1TA5
Treasure Magnet	H86LA2
Treasure x2	VM4TS9
Treasure x4	VLWEN3
Treasure x6	V84RYS
Treasure x8	A72E1M
Treasure x10	VI3PS8

ACHIEVEMENTS

UNLOCKABLE	HOW TO UNLOCK
A source of unspeakable power! (20)	Build 250 LEGO objects.
Bad dates! (20)	Give 20 bananas to monkeys.
Belloq's staff is too long. (10)	Complete the "City of Danger" level in Story mode.
Blow it up! (40)	Blow up 5 enemies with 1 explosion.
DON'T call me Junior! (10)	Complete the "Castle Rescue" level in Story mode.
Fortune & glory kid. (100)	Complete the game to 100%.
Goodbye Dr. Jones. (20)	Destroy Indy with Lao Che.
He chose... poorly. (10)	Complete the "Temple of the Grail" level in Story mode.
He no nuts. He's crazy!! (20)	Smash 250 LEGO objects.
Hey! You call him Dr. Jones! (20)	Create and name a custom build character.
How dare you kiss me! (15)	Use your whip to kiss Marion, Willie, and Elsa.
How we say goodbye in Germany. (20)	Access restricted enemy locations 50 times.
I had bugs for lunch! (10)	Complete the "Pankot Secrets" level in Story mode.
I hate these guys. (20)	Destroy 200 bad guys.
I step on fortune cookie! (20)	Destroy 50 creepy-crawlies.

UNLOCKABLE	HOW TO UNLOCK
It's not the years honey... (40)	Complete any level with out dying, without invincibility.
It's important Marion, trust me. (10)	Complete the "Into the Mountains" level in Story mode.
I'm making this up as I go along (10)	Complete the "Pursing the Ark" level in Story mode.
Kali Ma will rule the world! (10)	Complete the "Kali's Temple" level in Story mode.
Keep your eyes shut! (10)	Complete the "Opening the Ark" level in Story mode.
Nice try, Lao Che! (20)	Destroy Lao Che with Indy.
No ticket. (10)	Complete the "Trouble in the Sky" level in Story mode.
Oh it breaks the heart. (15)	Oh it breaks the heart.
Prepare to meet Kali! (10)	Complete the "Battle on the Bridge" level in Story mode.
Quit fooling around. (10)	Complete the "Free the Slaves" level in Story mode.
Short Round, step on it! (10)	Complete the "Shanghai Showdown" level in Story mode.
Show a little backbone will ya? (20)	Destroy 100 snakes.
Start the engines, Jock! (20)	Use a mechanic character's repair ability 50 times.
Take the left tunnel! (10)	Complete the "Escape the Mines" level in Story mode.
That belongs in a museum! (10)	Complete the "Young Indy" level in Story mode.
That's for blasphemy! (20)	Destroy Indy with Jones Senior.
The best digger in Cairo. (20)	Uncover 50 pieces of buried treasures using the excavation ability.
There is nothing to fear here. (10)	Complete the "The Lost Temple" level in Story mode.
They're well out of range dad. (10)	Complete the "Desert Ambush" level in Story mode.
This... this is history... (40)	Collect all artifacts.
Trouble with her is the noise. (20)	Destroy 50 objects or characters using the scream and super scream ability.
We're not going in the boat? (10)	Complete the "Motorcycle Escape" level in Story mode.
What a cautious fellow I am. (20)	Destroy 50 objects with a bazooka or other explosive device.
Where Forrestal cashed in. (30)	Collect 1,000,000 studs in the Ancient City level.
Why did it have to be snakes? (10)	Complete the "The Well of Souls" level in Story mode.
X marks the spot! (10)	Complete the "The Hunt for Sir Richard" level in Story mode.
You call this archaeology? (20)	Use a scholar character's academic ability 50 times.
You chose... wisely. (30)	Unlock all of the available characters.
You will become a true believer. (20)	Use a Thuggee Statue 20 times.
Your mail is on your desk. (40)	Post all parcels.

LEGO INDIANA JONES: THE ORIGINAL ADVENTURES (PlayStation 3)

CHARACTER CODES

Enter the codes on the blackboard in the math classroom of Barnett College (the 2nd door on the left in the main hallway).

EFFECT	CODE
Bandit	12N68W
Bandit Swordsman	1MK4RT
Barranca	04EM94
Bazooka Trooper (Crusade)	MK83R7
Bazooka Trooper (Raiders)	S93Y5R
Belloq	CHN3YU
Belloq (Jungle)	TDR197
Belloq (Robes)	VEO29L

British Officer	VJ5TI9
British Troop Commander	B73EUA
British Troop Soldier	DJ5I2W
Captain Katanga	VJ3TT3
Chatter Lal	ENW936
Chatter Lal (Thuggee)	CNH4RY
Chen	3NK48T
Colonel Dietrich	2K9RKS
Colonel Vogel	8EAL4H
Dancing Girl	C7EJ21
Donovan	3NFTU8
Elsa (Desert)	JSNRT9
Elsa (Officer)	VMJ5US
Enemy Boxer	8246RB
Enemy Butler	VJ48W3
Enemy Guard	VJ7R51
Enemy Guard (Mountains)	YR47WM
Enemy Officer	572 E61
Enemy Officer (Desert)	2MK450
Enemy Pilot	B84ELP
Enemy Radio Operator	1MF94R
Enemy Soldier (Desert)	4NSU7Q
Fedora	V75YSP
First Mate	0GIN24
Grail Knight	NE6THI
Hovitos Tribesman	H0V1SS
Indiana Jones (Desert Disguise)	4J8S4M
Indiana Jones (Officer)	VJ850S
Jungle Guide	24PF34
Kao Kan	WM046L
Kazim	NRH23J
Kazim (Desert)	3M29TJ
Lao Che	2NK479
Maharaja	NFK5N2
Major Toht	13NS01
Masked Bandit	N48SF0
Mola Ram	FJUR31
Monkey Man	3RF6YJ
Pankot Assassin	2NKT72
Pankot Guard	VN28RH
Sherpa Brawler	VJ37WJ
Sherpa Gunner	ND762W
Slave Child	0E3ENW
Thuggee	VM683E
Thuggee Acolyte	T2R3F9
Thuggee Slavedriver	VBS7GW
Village Dignitary	KD48TN
Village Elder	4682 E1
Willie (Dinner Suit)	VK93R7

EFFECT	CODE
Willie (Pajamas)	MEN4IP
Wu Han	3NSLT8

ITEM CODES

Enter the codes on the blackboard in the math classroom of Barnett College (the 2nd door on the left in the main hallway).

EFFECT	CODE
Artifact Detector	VIKED7
Beep Beep	VNF59Q
Character Treasure	VIES2R
Disarm Enemies	VKRNS9
Disguises	4ID1N6
Fast Build	V83SLO
Fast Dig	378RS6
Fast Fix	FJ59WS
Fertilizer	B1GW1F
Ice Rink	33GM7J
Parcel Detector	VUT673
Poo Treasure	WWQ1SA
Regenerate Hearts	MDLP69
Secret Characters	3X44AA
Silhouettes	3HE85H
Super Scream	VN3R7S
Super Slap	0P1TA5
Treasure Magnet	H86LA2
Treasure x2	VM4TS9
Treasure x4	VLWEN3
Treasure x6	V84RYS
Treasure x8	A72E1M
Treasure x10	VI3PS8

LEGO INDIANA JONES: THE ORIGINAL ADVENTURES (Wii)

CHARACTER CODES

Enter the codes in the math classroom (the 2nd door on the left in the main hallway). The characters still have to be purchased.

EFFECT	CODE
Bandit	12N68W
Bandit Swordsman	1MK4RT
Barranca	04EM94
Bazooka Trooper (Crusade)	MK83R7
Bazooka Trooper (Raiders)	S93Y5R
Belloq	CHN3YU
Belloq (Jungle)	TDR197
Belloq (Robes)	VEO29L
British Officer	VJ5TI9
British Troop Commander	B73EUA
British Troop Soldier	DJ5I2W
Captain Katanga	VJ3TT3
Chatter Lal	ENW936
Chatter Lal (Thuggee)	CNH4RY

Chen	3NK48T
Colonel Dietrich	2K9RKS
Colonel Vogel	8EAL4H
Dancing Girl	C7EJ21
Donovan	3NFTU8
Elsa (Desert)	JSNRT9
Elsa (Officer)	VMJ5US
Enemy Boxer	8246RB
Enemy Butler	VJ48W3
Enemy Guard	VJ7R51
Enemy Guard (Mountains)	YR47WM
Enemy Officer	572 E61
Enemy Officer (Desert)	2MK450
Enemy Pilot	B84ELP
Enemy Radio Operator	1MF94R
Enemy Soldier (Desert)	4NSU7Q
Fedora	V75YSP
First Mate	0GIN24
Grail Knight	NE6THI
Hovitos Tribesman	H0V1SS
Indiana Jones (Desert Disguise)	4J8S4M
Indiana Jones (Officer)	VJ850S
Jungle Guide	24PF34
Kao Kan	WM046L
Kazim	NRH23J
Kazim (Desert)	3M29TJ
Lao Che	2NK479
Maharaja	NFK5N2
Major Toht	13NS01
Masked Bandit	N48SF0
Mola Ram	FJUR31
Monkey Man	3RF6YJ
Pankot Assassin	2NKT72
Pankot Guard	VN28RH
Sherpa Brawler	VJ37WJ
Sherpa Gunner	ND762W
EFFECT	**CODE**
Slave Child	0E3ENW
Thuggee	VM683E
Thuggee Acolyte	T2R3F9
Thuggee Slavedriver	VBS7GW
Village Dignitary	KD48TN
Village Elder	4682 E1
Willie (Dinner Suit)	VK93R7
Willie (Pajamas)	MEN4IP
Wu Han	3NSLT8

ITEM CODES

Enter the codes on the blackboard in the math classroom of Barnett College (the 2nd door on the left in the main hallway).

EFFECT	CODE
Artifact Detector	VIKED7
Beep Beep	VNF59Q
Character Treasure	VIES2R
Disarm Enemies	VKRNS9
Disguises	4ID1N6
Fast Build	V83SLO
Fast Dig	378RS6
Fast Fix	FJ59WS
Fertilizer	B1GW1F
Ice Rink	33GM7J
Parcel Detector	VUT673
Poo Treasure	WWQ1SA
Regenerate Hearts	MDLP69
Secret Characters	3X44AA
Silhouettes	3HE85H
Super Scream	VN3R7S
Super Slap	0P1TA5
Treasure Magnet	H86LA2
Treasure x2	VM4TS9
Treasure x4	VLWEN3
Treasure x6	V84RYS
Treasure x8	A72E1M
Treasure x10	VI3PS8

LEGO INDIANA JONES: THE ORIGINAL ADVENTURES (DS)

CODES

EFFECT	CODE
All Characters Unlocked	X, Up, B, Down, Y, Left, START, Right, R, R, L, R, R, Down, Down, Up, Y, Y, Y, START, SELECT
All Episodes Unlocked + Free Play	Right, Up, R, L, X, Y, Right, Left, B, L, R, L, Down, Down, Up, Y, Y, X, X, B, B, Up, Up, L, R, START, SELECT
All Extras Unlocked	Up, Down, L, R, L, R, L, Left, Right, X, X, Y, Y, B, B, L, Up, Down, L, R, L, R, Up, Up, Down, START, SELECT
Start with 1,000,000 Studs	X, Y, B, B, Y, X, L, L, R, R, Up, Down, Left, Right, START, SELECT
Start with 3,000,000 Studs	Up, Up, B, Down, Down, X, Left, Left, Y, L, R, L, R, B, Y, X, START, SELECT

LEGO INDIANA JONES: THE ORIGINAL ADVENTURES (PSP)

CHARACTER CODES

Enter the codes on the blackboard in the math classroom of Barnett College(the 2nd door on the left in the main hallway).

EFFECT	CODE
Bandit	12N68W
Bandit Swordsman	1MK4RT
Barranca	04EM94
Bazooka Trooper (Crusade)	MK83R7
Bazooka Trooper (Raiders)	S93Y5R
Belloq	CHN3YU
Belloq (Jungle)	TDR197
Belloq (Robes)	VEO29L
British Officer	VJ5TI9
British Troop Commander	B73EUA

British Troop Soldier	DJ5I2W
Captain Katanga	VJ3TT3
Chatter Lal	ENW936
Chatter Lal (Thuggee)	CNH4RY
Chen	3NK48T
Colonel Dietrich	2K9RKS
Colonel Vogel	8EAL4H
Dancing Girl	C7EJ21
Donovan	3NFTU8
Elsa (Desert)	JSNRT9
Elsa (Officer)	VMJ5US
Enemy Boxer	8246RB
Enemy Butler	VJ48W3
Enemy Guard	VJ7R51
Enemy Guard (Mountains)	YR47WM
Enemy Officer	572 E61
Enemy Officer (Desert)	2MK450
Enemy Pilot	B84ELP
Enemy Radio Operator	1MF94R
Enemy Soldier (Desert)	4NSU7Q
Fedora	V75YSP
First Mate	0GIN24
Grail Knight	NE6THI
Hovitos Tribesman	H0V1SS
Indiana Jones (Desert Disguise)	4J8S4M
Indiana Jones (Officer)	VJ850S
Jungle Guide	24PF34
Kao Kan	WM046L
Kazim	NRH23J
Kazim (Desert)	3M29TJ
Lao Che	2NK479
Maharaja	NFK5N2
Major Toht	13NS01
Masked Bandit	N48SF0
Mola Ram	FJUR31
Monkey Man	3RF6YJ
Pankot Assassin	2NKT72
Pankot Guard	VN28RH
Sherpa Brawler	VJ37WJ
Sherpa Gunner	ND762W
Slave Child	0E3ENW
Thuggee	VM683E
Thuggee Acolyte	T2R3F9
Thuggee Slavedriver	VBS7GW
Village Dignitary	KD48TN
Village Elder	4682 E1
Willie (Dinner Suit)	VK93R7
Willie (Pajamas)	MEN4IP
Wu Han	3NSLT8

ITEM CODES

Enter the codes on the blackboard in the math classroom of Barnett College(the 2nd door on the left in the main hallway).

EFFECT	CODE
Artifact Detector	VIKED7
Beep Beep	VNF59Q
Character Treasure	VIES2R
Disarm Enemies	VKRNS9
Disguises	4ID1N6
Fast Build	V83SLO
Fast Dig	378RS6
Fast Fix	FJ59WS
Fertilizer	B1GW1F
Ice Rink	33GM7J
Parcel Detector	VUT673
Poo Treasure	WWQ1SA
Regenerate Hearts	MDLP69
Secret Characters	3X44AA
Silhouettes	3HE85H
Super Scream	VN3R7S
Super Slap	0P1TA5
Treasure Magnet	H86LA2
Treasure x2	VM4TS9
Treasure x4	VLWEN3
Treasure x6	V84RYS
Treasure x8	A72E1M
Treasure x10	VI3PS8

INVINCIBILITY

Enter the code on the blackboard of the math classroom.

EFFECT	CODE
Invincibility	B83EA1

SECRET LEVELS

UNLOCKABLE	HOW TO UNLOCK
Ancient City	Collect all of the artifacts in Temple of Doom.
Warehouse Level	Collect all of the artifacts in The Last Crusade.
Young Indy level	Collect all of the artifacts in Raiders of the Lost Ark.

LEGO INDIANA JONES: THE ORIGINAL ADVENTURES (PlayStation 2)

CHARACTER CODES

Enter the codes on the blackboard in the math classroom of Barnett College (the 2nd door on the left in the main hallway).

EFFECT	CODE
Bandit	12N68W
Bandit Swordsman	1MK4RT
Barranca	04EM94
Bazooka Trooper (Crusade)	MK83R7
Bazooka Trooper (Raiders)	S93Y5R
Belloq	CHN3YU
Belloq (Jungle)	TDR197
Belloq (Robes)	VEO29L
British Officer	VJ5TI9
British Troop Commander	B73EUA
British Troop Soldier	DJ5I2W

Captain Katanga	VJ3TT3
Chatter Lal	ENW936
Chatter Lal (Thuggee)	CNH4RY
Chen	3NK48T
Colonel Dietrich	2K9RKS
Colonel Vogel	8EAL4H
Dancing Girl	C7EJ21
Donovan	3NFTU8
Elsa (Desert)	JSNRT9
Elsa (Officer)	VMJ5US
Enemy Boxer	8246RB
Enemy Butler	VJ48W3
Enemy Guard	VJ7R51
Enemy Guard (Mountains)	YR47WM
Enemy Officer	572 E61
Enemy Officer (Desert)	2MK450
Enemy Pilot	B84ELP
Enemy Radio Operator	1MF94R
Enemy Soldier (Desert)	4NSU7Q
Fedora	V75YSP
First Mate	0GIN24
Grail Knight	NE6THI
Hovitos Tribesman	H0V1SS
Indiana Jones (Desert Disguise)	4J8S4M
Indiana Jones (Officer)	VJ85OS
Jungle Guide	24PF34
Kao Kan	WM046L
Kazim	NRH23J
Kazim (Desert)	3M29TJ
Lao Che	2NK479
Maharaja	NFK5N2
Major Toht	13NS01
Masked Bandit	N48SF0
Mola Ram	FJUR31
Monkey Man	3RF6YJ
Pankot Assassin	2NKT72
Pankot Guard	VN28RH
Sherpa Brawler	VJ37WJ
Sherpa Gunner	ND762W
Slave Child	0E3ENW
Thuggee	VM683E
Thuggee Acolyte	T2R3F9
Thuggee Slavedriver	VBS7GW
Village Dignitary	KD48TN
Village Elder	4682 E1
Willie (Dinner Suit)	VK93R7
Willie (Pajamas)	MEN4IP
Wu Han	3NSLT8

ITEM CODES

ENTER THE CODES ON THE BLACKBOARD IN THE MATH CLASSROOM OF BARNETT COLLEGE (THE 2ND DOOR ON THE LEFT IN THE MAIN HALLWAY).

EFFECT	CODE
Artifact Detector	VIKED7
Beep Beep	VNF59Q
Character Treasure	VIES2R
Disarm Enemies	VKRNS9
Disguises	4ID1N6
Fast Build	V83SLO
Fast Dig	378RS6
Fast Fix	FJ59WS
Fertilizer	B1GW1F
Ice Rink	33GM7J
Parcel Detector	VUT673
Poo Treasure	WWQ1SA
Regenerate Hearts	MDLP69
Secret Characters	3X44AA
Silhouettes	3HE85H
Super Scream	VN3R7S
Super Slap	0P1TA5
Treasure Magnet	H86LA2
Treasure x2	VM4TS9
Treasure x4	VLWEN3
Treasure x6	V84RYS
Treasure x8	A72E1M
Treasure x10	VI3PS8

LEGO INDIANA JONES 2: THE ADVENTURE CONTINUES (XBOX360)

CODES

EFFECT	CODE
Beep Beep	UU3VSC
Disguise	Y9TE98
Fast Build	SNXC2F
Fast Dig	XYAN83
Fast Fix	3Z7PJX
Fearless	TUXNZF
Hot Rod	YLG2TN
Ice Rink	TY9P4U
Indiana Jones: 1	PGWSEA
Indiana Jones: 2	DZFY9S
Indiana Jones: Desert	M4C34K
Indiana Jones: Disguised	2W8QR3
Indiana Jones: Kali	J2XS97
Indiana Jones: Officer	3FQFKS
Invincibility	6JBB65
Lao Che	7AWX3J
Mola Ram	82RMC2
Mutt	2GK562
Poo Money	SZFAAE

Professor Henry Jones	4C5AKH
Rene Belloq	FTL48S
Sallah	E88YRP
Score x2	U38VJP
Score x3	PEHHPZ
Score x4	UXGTB3
Score x6	XWJ5EY
Score x8	S5UZCP
Score x10	V7JYBU
Silhouettes	FQGPYH
Snake Whip	2U7YCV
Stud Magnet	EGSM5B
Willie: Singer	94RUAJ

LEGO INDIANA JONES 2: THE ADVENTURE CONTINUES (Wii)

CODES

EFFECT	CODE
Beep Beep	UU3VSC
Disguise	Y9TE98
Fast Build	SNXC2F
Fast Dig	XYAN83
Fast Fix	3Z7PJX
Fearless	TUXNZF
Hot Rod	YLG2TN
Ice Rink	TY9P4U
Indiana Jones: 1	PGWSEA
Indiana Jones: 2	DZFY9S
Indiana Jones: Desert	M4C34K
Indiana Jones: Disguised	2W8QR3
Indiana Jones: Kali	J2XS97
Indiana Jones: Officer	3FQFKS
Invincibility	6JBB65
Lao Che	7AWX3J
Mola Ram	82RMC2
Mutt	2GK562
Poo Money	SZFAAE
Professor Henry Jones	4C5AKH
Rene Belloq	FTL48S
Sallah	E88YRP
Score x2	U38VJP
Score x3	PEHHPZ
Score x4	UXGTB3
Score x6	XWJ5EY
Score x8	S5UZCP
Score x10	V7JYBU
Silhouettes	FQGPYH
Snake Whip	2U7YCV
Stud Magnet	EGSM5B
Willie: Singer	94RUAJ

CODES & CHEATS

LEGO RACER 2 (PlayStation 2)

Enter these codes at the Main menu.

UNLOCKABLE	CODE
Mars Tracks	⇦, ⇦, ⇨, ⇨, ⇦, ⇦, ⇨, ⇦, ⇩, ⇦, ⇨
Martian	⇨, ⇦, ⇨, ⇧, ⇩, ⇦, ⇨, ⇧, ⇧
Wide Angle	⇦, ⇦, ⇦, ⇨, ⇨, ⇨, ⇧, ⇧, ⇧, ⇩, ⇩, ⇩, ⇦, ⇦, ⇦, ⇨, ⇨, ⇨

LEGO ROCK BAND (DS

UNLOCK GUEST ARTISTS

Complete the following songs in Tour Mode to unlock the corresponding guest artist and their parts for use in your own band.

UNLOCKABLE	HOW TO UNLOCK
Blur	Beat "Song 2" in Tour.
David Bowie	Beat "Let's Dance" in Tour.
Iggy Pop	Beat "The Passenger" in Tour.
Queen	Beat "We Are The Champions" in Tour.

LEGO STAR WARS (XBOX)

To unlock characters for purchase in Free Play mode, go to Dexter's Diner, then the Codes menu, and enter the following.

UNLOCKABLE	CODE
Battle Droid	987UYR
Battle Droid (Commander)	EN11K5
Battle Droid (Geonosis)	LK42U6
Battle Droid (Security)	KF999A
Big Blasters	IG72X4
Boba Fett	LA811Y
Brushes	SHRUB1
Classic Blasters	L449HD
Clone	F8B4L6
Clone (Episode III)	ER33JN
Clone (Episode III, Pilot)	BHU72T
Clone (Episode III, Swamp)	N3T6P8
Clone (Episode III, Walker)	RS6E25
Count Dooku	14PGMN
Darth Maul	H35TUX
Darth Sidious	A32CAM
Disguised Clone	VR832U
Droideka	DH382U
General Grievous	SF321Y
Geonosian	19D7NB
Gonk Droid	U63B2A
Grievous' Bodyguard	ZTY392
Invincibility	4PR28U
Jango Fett	PL47NH
Ki-Adi Mundi	DP55MV
Kit Fisto	CBR954
Luminara	A725X4
Mace Windu (Episode III)	MS952L
Minikit Detector	LD116B
Moustaches	RP924W
Padme	92UJ7D
PK Droid	R840JU

Princess Leia	BEQ82H
Purple	YD77GC
Rebel Trooper	L54YUK
Royal Guard	PP43JX
Shaak Ti	EUW862
Silhouettes	MS999Q
Silly Blasters	NR37W1
Super Battle Droid	XZNR21
Tea Cups	PUCEAT

LEGO STAR WARS (PlayStation 2)

In Dexter's Diner, go to Codes and enter the following. This will unlock characters for purchase in Free Play mode.

CHARACTER	CODE
Battle Droid	987UYR
Battle Droid (Commander)	EN11K5
Battle Droid (Geonosis)	LK42U6
Battle Droid (Security)	KF999A
Big Blasters	IG72X4
Boba Fett	LA811Y
Brushes	SHRUB1
Classic Blasters	L449HD
Clone	F8B4L6
Clone (Episode III, Pilot)	BHU72T
Clone (Episode III, Swamp)	N3T6P8
Clone (Episode III, Walker)	RS6E25
Clone (Episode III)	ER33JN
Count Dooku	14PGMN
Darth Maul	H35TUX
Darth Sidious	A32CAM
Disguised Clone	VR832U
Droideka	DH382U
General Grievous	SF321Y
Geonosian	19D7NB
Gonk Droid	U63B2A
Grievous' Bodyguard	ZTY392
Invincibility	4PR28U
Jango Fett	PL47NH
Ki-Adi Mundi	DP55MV
Kit Fisto	CBR954
Luminara	A725X4
Mace Windu (Episode III)	MS952L
Minikit Detector	LD116B
Moustaches	RP924W
Padme	92UJ7D
PK Droid	R840JU
Princess Leia	BEQ82H
Purple	YD77GC
Rebel Trooper	L54YUK
Royal Guard	PP43JX
Shaak Ti	EUW862
Silhouettes	MS999Q
Silly Blasters	NR37W1

CHARACTER	CODE
Super Battle Droid	XZNR21
Tea Cups	PUCEAT

LEGO STAR WARS: THE COMPLETE SAGA (XBOX 360)

CHARACTERS

To use the codes, enter the Cantina, go to the bar, access the codes command, and type in the codes.

UNLOCKABLE CHARACTERS	CODES
Admiral Ackbar	ACK646
Battle Droid Commander	KPF958
Boba Fett (Boy)	GGF539
Boss Nass	HHY697
Captain Tarpals	QRN714
Count Dooku	DDD748
Darth Maul	EUK421
Ewok	EWK785
General Grievous	PMN576
Greedo	ZZR636
IG-88	GIJ989
Imperial Guard	GUA850
Indiana Jones	After you watch the trailer for the upcoming Indiana Jones game in the Bonus Room, Indy will become a playable character.
Jango Fett	KLJ897
Ki-Adi-Mundi	MUN486
Luminara	LUM521
Padmé	VBJ322
R2-Q5	EVILR2
Unlockable Characters	Codes
Sandtrooper	CBR954
Stormtrooper	NBN431
Super Battle Droid	XZNR21
Taun We	PRX482
Vulture Droid	BDC866
Watto	PLL967
Zam Wesell	584HJF

SHIPS

UNLOCKABLE SHIPS	CODES
Droid Trifighter	AAB123
Imperial Shuttle	HUT845
Slave I	Collect all 10 Minikits on each level.
TIE Fighter	DBH897
TIE Interceptor	INT729
Zam's Speeder	UUU875

SKILLS

UNLOCKABLE SKILLS	CODES
Disguise	BRJ437
Force Grapple Leap	CLZ738

LEGO STAR WARS: THE COMPLETE SAGA (PlayStation 3)

CHARACTERS

To use the codes, enter the Cantina, go to the bar, access the codes command, and type in the codes.

UNLOCKABLE CHARACTERS	CODES
Admiral Ackbar	ACK646
Battle Droid Commander	KPF958
Boba Fett (Boy)	GGF539
Boss Nass	HHY697
Captain Tarpals	QRN714
Count Dooku	DDD748
Darth Maul	EUK421
Ewok	EWK785
General Grievous	PMN576
Greedo	ZZR636
IG-88	GIJ989
Imperial Guard	GUA850
Indiana Jones	After you watch the trailer for the upcoming Indiana Jones game in the Bonus Room, Indy will become a playable character.
Jango Fett	KLJ897
Ki-Adi-Mundi	MUN486
Luminara	LUM521
Padmé	VBJ322
R2-Q5	EVILR2
Sandtrooper	CBR954
Stormtrooper	NBN431
Super Battle Droid	XZNR21
Taun We	PRX482
Vulture Droid	BDC866
Watto	PLL967
Zam Wesell	584HJF

SHIPS

UNLOCKABLE SHIPS	CODE/OBJECTIVE
Droid Trifighter	AAB123
Imperial Shuttle	HUT845
Slave I	Collect all 10 Minikits on each level.
TIE Fighter	DBH897
TIE Interceptor	INT729
Zam's Speeder	UUU875

SKILLS

UNLOCKABLE SKILLS	CODES
Disguise	BRJ437
Force Grapple Leap	CLZ738

LEGO STAR WARS: THE COMPLETE SAGA (Wii)

CHARACTERS

To use the codes, enter the Cantina, go to the bar, access the codes command, and type in the codes.

UNLOCKABLE CHARACTERS	CODES
Admiral Ackbar	ACK646

UNLOCKABLE CHARACTERS	CODES
Battle Droid Commander	KPF958
Boba Fett (Boy)	GGF539
Boss Nass	HHY697
Captain Tarpals	QRN714
Count Dooku	DDD748
Darth Maul	EUK421
Ewok	EWK785
General Grievous	PMN576
Greedo	ZZR636
IG-88	GIJ989
Imperial Guard	GUA850
Indiana Jones	After you watch the trailer for the upcoming Indiana Jones game in the Bonus Room, Indy will become a playable character.
Jango Fett	KLJ897
Ki-Adi-Mundi	MUN486
Luminara	LUM521
Padmé	VBJ322
R2-Q5	EVILR2
Sandtrooper	CBR954
Stormtrooper	NBN431
Super Battle Droid	XZNR21
Taun We	PRX482
Vulture Droid	BDC866
Watto	PLL967
Zam Wesell	584HJF

SHIPS

UNLOCKABLE SHIPS	CODES
Droid Trifighter	AAB123
Imperial Shuttle	HUT845
Slave I	Collect all 10 Minikits on each level.
TIE Fighter	DBH897
TIE Interceptor	INT729
Zam's Speeder	UUU875

SKILLS

UNLOCKABLE SKILLS	CODES
Disguise	BRJ437
Force Grapple Leap	CLZ738

LEGO STAR WARS II: THE ORIGINAL TRILOGY (XBOX 360)

DIFFERENT CHARACTERS

PASSWORD	EFFECT
Beach Trooper	UCK868
Ben Kenobi's Ghost	BEN917
Bespin Guard	VHY832
Bib Fortuna	WTY721
Boba Fett	HLP221
Death Star Trooper	BNC332
Emperor	HHY382
Ewok	TTT289

Gamorean Guard	YZF999
Gonk Droid	NFX582
Grand Moff Tarkin	SMG219
Han Solo with Hood	YWM840
IG-88	NXL973
Imperial Guard	MMM111
Imperial Officer	BBV889
Imperial Shuttle Pilot	VAP664
Imperial Spy	CVT125
Lobot	UUB319
Palace Guard	SGE549
Rebel Pilot	CYG336
Rebel Trooper from Hoth	EKU849
Red Noses on All Characters	NBP398
Santa Hat and Red Clothes	CL4U5H
Skiff Guard	GBU888
Snowtrooper	NYU989
Stormtrooper	PTR345
TIE Fighter	HDY739
TIE Fighter Pilot	NNZ316
TIE Interceptor	QYA828
Ugnaught	UGN694
Unlock Greedo	NAH118
Unlock Jawa	JAW499
Unlock Sandtrooper	YDV451
Unlock Tusken Raider	PEJ821
White Beard Extra	TYH319

LEGO STAR WARS II: THE ORIGINAL TRILOGY (DS)

Enter this password in the Cantina.

UNLOCKABLE	PASSWORD
10 extra studs	4PR28U

LEGO STAR WARS II: THE ORIGINAL TRILOGY (PSP)

PASSWORDS

Enter the following codes at the Mos Eisley Cantina to unlock the character for purchase in Free Play mode.

UNLOCKABLE	HOW TO UNLOCK
Beach Trooper	UCK868
Ben Kenobi's Ghost	BEN917
Bespin Guard	VHY832
Bib Fortuna	WTY721
Boba Fett	HLP221
Death Star Trooper	BNC332
Emperor	HHY382
Ewok	TTT289
Gamorean Guard	YZF999
Gonk Droid	NFX582
Grand Moff Tarkin	SMG219
Han Solo with Hood	YWM840
IG-88	NXL973

Imperial Guard	MMM111
Imperial Officer	BBV889
Imperial Shuttle Pilot	VAP66
Imperial Spy	CVT125
Lobot	UUB319
Palace Guard	SGE549
Rebel Pilot	CYG336
Rebel Trooper from Hoth	EKU849
Red Noses on All Characters	NBP398
Santa Hat and Red Clothes	CL4U5H
Skiff Guard	GBU888
Snow Trooper	NYU989
Stormtrooper	PTR345
TIE Fighter	HDY739
TIE Fighter Pilot	NNZ316
TIE Interceptor	QYA828
Ugnaught	UGN694
White Beard Extra	TYH319

UNLOCKABLE CHARACTERS

Complete challenge by collecting 10 Blue Minikits within the time limit allowed per level.

UNLOCKABLE	HOW TO UNLOCK
R4-P17, PK Droid	Episode 4, Chapter 2
Battle Droid, B. D. (Security), B. D. (Geonosis), B. D. (Commander)	Episode 4, Chapter 4
Chancellor Palpatine, General Grievous, Grievous' Bodyguard	Episode 6, Chapter 5
Clone (Episode III, Pilot)	Episode 4, Chapter 6
Clone (Episode III, Swamp)	Episode 5, Chapter 4
Clone, Clone (Episode III), Commander Cody, Clone (Episode III Walker)	Episode 6, Chapter 3
Disguised Clone, Boba Fett (Boy)	Episode 6, Chapter 1
Droideka	Episode 4, Chapter 5
Geonosian	Episode 5, Chapter 3
Jango Fett	Episode 6, Chapter 2
Luminara, Ki-Adi-Mundi, Kit Fisto, Shaak Ti	Episode 5, Chapter 1
Mace Windu, Mace Windu (Episode 3)	Episode 6, Chapter 6
Padmé (Battle), Padmé (Clawed), Padmé (Geonosis)	Episode 5, Chapter 2
Padmé, Anakin Skywalker (boy)	Episode 4, Chapter 3
Queen Amidala, Royal Guard, Captain Panaka	Episode 5, Chapter 6
Super Battle Droid	Episode 5, Chapter 5
TC-14	Episode 4, Chapter 1
Wookiee, Jar Jar Binks	Episode 6, Chapter 4

LEGO STAR WARS II: THE ORIGINAL TRILOGY (XBOX)

Enter these passwords in the Cantina.

UNLOCKABLE	PASSWORD
Beach Trooper	UCK868
Ben Kenobi (Ghost)	BEN917
Bespin Guard	VHY832
Bib Fortuna	WTY721

Boba Fett	HLP221
Death Star Trooper	BNC332
Ewok	TTT289
Gamorrean Guard	YZF999
Gonk Droid	NFX582
Grand Moff Tarkin	SMG219
Greedo	NAH118
Han Solo (Hood)	YWM840
IG-88	NXL973
Imperial Guard	MMM111
Imperial Officer	BBV889
Imperial Shuttle Pilot	VAP664
Imperial Spy	CVT125
Jawa	JAW499
Lobot	UUB319
Palace Guard	SGE549
Rebel Pilot	CYG336
Rebel Trooper (Hoth)	EKU849
Sandtrooper	YDV451
Skiff Guard	GBU888
Snowtrooper	NYU989
Stormtrooper	PTR345
The Emperor	HHY382
Tie Fighter	HDY739
Tie Fighter Pilot	NNZ316
Tie Interceptor	QYA828
Tusken Raider	PEJ821
Ugnaught	UGN694

LEGO STAR WARS II: THE ORIGINAL TRILOGY (PlayStation 2)

Enter these passwords in the Cantina.

UNLOCKABLE	PASSWORD
Beach Trooper	UCK868
Ben Kenobi (Ghost)	BEN917
Bespin Guard	VHY832
Bib Fortuna	WTY721
Boba Fett	HLP221
Death Star Trooper	BNC332
Ewok	TTT289
Gamorrean Guard	YZF999
Gonk Droid	NFX582
Grand Moff Tarkin	SMG219
Greedo	NAH118
Han Solo (Hood)	YWM840
IG-88	NXL973
Imperial Guard	MMM111
Imperial Officer	BBV889
Imperial Shuttle Pilot	VAP664
Imperial Spy	CVT125

Jawa	JAW499
Lobot	UUB319
Palace Guard	SGE549
Rebel Pilot	CYG336
Rebel Trooper (Hoth)	EKU849
Sandtrooper	YDV451
Skiff Guard	GBU888
Snowtrooper	NYU989
Stormtrooper	PTR345
The Emperor	HHY382
Tie Fighter	HDY739
Tie Fighter Pilot	NNZ316
Tie Interceptor	QYA828
Tusken Raider	PEJ821
Ugnaught	UGN694

LINE RIDER 2: UNBOUND (Wii)

UNLOCKABLES

Collecting the tokens in Story Mode allows you to unlock extra riders besides Bosh.

UNLOCKABLE	HOW TO UNLOCK
Bailey	Collect 20 Tokens.
Chaz	Collect 150 Tokens.
Classic Bosh	Collect all 260 Tokens.

LINE RIDER 2: UNBOUND (DS)

UNLOCKABLES

Collecting the tokens in Story Mode allows you to unlock extra riders besides Bosh.

UNLOCKABLE	HOW TO UNLOCK
Bailey	Collect 20 tokens.
Chaz	Collect 150 tokens.
Classic Bosh	Collect all 260 tokens.

LITTLE BIG PLANET (PlayStation 3)

COSTUMES

Complete the corresponding level without dying to unlock the following costumes.

UNLOCKABLE	HOW TO UNLOCK
Bunny Tail	The Collectors Lair
Chicken Beak	The Dancers Court
Chicken Gloves	Great Magicians Palace
Chicken Tail	Elephant Temple
Cowboy Boots and Leather Gloves	Boom Town
Cowboy Hat	Serpent Shrine
Dinosaur Mask	The Construction Site
Dinosaur Tail	Lowrider
Googly Eye Glasses	Sensei's Lost Castle
Green Sock Puppet	Subway
Japanese Festival Headband	The Terrible Oni's Volcano
Japanese Festival Robe	Endurance Dojo
Jeans with a Belt and Cowboy Bandana	The Mines

Moustache	Burning Forest
Neon Helmet	The Bunker
Pirate Hat	Skate to Victory
Pirate Hook and Pirate Eye Patch	First Steps
Pirate Waistcoat and Pirate Shorts	Get a Grip
Ringmaster Jacket	Swinging Safari
Ringmaster Top Hat and Gold Monocle	The Meerkat Kingdom
Roman Armor	The Darkness
Roman Helmet	Skulldozer
White Neon Eyes	The Frozen Tundra
Wooden Sword	The Wedding Reception
Yellow Head	The Collector

LEVEL COMPLETION PRIZES

Gain the following prizes by achieving 100% level completion (collect all the prize bubbles on that level).

UNLOCKABLE	HOW TO UNLOCK
Anteater concept and Anteater concept with frame	The Mines 100%
Bad Witch concept, Bad Witch concept with frame	The Bunker 100%
Big Cat and Big Cat concept with frame	Burning Forest 100%
UNLOCKABLE	**HOW TO UNLOCK**
Big Sumo, The Islands concept, and The Islands concept with frame	Sensei's Lost Castle 100%
Boom Town concept and Boom Town concept with frame	Boom Town 100%
Boss concept, Boss concept with frame, and a monster truck	The Construction Site 100%
Bunny Tail and The Gardens	Skate to Victory 100%
Circus concept, Circus concept with frame	The Frozen Tundra 100%
Costumes concept and Costumes concept with frame	Elephant Temple 100%
Early Sackboy and Early Sackboy with frame	Lowrider 100%
Fairy Tale concept and Fairy Tale concept with frame	Get a Grip 100%
Grabbing Machine, Rock God, and Rock God with frame	Subway 100%
Graveyard concept, The Wedding concept with frame, and Skulldozer	Skulldozer 100%
Jumping Tank, Very First LBP concept, Very First LBP concept with frame	The Collectors Lair 100%
LBP concept with frame, Background Environment concept	The Dancers Court 100%
LBP Cosmos concept, Magicians Box, and Cosmos concept with frame	Great Magicians Palace 100%
Savannah concept and Savannah concept with frame	Swinging Safari 100%
Sheriff Zapata's Explosives Machine, The Mines concept with frame, and The Mines concept	Serpent Shrine 100%
Temple concept, Temple concept with frame, and a Mystical Dragon	Endurance Dojo 100%
Terrible Oni, Islands City concept, and Islands City concept with frame	The Terrible Volcano 100%
The Collector Boss, The Collector's Pod, and the Collector	The Collector 100%
The Gardens concept and The Gardens concept with frame	First Steps 100%
The Savannah and The Pink Scarf	The Meerkat Kingdom 100%

UNLOCKABLE	HOW TO UNLOCK
Theme Characters concept with frame and Theme Characters Concept	The Darkness 100%
Wrestling Ring with frame and Wrestling concept	The Wedding Reception 100%

TROPHIES

Complete each condition to get the allotted Trophies. There are 36 Bronze Trophies, 8 Silver Trophies, 3 Gold Trophies, and 1 Platinum Trophy.

UNLOCKABLE	HOW TO UNLOCK
100% Complete (Platinum)	Earn all LittleBigPlanet trophies to unlock this platinum trophy
20X Multiplier! (Silver)	Get a 20X Multiplier
2X Multiplier! (Bronze)	Get a 2X Multiplier
8X Multiplier! (Bronze)	Get an 8X Multiplier
Artist (Bronze)	Place a sticker
Booty Master (Silver)	Collect all the prize bubbles on the story levels
Celebrity (Silver)	You were hearted by 5 or more people as a player
Cranium Collector (Bronze)	Kill 100 creatures across all levels
Create (Gold)	A level you published was hearted by 50 or more people and you were hearted by 30 or more people
Creator (Bronze)	Build and save a level with the thermometer more than 30% full
Crowd Pleaser (Silver)	A level you published was played by 50 or more people
Dr. Frankenstein (Silver)	Create a living creature with at least 2 eyes, 2 legs or wheels, and a brain
Expert Creator (Bronze)	Complete all levels in the Tutorials
Fashion Sense (Bronze)	Choose a costume for your sackperson with at least one item on your head, at least one item on your body, and a material
Feel the love (Silver)	A level you published was hearted by 10 or more people
FIRST! (Bronze)	Be among the first 10 people to complete a community level
Forager (Bronze)	Collect 25% of the prize bubbles on the story levels
Friendly (Bronze)	Complete a level with more than one player
Hi Score (Silver)	Collect 1,000,000 points over all levels you have played
Homemaker (Bronze)	Place 10 stickers or decorations in your pod
Incredible Height! (Bronze)	Travel to an incredible height
Incredible Speed! (Bronze)	Travel at incredible speed
Just Beginning (Silver)	Complete all the main path story levels
Look What I Made! (Bronze)	A level you published was played by 5 or more people
Neighbourhood (Bronze)	Watch heart 5 community levels
Networking (Bronze)	Heart 3 authors
Opinionated (Bronze)	Tag a community level
Party Person (Bronze)	Complete a level online with 3 other players who are on your friends list
Play (Gold)	Complete all story levels without dying, with the exception of those levels that only end when you die
Publisher (Bronze)	Publish a level
Sackbird (Bronze)	Spend 8 seconds or more in the air
Secret Stickerist (Bronze)	Unlock the race in First Steps
Share (Gold)	Play 150 community levels, tag 50 community levels and heart 10 community levels

Socialite (Bronze)	Complete a level online with 3 other players who are not on your friends list
Sticky Fingers (Bronze)	Collect 50% of the prize bubbles on the story levels
Talkative (Bronze)	Post a comment on a community level
Team Creator (Bronze)	Build and save a level with more than one player with the thermometer more than 30% full
The Canyons (Bronze)	Complete all levels in The Canyons
The Gardens (Bronze)	Complete all levels in The Gardens
The Islands (Bronze)	Complete all levels in The Islands
The Metropolis (Bronze)	Complete all levels in The Metropolis
The Savannah (Bronze)	Complete all levels in The Savannah
The Temples (Bronze)	Complete all levels in The Temples
The Wedding (Bronze)	Complete all levels in The Wedding
Top of the Class (Bronze)	Win a 4-player game
Traveller (Bronze)	Complete a community level
Treasure Hunter (Bronze)	Collect 75% of the prize bubbles on the story levels
Trendsetter (Bronze)	Place a sticker or a decoration on another player's sackperson

LITTLE KING'S STORY (Wii)

UNLOCKABLE

UNLOCKABLE	HOW TO UNLOCK
Tyrant Mode	Beat the game once.

LITTLEST PET SHOP: JUNGLE (DS)

CODES

Enter the following code in the options menu under the "Enter Passwords" section.

EFFECT	CODE
Giraffe	LPSTRU

LODE RUNNER (Wii)

UNLOCKABLES

UNLOCKABLE	HOW TO UNLOCK
Game Speed	Press SELECT to view current level. Hold SELECT and press Ⓑ to decrease game speed, or Ⓐ to increase game speed.
Level Select	Press select to view current level. Press SELECT then press Ⓐ to increase a level and Ⓑ to drop one.

LORD OF THE RINGS: CONQUEST (XBOX 360)

LEGENDARY DIFFICULTY

Beat the War of the Ring mode and the Rise of Sauron mode to unlock the Legendary difficulty for both.

LORD OF THE RINGS: CONQUEST (PlayStation 3)

UNLOCKABLES

UNLOCKABLE	HOW TO UNLOCK
Evil Campaign	Beat the Good Campaign on any difficulty.
Legendary Difficulty	Beat the Good campaign on Heroic Difficulty.

LORD OF THE RINGS, THE BATTLE FOR MIDDLE-EARTH II (XBOX 360)

UNLOCKABLE HEROES

UNLOCKABLE	HOW TO UNLOCK
Avatan	Win 10 capture and hold games

UNLOCKABLE	HOW TO UNLOCK
Brerthor	Complete the whole good campaign
Celebrim	Win 10 resource race games
Felek	Win 10 hero vs. hero games
Fhaleen	Win 10 king of the hill games
Hadhood	Complete level 1 of good campaign with all bonus objectives
Idrial	Complete level 8 of good campaign with all bonus objectives
Krashnack	Complete level 1 of dark campaign with all bonus objectives
Maur	Complete level 4 of the dark campaign with all bonus objectives
Mektar	Complete good campaign with no heroes dying
Ohta	Win 10 versus games
Olog	Complete level 8 of the dark campaign with all bonus objectives
Thrugg	Complete level 4 of the dark campaign with all bonus objectives
Tumna	Complete the whole bad campaign
Urulooke	Complete dark campaign with no heroes dying

LOST PLANET: EXTREME CONDITION (XBOX 360)

Enter these codes when the game is paused. They can be used only on Easy mode.

UNLOCKABLE	CODE
500 Thermal Energy	Up, Up, Down, Down, Left, Right, Left, Right, X, Y, RB, LB
Infinite Ammunition	LB, LT, RT, RB, Y, X, Right, Down, Left, LB, LT, RT, LT, LB, RB, X, Left, Down, X, RB, LB
Infinite Health	Down, Down, Down, Up, Y, Up, Y, Up, Y, Up, Up, Up, Down, X, Down, X, Down, X, Left, Y, Right, X, Left, Y, Right, X, RB, LB
Infinite Ammunition	RT, RB, Y, X, Right, Down, Left, LB, LT, RT, RB, Y, X, Right, Down, Left, LB, LT, RT, LT, LB, RB, X, Left, Down, X, RB, LB

LUMINOUS ARC (DS)

UNLOCKABLES

Completion bonuses are available after you finish the game by hitting ⓧ when "Fin" is on the screen after the credits. Save the game, and then replay with all of your attained levels and items, as well as being able to access "Mysteria Ruins" (north of the starting location), and extras such as music, sound effects, and character profiles.

MADAGASCAR (PlayStation 2)

Enter these codes while playing.

UNLOCKABLE	CODE
All power-ups	●,×,×,●,▲,L1,■,R1,L1
Invincibility	⇧,⇩,×,×,R1,L1,R2,L2,▲,■,●
Level select	R1,R1,●,L2,L1,×,▲,R1,▲

MADDEN NFL 2005 (DS)

CODES

Touch the small spot in the middle of the main menu to display the cheat entry box. Then enter one of the following codes to activate the corresponding cheat function:

CODE	EFFECT
SMASHMOUTH	Harder hits
SUPERSLICK	More fumbles
BADPASS	More interceptions
SAD SACK	More sacks
SHORTTIME	Opponent gets 3 downs
LONGTIME	You get 5 downs

MADDEN NFL 06 (XBOX)

To enter this code, go into My Madden, select Madden Cards, then select Enter Code.

UNLOCKABLE	CODE
1st and 5 Bronze	2Y7L8B
1st and 15 Bronze	2W4P9T
3rd Down Bronze	3F9G4J
5th Down Bronze	3E9R4V
Da Boot Bronze	3J3S9Y
Donovan McNabb Gold Card (alternate)	8Q2J2X
Extra Credit Bronze	3D3Q3P
Human Plow Bronze	3H3U7F
Super Dive Bronze	3H8M5U
Tight Fit Bronze	3D8X6T
Unforced Errors Bronze	2Z2F4H

MADDEN NFL 06 (PlayStation 2)

To enter this code, go into My Madden, select Madden Cards, then select Enter Code.

UNLOCKABLE	CODE
1st and 5 Bronze	2Y7L8B
1st and 15 Bronze	2W4P9T
3rd Down Bronze	3F9G4J
5th Down Bronze	3E9R4V
Da Boot Bronze	3J3S9Y
Donovan McNabb Gold Card (alternate)	8Q2J2X
Extra Credit Bronze	3D3Q3P

UNLOCKABLE	CODE
Human Plow Bronze	3H3U7F
Super Dive Bronze	3H8M5U
Tight Fit Bronze	3D8X6T
Unforced Errors Bronze	2Z2F4H

MADDEN NFL '07 (PlayStation 3)

CODES

CODE	EFFECT
XL7SP1	Cannot throw an INT or Fumble the ball for 1 half
WROAOR	QB will have 100% accuracy for 1 half
5LAWO0	The opponent throws lob passes for 1 half
B57QLU	Unlock the 1958 Colts Gold card
1PL1FL	Unlock the 1966 Packers Gold card
MIE6WO	Unlock the 1968 Jets Gold card
CL2TOE	Unlock the 1970 Browns Gold card
NOEB7U	Unlock the 1972 Dolphins Gold card
YOOFLA	Unlock the 1974 Steelers Gold card
MOA11I	Unlock the 1976 Raiders Gold card
C8UM7U	Unlock the 1977 Broncos Gold card
VIU007	Unlock the 1978 Dolphins Gold card
NLAPH3	Unlock the 1980 Raiders Gold card
COAGI4	Unlock the 1981 Chargers Gold card
WL8BRI	Unlock the 1982 Redskins Gold card
H0EW7I	Unlock the 1983 Raiders Gold card
M1AM1E	Unlock the 1984 Dolphins Gold card
QOETO8	Unlock the 1985 Bears Gold card
ZI8S2L	Unlock the 1986 Giants Gold card
SP2A8H	Unlock the 1988 49ers Gold card
2L4TRO	Unlock the 1990 Eagles Gold card
J1ETRI	Unlock the 1991 Lions Gold card
W9UVI9	Unlock the 1992 Cowboys Gold card
DLA3I7	Unlock the 1993 Bills Gold card
DR7EST	Unlock the 1994 49ers Gold card
F8LUST	Unlock the 1996 Packers Gold card
FIES95	Unlock the 1998 Broncos Gold card
S9OUSW	Unlock the 1999 Rams Gold card
YI8P8U	Unlock the Aloha Stadium Gold card
RLA9R7	Unlock the Super Bowl XLI Gold card
WRLUF8	Unlock the Super Bowl XLII Gold card
NIEV4A	Unlock the Super Bowl XLIII Gold card
M5AB7L	Unlock the Super Bowl XLIV Gold card

MADDEN NFL 07 (Wii)

To enter these codes, select My Madden, then select Madden Cards, and then select Madden Codes.

UNLOCKABLE	CODE
#220 Super Bowl XLI (Gold)	RLA9R7
#221 Super Bowl XLII (Gold)	WRLUF8
#222 Super Bowl XLIII (Gold)	NIEV4A

#223 Super Bowl XLIV (Gold)	M5AB7L
#224 Aloha Stadium (Gold)	YI8P8U
#225 '58 Colts (Gold)	B57QLU
#226 '66 Packers (Gold)	1PL1FL
#227 '68 Jets (Gold)	MIE6WO
#228 '70 Browns (Gold)	CL2TOE
#229 '72 Dolphins (Gold)	NOEB7U
#230 '74 Steelers (Gold)	YOOFLA
#231 '76 Raiders (Gold)	MOA11I
#232 '77 Broncos (Gold)	C8UM7U
#233 '78 Dolphins (Gold)	VIU007
#234 '80 Raiders (Gold)	NLAPH3
#235 '81 Chargers (Gold)	COAGI4
#236 '82 Redskins (Gold)	WL8BRI
#238 '84 Dolphins (Gold)	M1AM1E
#240 '86 Giants (Gold)	ZI8S2L
#241 '88 49ers (Gold)	SP2A8H
1985 Bears Gold card	QOETO8
1990 Eagles Gold card	2L4TRO
1991 Lions Gold card	J1ETRI
1992 Cowboys Gold card	W9UVI9
1993 Bills Gold card	DLA3I7
1994 49ers Gold card	DR7EST
1996 Packers Gold card	F8LUST
1998 Broncos Gold card	FIES95
1999 Rams Gold card	S9OUSW
Lame Duck card	5LAWO0
Mistake Free card	XL7SP1
QB On Target card	WROA0R
Pump up the crowd for the 49ers	KLOCRL
Pump up the crowd for the Bears	B1OUPH
Pump up the crowd for the Bengals	DRL2SW
Pump up the crowd for the Bills	1PLUYO
Pump up the crowd for the Broncos	3ROUJO
Pump up the crowd for the Browns	T1UTOA
Pump up the crowd for the Buccaneers	S9EWRI
Pump up the crowd for the Cardinals	57IEPI
Pump up the crowd for the Chargers	F7UHL8
Pump up the crowd for the Chiefs	PRI5SL
Pump up the crowd for the Colts	1R5AMI
Pump up the crowd for the Cowboys	Z2ACHL
Pump up the crowd for the Dolphins	C5AHLE
Pump up the crowd for the Eagles	PO7DRO
Pump up the crowd for the Falcons	37USPO
Pump up the crowd for the Giants	C4USPI
Pump up the crowd for the Jaguars	MIEH7E
Pump up the crowd for the Jets	COLUXI
Pump up the crowd for the Lions	3LABLU

UNLOCKABLE	CODE
Pump up the crowd for the Packers	4H07V0
Pump up the crowd for the Panthers	F2IASP

MADDEN NFL '07 (PSP)

PASSWORDS

Enter these names in the password section to get the Madden cards.

PASSWORD	EFFECT
B57QLU	1958 Colts Gold card
1PL1FL	1966 Packers Gold card
MIE6WO	1968 Jets Gold card
CL2TOE	1970 Browns Gold card
NOEB7U	1972 Dolphins Gold card
YOOFLA	1974 Steelers Gold card
MOA11I	1976 Raiders Gold card
C8UM7U	1977 Broncos Gold card
VIU007	1978 Dolphins Gold card
NLAPH3	1980 Raiders Gold card
COAGI4	1981 Chargers Gold card
WL8BRI	1982 Redskins Gold card
H0EW7I	1983 Raiders Gold card
M1AM1E	1984 Dolphins Gold card
QOETO8	1985 Bears Gold card
ZI8S2L	1986 Giants Gold card
SP2A8H	1988 49ers Gold card
2L4TRO	1990 Eagles Gold card
J1ETRI	1991 Lions Gold card
W9UVI9	1992 Cowboys Gold card
DLA3I7	1993 Bills Gold card
DR7EST	1994 49ers Gold card
F8LUST	1996 Packers Gold card
FIES95	1998 Broncos Gold card
S9OUSW	1999 Rams Gold card
YI8P8U	Aloha Stadium Gold card
5LAWO0	Lame Duck card
XL7SP1	Mistake Free card
XL7SP1	Mistake Free card, effective for one half
WROA0R	QB on Target card
WROA0R	Quarterback 100% Accuracy for one half
RLA9R7	Super Bowl XLI Gold card
WRLUF8	Super Bowl XLII Gold card
NIEV4A	Super Bowl XLIII Gold card
M5AB7L	Super Bowl XLIV Gold card
5LAQ00	Your opponent will have to throw Lob Passes for one half

MADDEN NFL '07 (XBOX)

Under Madden Cards, select Madden Codes to enter these passwords. Passwords are case sensitive.

UNLOCKABLE	PASSWORD
When this card is played, you can't fumble or throw interceptions for one half	XL7SP1
When this card is played, your opponent will throw a lob pass for one half	5LAWO0

When this card is played, your QB accuracy will be 100% for one half	WROA0R

MADDEN NFL '07 (PlayStation 2)

Under Madden Cards, select Madden Codes to enter these passwords. Passwords are case sensitive.

UNLOCKABLE	PASSWORD
When this card is played, you can't fumble or throw interceptions for one half	XL7SP1
When this card is played, your opponent will throw a lob pass for one half	5LAWO0
When this card is played, your QB accuracy will be 100% for one half	WROA0R

MADDEN NFL '08 (XBOX 360)

ACHIEVEMENTS

UNLOCKABLE	HOW TO UNLOCK
1 Catch by Seven Players (20)	Catch one pass with seven players.
2 TD Catches with One Player (10)	Get two touchdown catches with one player.
3 2pt Conversions Passing (35)	Pass for three two-point conversions in one game.
3 2pt Conversions Rushing (35)	Rush for three two-point conversions in one game.
3 Rushing TDs (15)	Get three rushing touchdowns with one player.
4 Sacks (10)	Get four sacks with one player in one game. Max 5min Qtr.
4 TD Passes (10)	Throw four touchdown passes in one game.
7 Sacks with One Player (35)	Sack the quarterback seven times with one player in one game.
8 Tackles with One Player (10)	Get eight tackles with one player in one game.
10 Catches in a Row (15)	Catch 10 passes in a row with one player. Max 5min Qtr.
10 Catches with One Player (15)	Get 10 receptions with one player.
20 Completions in a Row (25)	Get 20 completions in a row with one player.
40 Rush Attempts with One Player (15)	Attempt 40 rushes with one player in on game. Max 5min Qtr.
40 Yard Field Goal (15)	Kick a 40-yard or more field goal.
50 Yard Field Goal (20)	Kick a 50-yard or more field goal.
60 Yard Pass (15)	Complete a 60-yard pass.
60 Yard Run (15)	Complete a 60-yard run.
80 Percent Pass Completion (15)	Complete 80 percent of the attempted passes in one game.
80 Yard Run (35)	Complete an 80-yard run.
90 Yard Pass (30)	Complete a 90-yard pass.
100 Percent Pass Completion (25)	Get 100 percent pass completion.
100 Rec Yards with 2 Players (15)	Get 100 reception yards by two players.
100 Rush Yards with One Player (15)	Get 100 rushing yards with one player.
100 Rush Yards with Two Players (30)	Get 100 rushing yards with two players.
150 Receiving Yards (15)	Achieve 150 receiving yards with one player.
150 Rush Yards in One Qtr (25)	Get 150 yards or more rushing in one quarter with one player.
200 Kick Return Yards (20)	Achieve 200 kick return yards with one player. Max 5min Qtr.

UNLOCKABLE	HOW TO UNLOCK
200 Pass Yards (10)	Get 200 passing yards in a game.
200 Punt Return Yards (20)	Get 200 punt return yards in one game with one player.
200 Receiving Yards (25)	Get 200 receiving yards with one player.
200 Rush Yards (15)	Rush for 200 yards or more with one player in one game.
250 Rush Yards (25)	Rush for 250 yards with one player in one game.
300 Pass Yards (10)	Achieve 300 passing yards in one game.
400 Yards on Offense (10)	Achieve 400 yards of offense in one game. Max 5 min Qtr.
500 Pass Yards (30)	Pass for 500 yards in one game.
650 Yards on Offense (30)	Get 650 yards on offense. Max 5min Qtr.
Average 20 Yards Receiving (25)	Average 20 yards receiving with one player in one game.
Average 20 Yards Rushing (25)	Average 20 yards rushing per attempt with one player in one game.
Complete 25 Passes (30)	Complete 25 passes in one game.
Deflect 4 Passes (20)	Deflect four or more passes with one player.
Force 3 Fumbles (10)	Force three fumbles with one player.
Intercept 2 Passes (20)	Get two interceptions with one player.
Intercept 3 Passes (20)	Get three interceptions in one game.
Intercept 5 Passes (35)	Intercept five passes in one game.
No Dropped Passes (20)	Don't drop a pass for an entire game. Min 5min Qtr.
No Sacks Allowed (20)	Don't allow a sack for an entire game. Min 5min Qtr.
Recover 2 Fumbles (25)	Recover two fumbles in one game with one player.
Score 84 Points (35)	Score 84 or more points in one game. Max 5min Qtr.

MADDEN NFL 09 (PlayStation 2)

CODES

Go to the MyMadden Screen then the MaddenCards and finally the MaddenCodes screen and enter the codes. (Use capital letters.)

EFFECT	CODE
Coffin Corner — causes your punts to go out of bounds inside the 10-yard line	GCHTBE
Human Plow — increases your ability to break tackles by 75% for 1 game	PZS0TB
Lame Duck — causes your opponent's QB to throw lob passes for 1 game	7WWFMD
Penetration — increases you defensive line penetration by 75% for 1 game	FDJ0SW
Pocket Protectors — increases your offensive line's pass protection by 75% for 1 game	ZUJ7J7
Quarter Back on Target — QB hits target every time	F8571G

UNLOCKABLES

Play Fantasy Challenge mode to unlock the following teams.

UNLOCKABLE	HOW TO UNLOCK
AFC All Star	Beat them at the Supreme League or buy their card.
Deceivers	Beat them at the Supreme League.
Dummies	Beat them at the Supreme League.
Glaciers	Beat them at the Supreme League.
Kickers	Beat them at the Newbie League.
Manipulators	Beat them at the Black and Blue League.
Monsters	Beat them at the Powerhouse League.
NFC All Star	Beat them at the Supreme League or buy their card.
Tridents	Beat them at the Supreme League.

MADDEN NFL 10 (Wii)

CODES

From the "Extras" menu select "Enter Codes"

EFFECT	CODE
Franchise Mode	TEAMPLAYER
Master Code (unlocks everything)	THEWORKS
Situation Mode	YOUCALLIT
Superstar Mode	EGOBOOST
Unlocks Pro Bowl Stadium	ALLSTARS
Unlocks Super Bowl Stadium	THEBIGSHOW

MAGIC THE GATHERING: BATTLEGROUNDS (XBOX)

UNLOCKABLE	CODE
All Quest	During the Quest select, press LT+RT, Down, Up, L, White, Up, Right, Left, Down, LT+RT.
Secret Level for Vs. Mode	At the Arena select, press LT+RT, Left, Up, X, Up, RT, Y, LT+RT.
All Duelists in Arcade Mode	At the Character select screen, press LT+RT, Down, Up, X, White, Up, X, Black, Up, X, LT+RT.

MAGIC: THE GATHERING—DUELS OF THE PLANESWALKERS (XBOX 360)

CLAWS OF VENGEANCE

Win matches using this deck to unlock cards for it.

UNLOCKABLE	HOW TO UNLOCK
Angel's Feather	2nd win
Angel's Feather	10th win
Brion Stoutarm	9th win
Bull Cerodon	6th win
Cho Manno, Revolutionary	15th win
Dragon's Claw	7th win
Godsire	14th win
Knight of the Skyward Eye	11th win
Pariah	4th win
Sangrite Surge	8th win
Sigil B Blessinlessing	3rd win
Sigil Blessing	12th win
Woolly Thoctar	1st win
Wrath of God	13th win
Wurms Tooth	5th win

EARS OF ELVES

Win matches using this deck to unlock cards for it.

UNLOCKABLE	HOW TO UNLOCK
Coat of Arms	12th win
Elvish Champion	1st win
Elvish Champion	6th win
Eyeblight's Ending	13th win
mmaculate Magistrate	3rd win
Imperious Perfect	9th win
Jagged-Scar Archers	8th win
Lys Alana Scarblade	11th win
Nath of the Gilt-Leaf	14th win

UNLOCKABLE	HOW TO UNLOCK
Rhys the Exiled	4th win
Talara's Battalion	15th win
Wurm's Tooth	7th win
Wurm's Tooth	5th win
Wurm's Tooth	10th win
Wurm's Tooth	2nd win

EYES OF SHADOW

Win matches using this deck to unlock cards for it.

UNLOCKABLE	HOW TO UNLOCK
Ascendant Evincar	13th win
Corrupt	15th win
Crowd of Cinders	8th win
Deathmark	9th win
Deathmark	5th win
Demon's Horn	1st win
Demon's Horn	6th win
Demon's Horn	4th win
Demon's Horn	3rd win
Dread	16th win
Hollowborn Barghest	17th win
Mind Shatter	10th win
Mortivore	11th win
Nekrataal	14th win
Plague Wind	2nd win
Royal Assassin	12th win
Soot Imp	7th win

HANDS OF FLAME

Win matches using this deck to unlock cards for it.

UNLOCKABLE	HOW TO UNLOCK
Blaze	7th Win
Bloodmark Mentor	9th win
Cinder Pyromancer	3rd win
Cryoclasm	6th win
Cryoclasm	10th win
Dragon's Claw	5th win
Dragon's Claw	2nd win
Dragon's Claw	8th win
Dragon's Claw	12th win
Furnace of Rath	16th win
Hostility	17th win
Incinerate	4th win
Kamahl, Pit Fighter	13th win
Rage Reflection	14th win
Seismic Assault	11th win
Shivan Dragon	1st win
Shivan Hellkite	15th win

SCALES OF FURY

Win matches using this deck to unlock cards for it.

UNLOCKABLE	HOW TO UNLOCK
Blighting	3rd win
Broodmate Dragon	11th win
Crucible of Fire	4th win
Demon's Horn	5th win
Dragon Roost	6th win
Dragon's Claw	7th win
Fervor	13th win
Flameblast Dragon	1st win
Flameblast Dragon	14th win
Hellkite Overlord	15th win
Shivan Dragon	9th win
Threaten	8th win
Violent Ultimatum	12th win
Wurm's Tooth	10th win
Wurm's Tooth	2nd win

TEETH OF THE PREDATOR

Win matches using this deck to unlock cards for it.

UNLOCKABLE	HOW TO UNLOCK
Blanchwood Armor	1st win
Blanchwood Armor	11th win
Elvish Piper	14th win
Howl of the Night Pack	4th win
Karplusan Strider	12th win
Karplusan Strider	10th win
Karplusan Strider	6th win
Loxodon Warhammer	16th win
Molimo, Maro-Sorcerer	3rd win
Roughshod Mentor	7th win
Troll Ascetic	15th win
Troll Ascetic	9th win
Verdant Force	13th win
Vigor	17th win
Wurm's Tooth	8th win
Wurm's Tooth	5th win
Wurm's Tooth	2nd win

THOUGHTS OF WIND

Win matches using this deck to unlock cards for it.

UNLOCKABLE	HOW TO UNLOCK
Counterbore	4th win
Denizen of the Deep	16th win
Flashfreeze	10th win
Flashfreeze	6th win
Flow of Ideas	14th win
Kraken's Eye	5th win
Kraken's Eye	2nd win

UNLOCKABLE	HOW TO UNLOCK
Kraken's Eye	8th win
Kraken's Eye	12th win
Mahamoti Djinn	1st win
Mind Spring	11th win
Mind Spring	17th win
Put Away	7th Win
Thieving Magpie	13th win
Thieving Magpie	15th win
Thieving Magpie	3rd win
Thieving Magpie	9th win

WINGS OF LIGHT

Win matches using this deck to unlock cards for it.

UNLOCKABLE	HOW TO UNLOCK
Angel's Feather	2nd win
Angel's Feather	12th win
Angel's Feather	5th win
Angel's Feather	8th win
Angel's Feather	13th win
Luminesce	6th win
Mass Calcify	15th win
Paladin en-Vec	10th win
Purity	17th win
Reya Dawnbringer	16th win
Serra Angel	1st win
Serra's Embrace	3rd win
Skyhunter Skirmisher	7th win
Soul Warden	11th win
Spirit of the Hearth	14th win
Voice of All	4th win
Wrath of God	9th win

GAMER PICTURES

UNLOCKABLE	HOW TO UNLOCK
Jace Beleren gamer pic	Complete all Challenges in single-player campaign.
Chandra Nalaar gamer pic	Beat the single-player campaign on any difficulty.

MAGICIAN'S QUEST: MYSTERIOUS TIMES (DS)

UNLOCKABLES

UNLOCKABLE	HOW TO UNLOCK
Bug Wizard	Catch all bugs.
Evil Wizard	Cause mischief all around town.
Fish Wizard	Catch all fish.
Flower Wizard	Make 200 flowers bloom in your town.
Forgetful Wizard	Don't save four times and get this title.
Gallant Wizard	Talk to everyone for 10 consecutive days.
Love Wizard	Have 10 classmates confess love.
Skull Wizard	Kill 100 ghosts with the flatulence spell.
Wise Wizard	Finish all mystery cases.

Great Wizard	Win some tournaments during extracurricular lessons, then get evaluated by Principal Sol.
Righteous Wizard	Beat Captain Dot 20 Times.
Evil Wizard	Use Prank Magic on your classmates over 100 times.
A La Mode Wizard	Get 12 different hair styles.
Stylish Wizard	Change into four different sets of clothes every day for 10 days.

MAJOR LEAGUE BASEBALL 2K5: WORLD SERIES EDITION

(XBOX)

Create a new profile and enter the following names.

UNLOCKABLE	CODE
Unlock All Cheats	Ima Cheater
Unlock All Classic Teams	Old Timers
Unlock All Extras	Gimme Goods

MAJOR LEAGUE BASEBALL 2K5: WORLD SERIES EDITION

(PlayStation 2)

Create a new profile and enter the following names.

UNLOCKABLE	CODE
Unlock All Cheats	Ima Cheater
Unlock All Classic Teams	Old Timers
Unlock All Extras	Gimme Goods

MAJOR LEAGUE BASEBALL 2K7 (XBOX 360)

To enter these codes select My 2K7. Then select Enter Cheat Code.

UNLOCKABLE	CODE
Boosts a team's power rating by 25% for 1 inning	mightymick
Boosts the hitting of the 3, 4, 5 hitters in the lineup by 50% for 1 game	triplecrown
Boosts your ability to hit home runs during the game just like The Mick	m4murder
Mickey will pinch hit	phmantle
Unlocks everything	Derek Jeter
Unlocks Mickey Mantle in free agency	themick

MAJOR LEAGUE BASEBALL 2K7 (PlayStation 3)

To enter these codes select My 2K7. Then select Enter Cheat Code.

UNLOCKABLE	CODE
Boosts a team's power rating by 25% for 1 inning	mightymick
Boosts the hitting of the 3, 4, 5 hitters in the lineup by 50% for 1 game	triplecrown
Boosts your ability to hit home runs during the game just like The Mick	m4murder
Mickey will pinch hit	phmantle
Unlocks everything	Derek Jeter
Unlocks Mickey Mantle in free agency	themick

CODES

Enter the codes in the Codes menu located in the Trading Card Album.

EFFECT	CODE
Unlocks all of the American League Central Classic Jersey Trading Cards.	ALCENTRALCLASSICTHREADS08
Unlocks all of the American League East Classic Jersey Trading Cards.	ALEASTCLASSICTHREADS08

EFFECT	CODE
Unlocks all of the American League West Classic Jersey Trading Cards.	ALWESTCLASSICTHREADS08
Unlocks all of the National League Central Classic Jersey Trading Cards.	NLCENTRALCLASSICTHREADS08
Unlocks all of the National League East Classic Jersey Trading Cards.	NLEASTCLASSICTHREADS08
Unlocks all of the National League West Classic Jersey Trading Cards.	NLWESTCLASSICTHREADS08

MAJOR LEAGUE BASEBALL 2K7 (XBOX)

CODES

CODE	EFFECT
triplecrown	Increase ability of 3,4,5 hitters
Derek Jeter	Unlock everything (except the cheats you need special codes for)
themick	Unlock Mickey Mantle in free agency

MAJOR LEAGUE BASEBALL 2K7 (PlayStation 2)

To enter these codes, select My 2K7. Then select Enter Cheat Code.

UNLOCKABLE	CODE
Boosts a team's power rating by 25% for 1 inning	mightymick
Boosts the hitting of the 3, 4, 5 hitters in the lineup by 50% for 1 game	triplecrown
Boosts your ability to hit home runs during the game just like The Mick	m4murder
Mickey will pinch hit	phmantle
Unlocks everything	Derek Jeter
Unlocks Mickey Mantle in free agency	themick

MAJOR LEAGUE BASEBALL 2K8 (XBox 360)

CODES

Enter the codes in the Codes menu located in the Trading Card Album.

EFFECT	CODE
Unlocks all of the American League Central Classic Jersey Trading Cards.	ALCENTRALCLASSICTHREADS08
Unlocks all of the American League East Classic Jersey Trading Cards.	ALEASTCLASSICTHREADS08
Unlocks all of the American League West Classic Jersey Trading Cards.	ALWESTCLASSICTHREADS08
Unlocks all of the National League Central Classic Jersey Trading Cards.	NLCENTRALCLASSICTHREADS08
Unlocks all of the National League East Classic Jersey Trading Cards.	NLEASTCLASSICTHREADS08
Unlocks all of the National League West Classic Jersey Trading Cards.	NLWESTCLASSICTHREADS08

MAJOR LEAGUE EATING: THE GAME (Wii)

UNLOCKABLES

UNLOCKABLE	HOW TO UNLOCK
Joey Chestnut	Complete the Single-Player Mode with Patrick Bertoletti.
Patrick Bertoletti	Complete the Single-Player Mode with El Toro Jimenez.
Richard LeFevre	Complete the Single-Player Mode with Juliet Lee.
Sonya Thomas	Complete the Single-Player Mode with Erik "The Red" Denmark.
The Bear (only usable in Versus Mode)	Complete the Single-Player Mode with Patrick Bertoletti.

Tim Janus	Complete the Single-Player Mode with Crazy Legs Conti.

MANHUNT7 (PlayStation 2)

UNLOCKABLE	CODE
God Mode	After finishing the game on Fetish mode, enter ↓,↓,●,↑,■,▲,■,R2,↑,↑,L1,▲ at the Title Screen.

MARVEL NEMESIS: RISE OF THE IMPERFECTS (XBOX)

Enter these passwords in the Cheat menu under Options.

UNLOCKABLE	PASSWORD
All Fantastic Four comics	SAVAGELAND
All Tomorrow People comics	NZONE
Electra swimsuit card	THEHAND
Solara swimsuit card	REIKO
Storm's swimsuit card	MONROE

MARVEL NEMESIS: RISE OF THE IMPERFECTS (PlayStation 2)

To enter these passwords, go into the Options menu and select Cheats.

UNLOCKABLE	PASSWORD
Elektra swimsuit model card	THEHAND
Solara swimsuit model card	REIKO
Storm swimsuit model card	MONROE
Unlocks all Fantastic Four comics	SAVAGELAND
Unlocks all Tomorrow People comics	NZONE

MARVEL: ULTIMATE ALLIANCE (XBOX 360)

These codes need to be entered in different areas of the game. Enter these in the Team menu.

UNLOCKABLE	CODE
100k	↑, ↑, ↑, ←, →, ←, START
Level 99	↑, ←, ↑, ←, ↓, →, ↓, →

Enter these in the Character Selection screen.

UNLOCKABLE	CODE
All Character Code	↑, ↑, ↓, ↓, ←, ←, ←, START
All Costumes	↑, ↓, ↑, ↓, ←, →, ←, →, ↑, ↓, START
All Powers	←, →, ←, →, ↑, ↓, ↑, ↓, ←, →, START
Unlock Daredevil	←, ←, →, →, ↑, ↓, ↑, ↓
Unlock Silver Surfer	↓, ←, ←, ↑, →, ↑, ↓, ←

Enter these codes in the Review menu.

UNLOCKABLE	CODE
All Cinematics	↑, ←, ←, ↑, →, →, ↑
All Comics	←, →, →, ←, ↑, ↑, →
All Concept Art	↓, ↓, ↓, →, →, ←, ↓
All Wallpapers	↑, ↓, →, ←, ↑, ↑, ↓

Enter these codes while playing.

UNLOCKABLE	CODE
Filler	←, →, →, ←, ↑, ↓, ↓, ↑
God mode	↑, ↓, ↑, ↓, ↑, ←, ↓, →
Super Speed	↑, ←, ↑, →, ↓, →
Touch of Death	←, →, ↓, ↓, →, ←

Enter this code on the Comic Book missions.

UNLOCKABLE	CODE
The Courses	↑, →, ←, ↓, ↑, →, ←, ↓

MARVEL ULTIMATE ALLIANCE (PlayStation 3)

Enter these codes while playing.

UNLOCKABLE	CODE
God Mode	↑, ↓, ↑, ↓, ↑, ←, ↓, →, START
Super Speed	↑, ←, ↑, →, ↓, →, START
Touch of Death	←, →, ↓, ↓, →, ←, START

Enter these codes at the Team menu.

UNLOCKABLE	CODE
100K	↑, ↑, ↑, ←, →, ←, START
All Characters	↑, ↑, ↓, ↓, ←, ←, ←, START
All Costumes	↑, ↓, ↑, ↓, ←, →, ←, →, ↑, ↓, START
All Powers	←, →, ←, →, ↑, ↓, ↑, ↓, ←, →, START
Level 99	↑, ←, ↑, ←, ↓, →, ↓, →, START
Unlocks Daredevil	←, ←, →, →, ↑, ↓, ↑, ↓, START
Unlocks Silver Surfer	↓, ←, ←, ↑, →, ↑, ↓, ←, START

Enter these codes at the Review menu.

UNLOCKABLE	CODE
All Cinematics	↑, ←, ←, ↑, →, →, ↑, START
All Comics	←, →, →, ←, ↑, ↑, →, START
All Concept Art	↓, ↓, ↓, →, →, ←, ↓, START
All Wallpapers	↑, ↓, →, ←, ↑, ↑, ↓, START

MARVEL: ULTIMATE ALLIANCE (Wii)

Enter these codes while playing.

UNLOCKABLE	CODE
God Mode	↑, ↓, ↑, ↓, ↑, ←, ↓, →, ⊕
Fill Momentum	←, →, →, ←, ↑, ↓, ↓, ↑, ⊕
Super Speed	↑, ←, ↑, →, ↓, →, ⊕
Touch of Death	←, →, ↓, ↓, →, ←, ⊕

Enter these codes in the Team menu.

UNLOCKABLE	CODE
100k	↑, ↑, ↑, ←, →, ←, ⊕
Level 99	↑, ←, ↑, ←, ↓, →, ↓, →, ⊕

Enter these codes in the Team Selection screen.

UNLOCKABLE	CODE
All Characters	↑, ↑, ↓, ↓, ←, ←, ←, ⊕
Unlock All Costumes	↑, ↓, ↑, ↓, ←, →, ←, →, ↑, ↓, ⊕
Unlock All Powers	←, →, ←, →, ↑, ↓, ↑, ↓, ←, →, ⊕
Unlock Daredevil	←, ←, →, →, ↑, ↓, ↑, ↓, ⊕
Unlock Silver Surfer	↓, ←, ←, ↑, →, ↑, ↓, ←, ⊕

Enter these codes in the Review menu.

UNLOCKABLE	CODE
All Comics	←, →, →, ←, ↑, ↑, →, ⊕
All Concept Art	↓, ↓, ↓, →, →, ←, ↓, ⊕
All Wallpapers	↑, ↓, →, Z, ↑, ↑, ↓, ⊕
All Cinematics	↑, ←, ←, ↑, →, →, ↑, ⊕

MARVEL ULTIMATE ALLIANCE (PlayStation 2)

Enter these codes while playing.

UNLOCKABLE	CODE
God Mode	↑, ↓, ↑, ↓, ↑, ←, ↓, →, START
Super Speed	↑, ←, ↑, →, ↓, →, START
Touch of Death	←, →, ↓, ↓, →, ←, START

Enter these codes at the Team menu.

UNLOCKABLE	CODE
100K	↑, ↑, ↑, ←, →, ←, START
All Characters	↑, ↑, ↓, ↓, ←, ←, ←, START
All Costumes	↑, ↓, ↑, ↓, ←, →, ←, →, ↑, ↓, START
All Powers	←, →, ←, →, ↑, ↓, ↑, ↓, ←, →, START
Level 99	↑, ←, ↑, ←, ↓, →, ↓, →, START
Unlocks Daredevil	←, ←, →, →, ↑, ↓, ↑, ↓, START
Unlocks Silver Surfer	↓, ←, ←, ↑, →, ↑, ↓, ←, START
All Cinematics	↑, ←, ←, ↑, →, →, ↑, START
All Comics	←, →, →, ←, ↑, ↑, →, START
All Concept Art	↓, ↓, ↓, →, →, ←, ↓, START
All Wallpapers	↑, ↓, →, ←, ↑, ↑, ↓, START

MARVEL: ULTIMATE ALLIANCE 2 (XBOX 360)

CODES

Enter one of the following codes at the indicated screen (saving is disabled).

EFFECT	CODE
Fusion	Right, Right, Up, Down, Up, Up, Left, START
Heroes (All Characters)	Up, Up, Down, Down, Left, Left, Left, START
Hulk (Character)	Down, Left, Left, Up, Right, Up, Down, Left, START
Jean Grey (Character)	Left, Left, Right, Right, Up, Down, Up, Down, START
Money	Up, Up, Down, Down, Up, Up, Up, Down, START
Movies	Up, Left, Left, Up, Right, Right, Up, START
Skins (Costumes)	Up, Down, Left, Right, Left, Right, START
Thor (Character)	Up, Right, Right, Down, Right, Down, Left, Right, START

TEAM BONUSES

Certain character combinations unlock special boosts.

UNLOCKABLE	HOW TO UNLOCK
Agile Warriors: +2 all Attributes	Daredevil, Spider-Man, Deadpool, Iron Fist
Bruisers: +5 Striking	Juggernaut, Hulk, Thing, Luke Cage, Thor
Classic Avengers: +15% Max Stamina	Hulk, Thor, Iron Man, Captain America
Fantastic Four: +35% Fusion Gain	Mr. Fantastic, Human Torch, Thing, Invisible Woman
Femmes Fatales: +5% Damage	Jean Grey, Storm, Invisible Woman, Ms. Marvel
Martial Artists: +5 Striking	Daredevil, Wolverine, Iron Fist, Deadpool
Masters of Energy: +15% Max Health	Gambit, Iron Fist, Jean Grey, Ms. Marvel, Nick Fury, Penance
Natural Forces +5% Damage inflicted as Health Gain	Storm, Iceman, Thor, Human Torch
New Avengers: +10% to all resistances	Ms. Marvel, Spider-Man, Wolverine, Iron Man, Luke Cage, Iron Fist
Pro-Reg Heroes: +15% Max HP	Iron Man, Mr. Fantastic, Deadpool, Songbird, Ms Marvel, Spider-Man

UNLOCKABLE	HOW TO UNLOCK
Secret Avengers: +3 Teamwork	Captain America, Iron Fist, Luke Cage, Invisible Woman, Human Torch, Storm, Spider-Man
Shut Up Already! - 15% Extra Health	Play as a team of Spider-Man, Iceman, Deadpool, and Human Torch.
Think Tank: +15% Max HP	Mr. Fantastic, Iron Man, Green Goblin, Spider-Man, Hulk
Thunderbolts: +5% Damage	Green Goblin, Songbird, Venom, Penance
Weapon Specialists: +5% Criticals	Daredevil, Deadpool, Gambit, Thor, Green Goblin, Captain America
X-Men: +15% Max Stamina	Gambit, Jean Grey, Wolverine, Storm, Ice Man, Juggernaut (interchangeable)

SPECIAL CHARACTERS

Unlock the following characters by performing the actions listed.

UNLOCKABLE	HOW TO UNLOCK
Deadpool	Beat the D.C. Level
Green Goblin and Venom	Beat them at the end of Wakanda Act 3.
Hulk	Collect all five Gamma Regulators.
Iron Fist	Choose the Rebel side when faced with the choice.
Jean Grey	Collect all five M'Kraan Shards.
Ms. Marvel	Beat the NYC Level.
Nick Fury	Beat the game.
Penance	Defeat him in the portal room to the negative zone.
Songbird	Choose the Register side when faced with the choice.
Thor	Collect all five Asgardian Runes.

MARVEL: ULTIMATE ALLIANCE 2 (PlayStation 3)

CODES

Enter one of the following codes at the indicated screen (saving is disabled).

EFFECT	CODE
Diaries	←,→,→,←,↑,↑,→,START
Dossier	↓,↓,↓,→,→,←,↓,START
Fusion	→,→,↑,↓,↑,↑,←,START
Heroes (All Characters)	↑,↑,↓,↓,←,←,←,START
Hulk (Character)	↓,←,←,↑,→,↑,↓,←,START
Jean Grey (Character)	←,←,→,→,↑,↓,↑,↓,START
Money	↑,↑,↓,↓,↑,↑,↑,↓,START
Movies	↑,←,←,↑,→,→,↑,START
Power	↑,↑,↓,↓,←,→,→,←,START
Skins (Costumes)	↑,↓,←,→,←,→,START
Thor (Character)	↑,→,→,↓,→,↓,←,→,START

TEAM BONUSES

Certain character combinations unlock special boosts.

UNLOCKABLE	HOW TO UNLOCK
Agile Warriors: +2 all Attributes	Daredevil, Spider-Man, Deadpool, Iron Fist
Bruisers: +5 Striking	Juggernaut, Hulk, Thing, Luke Cage, Thor
Classic Avengers: +15% Max Stamina	Hulk, Thor, Iron Man, Captain America
Fantastic Four: +35% Fusion Gain	Mr. Fantastic, Human Torch, Thing, Invisible Woman

Femmes Fatales: +5% Damage	Jean Grey, Storm, Invisible Woman, Ms. Marvel
Martial Artists: +5 Striking	Daredevil, Wolverine, Iron Fist, Deadpool
Masters of Energy: +15% Max Health	Gambit, Iron Fist, Jean Grey, Ms. Marvel, Nick Fury, Penance
Natural Forces +5% Damage inflicted as Health Gain	Storm, Iceman, Thor, Human Torch
New Avengers: +10% to all resistances	Ms. Marvel, Spider-Man, Wolverine, Iron Man, Luke Cage, Iron Fist
Pro-Reg Heroes: +15% Max HP	Iron Man, Mr. Fantastic, Deadpool, Songbird, Ms Marvel, Spider-Man
Secret Avengers: +3 Teamwork	Captain America, Iron Fist, Luke Cage, Invisible Woman, Human Torch, Storm, Spider-Man
Shut Up Already! —15% Extra Health	Play as a team of Spider-Man, Iceman, Deadpool, and Human Torch.
Think Tank: +15% Max HP	Mr. Fantastic, Iron Man, Green Goblin, Spider-Man, Hulk
Thunderbolts: +5% Damage	Green Goblin, Songbird, Venom, Penance
Weapon Specialists: +5% Criticals	Daredevil, Deadpool, Gambit, Thor, Green Goblin, Captain America
X-Men: +15% Max Stamina	Gambit, Jean Grey, Wolverine, Storm, Ice Man, Juggernaut (interchangeable)

SPECIAL CHARACTERS

Unlock the following characters by performing the actions listed.

UNLOCKABLE	HOW TO UNLOCK
Deadpool	Beat the D.C. Level.
Green Goblin and Venom	Beat them at the end of Wakanda Act 3.
Hulk	Collect all five Gamma Regulators.
Iron Fist	Choose the Rebel side when faced with the choice.
Jean Grey	Collect all five M'Kraan Shards.
Ms. Marvel	Beat the NYC Level.
Nick Fury	Beat the game.
Penance	Defeat him in the portal room to the negative zone.
Songbird	Choose the Register side when faced with the choice.
Thor	Collect all five Asgardian Runes.

MARVEL: ULTIMATE ALLIANCE 2 (Wii)

CODES

Enter the following codes with the D-Pad

EFFECT	CODE
All Bonus Missions (at Bonus Missions screen)	↑, →, ↓, ←, ←, →, ↑, ↑
All Heroes (at Character Select screen)	↑, ↑, ↓, ↓, ←, ←, ←, →
Characters Advance 10 Levels (at Pause menu)	↓, ↑, ←, ↑, ←, ↑, ←, ↓
Fusion Power Always Four Stars	↓, ↑, ↑, ↓, ↓, ←, ←, ↓
God Mode (at Pause menu)	↓, ↑, ↑, ↓, ↓, ←, →, ↓

MARVEL VS. CAPCOM 2 (XBOX)

UNLOCKABLE	HOW TO UNLOCK
Attack After Fight Is Finished	After you win a fight, press start to attack the other person until the end of the match
Choose Character to Start Match With	At the beginning of a battle, hold a character's assist button, and he/she will be first instead
Use the Same Character 3x Per Team	Unlock all hidden characters and all extra costumes

NEW! A B C D E F G H I J K L M N O P Q R S T U V W X Y Z

MASS EFFECT (XBOX 360)

ACHIEVEMENTS

Complete each of the following achievements to get the allotted gamerscore.

UNLOCKABLE	HOW TO UNLOCK
AI Hacking Specialist (15)	Use AI hacking 75 times.
Asari Ally (20)	Complete the majority of the game with the Asari squad member.
Assault Rifle Expert (15)	Register 150 assault rifle kills.
Barrier Mastery (15)	Use Biotic Barrier 75 times.
Charismatic (10)	Use Charm or Intimidate to resolve an impossible situation.
Completionist (25)	Complete the majority of the game.
Council Legion of Merit (25)	Complete Virmire.
Damping Specialist (15)	Use Damping Field 75 times.
Distinguished Combat Medal (25)	Complete one Mass Effect playthrough on the Hardcore difficulty setting.
Distinguished Service Medal (25)	Complete Eden Prime.
Dog of War (25)	Register 150 organic enemy kills.
Extreme Power Gamer (50)	Reach 60th level with one character.
First Aid Specialist (15)	Use medi-gel 150 times.
Geth Hunter (25)	Register 250 synthetic enemy kills.
Honorarium of Corporate Service (25)	Complete Noveria.
Krogan Ally (20)	Complete the majority of the game with the Krogan squad member.
Lift Mastery (15)	Use Biotic Lift 75 times.
Long Service Medal (25)	Complete two playthroughs on any setting.
Medal of Exploration (50)	Land on an uncharted world.
Medal of Heroism (25)	Complete Feros.
Medal of Honor (100)	Complete one playthrough on any difficulty setting.
Medal of Valor (50)	Complete one playthrough on the Insanity difficulty setting.
Neural Shock Specialist (15)	Use Neural Shock 75 times.
Overlord Specialist (15)	Use Shield Overload 75 times.
Paragon (15)	Accumulate 75% of total Paragon points.
Paramour (10)	Complete any romance subplot.
Pistol Expert (10)	Register 150 pistol kills.
Power Gamer (20)	Reach 50th level with one character.
Quarian Ally (20)	Complete the majority of the game with the Quarian squad member.
Renegade (15)	Accumulate 75% of total Renegade points.
Rich (25)	Exceed 1,000,000 Credits.
Sabotage Specialist (15)	Use Sabotage 75 times.
Scholar (25)	Find all primary aliens: Council Races, Extinct Races, and Non-Council Races codex entries.
Search and Rescue (10)	Locate Dr. T'Soni in the Artemis Tau cluster.
Sentinel Ally (20)	Complete the majority of the game with the Alliance sentinel squad member.
Shotgun Expert (15)	Register 150 shotgun kills.

Singularity Mastery (15)	Use Biotic Singularity 75 times.
Sniper Expert (15)	Register 150 sniper rifle kills.
Soldier Ally (20)	Complete the majority of the game with the Alliance soldier squad member.
Spectre Inductee (15)	Become a Spectre.
Stasis Mastery (15)	Use Biotic Stasis 75 times.
Tactician (25)	Complete playthrough with shield damage greater than health damage.
Throw Mastery (15)	Use Biotic Throw 75 times.
Turian Ally (20)	Complete the majority of the game with the Turian squad member.
Warp Mastery (15)	Use Biotic Warp 75 times.

CHARACTER BENEFIT UNLOCKABLES

Attain certain achievements to gain benefits on future playthroughs.

UNLOCKABLE	HOW TO UNLOCK
+10% Experience Bonus	Complete 75% of game.
+10% Hardening Bonus	Complete 75% of game with Ashley in squad.
+10% Health Bonus	Kill 150 organic beings.
+10% Shield Bonus	Kill 250 synthetics.
+25% Marksman Cooldown Bonus	Attain 150 kills with pistol.
10% Reduced Cooldown for Barrier and Stasis	Complete 75% of game with Liara in squad.
10% Reduced Cooldown for Lift and Throw	Complete 75% of game with Kaiden in squad.
10% Reduced Cooldown for Overload and Damping	Complete 75% of game with Garrus in squad.
10% Reduced Cooldown for Sabotage and AI Hacking	Complete 75% of game with Tali in squad.
10% Shield Increase	Sustain more shield damage than health damage during one playthrough.
5% Increase in Weapon Damage	Complete the game twice on any difficulty.
Assault Rifle Skill for New Characters	Attain 150 kills with assault rifle.
Barrier Skill for New Characters	Use Barrier 75 times.
Decryption Skill for New Characters	Use Sabotage 75 times.
Electronics Skill for New Characters	Use Overload 75 times.
First Aid Skill for New Characters	Use medi-gel 150 times.
Hacking Skill for New Characters	Use AI Hacking 75 times.
Lift Skill (for non-biotics)	Use Lift 75 times.
Medicine Skill for New Characters	Use Neural Hacking 75 times.
Regenerate 1 Health per Second	Complete 75% of game with Wrex in squad.
Shielding Skill for New Characters	Use Dampening 75 times.
Shotgun Skill for New Characters	Attain 150 kills with shotgun.
Sniper Rifle Skill for New Characters	Attain 150 kills with sniper rifle.
Spectre Grade Weapons for Purchase	Attain 1,000,000 credits in your wallet.
Singularity Skill for New Characters	Use Singularity 75 times.
Statis Skill for New Characters	Use Statis 75 times.
Throw Skill for New Characters	Use Throw 75 times.
Warp Skill for New Characters	Use Warp 75 times.

UNLOCKABLE GAMER PICS

Complete the game on the Hardcore and Insanity difficulties to unlock two special gamer pics for your profile.

UNLOCKABLE	HOW TO UNLOCK
"N7" Gamer Pic	Gain the Medal of Valor achievement.
Saren Gamer Pic	Gain the Distinguished Combat Medal achievement.

UNLOCKABLES

Complete the game on Normal to unlock the secrets.

UNLOCKABLE	HOW TO UNLOCK
Hardcore Mode	Complete the game once.
Increased Level Cap (51–0)	Complete the game once.
Insane Difficulty	Beat the game on the Hardcore difficulty without changing the difficulty.
New Game +	Start a New Game, then select existing Career. You'll be playing with your older character (with all items and skills intact).

MASS EFFECT 2 (XBOX 360)

UNLOCKABLES

UNLOCKABLE	HOW TO UNLOCK
Bonus 25% Experience	Beat the game on any difficulty
200k Credits	Start New Game after 1 Playthrough
50k of each Resource	Start New Game after 1 Playthrough
New Colors for Party Members	Complete a party member's loyalty mission.
Unlock Loyalty Skills	Complete the Loyalty missions for each of your party members to unlock their individuals skills.

MAX PAYNE (XBOX)

UNLOCKABLE	OBJECTIVE
Additional Difficulty Settings—"Dead on Arrival" and "New York Minute"	Complete the game under the "Fugitive" difficulty setting.
Bonus Level	Complete the game in New York Minute mode to unlock a new bonus level in which you have to kill a lot of enemies, all in bullet time.
Cheat Mode	Start a game. Press BACK during gameplay to display the main menu. Then, hold LT + RT + click L + click R, and quickly press WHT, BLK, BLK, WHT, WHT, BLK at the main menu. A cheat option will appear.
Last Challenge Bonus Level	Complete the game under the "Dead on Arrival" difficulty setting.
Secret Programmer Room	Complete the Last Challenge level. The doors in the back of the room will open up to the Remedy Room.

MAX PAYNE (PlayStation 2)

UNLOCKABLE	CODE
All Weapons and Full Ammo	Pause the game and press L1, L2, R1, R2, ▲, ●, ×, ■.
Infinite Health	Pause the game and press L1, L1, L2, L2, R1, R1, R2, R2.
Level Select	Finish the first chapter of the Subway. Return to the Main Menu and press ↑, ↓, ←, →, ↑, ←, ↓, ●.
Slow Motion Sounds	Pause the game and press L1, L2, R1, R2, ▲, ■, ×, ●.
Unlimited Bullet Time	Pause the game and press L1, L2, R1, R2, ▲, ×, ×, ▲.

MAX PAYNE 2 (XBOX)

UNLOCKABLE	CODE
All Modes	At any time during the game, pause and enter X,X,X,A,LT,RT,LT,RT

MECH ASSAULT (XBOX)

UNLOCKABLE	CODE
Completion Bonuses	Complete the game to unlock Ragnarok in local multiplayer mode.

MEDAL OF HONOR: AIRBORNE (XBOX 360)

CODES

UNLOCKABLE	HOW TO UNLOCK
Enter Cheat menu	Press RB+LB, then press X,B,Y,A,A
Full Ammo	Press and hold LB+RB then press B,B,Y,X,A,Y
Full Health	Y,X,X,Y,A,B

MEDAL OF HONOR: AIRBORNE (PlayStation 3)

CODES

During gameplay, hold L1,R1 and push ■,●,▲,×,× to call up the code screen, then enter the codes below.

UNLOCKABLE	HOW TO UNLOCK
Health Restoration	Hold L1,R1 and push ▲,■,■,▲,×,●
Infinite Ammo	Hold L1,R1 and push ●,●,▲,■,×,▲

MEDAL OF HONOR: EUROPEAN ASSAULT (XBOX)

CODES

To enter Cheat mode, hold LT+RT then ↓, A, X, BLK, B, ←. Release LT+RT when entering the actual cheat.

EFFECT	CODE
Disable Shell Shock	X, Y, A, B, LT, X
Find OSS Document	A, B, RT, WHT, BLK, LT
Full Adrenaline	B, Y, →, X, A, X
God Mode	WHT, BLK, Y, WHT, LT, LT
Kill Nemesis	→, ←, RB, LB, X, Y, ↗
Suicide	X, RT, WHT, Y, LT, WHT
Turn off HUD	BLK, LT, BLK, RT, ↑, Y
Unlimited Ammo	LT, Y, B, ↑, A, A

MEDAL OF HONOR: EUROPEAN ASSAULT (PlayStation 2)

To unlock the ability to enter cheats, go to the Pause menu and enter the Activate Cheat Entry code.

UNLOCKABLE	CODE
Active Cheat Entry	Hold L1+R1 then press ●,●,←,▲,●,×
Player Suicide (SP only)	×,▲,●,→,▲,●
Hide HUD	●,↓,●,↑,▲,●
Kill Nemesis	↓,L2,R2,↑,■
Pickup OSS Document	↑,×,R2,R1,↑,■
Disable Shellshock	L2,R1,L2,▲,▲,▲

MEDAL OF HONOR: FRONTLINE (XBOX)

Enter these passwords in the Options menu.

UNLOCKABLE	PASSWORD
Achilles Mode	TODADOME
Bullet Shield	NOHITSFORU

UNLOCKABLE	PASSWORD
Full Bonus Menu	ENCHILADA
Gold on Previous Level	SALMON
Invisible Enemies	GHOSTSHOTS
M.O.H.ton Torpedo	TONSOFUN
Men with Hats	MERCER
Perfectionist Mode	ONEPMPCHMP
Rubber Grenades	ELASTIC
Silver Bullet Mode	KILLERSHOT
Sniper Mode	LONGVIEW

Pause the game to enter this code:

UNLOCKABLE	CODE
Invincibility	Ⓧ, LT, Ⓑ, RT, BACK, Ⓨ, Ⓧ

MEDAL OF HONOR: FRONTLINE (PlayStation 2)

Enter the following codes at the Enigma Machine. Green lights will confirm correct code entry. Select the "Bonus" option under the Enigma Machine to enable or disable the cheat.

DESCRIPTION	CODE
Achilles' Head mode (Nazis can be killed only with a headshot when this cheat is active.)	GLASSJAW
Bullet Shield Mode (Bullets will not damage you.)	BULLETZAP
Complete Current Mission with Gold Star	MONKEY
Complete Previous Mission with Gold Star	TIMEWARP
Invisible Enemies (You will see only your enemies' guns and helmets.)	WHERERU
Making of D-Day FMV Sequence	BACKSTAGEO
Making of Needle in a Haystack FMV Sequence	BACKSTAGER
Making of Rolling Thunder FMV Sequence	BACKSTAGEI
Making of Several Bridges Too Far FMV Sequence	BACKSTAGEF
Making of Storm in the Port FMV Sequence	BACKSTAGET
Making of The Horten's Nest FMV Sequence	BACKSTAGES
Master Code	DAWOIKS
Men with Hats (Characters will have various objects on their heads.)	HABRDASHR
Mission 2 (A Storm in the Port)	ORANGUTAN
Mission 3 (Needle in a Haystack)	BABOON
Mission 4 (Several Bridges Too Far)	CHIMPNZEE
Mission 5 (Rolling Thunder)	LEMUR
Mission 6 (The Horten's Nest)	GORILLA
Mohton Torpedoes (Your bullets will change into "photon torpedoes.")	TPDOMOHTON
Perfectionist (Nazis kill you with one shot.)	URTHEMAN
Rubber Grenade Mode	BOING
Silver Bullet Mode (Silver Bullet mode allows enemies to be killed with one shot.)	WHATYOUGET
Snipe-O-Rama Mode (All guns can zoom like a sniper rifle.)	LONGSHOT

Enter the following codes while the game is paused. The game will automatically resume after correct code entry.

UNLOCKABLE	CODE
Invincibility	■, L1, ●, R1, ▲, L2, SELECT, R2
Unlimited Ammunition	●, L2, ■, L1, SELECT, R2, ▲, SELECT

TO GET THE EA LA MEDAL OF VALOR, COMPLETE THE GAME WITH A GOLD STAR IN EVERY MISSION.

MEDAL OF HONOR: HEROES 2 (Wii)

MAP AWARDS

UNLOCKABLE	HOW TO UNLOCK
Base Demolition	Put a permanent end to the Further's pet project.
Beach Attack	Land on the beach with the 5th Rangers, and push through the German defenses.
Destroy the Guns	To protect Allied bombers, five Anti-Air gun batteries need to be knocked out.
Destroy Train	Fight your way through the fields to the Train Station. Whatever is on that train is too important to let go.
Monastery Assault	A key figure has set up a base of operation in a remote monastery. Crack the defenses and get whatever information you can.
Sink U-boats	Take out three U-boats in the port area.
Through the Sewers	The Germans have holed up underground. Go take them out while staying safe from Allied bombardment.

SPECIAL AWARDS

UNLOCKABLE	HOW TO UNLOCK
Combat Basic	Awarded for killing 100 enemy soldiers on the battlefield.
Combat Master	Awarded for killing 500 enemy soldiers on the battlefield.
Combat Senior	Awarded for killing 250 enemy soldiers on the battlefield.
Endurance	Awarded for completing a mission without being critically injured once.
Green Survivor	Awarded for completing a mission on Green without dying once.
Grenade Combat	Awarded for killing 25 enemy soldiers with grenades.
Hero Survivor	Awarded for completing a mission on Hero without dying once.
Heroism	Awarded for completing Campaign mode on the Hero difficulty setting.
LMG Combat	Awarded for killing 150 enemy soldiers with the BAR or STG44 light machine guns.
Machine Gun Combat	Awarded for killing 50 enemy soldiers with the MG42 machine gun.
Marksmanship	Awarded for completing a mission with 75 percent accuracy.
Melee Combat	Awarded for killing 25 enemy soldiers in melee combat.
Participant	Awarded for completing Campaign mode on the Green difficulty setting.
Pistol Combat	Awarded for killing 50 enemy soldiers with the Colt .45 or Luger pistol.
Rifle Combat	Awarded for killing 50 enemy soldiers with the M1 Garand or Karabiner 98K rifles.
Rocket Combat	Awarded for killing 25 enemy soldiers with the Bazooka or Panzerschrek rocket launcher.
Sharpshooter	Awarded for achieving 100 headshots on the battlefield.
Shotgun Combat	Awarded for killing 50 enemy soldiers with the shotgun.
SMG Combat	Awarded for killing 250 enemy soldiers with the Thompson or MP40 submachine guns.
Sniper Combat	Awarded for killing 50 enemy soldiers with the scoped Gewehr rifle or the scoped Springfield rifle.
eteran	Awarded for completing Campaign mode on the Veteran difficulty setting.
Veteran Survivor	Awarded for completing a mission in Veteran without dying once.
Weapon Expert	Awarded for getting at least one kill with each weapon in the game.

MEDAL OF HONOR: RISING SUN (XBOX)

UNLOCKABLE	CODE
God Mode	banner
Infinite Ammo	jawfish
All Missions	tuskfish

MEDAL OF HONOR: RISING SUN (PlayStation 2)

Go to the Options screen and select Password. Enter the following codes. You will hear a chime to confirm code entry.

UNLOCKABLE	CODE
All Missions	BUTTERFLY—Go to Mission Select and pick the desired level.
Invisible Soldiers	TRIGGER
Unlimited Ammo	GOBY

MEDAL OF HONOR: VANGUARD (Wii)

UNLOCKABLE	CODE
Cheat Menu (required for entering following codes)	In the pause menu, enter ↑, ↓, ↑, ↓
Extra Armor	→, ←, →, ↓, ↑, →
Invisibility	↑, →, ←, ↓, ↓, ↑

MEDAL OF HONOR: VANGUARD (PlayStation 2)

CODES

Pause the game and then enter ↑,↓,↑,↓ on the D-pad. If entered correctly a message will pop up saying "Enter Cheat Code," then enter the following codes.

EFFECT	CODE
Extra Armor	→,←,→,↓,↑,→
Invincibility	↑,→,←,↓,↓,↑

MEDIEVIL RESURRECTION (PSP)

To enter this code, pause the game.

UNLOCKABLE	CODE
Invincibility and All Weapons	Hold R, then press ↓, ↑, ■, ▲, ▲, ●, ↓, ↑, ■, ▲

MEGA MAN (Wii)

UNLOCKABLES

UNLOCKABLE	HOW TO UNLOCK
Select Trick	When using a weapon that goes through an enemy, press the SELECT button (this pauses the game without bringing up the weapon menu) when the weapon is making contact with the enemy. While the game is paused this way the enemy continues to flash. When the flashing has stopped, press the SELECT button again to un-pause the game and the weapon hits the enemy again, causing more damage. You can do this trick repeatedly with many of the bosses, making them very easy to beat.

MEGA MAN BATTLE NETWORK 5: DOUBLE TEAM (DS)

CODES

Highlight the corresponding program from the list and hold down the right button. Then push the following buttons to compress them by one block. To uncompress them, just repeat the above process again.

CODE	EFFECT
BLBABLBBAA	Air Shoes
RBBARBRARB	Anti-Damage

LLLRRBARBL	Attack MAX
RLRLRBBRAB	Auto Recover
AABRABRLLR	Battery
ABBRAABRBR	Beat
BARABRLRRA	Body Pack
BABLABRLRB	Bug Stop
LLRARLBLAR	Buster Pack
ALAARBRBAR	Charge MAX
RRBBRBRBAA	Chivalry
BRALARBAAB	Collect
AARLBABALB	Custom +1
BARLLRALBR	Custom +2
RLABBARALR	First Barrier
BABALRARAA	Fish
ALLBRLAAAL	Float Shoes
RRLBLLARBL	Giga Folder +1
BBRALBLARR	Giga Virus
ALRABLRALR	Hub Batch
ABLARABLRL	Humor
LRLABLBBLA	Jungle
LABBLBAALL	Mega Folder +2
BBABBRRLAR	Mega Folder +1
AABLARBLAA	Mega Virus
RLRARRLLLR	Millions
LBRARLABLB	Oil Body
LLRBLLAALB	Reflect
RBLRBRLLRL	Rush
ABARALRBBA	Shield
RLLALLBABB	Sneak Run
RARLLRRABA	Speed MAX
RABRALLRBA	Super Armor
LBLABLABAL	Tango
ARBBRLRALA	Undershirt

PRIZE CODES

Go to the numberman machine in Higsby's shop when it is placed there, and enter the passwords to get your prize. These codes can only be used for the DS version, they won't work on the GBA versions.

CODE	EFFECT
99428938	Area Steal
91182599	Dark Recovery
78234329	DoroTsunamiBall
01285874	Leaders Raid L
39285712	Lord of Chaos X
29387483	MagmaSeed
64836563	NumberBall
22323856	P. Battle Pack 1
66426428	P. Battle Pack 2
76820385	P.Attack+3
48582829	P.Chip+50
28475692	P.HP+100

CODE	EFFECT
53891756	P.HP+50
29486933	Super Kitakaze
12495783	Sword
85375720	TP Chip
19283746	Tsunami Hole
15733751	Unlocker

NUMBERMAN NAVI CUSTOMIZER PROGRAM CODES

Enter these codes in the Numberman Lotto Number to get a Navi customizer program.

CODE	EFFECT
25465278	Anti Aqua*
35607360	Anti Elec*
73877466	Anti Fire*
05068930	Anti Navi V
44213168	Anti Recovery P
10386794	Anti Sword R
10133670	Anti Wood*
63231870	Attack MAX (Yellow NCP)
79877132	BeatSupport NCP
30112002	BodyPack (Green)
50364410	Bug Fix*
80246758	BusterPack NCP
87412146	Charge MAX (White NCP)
15595587	Custom 2
07765623	Custom Bolt 3 G
68799876	Dark Invis*
52052687	Death Match 3 V
91098051	DjangoSP D
83143652	Fast Gauge*
12118790	Full Energy
90914896	Full Energy
68942679	Grab Revenge P
35321321	Gun Del Sol 3 O
90630807	HP+200 (Pink NCP)
48785625	HP+300 (Pink NCP)
13926561	HP+300 (White NCP)
03419893	HP+400 (Pink NCP)
45654128	HP+400 (Yellow)
31084443	HP+50 NCP
50906652	HP+500 (Pink)
72846472	HP+500 (White NCP)
29789661	Lock Enemy
97513648	Mega Folder 2 NCP
18746897	Recovery 300 Y
09609807	Rush (Yellow)
64892292	Sneakrun
28256341	SoulT+1 (Yellow)
36695497	Speed MAX (Pink NCP)

12541883	Spin Blue
78987728	Spin Green
30356451	Spin Red
48958798	Static S
54288793	Tango (Green)
73978713	Unlocker
28706568	Unlocker
64664560	Unlocker
00798216	Untrap

UNLOCKABLE PRIZES

Every time a Liberation Mission is completed, you get a prize depending on the number of phases you completed it in.

UNLOCKABLE	HOW TO UNLOCK
AntiNavi M	Beat Liberation 4 in 9–10
Anubis A	Beat Liberation 9 in 14 or less
BlackWing W	Beat Liberation 7 in 10 or less
BlizzardMan B	Beat Liberation 1 in 6–7
BlizzardManSP B	Beat Liberation 1 in 5 or less
CloudMan C	Beat Liberation 3 in 8–9
CloudManDS B	Beat Liberation 8 in 13–14
CloudManSP C	Beat Liberation 3 in 7 or less
Colonel C	Beat Liberation 6 in 9–10 (Colonel version only)
CosmoMan C	Beat Liberation 5 in 8–9
CosmoManDS	Beat Liberation 9 in 15–16
CosmoManSP C	Beat Liberation 5 in 7 or less
FullCust *	Beat Liberation 4 in 8 or less
Muramasa M	Beat Liberation 8 in 12 or less
ProtoMan B	Beat Liberation 6 in 9–10 (ProtoMan version only)
ShadeMan S	Beat Liberation 2 in 8–9
ShadeManDS S	Beat Liberation 7 in 11–12
ShadeManSP S	Beat Liberation 2 in 7 or less
Z-Saber Z	Beat Liberation 6 in 8 or less

MEGA MAN STAR FORCE: DRAGON (DS)

PASSWORDS

Compose a mail by pressing "X" in the mail screen, and send it to yourself. Type "Cipher" in the subject, then type the code in the body of the email. Send the email, and exit back to the main screen (Map screen). If you entered it correctly, it should give you a card.

PASSWORD	EFFECT
Let's combine our strength!	Brave Sword 3 Card
Dec. 17, 1986	ChainBubble3
ISNBDUBO	Cloaker
ILABCLERSAS	D. Energy
SIXGAME-O	D.Energy SubCard
CENCARLEBBUB	D.Eye Mega Weapon
KNIGSPIAREM	FlickrKck3
NGYNGIWCUS	GhostPulse2 B. Card
Legendary SP Card Master Shin	Grants DragonSky
ROHNATPE	Heatball3
Star Force, the ultimate power!	LeoKingdm SP

PASSWORD	EFFECT
KMALEETZCP	M. Breath (Mega Weapon) 1/2/1 Charge may Freeze or Bubble target
Ride On the Wave Road!	MopLance3
Go On Air battle card to trade info with friends.	PegasusMagic SP
Wave Change!	Porcupine Needle Mega Weapon, AT1|SP3|CH1 Geo Stellar, On, The Air!!
Brother Action RPG	QnOphiucaSP Card
AURIEFRUTS	Recovery 50 B. Card
PREOBCOPB	SearchEye SubCard
LAREBARAON	TimeBomb1 B. Card
Let's form a BrotherBand!	TimeBomb3
ALPTUNZLA	Unlocker
NROSIMAMSTU	Unlocker SubCard
DWOWOOLFS Subcard	Unlocks Cloaker
Fly away for skies unknown!	Unlocks Cygnus WingSP
NGAMEMA RESCAFROT	Unlocks D. Energy
Transers are really useful!	Unlocks FireBazooka3
How many more until you have all the cards?	Unlocks Freezenukle
Pegasus, Leo, Dragon - which is for you?	Unlocks Gatling3
Check out the Mega Man website!	Unlocks GhstPulse3
Get stronger through BrotherBands!	Unlocks GrndWave3
Only you can protect the Wave Road!	Unlocks JetAttack3
Win big with a Star Force Big Bang!	Unlocks PlasmaGun3
Mega Man 20th Anniversary Game	Unlocks Stikyrain3
I love Battle Network!	Unlocks SyncHook1
IPHAUEOEUNQC	Unlocks TailBurner3
Store info in your Transer!	Unlocks TaurusFireSP
Time to bust some EM viruses!	Unlocks WideWave3
OSLEGRATE	You get Heavy Cannon

MERCENARIES 2: WORLD IN FLAMES (XBOX 360)

UNLOCKABLE COSTUMES

To unlock costumes, you must complete Level 3 of a weapon challenge, which can be done by talking to Fiona at your PMC. Each time you complete a Level 3 weapon challenge, you receive one of three costumes.

MERCENARIES 2: WORLD IN FLAMES (PlayStation 2)

FACTION CODES

Codes must be entered in the Faction menu.
You'll get a confirmation sound if code was entered correctly.

EFFECT	CODE
One Million Dollars	→,↓,←,↑,↑,←,↓,→
Full Fuel	→,↓,←,↑,→,↓,←,↑
Infinite Ammo	→,←,→,→,←,→,←,←
Infinite Health	↑,↓,↑,↓,←,→,←,→
Reset All Factions to Neutral	↑,↑,↑,↑,↓,↓,→,←

MERCURY MELTDOWN REVOLUTION (Wii)

UNLOCKABLES

UNLOCKABLE	HOW TO UNLOCK
30mph Speed Limit Sign Skin	Collect the bonus points in each stage
Basketball Skin	Collect the bonus points in each stage
Black and White Cat's Face	Collect the bonus points in each stage
Brown and White Dog's Face	Collect the bonus points in each stage
Football Skin	Collect the bonus points in each stage
Smiley Face Skin	Collect the bonus points in each stage
Snooker Ball Skin	Collect the bonus points in each stage
Wheel Skin	Collect the bonus points in each stage

METAL GEAR ACID (PSP)

Enter the following in the Passwords menu through the Main menu.

CARD	PASSWORD
Gives Card No. 173 - Viper	Viper
Gives Card No. 178 - Mika Slayton	Mika
Gives Card No. 182 - Karen Houjou	Karen
Gives Card No. 184 - Jehuty	Jehuty
Gives Card No. 199 - XM8	Xmeight
Gives Card No. 200 - Kosaka Yuka	Kobe
Gives Card No. 201 - Asaki Yoshida	umeda
Gives Card No. 202 - Yu Saito	YEBISU
Gives Card No. 203 - Shibuya Eri	Roppongi

METAL GEAR ACID 2 (PSP)

Enter these passwords at the password screen. You'll obtain them as you load your saved games.

PASSWORD	EFFECT
Ronaldsiu	Banana Peel Card
Dcy	Card No. 203—Decoy Octopus
SONOFSULLY	Card No. 291—Jack
Vrs	Card No. 046—Strain (JP Version only)
Cct	Card No. 099—Gijin-san (JP Version only)
Konami	Card No. 119—Reaction Block
Viper	Card No. 161—Viper
Mika	Card No. 166—Mika Slayton
Karen	Card No. 170—Karen Houjou
Jehuty	Card No. 172—Jehuty
Xmeight	Card No. 187—XM8
Signt	Card No. 188—Mr. Sigint
Sgnt	Card No. 188—SIGINT (JP Version only)
Hrrr	Card No. 197—Sea Harrier (JP Version only)
Dcyctps	Card No. 203—Decoy Octopus (JP Version only)
Rgr	Card No. 212—Roger McCoy (JP Version only)
Xx	Card No. 281—Hinomoto Reiko (JP Version only)
Kinoshitaa	Card No. 285—Kinoshita Ayumi (JP Version only)
Shiimeg	Card No. 286—Ishii Meguru (JP Version only)
Nonat	Card No. 287—Sano Natsume (JP Version only)
No Place	Card No. 288—MGS4 (JP Version only)
Snake	Card No. 294—Solid Snake (MGS4)
Otacon	Card No. 295—Otacon (MGS4)

PASSWORD	EFFECT
shrrr	Card No. 197 Sea Harrier (US version)
Ginormousj	Emma's Parrot Card
Gekko	Gekko (US Version)
NEXTGEN	Get MGS4 card
shinta	Gives you card Gijin-san
nojiri	Gives you card Strand
mgr	Ishii Meguru
aym	Kinoshita Ayumi
mk2	Metal Gear MK. II (MGS4) Card unlocked
smoking	No Smoking card (US Version)
thespaniard	Possessed Arm card
gcl	Reaction Block 119 (Japanese version only)
tobidacid	Solid Eye card (US/UK Version)
ntm	Unlocks Natsume Sano Card an Solid Eye Video
Hnmt	Unlocks Reiko Hinomoto card
Mccy	Unlocks the Roger McCoy card

CARD PACK UPGRADES

Complete the game once. Load your finished game save and play through the game again. At the points where you received the card packs, they will be upgraded into newer versions.

UNLOCKABLE	HOW TO UNLOCK
Chronicle Unlimited Pack	Upgrade Chronicle Pack
MGS1 Integral Pack	Upgrade MGS1 Pack
MGS2 Substance Pack	Upgrade MGS2 Pack
MGS3 Subsistence Pack	Upgrade MGS3 Pack

UNLOCKABLE CARDS

Complete the game on any difficulty and get a certain rare card.

UNLOCKABLE	HOW TO UNLOCK
"E-Z Gun" Card	Beat 6 levels in Arena mode on Easy setting
"G36C" Card	Beat 6 levels in Arena mode on Extreme setting
"Stealth Camo" Card	Beat 6 levels in Arena mode on Normal setting
Metal Gear RAY	Beat Campaign mode twice
Metal Gear Rex	Complete game on Normal
MGS4	Complete game on Easy
Running Man Card	Complete 6 rounds in the Arena on Hard setting

METAL GEAR SOLID 4: GUNS OF THE PATRIOTS (PlayStation 3)

BONUS WEAPONS

UNLOCKABLE	HOW TO UNLOCK
Bandanna	Complete a single-player session, on any difficulty, without killing anyone (including bosses).
Desert Eagle, Long Barrel	Earn the Fox emblem on a single-player session.
Digital Camera	In the Nomad vehicle during the mission intermission; you can unlock a special photo by picking up this item in stage 4 instead of earlier.
Patriot Future Assault Weapon	Earn the Big Boss emblem on a single-player session.
Race (Ricochet) Gun	Clear the single-player game once.
Scanning Plug S	Log more than 10 hours of Metal Gear Online play time on the same profile as your Metal Gear 4 game. You purchase this from Drebin.

Solar Gun	Collect the five statues (those of the four Battle Beauties and the Frog Soldier/Haven Troopers in stage 1) using non-lethal means on their respective idols.
Stealth Item this	Complete a single-player session without instigating a single alert (caution is okay, but not alert). You can do on any difficulty.
Thor 45-70	Earn the Fox Hound emblem on a single-player session.
World War I Pistol	Earn the Hound emblem on a single-player session.

COMPLETION UNLOCKABLES

UNLOCKABLE	HOW TO UNLOCK
Big Boss Extreme Difficulty	Complete the single-player mode once (and saving the cleared data).
New Combat Vests	Clear the single-player game once.

COSTUMES

UNLOCKABLE	HOW TO UNLOCK
Altair	Obtain the Assassin emblem.
UNLOCKABLE	**HOW TO UNLOCK**
Civilian Disguise	Start Eastern Europe level.
Corpse Camo	Get 41 continues or more in a single playthrough to unlock this Octocamo.
Middle East Militia Disguise	Middle East in the Militia Safe House.
South American Rebel Disguise	South America (Cove Valley Village).
Suit	Clear the game once.

DOLLS/STATUES

UNLOCKABLE	HOW TO UNLOCK
Crying Wolf Doll/Statue	In a side of a building just where you start after killing her beast form
Frog Soldier Doll/Statue	At the garage at the end of the battle
Laughing Beast Doll/Statue	On a bed in a little room
Raging Raven Doll/Statue	On the upper floor on a corner
Screaming Mantis Doll/Statue	On the corridor where you started

FACE PAINT

UNLOCKABLE	HOW TO UNLOCK
Big Boss's	Earn the Big Boss emblem on a single-player session.
Crying Wolf	Defeat the Battle Beauty (human form) Crying Wolf by non-lethal means.
Drebin	Purchase and keep more than 60 different weapons.
FaceCamo	Defeat the Battle Beauty Laughing Octopus (the overall battle, no specifics involved).
Laughing Octopus	Defeat the Battle Beauty (human form) Laughing Octopus by non-lethal means.
Otacon	Shock Dr. Emmerich using the Metal Gear II during the intermission scene.
Raging Raven	Defeat the Battle Beauty (human form) Raging Raven by non-lethal means.
Raiden Mask A	Shock Sunny using the Metal Gear II during the intermission scene.
Raiden Mask B	Shock Dr. Naomi Hunter using the Metal Gear II during the intermission scene.
Roy Campbell	Shock Colonel Campbell using the Metal Gear II during the intermission scene.

UNLOCKABLE	HOW TO UNLOCK
Screaming Mantis	Defeat the Battle Beauty (human form) Screaming Mantis by non-lethal means.
Young Snake	Beat Act 2.
Young Snake with Bandana	Beat Act 2.

IPOD TUNES

Snake's iPod can download specific tunes throughout the course of the game. Some songs have an additional "secret" effect when it is played in the game.

UNLOCKABLE	HOW TO UNLOCK
Beyond the Bounds (increases power stun damage done by Snake from non-lethal weapons)	Stage 4 Shadow Moses, Tank Hangar. After is restored, backtrack to the upper catwalk and explore all rooms.
Big Boss (increases stun damage and increases Snake's accuracy when played)	Earn the Big Boss emblem.
Bio Hazard	Frisk the resistance fighter in Easter Europe.
Bio Hazard (cause soldiers held by Snake to scream in terror)	Stage 3 Europe, Midtown.
Boktai 2 Theme	Act 2, Mission Briefing, upstairs in the Nomad.
Bon Dance	Act 2, Marketplace.
Destiny's Call (causes soldiers held by Snake to go enraged)	A random gift from a militia or rebel soldier if Snake gives them a healing item.
Flowing Destiny (causes soldiers held by Snake to weep like a little girl)	Stage 4 Shadow Moses, Canyon. Before leaving the canyon area, examine the rocky walls for a hole hiding this item.
Fury, The (causes soldiers held by Snake to go enraged)	Stage 2 South America, Cove Valley Village. Inside the fire ravaged house.
Inorino Uta	Act 1, Mission Briefing.
Level 3 Warning	Act 1, Advent Palace.
Lunar Knights Main Theme	Act 4, Mission Briefing, upstairs in the Nomad.
Metal Gear 20 Years History: Part 2	Act 4, Warhead Storage Building B2.
Metal Gear 20 Years History: Part 3	Act 2, South America Confinement Facility. In room with beds inside the house.
Metal Gear Solid Main Theme (The Document Remix)	Act 5, under hatch to the left at the beginning of area.
MGS 4 Love Theme / Action (causes soldiers held by Snake to weep like a little girl)	A random gift from a militia or rebel soldier if Snake gives them a healing item.
On Alert	Act 3, Midtown N Sector.
One Night in Neo Kobe City (causes soldiers held by Snake to laugh)	Act 3, Midtown, hold-up PMC.
Opening—Old L.A. 2040 (increases Snake's accuracy)	Stage 4 Shadow Moses, Nuclear Warhead Storage B2. Input 78925 into Otacon's lab computer.
Policenaughts Ending (causes soldiers held by Snake to fall asleep on touch)	Stage 4 Shadow Moses, Nuclear Warhead Storage B2. Input 13462 into Otacon's lab computer.
Rock Me (increases Snake's amount of life recovered from items and other means)	Stage 2 South America, Confinement Facility. Island in the southeastern quadrant.
Sailor (increases Snake's amount of life recovered from items and other means)	Stage 2 South America, Vista Mansion. Between the east wall and a cargo container

Shin Bokura no Taiyou Theme	Act 3, Mission Briefing, upstairs in the Nomad.
Show Time (causes soldiers held by Snake to scream in terror)	A random gift from a militia or rebel soldier if Snake gives them a healing item.
Snake Eater (increase the life recovery rate of Snake through items and other actions)	Unlocked by earning all 40 game clear emblems.
Subsistence (increase Snake's accuracy)	Play at least one game of Metal Gear Online. You must start the match with at least two players.
Test Subject's Duality	Act 3, Midtown S Sector.
The Best Is Yet To Come	Act 4, Snow Field. Just before the "Disc Change" Codec scene.
The Essence of Vince	Act 3, Echo's Beacon.
The Fury	Act 2, in the Cave Valley Village in badly burned building.
Theme of Solid Snake	Act 1, Millennium Park.
Theme of Tara	Act 1, Militia Safehouse. Just before seeing the unmanned flying-bomber on the table.
Warhead Storage	Act 4, Tank Hanger. Upper floor ventilation shaft.
Yell (Dead Cell)	Act 4, Casting Facility North.
Zanzibarland Breeze	Act 1, Urban Ruins before cutscene.

UNLOCKABLE EMBLEMS

UNLOCKABLE	HOW TO UNLOCK
Ant Emblem	Shake 50 enemies for items.
Assassin's Emblem	Beat the game with 50+ knife kills, 50+ CQC holds, and 25 or less alerts.
Bear Emblem	Choke 100 enemies to death.
Bee Emblem	Use the Scanning Plug S or Syringe on 50 enemies.
Big Boss Emblem	Beat the game on the highest difficulty with no deaths, no alerts, no kills, no recovery items, no stealth suit, no bandana items, in under 5 hours.
Blue Bird Emblem	Give friendly soldiers 50 items.
Centipede	Get less than 75 alert phases, less than 250 kills, and over 25 continues.
Chicken	Get over 150 alert phases, over 500 kills, over 50 continues, use over 50 recovery items and finish the game in over 35 hours.
Cow	Activate over 100 alerts.
Crocodile	Have over 400 kills.
Eagle Emblem	Get 150 headshots.
Fox Emblem	Beat the game on Normal or higher with no deaths, 5 or less alerts, no kills, no recovery items, no stealth suit, no bandana items, in under 6 hours.
Fox Hound Emblem	Beat the game on Hard or higher with no deaths, 3 or less alerts, no kills, no recovery items, no stealth suit, no bandana items, in under 5.5 hours.
Frog Emblem	Dive or roll 200 times.
Gecko Emblem	Press against walls for a total of 1 hour.
Giant Panda Emblem	Complete the game after 30 cumulative hours of play.
Gibbon Emblem	Hold up 50 enemies.
Hawk Emblem	Be admired by 25 friendly soldiers.

UNLOCKABLE	HOW TO UNLOCK
Hog Emblem	Get 10 combat highs.
Hound Emblem	Beat the game on hard or higher with no deaths, 3 or less alerts, no kills, no recovery items, no stealth suit, no bandana items, in under 6.5 hours.
Hyena Emblem	Pick up 400 dropped weapons.
Inch Worm Emblem	Crawl on the ground for a total of 1 hour.
Jaguar	Get over 75 alert phases, less than 250 kills, and less than 25 continues.
Leopard	Get over 75 alert phases, less than 250 kills, and over 25 continues.
Little Gray Emblem	Collect all 69 weapons.
Lobster Emblem	Spend a total of 2.5 hours crouching.
Mantis	Finish the game with no alerts activated; no continues; no rations, noodles, or regains used; and in under 5 hours.
Octopus	Beat the game without activating any alert phases.
Panther	Get over 75 alert phases, over 250 kills, and less than 25 continues.
Pig	Use more than 50 recovery items.
Pigeon	Beat the game without killing a single person (Gekkos and Dwarf Gekkos don't count).
Puma	Get over 75 alert phases, over 250 kills, and over 25 continues.
Rabbit	Flick through 100 *Playboy* pages.
Rabbit Emblem	Look at 100 *Playboy* pages.
Raven	Beat the game in under 5 hours.
Scarab	Perform over 100 rolls.
Scorpion	Get less than 75 alert Phases, less than 250 kills, and less than 25 continues.
Spider	Get less than 75 alert phases, over 250 kills, and over 25 continues.
Tarantula	Get less than 75 alert phases, over 250 kills, and less than 25 continues.
Tortoise	Spend more than 60 minutes inside the drum can or cardboard box (this can be done throughout the game, not all at once),
Wolf	Beat the game with no continues and no rations, regains, or noodles used.

METAL MARINES (Wii)

CODES

CODE	EFFECT
Enter CSDV as a password	Start with more Money and Energy for each level
HBBT	Level 02
PCRC	Level 03
NWTN	Level 04
LSMD	Level 05
CLST	Level 06
JPTR	Level 07
NBLR	Level 08
PRSC	Level 09
PHTN	Level 10
TRNS	Level 11
RNSN	Level 12

ZDCP	Level 13
FKDV	Level 14
YSHM	Level 15
CLPD	Level 16
LNVV	Level 17
JFMR	Level 18
JCRY	Level 19
KNLB	Level 20

METAL SAGA (PlayStation 2)

UNLOCKABLES

Beat the game and load your save. This opens access to the Mysterious Cave where you can fight all the outlaws again.

METAL SLUG ANTHOLOGY (Wii)

UNLOCKABLES

UNLOCKABLE	HOW TO UNLOCK
Special Music	Complete Metal Slug 1-5 and X on Hard with limited continues and also complete Metal Slug 6 with limited continues
Tonko Art Gallery	Complete Metal Slug 1-5 and X on Easy with limited continues and also complete Metal Slug 6 with limited continues

MIDNIGHT CLUB 3: DUB EDITION (PSP)

Go into the Options menu, then into the Cheats menu to enter these passwords.

UNLOCKABLE	PASSWORD
Max Nitro	fillmeup
Unlock All Cities in Arcade Mode	crosscountry
Unlocks Atlanta & Detroit	roadtrip
Vehicles Take No Damage	ontheroad

MIDNIGHT CLUB 3 DUB EDITION (XBOX)

Enter these case sensitive passwords in the Cheats section under Options.

UNLOCKABLE	PASSWORD
All Cities Unlocked in Arcade Mode	crosscountry
Bunny Ears	getheadl
Chrome Body	haveyouseenthisboy
Faster Pedestrians/All Cities in Arcade Mode	urbansprawl
Flaming Head	trythisathome
Increase Car Mass in Arcade Mode	hyperagro
No Damage	ontheroad
Pumpkin Heads	getheadk
Skull Head	getheadn
Snowman Head	getheadm
Special Move Agro	dfens
Special Move Roar	Rjnr
Special Move Zone	allin
Unlock All Cities	roadtrip
Yellow Smile	getheadj

MIDNIGHT CLUB 3 DUB EDITION (PlayStation 2)

Enter these case sensitive passwords in the Cheats section under Options.

UNLOCKABLE	PASSWORD
All cities in arcade mode	crosscountry

UNLOCKABLE	PASSWORD
Bunny ears	getheadl
Chrome Body	haveyouseenthisboy
Faster pedestrians/All cities in arcade mode	urbansprawl
Flaming Head	trythisathome
Increase car mass in arcade mode	hyperagro
No damage	ontheroad
Pumpkin Heads	getheadk
Skull head	getheadn
Snowman head	getheadm
Special move Agro	dfens
Special move Roar	Rjnr
Special move Zone	allin
Unlock all cities	roadtrip
Yellow Smile	getheadj

MIGHT AND MAGIC: CLASH OF HEROES (DS)

UNLOCKABLES

As you complete each chapter in Story Mode, you will unlock the main characters' companions for use in Quick Battle and Multiplayer Modes. The new characters have new spells, as well.

UNLOCKABLE	HOW TO UNLOCK
Cyrus—Wizard—Staff of Explosia, Launches staff, which damages units it lands on, waits 3 turns, then explodes for more damage	Complete chapter 5 (Nadia)
Findan—Elf—Swift Strike, reduces charge time for all formations to 1	Complete chapter 1 (Anwen)
Jezebeth—Demon—Wall Crusher, explodes enemy walls and damages nearby units	Complete chapter 4 (Aidan)
Markal—Undead—Death March, instantly charges all Elite/Champion units	Complete chapter 3 (Fiona)
Varkas—Human—Elrath's Sword, sword tears through first two enemy rows	Complete chapter 2 (Godric)

MIGHTY BOMB JACK (Wii)

UNLOCKABLES

UNLOCKABLE	HOW TO UNLOCK
Skip Levels	To perform this trick, get to the first treasure room in Round 1. Grab any of the bombs. Immediately you see another bomb light up with a sparkle. Grab the other bombs in the treasure room, making sure to grab the lit bomb last. You're transported to the Round 2 treasure room! Use this trick to skip as many of the normal stages as you wish. However, if you lose a life in one of the treasure rooms, you're transported back to the last level you were on before entering a treasure room.

MILITARY MADNESS (Wii)

UNLOCKABLES

UNLOCKABLE	HOW TO UNLOCK
Alternate Colors	Power on the system, and hold SELECT to reset. While continuing to hold SELECT, choose the 1-player continue option and enter a map name.
Play as Axis	Select the new game or 1-player continue option on the title screen, then hold SELECT and press ①.
Switch Sides	Hold SELECT and press RUN before choosing the 1-player continue option.

PASSWORDS

PASSWORD	EFFECT
REVOLT	Level 01
ICARUS	Level 02
CYRANO	Level 03
RAMSEY	Level 04
NEWTON	Level 05
SENECA	Level 06
SABINE	Level 07
ARATUS	Level 08
GALIOS	Level 09
DARWIN	Level 10
PASCAL	Level 11
HALLEY	Level 12
BORMAN	Level 13
APOLLO	Level 14
KAISER	Level 15
NECTOR	Level 16
PASSWORD	EFFECT
MILTON	Level 17
IRAGAN	Level 18
LIPTUS	Level 19
INAKKA	Level 20
TETROS	Level 21
ARBINE	Level 22
RECTOS	Level 23
YEANTA	Level 24
MONOGA	Level 25
ATTAYA	Level 26
DESHTA	Level 27
NEKOSE	Level 28
ERATIN	Level 29
SOLCIS	Level 30
SAGINE	Level 31
WINNER	Level 32
ONGAKU	Sound Test

MILON'S SECRET CASTLE (Wii)

UNLOCKABLES

UNLOCKABLE	HOW TO UNLOCK
Continue Game	Hold down left and press START when you die after getting the first crystal

MIRROR'S EDGE (PlayStation 3)

UNLOCKABLES

Complete the game on any difficulty to unlock the "speedrun" option. This allows you to play through any chapter of the game like a time trial.

MISSION IMPOSSIBLE: OPERATION SURMA (XBOX)

UNLOCKABLE	CODE
Level Select	In the Profiles menu, highlight Jasmine Curry and press LT+RT+Ⓨ+Ⓑ. You will be able to choose your level from the Main menu.

MISTER MOSQUITO (PlayStation 2)

Enter these codes on the Selection menu. Hold L2 will entering the codes.

UNLOCKABLE	CODE
Doctor Mosquito	⇧, ⇨, ⇦, ⇩, ■, ■, R2, R2, R2
Mama Mosquito	⇧, ⇨, ⇦, ⇩, ■, ■, R1, R1, R1

MLB 06 (PlayStation 2)

Pause the game to enter this code.

UNLOCKABLE	CODE
Fart Mode	⇧,⇧,⇩,⇩,⇦,⇨,⇦,⇨

MLB 07: THE SHOW (PSP)

CODES

CODE	EFFECT
All Pitches Have Max Break	Pause during a game and enter: ⇨, ×, □, △, ×, ○, ○, △
All Pitches Have Max Speed	Pause during a game and enter: ⇧, ○, △, ×, ○, □, ○, △
Silver Era Team and Gold Era Team Unlocked	At the main menu: ⇦, ×, □, △, △, ○, ×, △

MOBILE SUIT GUNDAM: CROSSFIRE (PlayStation 3)

UNLOCKABLE	CODE
Amuro Ray	Beat EFF campaign on Very Hard mode once, and load the clear data
Char Aznable	Beat Zeon campaign on Very Hard mode once, and load the clear data
Fraw Bow	Beat any campaign on Very Hard and load the clear data
Gelgoog	Become Brigadier General and play on Very Hard mode, and just after you get the Hildolfr you should unlock the Gelgoog
Gundam	Reach the rank of Warrant General
Hildolfr	Become Brigadier General and play on Very Hard mode in early December before the unidentified enemy mission
Kai Shiden	Beat any campaign on Very Hard and load the clear data

MONSTER 4X4: WORLD CIRCUIT (Wii)

UNLOCKABLES

UNLOCKABLE	HOW TO UNLOCK
Reverse Tracks	Get first place on a track to get the same track in reverse

MONSTER MADNESS: BATTLE FOR SUBURBIA (XBOX 360)

At the pause screen press: ⇧,⇧,⇩,⇩,⇦,⇨,⇦,⇨,Ⓑ,Ⓐ. The typing console appears. Then type in the cheat.

CODE	EFFECT
patrickdugan	Animal sounds
ihatefunkycameras	Disable special tracking cameras
upthejoltcola	Faster music
MorgyTheMole	First person/headless

ArieannDeFazioWithFlair	Increase the size of Jennifer's chest
stevebrooks	Infinite secondary items
SouthPeak	Push objects away from player
reverb	Remove film grain
chipmunks	Squeaky voices

MORTAL KOMBAT: ARMAGEDDON (Wii)

KRYPT KODES (USING A GAMECUBE CONTROLLER)

Enter the following by choosing the "?" in the Krypt. Enter the Krypt and press L on the GameCube Controller 4 times and you'll see it in the bottom right corner.

CODE	EFFECT
L, →, A, R, ↑, ↑	Unlock Alternate Costume: Drahmin
↓, ↑, R, L, X, L	Unlock Alternate Costume: Frost
↓, L, ↑, L, L, →	Unlock Alternate Costume: Nitara
L, ←, ↑, X, ↑, L	Unlock Alternate Costume: Shang Tsung
↑, X, B, A, X, Y	Unlock Arena: Falling Cliffs
↑, X, R, ↑, A, A	Unlock Arena: General Reiko's Map Room
X, L, ↑, B, X, ↓	Unlock Arena: Krimson Forest
R, ←, ←, ↓, L, B	Unlock Arena: Nethership Interior
R, L, B, A, ↑, ↑	Unlock Arena: Pyramid of Argus
←, ←, X, ↑, Y, L	Unlock Arena: Shinnok's Spire
Y, B, ←, L, ←, X	Unlock Character: Blaze
L, L, Y, ↓, ↓, B	Unlock Character: Daegon
↑, B, B, X, X, ↑	Unlock Character: Meat
L, ←, ↑, ↑, X, ↓	Unlock Character: Taven
L, Y, L, L, R, B	Unlock Concept Art: Blaze
↑, A, ↑, ↓, L, A	Unlock Concept Art: Early Taven
↑, B, L, ↑, X, L	Unlock Concept Art: Firewall Arena
R, →, ↑, R, Y, ↑	Unlock Concept Art: Mileena's Car Design
Y, ←, ←, A, ↓, X	Unlock Concept Art: Pyramid Crack of Dawn
A, L, R, ↑, ↑, ↑	Unlock Concept Art: Pyramid of Argus
L, ←, ↑, X, ↑, L	Unlock Concept Art: Scorpion Throw Sketch
R, L, ←, A, ↑, R	Unlock Concept Art: Sektor's 2 Handed Pulse Blade
X, ↑, Y, ↓, X, ←	Unlock Concept Art: Unused Trap in Konquest Mode
↑, ↑, ↓, ↑, L, A	Unlock Movie: Armageddon Promo
←, L, ↑, ↓, ↑, L	Unlock Movie: Cyrax Fatality Blooper
Y, ↑, ↑, L, R, ↑	Unlock Movie: Motor Gameplay
A, B, ←, Y, B, A	Unlock Tune: Armory
L, ←, X, A, ↑, →	Unlock Tune: Lin Kuei Palace
↓, ←, ↑, L, ↑, L	Unlock Tune: Pyramid of Argus
↑, X, L, R, R, A	Unlock Tune: Tekunin Warship

KRYPT KODES (USING A WII REMOTE)

Enter the following by choosing the "?" in the Krypt. Enter the Krypt and press L on the GameCube Controller 4 times and you'll see it in the bottom right corner.

CODE	EFFECT
D-Pad Down, Nunchuk Right, D-Pad Down, Z, Nunchuk Up, Nunchuk Up	Unlock Alternate Costume: Drahmin
Nunchuk Down, Z, Z, D-Pad Down, D-Pad Right, D-Pad Down	Unlock Alternate Costume: Frost
Nunchuk Down, D-Pad Down, Nunchuk Up, D-Pad Down, D-Pad Down, Nunchuk Right	Unlock Alternate Costume: Nitara

CODE	EFFECT
✚↓, ◎←, ◎↑, ✚→, ◎↑, ✚↓	Unlock Alternate Costume: Shang Tsung
Z, ✚→, ✚←, ✚↓, ✚→, ✚↑	Unlock Arena: Falling Cliffs
Z, ✚↑, Z, ◎↑, ✚↓, ✚↓	Unlock Arena: General Reiko's Map Room
✚→, ✚↓, ◎↑, ✚←, ✚→, ◎↓	Unlock Arena: Krimson Forest
Z, ◎←, ◎←, ◎↓, ✚↓, ✚←	Unlock Arena: Nethership Interior
Z, ✚↓, ✚←, ✚↓, Z, ◎↑	Unlock Arena: Pryamid of Argus
◎←, ◎←, ✚→, ◎↑, ✚↑, ✚↓	Unlock Arena: Shinnok's Spire
✚↑, ✚←, ◎←, ✚↓, ◎←, ✚→	Unlock Character: Blaze
✚↓, ✚↓, ✚↑, ◎↓, ◎↓, ✚←	Unlock Character: Daegon
◎↑, ✚←, ✚←, ✚→, ✚→, ◎↑	Unlock Character: Meat
✚↓, ◎←, Z, ◎↑, ✚→, ◎↓	Unlock Character: Taven
✚↓, ✚↑, ✚↓, ✚↓, Z, ✚←	Unlock Concept Art: Blaze
◎↑, ✚↓, Z, ◎↓, ✚↓, ✚↓	Unlock Concept Art: Early Taven
◎↑, ✚←, ✚↓, Z, ✚→, ✚↓	Unlock Concept Art: Firewall Arena
Z, ◎→, ◎↑, Z, ✚↑, ◎↑	Unlock Concept Art: Mileena's Car Design
✚↑, ◎←, ◎←, ✚↓, ◎↓, ✚→	Unlock Concept Art: Pyramid Crack of Dawn
✚↓, ✚↓, Z, Z, ◎↑, ◎↑	Unlock Concept Art: Pyramid of Argus
✚↓, ◎←, ◎↑, ✚→, Z, ✚↓	Unlock Concept Art: Scorpion Throw Sketch
Z, ✚↓, ◎←, ✚↓, ◎↑, Z	Unlock Concept Art: Sektor's 2 Handed Pulse Blade
✚→, Z, ✚↑, ◎↓, ✚→, ◎←	Unlock Concept Art: Unused Trap in Konquest Mode
◎↑, ◎↑, ◎↓, ◎↑, ✚↓, ✚↓	Unlock Movie: Armageddon Promo
◎→, ✚↓, Z, ◎↓, ◎↑, ✚↓	Unlock Movie: Cyrax Fatality Blooper
✚↑, ◎↑, Z, ✚↓, Z, Z	Unlock Movie: Motor Gameplay
✚↓, ✚←, ◎←, ✚↑, ✚←, ✚↓	Unlock Tune: Armory
✚↓, ◎←, ✚→, ✚↓, Z, ◎→	Unlock Tune: Lin Kuei Palace
◎↓, ◎←, Z, ✚↓, ◎↑, ✚↓	Unlock Tune: Pyramid of Argus
◎↑, ✚→, ✚↓, Z, Z, ✚↓	Unlock Tune: Tekunin Warship

ALTERNATE COSTUMES

UNLOCKABLE	HOW TO UNLOCK
Ashrah's Alternate Costume	Defeat the Ice Beast you encounter in Arctika and open the chest that appears
Baraka's Alternate Costume	Kill all of the enemies in the final room of the Tekunin Warship and open the chest that appears
Bo'Rai Cho's Alternate Costume	Open the chest that appears after you defeat the Wraiths of Shinnok's Spire
Cyrax's Alternate Costume	Kill all of the enemies in the third room of the Tekunin Warship and open the chest that appears
Dairou's Alternate Costume	Open the chest at the end of the second ice hallway at the beginning of the Lin Kuei Temple Entrance
Darrius' Alternate Costume	In a chest behind a discolored wall at the beginning of the Lin Kuei Temple where you are attacked by Lin Kuei Archers
Drahmin's Alternate Costume	In the Netherrealm after you defeat Drahmin, shoot down the bat creature over the nearby cliff and open the chest that appears
Ermac's Alternate Costume	In a chest by the left wall in the room where you get attacked by the Red Commandos for the second time
Frost's Alternate Costume	Break all of the tombs lining the wall in the room where you meet Frost
Fujin's Alternate Costume	Defeat all of the Red Dragon Soldiers at the beginning of the Charred Mountain

Goro's Alternate Costume	In an invisible chest on the left side of the first area in Shao Khan's Fortress and directly to the right of a musical note
Havik's Alternate Costume	Defeat all of the demons in the second area of Shinnok's Spire
Hotaru's Alternate Costume	In a chest close to the wall in the second room of the Tekunin Warship
Hsu Hao's Alternate Costume	In a chest on the right walkway after you wake up on the Tekunin Warship
Jade's Alternate Costume	Defeat all of the Lin Kuei at the very beginning of the Lin Kuei Palace and open the chest that appears
Jarek's Alternate Costume	Open the right chest in the room where you fight with the Ice Scepter
Jax's Alternate Costume	Once you enter Arctika, turn around and go to the left to find an invisible chest
Johnny Cage's Alternate Costume	Defeat the Tengu Guards at the beginning of Arctika and open the chest that appears
Kai's Alternate Costume	In an invisible chest behind a breakable discolored wall to the right as you enter the third area of Lin Kuei Temple Entrance in Arctika
Kano's Alternate Costume	In an invisible chest to the left as you enter the last room of the Temple of Argus
Kenshi's Alternate Costume	Defeat all of the Tengu Ninjas with the given sword in Arctika
Kira's Alternate Costume	Step on the second Giant Spider in Botan Jungle and open the chest that appears
Kitana's Alternate Costume	Perform a Fatality on Wi Lae, leader of the Tengu Ninjas
Kobra's Alternate Costume	In an invisible chest behind the first monolith in the Botan Jungle
Kung Lao's Alternate Costume	Found in a chest to the right after you enter the Temple of Argus
Li Mei's Alternate Costume	In the second area of Shinnok's Spire, walk around the edge of the room until you find an invisible chest
Liu Kang's Alternate Costume	As you enter Shao Kahn's Fortress, turn around and run forward to find an invisible chest.
Mavado's Alternate Costume	Inside an invisible chest on the left part of the room where you do battle after you receive the Supermove: Time Stop
Mileena's Alternate Costume	After you defeat Mileena, hit the Ground Pound Switch in front of you and open the chest that appears
Motaro's Alternate Costume	After the third training obelisk, during the time you must gather crystals, go to the left side of this area and open the chest there
NightWolf's Alternate Costume	After you defeat the Giant Skulls in Edenia, travel up the path until all of the chests appear and open the first one on the right
Nitara's Alternate Costume	After you defeat the Undead Revenants for the first time in the Netherrealm, jump down the leftmost cliff instead of the right and open the nearby chest
Noob Saibot's Alternate Costume	Defeat all of the Shadow Ninjas the first time you encounter then in the Lin Kuei Palace and open the chest that appears
Quan Chi's Alternate Costume	Step on the rat in the tunnel after you travel through Door A1 in the Red Dragon Caverns and open the chest that appears
Raiden's Alternate Costume	When or after fighting the Shao Khan Colossus, go into the first room on the left

UNLOCKABLE	HOW TO UNLOCK
Rain's Alternate Costume	Open the chest at the end of the area in Arctika where you are attacked by Red Dragon Spies and before you meet Rain
Reiko's Alternate Costume	In a chest in Shao Khan's Fortress,; as you enter the first area with blades, travel down a hall to the left
Reptile's Alternate Costume	Defeat the Hybrid Dragons you encounter in the Red Dragon Caverns and open the chest
Sareena's Alternate Costume	Defeat Kai, Sareena, and Jatakka and open the chest that appears
Shang Tsung's Alternate Costume	At the beginning of Shao Khan's Fortress, hit the Ground Pound icon to the right and up the ramp
Shao Kahn's Alternate Costume	Open the chest that appears after you defeat Shao Khan's Statue
Shinnok's Alternate Costume	Once you get to the area in the Netherrealm with the falling rocks go to the leftmost side and open the chest
Shujinko's Alternate Costume	Hit the Ground Pound icon in one of the cells after you defeat The Executioner in Shao Khan's Dungeon
Sindel's Alternate Costume	Complete the third training obelisk
Smoke's Alternate Costume	Defeat Smoke and open the chest that appears
Sonya's Alternate Costume	In an invisible chest to the left of the gate in the area after you defeat Sonya
Stryker's Alternate Costume	Break the wall on the right of the hallway after the Shadow Stalkers, travel to the end of it, and open the chest in the left alcove
Sub-Zero's Alternate Costume	Open the chest to the right of the statue of your mother after your fight with Sub-Zero
Tanya's Alternate Costume	In Shao Khan's Dungeon, after you make it to the cell area, hit the Ground Pound icon and then go back to the third cell on the right
Taven's Alternate Costume	After you defeat the Giant Skulls in Edenia, travel up the path until all of the chests appear, and open the third one on the left

CHARACTERS

UNLOCKABLE	HOW TO UNLOCK
Blaze	Obtain 50 relics in Konquest
Daegon	Obtain 30 relics in Konquest
Meat	Obtain 10 relics in Konquest
Taven	Finish the storyline in Konquest

KONQUEST MODE UNLOCKABLE

UNLOCKABLE	HOW TO UNLOCK
+20,000 Koins	Obtain 20 relics in Konquest mode

KREATE-A-KHARACTER UNLOCKABLES

The following parts for kreate-a-kharacter are unlocked in Konquest mode.

UNLOCKABLE	HOW TO UNLOCK
Elder God Female Armor: Torso	Open the golden chest in the right path of the fork in the Red Dragon Caverns
Elder Gods Female Armor: Belt	Inside a golden chest in a locked gate in Arctika after the second obelisk that opens after you defeat the Tengu Ninjas
Elder Gods Female Armor: Boots	After the Shadow Stalkers, break the cracked wall to the left and travel down to the right alcove where you find the golden chest
Elder Gods Female Armor: Cape	Inside a golden chest in the area after you meet and defeat Sonya

Elder Gods Female Armor: Glove	Once you get to the flaming sword area of Shinnok's Spire, turn and run to your left and open the golden chest
Elder Gods Female Armor: Helmet	When or after fighting the Shao Khan Colossus, go into the second room on the right
Elder Gods Female Armor: Legs	Open the golden chest in the cave that gets opened after you defeat the undead of the Netherrealm after you get your gauntlets
Elder Gods Female Armor: Shoulders	In Shao Kahn's Dungeon, after you make it to the cell area, hit the Ground Pound icon and then go back to the first cell on the left
Elder Gods Male Armor: Belt	Inside of a golden chest to the right after you open the first door in the Tekunin Warship
Elder Gods Male Armor: Boots	After the Shadow Stalkers, break the second cracked wall on the right and travel down to the end and open the golden chest in the left alcove
Elder Gods Male Armor: Cape	When or after fighting the Shao Khan Colossus, go into the second room on the left
Elder Gods Male Armor: Glove	Inside of a golden chest after the second fallen log and to the right in Botan Jungle
Elder Gods Male Armor: Helmet	After you defeat the Giant Skulls in Edenia, travel up the path until you find a golden chest
Elder Gods Male Armor: Legs	In a golden chest in the left corner of the second area of Shinnok's Spire
Elder Gods Male Armor: Shoulders	Stand in the middle of the room after you free Shujinko, shoot a fireball at the nearby torch, and get the chest that appears
Elder Gods Male Armor: Torso	After you defeat the Tengu Leader, break open the discolored wall on the right in the blade trap area.

SOUNDTRACKS

All of the following soundtracks are unlocked in Konquest mode and found in the shape of a musical note.

UNLOCKABLE	HOW TO UNLOCK
Arctika Tune	As you enter the second area of the Lin Kuei Temple Entrance, destroy the discolored wall on the right and open the chest
Bo'Rai Cho's Brewery Tune	Get the musical note after the bridge and in the cave to the right in Botan Jungle
Botan Jungle Track Tune	Get the musical note right before the second fallen log in Botan Jungle
Goro's Lair Fight Tune	In Shujinko's cell when you release him
Hell Fight Tune	In Shao Khan's Dungeon, after you make it to the cell area, hit the Ground Pound icon and then go back to the second cell on the right
Konquest Final Battle Tune	In Shao Khan's Fortress as you run up to the first area with the blades, travel to the right to find the musical note in the next room
Lin Kuei Palace Tune	Get the musical note in the Lin Kuei Palace directly to your left after you punch down the Ice Door
Lin Kuei Raceway Tune	Get the musical note near the entrance in the final area of Arctika after you defeat all of the Lin Kuei Warriors and Archers
Lumbermill Fight Tune	Get the musical note after the second crusher when you return to Arctika after the second obelisk
Meteor Storm Fight Tune	Get the musical note after you defeat the Undead Revenants for the first time in the Netherrealm, jump down the leftmost cliff instead of the right

UNLOCKABLE	HOW TO UNLOCK
Outworld Refinery Tune	Get the musical note behind you after you fight Drahmin in the Netherrealm
Outworld Spire Fight Tune	Get the musical note on the right side of the first room as you enter Shinnok's Spire
Pyramid of Argus Tune	After you defeat the Giant Skulls in Edenia, travel up the path and find the musical note to the right of a golden chest
Reptile's Lair Fight Tune	Get the musical note in the hallway right before the final room of the Red Dragon Caverns, behind a grouping of three blue barrels
Soul Chamber Fight Tune	Once you get to the flaming sword area of Shinnok's Spire, turn around and get the musical note
Subway Fight Tune	Get the musical note after you defeat Sonya Blade in A rctika
Tekunin Prison Fight Tune	In Shao Khan's Fortress, after you open the main door and enter the second area, go to the upper left side and get the musical note
Tekunin Warship Tune	Get the musical note in the area where you get attacked by Black Dragon Thug's in the Botan Jungle
The Lost Pyramid Tune	Behind an explosive barrel in the battle after you gain the Supermove: Time Stop
Wastelands Fight Tune	On the left of the elevator you get into at the end of Shao Khan's Dungeon

UNLOCKABLE ARENAS

UNLOCKABLE	HOW TO UNLOCK
Artika Arena	Beat all 7 trials in Artika Obelisk
Edenian Ruins	After you defeat the Giant Skulls in Edenia, travel up the path until all of the chests appear and open the second one on the left
Netherrealm Cliffs	Defeat Drahmin in Konquest mode
Pyramid of Argus Arena	Collect 40 Relics in Konquest mode
Scorpion's Lair	After you defeat the Giant Skulls in Edenia,travel up the path until all of the chests appear and open the third one on the right

MORTAL KOMBAT: ARMAGEDDON (XBOX)

KRYPT KODES

Enter at the ? in the krypt.

UNLOCKABLE	HOW TO UNLOCK
Armageddon Promo Movie	Up, Up, Down, Up, WHT, A
Armory Music	A, X, Left, Y, X, A
Blaze	Y, X, Left, RT, Left, B
Concept Art Blaze	RT, Y, WHT, WHT, RT, X
Concept Art Early Taven	Up, A, WHT, Down, WHT, A
Concept Art Ed Boon Drawing	RT, Left, Up, B, WHT, RT
Concept Art Firewall Arena	Up, X, RT, WHT, B, RT
Concept Art Mileena's Car Design	WHT, Right, Up, RT, Y, Up
Concept Art Pyramid of Argus	A, RT, RT, WHT, Up, Up
Concept Art Pyramid of Argus	Y, Left, Left, A, Down, B
Concept Art Sektor's Pulse Blade	WHT, RT, Left, A, Up, RT
Concept Art Unused Konquest Trap	B, WHT, Y, Down, B, Left
Daegon	RT, RT, Y, Down, Down, X
Drahmin's Alternate Costume	WHT, Right, A, WHT, Up, Up
Ed Boon Drawing	RT, Left, Up, B, WHT, RT
Falling Cliffs Arena	WHT, B, X, A, B, Y

Frost's Alternate Costume	↓, WHT, RT, RT, B, WHT
General Reiko's Map Room Arena	WHT, Y, RT, ↑, A, A
Lin Kuei Palace Tune	WHT, ←, B, A, WHT, →
Meat	↑, X, X, B, B, ↑
Motor Gameplay Movie	Y, ↑, WHT, RT, RT, WHT
Nethership Interior Arena	RT, ←, ←, ↓, RT, X
Nitara's Alternate Costume	↓, RT, ↑, RT, RT, →
Pyramid of Argus Arena	RT, RT, X, A, WHT, ↑
Pyramid of Argus Music	↓, ←, WHT, WHT, ↑, RT
Red Dawn Arena	B, RT, ↑, X, B, ↓
Shang Tsung's Alternate Costume	RT, ←, ↑, B, ↑, WHT
Shinnok's Spire Arena	←, ←, B, ↑, Y, RT
Taven	RT, ←, WHT, ↑, B, ↓
Tekunin Warship Music	↑, B, RT, RT, A

MORTAL KOMBAT: DEADLY ALLIANCE (PlayStation 2)

UNLOCKABLE	CODE
Random Character Select	Highlight "Shang Tsung" (for player one) or "Quan Chi" (for player two) at the Character Selection screen, and then hold ↑+START.
Versus Mode Stage Select	Press R1 before either player chooses a character to get a screen with a screenshot of a stage. Press ← or → to change to the desired stage.
Versus Mode Skill Select	Press L2 before either player chooses a character.

FATALITIES!
YOU CAN DO FATALITIES FROM ANYWHERE ON SCREEN! PRESS L AT THE FINISH HIM/HER SCREEN TO CHANGE INTO YOUR FATALITY STANCE, OR YOU HAVE TO FIGURE OUT THE DISTANCE RANGE.

FATALITY	BUTTON COMBINATION
Bo Rai Cho (Belly Flop)	Press Away (x3), ↓, ●.
Cyrax (Smasher)	Press Toward (x2), ↑, ▲.
Drahmin (Iron Bash)	Press Away, Toward (x2), ↓, ×.
Frost (Freeze Shatter)	Press Toward, Away, ↑, ↓, ■.
Hsu Hao (Laser Slice)	Press Toward, Away, ↓, ↓, ▲.
Jax (Head Stomp)	Press ↓, Toward (x2), ↓, ▲.
Johnny Cage (Brain Ripper)	Press Away, Toward (x2), ↓, ▲.
Kano (Heart Grab)	Press Toward, ↑ (x2), ↓, ■.
Kenshi (Telekinetic Crush)	Press Toward, Away, Toward, ↓, ×.
Kitana (Kiss of Doom)	Press ↓, ↑, Toward (x2), ▲.
Kung Lao (Hat Throw)	Press ↓, ↑, Away, ×.
Li Mei (Crush Kick)	Press Toward (x2), ↓, Toward, ●.
Mavado (Kick Thrust)	Press Away (x2), ↑ (x2), ■.
Nitara (Blood Thirst)	Press ↑ (x2), Toward, ■.
Quan Chi (Neck Stretch)	Press Away (x2), Toward, Away, ×.
Raiden (Electrocution)	Press Away, Toward, Toward (x2), ×.
Reptile (Acid Shower)	Press ↑ (x3), Toward, ×.
Scorpion (Spear)	Press Away (x2), ↓, Away+●.
Shang Tsung (Soul Steal)	Press ↑, ↓, ↑, ↓, ▲.
Sonya (Kiss)	Press Away, Toward (x2), ↓, ▲.
Sub Zero (Spine Rip)	Press Away, Toward (x2), ↓, ×.

MORTAL KOMBAT: SHAOLIN MONKS (XBOX)

Enter to following codes for the fatalities for Kung Lao.

UNLOCKABLE	CODE
Arm Cutter	←, →, ←, ↓, Ⓧ
Body Slice Fatality	→, →, →, →, Ⓧ
Buzzsaw Fatality	→, →, ↑, ↑, Ⓧ
Friendly Rabbit Fatality	↑, ↑, ↑, ↓, Ⓧ
Hat Control Mutality	←, →, →, ←, Ⓨ
Head Toss Fatality	←, →, ←, ←, Ⓧ
Headache Fatality	↑, ↓, ↑, →, Ⓧ
Many Chops Fatality	↑, ↑, ←, ↑, Ⓧ
Mid-Air Slice Fatality	↑, ↑, ↑, →, Ⓧ
Razor Edge Brutality	←, ←, ↑, ↑, Ⓑ
Tornado Mutality	↑, →, ↓, ←, Ⓨ

Enter to following codes for the fatalities for Liu Kang.

UNLOCKABLE	CODE
Arm Rip Fatality	↓, ←, →, ↑, Ⓧ
Bonebreak Fatality	←, ↑, ↑, →, Ⓧ
Dragon Fatality	↓, →, ←, ←, Ⓧ
Dragon's Fury Mutality	←, →, ↑, ↑, Ⓨ
Fire Trails Mutality	↑, ↓, ↑, ↓, Ⓨ
Fire/Kick Combo Fatality	←, →, ↓, ↓, Ⓧ
Flipping Uppercut Fatality	↑, →, ↓, ←, Ⓧ
Headclap Fatality	→, ↑, →, ↑, Ⓧ
Rage Mode Brutality	→, ↑, ↓, ↓, Ⓑ
Shaolin Soccer Fatality	↓, ←, ↑, →, Ⓧ
Stomp Fatality	←, ←, ←, ↑, Ⓧ

Enter these codes at the Main menu.

UNLOCKABLE	CODE
Mortal Kombat 2	Ⓧ, ↑, ↓, →, ←, (RT), Ⓧ
Scorpion	Ⓧ, ↑, (LT), (RT), ←, →, Ⓧ
Sub-Zero	Ⓧ, ↓, ↑, (LT), (LT), ↑, Ⓧ

MORTAL KOMBAT VS. DC UNIVERSE (XBOX 360)

UNLOCKABLES

Both of these characters can be unlocked by beating story mode with a certain side. Hold down (RB) on character select.

UNLOCKABLE	HOW TO UNLOCK
Darkseid	Beat the DC side of story mode.
Shao Kahn	Beat the MK side of story mode.

MORTAL KOMBAT VS. DC UNIVERSE (PlayStation 3)

UNLOCKABLES

Both of these characters can be unlocked by beating story mode with a certain side. To play as these characters, hold down R1 on character select.

UNLOCKABLE	HOW TO UNLOCK
Darkseid	Beat the DC side of story mode.
Shao Kahn	Beat the MK side of story mode.

MOTO ROADER (Wii)

UNLOCKABLES

UNLOCKABLE	HOW TO UNLOCK
Get $50,000	Hold SELECT and press ② on the Course Selection screen
Music Select	Hold SELECT and press ① or ② while the game is paused
See Winning Time	Hold SELECT and press ➡ (D-pad right) on the Course Selection screen
Special Course	Hold SELECT and press ⬅ (D-pad left) on the Course Selection screen
Sound Test	Input MUSIC or ART88 as a player name

MOTOCROSS MANIA 3 (XBOX)

Enter these codes at the Main menu.

UNLOCKABLE	CODE
All bike upgrades	Up, Left, Down, Right, Up, Down, Down, Left, Down, Ⓧ
All bikes	Up, Left, Down, Right, Up, Left, Down, Up, Ⓧ
All levels	Up, Left, Down, Right, Up, Left, Down, Left, Left, Ⓧ
All weapons	Up, Left, Down, Right, Up, Left, Down, Left, Down, Ⓧ

MOTOR MAYHEM (PlayStation 2)

DESCRIPTION	CODE
Buzzsaw as a playable character	Beat the Deathmatch, Endurance, and Eliminator modes with the same character on either Hard or Very Hard difficulty.

MOTORSTORM (PlayStation 3)

Enter this code at the main menu.

UNLOCKABLE	CODE
Unlock Everything	Hold L1, L2, R1, R2, R2 pushed up, L2 pushed down

Enter this code while the game is paused.

UNLOCKABLE	CODE
Big Head on ATVs and Bikes	Hold L1, L2, R1, R2, R2 pushed right, L1 pushed left

MURAKUMO (XBOX)

UNLOCKABLE	OBJECTIVE
Expert mission	Complete scenario mode with all missions at A rank.
Free mission	Beat Scenario mode.
Sound Test mode	Beat Expert mode all with double S ranks.
"Special Art"	Beat expert mode with any rank.

MVP BASEBALL (PSP)

Under the "My MVP" menu, create a player named "Dan Carter." Once you do this, there will be a message indicating that the code was successful.

MX UNLEASHED (XBOX)

UNLOCKABLE	OBJECTIVE
All Bonuses	Enter clappedout under Career Completion in the cheats section.

MX UNLEASHED (PlayStation 2)

Go to Options and select Cheat Codes. Pick the cheat you want and press ● to enter the code.

UNLOCKABLE	CODE
500cc Bikes	BIGDOGS
50cc Bikes	SQUIRRELDOG

UNLOCKABLE	CODE
A.I. Bowling	WRECKINGBALL
All Bonuses/ Completion	CLAPPEDOUT
All Machines	MINIGAMES
Expert A.I.	OBTGOFAST
Freestyle Tracks	BUSTBIG
National Tracks	ECONATION
Pro Physics	SWAPPIN
Supercross Tracks	STUPERCROSS

MX VS. ATV UNLEASHED (XBOX)

Enter the codes in the Cheat menu.

UNLOCKABLE	CODE
50cc Bikes	Minimoto
All Freestyle Tracks	Huckit
Everything	Toolazy

MX VS. ATV UNLEASHED (PlayStation 2)

Enter in the Cheats menu.

UNLOCKABLE	CODE
50cc Bikes	Minimoto
Unlock all freestyle tracks	Huckit
Unlock Everything	Toolazy

MX VS. ATV UNTAMED (XBOX 360)

UNLOCKABLES

Type in the following codes in the cheats menu to unlock the gear.

UNLOCKABLE	HOW TO UNLOCK
All Handlebars	NOHANDS
FOX Riding Gear	CRAZYLIKEA

MX VS. ATV UNTAMED (PlayStation 3)

UNLOCKABLES

Type the following codes in the Cheats menu to unlock the gear.

UNLOCKABLE	HOW TO UNLOCK
All Handlebars	NOHANDS
FOX Riding Gear	CRAZYLIKEA

MX VS. ATV UNTAMED (Wii)

CODES

Go to the Options screen and go to the Cheat Code input screen.

EFFECT	CODE
1 Million Store Points	MANYZEROS
50cc Bike Class	LITTLEGUY
All Bikes	ONRAILS
All Challenges	MORESTUFF
All Gear	WELLDRESSED
All Machines	MCREWHEELS
All Riders	WHOSTHAT
Freestyle Tracks	FREETICKET
Paralyzer Monster Truck	PWNAGE
Unlock Everything	YOUGOTIT

MX VS. ATV UNTAMED (PlayStation 2)

UNLOCKABLES

Type in the following codes in the Cheats menu to unlock the gear.

UNLOCKABLE	HOW TO UNLOCK
All Handlebars	NOHANDS
FOX Riding Gear	CRAZYLIKEA

MYSIMS (Wii)

CODES

While running around town, pause the game, then push the following buttons on the Wiimote to get to the hidden password system: ②,①,↓,↑,↓,↑,←,←,→,→. A keyboard appears to allow you to type in the following case-sensitive codes.

UNLOCKABLE	HOW TO UNLOCK
Bunk Bed (Furniture)	F3nevr0
Camouflage Pants	N10ng5g
Diamond Vest (Outfit)	Tglg0ca
Genie Outfit	Gvsb3k1
Hourglass Couch	Ghtymba
Kimono Dress (Outfit)	I3hkdvs
Modern Couch	T7srhca
Racecar Bed (Furniture)	Ahvmrva
Rickshaw Bed	Itha7da
White Jacket	R705aan

TOOLS

Once you reach a certain level, you get a message saying you've earned the following new tools.

UNLOCKABLE	HOW TO UNLOCK
Blow Torch	Have your town reach four stars.
Crowbar	Have your town reach one star.
Pickaxe	Have your town reach three stars.
Saw	Have your town reach two stars.
Town Monument Blueprint	Have a five-star town.

UBER-SIMS

After getting your interest level to 100% in any of the six categories, you get a message about a special guest waiting for you in the hotel. Check the next day and find the following Sims.

UNLOCKABLE	HOW TO UNLOCK
Amazing Daryl	100% Fun Town
Chancellor Ikara	100% Tasty Town
Hopper	100% Cute Town
Mel	100% Spooky Town
Samurai Bob	100% Studious Town
Star	100% Geeky Town

MYSIMS AGENTS (Wii)

LEVEL SELECT

Do the specified objectives to gain a new recruit for your HQ. This can involve completing a part of a game, doing dispatch missions, etc.

UNLOCKABLE	HOW TO UNLOCK
Annie Radd	Complete dispatch mission "Roadie Despair."
Beebee	Complete the Snowy Mountains level.
Elmira Clamp	Complete dispatch mission "Assistant Librarian."

UNLOCKABLE	HOW TO UNLOCK
Gonk	Complete dispatch mission "Gonk Need Food, Badly."
Gordon	Complete the Boudreaux Mansion level.
Hopper	Complete dispatch mission "Tainted Broth."
King Mike	Complete the Jungle Temple level.
Leaf	During Evelyn's house robbery case, dig around one of the holes west of the Forest Park. If you dig in the right hole, Leaf will be found.
Liberty	Complete dispatch mission "Snake on the Loose!"
Lyndsay	Complete the Jungle Temple level.
Madame Zoe	Complete the Boudreaux Mansion level.
Magellan	Complete the Jungle Temple level.
Makoto	Complete dispatch missions "High School Yearbook" and "Prom Date."
Marlon	Complete dispatch missions "Magical Assistant" and "Magical Disaster."
Master Aran	Complete dispatch mission "Penguin Style."
Ms. Nicole Vogue	Complete the Boudreaux Mansion level.
Petal	Complete dispatch mission "Failing Forest."
Pinky	Complete dispatch mission "Blue Thing!"
Preston Winthrop	Complete the Snowy Mountains level.
Professor Nova	Complete the Snowy Mountains level.
Renée	Complete dispatch mission "Pig, Camera, Action!"
Roger	Complete the Evelyn robbery case.
Rosalyn P. Marshall	Complete the Snowy Mountains level.
Sir Spencer	Complete dispatch mission "H4XXOR3D!"
Sir Vincent Skullfinder	Complete the Jungle Temple level.
Star	Complete dispatch mission "Blade of Destiny."
Travis	Available to recruit by default once you become a special agent.
Trevor Verily	Complete the Boudreaux Mansion level.
Vic Vector	Complete the Snowy Mountains level.
Violet Nightshade	Complete the Boudreaux Mansion level.
Wendalyn	Complete dispatch mission "Reagent Run."
Wolfah	Complete the Snowy Mountains level.
Zombie Carl	Complete the Boudreaux Mansion level.

MYSIMS KINGDOM (Wii)

CODES

From the Pause menu enter the following codes to get the desired effect.

EFFECT	CODE
Detective outfit	←,→,←,→,←,→
Tattoo Vest outfit	Ⓒ,Ⓩ,Ⓒ,Ⓩ,Ⓑ,Ⓐ,Ⓑ,Ⓐ
Swordsman outfit	↓,↑,↓,↑,↓,↑,↓,↑

MYSIMS PARTY (Wii)

UNLOCKABLES

UNLOCKABLE	HOW TO UNLOCK
New inhabitants	Get at least 60 points in the minigame they're hosting.
New playable characters	Get at least 80 points in the minigame they're hosting.

MYSIMS RACING (Wii)

CODES

From the main menu go to Extras, then to Cheats. After entering the code a message will appear telling you that a new car part has been unlocked. Go to "Story Mode" and enter the garage to equip your new car part.

EFFECT	CODE
Unlocks Butterflies (Wheels)	z74hsv
Unlocks Holstein (Hood Ornament)	36mj5v
Unlocks Mega Spoiler (Rear Accessory)	k4c2sn

MY STREET (PlayStation 2)

DESCRIPTION	CODE
Custom Body Parts	Beat Story Mode once.

N+ (DS)

CODES

Hold Ⓛ and Ⓡ and insert the following code at the Unlockables menu.

EFFECT	CODE
Unlocks Atari Bonus Levels	Ⓐ,Ⓑ,Ⓐ,Ⓑ,Ⓐ,Ⓐ,Ⓑ

N+ (PSP)

CODES

Hold Ⓛ and Ⓡ and insert the following code at the Unlockables menu.

EFFECT	CODE
Unlocks Atari Bonus Levels	×,●,×,●,×,×,●

NAMCO MUSEUM ESSENTIALS (PlayStation 3)

DIG DUG UNLOCKABLES

UNLOCKABLE	HOW TO UNLOCK
Carrot	Grab the Carrot.
Complete Dig	Successfully dig the whole entire level.
Cucumber	Grab the Cucumber.
Eggplant	Grab the Eggplant.
Green Pepper	Grab the Green Pepper.
Mushroom	Grab the Mushroom.
No Dig	Complete the level without digging.
Pineapple	Grab the Pineapple.
Quad Squash	Successfully squash four enemies with one rock.
Tomato	Grab the Tomato.
Turnip	Grab the Turnip.
Watermelon	Grab the Watermelon.

DRAGON SPIRIT UNLOCKABLES

UNLOCKABLE	HOW TO UNLOCK
Earthquake	Collect the Earthquake power-up.
Endurance	Successfully survive against a boss under a timed limit without killing him.
Fire Breath	Collect the Fire Breath power-up.
Homing Fire	Collect the Homing Fire power-up.
Incubation	Collect the Incubation power-up.
Maximum	Successfully get three heads and six fire power orbs without getting hit.
Over The Jungle	Get to the Jungle Area.
Power Down	Collect the Power Down power-up.
Power Wing	Collect the Power Wing power-up.
Small Dragon	Collect the Small Dragon power-up.
Small N Wide	Collect the Small Dragon, followed by Wide Fire without getting hit.
Wide Fire	Collect the Wide Fire power-up.

GALAGA UNLOCKABLES

UNLOCKABLE	HOW TO UNLOCK
Blue Spaceship	Destroy the Blue Spaceship.
Boss Alien	Destroy the Boss Alien.
Destroy Fighter	Successfully destroy your captured ship.
Dragonfly	Destroy the Dragonfly.
Dual Fighter	Successfully destroy the enemy holding your ship captive.
Maple	Destroy the Maple.
Perfect	Win a perfect game in the Challenging Stage.
Scorpion	Destroy the Scorpion.
Stage 10	Reach Stage 10.
Stage 20	Reach Stage 20.
Stage 30	Reach Stage 30.
Stingray	Destroy the Stingray.

PAC-MAN STAMPS

UNLOCKABLE	HOW TO UNLOCK
1600	Eat all the ghosts after eating a single Power Pellet.
1600X2	Do the above task twice in one round.
Apple	Eat the Apple that appears in Round 5 or 6.
Bell	Eat the Bell that appears in Round 11 or 12.
Big Eater	Beat Round 21.
Cherry	Eat the Cherry that appears in Round 1.
Galboss	Eat the Galboss that appears in Round 9 or 10.
Intermediate	Beat Round 5.
Key	Eat the Key that appears after Round 13.
Melon	Eat the Melon that appears in Round 7 or 8.
Orange	Eat the Orange that appears in Round 3 or 4.
Strawberry	Eat the Strawberry that appears in Round 2.

TROPHIES

Complete each requirement to get the specified Trophy. There are 5 Bronze Trophies, 5 Silver Trophies and 1 Gold Trophy.

UNLOCKABLE	HOW TO UNLOCK
Dig Dug Rookie (Bronze)	Obtained four Dig Dug stamps.
Dig Dug Veteran (Silver)	Obtained all Dig Dug stamps.
Dragon Spirit Rookie (Bronze)	Obtained four Dragon Spirit stamps.
Dragon Spirit Veteran (Silver)	Obtained all Dragon Spirit stamps.
Galaga Rookie (Bronze)	Obtained four Galaga stamps.
Galaga Veteran (Silver)	Obtained all Galaga stamps.
Pac-Man Rookie (Bronze)	Obtained four Pac-Man stamps.
Pac-Man Veteran (Silver)	Obtained all Pac-Man stamps.
Xevious Resurrection Veteran (Gold)	Obtained all Xevious Resurrection stamps.
Xevious Rookie (Bronze)	Obtained four Xevious stamps.
Xevious Veteran (Silver)	Obtained all Xevious stamps.

XEVIOUS RESURRECTION UNLOCKABLES

UNLOCKABLE	HOW TO UNLOCK
100 Items	Collected 100 shield items.
4 At Once	Successfully destroy four ground enemies with one bomb.
All Clear	Destroyed the Final Boss.

UNLOCKABLE	HOW TO UNLOCK
Boss 12 Clear	Destroyed the Level 12 Boss.
Boss 9 Clear	Destroyed the Level 9 Boss.
Enemy Collector	Successfully shot or bombed all enemies.
Free Play	Play Xevious Resurrection 50 times.
Laser Cancel 100	Used your shields against lasers 100 times.
No Shield Clear	Successfully clear a level without using your shields.
No Weapon Clear	Successfully clear a level without shooting and bombing.
Sol Discovered	Successfully found the hidden Sol Citadel.
SP Flag Found	Successfully found the hidden SP Flag.

XEVIOUS UNLOCKABLES

UNLOCKABLE	HOW TO UNLOCK
Ace Pilot	Destroy 500 air enemies in a single playthrough.
Andor Genesis	See Andor Genesis at end of Area 4.
Area 16	Reach Area 16.
Area 4	Reach Area 4.
Area 8	Reach Area 8.
Backfire	Destroy an enemy while another one is behind your ship.
Blaster Master	Destroy 100 ground enemies in a single playthrough.
Destroy Grobda	Destroy one of the tanks that moves when shot at.
Full Destruction	Destroy every part of the Andor Genesis before defeating it.
Sheonite	See Sheonite at the end of Area 9.
Sol Citadel	Find a Sol Citadel.
Special Flag	Find a special flag.

NANO BREAKER (PlayStation 2)

Enter code during game.

UNLOCKABLE	CODE
Mini Map Shooter	⇧, ⇧, ⇩, ⇩, ⇦, ⇨, ⇦, ⇦, ⇦, ⇨, ×, ●.

NARUTO: CLASH OF NINJA REVOLUTION (Wii)

CHARACTERS

To unlock the following characters, beat the Mission mode at least once, then do the following:

UNLOCKABLE	HOW TO UNLOCK
Gaara	Beat Single Player mode with Naruto and Shikamaru.
Guy	Clear Mission 13.5.
Hinata Hyuuga	Beat Single Player mode with Neji.
Ino Yamanaka	Beat Single Player mode with Sakura.
Itachi Uchiha	Beat Mission "Rematch Itachi vs. Saskue," after unlocking all other starting characters plus Guy and Kankuro.
Kankuro	Clear Mission mode once.
Kisame	Beat Single Player mode with Naruto, Sasuke, Kakashi, Guy, and Jiraiya.
Orochimaru	Beat Single Player mode with Naruto, Sasuke, Kakashi, and Jiraiya.
Shino Aburame	Beat Arcade mode with Kankuro.
Temari	Beat Shikamaru's Single Player mode.
Tenten	Clear Mission 20.
Tsunade	Beat Single Player mode with Jiraiya.

NASCAR 08 (XBOX 360)

PASSWORDS

PASSWORD	EFFECT
checkered flag	All Chase mode cars unlocked
ea sports car	Unlocks the EA Sports car
race the pack	Unlocks the fantasy drivers
Walmart Everyday	Unlocks the Walmart car and track

NASCAR 08 (PlayStation 3)

PASSWORDS

Submit these cheats at the Cheat Code screen under Options at the main menu.

PASSWORD	EFFECT
checkered flag	Unlock all chase mode cars
EA SPORTS CAR	Unlock EA SPORTS CAR
race the pack	Unlock fantasy drivers
walmart everyday	Unlock Wal-Mart car and track

NASCAR 08 (PlayStation 3)

PASSWORDS

Submit these cheats at the Cheat Code screen under Options at the main menu.

PASSWORD	EFFECT
checkered flag	Unlock all chase mode cars
EA SPORTS CAR	Unlock EA SPORTS CAR
race the pack	Unlock fantasy drivers
walmart everyday	Unlock Wal-Mart car and track

NASCAR 09 (XBOX 360)

CODES

EFFECT	CODE
Unlocks All Fantasy Drivers	CHECKERED FLAG
Unlocks Walmart Track (Chicago Pier) and the Walmart Car	Walmart Everyday

NASCAR KART RACING (Wii)

CODES

EFFECT	CODE
Joey Logano as a driver	426378

NBA 07 (PlayStation 3)

To enter these passwords, select Options, then Trophy Room and then select Team Jerseys. While in Team Jerseys, press ■ to enter these passwords.

UNLOCKABLE	PASSWORD
Charlotte Bobcats Secondary Road Uniform	JKL846ETK5
New Jersey Nets Secondary Road Uniform	NB79D965D2
Utah Jazz Secondary Road Uniform	228GG7585G
Washington Wizards Secondary Road Uniform	PL5285F37F

NBA 09: THE INSIDE (PlayStation 3)

UNLOCK NEW JERSEYS

From Main Menu choose Progression, go to Extras, then Jerseys, press left or right to get to nba.com tab and press Square to enter code.

UNLOCKABLE	CODE
Eastern All-Stars 09 Jersey	SHPNV2K699
L.A. Lakers Latin Night Jersey	NMTWCTC84S
Miami Heat Latin Night Jersey	WCTGSA8SPD
Phoenix Suns Latin Night Jersey	LKUTSENFJH
San Antonio Spurs Latin Night Jersey	JFHSY73MYD
Western All-Stars 09 Jersey	K8AV6YMLNF

NBA 2K6 (XBOX 360)

Enter these passwords in the Codes menu from the Features menu.

UNLOCKABLE	PASSWORD
2K Sports Team	2KSPORTS
Air Zoom Kobe 1 Shoes	KOBE
Alt. All-Star Team Jerseys	fanfavorites
Boston, New York and Chicago St. Patricks Day Jerseys	gogreen
Celebrity Players Unlocked in 24/7 Mode	ballers
Champagne Uniform	sac 2nd
Dark Blue Uniform	den 2nd
Green Uniform	bos 2nd
Lebron James Summer Shoes	lebronsummerkicks
Lebron's Allstar shoes	lb allstar
Lebron's Birthday Shoes	lb bday
Lebron's Black and Crimson shoes	lb crimsonblack
Lebron's White and Gold shoes	lb whitegold
Navy Blue Uniform	cle 2nd
NBA 2K6 Team	NBA2K6
New Indiana Pacers Jerseys	31andonly
Nike Shoes	anklebreakers Uptempo
Red Pistons Uniform	det 2nd
Unlocks Chicago Bulls Throwback	chi retro
Unlocks Houston Rockets Throwback	hou retro
Unlocks L.A. Clippers Throwback	lac retro
Unlocks Memphis Grizzlies Throwback	mem retro
Unlocks Miami Heat Throwback	mia retro
Unlocks New Jersey Nets Throwback	nj retro
Unlocks New Orleans Hornets Throwback	no retro
Unlocks New York Knicks Throwback	ny retro
Unlocks Orlando Magic Throwback	orl retro
Unlocks Phoenix Suns Throwback	phx retro
Unlocks Seattle Sonics Throwback	sea retro
Unlocks Shawn Marions signature shoes "MTX"	crazylift
Unlocks Washington Wizards Throwback	was retro
Visual Concepts Team	vcteam

Enter these passwords at the Vending Machine located in "The Crib".

UNLOCKABLE	PASSWORD
+10 defensive awareness	lockdown
+10 offensive awareness	getaclue
No quick game fatigue	nrgmax
No quick game injuries	noinjury
Power bar tattoo in the create player mode	pbink

NBA 2K6 (XBOX)

From the Main menu, go to "Features," then "Codes" to enter the following codes.

UNLOCKABLE	CODE
2005-2006 Pacers Uniform	31andonly
2K Sports Team	2ksports
Nike Up Tempo Pro Shoes	anklebreakers
Nike Zoom Kobe 1 Shoes	kobe

From the Main menu, go to "Features," then "THE CRIB." Go to the PowerBar vending machine and enter the following codes.

UNLOCKABLE	CODE
+10 Bonus for Defensive Awareness	lockdown
+10 Bonus for Offensive Awareness	getaclue
Max Durability	noinjury
Powerbar Tattoo	pbink
Unlimited Stamina	nrgmax
Unlock All Items	criball

NBA 2K7 (XBOX 360)

Enter these passwords in the Codes menu under Features.

UNLOCKABLE	CODE
ABA Ball	payrespect
Defensive Awareness	getstops
Maximum Durability for One Game	ironman
Offensive Awareness	inthezone
All-Star Uniforms	syt6cii
Bobcats Secondary	bcb8sta
Jazz Secondary	zjb3lau
Nets Secondary	nrd4esj
Wizards Secondary	zw9idla
St. Patrick Day uniforms	tpk7sgn
International All-Stars	tns9roi
NBA 2K Team	bestsim
Superstar Team	rta1spe
Topps 2K Sports All-Stars	topps2ksports
2007 All-Star Ball	ply8mia
2007 All-Star Uniforms	syt6cii
New Orleans Hornets Uniforms (Valentine's Day)	vdr5lya

NBA 2K7 (PlayStation 3)

Enter these passwords in the Codes menu under Features.

UNLOCKABLE	CODE
ABA Ball	payrespect
Defensive Awareness	getstops
Maximum Durability for One Game	ironman
Offensive Awareness	inthezone
Unlimited Stamina for One Game	norest
All-Star Uniforms	syt6cii
UNLOCKABLE	CODE
Bobcats Secondary	bcb8sta
Jazz Secondary	zjb3lau
Nets Secondary	nrd4esj

UNLOCKABLE	CODE
Wizards Secondary	zw9idla
St. Patrick Day Uniforms	tpk7sgn
International All-Stars	tns9roi
NBA 2K Team	bestsim
Superstar Team	rta1spe
Topps 2K Sports All-Stars	topps2ksports
2007 All-Star Ball	ply8mia
2007 All-Star Uniforms	syt6cii
New Orleans Hornets Uniforms (Valentine's Day)	vdr5lya

NBA 2K8 (XBOX 360)

UNLOCKABLES

Go to the Features menu and select the Codes section to enter the following codes.

UNLOCKABLE	HOW TO UNLOCK
2008 All Star Jerseys	haeitgyebs
2K Sports Team	2ksports
ABA Ball	payrespect
Bobcats Racing Uniforms	agtaccsinr
Pacers' Secondary Road Uniforms	cpares
NBA Development Team	nba2k
St. Patrick's Day Uniforms	uclerehanp
Superstars Team	llmohffaae
Valentine's Day Uniforms	amcnreo
Visual Concepts team	vcteam

ACHIEVEMENTS

UNLOCKABLE	HOW TO UNLOCK
3 Online Ranked Streak (15)	Win three online ranked games in a row.
3-For-All (20)	Make at least 10 three-point FGs while shooting at least 45% from three-point range with any team.
3pt Shootout (25)	Win the three-point shootout.
5 Online Ranked Streak (20)	Win five online ranked games in a row.
5 Online Ranked Wins (15)	Win five online ranked games.
10 Online Ranked Wins (25)	Win 10 online ranked games.
15 Blocks (20)	Record 15 blocks or more with any team.
15 Steals (20)	Record 15 steals or more with any team.
15 Threes (15)	Make 15 three-pointers or more with any team.
20 Online Ranked Wins (35)	Win 20 online ranked games.
30 Assists (20)	Record 30 assists or more with any team.
2K Beats Playlist (10)	Create a 2K Beats playlist.
All-Heart (15)	Start the fourth period losing by 10 or more points and win the game with any team.
All-Hustle (15)	Record at least 10 offensive rebounds, five blocks, and five steals with any team.
Allen Iverson (25)	Record at least 30 points, 10 assists, and five steals with Allen Iverson.
Carmelo Anthony (25)	Record at least 40 points and eight rebounds with Carmelo Anthony.
Chris Bosh (25)	Record at least 30 points, 15 rebounds, and two blocks with Chris Bosh.

Chris Paul (25)	Record at least 25 points, 10 assists, and five steals with Chris Paul.
Create Player (10)	Use the Create Player feature.
Defensive FG% (15)	Hold the opposing team's FG% below 40% with any team.
Dwight Howard (25)	Record at least 20 points, 15 rebounds, and five blocks with Dwight Howard.
Dwyane Wade (25)	Record at least 30 points, nine rebounds, and nine assists with Dwyane Wade.
East vs. West (15)	User-controlled team must win this matchup on All-Star difficulty.
Gilbert Arenas (25)	Record at least 35 points, five steals, and five threes with Gilbert Arenas.
Good Hands (20)	Record 20 assists with no more than five turnovers with any team.
Ice Water (15)	FT% over 85% with at least 15 FTAs with any team.
Inside Domination (20)	Score at least 60 points in the paint with any team.
Kevin Garnett (25)	Record at least 25 points, 15 rebounds, and seven assists with Kevin Garnett.
Kobe Bryant (25)	Record at least 40 points, five rebounds, and five assists with Kobe Bryant.
Kobe Bryant Dunk-Off (35)	Defeat Kobe Bryant in a Dunk-Off.
Lakers vs. Clippers (15)	User-controlled team must win this matchup on All-Star difficulty.
LeBron James (25)	Record at least 35 points, seven rebounds, and seven assists with LeBron James.
Lights Out (15)	FG% over 55% for the game (minimum 40 FGAs) with any team.
Lockdown (20)	Record at least 10 blocks and 10 steals with any team.
Online Draft League (10)	Participate in an online draft.
Online League Game (15)	Complete an online league game.
Online Ranked Game (15)	Win one online ranked game.
Online Ranked NBA Blacktop Game (15)	Win one online ranked NBA Blacktop game.
Online Tournament Game (15)	Complete an online tournament game.
Pistons vs. Heat (15)	User-controlled team must win this matchup on All-Star difficulty.
Rebound Margin +7 (20)	Win the rebound battle by a margin of +7 with any team.
Second Unit (15)	Score at least 40 bench points with any team.
Sprite Slam Dunk (35)	Win the Sprite Slam Dunk Contest using LeBron James.
Spurs vs. Mavericks (15)	User-controlled team must win this matchup on All-Star difficulty.
Steve Nash (25)	Record at least 20 points and 15 assists with Steve Nash.
Suns vs. Lakers (15)	User-controlled team must win this matchup on All-Star difficulty.
Suns vs. Mavericks (15)	User-controlled team must win this matchup on All-Star difficulty.
Track Meet (15)	Score at least 15 fastbreak points with any team.
UNLOCKABLE	**HOW TO UNLOCK**
Trivia (35)	Answer 30 trivia questions correctly.
Yao Ming (25)	Record at least 30 points, 15 rebounds, and five blocks with Yao Ming.

NBA 2K8 (PlayStation 3)

UNLOCKABLES

Go to the Features menu and select the Codes section to enter the following codes.

UNLOCKABLE	HOW TO UNLOCK
2008 All-Star NBA Uniforms	haeitgyebs
2K Sports Team	2ksports
ABA Ball	payrespect
Bobcats Racing	agtaccsin
Bobcats Racing Uniform	agtaccsinr
NBA Development Team	nba2k
Pacers' Second Jersey	cpares
St. Patrick's Day Jerseys	uclerehanp
Valentine's Day Jerseys	amcnreo
Visual Concepts Team	vcteam

NBA 2K8 (PlayStation 2)

UNLOCKABLES

Go to the Features menu and select the Codes section to enter the following codes.

UNLOCKABLE	HOW TO UNLOCK
2K Sports Team	2ksports
ABA Ball	payrespect
CHA "Race Day" Uniform	agtaccsinr
IND Alternate Uniform	cpares
NBA Development Team	nba2k
St. Patrick's Day Uniforms (CHI/BOS/NY/TOR)	uclerehanp
Valentine's Day Uniforms (CLE/SEA)	amcnreo
Visual Concepts Team	vcteam

NBA 2K10 (XBOX 360)

CODES

Go into the Options menu and select the Codes section to enter these codes.

EFFECT	CODE
2K Sports team	2ksports
ABA ball	payrespect
Blazers "Rip City" Jersey	ycprtii
Cavs, Jazz, Magic, Raptors, T'Wolves, Trail Blazers, Warriors Hardwood Classic Jerseys Unlocked	wasshcicsl
Grizzlies, Hawks, Mavericks, and Rockets secondary road jerseys	eydonscar
Unlock the 2K China team	2kchina
Unlock the 2K development team	nba2k
Unlock visual concepts team	vcteam

NBA 2K10 (PlayStation 3)

CODES

Go into the Options menu and select the Codes section to enter these codes.

EFFECT	CODE
2K Sports team	2ksports
ABA ball	payrespect
Blazers "Rip City" Jersey	ycprtii

Cavs, Jazz, Magic, Raptors, T'Wolves, Trail Blazers, Warriors Hardwood Classic Jerseys Unlocked	wasshcicsl
Grizzlies, Hawks, Mavericks, and Rockets secondary road jerseys	eydonscar
Unlock the 2K China team	2kchina
Unlock the 2K development team	nba2k
Unlock visual concepts team	vcteam

NBA 2K10 (Wii)

CODES

Go into the Options menu and select the Codes section to enter these codes.

EFFECT	CODE
2K Sports team	2ksports
ABA ball	payrespect
Blazers "Rip City" Jersey	ycprtii
Cavs, Jazz, Magic, Raptors, T'Wolves, Trail Blazers, Warriors Hardwood Classic Jerseys Unlocked	wasshcicsl
Grizzlies, Hawks, Mavericks, and Rockets secondary road jerseys	eydonscar
Unlock the 2K China team	2kchina
Unlock the 2K development team	nba2k
Unlock visual concepts team	vcteam

NBA BALLERS: CHOSEN ONE (XBOX 360)

ACHIEVEMENTS

UNLOCKABLE	HOW TO UNLOCK
3-Pointer (25)	Defeat Episode 3.
Achiever (25)	Perform a Level 3 Shut 'Em Down move in any Ranked Match.
Big Air (50)	Make a 3-pt. shot in a 2v2 Match beyond the half-court line in Single Player Game modes.
Can't Stop the Reign (100)	Unlock all Super Dunks.
Dedicated (100)	Win 25 Ranked Matches.
Double Double (100)	Defeat every Episode of Story mode twice.
Dynasty! (40)	Defeat Episode 4.
Free Throw (25)	Defeat Episode 1.
Getting Into It (25)	Win 5 Ranked Matches.
Hall-of-Fame! (200)	Defeat Episode 6.
Jump Shot (25)	Defeat Episode 2.
Just Getting Started (20)	Complete your first chapter of Story mode.
Legend! (50)	Defeat Episode 5.
Own the Court (50)	Perform a 7-Move Combo String in Single Player game modes.
Pass the Rock! (20)	Complete an Alley-Oop from your Pass-To Buddy in a Single Player 1v1 or Xbox LIVE Match.
Show Off! (100)	Perform a Level 3 Shut 'Em Down move in a Single Match in Single Player game modes.
Show-n-Prove (25)	Perform a Shut 'Em Down move in a Ranked Match.
Takin' it Downtown (10)	Win Your First Ranked Match on Xbox LIVE.

NBA BALLERS: REBOUND (PSP)

Enter these passwords in the Phrase-ology under Inside Stuff.

UNLOCKABLE	PASSWORD
All Alternate Gear, Players, and Movies	NBA Ballers True Playa
Allen Iverson's Recording Studio	The Answer
Alonzo Mourning Alternate Gear	Zo
Ben Gordon's Yacht	Nice Yacht
Chris Weber's Alternate Gear	24 Seconds
Clyde Drexler's Alternate Gear	Clyde The Glide
Dikembe Mutumbo's Alternate Gear	In The Paint
Emanuel Ginobli Alternate Gear	Manu
Jerry Stackhouse Alternate Gear	Stop Drop And Roll
Julius Irving Alternate Gear	One On One
Kevin McHale Alternate Gear	Holla Back
Lebron James' Alternate Gear	King James
Magic Johnson Alternate Gear	Laker Legends
Nene's Hilarios Alternate Gear	Rags To Riches
Pete Maravich's Alternate Gear	Pistol Pete
Rasheed Wallace Alternate Gear	Bring Down The House
Rick Hamilton's Alternate Gear	Rip
Stephon Marbury's Alternate Gear	Platinum Playa
Steve Francis Alternate Gear	Ankle Breaker
Steve Francis' Alternate Gear	Rising Star
Tim Duncan Alternate Gear	Make It Take It
Wilt Chamberlain's Alternate Gear	Wilt The Stilt

NBA JAM (XBOX)

Create a new profile using these names.

UNLOCKABLE	CODE
Unlock Everything	-LPP-
Unlock the NBA Jam Development Team	CREDITS

NBA JAM (PlayStation 2)

Create a new profile using these names.

UNLOCKABLE	CODE
Unlock Everything	-LPP-
Unlock the NBA Jam Development Team	CREDITS

NBA LIVE 08 (PlayStation 3)

SHOES

From the main menu go to "My NBA Live" then "EA Sports Extras" then select "NBA Codes" and enter the following case-sensitive codes.

UNLOCKABLE	HOW TO UNLOCK
Adidas Gil-Zero (All-Star Edition)	23DN1PPOG4
Adidas Tim Duncan Stealth (All-Star Edition)	FE454DFJCC

NBA LIVE 08 (PlayStation 2)

SHOES

From the main menu, go to "My NBA Live" then select "NBA Codes" and enter the following codes.

UNLOCKABLE	HOW TO UNLOCK
Adidas GIL II ZERO: "Agent Zero" Shoe	ADGILLIT6BE
Adidas GIL II ZERO: "Black President" Shoe	ADGILLIT7BF
Adidas GIL II ZERO: "Cuba" Shoe	ADGILLIT4BC

Adidas GIL II ZERO: "Cust0mize" Shoe	ADGILLIT5BD
Adidas GIL II ZERO: "GilWood" Shoe	ADGILLIT1B9
Adidas GIL II ZERO: "TS Lightswitch Away" Shoe	ADGILLIT0B8
Adidas GIL II ZERO: "TS Lightswitch Home" Shoe	ADGILLIT2BA

NBA LIVE 10 (XBOX 360)

ALTERNATE JERSEYS

Go to the Main menu, My NBA Live 10, EA Sports Extras, NBA Codes and then input the code.

CODE	EFFECT
ndnba1rooaesdc0	Unlocks alternate jerseys.

NBA LIVE 10 (PlayStation 3)

ALTERNATE JERSEYS

Go to the Main menu, My NBA Live 10, EA Sports Extras, NBA Codes and then input the code.

CODE	FFECT
ndnba1rooaesdc0	Unlocks alternate jerseys.

NBA STREET: HOMECOURT (XBOX 360)

Enter these codes at the main menu.

UNLOCKABLE	CODE
All Courts	Hold LB and RB and press ↑, →, ↓, ←
Virtual Ball	Hold LB and RB and press ↑, ↓, ←, →

NBA STREET: HOMECOURT (PlayStation 3)

UNLOCKABLE	CODE
Brand Jordan Outfit 2	Get 10 blocks in a game
Brand Jordan Outfit 4	Get 10 steals in a game
Chicago All-Stars	Beat the Chicago Bulls in a Back to Basics game
Detroit All-Stars	Defeat the Detroit Pistons in a GB Battle
Jordan 9.5 Team	Win 5 Back to Basics games
Jordan 9.5 Team	Win 5 GB Battles
Jordan Hoops Lo	Win 15 GB Battles
Jordan Hoops Lo	Win 15 Back to Basics games
Jordan Laney 23	Win 30 Back to Basics games
Jordan Show Em Lo	Win 30 GB Battles
Jordan XXI PE	Win 100 Pick Up games
Los Angeles All-Stars	Defeat the Los Angeles Lakers in a Pick Up game
New Jersey All-Stars	Defeat the New Jersey Nets in a Trick Battle
New York All-Stars	Defeat the New York Knicks in a GB Battle
Oakland All-Stars	Defeat the Golden State Warriors in a Trick Battle
Jordan 9.5 Team	Win 5 Pick Up games
Jordan 9.5 Team	Win 5 Trick Battles
Jordan Hoops Lo	Win 15 Pick Up games
UNLOCKABLE	CODE
Jordan Hoops Lo	Win 15 Trick Battles
Jordan Laney 23	Win 30 Pick Up games
Jordan Show Em Lo	Win 30 Trick Battles

NCAA FOOTBALL 08 (XBOX 360)

ACHIEVEMENTS

Complete the following achievements to get the gamerscore.

UNLOCKABLE	HOW TO UNLOCK
1-Star into 6-Star (50)	Turn a one-star prestige school into a six-star prestige school in single team Dynasty mode.
2 Sack Player (10)	Make two sacks in a Play Now or Dynasty mode game with the same player.
5-Star Legend Prospect (20)	Create a five-star legend prospect.
50 Yard Field Goal (25)	Kick a 50 or more yard field goal in a Play Now or Dynasty mode game.
50 Yard Punt (15)	Punt the ball 50 or more net yards in a Play Now or Dynasty mode game.
100 Yard Receiver (10)	Gain 100 or more receiving yards with a single player in a Play Now or Dynasty mode game.
100 Yard Rusher (10)	Rush for 100 or more yards with a single player in a Play Now or Dynasty mode game.
200 Total Rushing Yards (15)	Rush for 200 or more total yards in a Play Now or Dynasty mode game.
350 Total Passing Yards (15)	Pass for 350 or more total yards in a Play Now or Dynasty mode game.
Allow No Sacks (15)	Do not give up any sacks in a Play Now or Dynasty mode game.
BCS Conference Invite (25)	Get an invite to a BCS conference in single team Dynasty mode.
Block a Field Goal (25)	Block a field goal in a Play Now or Dynasty mode game.
Block a Punt (25)	Block a punt in a Play Now or Dynasty mode game.
Bowl Win (10)	Win a bowl game in single team Dynasty mode or Campus Legend mode.
Break a 30 Yard Run (10)	Break a run for 30 or more yards in a Play Now or Dynasty mode game.
Break a 60 Yard Run (20)	Break a run for 60 or more yards in a Play Now or Dynasty mode game.
Complete a 30 Yard Pass (10)	Complete a pass for 30 or more yards in a Play Now or Dynasty mode game.
Complete a 60 Yard Pass (20)	Complete a pass for 60 or more yards in a Play Now or Dynasty mode game.
Conference Champs! (10)	Win a conference championship game in single team Dynasty mode or Campus Legend mode.
Develop New Pipeline State (25)	Develop a new pipeline state in single team Dynasty mode.
Fill Up Legend Meter (30)	Completely fill up the legend meter.
Heisman Memorial Trophy (25)	Win the Heisman Memorial Trophy in single team Dynasty mode or Campus Legend mode.
Held Under 100 Yards (25)	Hold the opposition to under 100 total yards in a Play Now or Dynasty mode game.
Held Under 200 Yards (10)	Hold the opposition to under 200 total yards in a Play Now or Dynasty mode game.
High Score —Option Dash (30)	Score 15,000 or more points in Option Dash.
Intercept 2 Passes (15)	Intercept two passes in a Play Now or Dynasty mode game.
Kickoff Return for TD (20)	Return a kickoff for a touchdown in a Play Now or Dynasty mode game.
Make 4 Sacks (20)	Sack the opposing quarterback four or more times in a Play Now or Dynasty mode game.
Make Promise to a Prospect (10)	Make a promise to a prospect in single team Dynasty mode.

Mr. February (30)	Have the number-one ranked recruiting class in a season in single team Dynasty mode.
National Champions! (30)	Lead your team to a BCS championship in single team Dynasty mode or Campus Legend mode.
No Interceptions in a Game (15)	Do not throw any interceptions in a Play Now or Dynasty mode game.
Old Spice Red Zone Perfection (15)	Complete a Play Now or Dynasty mode game with a Red Zone Efficiency rating of 100 percent.
Old Spice Red Zone Shutout (20)	Complete a Play Now or Dynasty mode game without giving up a touchdown while in the Red Zone.
Pass to 5 Different Receivers (10)	Complete a pass to five or more different receivers in a Play Now or Dynasty mode game.
Perfect Game (30)	Bowl a 300 game in a single player Bowling minigame.
Player Interception Record (25)	Break the game record for interceptions with one player (5) in a Play Now or Dynasty mode game.
Player Passing Record in a Game (25)	Break the game record for passing yards with one player (716) in a Play Now or Dynasty mode game.
Player Rushing Record in a Game (25)	Break the game record for rushing yards with one player (406) in a Play Now or Dynasty mode game.
Pontiac 4th Quarter Comeback (30)	Win a Play Now or Dynasty mode game when down by 14 to start the fourth quarter. (Min Difficulty: Varsity)
Punt Return for TD (15)	Return a punt for a touchdown in a Play Now or Dynasty mode game.
Ranked Game (10)	Play a ranked game.
Return Fumble for TD (20)	Score a touchdown after recovering a fumble on defense in a Play Now or Dynasty mode game.
Return Interception for a TD (20)	Return an interception for a touchdown on defense in a Play Now or Dynasty mode game.
Score 35 Points (15)	Score 35 points or more in a Play Now or Dynasty mode game.
Score a Safety (30)	Score a safety on defense in a Play Now or Dynasty mode game.
Shutout (30)	Prevent your opponent from scoring any points in a Play Now or Dynasty mode game.
Throw 4 TD Passes in a Game (15)	Throw four touchdown passes in a single Play Now or Dynasty mode game.
Win by 21 (10)	Win a Play Now or Dynasty mode game by 21 points or more.
Win Tug-of-War (30)	Win the Tug-of-War minigame.

NCAA FOOTBALL 08 (PlayStation 3)

RIVALRY TROPHIES

Play the corresponding games to unlock the trophy.

UNLOCKABLE	HOW TO UNLOCK
Administaff Bayou Bucket	Houston Vs. Rice
Anniversary Award	Bowling Green Vs. Kent State
Apple Cup	Washington Vs. Washington State
Backyard Bowl	West Virginia Vs. Pittsburgh
Battle for Illibuck	Ohio State Vs. Indiana
Battle for the Bell	Tulane Vs. Southern Miss
Battle of I-10	UTEP Vs. New Mexico State
Battle of I-25	New Mexico State Vs. New Mexico
Battle of I-75	Bowling Green Vs. Toledo
Bedlam Game	Oklahoma State Vs. Oklahoma
Beehive Bell	Utah Vs. Utah State
Beehive Boot	Utah State Vs. BYU or Utah
Big Game	Cal Vs. Stanford

UNLOCKABLE	HOW TO UNLOCK
Black and Blue Bowl	Southern Miss Vs. Memphis
Black Diamond Trophy	West Virginia Vs. Virginia Tech
Border War	Colorado State Vs. Wyoming
Civil War	Oregon State Vs. Oregon
Clean, Old-fashioned Hate	Georgia Vs. Georgia Tech
Commander in Chief Trophy	Air Force Vs. Navy or Army
Commonwealth Cup	Virginia Tech Vs. Virginia
Cy-Hawk Trophy	Iowa State Vs. Iowa
Deep South's Oldest Rivalry	Auburn Vs. Georgia
Egg Bowl	Ole Miss Vs. Mississippi
Florida-Georgia Game	Florida Vs. Georgia
Floyd of Rosedale	Minnesota Vs. Iowa
Fremont Cannon	UNKV Vs. Nevada
Golden Boot	Arkansas Vs. LSU
Governor's Victory Bell	Penn State Vs. Minnesota
Governor's Cup	Louisville Vs. Kentucky
Governor's Cup	Florida Vs. Florida State
Holy War	BYU Vs. Utah
Ireland Trophy	Boston College Vs. Notre Dame
Iron Bowl	Alabama Vs. Auburn
Iron Skillet	TCV Vs. SMU
Jefferson-Eppes Trophy	Florida State Vs. Virginia
Jewels Shillelagh	USC Vs. Notre Dame
Keg of Nails	Cincinnati Vs. Miami University
Legends Trophy	Stanford Vs. Notre Dame
Lone Star Showdown	Texas A&M Vs. Texas
Mayor's Cup	SMU Vs. Rice
Missouri-Nebraska Bell	Nebraska Vs. Missouri
Old Oaken Bucket	Purdue Vs. Indiana
Palmetto State	Clemson Vs. South Carolina
Paul Bunyan Trophy	Penn State Vs. Michigan State
Paul Bunyan's Axe	Wisconsin Vs. Minnesota
Peace Pipe	Western Michigan Vs. Miami University
Purdue Cannon	Purdue Vs. Illinois
Ram-Falcon Trophy	Colorado State Vs. Air Force
Red River Rivalry	Texas Vs. Oklahoma
Rocky Mountain Showdown	Colorado Vs. Colorado State
Seminole War Canoe	Florida Vs. Miami
Shillelagh Trophy	Purdue Vs. Notre Dame
Schwartzwaler Trophy	West Virginia Vs. Syracuse
Sweet Sioux Tomahawk	Northwestern Vs. Illinois
Telephone Trophy	Missouri Vs. Iowa State
Textile Bowl	Clemson Vs. NC State
The Big Game	Arizona Vs. Arizona State
Third Saturday in October	Alabama Vs. Tennessee
Tigers Rag	Tulane Vs. LSU
Victory Bell	Cincinnati Vs. Miami University

Victory Bell	Duke Vs. North Carolina
Wagon Wheel	Akron Vs. Kent State
Williams Trophy	Tulsa Vs. Rice

TROPHIES

UNLOCKABLE	HOW TO UNLOCK
AT&T Bowl	Win the AT&T Bowl.
Back-To-Back National Champs	Win two consecutive national championships.
BCS National Championship	Be the number-one ranked college football team.
Big East Championship	Have the most Big East conference wins.
C-USA Championship	Have the best conference wins in the C-USA conference.
Capital One Bowl	Win the Capitol One Bowl.
Chick-Fil-A Bowl	Win the Chick-Fil-A Bowl.
Davey O' Brien Award	Be the best quarterback.
Doak Walker Running Back Award	Be the number-one running back in the class, field, and community.
Gator Bowl Trophy	Win the Gator Bowl.
GMAC Bowl	Win the GMAC Bowl.
Hawaii Bowl	Win the Hawaii Bowl.
Heisman Memorial Trophy	Be the most outstanding college player in the United States.
Holiday Bowl	Win the Holiday Bowl.
Independence Bowl	Win the Independence Bowl.
Insight Bowl	Win the Insight Bowl.
Jim Thorpe Award	Be the number-one defensive back based on on-field performance, athletic ability, and character.
Las Vegas Bowl	Win the Las Vegas Bowl.
MAC Championship	Have the best conference wins in the MAC conference.
Maxwell Award	Be the college player of the year.
Meineke Car Care Bowl	Win the Meineke Car Care Bowl.
Motor City Bowl	Win the Motor City Bowl.
MWC Championship	Have the best conference wins in the MWC conference.
New Orleans Bowl	Win the New Orleans Bowl.
Orange Bowl Trophy	Win the Orange Bowl.
Receiver of the Year	Be the number-one wide receiver.
SEC Championship	Have the best conference wins in the SEC conference.
Sugar Bowl Trophy	Win the Sugar Bowl.
Sun Belt Championship	Have the best conference wins in the Sun Belt conference.
Three-In-A-Row National Champs	Win three consecutive national championships.
Tight End of the Year	Be the number-one tight end.
WAC Championship	Have the best conference wins in the WAC conference.

NCAA FOOTBALL 08 (PlayStation 2)

PENNANTS

In your Pennant Collection, press Select and then enter the codes.

UNLOCKABLE	HOW TO UNLOCK
#200, First and 15	Thanks
2004 All-American Team	Fumble
All-Time Alabama Team	Roll Tide
All-Time Arkansas Team	Woopigsooie
All-Time Auburn Team	War Eagle
All-Time Baylor Team	Sic Em
All-Time Clemson Team	Death Valley
All-Time Colorado Team	Glory
All-Time Florida State Team	Uprising
All-Time Florida Team	Great To Be
All-Time Georgia Team	Hunker Down
All-Time Illinois Team	Oskee Wow
All-Time Iowa Team	On Iowa
All-Time Kansas State Team	Victory
All-Time LSU Team	Geaux Tigers
All-Time Miami (Fl) Team	Raising Cane
All-Time Michigan Team	Go Blue
All-Time Mississippi State Team	Hail State
All-Time Missouri Team	Mizzou Rah
All-Time Nebraska Team	Go Big Red
All-Time North Carolina Team	Rah Rah
All-Time Notre Dame Team	Golden Domer
All-Time Ohio State Team	Killer Nuts
All-Time Oklahoma State Team	Go Pokes
All-Time Oklahoma Team	Boomer
All-Time Oregon Team	Quack Attack
All-Time Penn State Team	We Are
All-Time Pittsburgh Team	Lets Go Pitt
All-Time Purdue Team	Boiler Up
All-Time Syracuse Team	Orange Crush
All-Time Tennessee Team	Big Orange
All-Time Texas A&M Team	Gig Em
All-Time Texas Team	Hook Em
All-Time Texas Tech Team	Fight
All-Time UCLA Team	Mighty
All-Time USC Team	Fight On
All-Time Virginia Team	Wahoos
All-Time Virginia Tech Team	Tech Triumph
All-Time Washington Team	Bow Down
All-Time Wisconsin Team	U Rah Rah
Blink (referee spots the ball short for opponent)	For
Boing (opponent drops more passes)	Registering
Butter Fingers (opponent fumbles more often)	With EA
Crossed The Line #205 (QB can pass the line of scrimmage)	Tiburon
Cuffed #206 (you cannot throw interceptions or fumble)	EA Sports
Extra Credit (four point interceptions, three point sacks)	Touchdown
Helium #208 (more catches likely)	In The Zone
Hurricane (your team's pass rush improved for one game)	Turnover
Instant Freeplay (five downs instead of four)	Impact
Jumbalaya #211 (get points when your players are injured)	Heisman
Kicker Hex #229	Sideline

Michigan State Mascot Team	Mizzou Rah
Molasses (improve your opponent's fatigue for one game)	Game Time
Nike Free (increase ability to break tackles for one game)	Break Free
Nike Magnigrip (better chance your players will intercept)	Hand Picked
Nike Pro (increase your QB's accuracy for one game)	No Sweat
QB Dud #219	Elite 11
Steel Toe #221	Gridiron
Stiffed #222	NCAA
Super Dive	Upset
Tough as Nails #226	Offense
What a Hit #228	Blitz
Wyoming Mascot	All Hail
Zips Mascot	Hail WV

GLITCHES

To use an injured player on your roster, start the game normally, then after the first kickoff hit pause and click restart. Once the game has restarted, the injured players are available.

NCAA FOOTBALL '09 · (XBOX 360)

ACHIEVEMENTS

UNLOCKABLE	HOW TO UNLOCK
A/V Club President (20)	Upload a Video or Photo Highlight.
BCS Conference Invite (25)	Get an invite to a BCS conference in single-team Dynasty mode.
Break the Ice (10)	Make a Field Goal when "Iced."
Breaker Breaker 4-9 (20)	Break a run for 49 or more yards in a Play Now or Dynasty mode game.
Conference Champs! (10)	Play and win a conference championship game in single-team Dynasty mode or Campus Legend mode.
Create Stadium Sound (20)	Create a custom Stadium Sound event.
Cue the Fat Lady (10)	Win a Play Now or Dynasty mode game by 21 points or more.
Don't Mess with Texas (10)	While playing as the Texas Longhorns, celebrate a touchdown by running to your mascot.
Get Creative (30)	On a non-option play, score a TD with at least one lateral.
Go Deep for 50+ (20)	Complete a pass for 50 or more yards in a Play Now or Dynasty mode game.
Got Gator Bait? (10)	While playing as the Florida Gators, celebrate a touchdown by running to your mascot.
Heisman Memorial Trophy® (25)	Win the Heisman Memorial Trophy® in single-team Dynasty mode or Campus Legend mode.
High School Hero (20)	Become a 5-star legend prospect.
HIT STUCK (10)	Jar the ball loose with a User-Controlled Hit Stick tackle.
I'm Special! (20)	Take a punt or kickoff back to the house for a touchdown. Valid only in Play Now or Dynasty mode.
Ice in Your Veins (20)	Be the hero and win a game by taking the lead as time expires.
Is That Even Legal? (20)	Return a missed field goal for a touchdown. Only valid in Play Now or Dynasty mode.
Join the Ranks (10)	Play a ranked game.
Let the Air Out (15)	As the away team, get into the end zone in the first 30 seconds of the game.

UNLOCKABLE	HOW TO UNLOCK
Mmmmm...Donut (30)	Pitch a shutout by holding your opponent to zero points. Valid only in Play Now or Dynasty mode.
Mr. February (30)	Have the #1 ranked recruiting class in a season in single-team Dynasty mode.
National Champions! (30)	Play and win a BCS championship in single-team Dynasty mode or Campus Legend mode.
Oil Tycoon (25)	Develop a new pipeline state in single-team Dynasty mode.
Old Spice Red Zone Perfection (15)	Complete a Play Now or Dynasty mode game with a Red Zone Efficiency rating of 100%.
Old Spice Red Zone Shutout (5)	Complete a Play Now or Dynasty mode game without allowing a touchdown from the red zone.
On Lockdown (20)	Hold the opposition to under 100 total yards in a Play Now or Dynasty mode game.
Out on a High Note (10)	Play and win a bowl game in single-team Dynasty mode or Campus Legend mode.
Pick 6! (20)	Take an interception back to the house in a Play Now or Dynasty mode game.
Pick Two (15)	Intercept 2 passes in a Play Now or Dynasty mode game.
Pick-Free (15)	Do not throw any interceptions in a Play Now or Dynasty mode game.
Place at the Table! (10)	Become a starter in Campus Legend mode.
Play a Mascot Game (15)	Play a Mascot Game with any mascot teams.
Pontiac G8 4th Quarter Comeback (30)	Win a Play Now or Dynasty mode game when down by 14 to start the 4th qtr. (Min Difficulty: Varsity)
QB Quiz Success (10)	Successfully complete a quiz in the QB Challenge.
Reach Out and Crush Someone (30)	Join or host an Online Dynasty.
Record Breaker—Interceptions (25)	Break the game record for interceptions with one player (5) in a Play Now or Dynasty mode game.
Russell High School Champ (40)	Win the Russell High School Championship Game in any state.
Safety and Sound (30)	Force a safety in Play Now or Dynasty mode.
Scoop and Score! (20)	Scoop a fumble on defense and take it to the house in a Play Now or Dynasty mode game.
Sick 'Em Smokey (10)	While playing as the Tennessee Volunteers, celebrate a touchdown by running to your mascot.
Special Teams Challenge Winner (20)	Win the Special Teams Challenge mini-game.
Take Control in the Clutch (10)	Sack the QB with a user-controlled defender on 3rd down to force a punt situation.
That Just Happened! (25)	Score a rushing touchdown with your punter in a Play Now or Dynasty mode game.
The Legend of Campus Legend (100)	Earn more than 1,000 points in Campus Legend mode.
Tippy Toe! Lemon) Tree! (30)	Score a touchdown with your receiver by performing a toe-drag animation.
Triple Threat (20)	Score a receiving, rushing, and passing touchdown with one player.
Up and Over (10)	Take it up the middle in a goal line situation and dive into the end zone.
What Were You Thinking?!?! (5)	Throw the ball away on 4th down. Nice one.
Win at H _ _ _ _ (20)	Win the H.O.R.S.E mini-game/

NCAA FOOTBALL 10 (XBOX 360)

UNLOCKABLE

UNLOCKABLE	HOW TO UNLOCK
All 34 Championship Trophies—In 1 Dynasty!	Play Dynasty Mode through to the postseason. When you get to Week 1 of the Bowl Season, play and win each bowl game with any team. These will count on your profile, and when you finish every bowl (including the National Championship), you will get the Trophy!

NEED FOR SPEED CARBON (XBOX 360)

Enter at the main menu.

UNLOCKABLE	CODE
Infinite Crew Charge	↓, ↑, ↑, →, ←, ←, →, Ⓧ
Infinite NOS	←, ↑, ←, ↓, ←, ↓, →, Ⓧ
Infinite SpeedBreaker	↓, →, →, ←, →, ↑, ↓, Ⓧ
Need For Speed Carbon Logo Vinyls Unlocked	→, ↑, ↓, ↑, ↓, ←, →, Ⓧ
Need For Speed Carbon Special Logo Vinyls Unlocked	↑, ↑, ↓, ↓, ↓, ↓, ↑, Ⓧ

NEED FOR SPEED CARBON (PlayStation 3)

Enter at the main menu screen.

UNLOCKABLE	CODE
10K Booster	↓, ↑, ←, ↓, →, ↑, ■, ▲
Infinite Crew Charge	↓, ↑, ↑, →, ←, ←, →, ■
Infinite Nitrous	←, ↑, ←, ↓, ←, ↓, →, ■
Infinite SpeedBreaker	↓, →, →, ←, →, ↑, ↓, ■
Unlock Logo Vinyls	→, ↑, ↓, ↑, ↓, ←, →, ■
Unlock Special Logo Vinyls	↑, ↑, ↓, ↓, ↓, ↓, ↑, ■

NEED FOR SPEED CARBON (Wii)

UNLOCKABLE	CODE
Aston Martin DB9 (Exotic)	Defeat Wolf in Boss Battle mode
Dodge Charger RT Classic (Muscle)	Defeat the 21st Muscle Car Gang
Jaguar XK 2007 (Exotic)	Clear all three Turf War races
Mazda RX7 (Tuner)	Defeat Kenji in Boss Battle mode
Nissan 240SX (Tuner)	Clear all three Checkpoint challenges

NEED FOR SPEED CARBON (XBOX)

Enter at the main menu.

UNLOCKABLE	CODE
Extra Cash	↓, ↑, ←, ↓, →, ↑, Ⓧ, Ⓑ
Infinite Crew Charge	↓, ↑, ↑, →, ←, ←, →, Ⓧ
Infinite NOS	←, ↑, ←, ↓, ←, ↓, →, Ⓧ
Infinite SpeedBreaker	↓, →, →, ←, →, ↑, ↓, Ⓧ
Need For Speed Carbon Logo Vinyls Unlocked	→, ↑, ↓, ↑, ↓, ←, →, Ⓧ
Need For Speed Carbon Special Logo Vinyls Unlocked	↑, ↑, ↓, ↓, ↓, ↓, ↑, Ⓧ

NEED FOR SPEED CARBON (PlayStation 2)

Enter at the main menu.

UNLOCKABLE	CODE
Extra Money	↓, ↑, ←, ↓, →, ↑, ■, ▲
Infinite Crew Charge	↓, ↑, ↑, →, ←, ←, →, ■
Infinite NOS	←, ↑, ←, ↓, ←, ↓, →, ■

IUnlockable	Code
nfinite SpeedBreaker	⇩, ⇨, ⇨, ⇦, ⇨, ⇧, ⇩, ■
Need For Speed Carbon Logo Vinyls Unlocked	⇨, ⇧, ⇩, ⇧, ⇩, ⇦, ⇨, ■
Need For Speed Carbon Special Logo Vinyls Unlocked	⇧, ⇧, ⇩, ⇩, ⇩, ⇩, ⇧, ■

NEED FOR SPEED CARBON: OWN THE CITY (PSP)

UNLOCKABLE CARS

Beat the following bosses to unlock these cars:

UNLOCKABLE	HOW TO UNLOCK
911 Carrera S	Beat MK
Aston Martin DB9	Beat Jenna
Carrera GT and Lamborghini Gallardo	Beat Clutch
Chevy Cobalt SS and VW Golf GTI	Beat Marcus
Chrysler 300 and Pontiac GTO	Beat Layla 1
Firebird, Toyota MR2, and '67 Mustang	Beat Poorboy
Lotus Elise and Mustang GT	Beat Steve
Mercedes SL65, Corvette, and Ford GT	Beat Scotty
Mitsubishi Eclipse	Beat Sly
Nissan 350Z	Beat Daemon
Pontiac Solstice	Beat Striker
RX-7, Skyline GTR, and WRX STI	Beat Buddy
RX-8, Toyota Supra, and Audi TT	Beat Layla 3

NEED FOR SPEED: HOT PURSUIT 2 (XBOX)

UNLOCK ALL TRACKS

UNLOCKABLE	HOW TO UNLOCK
Unlock all tracks	Ⓧ, Ⓑ, Ⓑ, (LB), (LB), ⇧, ⇩, ⇨, ⇧

UNLOCKABLE CARS

UNLOCKABLE	HOW TO UNLOCK
Dodge Viper GTS	2,000,000 points
Ferrari F50	Lead a single race with full grid and advanced for 8 laps
Ford Crown Victoria	Complete Hot Pursuit Event 5
Lamborghini Murcielago	3,000,000 points
Lamborghini Diablo 6.0 VT	2,500,000 points
McLaren F1	4,000,000 points
McLaren F1 LM	5 million points OR win world championship
Mercedes CLK GTR	4,500,000 points
Porsche 911 Turbo	800,000 points
Porsche Carrera GT	3,500,000 points
Vauxhall VX220	Win a single race with first place in all laps

UNLOCKABLE TRACKS

Complete the following events to unlock the corresponding race tracks.

UNLOCKABLE	HOW TO UNLOCK
Alpine Trail	Championship event 22
Ancient Ruins II	Ultimate racer event 12
Autumn Crossing	Ultimate racer event 17
Autumn Crossing II	Ultimate racer event 14
Calypso Coast	Ultimate racer event 10
Calypso Coast II	Ultimate racer event 26

Coastal Parklands	Championship event 4
Desert Heat II	Championship event 25
Fall Winds II	Championship event 24
Island Outskirts II	Championship event 8
Mediterranean Paradise II	Championship event 14
National Forest	Ultimate racer event 1
National Forest II	Ultimate racer event 6
Outback	Championship event 11
Outback II	Ultimate racer event 25
Palm City Island	Ultimate racer event 28
Palm City Island II	Ultimate racer event 29
Rocky Canyons	Championship event 27
Rocky Canyons II	Championship event 9
Scenic Drive II	Championship event 6
Tropical Circuit	Championship event 29
Tropical Circuit II	Championship event 28

NEED FOR SPEED HOT PURSUIT 2 (PlayStation 2)

Enter these codes at the Main menu.

UNLOCKABLE	CODE
Aston Martin V12 Vanquish	R2,→,R2,→,▲,←,▲,←
BMW Z8	■,→,■,→,R2,▲,R2,▲
Cheat Mode	L2,R2,L2,R2,▲,■,▲,■
Ferrari F550	L1,■,L1,■,→,R1,→,R1
HSV Coupe GTS	L1,L2,L1,L2,R1,▲,R1,▲
Lamborghini Diablo 6.0 VT	→,R2,→,R2,R1,L1,R1,L1
Lotus Elise	▲,R2,▲,R2,←,■,←,■
McLaren F1 LM	■,L1,■,L1,▲,→,▲,→
Porsche Carrera GT	←,→,←,→,R1,R2,R1,R2

NEED FOR SPEED: MOST WANTED (XBOX 360)

All codes should be entered at the Start screen.

UNLOCKABLE	CODE
Unlocks Burger King Challenge Event (#69)	↑, ↓, ↓, ↓, ←, →, ←, →
Unlocks Free Engine Upgrade Bonus Marker (Can be used in the backroom of the customization shops)	↑, ↑, ↓, ↓, ←, →, ↑, ↓
Unlocks Special Edition Castrol Ford GT (Which is added to your bonus cars)	←, →, ←, →, ↑, ↓, ↑, ↓

NEED FOR SPEED: MOST WANTED (XBOX)

All codes should be entered at the Start screen.

UNLOCKABLE	CODE
Unlocks Burger King Challenge Event (#69)	↑, ↓, ↓, ↓, ←, →, ←, →
Unlocks Free Engine Upgrade Bonus Marker (Can be used in the backroom of the customization shops)	↑, ↑, ↓, ↓, ←, →, ↑, ↓
Unlocks Special Edition Castrol Ford GT (Which is added to your bonus cars)	←, →, ←, →, ↑, ↓, ↑, ↓

NEED FOR SPEED: MOST WANTED (PlayStation 2)

All codes should be entered at the Start screen.

UNLOCKABLE	CODE
Unlocks Burger King Challenge Event (#69)	↑, ↓, ↓, ↓, ←, →, ←, →

UNLOCKABLE	CODE
Unlocks Free Engine Upgrade Bonus Marker (Can be used in the backroom of the customization shops)	⇧, ⇧, ⇩, ⇩, ⇦, ⇨, ⇧, ⇩
Unlocks Special Edition Castrol Ford GT (Which is added to your bonus cars)	⇦, ⇨, ⇦, ⇨, ⇧, ⇩, ⇧, ⇩

NEED FOR SPEED: PROSTREET (XBOX 360)

CODES

Go to the "Enter Codes" section of the Career menu and enter the following codes.

UNLOCKABLE	HOW TO UNLOCK
5 Repair Tokens	SAFETYNET
Extra $2,000	1MA9X99
Extra $4,000	W2iOLL01
Extra $8,000	L1iS97A1
Extra $10,000	1Mi9K7E1
Extra $10,000	CASHMONEY
Extra $10,000 and Castrol Syntec Bonus Vinyl	CASTROLSYNTEC
Extra $10,000, unlocks Camaro concept, Mustang GT500, and r34 Skyline	REGGAME
Audi TT 3.2 Quattro (In Garage)	ITSABOUTYOU
Bonus Energizer Lithium Vinyl	ENERGIZERLITHIUM
K&N Bonus Vinyl	WORLDSLONGESTLASTING
Lancer Evo (In Garage)	MITSUBISHIGOFAR
Pre-tuned Grip Coke Zero Golf GTI (In Garage) and bonus Coke Zero Vinyl	ZEROZEROZERO
Re-Locks Everything Unlocked by "Unlockallthings"	LEIPZIG
Solstice GXP in Collectors Edition	collectorsed
Unlocks Acura Integra, NSX, Audi RS4, Lexus IS350, and Unlocks Engine Upgrades	HORSEPOWER
Unlocks Everything (maps, cars, parts)	UNLOCKALLTHINGS

KING CARS

After you beat each of the five Kings, you get their car as the reward.

UNLOCKABLE	HOW TO UNLOCK
06 Mustang GT (Karol Monroe)	Beat Drag King in Career mode.
08 Evo X (Ryo Watanabe)	Beat Showdown King in Career mode.
08 M3 E92 (Ray Krieger)	Beat Grip King in Career mode.
65 GTO (Nate Denver)	Beat Speed King in Career mode.
95 RX-7 (Aki Kimura)	Beat Drift King in Career mode.

ACHIEVEMENTS

UNLOCKABLE	HOW TO UNLOCK
8 Player Race (10)	Competed in an online multiplayer race against seven human opponents.
Beat Showdown 1 (25)	Awarded for beating Showdown 1 in Career.
Beat Showdown 2 (25)	Awarded for beating Showdown 2 in Career.
Beat Showdown 3 (25)	Awarded for beating Showdown 3 in Career.
Best Blueprint (50)	Your Blueprint is used by a player in the Top 100 on any weekly Freestyle Race Day leaderboard.
Blueprint Apprentice (15)	Awarded when your Blueprint has been shared five times.
Blueprint Master (25)	Awarded when your Blueprint has been shared 25 times.
Career Domination (125)	Dominated Career. Awarded for dominating all Career Race Days.

Clutch (15)	Won five times in a Drag event using Clutch.
Co-op Victory (20)	Achieved when all eight players in a multiplayer Race Day score a total of 10,000 points.
Community Race Day 1 (15)	Awarded for participating in the Community Race Day 1. Visit *www.NeedforSpeed.com* for details.
Community Race Day 2 (15)	Awarded for participating in the Community Race Day 2. Visit *www.NeedforSpeed.com* for details
Domination (15)	Awarded for dominating a Career Race Day.
Drag King (25)	Defeat the Drag King. Awarded for beating the Drag King in Career.
Drag Master (15)	Awarded for unlocking the Rogue Speed Org in Career.
Drift King (25)	Defeat the Drift King. Awarded for beating the Drift King in Career.
Drift Master (15)	Awarded for unlocking the Noise Bomb Org in Career.
EA Moderator (25)	Beat an EA Moderator in a Ranked Online Multiplayer race.
First Big Crash (5)	Awarded for crashing and totaling a car. Brought to you by Progressive Insurance!
Friction Fever (10)	Catch Friction Fever by playing an Online Grip race with an infected player.
Gear Strain (10)	Catch the Gear Strain by playing an Online Drag race with an infected player.
Grip King (25)	Defeat the Grip King. Awarded for beating the Grip King in Career.
Grip Master (15)	Awarded for unlocking the GEffect Org in Career.
Horsepower Challenge (10)	Increase your car's HP by 25. Brought to you by K&N—THE Performance Air Filter.
Keep on Wheelin' (5)	Wheelie 50 or more feet in a Wheelie Competition.
Manual Transmission (10)	Won five times in a non-Drag event using Manual Transmission.
Paparazzi (15)	Awarded when you upload your car photo to *NeedforSpeed.com*
Perfect Tire Grip (10)	Awarded for having maximum tire grip in drag staging.
Performance) Upgrade (10	Modify a Tier 1 car into a Tier 3 car. Brought to you by K&N—The Original High-Flow Air Filter.
Race Day Coordinator (15)	Awarded when your Race Day has been shared five times.
Race Day Leader (15)	Rank first on the leaderboard for a shared Race Day. Leaderboard must have at least three players.
Race Day Organizer (25)	Awarded when your Race Day has been shared 25 times.
Race Day Victory (10)	Awarded for winning a Career Race Day.
Ryo's Record 1 (15)	Beat Ryo's Record within Battle Machine at Grip at Chicago Airfield in Career.
Ryo's Record 2 (15)	Beat Ryo's Record within Battle Machine at Drift at Nevada Highway II in Career.
Ryo's Record 3 (15)	Beat Ryo's Record in Battle Machine at Half-Mile Drag at Portland International Raceway II in Career.
Ryo's Record 4 (15)	Beat Ryo's Record within React Team Sessions at Sector Shootout at Autopolis in Career.
Ryo's Record 5 (15)	Beat Ryo's Record within React Team Sessions at Drift at Tokyo Dockyard II in Career.
Ryo's Record 6 (15)	Beat Ryo's Record within React Team Sessions at Top Speed Run at Autobahnring II in Career.
Ryo's Record 7 (15)	Beat Ryo's Record within Super Promotion at Time Attack at Infineon II in Career.

UNLOCKABLE	HOW TO UNLOCK
Ryo's Record 8 (15)	Beat Ryo's Record within Super Promotion at Quarter-Mile Drag at Texas World Speedway in Career.
Ryo's Record 9 (15)	Beat Ryo's Record within Super Promotion at Wheelie Competition at Autobahnring II in Career.
Ryo's Record 10 (15)	Beat Ryo's Record within Super Promotion at Speed Challenge at Nevada Highway II in Career.
Safe Driver (50)	Finish five Career or Ranked Race Days with no car damage. Brought to you by Progressive Insurance!
Share a Blueprint (10)	Successfully share a Blueprint with another player.
Showdown King (75)	Defeat the Showdown King. Awarded for beating the Showdown King in Career.
Speed King (25)	Defeat the Speed King. Awarded for beating the Speed King in Career.
Speed Master (15)	Awarded for unlocking the Nitrocide Org in Career.

NEED FOR SPEED: PROSTREET (PlayStation 3)

CODES

Go to the "Enter Codes" section of the Career menu and enter the following codes.

UNLOCKABLE	HOW TO UNLOCK
Extra $2,000	1MA9X99
Extra $4,000	W2iOLLO1
Extra $8,000	L1iS97A1
Extra $10,000	1Mi9K7E1
Extra $10,000	REGGAME
Extra $10,000	CASHMONEY
Extra $10,000 and Castrol Syntec Bonus Vinyl	CASTROLSYNTEC
5 Repair Tokens	SAFETYNET
Audi TT 3.2 Quattro (In Garage)	ITSABOUTYOU
Bonus Energizer Lithium Vinyl	ENERGIZERLITHIUM
Dodge Viper (In Garage)	WORLDSLONGESTLASTING
K&N Bonus Vinyl	HORSEPOWER
Lancer Evo (In Garage)	MITSUBISHIGOFAR
Pre-tuned Grip Coke Zero Golf GTI (In Garage) and Bonus Coke Zero Vinyl	ZEROZEROZERO
Re-Locks Everything Unlocked by "Unlockallthings"	LEIPZIG
Unlocks Everything (maps, cars, parts)	UNLOCKALLTHINGS

NEED FOR SPEED: PROSTREET (Wii)

CODES

Go to the "Enter Codes" section of the Career menu and enter the following codes.

UNLOCKABLE	HOW TO UNLOCK
Audi TT 3.2 Quattro (In Garage)	ITSABOUTYOU
Bonus Energizer Lithium Vinyl	ENERGIZERLITHIUM
Dodge Viper (In Garage)	WORLDSLONGESTLASTING
Extra $2,000	1MA9X99
Extra $4,000	W2iOLLO1
Extra $8,000	L1iS97A1
Extra $10,000	1Mi9K7E1
Extra $10,000	REGGAME
Extra $10,000	CASHMONEY

Extra $10,000 and Castrol Syntec Bonus Vinyl	CASTROLSYNTEC
Five Repair Tokens	SAFETYNET
K&N Bonus Vinyl	HORSEPOWER
Lancer Evo (In Garage)	MITSUBISHIGOFAR
Pre-tuned Grip Coke Zero Golf GTI (In Garage) and Bonus Coke Zero Vinyl	ZEROZEROZERO
Re-Locks Everything Unlocked by "Unlockallthings"	LEIPZIG
Unlocks Everything (maps, cars, parts)	UNLOCKALLTHINGS

NEED FOR SPEED: PROSTREET (PlayStation 2)

CODES

Go to the "Enter Codes" section of the Career menu and enter the following codes.

UNLOCKABLE	HOW TO UNLOCK
Extra $2,000	1MA9X99
Extra $4,000	W2iOLL01
Extra $8,000	L1iS97A1
Extra $10,000	1Mi9K7E1
Extra $10,000	REGGAME
Extra $10,000	CASHMONEY
5 Repair Tokens	SAFETYNET
Castrol Syntec Vinyl	CASTROLSYNTEC
Dodge Viper SRT10 (Speed Races)	horsepower
Dodge Viper SRT10 (In Garage)	WORLDSLONGESTLASTING
Receive Bonus Vinyl Sticker	ENERGIZERLITHIUM
Receive Coke Zero Golf GTI in Career Mode	ZEROZEROZERO
Receive Mitsubishi Lancer Evolution in Career Mode	MITSUBISHIGOFAR
Unlock Map, Cars (Dodge Viper SRT10, 2004 Pontiac GTO, Chevrolet Cobalt SS, and Nissan 240SX), and Stage 4 Parts	UNLOCKALLTHINGS
Unlock Progressive Vinyl	ITSABOUTYOU

KING CARS

After you beat each of the five Kings, you get their car as the reward.

UNLOCKABLE	HOW TO UNLOCK
06 Mustang GT (Karol Monroe)	Beat Drag King in Career mode.
08 Evo X (Ryo Watanabe)	Beat Showdown King in Career mode.
08 M3 E92 (Ray Krieger)	Beat Grip King in Career mode.
65 GTO (Nate Denver)	Beat Speed King in Career mode.
95 RX-7 (Aki Kimura)	Beat Drift King in Career mode.

NEED FOR SPEED: UNDERCOVER (XBOX 360)

CODES

EFFECT	CODE
$10,000 in-game currency	$EDSOC
Die-Cast Lexus IS F bonus car	0;5M2;
Die-Cast Nissan 240SX (S13) bonus car	?P:COL
Die-Cast Volkswagen R32 bonus car	!2ODBJ:
NeedforSpeed.com Lotus Elise bonus car	-KJ3=E

NEED FOR SPEED: UNDERCOVER (PlayStation 3)

CODES

EFFECT	CODE
$10,000 in-game currency	$EDSOC
Die-Cast Lexus IS F Bonus Car	0;5M2;
Die-Cast Nissan 240SX (S13) Bonus Car	?P:COL
Die-Cast Volkswagen R32 Bonus Car	!20DBJ:
NeedforSpeed.com Lotus Elise Bonus car	-KJ3=E

NEED FOR SPEED: UNDERGROUND (XBOX)

Enter the following codes at the Main menu.

UNLOCKABLE	CODE
Circuit Tracks	↓,RT,RT,RT,BLK,BLK,X
Drift Tracks	←,←,←,←,→,BLK,RT,WHT
Drag Tracks	→,X,←,RT,X,LT,WHT,BLK
Sprint Tracks	↑,BLK,BLK,BLK,RT,↓,↓,↓

NEED FOR SPEED: UNDERGROUND (PlayStation 2)

At the Main menu:

UNLOCKABLE	CODE
Drift Physics in All Modes	R1,↑,↑,↑,↓,↓,↓,L1
Level 1 Performance Parts	R2,R2,R1,R1,←,→,←,→
Level 2 Performance Parts	R1,R1,R1,R1,R2,R2,←,→
Level 2 Visual Parts	↓,←,↑,↓,R1,R2,R2,■
Acura Integra	R2,R2,R1,R2,L2,L1,↓,↑
Acura RSX	R1,R2,↓,←,↑,→,←,→
Ford Focus	←,→,↑,R1,R2,R1,R2,↑
Honda S2000	↑,↑,↓,↓,↑,←,■,R2
Hyundai Tiburon	←,→,←,→,↑,↓,↑,↓
Lost Prophets Car	↑,↑,↑,→,↓,↓,↑,→
Mitsubishi Lancer	←,←,←,R1,R1,R2,R2,L2
Mystikal Car	↑,→,↑,↑,↓,→,↑,→
Nissan Nismo	↑,↓,↑,←,↓,↓,↑,→
Nissan 240SX	↑,↓,←,→,■,R1,L2,R1

At the Main menu:

UNLOCKABLE	CODE
Nissan 350Z	→,→,↓,↑,■,L1,R1,L2
Nissan Sentra	→,→,→,L2,L2,R2,R2,↑
Nissan Skyline	↓,↓,L1,L2,L1,L2,L1,↓
Petey Pablo Car	↑,↑,↑,↑,↓,↑,↑,→
Rob Zombie Car	↑,←,↑,↑,↓,←,↑,→
Subaru Impreza	↑,↓,↓,↑,L2,↑,L2,↓
Toyota Supra	R1,R1,R2,R1,R2,R1,L2,L1
All Circuit Tracks	↓,R1,R1,R1,R2,R2,R2,■
All Drag Tracks	→,■,←,R1,■,L1,L2,R2
All Drift Tracks	←,←,←,←,→,R2,R1,L2
All Sprint Tracks	↑,R2,R2,R2,R1,↓,↓,↓

NEED FOR SPEED: UNDERGROUND 2 (XBOX)

Codes are entered at the Main menu.

UNLOCKABLE	CODE
$1,000 for Career Mode	←,←,→,X,X,→,LT,RT

Best Buy Vinyl	↑,↓,↑,↓,↓,↑,→,←

NEED FOR SPEED: UNDERGROUND 2 (PlayStation 2)

Enter these codes at the Title screen.

UNLOCKABLE	CODE
$1000	←,←,→,■,■,→,L1,R1
All Circuit Tracks	↓,R1,R1,R1,R2,R2,R2,■
Best Buy Vinyl	↑,↓,↑,↓,↓,↑,→,←
Burger King Vinyl	↑,↑,↑,↑,↓,↑,↑,←
D3 GTO	↑,↓,→,↑,←,↓,→,→
Hummer H2 Capone	↑,←,↑,↑,↓,←,↓,←

NEO CONTRA (PlayStation 2)

Enter this code at the Title screen.

UNLOCKABLE	CODE
19 Lives	↑,↑,↓,↓,L1,R1,L1,R1,L3,R3

NEUTOPIA (Wii)

PASSWORDS

PASSWORD	EFFECT
5ltgaKyUFxsWssUkjzmVAkcQ	Begin game with 16 life bars
yP5ESDjsMwPB NDCYSzhXr%PP	End Level
KgKc%h5oFfep Qy1XwcjZXDVn	Level 4
rZtW68PjCG%L 1d9gSJ2uzn7r	Level 5
TQinHIUCDOQJ I$ZEhVQJNAwl	Super Password (5 medallions, 78 bombs)

NEUTOPIA II (Wii)

EVERYTHING COLLECTED

PASSWORD	EFFECT
At the Password screen, enter the following passwords: IbnoBJt$ AyUkJ7Wa XACpGDjm q1j1uR1Q M8ozNOQa cPUM&XcX	Puts you in the Town of Oasis ready to tackle the last dungeon, The Atra Labyrinth
Music_From_Neutopia	Sound Test
Thats_Entertainment_Neutopia	View Enemies

NEW ADVENTURE ISLAND (Wii)

UNLOCKABLES

UNLOCKABLE	HOW TO UNLOCK
Level Select	Press ←, ←, ①, →, →, ②, ↑, ↓, ↑, ↓
Level Skip	Insert a NEC Avenue 6 pad in 6-button mode into port 1

NFL STREET (XBOX)

Enter the following passwords as your User name.

UNLOCKABLE	CODE
NFL Legends	classic
Xecutioner Team	excellent
Kay Slay Team	kayslay
All Stadiums	travel

NFL STREET (PlayStation 2)

Enter these codes at the User Name screen.

UNLOCKABLE	CODE
All 8 Division All-Star Teams	AW9378
All Stadiums	Travel

UNLOCKABLE	CODE
All Star Teams	AW9378
KaySlay Team	KaySlay
NFL Legends Team	Classic
NFC West Team	NW9378
X-Ecutioners Team	Excellent

NFL STREET 2 (XBOX)

Enter these codes in the Cheats menu.

UNLOCKABLE	CODE
AFC East All-Stars	EAASFSCT
AFC North All-Stars	NAOFRCTH
AFC South All-Stars	SAOFUCTH
AFC West All-Stars	WAEFSCT
All players will have a maxed out catching stat	MagnetHands

NFL STREET 2 (PlayStation 2)

Create a profile then enter these case sensitive codes in the Cheats menu.

UNLOCKABLE	CODE
AFC East All-Stars	EAASFSCT
AFC North All-Stars	NAOFRCTH
AFC South All-Stars	SAOFUCTH
AFC West All-Stars	WAEFSCT
All players will have a maxed out catching stat	MagnetHands
NFC East All Stars	NNOFRCTH
NFC North All-Stars	NNAS66784
NFC South All Stars	SNOFUCTH
NFC West All Stars	ENASFSCT
EA Field	EAField
No Fumble Mode (Quick Game)	GlueHands
Reebok Team	Reebok

NFL STREET 2 UNLEASHED (PSP)

Enter the following in the Cheats menu.

UNLOCKABLE	CODES
AFC East All Stars	EAASFSCT
AFC North All Stars	NAOFRCTH
AFC South All Stars	SAOFUCTH
AFC West All Stars	WAEFSCT
EA Field	EAField
Fumble Mode (Other team fumbles)	GreasedPig
Gargantuan Players	BIGSmash
Max Catch	MagnetHands
NFC East All Stars	NNOFRCTH
NFC North All-Stars	NNAS66784
NFC South All Stars	SNOFUCTH
NFC West All Stars	ENASFSCT
No Fumble Mode	GlueHands
Reebok Team	Reebok
Unlimited Turbo	NozBoost

NHL 08 (XBOX 360)

GEAR

Enter the code in the RBK Edge Code option.

UNLOCKABLE	HOW TO UNLOCK
RBK Edge Jerseys	h3oyxpwksf8ibcgt

ALL JERSEYS

Under the Features menu, go to "Unlock 2007-2008 Uniforms" then enter the following case-sensitive password.

UNLOCKABLE	HOW TO UNLOCK
All Jerseys	S6j83RMK01
AHL Upset (25)	As the lead *NHL 08* Profile, beat an NHL team with an AHL team on Superstar mode.
Beating Tough Competition (100)	As the lead *NHL 08* Profile, beat an opponent ranked Online in the Top 50.
Create a Goalie (25)	As the lead *NHL 08* Profile, use a Created Goalie in a Play Now game.
Create a Skater (25)	As the lead *NHL 08* Profile, use a Created Skater in a Play Now game.
Create a Team (25)	As the lead *NHL 08* Profile, use a Created Team in a Play Now game.
Elite League Upset (25)	As the lead *NHL 08* Profile, beat an NHL team with an Elite League team on Superstar mode.
Fun for All (25)	As the lead *NHL 08* Profile, be on the winning team in an Online Team Play game.
Goalie's Nightmare (50)	As the lead *NHL 08* Profile, score 70 goals with one player in Dynasty mode.
He Shoots, He Scores (25)	As the lead *NHL 08* Profile, score a goal with the Goalie on Superstar mode.
Last Minute of Play (25)	As the lead *NHL 08* Profile, score a goal in the last minute of play on Superstar mode.
On a Roll (50)	As the lead *NHL 08* Profile, win five games in a row in the Playoffs in Dynasty mode.
Online All the Time (75)	As the lead *NHL 08* Profile, play 50 Online Ranked Versus games.
UNLOCKABLE	HOW TO UNLOCK
OT Winner (25)	As the lead *NHL 08* Profile, win an Online Ranked Versus game in Overtime.
Penalty Kill Special (25)	As the lead *NHL 08* Profile, score a goal when two men down on Pro mode.
Penalty Shot Hero (25)	As the lead *NHL 08* Profile, score a goal on the penalty shot in Pro mode.
Players of the Game (25)	As the lead *NHL 08* Profile, earn all three stars in Superstar mode.
Playing as a Team (50)	As the lead *NHL 08* Profile, win an Online Ranked Versus game with a friend on the same Xbox 360 console.
Regular Season Best (50)	As the lead *NHL 08* Profile, have your team finish the regular season with the best overall record.
Seeing Lots of Rubber (50)	As the lead *NHL 08* Profile, record 40 shots or more on goal in an Online Ranked Versus game.
Shoot It! (50)	As the lead*NHL 08* Profile, record 25 shots in one period of play on Superstar mode.
Shootout King (25)	As the lead *NHL 08* Profile, play 25 Online Ranked S hootout games.
Shootout Mastery (50)	As the lead *NHL 08* Profile, win an Online Ranked Versus game in Shootout Overtime.

Shorthanded, No Problem (25)	As the lead *NHL 08* Profile, score a Shorthanded Goal in an Online Ranked Versus game.
Shutting the Door (50)	As the lead *NHL 08* Profile, record a shutout in an Online Ranked Versus game.
Stay Out of the Box (25)	As the lead *NHL 08* Profile, play an entire game in Superstar mode without getting a penalty.
Tournament Champs (50)	As the lead *NHL 08* Profile, win the EA Sports World Tournament.

NHL 08 (PlayStation 3)

GEAR

At the in-game cheat menu, type in the following code.

UNLOCKABLE	HOW TO UNLOCK
RBK Edge Jerseys	h3oyxpwksf8ibcgt

NHL 0 (PlayStation 2)

GEAR

Enter the code at the EA Extras menu under RBK Edge.

UNLOCKABLE	HOW TO UNLOCK
RBK Edge Jerseys	h3oyxpwksf8ibcgt

NHL 10 (XBOX 360)

CODES

Enter the following code at the EA Extras screen

EFFECT	CODE
Unlocks third jerseys	rwyhafwh6ekyjcmr

NHL 10 (PlayStation 3)

CODES

Enter the following code at the EA Extras screen.

EFFECT	CODE
Unlocks third jerseys	rwyhafwh6ekyjcmr

NHL 2K6 (XBOX 360)

Enter this as a profile name. Case Sensitive.

UNLOCKABLE	PASSWORD
Unlock everything	Turco813

NHL 2K6 (XBOX)

Enter this as a profile name. Case Sensitive.

UNLOCKABLE	PASSWORD
Unlock everything	Turco813

NHL 2K6 (PlayStation 2)

Enter this as a profile name. Case Sensitive.

UNLOCKABLE	PASSWORD
Unlock everything	Turco813

NHL 2K9 (XBOX 360)

UNLOCKABLES

Go to Features, and enter the code into the Code menu. The code is case sensitive.

EFFECT	CODE
Unlocks the third jerseys	R6y34bsH52

NHL 2K9 (PlayStation 3)

UNLOCKABLES

Go to Features, and enter the code into the code menu. The code is case sensitive.

EFFECT	CODE
Unlocks the 3rd jerseys.	R6y34bsH52

NHL 2K10 (XBOX 360)

CODES

In the cheats/password option located in the extras menu enter the following codes.

EFFECT	CODE
2K/Visual Concepts developer teams	vcteam
The five alternates for this season	G8r23Bty56

NHL 2K10 (Wii)

CODES

In the cheats/password option located in the Extras menu, enter the following codes.

EFFECT	CODE
2K/Visual Concepts developer teams	vcteam
The five alternates for this season	G8r23Bty56

NINETY-NINE NIGHTS (XBOX 360)

UNLOCKABLES

UNLOCKABLE	HOW TO UNLOCK
Character Profiles	Clear all of a character's missions to unlock his or her profile
Special Stage	Complete each character's story and then play Inphyy's last stage again and you will travel to fight the King of Nights
Character: Aspharr	Clear Fort Wyandeek with Inphyy
Character: Dwingvatt	Clear all of Inphyy, Aspharr, and Myifee's missions
Character: Klarrann	Clear all of Dwingvatt's missions
Character: Myifee	Clear the Pholya Flatlands with Inphyy
Character: Tyurru	Clear all of Dwingvatt's missions
Character: Vigk Vagk	Clear all of Tyurru and Klarrann's missions

NINJA GAIDEN (Wii)

UNLOCKABLES

UNLOCKABLE	HOW TO UNLOCK
Sound Test	When the screen says Techmo Presents 1989: Hold Ⓐ+Ⓑ+Up+Down+SELECT, and press START
Extra Lives	In Area 5-3, there's a 1UP on the third floor of the tower. Go back down the ladder to the second floor, and then back up to the third floor. The 1UP has returned. You can do this as many timeş as you want.

NINJA GAIDEN II (XBOX 360)

ACHIEVEMENTS

UNLOCKABLE	HOW TO UNLOCK
Completed Chapter 5 (10G)	Clear Chapter 5, The Aqua Capita.
Completed Chapter 7 (10G)	Clear Chapter 7, The Flying Fortress Daedalus.
Completed Chapter 9 (10G)	Clear Chapter 9, Heart of Darkness.
Diffused the Lightening (15G)	Defeat Alexei for the second time.

UNLOCKABLE	HOW TO UNLOCK
Dragon Sword Master (5)	Complete the game using only the Dragon Sword.
Dual Katana Master (5)	Complete the game using only the Dragons Claw and Tigers Fang.
Eclipse Scythe Master (5)	Complete the game using only the Eclipse Scythe.
Eight of White (15G)	Beat the eighth Test of Valor.
Ended the Infernal Reign (15G)	Defeat High Infernal Priest, Dagra Dai.
Extinguished the Flame (15G)	Defeat Zedonius for the second time.
Falcon's Talons Master (5)	Complete the game using only the Falcon's Talons.
Feat of a Hundred Slashes (20)	Achieve a 100-hit combo with any weapon.
Feat of a Thousand Obliterations (20)	Defeat 1,000 enemies using Obliteration Techniques.
Feat of Ultimate Destruction (20)	Defeat 1,000 enemies using Ultimate Techniques.
Finished Chapter 1 (10)	Finish Chapter 1, "Sky City Tokyo."
Finished Chapter 2 (10)	Finish Chapter 2, "The Castle of the Dragon."
Finished Chapter 3 (10)	Finish Chapter 3, "Thunderclap of Catastrophe."
Five of Yellow (15G)	Beat the fifth Test of Valor.
Four of Green (15G)	Beat the fourth Test of Valor.
Indomitable Spirit (5G)	Choose to continue the game 100 times.
Karma of the Master Ninja (20)	Obtain all of the Crystal Skulls.
Karma of the Mentor (20)	Obtain 20 Crystal Skulls.
Karma of the Warrior (20)	Obtain 10 Crystal Skulls.
Kusari-gama Master (5)	Complete the game using only the Kusari-gama.
Lunar Staff Master (5)	Complete the game using only the Lunar Staff.
Mastered Counter Attack (5)	Successfully perform the Counter Attack Technique.
Mastered Flying Bird Flip (5)	Successfully perform the Flying Bird Flip Technique.
Mastered Flying Swallow (5)	Successfully perform the Flying Swallow Technique.
Mastered Furious Wind (5)	Successfully perform the Furious Wind Technique.
Mastered Invisible Path (5)	Successfully perform the Invisible Path Technique.
Mastered Obliteration Technique (5)	Successfully perform the Obliteration Technique.
Mastered Reverse Wind (5)	Successfully perform the Reverse Wind Technique.
Mastered Shadowless Footsteps (5)	Successfully perform the Shadowless Footsteps Technique.
Mastered Ultimate Guidance (5)	Successfully perform the Ultimate Guidance Technique.
Mastered Ultimate Technique (5)	Successfully perform the Ultimate Technique.
Mastered Unrivaled Soaring (5)	Successfully perform the Ultimate Soaring Technique.
Nine of Violet (15G)	Beat the last Test of Valor.
One of White (15)	Purify the site of the first Test of Valor.
Redeemed Genshin (15G)	Defeat Genshin for the last time.
Seven of Red (15G)	Beat the seventh Test of Valor.
Silenced the Storm (15G)	Defeat Volf for the second time.

Six of White (15G)	Beat the sixth Test of Valor.
Staunched the Blood (15G)	Defeat Elizébet for the second time.
The Art of Inferno (5)	Successfully perform the Art of the Inferno Ninpo.
The Art of the Flame Phoenix (5)	Successfully perform the Art of the Flame Phoenix Ninpo.
The Art of the Piercing Void (5)	Successfully perform the Art of the Piercing V oid Ninpo.
The Art of the Wind Blades (5)	Successfully perform the Art of the Wind Blades Ninpo.
Three of Blue (15G)	Beat the third Test of Valor.
Tonfa Master (5)	Complete the game using only the Tonfa.
Two of Black (15)	Purify the site of the second Test of Valor.
Vanquished Alexei (15)	Defeat Alexei in battle.
Vanquished Elizébet (15)	Defeat Elizébet in battle.
Vanquished Genshin (15)	Defeat Genshin in battle.
Vanquished Volf (15)	Defeat Volf in battle.
Vanquished Zedonius (15)	Defeat Zedonius in battle.
Vigoorian Flail Master (5)	Complete the game using only the Vigoorian Flail.
Way of the Acolyte (100)	Complete the game on the Path of the Acolyte.
Way of the Master Ninja (100)	Complete the game on the Path of the Master Ninja.
Way of the Mentor (100)	Complete the game on the Path of the Mentor.
Way of the Warrior (100)	Complete the game on the Path of the Warrior.

MISSION MODE ACHIEVEMENTS

Complete Mission mode with the following conditions met to unlock new Downloadable Content Achievements.

UNLOCKABLE	HOW TO UNLOCK
Acolyte of Missions (20)	Complete all Karma Attack Missions on Path of the Acolyte.
All Bronze (30)	Obtain all Bronze Medallions in the Survival Missions.
All Gold (30)	Obtain all Gold Medallions in the Survival Missions.
All Silver (30)	Obtain all Silver Medallions in the Survival Missions.
Eight Missions Completed (30)	Complete 8 Missions.
First Medallion (20)	Obtain a Medallion in a Survival Mission.
Four Missions Completed (30)	Complete 4 Missions.
Master Ninja of Missions (20)	Complete all Karma Attack Missions on Path of the Master Ninja.
Mentor of Missions (20)	Complete all Karma Attack Missions on Path of the Mentor.
Warrior of Missions (20)	Complete all Karma Attack Missions on Path of the Warrior.

UNLOCKABLES

UNLOCKABLE	HOW TO UNLOCK
Black Jaguar Costume	Complete Path of Mentor.
Camouflage Ninja Outfit	Complete the game on Warrior.
Gamerpic of Ryu	Complete the game on Path of the Master Ninja.
Gamerpic	Collect all 30 crystal skulls.
Golden Ninja Costume	Complete the game on Path of The Master Ninja.

UNLOCKABLE	HOW TO UNLOCK
Music Test	Clear the game on any difficulty.
New Game +	Complete the game and save after Credit Scroll.
Old Film Filter	Beat the game.
Path of the Master Ninja	Beat Path of the Mentor.
Path of the Mentor	Beat Path of the Warrior.
Red Ninja Outfit	Complete the game on Acolyte.

EASTER EGGS: HIDDEN SILVER XBOX

At the bottom of the Statue of Liberty diagonally across from where the save point there is a false wall. Inside of the breakable wall is a silver Xbox that will regenerate Ryu's health.

NINJA GAIDEN SIGMA (PlayStation 3)

MISSION MODE

To unlock Mission mode, beat the Normal difficulty setting in Story mode.

UNLOCKABLE DIFFICULTIES

UNLOCKABLE	HOW TO UNLOCK
Hard	Beat the game on Normal.
Master Ninja	Beat the game on Very Hard.
Ninja Dog	Die three times.
Very Hard	Beat the game on Hard.

EXTRA COSTUMES

UNLOCKABLE	HOW TO UNLOCK
Ashtar Ryu costume	Beat Story mode on the Hard difficulty setting.
Classic Ryuken costume	Beat Story mode on the Normal difficulty setting.

GOLDEN SCARAB REWARDS

Collect the Golden Scarabs and Muramasa the shop owner will reward you with the following items and weapons. There are 50 Golden Scarabs in the game, but they are not available when playing as Rachel.

UNLOCKABLE	HOW TO UNLOCK
Armlet of Benediction	Collect 30 Golden Scarabs.
Armlet of Celerity	Collect 25 Golden Scarabs.
Armlet of Fortune	Collect 40 Golden Scarabs.
Armlet of Potency	Collect 5 Golden Scarabs.
Dabilahro	Collect 20 Golden Scarabs.
Great Spirit Elixir	Collect 35 Golden Scarabs.
Jewel of the Demon Seal	Collect 45 Golden Scarabs.
Life of Gods	Collect 1 Golden Scarab.
Lives of the Thousand Gods	Collect 10 Golden Scarabs.
Plasma Saber MkII	Collect 50 Golden Scarabs.
Spirit of the Devils	Collect 15 Golden Scarabs.

GOLDEN SCARAB REWARDS—HARD MODE

UNLOCKABLE	HOW TO UNLOCK
Armlet of Benediction	Collect 40 Scarabs.
Armlet of Celerity	Collect 30 Scarabs.
Armlet of Fortune	Collect 45 Scarabs.
Dabilahro	Collect 25 Scarabs.
Dark Dragon Blade	Collect 50 Scarabs.
Plasma Saber MkII	Collect 49 Scarabs.
Spear Gun	Collect 35 Scarabs.
Technique Scroll—Counter Attacks	Collect 1 Scarab.

Technique Scroll—Guillotine Throw	Collect 10 Scarabs.
Technique Scroll—Izuna Drop	Collect 5 Scarabs.
Windmill Shuriken	Collect 15 Scarabs.
Wooden Sword	Collect 20 Scarabs.

GOLDEN SCARAB REWARDS—MASTER NINJA DIFFICULTY

UNLOCKABLE	HOW TO UNLOCK
Ayane's Ration	Collect 30 Golden Scarabs.
Ayane's Ration Bundle	Collect 40 Golden Scarabs.
Dark Dragon Blade	Collect 50 Golden Scarabs.
Elixir of Spiritual Life	Collect 5 Golden Scarabs.
Elixir of the Devil Way	Collect 15 Golden Scarabs.
Fragrance Hydrangea	Collect 45 Golden Scarabs.
Fragrance of Dayflower	Collect 35 Golden Scarabs.
Great Devil Elixir	Collect 20 Golden Scarabs.
Great Spirit Elixir	Collect 10 Golden Scarabs.
Plasma Saber MkII	Collect 49 Golden Scarabs.
Smoke Bomb	Collect 25 Golden Scarabs.
Smoke Bomb	Collect 1 Golden Scarab.

GOLDEN SCARAB REWARDS—VERY HARD DIFFICULTY

UNLOCKABLE	HOW TO UNLOCK
Armlet of Fortune	Collect 30 Golden Scarabs.
Art of Inazuma	Collect 40 Golden Scarabs.
Art of the Ice Storm	Collect 10 Golden Scarabs.
Art of the Inferno	Collect 1 Golden Scarab.
Dark Dragon Blade	Collect 50 Golden Scarabs.
Jewel of the Demon Seal	Collect 25 Golden Scarabs.
Jewel of the Demon Seal	Collect 15 Golden Scarabs.
Jewel of the Demon Seal	Collect 35 Golden Scarabs.
Plasma Saber MkII	Collect 49 Golden Scarabs.
Spirit of the Devils	Collect 20 Golden Scarabs.
Spirit of the Devils	Collect 5 Golden Scarabs.
Spirit of the Devils	Collect 45 Golden Scarabs.

NO MORE HEROES 2: DESPERATE STRUGGLE (Wii)

UNLOCKABLES

UNLOCKABLE	HOW TO UNLOCK
Bitter Mode	Complete the game on Mild.
BJ5 Video	Beat BJ5 game, then select from TV menu.
Deathmatch (Boss Rush)	Beat the game, then select from Main menu.
E3 Trailer	Beat the game, then select from TV menu.
No Jacket	Complete all the "Revenge" missions.
New Game +	Beat the game and save your data. When you start No More Heroes 2 again you will be brought to the intro fight where you have all of your old equipment and items from the previous game.

ODDWORLD: MUNCH'S ODDYSEE (XBOX)

UNLOCK ALTERNATE ENDINGS

The game endings below can be obtained depending on your Quarma level near the end of the game. You can check your detailed Quarma level on the Quarma Bar in the Pause menu.

UNLOCKABLE	HOW TO UNLOCK
Angelic Quarma Ending	Beat the game with the Quarma Bar filled higher that 75%
Bad Quarma Ending	Beat Level 23 with the Quarma Bar filled less than 50%
Neutral Quarma Ending	Beat the game with the Quarma Bar filled between 50% and 75%

ODDWORLD STRANGER'S WRATH (XBOX)

CODES

This is all done in game, with no need to pause. Insert a second controller into port #2 on your Xbox. Remove the second controller. On controller 1, press Ⓧ, Ⓧ, Ⓨ, Ⓨ, Ⓑ, Ⓑ, Ⓐ, Ⓐ to activate Cheat mode. You hear a sound confirming that Cheat mode has been activated.

UNLOCKABLE	HOW TO UNLOCK
1,000 Extra Moolah	Ⓛ, Ⓛ, Ⓡ, Ⓡ, Ⓛ, Ⓛ, Ⓡ, Ⓡ
Invincibility	Ⓧ, Ⓨ, Ⓐ, Ⓑ, Ⓧ, Ⓨ
Level Select	Start a new game and enter the following Player Name: ©@®&
New Yolk City's Black Market	After bagging X'Plosives but before taking on a new bounty, Stranger can ask townfolk about where X got all his weapons. On the side of the road is a female clakker who knows about a black market in town, and she then tells you the password. The Black Market is located up a rope across from the Bounty Store. Go down the hallway, recite the password, and gain access. The store's items include: Bola Blasts, Wasps, Regen Upgrade, Stamina Upgrade, and Steel Knuckles.
Secret Grubb Statue	When you complete the Eugene Ius bounty you end up in a Grubb village. Proceed into the village by jumping across the rooftops. Turn right and keep going forward and you see a break to the right, leading to a little maze-like area. Turn right and there's a small forked path. Go left and you're right next to a rope. Climb it and jump on to the roof. You can see another rope that you have to jump onto. When you jump on it you can see a boarded-up window. Break it by shooting it or meleeing it. When you enter the room there is a shiny Grubb statue. It's worth a bit of moolah.
Sepia Graphics Filter	This code makes the graphics a brownish-yellow color that's synonymous with the western theme seen in Stranger's Wrath. While in-game and only one controller is plugged in (the first port), press LT, Ⓛ, Ⓡ, Ⓐ, Ⓑ, RT, Ⓑ, Ⓐ, Ⓡ, Ⓛ, LT After entering this, take a second controller, plug it into the fourth controller slot, then pull it back out. If done correctly, you will see the graphics filter change. To deactivate the code, repeat this process.

ONE PIECE: UNLIMITED ADVENTURE (Wii)

UNLOCKABLE CHARACTERS

UNLOCKABLE	HOW TO UNLOCK
Unlock Survival Mode	Unlock the following characters in Vs. mode. All characters must be defeated to unlock them. All locations given are the first location you encounter each enemy.
Bazooka Marine	Defeat one in the Seaside Zone
Blue Demon General	Defeat one in the Cave Zone
Cluster Demon Soldier	Defeat one in the Cave Zone
Crimson Demon General	Defeat one in the Cave Zone
Knuckle Pirate	Defeat one in the Ruins Zone
Marine Corps Chief	Defeat one in the Jungle Zone
Normal Marine	Defeat one in the Seaside Zone
Pistol Pirate	Defeat one in the Jungle Zone
Sabre Pirate	Defeat one in the Jungle Zone
Sword Demon Soldier	Defeat one in the Cave Zone
World Government Agent	Defeat one in the Ruins Zone
Transform into Overlimit Chopper in Story Mode	Defeat Overlimit Chopper in Story mode and create the Rumble Ball. You are now eligible to transform into Overlimit Chopper. To do so, you first must be in a boss fight. While in the fight you have to use two Rumble Balls (wait for one to run out, heal SP gauge, take another one). While you are using the second Rumble Ball, the enemy has to kill Chopper. Instead of dying, as he normally would, a cinema scene occurs. The scene shows Chopper taking a third Rumble Ball and he transforms into his Overlimit form. He gains a new HP and SP bar. He can't use items.

ONIMUSHA: DAWN OF DREAMS (PlayStation 2)

Input these codes by going into the Special menu, highlighting exit, and entering a code.

UNLOCKABLE	CODE
Gives Jubei a Racket	L1, R1, ⇨, L2, ▲, ⇨, L1, ⇨, L3, R1
Gives Jubei Cammy's Costume	L2, L2, ⇨, ⇨, L3, ▲, ⇦, L1, L2, ■
Gives Ohatsu Chun-Li's Costume	R3, ⇨, L2, ⇦, ⇦, R3, L1, R1, ⇨, R3

Input these codes by going into the Special menu, highlighting exit, and entering a code.

UNLOCKABLE	CODE
Gives Ohatsu a Piggy Bank	⇨, ▲, ⇦, L3, L1, ▲, ■, R2, ■, R2
Gives Roberto Boxing Gloves	▲, R3, ▲, ⇨, R1, L3, ▲, L1, ⇨, L3
Gives Roberto Guile's Costume	R2, L2, ⇦, L1, ⇦, ⇨, R3, ■, ■, ▲
Gives Soki a Steel Pipe	L2, ■, ▲, R1, R1, R3, ⇦, ■, L1, ▲
Gives Soki Ryu's Costume	⇦, ▲, R2, R3, ■, R1, R1, ⇨, ⇦, L2

UNLOCKABLE	CODE
Gives Tenkai a Microphone Stand	R2, R3, ■, ⇦, ⇦, ⇨, L2, ⇦, R2, ⇦
Gives Tenkai Ken's Costume	L3, L3, R3, R3, R3, ⇦, R2, L1, ■, ⇨

ONSLAUGHT (Wii)

STAGES

In addition to the three difficulty settings available from the start, there are two unlockable difficulty settings.

UNLOCKABLE	HOW TO UNLOCK
Expert difficulty	Finish the game on Hard difficulty.
Ultra difficulty	Finish the game on Expert difficulty.

UPGRADE LOCATIONS

Each weapon has 2 upgrades that count as additional weapons.

UNLOCKABLE	HOW TO UNLOCK
2nd level Assault Rifle	Box in Mission 5.
2nd level Grenades	Clear Missions 1, 2, and 3 in Normal difficulty (S rank).
2nd level Rocket Launcher	Clear Missions 9, 10, and 11 in Normal difficulty (S rank).
2nd level Shotgun	Box in Mission 11.
2nd level SMG	Box in Mission 3.
2nd level Whip	Clear Missions 5, 6, and 7 in Normal difficulty (S rank).
3rd level Assault Rifle	Beat the game in Ultra difficulty.
3rd level Grenades	Clear Missions 1 to 8 in Hard difficulty (S rank).
3rd level Rocket Launcher	Clear Missions 1 to 12 in Ultra difficulty (S rank).
3rd level Shotgun	Beat the game in Expert difficulty.
3rd level SMG	Beat the game in Hard difficulty.
3rd level Whip	Clear Missions 1 to 8 in Expert difficulty (S rank).

OPEN SEASON (Wii)

UNLOCKABLE MINIGAMES

UNLOCKABLE	HOW TO UNLOCK
Duck Chorus	Complete "Crazy Quackers"
Flowers for My Deer	Complete "Meet the Skunks"
Rise, Rise to the Top!	Complete "Beaver Damage"
Shake That Butt!	Complete "Hunted"
Wild Memory	Complete "Shaw's Shack"

OPEN SEASON (XBOX)

UNLOCKABLE MINIGAMES

UNLOCKABLE	HOW TO UNLOCK
Duck Chorus	Complete "Crazy Quackers"
Flowers for My Deer	Complete "Meet the Skunks"
Rise, Rise to the Top!	Complete "Beaver Damage"
Shake That Butt!	Complete "Hunted"
Wild Memory	Complete "Shaw's Shack"

OPERATION FLASHPOINT: DRAGON RISING (XBOX 360)

CODES

EFFECT	CODE
Unlocks "Ambush" mission	AmbushU454
Unlocks "Close Quarters" mission	CloseQ8M3
Unlocks "Coastal Stronghold" mission	StrongM577
Unlocks "F.T.E." mission	BLEEDINGBADLY
Unlocks "Night Raid" mission	RaidT18Z
Unlocks "Debris Field" mission	OFPWEB2
Unlocks "Encampment" mission	OFPWEB1

OPOONA (Wii)

UNLOCKABLES

UNLOCKABLE	HOW TO UNLOCK
Fifth Citizen Ranking Star	Acquire the Five-Star Landroll Ranger License. Must be done before talking to woman for Sixth Star.
Five-Star Landroll Ranger License	Win 100 battles in the Intelligent Sea server room.

Sixth Citizen Ranking Star	Talk to a woman on the bottom floor of the Moon Forest Tokione Hotel after spending the night.

ORDYNE (Wii)

UNLOCKABLES

UNLOCKABLE	HOW TO UNLOCK
Continue Game	While falling, hold ① and press RUN
Princess Mode	At the title screen, hold ① for about 10 seconds
Secret Test Mode	At the title screen, hold down RUN while pressing SELECT, SELECT, SELECT, SELECT, SELECT, SELECT, then release. Hold down ①+②+Up+Left, then press RUN. Press SELECT and RUN simultaneously to reach each part of the Secret Test mode. You can access a Sound Test, select your starting stage and your starting number of ships, among other things.

OUTLAW GOLF (XBOX)

UNLOCKABLE	OBJECTIVE
Atlas Driver	Complete the Stroke Me event.
Atlas Fairway Woods	Complete the Not-So-Goodfellas event.
Atlas Irons	Complete the High Rollers event.
Atlas Putter (Black)	Complete the All the Marbles event.
Atlas Putter Gold	Complete the Suave's Revenge event.
Atlas Wedge	Complete the Pretty in Pink event.
Boiler Maker Fairway Woods	Complete the Hole Lotta Luv event.
Boiler Maker Irons	Complete the Jersey Ball Bash event.
Boiler Maker Putter	Complete the Sun Stroke event.
Boiler Maker Wedge	Complete the Back 9 Shuffle event.
Bonus Costumes	Hold LT and press Y, Y, White, Y, Black, Y at the character selection screen.
C.C.	Complete the Hot, Hot, Hot event.
Cincinnati Balls	Complete the Rough Riders event.
Cincinnati Driver	Complete the Ol' Blood and Guts event.
Cincinnati Fairway Woods	Complete the Full Frontal event.
Cincinnati Irons	Complete the Stroke Me Again event.
Cincinnati Wedge	Complete the Blister in the Sun event.
Coiler Maker Driver	Complete the Money Talks event.
Distract Opponent	Start a game with two or more players. While the other person is hitting the ball, press A to say things to distract them.
Doc Diggler	Complete the Ladies Night event.
Ecstasy Balls	Complete the Scorched Earth Classic event.
Ecstasy Putter	Complete the Motley Crew event.
Killer Miller	Complete the Test Drive event.
Master Code	Start a new game and enter Golf_Gone_Wild as a case-sensitive name, including underscores, to unlock all characters, clubs, and stages.
Nelson Balls	Complete the Different Strokes event.
Python Driver	Complete the Heat Rash Invitational event.
Python Fairway Woods	Complete the Tough Crowd event.
Python Irons	Complete the A Hole in the Sun event.
Python Wedge	Complete the Garden State Stroke Fest event.
Scrummy	Complete the Odd Ball Classic event.
Suave's Balls	Complete the Garden State Menage a Trois event.
Suki	Complete the Baked on the Bone event.
Trixie	Complete the Chicks with Sticks event.

OUTLAW GOLF 2 (XBOX)

UNLOCKABLE	CODE
Big Head Mode	At any time during the game, hold LT and press B, A, B, Y, ↓, ←.
Everything	Enter I Have No Time as your name.

OUTLAW GOLF 2 (PlayStation 2)

UNLOCKABLE	OBJECTIVE
Everything unlocked	Enter I Have No Time as a profile name.

OUTLAW VOLLEYBALL (XBOX)

UNLOCKABLE	CODE
All Characters	At the character select screen, hold LT and press ←, WHT, →, WHT.
All Courts	On Court Selection Screen, hold LT and press ↑, ↓, ↑, ↓, ←, ←, →, →.
Big Head Mode	During gameplay, hold LT and press B, A, B, Y.
Maximum Stats	In Exhibition mode, hold RT and press ←, WHT, →, WHT.
Time Bombs	In Exhibition mode, hold LT and press A, B, B, Y, and A+X together.

OUTLAW VOLLEYBALL REMIXED (PlayStation 2)

Enter these codes at the Exhibition Court Select screen.

UNLOCKABLE	CODE
Hell Pit court	Hold R1 and press ■, ■, ■, ■, ■, ■, ▲, ▲, ▲, ▲, ▲, ▲, L2, L2, L2, L2, L2, L2
Warehouse court	Hold L1 and press ↑, ■, ■, ▲, ▲, ↓

Enter this at the Character Select screen.

UNLOCKABLE	CODE
Better Stats	Hold R1 and press ←, L2, →, L2

Enter this code during gameplay.

UNLOCKABLE	CODE
Big Heads	Hold L1 and press ●, ×, ●, ▲

OUTRUN 2 (XBOX)

To enter these codes, select Outrun Challenge, then select Gallery, and last, select Enter Code.

UNLOCKABLE	CODE
All Cars	DREAMING
All Mission Stages	THEJOURNEY
All Music	RADIOSEGA
Bonus Tracks	TIMELESS
Original Outrun	NINETEEN86
Reverse Tracks	DESREVER

OUTRUN 2006: COAST TO COAST (XBOX)

To enter these passwords create a license. Then go into Edit License and change the name to the password. Do not press the Done button—instead, press the B to back out of the screen.

UNLOCKABLE	PASSWORD
100% Complete	ENTIRETY
1,000,000 Outrun Miles	MILESANDMILES

OVER THE HEDGE (XBOX)

UNLOCK MINIGAMES AND ATTACKS

UNLOCKABLE	HOW TO UNLOCK
Unlock Attack: Finishing Moves	Complete 20 Objectives
Unlock Attack: Ground Pound	Complete 50 Objectives
Unlock Minigame: Bumper Carts 1	Complete 15 Objectives
Unlock Minigame: Bumper Carts 2	Complete 45 Objectives
Unlock Minigame: Race Track 1	Complete 25 Objectives
Unlock Minigame: Race Track 2	Complete 60 Objectives
Unlock Minigame: Range Driver 1	Complete 10 Objectives
Unlock Minigame: Range Driver 2	Complete 40 Objectives

OVERRIDE (Wii)

LEVELS

Enter the "Level Select mode" code before entering any of the level passwords.

CODE	EFFECT
Level Select Mode	Hold RUN and press SELECT 10 times
Level 2	↑, SELECT, RUN
Level 3	→, SELECT, RUN
Level 4	↓, SELECT, RUN
Level 5	←, SELECT, RUN
Level 6	↑, →, SELECT, RUN

UNLOCKABLES

UNLOCKABLE	HOW TO UNLOCK
Ending	Holding ↖+①+②+SELECT, press RUN
Invincibility	Press RUN, then quickly press and hold ①+②+SELECT+RUN
Sound Test	Hold SELECT and press RUN

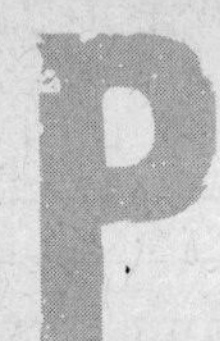

PAC-MAN WORLD 3 (PSP)

Enter this code at the main menu.

UNLOCKABLE	CODE
Unlock levels and mazes	⇦, ⇨, ⇦, ⇨, ●, ⇧

PARIAH (XBOX)

To enter these codes go to the Codes option.

UNLOCKABLE	CODE
EB Games Multiplayer Level	WHT, Y, X, BLK
Gamestop Multiplayer Level	←, LT, X, ←

Enter these codes in the Cheat Codes menu under "settings."

UNLOCKABLE	CODE
All Ammo	↓, ↑, ↓, Y
God Mode	↑, LT, X, LT

PATAPON 2 (PSP)

UNLOCKABLES

Complete the following tasks to gain the corresponding miracles.

UNLOCKABLE	HOW TO UNLOCK
Attack Miracle	Beat invincible Dragon Majidonga Level 3
Blizzard Miracle	Finish Watchtower and Two Karmen Mission.
Defense Miracle	Beat Fearful Tentacle Monster Darachura Level 3.
Earthquake Miracle	Beat Living Fortress Cannodears Level 3.
Rain Miracle	Finish Mushroom shroom shroom Nyokiri Swamp Mission in the Second Time.
Storm Miracle	Beat God General of Staff Hookmen.
Tailwind Miracle	Finish Mystery of the Desert's Sandstorm Mission in the Second Time.

PHANTASY STAR ONLINE: EPISODE I AND II (XBOX)

UNLOCKABLE	OBJECTIVE
Open the Dressing Room	Have 10,000 Meseta on your character (not in the bank) when you start the game.
Hard Mode (offline)	Beat Normal Mode.
Hard Mode (online)	Get to level 20.
Ultimate Mode (offline)	Beat Very Hard Mode.
Ultimate Mode (online)	Get to level 80.
Very Hard Mode (offline)	Beat Hard Mode.
Very Hard Mode (online)	Get to level 40.

PHANTASY STAR UNIVERSE: AMBITION OF THE ILLUMINUS (XBOX 360)

ACHIEVEMENTS

UNLOCKABLE	HOW TO UNLOCK
De Rol Le Slayer (40 points)	Defeat De Rol Le
Mother Brain Slayer (50 points)	Defeat Mother Brain
Slterazgohg Slayer (40 points)	Defeat Slterazgohg

PHANTOM BRAVE: WE MEET AGAIN (Wii)

UNLOCKABLES

UNLOCKABLE	HOW TO UNLOCK
New Game Plus	Once you clear the game, go to the Phantom Island and speak to the black spirit. Pick the first choice.

PINBALL HALL OF FAME (PSP)

Enter these passwords on the Password screen.

UNLOCKABLE	PASSWORD
999 Credits	JAT
Freeplay on Big Shot	UJP
Freeplay on Black Hole	LIS
Freeplay on Goin' Nuts	PHF
Freeplay on Love Meter	HOT

Enter these passwords on the Password screen.

UNLOCKABLE	PASSWORD
Freeplay on Tee'd Off	PGA
Freeplay on Xolten	BIG
Unlocks Payout mode	WGR
Unlocks Aces High for freeplay	UNO
Unlocks Central Park for freeplay	NYC
Unlocks custom balls in Options	CKF
Unlocks freeplay on Strikes 'N Spares	PBA
Unlocks optional tilt in Options	BZZ
Unlocks Play Boy table for freeplay	HEF

PIRATES OF THE CARIBBEAN: AT WORLD'S END (DS)

UNLOCKABLES

UNLOCKABLE	HOW TO UNLOCK
Secret Cove	Collect all 7 Secret Map Fragments in Shipwreck Cove.

PITFALL: THE LOST EXPEDITION (XBOX)

Enter the following codes at the Main menu while holding LT+RT.

UNLOCKABLE	CODE
Bottomless Canteen	←,X,B,↓,X,A,X,B
Original Pitfall	B,B,←,→,B,X,A,↑,B
Play as Nicole	←,↑,↓,↑,B,↑,↑
Punch Mode	←,→,B,↑,B,→,←

PITFALL: THE LOST EXPEDITIONS (PlayStation 2)

Enter the following codes at the Title Screen. If you entered the code correctly, a message will appear.

UNLOCKABLE	CODE
Hyper Punch Mode	Hold L1+R1, then press →,←,●,↑,●,→,←
Original Pitfall game	Hold L1+R1, then press ●,●,←,→,●,■,×,↑,●
Original Pitfall 2: Lost Caverns game	Hold L1+R1, then press ←,→,←,→,▲,▲,▲
Play as Nicole	Hold L1+R1, then press ←,↑,↓,↑,●,↑,↑
Unlimited Water in Canteen	Hold L1+R1, then press ←,■,●,↓,■,×,■,●

PIXELJUNK EDEN (PlayStation 3)

CUSTOM SOUNDTRACK

Find all 50 spectra to unlock in-game custom soundtrack.

NEW! A B C D E F G H I J K L M N O P Q R S T U V W X Y Z

TROPHIES

UNLOCKABLE	HOW TO UNLOCK
500 Dead Pollen Prowlers (Bronze)	500 Pollen Prowlers killed.
All Gardens Clear (Bronze)	Get a Spectra in each garden.
All Seeds 01 (Bronze)	Open all seeds in garden 01.
All Seeds 02 (Bronze)	Open all seeds in garden 02.
All Seeds 03 (Bronze)	Open all seeds in garden 03.
All Seeds 04 (Bronze)	Open all seeds in garden 04.
All Seeds 05 (Bronze)	Open all seeds in garden 05.
All Seeds 06 (Bronze)	Open all seeds in garden 06.
All Seeds 07 (Bronze)	Open all seeds in garden 07.
All Seeds 08 (Bronze)	Open all seeds in garden 08.
All Seeds 09 (Bronze)	Open all seeds in garden 09.
All Seeds 10 (Bronze)	Open all seeds in garden 10.
All Spectra Found (Silver)	Get all the Spectra in all gardens.
Combo Fifteen (Bronze)	Pollen Prowler combo x 15.
Combo Ten (Bronze)	Pollen Prowler combo x 10.
Fifteen Crystals (Bronze)	Get 15 crystals in a single jump.
Ten Minute Grimp (Bronze)	Get all 5 Spectra from a garden within 10 minutes.
The Hundred Thousander (Bronze)	Get 100,000 pollen in one garden.
Three Play Ping Pong (Bronze)	In 3p mode, trapeze jump between two swinging Grimps.
Zero Wasted Pollen (Bronze)	Open all seeds in a garden without missing any pollen.

POPULOUS DS (DS)

ADDITIONAL LEVELS AND FEATURES

To unlock the generic levels (levels 1-8) clear 3 of the 5 stages from the previous level.

UNLOCKABLE	HOW TO UNLOCK
Bonus Challenge Stage 41	Get Gold or better on Warrior Hunt Level 1.
Bonus Challenge Stage 42	Get Gold or better on Warrior Hunt Level 2.
Bonus Challenge Stage 43	Get Gold or better on Warrior Hunt Level 3.
Bonus Challenge Stage 44	Get Gold or better on all levels of Warrior Hunt.
Bonus Challenge Stage 45	Get Platinum on all levels of Warrior Hunt.
Extra Challenge Stages 46-50	Clear All 40 stages in Challenge mode Levels 1-8.
Infinite Psyche Energy in Free Play Mode	Clear all Extra Challenge stages.

GODS

UNLOCKABLE	HOW TO UNLOCK
God of Fire	Beat the Demon of Harvest once in Challenge Mode.
God/Goddess of Wind	Beat the Demon of Water once in Challenge Mode.
Goddess of Harvest	Clear Tutorial Stage 5.
Goddess of Water	Beat the Demon of Fire once in Challenge Mode.

LANDSCAPES

UNLOCKABLE	HOW TO UNLOCK
8-Bit Plain	Clear Challenge Stage 26 (Level 6).
Fairytale	Clear Challenge Stage 2 (Level 1).
Hanging Gardens	Clear Challenge Stage 27 (Level 6).
Horror	Clear Challenge Stage 11 (Level 3).
Magma	Clear Challenge Stage 7 (Level 2).

Outer Space	Clear Challenge Stage 16 (Level 4).
Persia	Clear Challenge Stage 6 (Level 2).
Snowfield	Clear Challenge Stage 21 (Level 5).
Yamato (Japanese landscape)	Clear Challenge Stage 3 (Level 1).

PORTAL: STILL ALIVE (XBOX 360)

UNLOCKABLES

UNLOCKABLE	HOW TO UNLOCK
Portal Gamer picture	In test chamber 17, incinerate the companion cube.
Portal Gamer picture (2)	Defeat GLaDOS and escape

POWER GOLF (Wii)

UNLOCKABLES

UNLOCKABLE	HOW TO UNLOCK
Left-handed Golfer	Hold ✜ and press ① when selecting a golfer

PRINCE OF PERSIA (XBOX 360)

UNLOCKABLE

UNLOCKABLE	HOW TO UNLOCK
Altair Skin	At the main menu, press "Y" for Exclusive Content. Create an Ubisoft account. Then select "Altair Skin for Prince" to unlock.

CODES

EFFECT	CODE
Classic Prince	52585854

PRINCE OF PERSIA (PlayStation 3)

UNLOCKABLE

To unlock the Altair Costume, sync your Ubisoft account with your PSN and it will be available in the Skins Manager menu in the Extras.

UNLOCKABLE	HOW TO UNLOCK
Altair Skin	At the Main Menu, press Y for Exclusive Content. Create an Ubisoft account. Then select "Altair Skin for Prince" to unlock.

CODES

Go to Skins Manager on Extras, press Triangle and enter 525858542 to unlock the Classic Prince.

EFFECT	CODE
Classic Prince	52585854

PRINCE OF PERSIA (XBOX)

UNLOCKABLE	OBJECTIVE
Original Prince of Persia	Complete the game and you will open up the very first Prince of Persia.

PRINCE OF PERSIA: CLASSIC (XBOX 360)

PASSWORDS

PASSWORD	EFFECT
73232535	Level 2
96479232	Level 3
53049212	Level 4
51144526	Level 5
18736748	Level 6
42085223	Level 7
98564243	Level 8
51139315	Level 9

PASSWORD	EFFECT
53246739	Level 10
32015527	Level 11
44153123	Level 12
96635134	Level 13
75423134	Level 14
89012414	End

PRINCE OF PERSIA: RIVAL SWORDS (Wii)

While in the Pause menu, use the d-pad to enter these codes.

UNLOCKABLE	CODE
Unlock the Baby Toy Weapon	←, ←, →, →, Z, Nunchuck down, Nunchuck down, Z, ↑, ↓
Unlock Telephone Sword	→, ←, →, ←, ↓, ↓, ↑, ↑, Z, Nunchuck down, Z, Z, Nunchuck down, Nunchuck down
Unlock Swordfish Weapon	↑, ↓, ↑, ↓, ←, →, ←, →, Z, Nunchuck down, Z, Nunchuck down
Unlock Chainsaw	↑, ↑, ↓, ↓, ←, →, ←, →, Z, Nunchuck down, Z, Nunchuck down

PRINCE OF PERSIA: THE SANDS OF TIME (PlayStation 2)

UNLOCKABLE	CODE
Unlock the first Prince of Persia	Start a new game and stay on the balcony, press L3 and quickly enter ×, ■, ▲, ●, ▲, ×, ■, ●.

PRINCE OF PERSIA: THE TWO THRONES (XBOX)

EXTRA SECONDARY WEAPONS

Pause the game while you have a secondary weapon equipped and ready.

UNLOCKABLE	HOW TO UNLOCK
Chainsaw	↑, ↑, ↓, ↓, ←, →, ←, →, Y, X, Y, X
Phone	→, ←, →, ←, ↓, ↓, ↑, ↑, Y, X, Y, Y, X, X
Rattle	←, ←, →, →, Y, X, X, Y, ↑, ↓
Swordfish	↑, ↓, ↑, ↓, ←, →, Y, X, Y, X

SAND GATE REWARDS

UNLOCKABLE	HOW TO UNLOCK
100 Sand Credits	Deactivate Two Sand Gates
150 Sand Credits	Deactivate Five Sand Gates
200 Sand Credits	Deactivate Eight Sand Gates
Eye of the Storm Power	Deactivate Three Sand Gates
Fifth Sand Tank	Deactivate Four Sand Gates
Fourth Sand Tank	Deactivate One Sand Gate
Sand Storm Attack	Deactivate Nine Sand Gates
Sixth Sand Tank	Deactivate Seven Sand Gates
Winds of Sand Attack	Deactivate Six Sand Gates
Video Gallery	Successfully complete the game

PRINCE OF PERSIA: WARRIOR WITHIN (XBOX)

REFILL SAND TANKS

CODE	EFFECT
Refills Sand Tanks	(Hold Left Analog Stick Down) B, B, A, X, X, A, Y, Y

HIDDEN BONUS: INDESTRUCTIBLE WEAPONS

At certain points throughout the game you find Weapon Racks containing "unique" weapons. These weapons are indicated in the Secondary Weapon Display with a question mark icon and are indestructible, unlike other secondary weapons. There are five of these weapons in all. For all but the Giant Hand, you need the Scorpion Sword. The Garden Flamingo and Teddy Bear must be completed before you find the Mask, and require you to backtrack along the path you would take when trying to complete the towers in which they are located. The Teddy Bear also requires you to break a wall during the Dahaka chase zone in that area. You get one chance only to find the Giant Hand and Glowing Sword.

UNLOCKABLE	HOW TO UNLOCK
Garden Flamingo	Hanging Garden (present)—Behind a wall in the first alcove you reach if you were trying to reach the giant ladder in the past.
Giant Hand (little	During the escape from the Tomb, find it in a small alcove to **damage, instant** your left during the second (or third) Dahaka chase (depending **knock down)** on how you play).
Glowing Sword (Very high stats, also damages Prince)	Behind a wall in a pit immediately after the room covered in fog.
Hockey Stick	Central Hall (past), rotate the switch toward the Hourglass Room. Use the new path to reach a breakable wall at the bottom of the room.
Teddy Bear (little damage, heals the Prince with each hit)	Mechanical Pit (present), in the area where you fought the second Brute, take the stairs up and look for a breakable wall in the water-filled pit.

SECRET ENDING

UNLOCKABLE	HOW TO UNLOCK
Secret Ending	Collect all 9 life upgrades. Then go to the hourglass room as you would normally would, get the Water Sword from Kaileena, and beat a secret final boss.

PRO EVOLUTION SOCCER 2008 (XBOX 360)

UNLOCKABLES

UNLOCKABLE	HOW TO UNLOCK
Classic Argentina	Win the World Cup with Argentina.
Classic Brazil	Win the World Cup with Brazil.
Classic England	Win the World Cup with England.
Classic France	Win the World Cup with France.
lassic Germany	Win the World Cup with Germany.
Classic Italy	Win the World Cup with Italy.
Classic Netherlands	Win the World Cup with Netherlands.
Classic Players 1	At the Master League, win the Division 1 League.
Classic Players 2	At the Master League, win the Division 1 Cup.
Classic Players 3	Win the European League.
Classic Players 4	At the Master League, win the European Cup.
Classic Players 5	Win the England League.
Classic Players 6	Win the France League.
Classic Players 7	Win the Italy League.
Classic Players 8	Win the Netherlands League.
Classic Players 9	Win the Spanish League.
Classic Players 10	Win the European Cup.
CClassic Players 11	Win the African Cup.
Classic Players 12	Win the American Cup.
Classic Players 13	Win the Asia/Oceania Cup.

ACHIEVEMENTS

UNLOCKABLE	HOW TO UNLOCK
100 Matches (25)	Play 100 matches.
100 Wins (20)	Win 100 matches.
Ace Striker (30)	Score an average of two goals in the last five games. Can only be achieved after playing 20 games.
Attacking Midfielder (30)	Get your successive pass ratio to 85% in the last 10 matches. Can only be achieved after playing 100 games.
Brick Wall (30)	Keep 100 clean sheets.
England League Dominated (25)	Defeat all England League teams.
Eredivisie Dominated (25)	Defeat all Eredivisie teams.
First Glory (10)	Achieved with your first victory.
FK Goal (50)	Score a direct free kick in a Xbox LIVE Ranked match.
Gentleman (25) matches.	Get your foul per match ratio below 1 in the last 10
Goal Getter (25)	Score 100 goals.
Hat-trick Hunter (15)	Achieved after scoring five hat-tricks.
Hat-trick Hunter (Xbox LIVE) (50)	Score a hat-trick in an Xbox LIVE Ranked Match.
High Win Ratio (100)	Win 75% of your last 20 Xbox LIVE Ranked matches
Liga Espanola Dominated (25)	Defeat all Liga Espanola teams.
Ligue 1 Dominated (25)	Defeat all Ligue 1 teams.
Long Ranger (30)	Score from a distance greater than 35 meters.
National Teams) Dominated (40	Defeat all national teams.
Owner (25)	Ball possession must be above 60% in the last 10 matches.
PK Master (20)	Win at least 10 penalty shootouts following regulation time.
Serie A Dominated (25)	Defeat all Serie A teams.
Silver Service (25)	Make 100 assists.
Sniper (40)	Get your successive shot ratio to 70% in the last 10 matches. Can only be achieved after playing 100 games.
Super Striker (40)	Score an average of 2+ goals in the last five games. Can only be achieved after playing 100 games.
Ultimate Player (100)	Unlocked when you have played 500 matches, scored 1,000 goals, and won all leagues and cups.
Winning Streak (50)	Win 10 consecutive games.
Winning Streak (Xbox LIVE) (70)	Win five successive Ranked Matches on Xbox LIVE.
World Traveler (20)	Play a game in every stadium in the game.

PRO EVOLUTION SOCCER 2008 (Wii)

UNLOCKABLES

UNLOCKABLE	HOW TO UNLOCK
Classic Argentina	Win the World Cup with Argentina.
Classic Brazil	Win the World Cup with Brazil.
Classic England	Win the World Cup with England.
Classic France	Win the World Cup with France.
Classic Germany	Win the World Cup with Germany.
Classic Italy	Win the World Cup with Italy.
Classic Netherlands	Win the World Cup with the Netherlands.
Mii Match Mode	Finish top of the practice league in the Champions Road.

PRO EVOLUTION SOCCER 09 (XBOX 360)

UNLOCKABLES

UNLOCKABLE	HOW TO UNLOCK
Classic Argentina	Win the international cup with Argentina.
Classic Brazil	Win the international cup with Brazil.
Classic England	Win the international cup with England.
Classic France	Win the international cup with France.
Classic Germany	Win the international cup with Germany.
Classic Italy	Win the international cup with Italy.
Classic Netherlands	Win the international cup with the Netherlands.

PRO WRESTLING (Wii)

UNLOCKABLES

UNLOCKABLE	HOW TO UNLOCK
Battle the Great Puma	Once you are VWA Champion, defend your title for 10 matches. Then you will have a match with the Great uma.

PROFESSOR LAYTON AND THE DIABOLICAL BOX (DS)

UNLOCKABLES

After beating the game, go to the Top Secret section of the Bonuses menu to access the following unlockables.

UNLOCKABLE	HOW TO UNLOCK
Art Gallery	Beat the game.
Character Profiles List	Beat the game.
Layton's Challenges: The Sweetheart's House	Beat the game.

PROJECT GOTHAM RACING (XBOX 360)

From the simple to the complex, these badges are your rewards for what you can accomplish as a driver.

RACE CRAFT BADGES

UNLOCKABLE BADGE	OBJECTIVE
3 Back-to-Back Wins	Successfully complete three races in a row.
5 Back-to-Back Wins	Successfully complete five races in a row.
10 Back-to-Back Wins	Successfully complete ten races in a row.
10 Races with No Penalties	Keep it clean by completing 10 races in a row without hitting another car or the barrier.
20m Power Slide	Complete a 20 meter powerslide anywhere on the track.
30m Power Slide	Complete a 30 meter powerslide anywhere on the track.
50m Power Slide	Complete a 50 meter powerslide anywhere on the track.
All Kudos Maneuvers in Game	In a single race, complete every type of Kudos maneuver there is!
All Slide Types in Race	Perform every type of slide-based Kudo maneuver there is in a race.
Big Air	Hit an incline and stay in the air for two seconds or more.
Millionaire Badge	Spend one million credits on cars.
My First Win	Finish in first place in any street race.
No Penalties	Successfully complete a race without smashing into either the barriers or another car.
X3 Combo	Complete three Kudos maneuvers in a row.
X5 Combo	Complete five Kudos maneuvers in a row.
X10 Combo	Perform 10 Kudos maneuvers in a row to earn this badge.

Career Badges focus on your victories in Gotham Career mode.

CAREER BADGES

UNLOCKABLE BADGE	OBJECTIVE
All Bronze	Win every match in Gotham Career mode on Easy difficulty.
All Gold	Win every match in Gotham Career mode on Hard difficulty.
All Platinum	Win every match in Gotham Career mode on Hardcore difficulty.
All Silver	Win every match in Gotham Career mode on Medium difficulty.
All Steel	Win every match in Gotham Career mode on Novice difficulty.
Complete a Championship in Manual	Drive a stick for an entire tournament.
First Medal	Earn your first medal in Gotham Career mode.
First Platinum Medal	Earn one platinum medal.
First Platinum Trophy	Complete every race in a tournament on Hardcore difficulty.
First Trophy	Win your first championship in Career mode.
Own a Car from Each Group	Buy a car from each of the five car classes.
Own All Cars	Collect every car in the game.
Pro Racer	Complete any championship on Hardcore difficulty using only a car with a manual transmission.
Race King	Complete all the wheel-to-wheel championships.
Style King	Complete all the style-based championships.
Time King	Complete all the time-based championships.

Online badges are rewarded based on your performance in Online Career mode.

ONLINE BADGES

UNLOCKABLE BADGE	OBJECTIVE
Clean Racer	Complete a race in Online Career mode without hitting another car or a barrier.
Complete 25 Races	Complete 25 races in Online Career mode.
Complete 50 Races	Complete 50 races in Online Career mode.
Complete 100 Races	Complete 100 races in Online Career mode.
Earn 250 Kudos in One Race	Earn 250 Kudos in a single online race.
Earn 500 Kudos in One Race	Earn 500 Kudos in one race while in Online mode.
Earn 1,000 Kudos in One Race	Earn 1,000 Kudos in a single race in Online mode.
Earn 10,000K Online	Gather more than 10,000 Kudos in the Online Career mode.
Earn 25,000K Online	Gather more than 25,000 Kudos in the Online Career mode.
Earn 100,000K Online	Gather more than 100,000 Kudos in the Online Career mode.
First Online Win	Win one race on Xbox Live.
Start Last, Finish First	Overcome your tragic handicap to win this badge.
Win in Each Online Scenario	Try all of the Online Career scenarios and win at least once each.
Winning Streak X3	Win three races in a row.
Winning Streak X5	Win five races in a row.
Winning Streak X10	Win ten races in a row.

PROJECT GOTHAM RACING (XBOX)

UNLOCKABLE	CODE
All Cars and Courses	Enter the name Nosliw.

PROJECT GOTHAM RACING 2 (XBOX)

BONUS CARS

UNLOCKABLE	HOW TO UNLOCK
Delfino Feroce	Beat Kudos Challenge on Steel
Ferrari 250 GTO	Beat Kudos Challenge on Bronze
Mercedes CLK-GTR	Beat Kudos Challenge on Gold
Porsche 911 GT1	Beat Kudos Challenge on Silver
TVR Cerbera Speed 12	Beat Kudos Challenge on Platinum

UNLOCKABLES

UNLOCKABLE	HOW TO UNLOCK
Geometry Wars	Access this minigame by going into the Garage. While you're in Walk mode, go over to the arcade machine and press Ⓐ.
Reverse	On any track in online Xbox Live play, you can drive backward, but it takes 2 laps for every actual lap. So 3 laps is really 6 laps. Drive over the start line, do a U-turn, and go. Whoever crosses the finish line first, (sixth place) is first on the leaderboard and gets the bonus kudos as well.

PROTOTYPE (XBOX 360)

CODES

Select "Extras" from the Main menu and go to "Cheats."

EFFECT	CODE
Unlock Body Surf Ability	→,→,←,↓,↑,↑,↑,↓

PROTOTYPE (PlayStation 3)

CODES

Select "Extras" from the Main Menu and go to "Cheats."

EFFECT	CODE
Unlock Body Surf Ability	→,→,←,↓,↑,↑,↑,↓

PRYZM CHAPTER 1: THE DARK UNICORNS (PlayStation 2)

UNLOCKABLE	CODE
Complete current level	←, →, ←, →, ↑, ↓, ↑, ↓
Invincibility, unlimited magic, and all levels	Start a new game and enter as your name SUPREMEMAGIC

PULSEMAN (Wii)

UNLOCKABLES

UNLOCKABLE	HOW TO UNLOCK
Level SELECT	At the Sega logo, press (in joystick 2): Ⓐ, Ⓑ, Ⓒ, Ⓒ, Ⓑ, Ⓐ. After this, go to Options and use the Map option.

THE PUNISHER (XBOX)

Enter V Pirate as a Profile Name to unlock everything except Upgrades.

THE PUNISHER (PlayStation 2)

EFFECT	CODE
Everything Unlocked (except upgrades)	V Pirate as a Profile Name.

THE PUNISHER: NO MERCY (PlayStation 3)

ACTIVE MODS

Complete the tasks to unlock the following active mods.

UNLOCKABLE	HOW TO UNLOCK
Invisibility	Perform 300 kills as Jigsaw in multiplayer.
Invulnerability	Perform 300 kills as Silver Sable in multiplayer.
Regenerator	Perform 225 kills as Barracuda in multiplayer.
Sprint for Life	Complete Story Mode Level 1.
Weapon Upgrade	Complete Story Mode Level 3.

CHARACTERS

Complete the levels to unlock the following characters.

UNLOCKABLE	HOW TO UNLOCK
Barracuda, Bushwacker, Silver Sable	Complete Story Mode Level 1.
Finn Cooley	Complete Story Mode Level 2.
Jenny Cesare, Microchip	Complete Story Mode Level 3.
Jigsaw	Complete Story Mode Level 4.

COSTUMES

Complete the tasks to unlock the following costumes.

UNLOCKABLE	HOW TO UNLOCK
Barracuda (1)	Perform 60 kills using the Mark 07 SSMG in multiplayer.
Barracuda (2)	Perform 150 kills using the Mark 07 SSMG in multiplayer.
Barracuda (3)	Perform 270 kills using the Mark 07 SSMG in multiplayer.
Barracuda (4)	Kill 50 Silver Sable in multiplayer
Bushwacker (1)	Perform 75 kills as Bushwacker in multiplayer.
Bushwacker (2)	Perform 150 kills as Bushwacker in multiplayer.
Bushwacker (3)	Perform 225 kills as Bushwacker in multiplayer.
Finn Cooley (1)	Perform 75 kills using the Disruptor ML76 in multiplayer.
Finn Cooley (2)	Perform 150 kills using the Disruptor ML76 in multiplayer.
Finn Cooley (3)	Perform 225 kills using the Disruptor ML76 in multiplayer.
Finn Cooley (4)	Perform 300 kills using the Disruptor ML76 in multiplayer.
Jenny Cesare (1)	Die 30 times as Jenny Cesare in multiplayer.
Jenny Cesare (2)	Die 90 times as Jenny Cesare in multiplayer.
Jenny Cesare (3)	Die 180 times as Jenny Cesare in multiplayer.
Jigsaw (1)	Perform 25 head shots in multiplayer.
Jigsaw (2)	Perform 50 head shots in multiplayer.
Jigsaw (3)	Perform 75 head shots in multiplayer.
Jigsaw (4)	Perform 100 head shots in multiplayer.
Jigsaw (5)	Kill 75 Punisher in multiplayer.
Microchip (1)	Perform 75 kills using the Enforcer M8 in multiplayer.
Microchip (2)	Perform 150 kills using the Enforcer M8 in multiplayer.
Microchip (3)	Perform 225 kills using the Enforcer M8 in multiplayer.
Silver Sable (1)	Perform 75 kills as Silver Sable in multiplayer
Silver Sable (2)	Perform 150 kills as Silver Sable in multiplayer.
The Punisher (1)	Kill 15 Barracuda in multiplayer.
The Punisher (2)	Kill 25 Bushwacker in multiplayer.
The Punisher (3)	Kill 35 Finn Cooley in multiplayer.
The Punisher (4)	Kill 50 Jigsaw in multiplayer.

PASSIVE MODS

Complete the tasks to unlock the following passive mods.

UNLOCKABLE	HOW TO UNLOCK
Berserk	Perform 250 kills using the Rhino in multiplayer
Blood Gain	Perform 150 kills using the CMG in multiplayer.
Link Feeder	Perform 300 kills using the Enforcer M8 in multiplayer.
Motion Sensor	Perform 175 kills as Microchip in multiplayer.
Rampage	Perform 275 head shots in multiplayer.
Thick Plates	Complete Story Mode Level 2

WEAPONS

Complete the tasks to unlock the following weapons.

UNLOCKABLE	HOW TO UNLOCK
AKS-49	Perform 150 kills using CMG in multiplayer.
ARM-5	Complete Story Mode Level 3.
Bushwacker LMG	Perform 400 kills as Bushwacker.
Bushwacker ML	Perform 400 kills as Bushwacker.
Bushwacker Slug	Perform 400 kills as Bushwacker.
CMG	Perform 150 kills using ARM-5 in multiplayer.
D2 Crossbow	Perform 275 head shots in multiplayer.
Disruptor ML76	Complete Story Mode Level 4.
Enforcer M8	Complete Story Mode Level 2.
GL32	Perform 150 kills playing Finn Cooley in multiplayer.
HSK PSU .45	Complete Story Mode Level 1.
Rhino	Perform 150 kills using the HSK PSU .45 in multiplayer.

PUYO POP FEVER (DS)

To enter this code, go into Options, then Gallery, then highlight Cutscene Viewer.

UNLOCKABLE	CODE
Unlock all characters and cutscenes	Hold ⓧ and press ↑, ↓, ←, →

NEW! A B C D E F G H I J K L M N O P Q R S T U V W X Y Z

QUAKE 3: REVOLUTION (PlayStation 2)

Enter the following code during gameplay.

UNLOCKABLE	CODE
Level Skip	Hold L1+R1+R2+SELECT, then press ×,●,■,▲,×,●,■,▲

QUAKE 4 (XBOX 360)

To enter these codes, press the Back button while playing.

UNLOCKABLE	CODE
Ammo Refill for All Weapons	B, A, X, Y, Left, Right, Left
Full Health Refill	B, A, B, A, Up, Up, Down, X

QUANTUM REDSHIFT (XBOX)

Enter Cheat as your name, then in the Options menu, select the Cheats menu to enter these codes. Codes are case sensitive.

UNLOCKABLE	CODE
All Characters	Nematode
All Speeds	zoomZOOM
Infinite Turbo	FishFace
Infinite Shields	ThinkBat
Upgrade All Characters	RICEitup

R

R-TYPE (Wii)

UNLOCKABLES

UNLOCKABLE	HOW TO UNLOCK
Extra Credits	Set the turbo switch for I to full. Then, hold SELECT+① and press RUN on the title screen.

PASSWORDS

PASSWORD	EFFECT
CPL-3590-CM	Hard mode

R-TYPE 2 (Wii)

PASSWORDS

PASSWORD	EFFECT
JJL-6589-MB	All items and 99 lives

R-TYPE 3 (Wii)

UNLOCKABLES

UNLOCKABLE	HOW TO UNLOCK
Level Select	At the continue screen, press →, →, →, →, →, →, →, →, →, ↓ then press ← one or more times, then press START (the number of times L is pressed dictates the level you skip to

R-TYPE FINAL (PlayStation 2)

Pause the game and enter the following (you will hear a sound if you entered the code correctly):

UNLOCKABLE	CODE
99.9% Charge Dose	Hold L2 and press R2, R2, ←, →, ↑, ↓, →, ←, ↑, ↓, ▲.
Curtain Call Ship (#100)	In the R's Museum, enter 1009 9201 as a password.
Full Blue Power, Missiles, and Bits	Hold L2 and press R2, R2, ←, →, ↑, ↓, →, ←, ↑, ↓, ●.
Full Red Power, Missiles, and Bits	Hold L2 and press R2, R2, ←, →, ↑, ↓, →, ←, ↑, ↓, ■.
Full Yellow Power, Missiles, and Bits	Pause the game, then hold L2 and press R2, R2, ←, →, ↑, ↓, →, ←, ↑, ↓, ×.
Invincibility	Hold L2 and press →, →, ←, →, ←, ←, →, ←, L1, ↑, ↑, ↓, ↓, ↑, ↓, ↑, ↓, L1.
Lady Love Ship (#3)	In the R's Museum, enter 5270 0725 as a password.
Mr. Heli Ship (#59)	In the R's Museum, enter 1026 2001 as a password.
Strider Ship (#24)	In the R's Museum, enter 2078 0278 as a password.

RAIDEN FIGHTERS JET (XBOX 360)

SECRET PLANES

UNLOCKABLE	HOW TO UNLOCK
Fairy	On the ship select screen hold B on Miclus and then press A (B must still be held down).
Slave	On the ship select screen Hold B on any ship except Miclus and then press A (while B is still held down).

RAMPAGE: TOTAL DESTRUCTION (Wii)

At the main menu, press the ⊖+⊕ to open the Password screen.

UNLOCKABLE	PASSWORD
All Monsters Unlocked	141421
Demo Mode with Two Random Monsters	082864
Disable All Active Codes	000000
Display Game Version	314159
Instant Demo Mode with Two Random Monsters	874098
Invincible to Military Attacks, Bombers, Infantry, Tanks, Etc.	986960
Obtain All Ability Upgrades	011235
One Hit Destroys a Building	071767
Unlock All Cities	271828
View Credits	667302
View Ending Theme	667301
View Opening Theme	667300

RAPALA TOURNAMENT FISHING (Wii)

UNLOCKABLE	HOW TO UNLOCK
DT Flat Sure Set Series	Correctly answer 20 questions
Glass Shad Rap Lure	Correctly answer 10 questions
Lauri Rapala 100th Anniversary Lure	Correctly answer 40 questions
X-Rap Jointed Shad Lure	Correctly answer 30 questions
Video 1	Answer 5 questions correctly
Video 2	Answer 15 questions correctly
Video 3	Answer 25 questions correctly
Video 4	Answer 35 questions correctly
Video 5	Answer every question correctly

RATATOUILLE (XBOX 360)

PASSWORDS

PASSWORD	EFFECT
SPEEDY	Unlimited running
MATTELME	Unlock all single player and multiplayer minigames

RATATOUILLE (PlayStation 3)

PASSWORDS

Load a saved profile or create a new profile. Then, select the "Extras" option at the main menu. Choose the "Gusteau's Shop" option, then select the "Secrets" option. Choose a "Code [number]" option and enter the corresponding cheat code to unlock that option. After a cheat option is unlocked, click on its name to enable it. Unlocked and enabled cheat options are saved with the current profile. However, some cheat options cannot be disabled.

* Codes marked with an asterisk cannot be unlocked until they are bought with Gusteau points earned during Story mode.

PASSWORD	EFFECT
Code 01 / Pieceocake	Very Easy difficulty *
Code 02 / Myhero	No impact or damage from enemies, but still take water and falling damage *
Code 03 / Shielded	No damage from enemies, but still take water and falling damage *
Code 04 / Spyagent	Move undetected by enemies *

Code 05 / Ilikeonions	Fart when jumping
Code 06 / Hardfeelings	Head butt when attacking instead of tailswipe
Code 07 / Slumberparty	Multiplayer mode
Code 08 / Gusteauart	All concept art
Code 09 / Gusteauship	All four championship modes
Code 10 / Mattelme	All single player and multiplayer minigames
Code 11 / Gusteauvid	All videos
Code 12 / Gusteaures	All bonus artworks
Code 13 / Gusteaudream	All Dream Worlds in Gusteau's Shop
Code 14 / Gusteauslide	All slides in Gusteau's Shop
Code 15 / Gusteaulevel	All single player minigames
Code 16 / Gusteaucombo	All items in Gusteau's Shop
Code 17 / Gusteaupot	+5,000 Gusteau points
Code 18 / Gusteaujack	+10,000 Gusteau points
Code 19 / Gusteauomni	+50,000 Gusteau points

RATATOUILLE (PSP)

CODES

Select "Options" at the main menu, then "Extras," and finally "Cheats." Enter one of the following codes to activate the corresponding cheat function. A sound confirms correct code entry. Make sure you enter the codes in lowercase.

CODE	EFFECT
saycheese	9,999 Cheese
anyonecancook	All recipes
gusteauvid	All videos
itscake	Any health restored to full
boingspawn	Bouncy cheese
skycan	Can all blue cheese
pieceocake	Easy enemies
myhero	Enemies cause no damage
deepfryer	Hard enemies

RATCHET AND CLANK FUTURE: A CRACK IN TIME (PlayStation 3)

SKILL POINTS

UNLOCKABLE	HOW TO UNLOCK
Agorian Battleplex—Flawless	Finish last challenge without getting hit.
Agorian Battleplex—Impatient Champion	Finish "Gone in 60 Seconds" in less than 45 seconds.
Agorian Battleplex—Interception!	Catch an Agorian Bomb out of the air.
Agorian Battleplex—Lifted and Gifted	Complete a Battleplex challenge entirely on hoverboots.
Agorian Battleplex—seconds Master Blaster	Keep your blaster in the hot state for 60 in My Blaster Runs Hot.
Agorian Battleplex—Praetorian Guard	Destroy the Hydra Tank using only your wrench.
Axiom City—Baggage Handler	Destroy all luggage in Axiom City.
Axiom City—Terachnoid Rave	Get 12 Terachnoids in Axiom City to dance.
Bernilius Sector—Hit and Run	Destroy 10 enemies by ramming them with the Quantum Reflector.
Destruction—Air Lombax	Defeat 50 enemies while the player is in midair.
Destruction—Champion Bowler	Defeat 10 enemies with one dynamo.

UNLOCKABLE	HOW TO UNLOCK
Destruction—Friend of Fred	Defeat 10 enemies with one shot of the Rift Inducer 5000.
Destruction—Magic Bullet	Defeat two enemies with one bullet.
Destruction —Negative, Ghostrider	Shoot down five dropships before they can drop off their passengers.
Destruction—Regifter	Destroy two enemies with one deflection.
Destruction—Shock Therapy using	Defeat an enemy trapped by the Mag-Net the Telsa Spike.
Gadget—Head Like a Rock	Cannonball through 100 crates while on your hoverboots.
Gadget—Orvus' Son	Timebomb 250 projectiles.
Gadget—You're Fired	Maintain an oil fire for at least 30 seconds.
Korthos Sector—The Samaritan	Complete all the missions in this sector.
Krell Canyon—Bug Bait	Take damage from every tetramite swarm without dying.
Krell Canyon—Treasure Hunter	Destroy every camo crate in the level.
Molonoth Fields—Son of Kaden	Complete the hoverboot course in less than 45 seconds.
Molonoth Fields—Spring Cleaning	Destroy every junk pile in Molonoth.
Nefarious Space Station—Pest Control	Defeat all Teratropes in the outer perimeter with the Hyper Strike.
Phylax Sector—I Think I'm Gonna Be Sick	Do five U-turns within 20 seconds.
Phylax Sector—Stockpiler	Destroy 20 fighters in a row without firing a missile.
Skill—Ace Pilot	Destroy 20 fighters without getting hit.
Skill—Custodian of Time	Fix 50 repairable objects in the Great Clock.
Skill—Dance, Monkey, Dance	Get eight monkeys to dance simultaneously.
Skill—Master of Time	Reach round 30 in the fix-time minigame.
Skill—Subzero Hero	Freeze four enemies simultaneously using the CryoMine Glove.
The Great Clock—Braniac	Complete the last time puzzle room in 40 seconds or less.
The Great Clock—Outta Time	Complete the first level within 300 seconds.
The Great Clock—Temporal Pacifism	Complete Quantum Annex 3 without harming a Teratrope.
The Great Clock —What Goes Up	Keep a crate suspended in midair for more than 3 seconds.
Vela Sector—Chasing Tail	Stay behind comet for 15 seconds.
Vela Sector—No Respect for the Dead	Destroy every ship in the graveyard.
Weapons—Longshot	Shoot 30 enemies in their weak spots using the Plasma Striker.
Weapons—Party Crasher	Defeat 50 dancing enemies.
Weapons—Round Trip	Defeat an enemy with the Spiral of Death while he energy spiral is returning.
Weapons—Sonic Assassin	Fire the Sonic Eruptor perfectly 50 times.
Weapons—The Simple Art of Armageddon	Defeat 15 enemies with the RYNO V without releasing the trigger.
Weapons—Wrenchmaster	Defeat 3 enemies with a single wrench throw.
Zolar Forest—Cold Killer	Destroy 100 zyphoids in Zolar Forest.
Zolar Forest—Terrible Tourist	Destroy every breakable object in the Fongoid Village.

BONUSES

If you have save files for Ratchet and Clank Future: Tools of Destruction and Ratchet and Clank Future: Quest for Booty on your system, you can unlock in-game perks that enhance your gameplay.

UNLOCKABLE	HOW TO UNLOCK
Discount at Weapon Vendors	Have a Ratchet and Clank Future: Tools of Destruction save.
Pirate Hat Skin	Have a Ratchet and Clank Future: Quest for Booty save.

RATCHET & CLANK FUTURE: TOOLS OF DESTRUCTION (PlayStation 3)

EXTRA MODES

UNLOCKABLE	HOW TO UNLOCK
Challenge Mode	Beat the game.

EXTRAS AND CONCEPT ART

Obtain the number of skill points listed below to unlock the art or the extra feature.

UNLOCKABLE	HOW TO UNLOCK
2006 GDC Trailer	150 SP
2007 E3 Trailer	25 SP
Big Head Enemies	100 SP
Big Head Mode (Ratchet only)	50 SP
Character Concept Art	75 SP
Environment Concept Art	250 SP
James the Galactic Defender	400 SP
Levels Are Mirrored	500 SP
Ratchet Drawing Tutorial	350 SP
Script to Screen	600 SP
Tools of Production	200 SP
Weapon Concept Art	450 SP
Wrench Replacement	300 SP

SKILL POINTS

UNLOCKABLE	HOW TO UNLOCK
Alphabet City	Teleport to each of the six asteroids in alphabetical order.
Been Around	Take off from every robo-wing pad in Stratus City.
Bolts in the Bank	Sell 20 Leviathan Souls to the Smuggler.
Can't Touch This	Don't take damage before fighting Greasepalms McGee.
Cheapskate	Purchase a single Combuster shot.
Chorus Line	Make 11 enemies dance together.
Collector's Addition	Collect all cargo containers.
Dancin' with the Stars	Make five enemies dance at once on an asteroid.
Dancing on the Ceiling	Successfully use the Groovitron on a Gravity Ramp.
Disco Inferno	Use the Groovitron followed by the Pyro Blaster.
Even Better the Second Time	Complete Challenge mode.
Everybody Dance Now	Make every type of enemy in the game dance.
Expert Marksman	Kill 75 percent of all the enemies.
Extinction	Kill all the Sargasso Grunthors.
Fast and Firey-ous	Use the charge boots to cross the bridge to the arena without being burned.
Fire With Fire	Kill two Kerchu Pyroguards with the Pyro Blaster.
For the Hoard!	Get every device.
Giant Hunter	Kill all Basilisk Leviathans in the Cobalia wilderness.

UNLOCKABLE	HOW TO UNLOCK
Global Thermonuclear War	Get every weapon.
Golden Children	Get all gold bolts.
Gotta Catch Them All	Hit all Cragmite soldiers with the Mag-Net Launcher.
Happy Feat	Get nine penguins dancing on screen.
Head Examiner	Land on all of the Troglosaur heads.
I Should Have Gone Down in a Barrel	Jump into each of the two gelatonium waterfalls in the Cobalia gelatonium plant.
I Think I'm Going To Be Sick	Ride the Ferris wheel five times without taking damage.
I've Got Places to Be	Destroy Iron Crotch Caruso in under 2:30.
It Sounded Like a Freight Train	Get 11 Anthropods in one tornado.
It's a Mutiny Cap'n!	Change five pirates into penguins in one shot.
It's Like the South Pole Here	Turn at least 15 enemies or citizens into penguins at one time.
It's Even Better the Second Time	Complete Challenge mode.
Knock You Down to Size	Wrench slam five Cerullean Centipedes.
Live Strong	Complete the Gyro-Cycle area in under 1:45.
Lombaxes Don't Like Cold	Break all the breakable icicles.
Low Flying Owls	Fly underneath an electrified barrier in the robo-wing segment.
Minesweeper	Clear out 10-15 mines.
Mow Down Hoedown	Use turrets to destroy 10 dancing pirates.
No, Up YOUR Arsenal	Upgrade every weapon to the max.
Now Boarding...	Complete the Gyro Cycle area in 0:55 seconds.
Nowhere to Hide	Destroy every piece of breakable cover.
One Heckuva Peephole	Use the Geo-Laser to blast through the wall.
Preemptive Strike	Destroy five of the Thwogs while they are still sleeping.
Pretty Lights	Don't destroy any Snatchers.
Promoted to Inspector	Get every gadget.
Pyew Pyew	Complete Verdigris Black Hole without secondary fire.
Roflcopter	Turn an enemy into a penguin, then use the Visi copter to destroy the penguin.
Say Hello to My Little Friend	Kill 15 enemies with one RYNO shot.
Seared Ahi	Use the Pyro Blaster on three Drophyds after freeing them from their robotic suits.
Six Gun Salute	Get six pirates in a row to salute Ratchet while wearing the Holo-Pirate disguise.
Smashing Good Time	Destroy all crates and consumer robots on port and gel factory.
Stay Still So I Can Shoot You!	Use strafe flip 10 times while fighting.
Surface-to-air Plasma Beasts	Take out three flying targets using the Plasma Beasts.
Taste O' Yer Own Medicine	Destroy all Corsairs with the Combuster.
The Consumer Is Not (Always) Right	Destroy 18 consumer robots.
The Hardest Core	Get everything else in the game.
Untouchable	Don't take damage in the Gyro-Cycle.
We Don't Need No Stinkin' Bridges!	Cross the tripad sequence without activating the bridge.
Whats That, R2?	Barrel roll 10 times.
Wrench Ninja 3	Use only the wrench to make it to the robo-wings segment.
You Sunk My Battleship!	Shoot down at least 75 percent of the flying ships.

RATCHET AND CLANK: UP YOUR ARSENAL (PlayStation 2)

UNLOCKABLE	CODE
Duel Blade Laser Sword	Pause the game and press ●,■,●,■,↑,↓,←,←.
Sly 2: Band of Thieves Demo	At the Title Screen, hold L1+L2+R1+R2.

RAYMAN ARENA (PlayStation 2)

Enter these codes as a name, then press L2+●+■ to activate it.

UNLOCKABLE	CODE
3D Mode	3DVISION
Every Battle Mode Unlocked	ALLFISH
Every Character Unlocked	PUPPETS
Every Mode Unlocked	ALLRAYMANM
Every Skin Unlocked	CARNIVAL
Every Battle Level Unlocked	ARENAS
Every Level Unlocked	FIELDS
Every Race Level Unlocked	TRACKS
Monochrome Mode	OLDTV

RAYMAN RAVING RABBIDS (Wii)

UNLOCKABLES

UNLOCKABLE	HOW TO UNLOCK
Alternate Ending	Score at least 1,000,000 points in Score mode
Artwork 1	5,000 Points
Artwork 2	93,000 Points
Bunnies Can't Cook Eggs	84,000 Points
Bunnies Can't Infiltrate Games Convention	48,000 Points
Bunnies Can't Play Soccer	138,000 Points
Bunnies Don't Do Vacuum Cleaning	21,000 Points
Bunnies Don't Like Taking a Bath	9,000 Points
Bunnies Never Close Doors	111,000 Points
Bunny Costume	Clear all games on day 12
Bunny Hunt Survival Mode	Clear all games on Bunny Hunt Time mode at least once
Bunny Hunt Time Mode	Clear all games on Bunny Hunt Score mode at least once
Caramba Costume	Clear all games on day 08
Challenge Mode	Complete Story mode
"Dark Iron Bunnies" for the Jukebox	Clear all games on day 11
Dee-Jay Costume	Clear all games on day 02
French Bastille Day	57,000 Points
Gold Cow Trophy on Top of the Wardrobe	Clear all games on day 15
"Girls Just Want To Have Fun" for the Jukebox	Clear all games on day 05
"Good Time" for the Jukebox	Clear all games on day 03
Gothic Costume	Clear all games on day 04
"Hip Hop Hooray" for the Jukebox	Clear all games on day 07
"La Bamba" for the Jukebox	Clear all games on day 09
"Misirlou" for the Jukebox	Clear all games on day 01
Raymaninho Costume	Clear all games on day 10
Rock 'n Roll Costume	Clear all games on day 06
"The Butcher Deejay" for the Jukebox	Clear all games on day 13

UNLOCKABLE	HOW TO UNLOCK
"Ubisoft Montpellier Choir" for the Jukebox	Clear all games on day 14
US Independence Day	165,000 Points

RED CARD 2003 (XBOX)

UNLOCKABLE	OBJECTIVE
Apes Team and Victoria Falls Stadium	Defeat the Apes team in World Conquest mode.
Dolphins Team and Nautilus Stadium	Defeat the Dolphins team in World Conquest mode.
Finals Mode	Win all matches in World Conquest mode.
Martians Team and USAFB001 Stadium	Defeat the Martians team in World Conquest mode.
Matadors Team and Coliseum Stadium	Defeat the Matadors team in World Conquest mode.
Samurai Team and Youhi Gardens Stadium	Defeat the Samurai team in World Conquest mode.
SWAT Team and Nova City Stadium	Defeat the SWAT team in World Conquest mode.
Cheat Mode	Enter BIGTANK as a name to unlock all teams, stadiums, and finals mode.

RED FACTION 2 (XBOX)

Input the following codes at the Cheat menu.

UNLOCKABLE	CODE
Bouncy Grenades	BLK, BLK, BLK, BLK, BLK, BLK, BLK, BLK
Bullet Gibs	BLK, BLK, BLK, BLK, WHT, X, BLK, BLK
Bullets Instantly Gib	X, X, X, X, Y, BLK, X, X
Directors Cut	Y, X, BLK, WHT, BLK, X, Y, WHT
Explosives Instantly Gib	WHT, BLK, X, Y, WHT, BLK, X, Y
Fat Mode	BLK, BLK, BLK, BLK, WHT, X, BLK, BLK
Fire Bullets	Y, Y, Y, Y, Y, Y, Y, Y
Hidden Message	Y, X, Y, X, Y, X, Y, X
Rapid Rails	BLK, Y, BLK, Y, X, X, WHT, WHT
Super Health	X, X, Y, WHT, Y, WHT, BLK
Unlimited Ammo	Y, WHT, X, BLK, Y, BLK, X, WHT
Unlimited Grenades	BLK, X, BLK, Y, X, WHT, X, BLK
Everything	WHT, WHT, X, X, Y, BLK, Y, BLK
Wacky Deaths	WHT, WHT, WHT, WHT, WHT, WHT, WHT, WHT
Zombie Walk	X, X, X, X, X, X, X, WHT

RED FACTION 2 (PlayStation 2)

Enter the following codes at the Cheats screen under the Options menu.

UNLOCKABLE	CODE
Bouncy Grenades	●,●,●,●,●,●,●,●
Directors Cut	■,×,●,▲,●,×,■,▲
Gibby Bullets	●,●,●,●,▲,×,●,●
Gibby Explosions	▲,●,×,■,▲,●,×,■
Instagib Ammunition	×,×,×,×,■,●,×,×
Joke Message	■,×,■,×,■,×,■,×
Level Select	●,■,×,▲,■,●,×,×
Master Code unlocks all normal game options.	▲,▲,×,×,■,●,■,●
Master Cheat Code	■,●,▲,●,■,×,▲,×
Rain of Fire	■,■,■,■,■,■,■,■
Rapid Rails	●,■,●,■,×,×,▲,▲

Super Health	×,×,■,▲,■,▲,●
Unlimited Ammunition	■,▲,×,●,■,●,×,▲
Unlimited Grenades	●,×,●,■,×,●,×,●
Wacky Deaths	▲,▲,▲,▲,▲,▲,▲,▲
Walking Dead	×,×,×,×,×,×,×,×

RED FACTION: GUERRILLA (XBOX 360)

CODES

Fom the main menu select "Options," then "Extras," then enter code.

EFFECT	CODE
Bonus multiplayer map pack featuring four maps	MAPMAYHEM
Unlocks golden sledgehammer for single-player use	HARDHITTER

RED FACTION: GUERRILLA (PlayStation 3)

CODES

Fom the main menu select "Options," then "Extras," then enter code.

EFFECT	CODE
Bonus multiplayer map pack featuring four maps	MAPMAYHEM
Unlocks golden sledgehammer for single-player use	HARDHITTER

RED STEEL (Wii)

UNLOCKABLES

UNLOCKABLE	HOW TO UNLOCK
Secret Staff Photos	When you first find the geishas on the mission Reiko sends you on, you'll see some lockers near them. Open the one with a darker door to see photos of the developers wearing blonde wigs.

REIGN OF FIRE (PlayStation 2)

UNLOCKABLE	CODE
Level Select	At Main menu, enter ↑, ←, ●, ●, ←, ←, ■, ↓, ↑, ●

RESERVOIR DOGS (XBOX 360)

CODES

UNLOCKABLE	HOW TO UNLOCK
Adrenaline Rush—Infinite Adrenaline	A, LT, Y, A, LT, A, START
Battering Ram—Instant Crash	BLK, BLK, A, A, Y, WHT, START
Bulletproof—Infinite Health	LT, RT, Y, Y, RT, WHT, START
Fully Loaded—Infinite Ammo	WHT, BLK, Y, BLK, A, WHT, START
Magic Bullet—One Shot Kills	RT, BLK, Y, A, RT, A, START
Time Out—Infinite Timer	RT, RT, WHT, Y, A, BLK, START
Unlock All Levels	BLK, WHT, BLK, WHT, LT, RT, START
Unlock Art Gallery	Y, A, BLK, WHT, Y, A, START
Unlock Movie Gallery	LT, LT, Y, A, LT, RT, START

UNLOCKABLES

UNLOCKABLE	HOW TO UNLOCK
Battering Ram	Successfully complete the game with the Professional ranking to unlock the Battering Ram cheat under the Extra menu.
Bulletproof	Successfully complete the game with the Professional ranking to unlock the Bulletproof cheat under the Extra menu.
Fully Loaded	Successfully complete the game with the Psychopath ranking to unlock the Fully Loaded cheat under the Extra menu.
Time Out	Successfully complete the game with the Career Criminal ranking to unlock the Time Out cheat under the Extra menu.

NEW! A B C D E F G H I J K L M N O P Q R S T U V W X Y Z

RESERVOIR DOGS (PlayStation 2)

Enter these codes in the Cheats menu under extras.

UNLOCKABLE	CODE
All levels	L2, R2, L2, R2, L1, R1, START
Art gallery	●, ×, L2, R2, ●, ×, START
Movie gallery	L1, L1, ●, ×, L1, R1, START
Unlimited ammo	R2, L2, ●; L2, ×, R2, START

RESIDENT EVIL 5 (PlayStation 3)

REGENERATE ITEMS

In Chapter 2-1, take all the items at the beginning and then quit the game. Resume the game by pressing "Continue" to start Chapter 2-1 again. This time you will have items you got before you quit the game in your inventory, however, new sets of the items are there for you to collect. Repeat the process to get as many as you like. This glitch is also available in Chapter 3-1.

RESIDENT EVIL: THE UMBRELLA CHRONICLES (Wii)

UNLOCKABLES

UNLOCKABLE	HOW TO UNLOCK
Unlimited Ammo	Gain an S rank in all missions on Hard difficulty.

EXTRA SCENARIOS

To unlock the extra scenarios, complete the following scenarios with the corresponding ranks.

UNLOCKABLE	HOW TO UNLOCK
Beginnings 1	Beat Train Derailment 3.
Beginnings 2	Beat Beginnings 1 with an A rank or higher.
Dark Legacy 1	Complete Fall of Umbrella 3.
Dark Legacy 2	Complete Death's Door and Nightmare 2.
Death's Door	Beat Raccoon's Destruction 3 with an A rank.
Fourth Survivor	Complete Dark Legacy 2.
Nightmare 1	Complete Mansion Incident 1.
Nightmare 2	Beat Nightmare 1 with an A rank or higher.
Rebirth 1	Beat Mansion Incident 3.
Rebirth 2	Beat Rebirth 1.

PAST ITEMS

To unlock items from past *Resident Evil* games, complete the following chapters and gain the corresponding rank.

UNLOCKABLE	HOW TO UNLOCK
Battery	Complete Dark Legacy 2 with S rank.
Blue/Green Leech Charm	Complete Train Derailment 3 with A rank.
Blue/Red/Green Chemical	Complete Umbrella's End 2 with A rank.
Blue/Red/Yellow Gemstone	Complete Rebirth 2 with A rank.
Book of Wisdom/Future Compass	Complete Raccoon's Destruction 1 with S rank.
Briefcase	Complete Train Derailment 1 with S rank.
Chronos Key	Complete Raccoon's Destruction 3 with S rank.
Clark/Gail X-Ray	Complete Rebirth 1 with A rank.
Crystal/Obsidian/Amber Ball	Complete Raccoon's Destruction 3 with A rank.
Cylinder Shaft	Complete Nightmare 1 with A rank.
Death Mask	Complete Rebirth 2 with S rank.
Eagle/Serpent/Jaguar Stone	Complete Fourth Survivor with S rank.
Emblem/Gold Emblem	Complete Nightmare 2 with S rank.
Film A/B/C/D	Complete Umbrella's End 1 with S rank.

Fire/Water Key	Complete Beginning 2 with A rank.
Fuel Canteen	Complete Mansion Incident 3 with S rank.
G-Virus	Complete Fourth Survivor with A rank.
Hex Crank	Complete Nightmare 1 with S rank.
Ink Ribbon	Complete Umbrella's End 3 with S rank.
Joint N/S Plug	Complete Raccoon's Destruction 2 with A rank.
King/Knight/Bishop/Rook Plug	Complete Dark Legacy 1 with A rank.
Last Book, Vol. 1/2	Complete Nightmare 2 with A rank.
Lighter Fluid	Complete Raccoon's Destruction 2 with S rank.
Medium Base	Complete Dark Legacy 1 with S rank.
Microfilm A/B	Complete Beginning 2 with S rank.
Mixing Set	Complete Train Derailment 1 with A rank.
MO Disk	Complete Mansion Incident 3 with A rank.
Motherboard	Complete Beginning 1 with A rank.
Picture (Ada and John)	Complete Death's Door with A rank.
Plastic Bomb/Detonator	Complete Umbrella's End 1 with A rank.
Relief of Discipline/ Obedience/Unity	Complete Train Derailment 2 with S rank.
S.T.A.R.S. Card (Brad's)	Complete Death's Door with S rank.
S.T.A.R.S. Card (Jill's)	Complete Raccoon's Destruction 1 with A rank.
Slide Cartridge	Complete Rebirth 1 with S rank.
Spade/Diamond/Club/Heart Key	Complete Dark Legacy 2 with A rank.
Square Crank	Complete Umbrella's End 2 with S rank.
Statue of Good/Evil	Complete Train Derailment 2 with A rank.
Sterilizing Agent	Complete Train Derailment 3 with S rank.
Sun/Star/Moon Crest	Complete Mansion Incident 2 with A rank.
V-Jolt	Complete Mansion Incident 2 with S rank.
Vaccine	Complete Umbrella's End 3 with A rank.
Valve Handle	Complete Beginning 1 with S rank.

RESISTANCE 2 (PlayStation 3)

COOPERATIVE MEDIC UNLOCKABLES

Reach the corresponding level to unlock.

UNLOCKABLE	HOW TO UNLOCK
Phoenix (Weapon)	Level 1
Ring of Life (Berserk)	Level 1
Rossmore 238 (Weapon)	Level 10
Phoenix Ash (Berserk)	Level 12
Air Fuel Grenades	Level 12 Medic
Bioplasm Tracking Tech	Level 14
Assault Pack	Level 16
HE .44 Magnum (Weapon)	Level 18
M5A2 Carbine (Weapon)	Level 2
Bio-amp Scope	Level 22
Voltaic Body Armor	Level 24
Leech Barrel	Level 26
V7 Splicer (Weapon)	Level 28
Psychokinetic Helmet	Level 30
Chloroform (Berserk)	Level 4

UNLOCKABLE	HOW TO UNLOCK
Kinetic Gloves	Level 6
High Density Bioplasm Chamber	Level 8

COOPERATIVE SOLDIER UNLOCKABLES

Reach the corresponding level to unlock.

UNLOCKABLE	HOW TO UNLOCK
HVAP Wraith (Weapon)	Level 1
Ironheart (Berserk)	Level 1
Auger (Weapon)	Level 10
Air Fuel Grenades (Weapon: Grenades)	Level 12
Backlash (Berserk)	Level 12
Advanced Timing Motor	Level 14
Assault Pack	Level 16
Bullseye (Weapon)	Level 18
Rossmore 238 (Weapon)	Level 2
Voltaic Body Armor	Level 24
Precision Scope	Level 26
Laark (Weapon)	Level 28
Psychokinetic Helmet	Level 30
Overload (Berserk)	Level 4
Kinetic Gloves	Level 6
High Capacity Ammo Belt	Level 8
Titanium Barrels	Level 22

COOPERATIVE SPEC. OPS. UNLOCKABLES

Reach the corresponding level to unlock.

UNLOCKABLE	HOW TO UNLOCK
Marksmen (Weapon)	Level 1
Prototype Ammo (Berserk)	Level 1
Proximity Mines (Weapon: Alternate to Ammo)	Level 10
Snake Eyes (Berserk)	Level 12
L23 Fareye (Weapon)	Level 12
Shock Suppressor	Level 14
Assault Pack	Level 16
Auger (Weapon)	Level 18
Bullseye (Weapon)	Level 2
Hawkeye Scope	Level 22
Voltaic Body Armor	Level 24
Mag-Propulsion Barrel	Level 26
Bellock (Weapon)	Level 28
Psychokinetic Helmet	Level 30
Invisibility (Berserk)	Level 4
Kinetic Gloves	Level 6
High Density Ammo Chamber	Level 8

RETURN TO CASTLE WOLFENSTEIN: TIDES OF WAR (XBOX)

UNLOCKABLE	CODE
Wolfenstein 3D	Beat the single player Campaign mode.

REZ HD (XBOX 360)

BEYOND MODE VIEWPOINTS

There are four extra unlockable "views" in Beyond mode. Unlock them by doing the following.

UNLOCKABLE	HOW TO UNLOCK
Dynamic View	Get first place in four Areas in Score Attack mode.
Far View	Get first place in three Areas in Score Attack mode.
First Person View	Get first place in five Areas in Score Attack mode.
Near View	Get first place in two Areas in Score Attack mode.

BEYOND MODE FORMS

Successfully complete the following tasks to unlock the corresponding form.

UNLOCKABLE	HOW TO UNLOCK
Fifth Form	Four areas 100 percent shot down (Play mode)/Play time more than eight hours.
Final Form	All areas 100 percent shot down (Play mode)/Play time more than nine hours.
Fourth Form	Three areas 100 percent shot down (Play mode)/Play time more than seven hours.
Morolian Form	All areas 100 percent shot down, 100 percent Support Item (Play mode)/Play time more than 10 hours.
Third Form	Two areas 100 percent shot down (Play mode)/Play time more than six hours.
Zero Form/Second Form	One area 100 percent shot down (Play mode)/Play time more than five hours.

ACHIEVEMENTS

UNLOCKABLE	HOW TO UNLOCK
Eden (20)	Clear Play mode area 5.
Firewall Buster (15)	Get a local ranking of first in boss rush.
Laser Assassin (15)	Shot down over 95 percent in area 1-5.
Power Breaker (10)	Clear score attack over 30 times.
The EARTH (20)	Clear Play mode area 1.
The Forgotten (15)	Get a local raking of first in lost area.
The MARS (20)	Clear Play mode area 2.
The Rezident (15)	Achieve 100 percent shot down and support items in areas 1-5, or play for over 10 hours.
The URANUS (20)	Clear Play mode area 4.
The VENUS (20)	Clear Play mode area 3.
Trance Hacker (15)	Clear direct assault (trance).
Ultimate Cracker (15)	Get a local ranking of first in all five areas in score attack.

BEYOND OPTIONS

UNLOCKABLE	HOW TO UNLOCK
Overdrive Infinity	Rank first in boss rush.

RIDGE RACER 7 (PlayStation 3)

UNLOCKABLE	HOW TO UNLOCK
Auto Rocket Start System	100 Points with Zolgear
Collision Decreaser	100 Points with all tyre and suspension manufacturers
Down Force Control System	100 Points with Bosconian
Nitrous Tank 100	100 Points with all nitrous manufacturers
Over Limit Start System	100 Points all engine tune up manufacturers
Prize Money x2	100 Points with all manufacturers

UNLOCKABLE	HOW TO UNLOCK
Race Data Analyzer	100 Points with Galaxian
SS Booster	100 Points with Arkbird
SS Canceler	100 Points all exterior parts manufacturers
10&20% discount and special Age machine	Obtain 100 Manufacturer Points from Age
10&20% discount and special Assoluto machine	Obtain 100 Manufacturer Points from Assoluto
10&20% discount and special Danver machine	Obtain 100 Manufacturer Points from Danver
10&20% discount and special Gnade machine	Obtain 100 Manufacturer Points from Gnade
10&20% discount and special Himmel machine	Obtain 100 Manufacturer Points from Himmel
10&20% discount and special Kamata machine	Obtain 100 Manufacturer Points from Kamata
10&20% discount and special Namco machine	Obtain 100 Manufacturer Points from Namco
10&20% discount and special SinseongMotors machine	Obtain 100 Manufacturer Points from SinseongMotors
10&20% discount and special Soldat machine	Obtain 100 Manufacturer Points from Soldat
10&20% discount and special Terrazi machine	Obtain 100 Manufacturer Points from Terrazi

RISE OF KASAI (PlayStation 2)

Enter the following codes at the Press Start screen.

UNLOCKABLE	CODE
Invincible Rau	■, ●, ×, ■, ●, ■, ×, ●, ×, ■, ●, ×
Infinite Ammunition	×, ●, ■, ■, ×, ■, ●, ●, ×, ■, ■, ×
Weaker Enemies	×, ●, ●, ■, ×, ■, ■, ●

RISE TO HONOR (PlayStation 2)

UNLOCKABLE	OBJECTIVE
Extra Costumes	Complete the game.
Hard Mode	Complete the game on Normal.
Kit Yun and Michelle's FMV	Complete the game.

RISTAR (Wii)

PASSWORDS

PASSWORD	EFFECT
STAR	A shooting star goes across the background (JP)
MUSEUM	Boss Rush mode
XXXXXX	Clears/Deactivates the current password
AGES	Copyright info is displayed
MIEMIE	Hidden items' grab points are shown with a blue star
FEEL	ILOVEU, MIEMIE, CANDY active all at once (JP)
CANDY	Invincibility (JP)
MACCHA	Mentions Miyake color (JP)
MASTER	Mentions next game (JP)
AAAAAA	No Continue limit (JP)
MAGURO	Onchi Music mode and credits music in sound test
HETAP	Reverses the high score in Demo mode (JP)
VALDI	Shows the solar system (JP)

ILOVEU	Stage select
SUPERB	Super Difficulty mode
SUPER	Super Hard mode
DOFEEL	Time Attack mode

RIVER CITY RANSOM (Wii)

PASSWORDS

PASSWORD	EFFECT
XfMdZTHwiR3 jaj6jfRUDEt tilm2tWRo8b	Final Boss, with Max Stats, Dragon Feet, Stone Hands, Grand Slam, and Texas Boots
XfMdZTHUPR3 rztzPeQUCTt 61lxhtWRo2b	Final Boss, with Max Stats, Stone Hands, Dragon Feet, Acro Circus, Grand SlaM, 4 Karma Jolts, and $999.99 cash
t1izvpdOZnZ JxNkJp7Cpub XMPQgXErSMF	Ivan Beaten, High School Open
w412ysgtMqc MUSjKm2PqtE UJMNdUTGOQC	Power Up
jrYplfTgbdj nOorLTIYXwR SjTuqpilUHP	Start with all abilities and $500 in cash
fHUFBbvcnpa MS8iPplCZJP VKNOeVRQPDD	Strange item in inventory that gives stat increases

UNLOCKABLES

UNLOCKABLE	HOW TO UNLOCK
Change Character Names	On the Character Select screen, press SELECT on the controller to go to a screen where you can change Alex and Ryan's names to whatever you want.
Merlin's Mystery Shop	To find Merlin's Mystery Shop go to the Armstrong Thru-Way. Once inside, press up at the top wall and the wall opens. Inside you can buy the best items in the game.

ROADKILL (XBOX)

Enter the following codes at the map screen when paused.

UNLOCKABLE	CODE
Restore Health	Ⓧ,Ⓑ,Ⓧ,Ⓑ,Ⓧ,Ⓑ,Ⓧ,Ⓑ
More Money	Ⓨ,Ⓑ,Ⓨ,Ⓑ,Ⓧ,Ⓐ,Ⓧ,Ⓐ,↓,↑
Infinite Ammo	Ⓨ,Ⓧ,Ⓧ,Ⓑ,Ⓨ,Ⓧ,Ⓧ,Ⓑ

ROADKILL (PlayStation 2)

Pause the game on the Map screen then enter the following codes.

UNLOCKABLE	CODE
All Weapons	▲, ×, ×, ▲, ■, ●, ●, ■, ×, ■, ●, ▲
All Vehicles	↑, ↓, ↑, ↓, ▲, ×, ▲, ×, ■, ●, ●, ■
Health	■, ●, ■, ●, ■, ●, ■, ●
Infinite Ammo	▲, ■, ■, ●, ▲, ■, ■, ●
More Money	▲, ●, ▲, ●, ■, ×, ■, ×, ↓, ↑

ROBOTS (XBOX)

Pause the game to enter these codes.

UNLOCKABLE	CODE
Give Rodney a Big Head	↑,↓,↓,↑,→,→,←,→
Unlimited Health	↑,→,↓,↑,←,↓,→,←
Unlimited Scrap	↓,↓,←,↑,↑,→,↑,↓

ROCK BAND (XBOX 360)

UNLOCK ALL

Enter quickly at the "Rock Band" title screen (disables saving).

CODE	EFFECT
Red, Yellow, Blue, Red, Red, Blue, Blue, Red, Yellow, Blue	Unlock All Songs

ROCK BAND (Wii)

CODES

Using the colored fret buttons on the guitar, enter these codes QUICKLY on the title screen.

EFFECT	CODE
Unlock All Songs (Disable Saving)	R, Y, B, R, R, B, B, R, Y, B

ROCK BAND 2 (XBOX 360)

CODES

Go to the "Extras" option in the main menu. Choose "Modify Game," then input the following codes. All codes disable saving.

EFFECT	CODE
Awesome Detection	Yellow, Blue, Orange, Yellow, Blue, Orange, Yellow, Blue, Orange
Stage Mode	Blue, Yellow, Red, Blue, Yellow, Red, Blue, Yellow, Red
Unlock All Songs	Red, Yellow, Blue, Red, Red, Blue, Blue, Red, Yellow, Blue
Venue Select: Unlock All Venues	Blue, Orange, Orange, Blue, Yellow, Blue, Orange, Orange, Blue, Yellow

THE BEATLES: ROCK BAND (XBOX 360)

CODES

Enter quickly at the "The Beatles Rock Band" title screen.

EFFECT	CODE
Unlocks set of bonus photos	Blue, Yellow, Orange, Orange, Orange, Blue, Blue, Blue, Yellow, Orange

UNLOCKABLES

UNLOCKABLE	HOW TO UNLOCK
Ringo Starr Gamer Picture	Earn Achievement: "And the Band Begins to Play."
John Lennon Gamer Picture	Earn Achievement: "Better Free Your Mind Instead."
George Harrison Gamer Picture	Earn Achievement: "No One's Frightened of Playing."
Paul McCartney Gamer Picture	Earn Achievement: "Things That Money Just Can't Buy."
Gold Plate (for your instruments)	Earn 30 Achievements.
Platinum Plate (for your instruments)	Earn 50 Achievements.
Silver Plate (for your instruments)	Earn 15 Achievements.

THE BEATLES: ROCK BAND (Wii)

CODES

Enter quickly atThe Beatles Rock Band title screen

EFFECT	CODE
Unlocks set of bonus photos	Blue, Yellow, Orange, Orange, Orange, Blue, Blue, Blue, Yellow, Orange

ROCKSTAR GAMES PRESENTS TABLE TENNIS (Wii)

UNLOCKABLE SHIRTS

UNLOCKABLE	HOW TO UNLOCK
Carmen's blue/green/gray Shirt	Win a match using a heavy leftspin shot.
Carmen's dark blue shirt	Win a match using a heavy topspin shot.
Carmen's grey shirt	Shut out the CPU in at least one game in the match.

Cassidy's brown shirt	Win a match using a heavy backspin shot.
Cassidy's dark blue shirt	Win a match using a heavy rightspin shot.
Cassidy's yellow/white shirt	Win a match by making the ball bounce 2or more times on the CPU's side of the table.
Liu Ping's green shirt	Win a match using a late swing.
Liu Ping's red/white shirt	Win a match by returning a shot from the CPU that dropped short.
Liu Ping's yellow shirt	Win a match using a forehand shot.
Solayman's dark blue shirt	Win a match with a 4-point deficit comeback.
Solayman's green shirt	Win a match using a backhand shot.
Solayman's gray shirt	Win a match using a smash shot.

ROGUE TROOPER (XBOX)

CODES

To activate these codes, enter them while in the "Extras" Menu. You can then select them from the "Cheats" menu.

UNLOCKABLE	HOW TO UNLOCK
Extreme Ragdoll	Up, Up, Up, BLK, BLK, BLK, Up
Hippy Blood	WHT, Left, B, Down, RB, BACK
Infinite Health	Left, Right, Up, Down, L, X
Infinite Supplies	BACK, RB, LB, BACK, R, LB
Low Gravity Ragdoll	X, X, X, B, B, B, Up, Down

UNLOCKABLES

UNLOCKABLE	HOW TO UNLOCK
All Weapons and Upgrades	Complete the game. Instead of starting a new game, use the Level Select cheat and start on the first level to keep everything you unlocked.
Extreme Ragdoll	Complete the game on any difficulty, start a new game, enter the Options menu, select Cheats.
Hippy Blood (Changes blood into colorful flowers)	Complete the game on any difficulty, start a new game, enter the Options menu, select Cheats.
Level Select	Successfully complete a level to unlock it at the Cheats menu.
Low Gravity Ragdoll (Enemies fly away when killed)	Complete the game on any difficulty, start a new game, enter the Options menu, select Cheats.
Massacre Mode	Complete the game on any difficulty setting to unlock the Massacre difficulty setting.

ROGUE TROOPER (PlayStation 2)

Enter these codes in the Extras menu.

UNLOCKABLE	CODE
Extreme Ragdoll Physics	Up, Up, Up, R2, R2, Up
Hippy Blood	L2, Right, ●, Down, R1, SELECT
Infinite Health	Left, Right, Up, Down, , ■
Infinite Supplies	SELECT, R1, L1, SELECT, , L1
Low Gravity Ragdoll Physics	■, ■, ●, ●, Up, Down

ROMANCE OF THE THREE KINGDOMS IV: WALL OF FIRE (Wii)

UNLOCKABLES

UNLOCKABLE	HOW TO UNLOCK
Form Anti-Dong Zhuo Coalition	Select the first scenario (Dong Zhuo Triumphs in Luo Yang), then select Cao Cao as your leader. On your very first turn, move some generals and troops to Xu Chang. A few months later, Cao Cao will call a meeting, asking all the other leaders to form an alliance against Dong Zhuo. If Yuan Shao joins, he will become

	leader; otherwise, Cao Cao will become leader. This makes defeating Dong Zhuo a bit easier, depending on who joins you (such as Yuan Shao or Ma Teng).
Unlimited Soldiers	Use the War command and select a general to go into battle. Assign the maximum number of men to his unit. When they asked for confirmation for going to war select the "No" option. Remove the general from the list of commanders and reassign him to the post. Return to the troop assignment screen. The number of men available should be multiplied by the number that was assigned earlier. Repeat this process to increase the number of men, but don't go back to the main menu.

ROOGOO (XBOX 360)

ACHIEVEMENTS

UNLOCKABLE	HOW TO UNLOCK
Acc-ROO-acy (10)	Score 100% accuracy on any 10 levels.
Bat Attack (35)	Score 100% accuracy on Bat Attack.
Bonus Drop (10)	Score perfect on any bonus stage.
Comeback ROO (13)	Win a multiplayer match with only one shape to lose remaining.
Fly Butterfly (20)	Score 100% accuracy on Fly Butterfly.
Meemoo Headache (7)	Knock off 7 consecutive Meemoo on a platform.
Meemoo Savvy (10)	Don't miss any shapes after the first Meemoo attack.
One Track Mind (5)	Only rotate in one direction for any 5 levels.
ROO-Race (15)	Win a multiplayer match on Bursting EX.
ROO-Worthy (10)	Unlock the first 10 levels.
Roogoo Guru (50)	Achieve par time on all levels.
Tower of Moo (15)	Beat par time on Tower of Moo.

RUN LIKE HELL (XBOX)

UNLOCKABLE	CODE
Breaking Benjamin Video	←, B, A, LT, RT, ↑
Baby Nick	B, A, B, Y, ↓, ↓
Max Assault Rifle Damage	←, B, →, X, ↓, Y, ↑, A
Max Bolt Thrower Damage	X, Y, B, WHT, B, Y, X, BLK
Max Pulse Rifle Damage	B, ↓, ←, A, WHT, BLK, X, Y
Max Repeater Rifle Damage	←, Y, →, A, ↑, X, ↓, B
Max Rifle Damage	L, L, X, Y, B, A, R, R
Max Shotgun Damage	A, A, L, R, ↑, ↓, ←, →
Refill Armor	A, Y, B, X, Y, A, LT, RT
Refill Health	↑, ↓, ←, →, ←, →, A, B
Show Credits	X, B, A, ↑, ↓, Y

RUNE FACTORY 2: A FANTASY HARVEST MOON (DS)

UNLOCKABLES

These are only accessible in the Second Generation, from the dresser on the left side of the second floor of the house.

UNLOCKABLE	HOW TO UNLOCK
Handsome Armor	Win the Adventure Contest.
Monster Costume	Win the Monster Taming Contest.

RUSH 'N ATTACK (XBOX 360)

CODES

A meow confirms that the code was entered correctly.

CODE	EFFECT
At the main menu, using the D-pad, press ↑/↑/↓/↓/←/→/←/→/B/A	Alternate Sound FX

'SPLOSION MAN (XBOX 360)

UNLOCKABLES

UNLOCKABLE	HOW TO UNLOCK
'Splosion Man Gamer Pic	Beat Single Level 1–4
'Splosion Man Premium Theme	Beat Single Level 3–18
Scientist Gamer Pic	Beat Multiplayer Level 1–4
Cowards' Way Out (Level skip feature)	Kill yourself repeatedly by holding right trigger until it unlocks.

SAINTS ROW (XBOX 360)

CODES

Dial the following phone numbers in the phone book to get the corresponding effects.

EFFECT	CODE
12 Gauge	#920
1,000 dollars	#cashmoneyz
.44 Cal	#921
Add Gang Notoriety	#35
Add Police Notoriety	#4
Annihilator RPG	#947
AR-200	#922
AR-50	#923
AR-50 with Grenade launcher	#924
AS14 Hammer	#925
Baseball Bat	#926
Car Mass Increased	#2
Chainsaw	#927
Clear Sky	#sunny
Crowbar	#955
Drunk Pedestrians	#15
Everybody Is Shrunk	#202
Evil Cars	#16
Fire Extinguisher	#928
Flame Thrower	#929
Flashbang	#930
Full Health	#1
GAL 43	#931
GDHC	#932
Get Horizon	#711
Get Snipes 57	#712
Get Tornado	#713
Get Wolverine	#714
Giant	#200
Grenade	#933

EFFECT	CODE
Gyro Daddy Added to Garage	#4976
Heaven Bound	#12
Itty Bitty	#201
KC	#935
Knife	#936
Kobra	#934
Lighting Strikes	#666
Low Gravity	#18
Machete	#937
McManus 2010	#938
Milk Bones	#3
Mini-Gun	#939
Molotov	#940
Never Die	#36
Nightstick	#941
No Cop Notoriety	#50
No Gang Notoriety	#51
NR4	#942
Pedestrian Wars	#19
Pepper Spray	#943
Pimp Slap	#969
Pimpcane	#944
Pipe Bomb	#945
Player Pratfalls	#5
Raining Pedestrians	#20
RPG	#946
Samurai Sword	#948
Satchel Charge	#949
Shock Paddles	#950
SKR-9	#951
Sledge Hammer	#952
Stun Gun	#953
Super Explosions	#7
Super Saints	#8
TK3	#954
Tombstone	#956
Unlimited Ammo	#11
Unlimited Clip	#9
Unlimited Sprint	#6
Unlock D-STROY UFO	#728237
Unlock Peewee Mini Bike	#7266837
Vice 9	#957
XS-2 Ultimax	#958

UNLOCKABLES

UNLOCKABLE	HOW TO UNLOCK
75% Mechanic Discount	Complete all 5 Chop Shop lists
Bodyguards and Ninjas	Game Progression
Brotherhood Gang Cars	Complete Last Mission for the Brotherhood

Brotherhood Melee	Complete Brotherhood Mission 6
Buggy	Complete Truck Yard Chop Shop list
Chainsaw in Weapon Cache	Complete Crowd Control (Marina) Level 6
Clothing Store Discount	Crowd Control Level 3 (Suburbs)
Crib Customization Discount	Mayhem Level 3 (Red Light)
Demo Derby Vehicles	Complete Demo Derby Level 6
Donnie's Vehicle	Complete Brotherhood Mission 2
Explosion Damage -5%	Level 3, Trail Blazing (Downtown)
Gang Customization Cars	15% hoods conquered
Gang Customization Cars	45% hoods conquered
Health Regeneration 2x	Snatch Level 3 (Chinatown)
Health Regeneration 3x	Snatch Level 6 (Chinatown)
Infinite Respect	Raise your respect past level 99
Infinite SMG Ammo	Successfully complete Snatch Level 6 Downtown
Kobra (Pistol)	Fuzz Level 3 (Projects)
Legal Lee	Beat Stilwater Prison Fight Club Level 3
Mechanic Discount	Complete Demo Derby Level 3
One Follower	Complete Prologue Mission 4
Pepper Spray in Weapon Cache	Complete Crowd Control (Marina) Level 3
Police Notoriety Reduced	Complete FUZZ Level 3, Suburbs
Police Notoriety Reduced 2	Complete FUZZ Level 6, Suburbs
Pumped Up	Fight Club Level 6 (Arena)
Pumped Up	Fight Club Level 3 (Arena)
Red Light Apartment Crib	Complete Prologue Mission 2
Reduced Bullet Damage	Heli assault Level 3 (Bario)
Ronin Gang Cars	Complete Last Mission for the Ronin
Ronin Melee	Complete Ronin Mission 6
Ronin Notoriety Reduced	Drug Trafficking Level 3 (Hotel and Marina)
Saints Hideout	Complete Prologue Mission 3
Sons of Samedi Gang Cars	Complete Last Mission for Sons of Samedi
Sons of Samedi Melee	Complete Mission "Bad Trip"
Sons of Samedi Notoriety Reduced	Complete Escort Level 3, University
Sprint Increased	Insurance Fraud level 3 (Factories)
Sprint Increased (Unlimited)	Insurance Fraud Level 6 (Factories)
The News Helicopter	Complete Sons of Samedi Mission 3
Three Followers	50% hoods conquered
Tobias	Complete Sons of Samedi Mission 3
Troy	Beat Stilwater Prison Fight Club Level 6
Two Followers	25% hoods conquered
Unlimited Pistol Ammo	Fuzz Level 6 (Projects)
Vehicle Delivery	Escort Level 3 (Red Light)
X2 Ultimax (Shotgun)	Drug Trafficking Level 3 (Airport)
Zombie Carlos	Call eye for an eye after you complete the brother hood story

SAINTS ROW (PlayStation 3)

CODES

Dial the following phone numbers to get the corresponding effects.

EFFECT	CODE	EFFECT	CODE
1,000 dollars	#2274666399	**.44 Cal**	#921
12 Gauge	#920	**Add Gang Notoriety**	#35

NEW! A B C D E F G H I J K L M N O P Q R S T U V W X Y Z

EFFECT	CODE
Add Police Notoriety	#4
Annihilator RPG	#947
AR-200	#922
AR-50	#923
AR-50 with Grenade Launcher	#924
AS14 Hammer	#925
Baseball Bat	#926
Car Mass Increased	#2
Chainsaw	#927
Crowbar	#955
Drunk Pedestrians	#15
Everybody Is Shrunk	#202
Evil Cars	#16
Fire Extinguisher	#928
Flame Thrower	#929
Flashbang	#930
Full Health	#1
GAL 43	#931
GDHC	#932
Get Horizon	#711
Get Snipes 57	#712
Get Tornado	#713
Get Wolverine	#714
Giant	#200
Grenade	#933
Gyro Daddy Added to Garage	#4976
Heaven Bound	#12
Itty Bitty	#201
K6	#935
Knife	#936
Kobra	#934
Lighting Strikes	#666
Low Gravity	#18
Machete	#937
McManus 2010	#938

EFFECT	CODE
Milk Bones	#3
Mini-Gun	#939
Molotov	#940
Never Die	#36
Nightstick	#941
No Cop Notoriety	#50
No Gang Notoriety	#51
NR4	#942
Pedestrian Wars	#19
Pepper Spray	#943
Pimp Slap	#969
Pimpcane	#944
Pipe Bomb	#945
Player Pratfalls	#5
Raining Pedestrians	#20
RPG	#946
Samurai Sword	#948
Satchel Charge	#949
Shock Paddles	#950
SKR-9	#951
Sledge Hammer	#952
Stun Gun	#953
Super Explosions	#7
Super Saints	#8
TK3	#954
Tombstone	#956
Unlimited Ammo	#11
Unlimited Clip	#9
Unlimited Sprint	#6
Unlock D-STROY UFO Bike	#728237
Unlock Peewee Mini #7266837	
Vice 9	#957
XS-2 Ultimax	#958

UNLOCKABLES

UNLOCKABLE	HOW TO UNLOCK
75% Mechanic Discount	Complete all 5 Chop Shop lists
Bodyguards and Ninjas	Game Progression
Brotherhood Gang Cars	Complete Last Mission for the Brotherhood
Brotherhood Melee	Complete Brotherhood Mission 6
Buggy	Complete Truck Yard Chop Shop list
Chainsaw in Weapon Cache	Complete Crowd Control (Marina) Level 6
Clothing Store Discount	Crowd Control Level 3 (Suburbs)
Crib Customization Discount	Mayhem Level 3 (Red Light)
Demo Derby Vehicles	Complete Demo Derby Level 6
Donnie's Vehicle	Complete Brotherhood Mission 2

UNLOCKABLE	HOW TO UNLOCK
Explosion Damage -5%	Level 3, Trail Blazing (Downtown)
Gang Customization Cars	15% hoods conquered
Gang Customization Cars	45% hoods conquered
Health Regeneration 2x	Snatch Level 3 (Chinatown)
Health Regeneration 3x	Snatch Level 6 (Chinatown)
Infinite Respect	Raise your respect past Level 99
Infinite SMG Ammo	Successfully complete "Snatch" Level 6 Downtown
Kobra (Pistol)	Fuzz Level 3 (Projects)
Legal Lee	Beat Stilwater Prison Fight Club Level 3
Mechanic Discount	Complete Demo Derby Level 3
One Follower	Complete Prologue Mission 4
Pepper Spray in Weapon Cache	Complete Crowd Control (Marina) Level 3
Police Notoriety Reduced	Complete FUZZ Level 3, Suburbs
Police Notoriety Reduced 2	Complete FUZZ Level 6, Suburbs
Pumped Up	Fight Club Level 6 (Arena)
Pumped Up	Fight Club Level 3 (Arena)
Red Light Apartment Crib	Complete Prologue Mission 2
Reduced Bullet Damage	Heli Assault Level 3 (Bario)
Ronin Gang Cars	Complete Last Mission for the Ronin
Ronin Melee	Complete Ronin Mission 6
Ronin Notoriety Reduced	Drug Trafficking Level 3 (Hotel and Marina)
Saints Hideout	Complete Prologue Mission 3
Sons of Samedi Gang Cars	Complete Last Mission for Sons of Samedi
Sons of Samedi Melee	Complete Mission Bad Trip
Sons of Samedi Notoriety Reduced	Complete Escort Level 3, University
Sprint Increased	Insurance Fraud Level 3 (Factories)
Sprint Increased (Unlimited)	Insurance Fraud Level 6 (Factories)
The News Helicopter	Complete Sons of Samedi Mission 3
Three Followers	50% hoods conquered
Tobias	Complete Sons of Samedi Mission 3
Troy	Beat Stilwater Prison Fight Club Level 6
Two Followers	25% hoods conquered
Unlimited Pistol Ammo	Fuzz Level 6 (Projects)
Vehicle Delivery	Escort Level 3 (Red Light)
X2 Ultimax (Shotgun)	Drug Trafficking Level 3 (Airport)
Zombie Carlos	Call eye for an eye after you complete the brother hood story

SAMURAI WARRIORS: KATANA (Wii)

CHAOS DIFFICULTY

UNLOCKABLE	HOW TO UNLOCK
Chaos Difficulty	Complete all missions with an S rank.

SCALER (XBOX)

Enter these codes while the game is paused. Select Options, then Audio, and then enter these codes.

UNLOCKABLE	CODE
200,000 Klokkies	LT, LT, RT, RT, Y, X, Y
Full Health	RT, LT, RT, LT, Y, Y, X, X, RT, X
Infinite Electric Bombs	RT, RT, LT, LT, Y, Y, X

SCARFACE (XBOX)

Enter these on the Cheats screen of the Pause menu.

UNLOCKABLE	PASSWORD
1,000 Balls	FPATCH
Antique Racer	OLDFAST
Bacinari	666999
Black Suit	BLACK
Blue Suit	BLUE
Blue Suit w/shades	BLUESH
BReal "The World Is Track Yours" Music	TUNEME
Bulldozer	DOZER
Change Time of Day	MARTHA
Decrease Cop Heat	FLYSTRT
Decrease Gang Heat	NOBALLS
Dump Truck	DUMPER
Fill Ammo	AMMO
Fill Health	MEDIK
Grey Suit	GREY
Grey Suit w/shades	GREYSH
Increase Cop Heat	DONUT
Increase Gang Heat	GOBALLS
Lightning	SHAZAAM
Rain	RAINY
Sandy Shirt	TANSHRT
Sandy Shirt w/shades	TANSH
Stampede	BUMMER
Tiger Shirt	TIGSHRT
Tiger Shirt w/shades	TIGERSH
Vehicle Repair	TBURGLR
White Suit	WHITE
White Suit w/shades	WHITESH

SCARFACE (PlayStation 2)

Enter these on the Cheats screen of the Pause menu.

UNLOCKABLE	PASSWORD
1,000 Balls	FPATCH
Antique Racer	OLDFAST
Bacinari	666999
Black Suit	BLACK
Blue Suit	BLUE
Blue Suit w/shades	BLUESH
BReal "The World Is Yours" Music Track	TUNEME
Bulldozer	DOZER
Change Time of Day	MARTHA
Decrease Cop Heat	FLYSTRT
Decrease Gang Heat	NOBALLS
Dump Truck	DUMPER
Fill Ammo	AMMO
Fill Health	MEDIK
Grey Suit	GREY
Grey Suit w/shades	GREYSH

Increase Cop Heat	DONUT
Increase Gang Heat	GOBALLS
Lightning	SHAZAAM
Rain	RAINY
Sandy Shirt	TANSHRT
Sandy Shirt w/shades	TANSH
Stampede	BUMMER
Tiger Shirt	TIGSHRT
Tiger Shirt w/shades	TIGERSH
Vehicle Repair	TBURGLR
White Suit	WHITE
White Suit w/shades	WHITESH

SCARFACE: THE WORLD IS YOURS (Wii)

PASSWORDS

PASSWORD	EFFECT
OLDFAST	Antique racer
666999	Bacinari
BLACK	Black suit
BLUESH	Blue suit with shades
DOZER	Bulldozer
MARTHA	Change time of day
NOBALLS	Decrease Gang Heat
FLYSTRT	Decreases Cop Heat
DUMPER	Dump truck
FPATCH	Fill Balls Meter
GRAYSH	Gray suit Tony with sunglasses
HAWAII	Hawaii print shirt
HAWAIIG	Hawaii print shirt with sunglasses
DONUT	Increase Cop Heat
GOBALLS	Increase Gang Heat
AMMO	Max Ammo
TUNEME	Real "The World Is Yours" music track
MEDIK	Refill health
TBURGLR	Repairs car
BUMMER	Stampede
RAINY	Toggle rain
WHITE	White suit
WHITESH	White suit with shades

SCARFACE: THE WORLD IS YOURS (XBOX)

PASSWORDS

PASSWORD	EFFECT
BUMMER	4x4 Stampede vehicle
S13	Babylon Club Redux
DW_fron	Cabana Cigar/Oakly drive in
FLYSTRT	CHEAT: Decrease Cop Heat
NOBALLS	CHEAT: Decrease Gang Heat
FPATCH	CHEAT: Fill Balls Meter
DONUT	CHEAT: Increase Cop Heat
GOBALLS	CHEAT: Increase Gang Heat
KILLTONY	CHEAT: Kill Tony

PASSWORD	EFFECT
AMMO	CHEAT: Max Ammo
MEDIK	CHEAT: Refill Health
BLACK	Clothing: Black Suit Tony
BLUESH	Clothing: Blue Suit Tony with Sunglasses
GRAY	Clothing: Gray Suit Tony
GRAYSH	Clothing: Gray Suit Tony with Sunglasses
S12	Deliver
S07A	Freedom town redux
F_M_SHA	Havana Storehouse
HAWAII	Hawaiian shirt Tony
HAWAIIG	Hawaiian shirt Tony w/shades
F_M_SHC	Leopard Storage
F_M_SHB	Marina Storage
TUNEME	Music Track: "The World Is Yours"
S09	Nacho Contreras
S10	Nacho's Tanker
DW_fron	Ogrady's
TBURGLR	Repair Tony's Vehicle
SANDY	Sandy shirt Tony
SANDYSH	Sandy shirt Tony w/shades
F_M_SHD	Shoreline Storage
A51	The Dock Boss
S18	The End
A22	The Plantation
A23	Tranquilandia
S11	Un-Load
OLDFAST	Vehicle: Spawn Ariel MK III
666999	Vehicle: Spawn Bacinari
DOZER	Vehicle: Spawn Bulldozer
MARTHA	Weather Modifier: Change Time of Day
SHAZAAM	Weather Modifier: Toggle Lightning
RAINY	Weather Modifier: Toggle Rain
WHITE	White suit Tony
WHITESH	White suit Tony w/shades

SCHIZOID (XBOX 360)

ACHIEVEMENTS

UNLOCKABLE	HOW TO UNLOCK
21st Century Schizoid Man (15)	Complete level 21 ("Tyger Tyger") either in Local Co-Op, Xbox LIVE, or Uberschizoid.
Barber of Schizzville (20)	Shave the Orbiddles from 8 Astramoebas on a level, without destroying Astramoebas or losing a life.
Corpus Callosum Severed (20)	Complete level 119 ("Ragnarok") in Uberschizoid mode.
Flitt Breeder (10)	Get a gold medal on level 5 ("My Man Flitt") without destroying any Flitts.
Huevos Done Naked (20)	Gold level 47 ("Los Huevos") without activating any power-ups.
One Mind, Two Goals (20)	Earn 20 silver or gold medals in Uberschizoid mode.
Playing the Field (15)	Play a game in each mode: Xbox LIVE, Local Co-Op, Wingman Bot Training, and Uberschizoid.

Schiz Hunter (20)	Destroy 30 Schizzes on a single level, using power-ups and without losing any lives.
Schizoid Sensei (20)	Earn 10 medals (any combination of gold, silver, and bronze) over Xbox LIVE.
Seafood Buffet (20)	Destroy 2,500 Scorpios.
Sploderific (10)	Destroy all enemies on level 12 ("Smartbomb") with a single smartbomb.
Wired (10)	Destroy an enemy with a razorwire.

SCRIBBLENAUTS (DS)

GOLD STAR RANKING

After you've completed a given puzzle, you'll be awarded a Silver Star on the puzzle selection screen to indicate your success. However, you can get a higher ranking. Retrying the same puzzle activates Advance Mode, which is a bonus challenge. You have to beat the same level three times in a row, and with different objects each time. If you restart, you'll have to begin the challenge from the beginning. If you successfully complete the Advance Mode version of a puzzle, you'll be awarded a Gold Star on the selection screen.

MERITS

Merits are awards/achievements you can earn by doing different things in a given level. However, you need to complete the level to get them.

UNLOCKABLE	HOW TO UNLOCK
5th Cell	Spawn a 5th Cell employee.
All New	Complete a level with objects you've never used before.
Architect	Write two buildings.
Arrrrrr	Attach the Jolly Roger to a flagpole.
Audiophile	Write two or more instruments or audio objects.
Bioterrorist	Introduce the plague and infect two or more people.
Botanist	Write two or more plants.
Chauffeur	Drive a vehicle with more than one passenger.
Chef	Write two or more foods.
Closet	Write two or more clothes.
Combo	Combine any two objects together.
Cupid	Shoot a humanoid with Cupid's arrow.
Decorator	Write two furniture objects.
Electrolysis	Shock someone with electricity.
Elemental	Write more than one element.
Entertainer	Write two or more entertainment objects.
Entomologist	Spawn two or more insects.
Environmentalist	Write two or more environmental objects.
Explosive	Spawn two or more objects that explode.
Exterminator	Two or more humanoids or animals start a level and are destroyed.
Fantasynovel	Write two fantasy objects.
Fashion Designer	Clothe Maxwell's head, body, legs, feet and give him an accessory.
Firefighter	Put out at least two fires.
Genius	Complete a level twice in a row.
Glutton	Feed someone or something three times in a row.
Gold Digger	Spawn three or more precious stones.
Grab and Go	Write two or more grabbing tool objects.
Haxxor	Write five or more developers.
Healer	Spawn two or more medical objects.
Herpetologist	Write two or more reptiles.
Humanitarian	Write two or more humans.

UNLOCKABLE	HOW TO UNLOCK
IUnlockable	How to Unlock
nfected	Spawn a zombie and make it infect at least two humanoids.
Janitor	Spawn two or more cleaning objects.
Jockey	Use an animal as a vehicle.
Joust	Defeat a knight while Maxwell is mounted.
Knight School	Kill a dragon using a melee weapon.
Luddite	Short out three or more objects.
Lumberjack	Cut down three or more trees.
Mad Hatter	Place a hat on four or more humanoids or ànimals.
Magician	Use the magic wand to turn something into a toad.
Marine Biologist	Write two or more fish.
Mechanic	Jump-start a vehicle.
Messiah	Turn a humanoid into a deity.
Militant	Use two weapons and one weaponized vehicle.
Miner 49er	Dig a massive hole.
Miser	Obtain a total of 300,000 or more Ollars.
New Object	Write a completely new item.
No Weapons	Don't write a weapon to complete a level.
Novice Angler	Catch a fish with a fishing pole.
Old School	Write two or more classic video game objects.
Organ Donor	Spawn two or more organs.
Ornithologist	Write two or more birds.
Paleontologist	Spawn two ore more dinosaurs.
Pariah	Make three humanoids or animals flee.
Pi	Earn exactly 314 Ollars in a level.
Picasso	Write two or more drawing object tools.
Pilot	Spawn two or more aircraft.
Prodigy	Complete a level three times in a row.
Pyromaniac	Set at least four objects on fire in a level.
Reanimator	Bring a corpse back to life.
Roped In	Write two or more rope objects.
Russian Doll	Place an object inside another object, and then place that object into a third object.
Savior	Two or more humanoids or animals start and finish a level alive.
Sea Two	Write two or more sea vehicles.
Series of Tubes	Spawn "tube" five times.
Shoveler	Spawn two or more digging objects.
Smasher	Write two or more melee weapons.
Smuggler	Hide an item in a container.
Split Personality	Write two or more cutting or splitting tool objects.
Stealth	Destroy a security camera.
Sweet Tooth	Write two or more junk foods.
Tooling Around	Write two or more tool objects.
Washington	Chop down a cherry tree.
Water Jockey	Use a sea animal as a vehicle.
Whisperer	Ride a hostile animal.
Zookeeper	Write two or more animals.

HIDDEN LEVELS

If you spawn a teleporter and use it, it takes you to one of three secret levels.

GLITCH

Challenge Mode encourages you to get creative by not allowing you to use the same words in three separate trials. If you are feeling uncreative, you can take advantage ofThe Great Adjective Exploit to bypass this entirely: just add an adjective (or gibberish) in front of a word and the game will give you a free pass to use it again. You can clear a stage three times by typing "Wings" the first time, "Big Wings" the second time and "Small Wings" the third time; you'll simply get the Wings all three times, but the game will register three different words and will allow it.

BACKGROUND SCREEN

When you're at the title screen (Sandbox Mode), you can unlock 14 more backgrounds by typing words that fall into certain categories. These are some words that unlock the backgrounds.

UNLOCKABLE	HOW TO UNLOCK
Background 02	Type "cat."
Background 03	Type "car."
Background 04	Type "bee."
Background 05	Type "tree."
Background 06	Type "woman."
Background 07	Type "coffin."
Background 08	Type "vibes."
Background 09	Type "coin."
Background 10	Type "chair."
Background 11	Type "zombie."
Background 12	Type "court."
Background 13	Type "rain" and select "rain(water)."
Background 14	Type "it."
Background 15	Type "pc.

SD GUNDAM: SCAD HAMMERS (Wii)

UNLOCKABLES

UNLOCKABLE	HOW TO UNLOCK
Unlock Turn A Gundam	Fill up the Data Accumulation gauge (the one with the picture of a mobile suit beside it) under the Educational Data/Analysis Situation menu to 100%, then beat the Side 3 stage (Lv. 10 Ki mama ni Hammer 50) to unlock the Turn A Gundam

SECTION 8 (XBOX 360)

CODES

At the main menu go to dropship and enter the following codes. Entering the Captain's Armor code twice disables the code.

EFFECT	CODE
Chrome Assault Rifle	68432181
Unlock Black Widow auto-pistol	13374877
Unlock Captain's Armor	17013214

SERIOUS SAM (XBOX)

Cheat Mode: Click and hold (L), and press (BLK), (WHT), (Y) at the main menu. A "Cheats" option now appears at the main menu. After enabling Cheat mode, press (START) during gameplay to access the Cheat menu. You can restore lives and ammunition to avoid dying.

UNLOCKABLE	OBJECTIVE
Hidden Level	Destroy all the statues in the "Valley of the Kings" level.
Mental Mode (Mental fades in and out under Serious. In Mental mode, all the enemies appear and disappear.)	Complete the game in Serious mode, and start a new game.

SERIOUS SAM 2 (XBOX)

Enter this code while the game is paused.

UNLOCKABLE	CODE
Unlock Cheat Menu	Hold RT, then keep pressing BLK, WHT, BLK, WHT until the Cheat menu appears at the bottom of the screen.

SHADOW DANCER (Wii)

UNLOCKABLES

UNLOCKABLE	HOW TO UNLOCK
Earning 200,000 points	When you battle any boss (except Stavros) reduce your foe to within a flame or two of destruction, then stay out of reach until the last 10 seconds. At the very last second, use ninja magic to destroy the boss.
Practice on Any Stage	Enter the following code at the Title screen: Ⓐ+Ⓑ+Ⓒ+START. A new option appears, allowing you to practice on any level.
Extra Life	In the bonus round where you have to shoot the ninjas, kill either all ninjas or none of them.

SHADOW LAND (Wii)

SECRET PASSWORD SCREEN

UNLOCKABLE	HOW TO UNLOCK
Password Screen	At the title screen hold ①+②+SELECT and press RUN

PASSWORDS

PASSWORD	EFFECT
PC-ENGINE	(message)
NAMCO	(message)
NAMCOT	(message)
6502	(message)
6809	(message)
68000	(message)
756-2311	(message)
YAMASHITA	(message)
AKIRA	(message)
KOMAI	(message)
KAZUHIKO	(message)
KAWADA	(message)
SPEED-UP (4 way split screen)	Reset after entering the password
S.62.08.22 (Start from level 5)	Reset after entering the password

SHADOW OPS: RED MERCURY (XBOX)

Enter the following codes at the Password screen.

UNLOCKABLE	OBJECTIVE
All Co-op Levels	wanderlust
All Single Player Missions	happycamper

SHARK TALE (PlayStation 2)

During gameplay, press SELECT, hold L1, and enter code. After you enter the code, release L1 to activate the cheat.

UNLOCKABLE	CODE
Attack Mode	●,●,●,●,×,●,●,●,●
Extra Clams and Fame	●,●,×,×,●,×,●,●
Replace All Pearls with Fish King Coins	●,×,●,●,●,×,●,●

SHELLSHOCK: NAM '67 (PlayStation 2)

Enter the following codes at the Title screen (Press Start Button screen):

UNLOCKABLE	CODE
Add Weapon Option	↑,↓,←,→,●,■,↑,↓,←,→,●,■
All Missions and Pictures	L2,R2,L1,R1,L1,L2,L2,R2,L1,R1,R1,R2
God Mode	R3, L3,→,←,L1,R1, R3, L3,→,←,L1,R1
Infinite Ammunition	R2,R1,▲,L2,L1,↑,R2,R1,▲,L2,L1,↑
Psychedelic Mode	↑,R2,●,←,▲,■,L2,L1,●,R1

SHIN MEGAMI TENSEI: PERSONA 3 FES (PlayStation 2)

UNLOCKABLE

To unlock a new game with all of your items, equipment, status, etc., beat The Journey once through, and then create a new save game using your old save's information.

SHINING FORCE (Wii)

UNLOCKABLES

UNLOCKABLE	HOW TO UNLOCK
Control All Opponents (JP Version Only)	When the battle begins, quickly tap Ⓐ, Ⓑ, Ⓒ, ✜, Ⓐ, Ⓒ, Ⓐ, Ⓑ, Ⓐ
Fight Any Battle (JP Version Only)	Hold START on controller 2 then reset the system. Let go of START and hold Ⓐ+Ⓑ on controller 2. Select continue and wait until the girl says good luck. At that instant hold Ⓐ on controller 1 while continuing to hold Ⓐ+Ⓑ on controller 2.
Name Characters	Start a new game (must have completed game first) and go to the Name Your Character screen. Put the cursor on end and hold START+Ⓐ+Ⓑ+Ⓒ on controller 2 while holding: START+Ⓐ+Ⓒ on controller 1. You will see another character. Continue this to name all characters.

OTHER UNLOCKABLES

UNLOCKABLE	HOW TO UNLOCK
2 Jogurts	If you put jogurt in your army and kill an enemy with him, you get a jogurt ring item. Use this in battle on any character to make that character look like a jogurt! Repeat as many times as you want, but you will have to get another ring when it breaks.
Anri's Alternate Costume	During the Laser Eye battle in Chapter 3, search to the left of the three dark elves. You'll receive a hidden item called Kitui Huku ("tight clothes" in Japanese). Give it to Anri and she'll have a new outfit.
Tao's Alternate Costume	In Chapter 3, after fighting the first battle to get the Moon Stone, go inside the cave and search the walls for a secret item called the Sugoi Mizugi. Give it to Tao and she will have an alternate costume.

SHINING IN THE DARKNESS (Wii)

UNLOCKABLES

UNLOCKABLE	HOW TO UNLOCK
Rename All Characters	At the Name Entry screen, input a name that takes up all the available spaces (5 letter spaces). Then, select the forward button and you can enter another name for the next character! This works for all the characters!

SHINOBI III: RETURN OF THE NINJA MASTER (Wii)

UNLOCKABLES

UNLOCKABLE	HOW TO UNLOCK
Bonus Points	Complete a level without throwing any shuriken to get 30,000 bonus points

UNLOCKABLE	HOW TO UNLOCK
Invincibility	Choose BMG selection on the options menu, then, press Ⓑ to select the following songs in order: He runs, Japonesque, shinboi walk, sakura, getufu
Unlimited Shuriken	Set the number of shuriken to 0 on the Options menu and set the sound effects option to Shuriken. Highlight the Shuriken option and keep it there, and the 0 will change into the symbol for infinity.

SHOCKMAN (Wii)

UNLOCKABLES

Enter these cheats when the game is paused.

UNLOCKABLE	HOW TO UNLOCK
Invincibility	Up, Up, SELECT, Down, ②, SELECT
Level Skip	Left, Down, SELECT, Right, Left, SELECT, SELECT
Refill Life Meter	Left, SELECT, ②
Suicide	Right, SELECT, Left, SELECT, SELECT

SHREK 2 (XBOX)

CODES

Press Start during game play to access the Scrapbook, enter a code here.

CODE	EFFECT
Left, Up, A, B, Left, Up, A, B, Left, Up, A, B, B, B, B, B, B	1,000 Coins
Left, Up, A, B, Left, Up, A, B, Left, Up, A, B, X, B, X, B, X, B	Bonus game (Found under "bonus")

UNLOCKABLE BONUSES

The following bonuses will be unlocked depending on the number of missions you have completed in *Shrek 2*.

UNLOCKABLE	HOW TO UNLOCK
Cage Drop	59 missions completed
Cloud Maze	45 missions completed
Floating Floor	31 missions completed
Movie Stills and Crash Coliseum	70 missions completed
Ring Coliseum	21 missions completed

SHREK 2 (PlayStation 2)

During gameplay, pause the game. Then select the Scrapbook and enter the following:

UNLOCKABLE	CODE
1,000 Coins	←,↑,×,●,←,↑,×,●,←,↑,×,●,↑,→,↓,←,↑
Bonus Games	←,↑,×,●,←,↑,×,●,←,↑,×,●,■,●,■,●,■,●
Full Health	←,↑,×,●,←,↑,×,●,←,↑,×,●,↑,→,↓,←,↑
Level Select	←,↑,×,●,←,↑,×,●,←,↑,×,●,↑,↑,↑,↑,↑

SHREK SUPER SLAM (XBOX)

Enter these codes at the Title screen.

UNLOCKABLE	CODE
Pizza One mini game	Up, Up, Y, Y, Right, Right, B, B, Down, Down, LT, RT, Left, Left, X, X, LT, RT
Pizza Two mini game	Down, Down, Right, B, Up, Y, Left, X, LT, LT
Pizza Three mini game	B, B, X, X, RT, RT, Left, Left, LT, LT
Slammageddon	Up, Up, Down, Down, Left, Right, Left, Right, Y, X, X, LT, RT
Super Speed Modifier	LT, LT, RT, RT, LT, RT, LT, RT, X, B, Y, Y
Unlock All Challenges	Y, Y, Y, B, B, B, Y, X, B, X, X, X, Up, Down, Left, Right, LT, RT

SHREK SUPER SLAM (PlayStation 2)

Enter these codes at the Title screen.

UNLOCKABLE	CODE
Pizza One mini game	↑, ↑, ▲, ▲, →, →, ●, ●, ↓, ↓, L1, R1, ←, ←, ■, ■, L1, R1
Pizza Two mini game	●, ●, ■, ■, →, →, ←, ←, L1, L1
Pizza Three mini game	↓, ↓, →, ●, ↑, ▲, ←, ■, L1, L1
Slammageddon	↑, ↑, ↓, ↓, ←, →, ←, →, ▲, ■, ■, L1, R1
Super Speed Modifier	L1, L1, R1, R1, L1, R1, L1, R1, ■, ●, ▲, ▲
Unlock All Challenges	▲, ▲, ▲, ●, ●, ●, ▲, ■, ●, ■, ■, ■, ↑, ↓, ←, →, L1, R1

SHREK THE THIRD (XBOX 360)

GOLD

CODE	EFFECT
D-pad up B, D-pad down, D-pad up, D-pad right, D-pad left	Receive 10,000 gold coins

SHREK THE THIRD (Wii)

UNLOCKABLES

UNLOCKABLE	HOW TO UNLOCK
10,000 Bonus Coins	Press D-pad up, D-pad up, D-pad down, D-pad up, D-pad right, D-pad left at the Gift Shop
Bonus Damage	Buy at the Gift Shop for 10,500
Bonus Fairy Dust	Buy at the Gift Shop for 7,700
Academy Grounds Commentary	Buy at the Gift Shop for 1,500
Catacombs Commentary	Buy at the Gift Shop for 5,000
Docks Commentary	Buy at the Gift Shop for 1,000
Evil Queen's Castle Commentary	Buy at the Gift Shop for 5,000
Ice Lake Commentary	Buy at the Gift Shop for 3,000
Merlin's Hills Commentary	Buy at the Gift Shop for 4,000
Prison Cell Blocks Commentary	Buy at the Gift Shop for 2,000
Rundown Streets Commentary	Buy at the Gift Shop for 6,000
Stromboli's Workshop Commentary	Buy at the Gift Shop for 5,000
Donkey: Dragon Disguise	Buy at the Gift Shop for 3,650
Fiona: Funeral Dress	Buy at the Gift Shop for 2,150
Puss: Evil Knight Disguise	Buy at the Gift Shop for 2,850
Shrek: Knight Armor	Buy at the Gift Shop for 3,500
Shrek: Pirate Outfit	Buy at the Gift Shop for 4,250
Shrek: Regal	Buy at the Gift Shop for 3,200
Shrek: Swim Trunks	Buy at the Gift Shop for 3,350
Sleeping Beauty: Gown	Buy at the Gift Shop for 2,500
Charming	Buy at the Gift Shop for 15,500
Grimm	Buy at the Gift Shop for 1,500
Cyclops (Character)	Buy at the Gift Shop for 1,500
Dragon Keep (Castle)	Buy at the Gift Shop for 1,600
Dragon Keep (Map)	Buy at the Gift Shop for 1,350
Dwarves (Character)	Buy at the Gift Shop for 2,400

SID MEIER'S PIRATES (XBOX)

Enter these as names for the desired effects.

UNLOCKABLE	PASSWORD
Begin game with the best ship in the game and a full crew	D.Gackey
Bonus Frag	Snappy Dresser
Dueling Invincibility	Dragon Ma
Food Never Dwindles	Sweet Tooth

UNLOCKABLE	PASSWORD
Invincibility in Ship Battles	Bloody Bones Baz
The Governor's daughters always love you no matter how badly you dance	Scooter
Your crew is always at highest possible morale	B.Caudizzle
Your fleet sails twice as fast	Sprinkler

SILENT HILL: SHATTERED MEMORIES (Wii)

UFO ENDING

UNLOCKABLE	HOW TO UNLOCK
UFO ending	Photograph 13 hidden UFOs.

EASTER EGG

Press 1 on the Wii Remote, go to "Hints," click on "Cell Phone Calls," on the picture of Harry's phone with a number. Dial the number on your phone to call Konami Customer Service. Unfortunately, they are unable to help you due to the fact you're in Silent Hill.

SILENT HILL 2 (XBOX)

Completion Bonuses: Complete the game. Start another game and enter the Extra Options menu to access new features. You can set a "Bullet Adjust" option, allowing the normal amount of ammunition found at a location to double or triple. You can toggle a "Noise Effect" option. Another new option you can toggle allows you to view scenes without distortion.

UNLOCKABLE	OBJECTIVE
Additional Riddle Difficulty	Complete the game under the Easy, Normal, and Hard riddle difficulty settings. Select the Hard riddle difficulty again, and begin a new game with a new combination of riddles.
Book of Lost Memories	Complete the game. Start a new game and look for the newspaper stand near the Texxon Gas Station. Find the Book of Lost Memories inside.
Book of the Crimson Ceremony	Find this book in the reading room on the second floor of the Nightmare hotel.
Chainsaw	Complete the game under the Normal difficulty and Normal riddle difficulty settings. Start a new game to find the Chainsaw among logs before the cemetery.
Dog Key	Complete the game with the "Rebirth" ending. Start a new game and a doghouse appears near Jack's Inn and the gas station. Look inside the doghouse to find the Dog Key. Use it to open the observation room in the Nightmare hotel.
Hyper Spray	Complete the game two times. Start a new game to find the Hyper Spray on the south side of the motor home.
Introduction FMV Sequence Audio	If you wait at the title screen for a while, the introduction FMV sequence begins. In some scenes, there will be no audio. Complete the game one time to restore the audio to those.
Joke Ending	To view the sixth secret joke ending, use the Blue Gem at Alternate Brook Haven Hospital's garden, the dock before getting on the boat, and room 312 in the Lakeview Hotel. Once you use it in room 312, the game ends and the joke ending appears.
Obsidian Goblet	Complete the game. Start a new game, and enter the Historical Society building. Find the Obsidian Goblet on a shelf.
Reveal Signs	Unlock all five endings, and start a new game. All signs are now revealed.
White Chrism	Complete the game. Start a new game to find the White Chrism vial in the kitchen of apartment 105 in Blue Creek Apartments.

SILENT SCOPE 3 (PlayStation 2)

UNLOCKABLE	OBJECTIVE
Real-Time Window Option	Complete the indoor shooting range with an "S" or better rank to unlock the "Real-Time Window" option at the EX Options menu.

SIMCITY (Wii)

UNLOCKABLES

UNLOCKABLE	HOW TO UNLOCK
$999,999	At any time while playing a city, spend all of your money. When the tax screen appears at the end of December, hold down L. Select "Go with Figures" and then go back to the tax screen. Turn all of the dues to 100% and exit still holding L. When you release L your money will be at $999,999.
999 Extra City Maps	Start a new city, and choose any map number, then start the game. Now select the "Go to Menu" icon at the screen's top, and choose Start New City without saving. After a short time, the map will change, but the number won't.
Freeland	Beat the Las Vegas scenario
Las Vegas Scenario	Beat the six game scenarios and have at least one city with over 100,000 citizens living in it saved to the game.

SIMCITY CREATOR (Wii)

NEW BUILDING SETS

Name your city one of the following names in order to unlock the corresponding building set.

UNLOCKABLE	HOW TO UNLOCK
Egyptian Building Set	Name your city "Mummy's desert."
Greek Building Set	Name your city "Ancient culture."
Jungle Building Set	Name your city "Become wild."
Sci-Fi Building Set	Name your city "Future picture."

NEW BUILDINGS

UNLOCKABLE	HOW TO UNLOCK
Art museum	Raise education level to 90.
Basketball court	Build 2 of each: tennis courts, baseball fields, and playgrounds.
Bus stop	Reach 1920.
High school	Raise education level to 75.
House of worship	Have a population of 4,000.
Large Garden	Build 4 small gardens and have a population of 50,000.
Large Park	Build 4 small parks and have a population of 50,000.
Museum	Raise education level to 100.
Nuclear Power Station	Raise education level to 115.
Opera House	Build 3 museums and 3 art museums.
Recycling Plant	Build one landfill zone.
Solar Power Plant	Reach year 2000.
Stadium	Have a population of 350,000.
TV station	Have a population of 350,000.
University	Raise education level to 90.
Wind Power Plant	Reach 1985.

SIMCITY DS (DS)

PASSWORDS

At the main menu, go to "Museum" then select "Landmark Collection," and finally "Password," then enter the following codes.

UNLOCKABLE	CODE
Anglican Cathedral (UK)	kipling
Arc de Triomphe (France)	gaugin
Atomic Dome (Japan)	kawabata
Big Ben (UK)	orwell

UNLOCKABLE	CODE
Bowser Castle (Nintendo)	hanafuda
Brandenburg Gate (Germany)	gropius
Coit Tower (USA)	kerouac
Conciergerie (France)	rodin
Daibutsu (Japan)	mishima
Edo Castle (Japan)	shonagon
Eiffel Tower (France)	camus
Gateway Arch (USA)	twain
Grand Central Station (USA)	f.scott
Great Pyramids (Egypt)	mahfouz
Hagia Sofia (Turkey)	ataturk
Helsinki Cathedral (Finland)	kivi
Himeji Castle (Japan)	hokusai
Holstentor (Germany)	durer
Independence Hall (USA)	mlkingjr
Jefferson Memorial (USA)	thompson
Kokkai (Japan)	soseki
LA Landmark (USA)	hemingway
Lincoln Memorial (USA)	melville
Liver Building (UK)	dickens
Melbourne Cricket Ground (Australia)	damemelba
Metropolitan Cathedral (UK)	austen
Moai (Chile)	allende
Mt. Fuji (Japan)	hiroshige
National Museum (Taiwan)	yuantlee
Neuschwanstein Castle (Germany)	beethoven
Notre Dame (France)	hugo
Palace of Fine Arts (USA)	bunche
Palacio Real (Spain)	cervantes
Paris Opera (France)	daumier
Parthenon (Greece)	callas
Pharos of Alexandria (Egypt)	zewail
Rama IX Royal Park (Thailand)	phu
Reichstag (Germany)	goethe
Sagrada Famillia (Spain)	dali
Shuri Castle (Japan)	basho
Smithsonian Castle (USA)	pauling
Sphinx (Egypt)	haykal
St. Paul's Cathedral (UK)	defoe
St. Basil's Cathedral (Russia)	tolstoy
St. Stephen's Cathedral (Austria)	mozart
Statue of Liberty (USA)	pollack
Stockholm Palace (Sweden)	bergman
Sydney Opera House Landmark # 12 (Australia)	bradman
Taj Mahal (India)	tagore
Tower of London (UK)	maugham
Trafalgar Square (UK)	joyce
United Nations (USA)	amnesty
United States Capitol (USA)	poe
Washington Monument (USA)	capote

Westminster Abbey (UK)	greene
White House (USA)	steinbeck

UNLOCKABLE BUILDINGS FROM POPULATION GROWTH

When your city reaches a certain number of people, Dr. Simtown unlocks buildings that help your city.

UNLOCKABLE	HOW TO UNLOCK
Center for the Arts	Reach a population of 100,000.
Court House	Reach a population of 25,000.
Mayor's House	Reach a population of 5,000.
Medical Research Lab	Have a population of 80,000 when you reach year 1999.
Museum	Reach a population of 3,000.
Post Office	Reach a population of 100.

THE SIMPSONS GAME (XBOX 360)

UNLOCKABLES

Go into the "Extras" section of the main menu and insert the following codes. If the code is accepted, you hear a sound effect.

UNLOCKABLE	HOW TO UNLOCK
All Homer's Costumes and Trophies	→,←,X,X,Y,R3
All Lisa's Costumes and Trophies	←,→,Y,Y,X,L3
All Marge's Costumes and Trophies	X,Y,X,X,Y,L3
All Bart's Costumes and Trophies	Y,X,Y,Y,X,R3

ACHIEVEMENTS

UNLOCKABLE	HOW TO UNLOCK
A Passive Fish (15)	Finish The Day of the Dolphin.
Back to the Futurama (5)	Win time challenge for Five Characters in Search of an Author.
Burger Victory (10)	Finish Around the World in 80 Bites.
Burns Baby Burns (10)	Finish Lisa the Tree Hugger.
Challenger (50)	Win every time challenge.
Chocolate Heaven (5)	Win time challenge for The Land of Chocolate.
Chocolate Victory (10)	Finish The Land of Chocolate.
Cloud Nine (100)	Finish Game Over.
Clown Around (5)	Win time challenge for Shadow of the Colossal Donut.
Complete Package (150)	Finish every episode, find every collectible, and discover every Video Game Cliché Moment.
Doggie Dazed (25)	Finish Grand Theft Scratchy.
Doll Crazy (50)	Find all of Lisa's Malibu Stacy Seals.
Dragon Slayer (25)	Finish NeverQuest.
Dufftacular Finish (50)	Find all of Homer's Duff Bottle Caps.
Engine Fun (5)	Win time challenge for Enter the Cheatrix.
Fast Times (50)	Beat every episode target time.
Fight the Power (10)	Finish Mob Rules.
Goes to 11 (30)	Find all of the collectibles in Springfield.
Hairs to You (50)	Find all of Marge's Try-n-Save Coupons.
Heavenly Joy (5)	Win time challenge for Game Over.
Heavenly Score (20)	Get a perfect score on the final Boss battle.
Heist Hijinx (10)	Finish Bartman Begins.
Hot Coffee (5)	Win time challenge for Grand Theft Scratchy.
Maki Roll Mania (5)	Win time challenge for Big Super Happy Fun Fun Game.
Mall Rising (5)	Win time challenge for Invasion of the Yokel-Snatchers.

UNLOCKABLE	HOW TO UNLOCK
Mmm Donut (15)	Finish Shadow of the Colossal Donut.
My Precious (5)	Win time challenge for NeverQuest.
Nice Cans! (5)	Win time challenge for The Day of the Dolphin.
On the Matt (40)	Finish Five Characters in Search of an Author.
Poster Paster (50)	Find all of Bart's Krusty Kollectible Koupons.
Power Up! (15)	Finish Enter the Cheatrix.
Press START to Play (5)	Easiest achievement...ever.
Pwnd (0)	Dude, need help? You've died, like, 10 times...
Save the Simpsons (15)	Finish Bargain Bin.
Shooters Rejoice (5)	Win time challenge for Medal of Homer.
Sim Sandwich (5)	Win time challenge for Bargain Bin.
Sparkling Defeat (25)	Finish Big Super Happy Fun Fun Game.
Steady Mobbin' (5)	Win time challenge for Mob Rules.
Table Smasher 2000 (5)	Win time challenge for Around the World in 80 Bites.
The Alienator (15)	Finish Invasion of the Yokel-Snatchers.
Up and Atom (5)	Win time challenge for Bartman Begins.
Victory at Sea! (25)	Finish Medal of Homer.
Wood Chippin' (5)	Win time challenge for Lisa the Tree Hugger.
Worst Cliché Ever (50)	Find all of the Video Game Cliché Moments.

THE SIMPSONS GAME (Wii)

CODES

Go into the "Extras" section of the main menu and insert the following codes. If the code is accepted, you hear a sound effect.

UNLOCKABLE	HOW TO UNLOCK
Unlimited Power for All Characters	⊕,Left,Right,⊕,⊖,Z
All Cliches	Left,⊖,Right,⊕,Right,Z
All Movies	⊖,Left,⊖,Right,⊕,C

THE SIMPSONS GAME (PSP)

CODES

Go into the "Extras" section of the main menu and insert the following codes. If your code is accepted, you hear a sound effect.

All Movies	⇦,■,⇨,▲,⇨,L
All Clichés	■,⇦,■,⇨,▲,R
Unlimited Power for All Characters	▲,⇦,⇨,▲,■,L

THE SIMPSONS GAME (PlayStation 2)

CODES

Go into the "Extras" section of the main menu and insert the following codes. If the code is accepted, you should hear a sound effect.

UNLOCKABLE	HOW TO UNLOCK
Unlimited Power for all characters	●,⇦,⇨,●,■,L1
All Cliché	⇦,■,⇨,●,⇨,L1
All Movies	■,⇦,■,⇨,●,R1

THE SIMPSONS: HIT AND RUN (XBOX)

Pause the game and enter the Option menu, then hold LT+RT and enter the code.

UNLOCKABLE	CODE
All cars for new game (must be typed in with complete save loaded)	A,B,A,B

One hit kills (all cars will explode if you ram them or if they ram you, including cops and bosses)	Y,Y,X,X
Press your horn for high flying jumps	X,X,X,Y
Secret cars replaced by red box racer	B,B,Y,X
Show grid view	B,A,B,Y
Show speedometer	Y,Y,B,X
Super fast Cars	X,X,X,X
Your car is invincible	Y,A,Y,A
Your cars are 5 times faster than normal	Y,Y,Y,Y

THE SIMPSONS: HIT AND RUN (PlayStation 2)

From the Main menu, go to Options. Hold L1+R1 and enter the following:

UNLOCKABLE	CODE
Blurry View	▲,●,▲,●
Explode on Impact Cars	▲,▲,■,■
Fast Cars	■,■,■,■
Grid View	●,×,●,▲
Invincible Car	▲,×,▲,×
Jumping Car	■,■,■,▲
Speedometer	▲,▲,●,■
Very Fast Cars	▲,▲,▲,▲

CHANGE THE DATE OF THE PLAYSTATION 2 TO HALLOWEEN, THANKSGIVING, AND CHRISTMAS TO SEE NEW LIVING ROOM DECORATIONS.

THE SIMPSONS: ROAD RAGE (XBOX)

CODES

In the Options menu, hold both triggers and press the following buttons:

CODE	EFFECT
X, X, X, X	2D Cardboard People
Y, Y, Y, Y	Cars in Slow Motion
B, B, X, B	Christmas Apu
B, B, A, A	Debug Mode
A, A, A, A	Drive at Night
B, B, Y, A	Drive Nuclear Bus
B, B, Y, X	Drive Red Soapbox Car
B, B, X, A	Halloween Bart
B, B, X, Y	Happy New Year Krusty!
B, B, X, X	Marge's Thanksgiving Car
Y, Y, Y, Y	More Camera Views
X, X, X, Y	Overhead View
B, B, Y, Y	Play as Smithers
X, B, Y, A	Stop Watch Mode
New Car for Homer	Play through and complete all missions and you get "The Car Built for Homer" from the episode where Homer and his brother designed a car for his brother's company.
Play as Frankenstein Bart	Set the system date/clock to Halloween (October 31st).
Play as Pilgrim Marge	Set the system date/clock to Thanksgiving (3rd Thursday of November).
Play as a Santa Apu	Set the system date/clock to Christmas (December 25th).
Play as Tuxedo Krusty	Set the system date/clock to New Year's Day (January 1st).

CODE	EFFECT
Skip Missions	Skip every mission (play the mission by trying it 5 times) and then beat the 10th mission. Then you will have beaten every mission and get the car built for Homer.

THE SIMPSONS: ROAD RAGE (PlayStation 2)

Change the date of the PlayStation 2 to the following to unlock secret characters:

UNLOCKABLE	CODE
New Year's Barney	Jan 1
Halloween Bart	Oct 31
Thanksgiving Marge	Nov 22
Christmas Apu	Dec 25

THE SIMPSONS SKATEBOARDING (PlayStation 2)

Enter these codes in the Character Selection screen while holding R1+R2+L1+L2.

UNLOCKABLE	CODE
$99.00	▲, ×, ●, ■
Add Money	▲, ×, ●, ■
Ballerina Nelson	▲, ■, ×, ●
Big-Head Bart	×, ■, ●, ▲
Big-Head Frink	■, ×, ▲, ●
Big-Head Homer	●, ×, ▲, ■
Big-Head Lisa	■, ▲, ×, ●
Big-Head Nelson	▲, ■, ●, ×
Big-Head Wiggum	×, ●, ■, ▲
Demon Marge	×, ■, ▲, ●
Fuzzy Skaters	×, ▲, ■, ●
Gangsta' Bart	●, ×, ■, ▲
Gangsta' Lisa	■, ▲, ●, ×
Groovy Frink	×, ●, ▲, ■
Man-Eater Wiggum	▲, ●, ■, ×
Men in Black Otto	■, ×, ●, ▲
Tightie-whitie Homer	▲, ●, ×, ■
Transvestite Nelson	▲, ■, ×, ●
Tuxedo Krusty	●, ▲, ■, ×
Unlock All Boards	×, ▲, ●, ■
Unlock All Levels	▲, ×, ■, ●
Unlock All Skaters	●, ▲, ×, ■

THE SIMS (XBOX)

Press both LT + RT to call up a cheat menu, then enter the codes below.

UNLOCKABLE	CODE
2 Player mode	MIDAS
First person View (press Black)	FISH EYE
Free Items	FREEALL
Party Motel in 2 Player Mode	PARTY M
Play the Sims Mode	SIMS

THE SIMS 2 (DS)

MUSIC STUFF

UNLOCKABLE	HOW TO UNLOCK
Custom Music in Music Panels and Radios	Record music in one of the lounges and save it. It will now be available in music panels and radios.
Tunes from Music Mixer in Music Panels and Radios	Mix up music in the music mixer (in one of the lounges) and save it.

NEW SONGS

UNLOCKABLE	HOW TO UNLOCK
"Combat Mode"	Collect 12 license plates.
"Credits Theme"	Beat the game.
"Razor Burn"	Collect 24 license plates.

THE SIMS 2 (XBOX)

CODES

Enter these codes in game. Most codes require the player to enter the master code (LB, RB, ↑, A, BLK) first.

CODE	EFFECT
LB, RB, ↑, A, BLK	Master code
↑, B, ↑, →, WHT	Max all motives
→, ↑, →, ↓, →, ↑, ↓, ←	Remove messages
Y, B, X, BLK, ←	Change any Sim's skill
RB, LB, BLK, →, ←	Give the household §10,000
B, X, LB, ↑, ↓	Go six hours forward in time
B, WHT, ←, ↑, B	Unlock all Story mode locations
X, BLK, ↓, →, X	Unlock all clothes
WHT, B, ↓, ←, ↑	Unlock all objects
BLK, X, ↑, ↓, →, A	Unlock all recipes
B, WHT, ←, B, ↑, B	Unlocks all lots/locations

UNLOCK LOCATIONS

To Unlock New Locations, complete all of your Gold and Platinum goals. Do not worry too much with the Green ones. You also need to complete your roommates' Gold and Platinum goal.

UNLOCKABLE	HOW TO UNLOCK
Alien Crash Site	Help XY-XY. Fulfill all Aspirations and become friends with Jonas.
Bio Dome	Have Noelle complete one full career.
Cliffside Retreat	Fulfill all of Isabella's Wants, but it might take a while for her to make a sandwich.
HMS Armore	Fulfill all of Betty's Wants until she is in a Platinum mood. Then marry Captain Nelson.
Jugen House	Fulfill Toothless Joe's Aspirations until your Sim gets "Visit New Location" as an Aspiration. Go back to Tranquility Falls, and help Chantel
Mesa Gallery	Help Hector complete his goals at HMS Amore.
Orbit Room	Become friends with Red S. and serve him food. Move back to Sunset Canyon and make Red S. and Helga get married and get Red S. in Platinum mood.
Rockwall Acres	Follow instructions on what it says
Shoreline Trails	Buy a foosball table and defeat Torin
Sunset Canyon	Bring Helga, Billy, and Sheila back to life, make a kitchen, clean up mess, buy them beds, and build bathroom
Tranquility Falls	Fulfill Larry's Want and put him in Platinum mood, same with Chantel.

THE SIMS 2: PETS (Wii)

UNLOCKABLES

UNLOCKABLE	HOW TO UNLOCK
10,000 Simoleons	Hold Ⓑ, press ↑, ←, ↓, ↓
Advance 6 Hours	→, →, →, →, →, ←
Change Skills	↓, ↓, ↓, ↑, ↑, ↑

SKATE (XBOX 360)

BEST BUY CLOTHES

CODE	EFFECT
↑, ↓, ←, →, Ⓧ, RB, Ⓨ, LB	Unlock exclusive Best Buy clothes

UNLOCK DEM BONES CHARACTER

UNLOCKABLE	HOW TO UNLOCK
Dem Bones	Break each bone in your body at least 3 times

SKATE (PlayStation 3)

CODE

Enter code at main menu.

CODE	EFFECT
↑, ↓, ←, →, ■, R1, ▲, L1	Unlock Best Buy clothes in store

SKATE 2 (XBOX 360)

CODES

Enter the code in the code entry screen in the "Extras" menu. The code for 3-D requires that you have 3-D glasses.

EFFECT	CODE
Turns the Game 3-D	Strangeloops
Unlocks Big Black as a playable character	letsdowork

UNLOCKABLES

UNLOCKABLE	HOW TO UNLOCK
GvR Plaza	Complete all Street Challenges to unlock the Etnies GvR Plaza.
King of the Mountain Crown	Beat all of the Races in Career mode (not the bonus races, though).
Legend Crown	Reach Legend level online.
Monster Skate Park	Get Sponsored and complete Team Film Challenges until you get a demo session with Rob Drydek; after completing this earn $200,000 to buy the park.
S.V. Dam	Complete all the Thrasher Mag challenges to drain the dam.
S.V. Stadium	Complete all Tranny Contests to unlock the S.V. Mega-Ramp Stadium.
S.V. Summit	Complete all the Death Races to unlock the peak of Cougar Mountain.
Training Park	Complete all Team Film Challenges to unlock the Training Park.

SKATE 2 (PlayStation 3)

CODES

Enter the code in the code entry screen in the "Extras" menu. The code for 3-D requires that you have 3-D glasses.

EFFECT	CODE
Turns The Game 3-D	Strangeloops
Unlocks Big Black as a playable character	letsdowork

SKATE IT (Wii)

UNLOCKABLES

These characters are unlocked during the career mode after you complete their sponsorship challenges.

UNLOCKABLE	HOW TO UNLOCK
Skeleton pants and skeleton shirt	Kill all story mode missions and complete all milestones.
Chris Haslam	Complete the Almost sponsorship challenge in career mode.
Danny Way	Complete the Plan B sponsorship challenge in career mode.
Eric Koston	Complete the Lakai sponsorship challenge in career mode.
Jake Brown	Complete the Blind sponsorship challenge in career mode.
Lucas Puig	Complete the Cliche sponsorship challenge in career mode.
Mike Carroll	Complete the Girl sponsorship challenge in career mode.
Rob Dyrdek	Complete the Alien Workshop sponsorship challenge in career mode.
Terry Kennedy	Complete the Baker sponsorship challenge in career mode.

SLY COOPER AND THE THIEVIUS RACCOONUS (PlayStation 2)

UNLOCKABLE	OBJECTIVE
Ending Bonuses	Get all the bottles hidden in a level to unlock an FMV sequence, special move, or background information.

SMALL ARMS (XBOX 360)

UNLOCKABLES

UNLOCKABLE	HOW TO UNLOCK
Shooting Range Practice	Beat Mission mode
Billy Ray Logg	Beat him in Mission mode with any character
ISO-7982	Complete Mission mode
Mousey McNuts	Beat him in Mission mode with any character
Professor Von Brown	Beat him in Mission mode with any character

SMASH T (XBOX 360)

INVINCIBILITY

CODE	EFFECT
Press Ⓐ+Ⓨ	Become invincible. This code must be entered in every room. You can move around and change the angle of your shooting. If you stop shooting, the code deactivates. Don't stop shooting unless you want to pick up a new weapon or prize.

SMASHING DRIVE (XBOX)

UNLOCKABLE SHIFT	OBJECTIVE
Dusk and Wired Shift	Complete the Night Owl shift.
Night Owl Shift	Complete the Rush Hour shift.
Rush Hour Shift	Complete the Early Bird shift.

SMUGGLER'S RUN (PlayStation 2)

To access the following unlockables, pause the game, then enter code. A sound confirms correct entry.

UNLOCKABLE	CODE
Invisibility	R1, L1, L1, R2, L1, L1, ↙
Less Time Warp	R2, L2, L1, R1, ←, ←, ←
Light Cars	L1, R1, R1, L2, R2, R2
More Time Warp	R1, L1, L2, R2, →, →, →
No Gravity	R1, R2, R1, R2, ↑, ↑, ↑

TO UNLOCK VEHICLES FROM MIDNIGHT CLUB: STREET RACING, USE A SAVED GAME FROM MIDNIGHT CLUB: STREET RACING. NOW YOU ARE ABLE TO USE VEHICLES FROM THAT GAME.

SMUGGLER'S RUN 2 HOSTILE TERRITORY (PlayStation 2)

Enter these codes after pausing the game.

UNLOCKABLE	CODE
Antigravity for ambient vehicles	R1, R2, R1, R2, ↑, ↑, ↑
Double the frame rate	R3, L3, L3, R3, ←, ●, ←, ●
Fast Motion	R1, L1, L2, R2, →, →, →
Glass Car	←, ↑, →, ↓, →, ↑, ←, L2
Increase Speed	R1, L1, L2, R2, →, →, →
Invisibility	R1, L1, L1, R2, L1, L1, L2
Level select and all cars	L2, R2, R2, L2, R1, L2, L1, ←, →, L2, ↓, R2
Low Gravity	L1, R1, R1, L2, R2, R2
Slow Motion	R2, L2, L1, R1, ←, ←, ←
Unlimited Countermeasures	R3, R3, R3, R1, R1, R2, R2

SOLDIER BLADE (Wii)

CODES

EFFECT	CODE
Level Select	Hold ↑, press SELECT, hold ↓, press SELECT, hold ←, press SELECT, hold →, press SELECT

SOLDIER OF FORTUNE II: DOUBLE HELIX (XBOX)

While playing, click in the left analog stick, then enter these codes.

UNLOCKABLE	CODE
All Weapons	X, Y, A, B
God Mode	B, A, Y, X
Level select	BLK, B, A, WHT
Unlimited Ammo	BLK, A, Y, WHT

SOLOMON'S KEY (Wii)

UNLOCKABLES

UNLOCKABLE	HOW TO UNLOCK
Continue Game	At the "Game Deviation Value" screen, hold ↑+Ⓐ+Ⓑ

SONIC 3D BLAST (Wii)

UNLOCKABLES

UNLOCKABLE	HOW TO UNLOCK
Level Select	Go to the Press Start screen and enter Ⓑ, Ⓐ, →, Ⓐ, Ⓒ, ↑, ↓, Ⓐ (or baracuda). You're taken to the main screen. Press the Start option and the level select appears.
Quick Emerald Gain	Enter the Level Select code twice, and go to a level/act with Knuckles or Tails in it. Enter one of their bonus levels by collecting 50 rings. When the bonus level begins, press Ⓐ+ START and you will receive the emerald for the bonus level.
Skip Levels	Do the Level Select code and start the game in any level. To skip levels, pause the game and press Ⓐ.
Stage Select (Alternative)	Beat the entire game with all the Chaos Emeralds. After the credits, the stage select is on.

SONIC AND THE SECRET RINGS (Wii)

UNLOCKABLE	CODE
Bookworm	Play a total time of 24 hours
Celebrity	Play attractions 35 times
Champion	Win 1st in 120 Party Games
Dark Master	Beat 20 missions using at least 5 Dark skills and no Wind/Fire skills
Dealer	Win World Bazaar 7 times
Explorer	Win at Treasure Hunt 7 times
Extreme Speeder	Use Speed Break 50 times
Flame Master	Beat 20 missions using at least 5 Fire skills and no Wind/ Dark skills
Genie Buster	Defeat 1,000 Genies
Grind Performer	Grind a distance of 30 km (18.64 miles)
Hero	Defeat Erazor Djinn
Pirate	Win at Pirates Coast 7 times
Rebellion	Beat Erazor Djinn at level 25 or lower
Record Buster	Set records for all party games that have records
Ring Catcher	Collect 10,000 Rings
Skill Collector	Unlock every skill available
Skill Quinti	Beat 20 missions using 4 or fewer skills
Skill Saver	Beat 30 missions using fewer than 100 SP
Sonic Freak	Use Sonic 30 times in Party mode
Soul Collector	Collect every Fire Soul
Star	Play party games 200 times
Super	Reach level 99
The Ultimate	Collect all Gold Medals
Thief	Win at Genie's Lair 7 times
Time Controller	Use Time Break for 300 seconds
Trier	Win Tournament Palace 7 times
True Hero	Defeat Alf Layla wa Layla
Wind Master	Beat 20 missions using at least 5 Wind skills and no Fire/Dark skills
World Traveler	Travel 500 km (310.7 miles)

SONIC HEROES (XBOX)

UNLOCKABLE	OBJECTIVE
2 Player Team Battle Mode	Collect 20 Emblems.
2 Player Special Stage Mode	Collect 40 Emblems.
2 Player Ring Race Mode	Collect 60 Emblems.
2 Player Bobsled Race Mode	Collect 80 Emblems.
2 Player Quick Race Mode	Collect 100 Emblems.
2 Player Expert Race Mode	Collect 120 Emblems.
Last Song and Movie	Complete the Last Story.
Last Story Mode	Complete Story Mode with all four teams and all Choas Emeralds.
Metal Characters	Press Ⓐ+Ⓨ after you chose a level for 2 players.
Super Hard Mode	Collect 141 Emblems and have all A ranks.
Team Chaotix Song and Movie	Complete Story Mode with Team Chaotix.
Team Dark Song and Movie	Complete Story Mode with Team Dark.

UNLOCKABLE	OBJECTIVE
Team Rose Song and Movie	Complete Story Mode with Team Rose.
Team Sonic Movie and Song	Complete Story Mode with Team Sonic.

SONIC RUSH ADVENTURE (DS)

UNLOCKABLES

UNLOCKABLE	HOW TO UNLOCK
Blaze the Cat	Defeat the Kraken boss in Coral Cave to unlock Blaze as a playable character.
Deep Core: Final extra boss stage	Collect all Sol Emeralds and Chaos Emeralds.

SONIC SPINBALL (Wii)

UNLOCKABLES

UNLOCKABLE	HOW TO UNLOCK
Level Select	Access the Options from the title screen, take controller 1, and press: Ⓐ, ↓, Ⓑ, ↓, Ⓒ, ↓, Ⓐ, Ⓑ, ↑, Ⓐ, Ⓒ, ↑, Ⓑ, Ⓒ, ↑. If you did it correctly, you hear a special sound. Go back to the title screen and hold Ⓐ and press START to begin on Level 2, Ⓑ and press START for Level 3, and ↓ and press START for level 4.
Multi-Ball Stage	Collect every ring in any stage.
Stop the Platform in The Machine	In Level 3, The Machine, a moving platform takes you to either side of the area. Stand on the platform and press up or down to make the platform stop, allowing you to get a good look around or plan your jump carefully.

SONIC THE HEDGEHOG (PlayStation 3)

UNLOCKABLE	HOW TO UNLOCK
Last Episode	Beat Sonic's Episode, Shadow's Episode, and Silver's Episode
Audio Room	Complete Sonic, Shadow, or Silver's story 100%
Theater Room	Complete Sonic, Shadow, or Silver's story 100%
Shadow the Hedgehog	Complete "Crisis City" with Sonic
Silver the Hedgehog	Complete "Silver the Hedgehog" boss battle with Sonic

SONIC THE HEDGEHOG (Wii)

UNLOCKABLES

UNLOCKABLE	HOW TO UNLOCK
Config Mode	There is a code called Control mode, which is required before activating this code. To activate Control mode, press ↑, Ⓒ, ↓, Ⓒ, ←, Ⓒ, →, Ⓒ at the title screen, but before pressing START to begin the game, hold Ⓐ as you hit START. Now, rather than just being in Control mode, you can enable Config mode by pressing Ⓑ. Sonic will morph into a ring, and the arrows can move him anywhere, even in the air, or through obstacles such as walls, floors, or even ceilings. You can change the item Sonic appears as by hitting Ⓐ while in Config mode. Ⓑ makes Sonic normal again, and ↓ will place the sprite that you have selected for Sonic to appear as. For example, you press Ⓑ, and Sonic becomes a ring, press ↓ to make a ring appear exactly where the ring icon is. WARNING!: This distorts several different things, such as the score, time, and other various icons throughout the game such as the finish signs at the end of the first two acts of each zone that spin when Sonic shoots past them, and the small score icons that appear whenever Sonic jumps high enough after finishing a level.
Drunk Sonic	During the demo, hold ↓. Sonic will crash into walls and get hit by enemies.
Level Select	At the title screen, press ↑, ↓, ←, ↓. You should hear a noise like a ring being collected. Then, hold Ⓐ and press START for a level select!

Secret Game Message	At the title screen, press Ⓒ, Ⓒ, Ⓒ, Ⓒ, Ⓒ, Ⓒ, ↑, ↓, ←, ↓. When the demo starts, hold Ⓐ+Ⓑ+Ⓒ+↓ then press START. Instead of the Sonic Team logo, you will see a list of the game's evelopers in Japanese. When the title screen appears, a flashing "Press Start Button" will be there under Sonic's head.
Different Ending	Beat game with all Chaos Emeralds.

SONIC THE HEDGEHOG 2 (XBOX 360)

CODE	EFFECT
17	Play Invincibility Music
65	Plays a Shifting Sound
09	Plays Casino Night Zone 1-Player Music
19	Plays Sonic 2 Theme

SONIC THE HEDGEHOG 2 (Wii)

UNLOCKABLES

UNLOCKABLE	HOW TO UNLOCK
Level Select	Some other cheats require you to enable this one first. Go to the Options menu from the main screen. From there, head to the Sound Select menu and play the following sounds: 19, 65, 09, 17. Once you have played each (1 time only), press ↓ and then press START to be brought back to the title screen. Now, when you see Sonic and Tails (Miles) appear on screen, hold Ⓐ and press START to finish off the code. You're brought to a menu where you have access to any level in the game, whether you've completed the level or not.
14 Continues	Go to the sound test (not the one on the level select) and put in 19, 65, 09, 17, 01, 01, 02, 04 (press Ⓐ after each one). There won't be a confirmation sound. Start the game by pressing START on the first option (character select) and you have 14 continues.
All 7 Chaos Emeralds	This code only works for Sonic. First, do the Level Select cheat. In the Level Select menu, go to Sound Test and play the sounds 04, 01, 02, 06. If done correctly, you'll hear a Chaos Emerald sound effect. Now, select any stage from this menu and you can turn into Super Sonic with 50 rings plus you'll get Sonic's second ending after beating Death Egg Zone.
Change Tails' Name to Miles	Press ↑, ↑, ↑, ↓, ↓, ↓, ↑ at the title screen.
Debug Mode	First enter the Level Select code. Now, go to Sound Test option, and play the following tunes: 01, 09, 09, 02, 01, 01, 02, 04. It should make a ring sound when track 4 is played to signify you've entered it correctly. Now select the stage you want to go to, and press START while holding Ⓐ until the stage starts, and you'll have debug activated. Press Ⓑ to turn Debug on/off, Ⓐ to switch object, and ↓ to put down object selected. Pressing Ⓐ while the game is paused will cause the game to reset.
Debug Mode (Alternate)	At Sound Test, enter: 19, 65, 09, 17, then press Ⓐ+START, then when Sonic and Tails pop up, press Ⓐ+START to go to the Level Select screen. On the Sound Test area, enter 01, 09, 09, 02, 01, 01, 02, 04, and then press Ⓐ+START.
Debug Mode and All Emeralds (when locked-on to Sonic and Knuckles)	First activate and go to the Stage Select. Play the following tracks in Sound Test with Ⓑ: 01, 09, 09, 04, 01, 00, 01, 08. This enables the Debug code, and you should hear a ring chime if the code is entered correctly. Start the selected level with Ⓐ+START. To get all 7 Chaos Emeralds, input this code the same way: 01, 06, 07, 07, 07, 02, 01, 06. You should hear the Emerald chime. Note: this code may not work without the Debug code.

CODES & CHEATS

UNLOCKABLE	HOW TO UNLOCK
Enable Super Sonic	First, head to the Options menu from the title screen, and then into the Sound Select menu from there. Play the following sounds in this order: 19, 65, 09, 17. After that, press ↓, START. You will be taken back to the title screen. Now, when you see Sonic and Tails (Miles) appear on the screen, press and hold Ⓐ and press START to be taken to the Level Select menu. From this menu, enter the Sound Test feature, and play the following sounds: 04, 01, 02, 06. If done correctly, a familiar tune plays. Exit this menu and start the game as normal. Once you collect a minimum of 50 coins in any level, Jump (Press Ⓐ) to activate the Super Sonic code.
Get Super Sonic on Emerald Hill	First, enter the Stage Select code, shown above. Then you go into the Special Stage in the Stage Select menu. Every time you finish the special stage, press reset and go back to the special stage. Keep doing this until you get the sixth emerald. Then don't press reset. It zaps you with your 6 emeralds into Emerald Hill. Get the last emerald on Emerald Hill, get 50 rings, and jump to be Super Sonic. Don't run out of rings or you will change into Sonic again. The rings start disappearing when you are Super Sonic.
Infinite Lives	First, enable the Level Select cheat and the Debug mode. Choose Sonic and Tails as the players. After entering the codes, choose any stage from the Level Select menu (preferably stage 1). As soon as you can move Sonic, hold ↓ and press Ⓐ (don't let go of down on the D-pad). This activates Sonic's spin; Tails will copy the Sonic spin also. Press Ⓑ and Sonic will become the Debug cursor. (Tails will be locked in the Sonic spin move). Press Ⓐ until the debug cursor displays an enemy sprite, like the monkey or that bee robot. Now that the debug cursor displays an enemy sprite, move the debug cursor to where Tails is, and repeatedly tap ↓. This produces enemies where Tails is, and because Tails is locked in the Sonic spin move, he destroys the enemies. As Tails destroys enemies in this position, press ↓ more until the score for destroying an enemy increases from 100 to 8,000 to a 1Up. Once you have enough 1Ups, press Ⓑ again to revert to Sonic.
Level Select (When Locked-On to Sonic and Knuckles)	At the title screen, press ↑, ↑, ↑, ↓, ↓, ↓, ←, →, ←, ↓. Then, hold Ⓐ and press START to be taken to the Level Select menu.
Night Mode	Activate level select and hold ↓ while selecting a stage to darken the level. The effect wears off when you die or when you beat the level.
Level Select Screen	At the title screen, select Options. Highlight Sound Test then play the following music and sounds: 19, 65, 09, and 17. You hear a ring-collecting sound for correct code entry. Then press START to return to the title screen. Highlight 1-Player, hold Ⓐ, and press START. You are directed to Level Select screen. Choose a level then press START to begin.
Slow Motion	First, enter the Level Select code. Then start your game in any level. When you start, press pause. Then hold Ⓑ and try to do anything with Sonic. The game plays in slow motion as long as you hold down Ⓑ.
Oil Ocean Music Forever	Go to the Sound Test in the Options menu and put in the sounds, 02, 01, 02, 04, and hold Ⓐ and press START. The Oil Ocean music will now be playing constantly, no matter what stage.
Pseudo Super Sonic	In Oil Ocean Zone, if you manage to take a hit and end up landing in one of those green-and-gold checkered cannons, you'll fall right out, but you'll be moving at twice your normal speed as well as jumping twice your normal height (with twice as much gravity). A good place for doing this would be in Oil Ocean Zone, Act 2, near the first set of pop-tops and cannons. Just jump into the semi-hidden bed of spikes on the right and land in the cannon. Note: Moving at twice normal velocity can often get you stuck in a wall. Also, this wears off if you Super Spin Dash or Spin Dash. It also only lasts for that act.

Super Tails	Normally, when you turn into Super Sonic you lose Tails behind you all the time. Well, after you put in the debug cheat and have started a level (preferably Emerald Hill), turn yourself into a box and place it somewhere on the floor while you are Super Sonic. It should be a switch places box. Hit it and Tails has a permanent invincible circle around him. He stays like this through the whole level.
Unlimited Speed Shoes in 2-Player vs. Mode	In 2-Player vs. mode, get speed shoes and die (while you still have them) and you get to keep your speed shoes until the end of the level.

CODES

CODE	EFFECT
17	Play Invincibility Music
65	Plays a Shifting Sound
09	Plays Casino Night Zone 1-Player Music
19	Plays Sonic 2 Theme

SONIC THE HEDGEHOG 3 (Wii)

UNLOCKABLES

UNLOCKABLE	HOW TO UNLOCK
All 7 Chaos Emeralds and Super Sonic	To get all 7 Chaos Emeralds without having to complete their Special Stages, first enter the Level Select and Sound Test codes. Go to the Sound Test and play the following tunes in order: 02, 04, 05, 06. You will hear an emerald sound if the code is entered correctly. To get Super Sonic after entering the previous code, just select any level from the level select and start it. Once you acquire 50 Rings, do a double-jump to become Super Sonic.
Control Tails in a 1-Player Game	Start a 1-player game with Sonic and Tails as the characters. With controller 2, you can take control of Tails while also using Sonic.
Hidden Special Stage	On the Level Select menu, play sounds 01, 03, 05, 07. Highlight Special Stage 2 and press Ⓐ+START.
Infinite Lives	Get up to Launch Base Zone. Sound any of the alarms, so that the Kamikaze birds come after you. Charge up a Super Sonic Dash in between the alarm, but do not let go of the button. The birds continually crash into you. After about 30 seconds, you have gained enough points to get an extra life. Continue the process for as many lives as you want.
Level Select (When Locked-On to Sonic and Knuckles)	Start a game and go to Angel Island Zone, Act 1. Go to one of the swings that you hang from and grab on. While Sonic is swinging, press ←, ←, ←, →, →, →, ↑, ↑, ↑. You will hear a ring if you entered the code correctly. Pause the game and press Ⓐ to take you back to the title screen. Press ↓, ↓ to find the newly unlocked Sound Test menu. Enter it, where you can play all of the sounds/music in the game and warp to any level.
Turn into Super Sonic	After entering the Level Select and Debug code, you can use the debug to turn yourself into Super Sonic without getting all of the Chaos Emeralds. With the debug on, go into any level and press Ⓑ to turn yourself into a ring. Then press Ⓐ to turn yourself into a monitor. Now, press ↓ to duplicate the monitor, and then Ⓑ again to change back into Sonic. Jump on the monitor and you will become Super Sonic.
Level Select	When the "SEGA" screen fades, quickly press ↑, ↑, ↓, ↓, ↑, ↑,↑, ↑. If you have done this right, you should be able to scroll down to "Sound Test" below "Competition."
Sonic and Knuckles Mini-Boss Music	Get to the end of Act 1 of Hydrocity Zone (Zone 2). When facing the mini-boss, keep yourself underwater until the water warning music plays. Then jump out of the water. The game should now be playing the mini-boss music from Sonic and Knuckles, which wasn't out at the time (the music was evidently included in *Sonic 3* to make the backward compatibility feature easier).

UNLOCKABLE	HOW TO UNLOCK
Walk Thru Walls	In the Icecap Zone, Act 1, when you come to a wall that only Knuckles can bust through, hold ✚ until Sonic or Tails looks down, and the screen pans all the way down. Then press ✚ and jump at the same time. The screen starts to rotate. Walk in the direction of the wall and you will walk right through it.
100,000 Points	Beat a stage at with your time at exactly 9:59.
Frame by Frame	When playing a level after enabling the Level Select cheat, pause the game, then press ✚ to advance the game by one frame.
Slow Motion Mode	When playing any level that you have accessed using the Cheat menu, pause the game and hold Ⓑ. While Ⓑ is held down, the game plays in Slow Motion mode.

CODES

CODE	EFFECT
Hold Ⓑ and press ✚	Your character shows all of his sprite animations
Hold Ⓑ and press ✚ again activated	Your character stops the sprite show if it is

THE SOPRANOS: ROAD TO RESPECT (PlayStation 2)

Enter these codes while playing.

UNLOCKABLE	CODE
Infinite Ammo	Hold L2 and R2 and press ●, ■, ×, ■, ▲, ▲
Infinite Respect	Hold L2 and R2 and press ×, ■, ×, ■, ▲, ▲

SOUL CALIBUR: BROKEN DESTINY (PSP)

UNLOCKABLE HONORS

View unlocked Honors in the Records menu.

UNLOCKABLE	HOW TO UNLOCK
Black Sword Valor	Execute a combination of 30 Side Dash Counters and Back Dash Counters.
Boundless Spirit	Guard 10 times in a single match.
Chosen Child	Execute a Just Impact.
Daybreak	Clear all missions up to Chapter 3 in the Gauntlet.
Elation of Chance	Execute a Throw Escape.
End of Tests	View Chapter 34 "Finale" in the Gauntlet.
Expert Dancer	Execute a 7+ combo
Fearful Hero	Clear Trial of Defense with more than 2,400,000 points.
Fierce Blade	Execute five Side Dash Counters and Back Dash Counters in a single match.
First Gate	Play the Gauntlet
Greedy Fool	Achieve Score Magnification x1,000% in Trials.
Hidden Fierceness	Execute a Throw.
Innocent Artist	Create a character with no equipment
Iron Soldier	Hit the opponent into the wall five times.
Loser's Lament	Win with a Ring Out.
Painted Illusion	Take a photo using frame decorations and backgrounds for thumbnail photographs in Creation.
Passionate Artist	Take five photos during one session in Creation's thumbnail photograph.
Ranging Dash	Clear Trial of Attack with more than 1,600,000 points.
Rebel Beacon	Execute a Guaranteed Hit.
Rebel Disciple	Execute 30 Guaranteed Hits.
Waking Art	Create your first original character in Creation

SOULCALIBUR IV (XBOX 360)

ITEMS/WEAPONS

UNLOCKABLE	HOW TO UNLOCK
Advanced Equipment	Achieve 20 achievements.
All Weapons for a Character	Clear Story mode with that character.
Animal Head Equipment	Achieve 25 achievements.
Basic Equipment	Achieve 5 achievements.
Intermediate Equipment	Achieve 15 achievements.
Leviathan and Voodoo Equipment	Achieve 30 achievements.
More Equipment	Achieve 10 achievements.

CHARACTERS

UNLOCKABLE	HOW TO UNLOCK
Algol	Beat Story mode with a character that faces him as the last boss (Mitsurugi, Taki, etc.).
Amy	Purchase her in the Character Creation for 4,000 gold.
Angol Fear	Defeat her in Story mode.
Ashlotte	Defeat her in Story mode.
Cervantes	Purchase him in the Character Creation for 4,000 gold.
Hong Yun-seong	Purchase him in the Character Creation for 4,000 gold.
Kamikirimusi	Defeat her in Story mode.
Lizardman	Buy for 4,000 gold.
Rock	Purchase him in the Character Creation for 4,000 gold.
Scheherazade	Defeat her in Story mode.
Seong Mi Na	Highlight and purchase for 4,000 gold.
Setsuka	Highlight and purchase for 4,000 gold.
Shura	Defeat her in Story mode.
Sophitia	Purchase her in the Create a Soul mode for 4,000 Gold.
Talim	Buy her for 4,000 gold in Character Creation mode.
The Apprentice	Beat Arcade mode with Yoda.
Yoshimitsu	Highlight and purchase for 4000 gold.
Zasalamel	Buy him for 4,000 gold in Character Creation mode.

TOWER OF LOST SOULS HIDDEN ITEMS (ASCENDING)

UNLOCKABLE	HOW TO UNLOCK
01f Soldier's Hat	Clear stage while taking no damage.
02f Warrior Trousers	Clear stage with no ring outs from either side.
03f Pauldron	Switch with ally more than 2 times.
04f Warlord's Belt	Perform 3 attack throws.
05f Clergy Clothes	Defeat an enemy with a ring out.
06f Wonder Jacket	Throw an opponent.
07f Warrior Trousers	Clear the stage without missing any attacks.
08f Armor Ring: Ice Mirror	Switch characters twice.
09f Scarlett Blossoms	Guard against the opponent's attack 3 times in a row.
10f Silver Boots	Guard the opponent's attack 10 times in a row.
11f Grim Horn	Defeat all enemies with a critical finish.
12f Magus Cloth	Defeat all enemies with ring outs.
13f Pegasus Sallet	Destroy all the walls.
14f Stage: Phantom Pavilion Seesaw	Perform guard impact more than 3 times.

UNLOCKABLE	HOW TO UNLOCK
15f Submissions Belt	Clear the stage using only the A and G buttons.
16f Warlord's Belt	Clear the stage with 0 time remaining.
17f Arm Bandages	Execute a 5+ combo.
18f Kouchu Kabuto	Stand on all corners of the stage.
19f Longhua Qippo	Switch with ally more than 5 times.
20f Life Gem: Sun	Clear the stage with a critical finish.
21f Longhua Qippo	Voluntarily ring yourself out.
22f Honor Boots	Perform more than 4 counter hits.
23F Frilled Skirt	Guard more than 3 times in a row.
24f Protect Gem: Cardinal Directions	Perform a combo with more than 240 damage.
25f Zhuque Changpao	Throw more than 5 times.
26f Warthog Cuirass	Execute a 10+ combo.
27f Iron Gauntlets	Clear the stage with no damage taken.
28F Aculeus Suit	Opponent guards a guard break attack at least twice.
29f Menghu Boots	Switch with ally 5+ times.
30f Spirit Gem: Noniple Heads	Clear stage without guarding.
31f Longming Qippo	Perform 5+ Just Inputs.
32f Vane Mask	Perform a low throw.
33f Battle Dress	Perform 3 attack throws.
34f Power Gem: Warrior Princess	Perform guard impact 3+ times.
35f Warthog Pauldrons	Clear without switching.
36f Parlor Blouse	Clear stage with 0 time remaining.
37f Siren's Helm	Defeat all enemies with critical finishes.
38f Gorgon Fauld	Defeat all enemies with ring out.
39f Kingfisher Greaves	Clear the stage without changing position.
40f Deer Head	Execute a 5+ combo.
41f Minotaur	Perform 5+ Just Inputs.
42f Demonic Gloves	Clear the stage without letting opponents invoke a skill.
43f Repel Gem: Iron Shell	Perform an over the back throw.
44f War Cloak	No ring outs either side.
45f Tiger Lily Kabuto	Defeat enemies without using any skills.
46f Butterfly Salet	Defeat enemies without using any skills.
47f Succubus Boots	Throw 5 times.
48f Life Dem: Jade	Clear stage with a character equipped with the "invisible" skill.
49f Horns of Calamity	Clear stage with no attacks missing.
50f Tiger Lily Breastplates	Execute a 10+ combo.
51f Tiger Lily Fauld	Perform more than 4 counter hits.
52f Feathered Wings	Clear stage with a critical finish.
53f Blade Ring: Demon Lord	Defeat all enemies with a ring out.
54f Leviathan Pauldron	Destroy all the walls.
55f Priestess Kimono	Perform 3 attack throws.
56f Leviathan Burgonet	Perform a combo with more than 240 damage.
57f Voodoo Armlets	Voluntarily perform a ring out.
58f Tiger Pauldrons	Defeat all enemies without any skills equipped.
59f Voodoo Greaves	Guard an enemy's attack 10 times in a row.
60f Voodoo Breastplate	Clear the stage without switching character.

TOWER OF LOST SOULS REWARD ITEMS (DESCENDING)

UNLOCKABLE	HOW TO UNLOCK
B05	Dark Knight's Cloak
B10	Blade Ring: Raging Thunder
B15	Lapin Chapeau
B20	Repel Gem: Fox Demon
B25	Succubus Gauntlets
B30	Demonic Armor
B35	Demonic Pauldrons
B40	Voodoo Crown

CREATE-A-SOUL ITEMS/WEAPONS

UNLOCKABLE	HOW TO UNLOCK
Advanced Equipment	Achieve 20 achievements.
All Weapons for a Character	Clear Story mode with that Character.
Animal Head Equipment	Achieve 25 achievements.
Basic Equipment	Achieve 5 achievements.
Intermediate Equipment	Achieve 15 achievements.
Leviathan and Voodoo Equipment	Achieve 30 achievements.
More Equipment	Achieve 10 achievements.

EASTER EGGS

UNLOCKABLE	HOW TO UNLOCK
Metallic Characters	At the Character Select screen, hold down (RT) and choose a character by pressing (A). When the battle begins, your character is metallic.

ACHIEVEMENTS

UNLOCKABLE	HOW TO UNLOCK
Apprentice (5)	Play 3 characters in any mode.
Art Connoisseur (5)	Explore the different areas in the museum.
Champion (25)	Beat Time Attack mode in under 4 minutes.
Close Call (15)	Defeat an opponent under adverse conditions.
Conqueror (25)	Beat 25 opponents in Extra Survival mode.
Edge Master (30)	Beat Arcade mode with all characters.
Guardian (15)	Perform 25 consecutive bursts with Freestyle set to Guard Impact in Practice mode.
Noble Soul (25)	Beat the game in Ultra Hard without losing a round.
Ring Out (15)	Finish Time Attack mode with all Ring Outs.
Summon Suffering (20)	Perform the move Summon Suffering with Ivy.
Warrior (10)	Complete Arcade mode.
Zen Warrior (10)	Play 3 characters in any mode.

SPACE GIRAFFE (XBOX 360)

SUPER OX MODE

Do this after finishing the game once, when the game asks you to choose between tutorial or main game mode.

CODE	EFFECT
Hold (Y), then push (A)	Play an extra 100 levels

SPAWN: ARMAGEDDON (XBOX)

Enter the following codes any time during the game (when paused).

UNLOCKABLE	CODE
All Comics	Up, Down, Left, Right, Right, Left, Left, Up

UNLOCKABLE	CODE
All Weapons	↑,↓,←,→,←,→,←,←
Infinite Health and Necroplasm	↑,↓,←,→,→,←,↓,↑
Infinite Ammo	↑,↓,←,→,↑,←,↓,→

SPAWN: ARMAGEDDON (PlayStation 2)

Pause the game and enter the following:

UNLOCKABLE	CODE
All Comics	↑,↓,←,→,→,←,←,↑
All Missions	↑,↓,←,→,←,←,→,→
All Weapons	↑,↓,←,→,←,→,←,←
No Blood	↑,↓,←,→,↑,↑,↑,↑
Open Encyclopedia	↑,↓,←,→,←,→,↓,↑
Unlimited Ammo	↑,↓,←,→,↑,←,↓,→
Unlimited Health/ Necroplasm	↑,↓,←,→,→,←,↓,↑
Unlimited Necroplasm	↑,↓,←,→,↓,←,↑,→

SPEED RACER (Wii)

CODES

Enter the following codes in the "Enter Code" section of the "Options" menu. Enter the codes again to disable them.

EFFECT	CODE
Aggressive Opponents	↑,←,↓,→,↑,←,↓
Granite Car	B,↑,−,+,1,↑,+
Helium	−,↑,−,2,−,↑,−
Invulnerability	A,B,A,↑,←,↓,→
Monster Truck	B,↑,−,2,B,↑,−
Moon Gravity	↑,+,↑,→,−,↑,−
Overkill	A,−,+,↓,↑,+,1
Pacifist Opponents (other racers don't attack you)	↑,→,↓,←,↑,→,↓
Psychedelic	←,A,→,↓,B,↑,−
Tiny Opponents	B,A,←,↓,−,↑,−
Unlimited Boost	B,A,↓,↑,B,A,↓
Unlock the Last 3 Cars	1,2,1,2,B,A,+

UNLOCKABLES

Complete the championships with a ranking of 3rd or higher to unlock the corresponding racer.

UNLOCKABLE	HOW TO UNLOCK
Booster Mbube	Complete Class 2, Championship 6.
Colonel Colon	Complete Class 3, Championship 4.
Delila	Complete Class 3, Championship 3.
Denise Mobile	Complete Class 3, Championship 6.
Esther "Rev" Reddy	Complete Class 3, Championship 7.
Gothorm Danneskjblo	Complete Class 3, Championship 2.
Grey Ghost	Complete Class 1, Championship 3.
Kellie "Gearbox" Kalinkov	Complete Class 2, Championship 4.
Mariana Zanja	Complete Class 3, Championship 5.
Nitro Venderhoss	Complete Class 2, Championship 5.
Pitter Pat	Complete Class 3, Championship 1.
Prince Kabala	Complete Class 2, Championship 3.
Rosey Blaze	Complete Class 1, Championship 1.
Snake Oiler	Complete Class 1, Championship 2.
Sonic "Boom Boom" Renaldi	Complete Class 2, Championship 2.
Taejo Togokahn	Complete Class 2, Championship 1.

SPIDER-MAN: FRIEND OR FOE (XBOX 360)

CODES

Venom and new Green Goblin (from the movie) can be unlocked by entering the following codes using the d-pad when standing in the Helicarrier in between levels. You hear a tone if you entered the code correctly, and they are then be selectable from the sidekick select console.

CODE	EFFECT
↑, ↑, ↓, ↓, ←, →	Gain 5,000 upgrade points
←, ↓, →, →, ↓, ←	New Green Goblin
←, ←, →, ↑, ↓, ↓	Venom

SPIDER-MAN: FRIEND OR FOE (Wii)

CODES

CODE	EFFECT
5,000 Tech Tokens, One Time Only	↑, ↑, ↓, ↓, ←, ↓
Unlock New Goblin	←, ↓, →, →, ↓, ←
Unlock Sandman	→, →, →, ↑, ↓, ←
Unlock Venom	←, ←, →, ↑, ↓, ↓

SPIDER-MAN 2 (PSP)

Go to Options, Special, and Cheats on the Main menu, and then type in the following passwords.

UNLOCKABLE	PASSWORD
All Levels Unlocked	WARPULON
All Moves Purchased	MYHERO
All Movies Unlocked	POPPYCORN
Enemies Have Big Heads and Feet	BAHLOONIE
Infinite Health	NERGETS
Infinite Webbing	FILLMEUP
Spidey Has Big Head and Feet	HEAVYHEAD
Tiny Spider-Man	SPIDEYMAN
Unlock All Production Art	SHUTT
Unlock Storyboard Viewer	FRZFRAME

SPIDER-MAN 2 (XBOX)

Type in HCRAYERT as a name to gain upgrades, a lot of Hero Points, and 44% game completion.

SPIDER-MAN 2 (PlayStation 2)

Start a New Game and enter HCRAYERT as a name. Go back and enter any name of your choice. This cheat will start in progress, with over 40% completion, 201,000 Hero points, upgrades, and other goodies!

SPIDER-MAN 3 (Wii)

UNLOCKABLES

UNLOCKABLE	HOW TO UNLOCK
Collect all 50 Spider Emblems	Unlock black suit Spider-man after you destroy the suit

SPLASHDOWN RIDES GONE WILD (PlayStation 2)

Enter codes in the Options menu screen.

UNLOCKABLE	CODE
50,000 Warehouse Points	↑, ↑, ↓, ↓, ←, →, ←, →, ■, ●
All Warehouse Items	↑, ↓, ↑, ↓, ←, →, ←, →, ←, ↓, →, ↑, →, ↓, ←, ↑

SPLATTERHOUSE (Wii)

UNLOCKABLES

UNLOCKABLE	HOW TO UNLOCK
Hard Mode screen	At the title screen, hold SELECT until "HARD" appears on the
Sound Test	First enter the code to access the Stage Select option. When the screen comes up and asks you to select what stage you want to start on, press and hold the select button. After a second or two, the Stage Select option becomes a Sound Test menu, allowing you to listen to various "songs" and sound effects. Hold select again to change it back to the Stage Select menu.
Stage Select	When the prologue starts up and there's a house in the rain, press SELECT, SELECT, SELECT, hold ✜ and then press ① or ②. It brings up the option to select a level.

SPONGEBOB SQUAREPANTS BATTLE FOR BIKINI BOTTOM (XBOX)

Pause the game and hold Ⓛ+Ⓡ, then input the code. You must do this quickly. You'll hear a sound if you entered the code correctly.

UNLOCKABLE	CODE
10 Spatulas	Ⓧ, Ⓨ, Ⓨ, Ⓧ, Ⓧ, Ⓨ, Ⓨ, Ⓧ
1000 Shiny Objects	Ⓨ, Ⓧ, Ⓧ, Ⓨ, Ⓨ, Ⓧ, Ⓧ, Ⓨ
All monsters in Monster Gallery (Police Station)	Ⓧ, Ⓨ, Ⓧ, Ⓨ, Ⓨ, Ⓧ, Ⓨ, Ⓧ
Big Plankton	Ⓨ, Ⓨ, Ⓨ, Ⓨ, Ⓧ, Ⓨ, Ⓧ, Ⓨ, Ⓧ, Ⓧ, Ⓧ, Ⓧ
Bubble Bowl Power Up	Ⓧ, Ⓨ, Ⓧ, Ⓨ, Ⓧ, Ⓧ, Ⓨ, Ⓨ
Cruise Bubble Bowl Power Up	Ⓨ, Ⓧ, Ⓨ, Ⓧ, Ⓨ, Ⓨ, Ⓧ, Ⓧ
Cruise Bubble has Cruise Control	Ⓧ, Ⓧ, Ⓧ, Ⓧ, Ⓨ, Ⓨ, Ⓧ, Ⓧ, Ⓨ, Ⓧ, Ⓨ, Ⓨ
Invert Camera Controls (Left/Right)	Ⓨ, Ⓨ, Ⓧ, Ⓧ, Ⓧ, Ⓧ, Ⓨ, Ⓨ
Invert Camera Controls (Up/Down)	Ⓨ, Ⓧ, Ⓧ, Ⓧ, Ⓧ, Ⓧ, Ⓧ, Ⓨ
Restore health	Ⓧ, Ⓧ, Ⓧ, Ⓧ, Ⓨ, Ⓧ, Ⓨ, Ⓧ, Ⓨ, Ⓨ, Ⓨ, Ⓨ
Small Patrick, Mr. Crab, Squidword, Squirrel Girl in Astronaut Costume	Ⓨ, Ⓨ, Ⓨ, Ⓨ, Ⓧ, Ⓨ, Ⓧ, Ⓨ, Ⓨ, Ⓨ, Ⓨ, Ⓨ
Small Towns People	Ⓨ, Ⓨ, Ⓨ, Ⓨ, Ⓨ, Ⓧ, Ⓨ, Ⓨ, Ⓧ, Ⓨ, Ⓧ
Sponge Bob No Pants	Ⓧ, Ⓧ, Ⓧ, Ⓨ, Ⓧ, Ⓧ, Ⓨ, Ⓧ, Ⓨ, Ⓨ, Ⓧ
Townspeople are Thieves (Shiny Objects)	Ⓨ, Ⓨ, Ⓨ, Ⓨ, Ⓨ, Ⓧ, Ⓨ, Ⓧ, Ⓨ, Ⓨ, Ⓧ, Ⓧ
Unlock Art Gallery (Theatre)	Ⓨ, Ⓧ, Ⓨ, Ⓧ, Ⓧ, Ⓨ, Ⓧ, Ⓨ

SPONGEBOB SQUAREPANTS: CREATURE FROM THE KRUSTY KRAB (Wii)

PASSWORDS

PASSWORD	EFFECT
ROCFISH	30,000 Z-Coins
HOVER	Alternate Plankton hovercraft
ROBOT	Astronaut suit for Plankton in Revenge of the Giant Plankton
LASER	Extra laser color in Revenge of the Giant Plankton level
ROCKET	Extra rocket for Patrick in Hypnotic Highway level
PILOT	Get Aviator SpongeBob costume
BRAIN	Get Exposed-Brain SpongeBob costume
INVENT	Get Inventor Plankton costume
SPIN	Get Patrick's different POW! effect
BUNRUN	Get Patrick's purple rocket
SAFARI	Get Safari Patrick costume
BONES	Get Skeleton Patrick costume

KRABBY	Get Skeleton SpongeBob costume
FLAMES	Get SpongeBob's flame effect color
HYPCAR	Get SpongeBob's Hypnotic car skin
DUCKGUN	Get SpongeBob's Squeaky Duck Gun
GASSY	Infinite Fuel (in Flying levels)
VIGOR	Infinite Health (in platforming levels)
SCOOTLES	Obtain all sleepy seeds
TISSUE	Obtain Sleepy Seed Detector
PIRATE	Play as Pirate Patrick in Rooftop Rumble level
SPONGE	Play as Punk SpongeBob in Diesel Dreaming level
PANTS	Play as SpongeBob Plankton in Super-Size Patty level
HOTROD	Unlock a bonus vehicle in the Diesel Dreaming level
PORKPIE	Unlock all bonus games
GUDGEON	Unlock all levels
SPACE	Unlock bonus ship in the Rocket Rodeo level
PATRICK	Unlock tuxedo for Patrick in Starfishman to the Rescue

SPONGEBOB SQUAREPANTS: THE MOVIE (XBOX)

Pause the game, hold LT+RT to enter the following codes.

UNLOCKABLE	CODE
All Health	Y,Y,Y,Y,X,Y,X,Y
All Moves	X,X,Y,X,Y,Y,X,X
All Moves to Macho	X,X,Y,X,Y,Y,X,Y
All Tasks	Y,X,Y,Y,X,Y,X,X

SPYHUNTER (PlayStation 2)

At the screen where you enter a name, enter this password. The sound of a chicken clucking will confirm that you have entered the code correctly.

UNLOCKABLE	CODE
Unlock Saliva Video	GUNN
View Concept Art	SCW823
View Making of FMV	MAKING
View Spy Hunter Theme FMV	SALIVA
View Test Animatic FMV	WWS413

SPY HUNTER 2 (XBOX)

To access the following codes, pause gameplay at any time during the game and enter code.

UNLOCKABLE	CODE
God Mode	LT,LT,LT,BLK,LT,RT,RT,LT,BLK
Infinite Ammo	RT,LT,BLK,BLK,WHT,RT,LT,BLK,WHT

SPY HUNTER 2 (PlayStation 2)

UNLOCKABLE	CODE
All Missions and Weapons	In the Main Menu, press L1,R2,L2,R1,R1,L2,R2,L1.
Infinite Ammo	Pause the game and press R1,L1,R2,R2,L2,R1,L1,R2,L2. Enter the code again to deactivate it.
Invincibility	Pause the game and press L1,L1,L1,R2,L1,R1,R1,L1,R2. Enter the code again to deactivate it.

SSX 3 (XBOX)

UNLOCKABLE	CODE
Snow Boards	graphicdelight
Videos	myeyesaredim
Hiro	slicksuit
Stretch	windmilldunk
Alternate Costumes	To earn more costumes, complete all chapters in your trick book. To unlock the final chrome costume, complete World Circuit mode with a "Master" rank.
Fugi Board	Get a gold medal on every course with all boarders with their überboards to unlock a Fugi board.

SSX 3 (PlayStation 2)

From the Main menu, go to Options. Select "Enter Cheat" and enter the following codes (these codes are case-sensitive):

UNLOCKABLE	CODE
All Artwork	naturalkoncept
All Boards	graphicdelight
All Peaks	biggerthank7
All Playlist Songs	djsuperstar
All Posters	postnobills
All Toys	nogluerequired
All Trading Cards	gotitgotitneedit
All Videos	myeyesaredim
Brodi	zenmaster
Bunny San	wheresyourtail
Canhuck	greatwhitenorth
Churchill	tankengine
Cudmore the Cow	milkemdaisy
Eddie	worm
Gutless	boneyardreject
Hiro	slicksuit
Lodge One Clothes	shoppingspree
Luther	bronco
Jurgen	brokenleg
Marty	back2future
North West Legend	callhimgeorge
Snowballs	betyouneverseen
Stretch	windmilldunk
Svelte Luther	notsosvelte
Unknown Rider	finallymadeitin

SSX BLUR (Wii)

In the Options menu, select Cheat to enter this code.

UNLOCKABLE	CODE
All Characters Unlocked	NoHolds

SSX ON TOUR (XBOX)

Enter these passwords at the Cheats menu.

UNLOCKABLE	PASSWORD
All Clothing	FLYTHREADS
All Levels	BACKSTAGEPASS
All Movies	THEBIGPICTURE

UNLOCKABLE	PASSWORD
Extra Cash	LOOTSNOOT
Infinite Boost	ZOOMJUICE
Monster Tricks	JACKALOPESTYLE
Snowball Fight	LETSPARTY
Stat Boost	POWERPLAY
Unlock Characters	ROADIEROUNDUP
Unlock Conrad (the MiniViking)	BIGPARTYTIME
Unlock Mitch Koobski (the Unicorn)	MOREFUNTHANONE
Unlock Nigel (Rocker)	THREEISACROWD
Unlock Ski Patrol Character	FOURSOME

SSX ON TOUR (PlayStation 2)

Enter these passwords at the Cheats menu.

UNLOCKABLE	CODE
All Clothing	FLYTHREADS
All Levels	BACKSTAGEPASS
All Movies	THEBIGPICTURE
Extra Cash	LOOTSNOOT
Infinite Boost	ZOOMJUICE
Monster Tricks	JACKALOPESTYLE
Snowball Fight	LETSPARTY
Stat Boost	POWERPLAY
Unlock Characters	ROADIEROUNDUP
Unlock Conrad (The MiniViking)	BIGPARTYTIME
Unlock Mitch Koobski (The Unicorn)	MOREFUNTHANONE
Unlock Nigel (Rocker)	THREEISACROWD
Unlock Ski Patrol Character	FOURSOME

SSX TRICKY (XBOX)

UNLOCKABLE	OBJECTIVE
Pipedream Course	Win a medal on all Showoff courses.
Play as Brodi	Win a gold medal in World Circuit mode.
Play as JP	Win three gold medals in World Circuit mode.
Play as Kaori	Win four gold medals in World Circuit mode.
Play as Luther	Win eight gold medals in World Circuit mode.
Play as Marisol	Win five gold medals in World Circuit mode.
Play as Psymon	Win six gold medals in World Circuit mode.
Play as Seeiah	Win seven gold medals in World Circuit mode.
Play as Zoe	Win two gold medals in World Circuit mode.
Überboards	Unlock all of the tricks for a character to get his or her überboard, which is that character's best board.
Untracked Course	Win a medal on all Race courses.

Input these codes at the main options screen, with the "Start Game" and "DVD Extras" option. Listen for the sound to confirm correct code entry.

UNLOCKABLE	CODE
Annette Board	Hold LT + RT and press X, A, →, X, A, ↓, X, A, ←, X, A, ↑, then release LT + RT. Choose Kaori and start a track. Kaori will have a full Tricky meter, and a faster board.
Full Stat Points	Hold LT + RT and press Y, Y, →, Y, Y, ↓, A, A, ←, A, A, ↑. (All the boarders will have full stat points.)

UNLOCKABLE	CODE
Mallora Board	Hold LT + RT and press Ⓐ, Ⓐ, →, Ⓑ, Ⓑ, ↓, Ⓨ, Ⓨ, ←, Ⓧ, Ⓧ, ↑, then release LT + RT. Choose Elise and start a track. Elise will have the Mallora Board and a blue outfit. This code only works for Elise.
Master Code	Hold LT + RT and press Ⓐ, Ⓨ, →, Ⓑ, Ⓧ, ↓, Ⓨ, Ⓧ, ←, Ⓑ, Ⓐ, ↑, then release LT + RT.
Mix Master Mike	Hold LT + RT and press Ⓐ, Ⓐ, →, Ⓐ, Ⓐ, ↓, Ⓐ, Ⓐ, ←, Ⓐ, Ⓐ, ↑, then release LT + RT. Choose any boarder at the character selection screen, and he or she will be replaced by Mix Master Mike on the course, with the number of the character that was originally selected. He has decks on his back and a vinyl board. Repeat the code to disable its effect.
Sticky Boards	Hold LT + RT and press Ⓧ, Ⓧ, →, Ⓨ, Ⓨ, ↓, Ⓑ, Ⓑ, ←, Ⓐ, Ⓐ, ↑, then release LT + RT.

SSX TRICKY (PlayStation 2)

UNLOCKABLE	OBJECTIVE
Alternate Costumes	To earn more costumes, complete all chapters in your trick book. To unlock the final chrome costume, complete World Circuit mode with a Master rank.
Fugi Board	Get a gold medal on every course with all boarders with their uberboard to unlock a Fugi board.
Pipedream Course	Win a medal on all Showoff courses.
Play as Brodi	Win a gold medal in World Circuit mode.
Play as JP	Win three gold medals in World Circuit mode.
Play as Kaori	Win four gold medals in World Circuit mode.
Play as Luther	Win eight gold medals in World Circuit mode.
Play as Marisol	Win five gold medals in World Circuit mode.
Play as Psymon	Win six gold medals in World Circuit mode.
Play as Seeiah	Win seven gold medals in World Circuit mode.
Play as Zoe	Win two gold medals in World Circuit mode.
Uberboards	Unlock all of the tricks for a character to get their uberboard, which is their best board.
Untracked Course	Win a medal on all Race courses.

To access the following unlockable, go to the Title screen and hold L1+R1, enter code, then release L1+R1. A sound will confirm correct code entry.

UNLOCKABLE	CODE
Full Stat Points	▲,▲,→,▲,▲,↓,×,×,←,×,×,↑—all the boarders will have full stat points.
Mallora Board	×,×,→,●,●,↓,▲,▲,←,■,■,↑—choose Elise and start a track. Elise will have the Mallora Board and a blue outfit.
Master Code	×,▲,→,●,■,↓,▲,■,←,●,×,↑
Mix Master Mike	×,×,→,×,×,↓,×,×,←,×,×,↑—(See below for more info)
Running Man Mode	■,▲,●,×,■,▲,●,×—enter at the Options screen.
Sticky Boards	■,■,→,▲,▲,↓,●,●,←,×,×,↑

FOR THE MIX MASTER MIKE UNLOCKABLE, ONCE YOU'VE INPUT THE CODE, CHOOSE ANY BOARDER AT THE CHARACTER SELECTION SCREEN AND HE OR SHE WILL BE REPLACED BY MIX MASTER MIKE ON THE COURSE. HE HAS DECKS ON HIS BACK AND A VINYL BOARD. REPEAT THE CODE TO DISABLE ITS EFFECT.

STAR SOLDIER (Wii)

UNLOCKABLES

UNLOCKABLE	HOW TO UNLOCK
Powered Up Ship	At the title screen, press SELECT 10 times on controller 1. Then, hold ↓+↓ on controller 2. Then, hold ↑+←+Ⓐ+Ⓑ on controller 1, finally press START, START on controller 1.

STAR TREK: LEGACY (XBOX 360)

UNLOCKABLE	HOW TO UNLOCK
Unlock the U.S.S. Legacy	To unlock the secret ship (and receive the achievement), beat the game once on any difficulty, then load your game. When you do, you should be on the ship buying screen right before the final mission. From there; sell and/or buy ships to make sure you have 3 Sovereign-class ships. The final ship you buy will be the U.S.S. Legacy.

STAR TREK: SHATTERED UNIVERSE (XBOX)

Enter these codes at the Main Menu.

UNLOCKABLE	CODE
All Medals and Ranks Awarded	BLK, LT, RT, B, RT, Y, LT, WHT
All Missions Open	BLK, RT, LT, B, X, LT, RT, Y, WHT
All Ships Open	BLK, LT, X, LT, X, RT, RT, B, WHT
Invincibility	BLK, LT, B, LT, RT, Y, Y, B, WHT
Kobayashi Maru Open	BLK, LT, Y, LT, LT, X, Y, Y, RT, WHT

STAR WARS BATTLEFRONT (XBOX)

UNLOCKABLE	CODE
All Missions	In Historical Campaign, press X,Y,X,Y at the Level Select screen.

STAR WARS BATTLEFRONT (PlayStation 2)

UNLOCKABLE	CODE
All Planets	Choose Historical Campaign, then press ■,●,■,● at the Planet Selection screen.

STAR WARS BATTLEFRONT II (PSP)

Pause the game and enter this code.

UNLOCKABLE	CODE
Invincibility	↑, ↑, ↑, ←, ↓, ↓, ↓, ←, ↑, ↑, ↑, ←, →

STAR WARS BATTLEFRONT II (XBOX)

During gameplay, pause the game. Enter the following codes. There will be a sound if done correctly.

UNLOCKABLE	CODE
Disable HUD	↑, ↑, ↑, ↑, ←, ↑, ↑, ↓, ←, ↓, ↑, ↑, ←, →
Lower Resolution Soldiers	↓, ↓, ↓, ↑, ↑, ←, ↓, ↓, ↓, ↓, ↓, ←, ↑, ↑, ↑, ←, →
Invulnerable	↑, ↑, ↑, ←, ↓, ↓, ↓, ←, ↑, ↑, ↑, ←, →
Slow Motion Sound Effects	↑, ↑, ↑, ←, ↑, ↓, ↑, ↑, ←, ↓, ↓, ↓, ←, ↑, ↓, ↓, ←, →
Weird Captions	↑, ↓, ←, ↓, ←, →

STAR WARS BOUNTY HUNTER (PlayStation 2)

Enter the following sequences as codes.

UNLOCKABLE	CODE
Chapter 1	SEEHOWTHEYRUN
Chapter 2	CITYPLANET
Chapter 3	LOCKDOWN
Chapter 4	DUGSOPLENTY
Chapter 5	BANTHAPOODOO
Chapter 6	MANDALORIANWAY
Concept Art	R ARTISTS ROCK
Mission 1	BEAST PIT
Mission 2	GIMMEMY JETPACK

UNLOCKABLE	CODE
Mission 3	CONVEYORAMA
Mission 4	BIGCITYNIGHTS
Mission 5	IEATNERFMEAT
Mission 6	VOTE4TRELL
Mission 7	LOCKUP
Mission 8	WHAT A RIOT
Mission 9	SHAFTED
Mission 10	BIGMOSQUITOS
Mission 11	ONEDEADDUG
Mission 12	WISHIHADMYSHIP
Mission 13	MOS GAMOS
Mission 14	TUSKENS R US
Mission 15	BIG BAD DRAGON
Mission 16	MONTROSSISBAD
Mission 17	VOSAISBADDER
Mission 18	JANGOISBADDEST
TGC Cards	GO FISH

STAR WARS: EPISODE I OBI-WAN (XBOX)

UNLOCKABLE	CODE
Additional Versus Mode Characters	Defeat a character in the Jedi Arena during gameplay to unlock him or her in Versus mode.
All levels until Darth Maul	Enter M1A2U3L4!? as a saved game name
Battle Royal Mission (You have to fight eight other Jedi Masters in the Saber Arena.)	Defeat Darth Maul in Level 25.
Level Select (All levels, including the bonus levels, will be unlocked.)	Select the "New Game" option at the main menu, then enter GREYTHERAT as saved game name.

STAR WARS: EPISODE III REVENGE OF THE SITH (XBOX)

These codes can be entered in the Codes section of the Options menu.

UNLOCKABLE	CODE
All Attacks and Force Power Upgrades Activated	JAINA
All Bonus Missions Unlocked NARSHADDAA	
All Concept Art Unlocked AAYLASECURA	
All Duel Arenas Unlocked	TANTIVEIV
All Duelist Unlocked	ZABRAK
All Story Missions Unlocked	KORRIBAN
Fast Force Energy and Health Regeneration Activated	BELSAVIS
Infinite Force Energy Activated	KAIBURR
Infinite Health Activated	XUCPHRA

STAR WARS: EPISODE III REVENGE OF THE SITH (PlayStation 2)

Enter the following codes in the Codes section of the Options menu.

UNLOCKABLE	CODE
All Attacks and Force Power Upgrades Activated	JAINA
All Bonus Missions Unlocked	NARSHADDAA
All Concept Art Unlocked	AAYLASECURA
All Duel Arenas Unlocked	TANTIVEIV
All Duelist Unlocked	ZABRAK

All Story Missions Unlocked	KORRIBAN
Fast Force Energy and Health Regeneration Activated	BELSAVIS
Infinite Force Energy Activated	KAIBURR
Infinite Health Activated	XUCPHRA

STAR WARS: JEDI KNIGHT II: JEDI OUTCAST (XBOX)

PASSWORDS

PASSWORD	EFFECT
DINGO	All Levels
BUBBLE	God Mode
BISCUIT	Infinite Ammo
PEEPS	Multiplayer Characters
DEMO	Play Bonus Level
Fudge	Start With Lightsaber
SCOOTER	Unlimited Force
CHERRY	Unlock First Seven Levels

UNLOCKABLES

UNLOCKABLE	HOW TO UNLOCK
Fight Desann Twice	When you are in Yavin Courtyard, run as fast as you can to the room with the Seeker Drones. Push the red button on the right wall 5 times and Desann appears. He is easier to fight right now than when you fight him at Yavin FinalConflict.

STAR WARS: JEDI STARFIGHTER (PlayStation 2)

Enter the following in the Codes section of the Options menu.

UNLOCKABLE	CODE
Invincibility	QUENTIN
Fly-By Mode	DIRECTOR
No Hud	NOHUD

STAR WARS: KNIGHTS OF THE OLD REPUBLIC (XBOX)

Unlock the Hidden Ending: Before the final battle with Darth Malak press LT + RT + Y on all controllers (you need to have more than one) that you have plugged into the Xbox. This must be done before you enter the door to face Darth Malak. If you did it right, your Jedi takes out her/his lightsaber. Then open the door and walk up to Malak and talk to him.

STAR WARS: REPUBLIC COMMANDO (XBOX)

Enter this code while the game is paused.

UNLOCKABLE	CODE
Refill Ammo (refills the weapon equipped)	Y, Y, X, ↓, RT, LT, RT, ↑

STAR WARS STARFIGHTER (PlayStation 2)

To access the following unlockables, go to the Code screen (via the Options menu) to enter the sequence.

UNLOCKABLE	CODE
Default Message	SHOTS (or SIZZLE)
Director Mode	DIRECTOR
Hidden Christmas Video	WOZ
Hidden Message	LTDJGD
Invincibility	MINIME
Jar Jar Mode	JARJAR
My Day at Work (short slideshow)	JAMEZ
No Heads Up Display	NOHUD

NEW! A B C D E F G H I J K L M N O P Q R S T U V W X Y Z

UNLOCKABLE	CODE
Everything	OVERSEER
Experimental N-1 Fighter	BLUENSF
Multiplayer Mode	ANDREW
Gallery	SHIPS
View Character Sketches	HEROES
View Hidden Picture	SIMON—you'll see a picture of the LEC team.
View Planet Sketch-Work	PLANETS
View the Credits	CREDITS
View the Dev Team	TEAM

STAR WARS STARFIGHTER: SPECIAL EDITION (XBOX)

Enter the following as codes to access the specified unlockable.

UNLOCKABLE	CODE
Alternate Camera Angles	DIRECTOR—the message "Director Mode" confirms correct code entry.
Bruiser Gun	BRUISER
Default Screen	SIZZLE
Disable Cockpit Displays	NOHUD
Enemy Ship Gallery	SHIPS
Invincibility	EARCHIPS—the message "Invincibility" confirms correct code entry.
Master Code (Everything except the multiplayer levels will be unlocked.)	EUROPA
Pre-Production Art	PLANETS
Programmer FMV Sequence	LATEAM
Reversed Controls	JARJAR—the message "Jar Jar Mode" confirms correct code entry.
Secret Level Programmers	SLTEAM
Secret Spaceship for Bonus Missions (Unlock the Experimental N-1 Fighter.)	FSNEULB
Spaceship and Cast Pictures	HEROES
Trade Federation Freighter	UTILITY
View Credits	CREDITS
Canyon Sprint Mission	Earn a silver medal in the Naboo Proving Grounds, the Royal Escort, Taking the Offensive, Midnight Munitions Run, Rescue on the Solleu, and the Final Assault missions.
Charm's Way Mission	Earn a bronze medal in the Royal Escort, Contract Infraction, Piracy above Lok, Taking the Offensive, the New Resistance, and the Final Assault missions.
Darth Maul's Infiltrator Ship	Earn a gold medal in all default missions.
Guardian Mantis Ship	Earn a gold medal in the Contract Infraction, Secrets on Eos, and the New Resistance missions.
Havoc Ship	Earn a gold medal in the Piracy above Lok, Valuable Goods, Eye of the Storm, the Crippling Blow, and Last Stand on Naboo missions.
Outpost Attack Mission	Earn a bronze medal in all default missions.
Secret Spaceship for Bonus Missions (Unlock the Experimental N-1 Fighter.)	Earn a gold medal in the Naboo Proving Grounds, the Royal Escort, Taking the Offensive, Midnight Munitions Run, Rescue on the Solleu, and the Final Assault missions.

Space Sweep Mission	Earn a silver medal in all default missions.

STAR WARS: THE CLONE WARS (XBOX)

UNLOCKABLE	CODE
All Bonus Menu Items	IGIVEUP
All Multiplayer Levels	LETSDANCE
Earn the three bonus objectives	ALITTLEHELP
Get All FMV Movies	GOTPOPCORN
Invincibility	LORDOFSITH
Team Photos	YOURMASTERS
Unlimited Ammo	NOHONOR

STAR WARS: THE CLONE WARS (PlayStation 2)

Enter the following as codes.

UNLOCKABLE	CODE
Unlock Clone Trooper in Academy Geonosis Level	FAKE FETT
All FMV Sequences	12 PARSECS
Campaign Level Select	DOORDONOT
Invincibility	DARKSIDE
Multiplayer Level Select	JORG SACUL
Programming Team Photographs (viewable after Sketchbook open)	JEDICOUNCIL
Three Bonus Objectives for Current Mission Marked Complete	GIMME
Unlimited Secondary and Special Weapon	SUPERLASER
Battle Droid in Academy Geonosis Level	TRADEFED
Next Level	THRISNOTRY
Padme Amidala in Academy Geonosis Level	NATALIE
Wookie in Academy Geonosis Level	NERFHERDER

STAR WARS THE CLONE WARS: LIGHTSABER DUELS (Wii)

CONCEPT ART

UNLOCKABLE	HOW TO UNLOCK
Character Costumes	Beat 27 Challenges.
Early Work	Beat 9 Challenges.
Evolution of the EG-5 Jedi Hunter Droid	Beat 40 Challenges.
Level Design	Beat 18 Challenges.

COSTUMES

UNLOCKABLE	HOW TO UNLOCK
Ahsoka Tano: Ilum Battle Gear	Beat 32 Challenges.
Ahsoka Tano: Padawan Robes	Beat Challenge mode as Ahsoka.
Ahsoka Tano: Training Gear	Beat Battle mode as Ahsoka.
Anakin Skywalker: ARC Battle Gear	Beat 32 Challenges.
Anakin Skywalker: Jedi Knight Robes	Beat Challenge mode as Anakin.
Anakin Skywalker: Tatooine Battle Gear	Beat Battle mode as Anakin.
Asajj Ventress: Acolyte Robes	Beat Challenge mode as Ventress.
Asajj Ventress: Assassin Battle Gear	Beat Battle mode as Ventress.
Asajj Ventress: Gladiatorial Outfit	Beat 36 Challenges
Count Dooku: Confederacy Battle Gear	Beat Battle mode as Dooku.
Count Dooku: Separatist Uniform	Beat 36 Challenges.
Count Dooku: Sith Robes	Beat Challenge mode as Dooku.

UNLOCKABLE	HOW TO UNLOCK
EG-1 Jedi Hunter Droid	Beat 36 Challenges.
EG-3 Jedi Hunter Droid	Beat Battle mode as EG-5 Droid.
EG-4 Jedi Hunter Droid	Beat Challenge mode as EG-5 Droid.
General Grievous: Kaleesh Markings	Beat 36 Challenges.
General Grievous: Sith Markings	Beat Challenge mode as Grievous.
General Grievous: Supreme General Battle Gear	Beat Battle mode as Grievous
Kit Fisto: High General Robes	Beat Battle mode as Kit.
Kit Fisto: Jedi Council Robes	Beat Challenge mode as Kit.
Kit Fisto: Jedi Taskforce Robes	Beat 40 Challenges.
Mace Windu: Jedi Council Robes	Beat Challenge mode as Mace.
Mace Windu: Jedi Master Robes	Beat Battle mode as Mace.
Mace Windu: Jedi Taskforce Robes	Beat 40 Challenges.
Obi-Wan Kenobi: ARC Battle Gear	Beat 32 Challenges.
Obi-Wan Kenobi: Kashyyyk Battle Gear	Beat Challenge mode as Obi-Wan.
Obi-Wan Kenobi: Tatooine Battle Gear	Beat Battle mode as Obi-Wan.
Plo Koon: Jedi Council Robes	Beat Challenge mode as Plo.
Plo Koon: Jedi Master Robes	Beat Battle mode as Plo.
Plo Koon: Kel Dorian Robes	Beat 40 Challenges.

UNLOCKABLES

UNLOCKABLE	HOW TO UNLOCK
Ahsoka Tano for Challenge	Clear Campaign.
Count Dooku for Challenge	Clear Campaign.
Credits	Clear Campaign.
EG-5 Jedi Hunter Droid for Challenge	Clear Campaign.
General Grievous for Challenge	Clear Campaign.
Kit Fisto for Challenge	Unlock Kit Fisto.
Mace Windu for Challenge	Unlock Mace Windu.
Movies	Clear Campaign.
Obi-Wan Kenobi for Challenge	Clear Campaign.
Plo Koon for Challenge	Unlock Plo Koon.

SECRET CHARACTERS

UNLOCKABLE	HOW TO UNLOCK
Count Dooku	Clear Campaign.
EG-5 Jedi Hunter Droid	Clear Campaign.
General Grievous	Clear Campaign.
Kit Fisto	Beat 9 Challenges.
Mace Windu	Beat 18 Challenges.
Plo Koon	Beat 27 Challenges.

STAGES

UNLOCKABLE	HOW TO UNLOCK
Mustafar	Beat 32 Challenges.
Raxus Prime	Beat 13 Challenges.
Sarlacc Pit	Beat 22 Challenges.
Separatist Droid Factory	Beat 4 Challenges.
Separatist Listening Post	Clear Campaign.
Tatooine Dune Sea	Clear Campaign.
Teth Castle Ramparts	Clear Campaign.
The Malevolence	Clear Campaign.

UNLOCKABLE	HOW TO UNLOCK
The Negotiator	Clear Campaign.
The Tranquility	Clear Campaign.

STAR WARS: THE CLONE WARS—REPUBLIC HEROES (XBOX 360)

ULTIMATE LIGHTSABER

EFFECT	CODE
Unlock Ultimate Lightsaber	→,↓,↓,↑,←,↑,↑,↓

STAR WARS: THE CLONE WARS—REPUBLIC HEROES (Wii)

CONCEPT ART

UNLOCKABLE	HOW TO UNLOCK
Character Costumes	Beat 27 Challenges.
Early Work	Beat nine Challenges.
Evolution of the EG-5 Jedi Hunter Droid	Beat 40 Challenges.
Level Design	Beat 18 Challenges.

COSTUMES

UNLOCKABLE	HOW TO UNLOCK
Ahsoka Tano: Ilum Battle Gear	Beat 32 Challenges.
Ahsoka Tano: Padawan Robes	Beat Challenge Mode as Ahsoka.
Ahsoka Tano: Training Gear	Beat Battle Mode as Ahsoka.
Anakin Skywalker: ARC Battle Gear	Beat 32 Challenges.
Anakin Skywalker: Jedi Knight Robes	Beat Challenge Mode as Anakin.
Anakin Skywalker: Tatooine Battle Gear	Beat Battle Mode as Anakin.
Asajj Ventress: Acolyte Robes	Beat Challenge Mode as Ventress.
Asajj Ventress: Assassin Battle Gear	Beat Battle Mode as Ventress.
Asajj Ventress: Gladiatorial Outfit	Beat 36 Challenges.
Count Dooku: Confederacy Battle Gear	Beat Battle Mode as Dooku.
Count Dooku: Separatist Uniform	Beat 36 Challenges.
Count Dooku: Sith Robes	Beat Challenge Mode as Dooku.
EG-1 Jedi Hunter Droid	Beat 36 Challenges.
EG-3 Jedi Hunter Droid	Beat Battle Mode as EG-5 Droid.
EG-4 Jedi Hunter Droid	Beat Challenge Mode as EG-5 Droid.
General Grievous: Kaleesh Markings	Beat 36 Challenges.
General Grievous: Sith Markings	Beat Challenge Mode as Grievous.
General Grievous: Supreme General Battle Gear	Beat Battle Mode as Grievous.
Kit Fisto: High General Robes	Beat Battle Mode as Kit.
Kit Fisto: Jedi Council Robes	Beat Challenge Mode as Kit.
Kit Fisto: Jedi Taskforce Robes	Beat 40 Challenges.
Mace Windu: Jedi Council Robes	Beat Challenge Mode as Mace.
Mace Windu: Jedi Master Robes	Beat Battle Mode as Mace.
Mace Windu: Jedi Taskforce Robes	Beat 40 Challenges.
Obi-Wan Kenobi: ARC Battle Gear	Beat 32 Challenges.
Obi-Wan Kenobi: Kashyyyk Battle Gear	Beat Challenge Mode as Obi-Wan.
Obi-Wan Kenobi: Tatooine Battle Gear	Beat Battle Mode as Obi-Wan.
Plo Koon: Jedi Council Robes	Beat Challenge Mode as Plo.
Plo Koon: Jedi Master Robes	Beat Battle Mode as Plo.
Plo Koon: Kel Dorian Robes	Beat 40 Challenges.

MISCELLANEOUS

UNLOCKABLE	HOW TO UNLOCK
Ahsoka Tano for Challenge	Clear the Campaign
Count Dooku for Challenge	Clear the Campaign
Credits	Clear Campaign
EG-5 Jedi Hunter Droid for Challenge	Clear the Campaign
General Grievous for Challenge	Clear the Campaign
Kit Fisto for Challenge	Unlock Kit Fisto.
Mace Windu for Challenge	Unlock Mace Windu.
Movies	Clear the Campaign.
Obi-Wan Kenobi for Challenge	Clear the Campaign.
Plo Koon for Challenge	Unlock Plo Koon.

SECRET CHARACTERS

UNLOCKABLE	HOW TO UNLOCK
Count Dooku	Clear the Campaign.
EG-5 Jedi Hunter Droid	Clear the Campaign.
General Grievous	Clear the Campaign.
Kit Fisto	Beat nine Challenges.
Mace Windu	Beat 18 Challenges.
Plo Koon	Beat 27 Challenges.

STAGES

UNLOCKABLE	HOW TO UNLOCK
Mustafar	Beat 32 Challenges
Raxus Prime	Beat 13 Challenges.
Sarlacc Pit	Beat 22 Challenges.
Separatist Droid Factory	Beat 4 Challenges.
Separatist Droid Factory	Beat 4 Challenges.
Separatist Listening Post	Clear the Campaign.
Tatooine Dune Sea	Clear the Campaign.
Teth Castle Ramparts	Clear the Campaign.
The Malevolence	Clear the Campaign.
The Negotiator	Clear the Campaign.
The Tranquility	Clear the Campaign.

STAR WARS: THE FORCE UNLEASHED (XBOX 360)

CODES

Input the following codes at the "Input Code" screen.

EFFECT	CODE
All Databank Entries Unlocked	OSSUS
All Force Push Ranks Unlocked	EXARKUN
All Saber Throw Ranks Unlocked	ADEGAN
All Talents Unlocked	JOCASTA
Combo Unlock	RAGNOS
Incinerator Trooper	PHOENIX
Makes Levels Mirrored	MINDTRICK
New Combo	FREEDON
New Combo	LUMIYA
New Combo	MARAJADE
New Combo	MASSASSI

New Combo	SAZEN
New Combo	YADDLE
Proxy Skin Code	PROTOTYPE
Shadowtrooper Costume	BLACKHOLE
Snowtrooper	SNOWMAN
Stormtrooper Commander Costume	TK421BLUE
Unlock All Lightsaber Crystals	HURRIKANE
Unlock Emperor Costume	MASTERMIND
Unlocks All 32 Costumes	SOHNDANN
Unlocks All Force Combos	MOLDYCROW
Unlocks Bail Organa Costume	VICEROY
Unlocks Deadly Saber	LIGHTSABER
Unlocks Kashyyyk Trooper Costume	TK421GREEN
Unlocks Maximum Force Powers	KATARN
Unlocks Maximum Force Repulse Ranks	DATHOMIR
Unlocks Scout Trooper Costume	FERRAL
Unlocks Sith Master difficulty	SITHSPAWN
Unlocks Stormtrooper Costume	TK421WHITE
Unlocks the Aerial Ambush Combo	VENTRESS
Unlocks the Aerial Assault Combo	EETHKOTH
Unlocks the Ceremonial Jedi Robes	DANTOOINE
Unlocks the Devastating Lightsaber Impale	BRUTALSTAB
Unlocks the Drunken Kota Costume	HARDBOILED
Unlocks the Jedi Adventure Robes	HOLOCRON
Unlocks the Master Kento Costume "The Apprentice's Father"	WOOKIEE
Unlocks the Rahm Kota Costume	MANDALORE
Unlocks the Saber Slam Combo	PLOKOON
Unlocks the Saber Sling Combo	KITFISTO
Unlocks the Sith Slash Combo	DARAGON
Unlocks the Sith Stalker Armor	KORRIBAN

STAR WARS: THE FORCE UNLEASHED (PlayStation 3)

CODES

From the pause menu go to the "Input Code" option then enter the following codes for the corresponding effect.

EFFECT	CODE
All Databank Entries Unlocked	OSSUS
All Force Push Ranks Unlocked	EXARKUN
All Saber Throw Ranks Unlocked	ADEGAN
All Talents Unlocked	JOCASTA
Combo Unlock	RAGNOS
Incinerator Trooper	PHOENIX
Makes Levels Mirrored	MINDTRICK
New Combo	FREEDON
New Combo	MASSASSI
New Combo	MARAJADE
New Combo	SAZEN
New Combo	LUMIYA
New Combo	YADDLE

EFFECT	CODE
Proxy Skin Code	PROTOTYPE
Shadowtrooper Costume	BLACKHOLE
Snowtrooper	SNOWMAN
Stormtrooper Commander Costume	TK421BLUE
Unlocks All Lightsaber Crystals	HURRIKANE
Unlocks Emperor Costume	MASTERMIND
Unlocks All 32 Costumes	SOHNDANN
Unlocks All Force Combos	MOLDYCROW
Unlocks Bail Organa Costume	VICEROY
Unlocks Deadly Saber	LIGHTSABER
Unlocks Kashyyyk Trooper Costume	TK421GREEN
Unlocks Maximum Force Powers	KATARN
Unlocks Maximum Force Repulse Ranks	DATHOMIR
Unlocks Scout Trooper Costume	FERRAL
Unlocks Sith Master Difficulty	SITHSPAWN
Unlocks Stormtrooper Costume	TK421WHITE
Unlocks the Aerial Ambush Combo	VENTRESS
Unlocks the Aerial Assault Combo	EETHKOTH
Unlocks the Ceremonial Jedi Robes	DANTOOINE
Unlocks the Devastating Lightsaber Impale	BRUTALSTAB
Unlocks the Drunken Kota Costume	HARDBOILED
Unlocks the Jedi Adventure Robes	HOLOCRON
Unlocks the Master Kento Costume "The Apprentice's Father"	WOOKIEE
Unlocks the Rahm Kota Costume	MANDALORE
Unlocks the Saber Slam Combo	PLOKOON
Unlocks the Saber Sling Combo	KITFISTO
Unlocks the Sith Slash Combo	DARAGON
Unlocks the Sith Stalker Armor	KORRIBAN

STAR WARS: THE FORCE UNLEASHED (Wii)

CODES

From the "Extras" menu inside the Rogue Shadow, select "Cheat Codes" and enter the following codes.

EFFECT	CODE
1,000,000 Force Points	SPEEDER
God Mode	CORTOSIS
Max All Force Powers	KATARN
Max Combos	COUNTDOOKU
Unlimited Force Power	VERGENCE
Unlock All Force Powers	TYRANUS
Your Lightsaber One Hit Kills All Normal Enemies	LIGHTSABER

SKIN CODES

EFFECT	CODE
Aayla Secura	AAYLA
Admiral Ackbar	ITSATWAR
Anakin Skywalker	CHOSENONE
Asajj Ventress	ACOLYTE
Chop'aa Notimo	NOTIMO

Classic Stormtrooper	TK421
Clone Trooper	LEGION
Count Dooku	SERENNO
Darth Desolus	PAUAN
Darth Maul	ZABRAK
Darth Phobos	HIDDENFEAR
Darth Vader	SITHLORD
Drexl Roosh	DREXLROOSH
Emperor Palpatine	PALPATINE
Episode IV Luke Skywalker	YELLOWJCKT
Episode VI Luke Skywalker	T16WOMPRAT
Imperial Shadow Guard	INTHEDARK
Juno Eclipse	ECLIPSE
Kleef	KLEEF
Lando Calrissian	SCOUNDREL
Mace Windu	JEDIMASTER
Mara Jade	MARAJADE
Maris Brood	MARISBROOD
Navy Commando	STORMTROOP
Obi-Wan Kenobi	BENKENOBI
PROXY	HOLOGRAM
Qui-Gon Jinn	MAVERICK
Rahm Kota	MANDALORE
Shaak Ti	TOGRUTA

EXTRA COSTUMES

EFFECT	CODE
Ceremonial Jedi Robes	DANTOOINE
Kento Marek's Robes	WOOKIEE
Sith Stalker Armor	KORRIBAN
Unlocks All Costumes	GRANDMOFF

STAR WARS: THE FORCE UNLEASHED (DS)

CODES

From the main menu select "Extras," then "Unleashed Codes," and then enter the codes.

EFFECT	CODE
Uber Lightsaber	lightsaber
Rahm Kota's costume	mandalore
Sith Robes	holocron
Starkiller's Father's Robes	wookiee

STAR WARS: THE FORCE UNLEASHED (PSP)

CODES

From the "Extras" menu inside the Rogue Shadow, select "Cheat Codes" and enter the following codes. Specific skin codes are not necessary after you enter the "Unlock All Costumes" code.

EFFECT	CODE
1,000,000 Force Points	SPEEDER
All Combos at Maximum Level	COUNTDOOKU
All Force Powers	TYRANUS
All Force Powers at Maximum Level	KATARN

EFFECT	CODE
Amplified Lightsaber Damage	LIGHTSABER
Immunity to All Damage	CORTOSIS
Unlimited Force Power	VERGENCE
Unlock All Costumes	GRANDMOFF

SKIN CODES

EFFECT	CODE
501st Legion	LEGION
Aayla Secura	AAYLA
Admiral Ackbar	ITSATWAP
Anakin Skywalker	CHOSENONE
Asajj Ventress	ACOLYTE
Ceremonial Jedi Robes	DANTOOINE
Chop'aa Notimo	NOTIMO
Classic Stormtrooper	TK421
Count Dooku	SERENNO
Darth Desolous	PAUAN
Darth Maul	ZABRAK
Darth Phobos	HIDDENFEAR
Darth Vader	SITHLORD
Drexl Roosh	DREXLROOSH
Emperor Palpatine	PALPATINE
General Rahm Kota	MANDALORE
Han Solo	NERFHERDER
Heavy Trooper	SHOCKTROOP
Juno Eclipse	ECLIPSE
Kento's Robe	WOOKIEE
Kleef	KLEEF
Lando Calrissian	SCOUNDREL
Luke Skywalker	T16WOMPRAT
Mace Windu	JEDIMASTER
Mara Jade	MARAJADE
Maris Brood	MARISBROOD
Navy Commando	STORMTROOP
Obi-Wan Kenobi	BENKENOBI
PROXY	HOLOGRAM
Qui-Gon Jinn	MAVERICK
Shaak Ti	TOGRUTA
Shadowtrooper	INTHEDARK
Sith Robes	HOLOCRON
Sith Stalker Armor	KORRIBAN
Twi'lek	SECURA
Yavin Luke	YELLOWJCKT

STAR WARS: THE FORCE UNLEASHED (PlayStation 2)

CODES

From the main menu go to "Options," then select "Enter Code." You can also do this from the "Extras" menu inside the Rogue Shadow.

EFFECT	CODE
1,000,000 Force Points	SPEEDER
Admiral Ackbar	ITSATWAP
All Combos at Maximum Level	COUNTDOOKU

All Force Powers	TYRANUS
All Force Powers at Maximum Level	KATARN
Amplified Lightsaber Samage	LIGHTSABER
Asajj Ventress	ACOLYTE
Chop'aa Notimo	NOTIMO
Classic Stormtrooper	TK421
Count Dooku	SERENNO
Heavy Trooper	SHOCKTROOP
Immunity to All Damage	CORTOSIS
Lando Calrissian	SCOUNDREL
Play as Captain Juno Eclipse	ECLIPSE
Qui-Gon Jinn	MAVERICK
Twi'lek	SECURA
Unlimited Force power	VERGENCE
Unlock Aayla Secura Costume	AAYLA
Unlock All Costumes	GRANDMOFF
Unlock Anakin Skywalker costume	CHOSENONE
Unlock Ceremonial Jedi Robes Costume	DANTOOINE
Unlock Darth Desolous Costume	PAUAN
Unlock Darth Phobos Costume	HIDDENFEAR
Unlock Drexl Roosh Costume	DREXLROOSH
Unlock Emperor Palpatine Costume	PALPATINE
Unlock General Rahm Kota Costume	MANDALORE
Unlock Han Solo Costume	NERFHERDER
Unlock Kento's Robe Costume	WOOKIE
Unlock Luke Skywalker Costume	T16WOMPRAT
Unlock Mace Windu Costume	JEDIMASTER
Unlock Mara Jade Costume	MARAJADE
Unlock Maris Brood Costume	MARISBROOD
Unlock Navy Commando Costume	STORMTROOP
Unlock Obi-Wan Kenobi Costume	BENKENOBI
Unlock PROXY Costume	HOLOGRAM
Unlock Shaak Ti Costume	TOGRUTA
Unlock Shadowtrooper Costume	INTHEDARK
Unlock Sith Robe Costume	HOLOCRON
Unlock Sith Stalker Armor Costume	KORRIBAN
Unlock Yavin Luke Costume	YELLOWJCKT
Unlocks Darth Maul as a Skin	ZABRAK
Unlocks the Darth Vader Costume	SITHLORD

STARSKY AND HUTCH (XBOX)

UNLOCKABLE	CODE
Everything	Enter VADKRAM as a profile name.

STARSKY AND HUTCH (PlayStation 2)

Type in VADKRAM as your Profile Name to unlock everything.

STOLEN (XBOX)

Enter this code in the Equipment screen.

UNLOCKABLE	CODE
99 of all equipment items	(RT), (LT), ✚▶

STRANGLEHOLD (XBOX 360)

ACHIEVEMENTS

UNLOCKABLE	HOW TO UNLOCK
Asplosion (20)	In multiplayer, kill an opponent with an explosive in Slums Downpour.
Barrage Specialist (10)	Use the Barrage special move with every weapon.
Be the Master (20)	Kill 100 opponents as John Woo in Multiplayer matches.
Boomtown (20)	In multiplayer, kill an opponent with an explosion in Slums Courtyard.
Bullet Ballet (20)	Kill 50 opponents while in Tequila Time in Multiplayer matches.
Bulletproof (40)	Win a multiplayer match without using a health pack.
Castaway (20)	In multiplayer, kill an opponent on the Heavy Machine Gun platform in Tai O Settlement.
Chicago History Museum Completed (20)	Complete the Chicago History Museum level on any difficulty setting.
Chow Would Be Proud (15)	Kill 10 enemies with a five-star kill rating.
Deadly World (25)	Kill 50 enemies by using the environment instead of guns.
Death by Swing (25)	Kill 50 enemies while hanging from a chandelier.
Death from Above (20)	In multiplayer, kill an opponent with a falling object in Kowloon Market.
Diplomatic Immunity (20)	In multiplayer, kill an opponent in the hull of the ship in Naval Exercise.
Fisticuffs (10)	In multiplayer, kill an opponent with a melee attack.
Freedom! (10)	Purchase all of the Multiplayer characters in the Unlock Shop.
Game Completed —Casual (40)	Complete the entire game on the Casual difficulty setting.
Game Completed —Hard (60)	Complete the entire game on the Hard difficulty setting.
Game Completed —Hard Boiled (70)	Complete the entire game on the Hard Boiled difficulty setting.
Game Completed— Normal (50)	Complete the entire game on the Normal difficulty setting.
Geronimo! (15)	Host and complete 10 multiplayer matches on the Totem Pole Gallery map.
God of Guns (40)	Win a multiplayer match without using a Tequila Bomb.
Hardboiled Killer (20)	Kill 307 opponents in Multiplayer matches.
Having a Blast (20)	In multiplayer, kill an opponent with an explosion in Fisherman's Cove.
Hong Kong Marketplace Completed (10)	Complete the Hong Kong Marketplace level on any difficulty setting.
I Don't Know How to Play Those (20)	In The Mega Restaurant level, complete the Casino or the Restaurant without using the Guitar Cases.
It's All Mine... (30)	Purchase every item in the Unlock Shop.
Jurassic Battle (15)	Host and complete 10 multiplayer matches on the Dinosaur Rotunda map.
Killing Spree (20)	Get five kills in a row without dying in a Multiplayer ranked match.
Lounge Lizard (15)	Host and complete 10 multiplayer matches on the Mega Lounge map.
Massive D (20)	Cause at least $75,000,000 of damage.
Master of Barrage (25)	Kill 100 enemies with the Barrage special move.

Master of Precision Aim (25)	Kill 50 enemies with the Precision Aim special move.
Master of Spin Attack (25)	Kill 100 enemies with the Spin Attack special move.
Meet John Woo (5)	Visit the Unlock Shop.
Mega Jackpot (15)	Host and complete 10 multiplayer matches on the Golden Dragon Casino map.
Movin' on Up (15)	Host and complete 10 multiplayer matches on the Chicago Penthouse map.
Nobody Has That Much Style... (60)	Acquire 5,000 total Style Points.
Old School (25)	On any difficulty setting, complete a level without using any of the Tequila Bomb special moves.
One Gun To Rule Them All (10)	Finish in first place in a Multiplayer ranked match.
Origami Master (35)	Collect 250 Origami Cranes.
Paleontologist (10)	In the Chicago History Museum level, completely destroy the Brachiosaurus or the T-Rex.
Rolling Death (25)	Kill 50 enemies while riding on a roll cart.
Ruthless (30)	Perform a 50 star Style Combo.
Sea Food (15)	Host and complete 10 multiplayer matches on the Tai O Drug Labs map.
Slums of Kowloon Completed (20)	Complete the Slums of Kowloon level on any difficulty setting.
Stay Dry (10)	In the Slums of Kowloon level, stay along the top pathway in the crumbling sewer area.
Tai O Completed (10)	Complete the Tai O level on any difficulty setting.
Tea Party (15)	Host and complete 10 multiplayer matches on the Kowloon Teahouse map.
Testikill (40) shot.	In multiplayer, kill an opponent with a precision aim crotch
The Killer (10)	Fire 10,000 times.
The Mega Restaurant Completed (15)	Complete The Mega Restaurant level on any difficulty setting.
Untouchable (10)	On any difficulty setting, complete a Standoff by defeating all enemies without taking any damage.
Winner Takes All (20)	Kill 50 opponents using Tequila Bombs in Multiplayer matches.
Wong's Estate Completed (25)	Complete the Wong's Estate level on any difficulty setting.
Zakarov's Penthouse Completed (15)	Complete the Zakarov's Penthouse level on any difficulty setting.

STRANGLEHOLD (PlayStation 3)

DIFFICULTIES

UNLOCKABLE	HOW TO UNLOCK
Hard Boiled Difficulty	Complete the game on Casual mode once to unlock this difficulty.

EASTER EGGS

UNLOCKABLE	HOW TO UNLOCK
Movie Theater Trailers	In the first chapter in the Hong Kong Marketplace, go into the Ambushed section. When you finish killing everyone, go into the building. Break the door, and follow the corridor until you reach a movie theater. The screen is showing trailers for *Wheelman* and *Blacksite*.

STREET FIGHTER 4 (XBOX 360)

CHARACTERS

UNLOCKABLE	HOW TO UNLOCK
Akuma	After unlocking Sakura, Dan, Cammy, Fei Long, Gen, and Rose, fight him on arcade mode; to do that, get at least 2 perfects and 2 Ultra Finishes.
Cammy	End the arcade mode with Crimson Viper.
Dan	End the arcade mode with Sakura.
Fei Long	End the arcade mode with Abel.
Gen	End the arcade mode with Chun-Li.
Gouken	After unlocking Akuma, Sakura, Dan, Cammy, Fei Long, Gen, and Rose, fight him on arcade mode; to do that, get at least 2 perfects and 3 Ultra Finishes.
Rose	End the arcade mode with M. Bison.
Sakura	End the arcade mode with Ryu.
Seth	End the game with all the other characters.

COLORS

To unlock every color in the game you have to play the Time Trial and Survival modes in order. Don't skip to the challenges where the colors are. Once completed you gain the colors for every fighter on the roster.

UNLOCKABLE	HOW TO UNLOCK
Color 10	Survival Normal 16
Color 3	Time Attack Normal 1
Color 4	Survival Normal 1
Color 5	Time Attack Normal 6
Color 6	Survival Normal 6
Color 7	Time Attack Normal 11
Color 8	Survival Normal 11
Color 9	Time Attack Normal 16

PERSONAL ACTIONS

UNLOCKABLE	HOW TO UNLOCK
Personal Action 2	Beat Time Attack Normal level 2
Personal Action 3	Beat Survival Normal level 2
Personal Action 4	Beat Time Attack Normal level 7
Personal Action 5	Beat Survival Normal level 7
Personal Action 6	Beat Time Attack Normal level 12
Personal Action 7	Beat Survival Normal level 12
Personal Action 8	Beat Time Attack Normal level 17
Personal Action 9	Beat Survival Normal level 17
Personal Action 10	Beat Time Attack Normal level 20

SPECIAL VIDEOS

You must complete arcade mode with the two characters that are in each special video.

UNLOCKABLE	HOW TO UNLOCK
Seth Vs. M. Bison video	Beat the game with M. Bison and Seth.
The Chun Li Vs. Crimson Viper video	Beat arcade mode with Chun Li and Crimson Viper.
The Gouken Vs. Akuma video	Beat Arcade mode with Gouken and Akuma.
The Guile Vs. Abel video	Beat arcade mode with Guile and Abel.
The Ryu Vs. Ken video	Beat arcade mode with Ryu and Ken.

CHARACTER ARTWORK

Complete each character's Trials in Challenge mode to unlock their respective artwork in the gallery option.

CHARACTER SPECIFIC TITLES

In Challenge mode, each time you beat a challenge you get a character-specific title. Challenges must be played in order.

UNLOCKABLE	HOW TO UNLOCK
Amigo	Beat El Fuerte's 1st Hard challenge.
Anti ShoRyuKen	Beat Sagat's 1st Hard challenge.
Bath Time	Beat E. Honda's 1st Hard challenge.
Blonde Arrow	Beat Cammy's 5th Hard challenge.
Delta Red	Beat Cammy's 1st Hard challenge.
Doofus	Complete Rufus's 3rd Hard challenge.
Family Man	Beat Guile's 5th Hard challenge.
Fists of Fire	Beat Ken's 5th Hard challenge.
Fists of Wind	Beat Ryu's 5th Hard challenge.
Flashy Fighter	Beat Fei Long's 5th Hard challenge.
Heavenly Sky	Beat Akuma's 5th Hard challenge.
High School Girl	Beat Sakura's 5th Hard challenge.
Hitenryu Kung fu	Beat Fei Long's 1st Hard challenge.
Hope You're Ready!	Beat Chun Li's 1st Hard challenge
I love Candy	Complete Rufus's 2nd Hard challenge.
I wish I had a family	Beat Abel's 5th Hard challenge.
I'm Number One	Complete Rufus's 5th Hard challenge.
I'm Ready For Ya!	Beat Ken's 1st Hard challenge.
Invincible Tiger	Beat Sagat's 5th Hard challenge.
Jimmy	Beat Blanka's 5th Hard challenge.
Jungle Boy	Beat Blanka's 1st Hard challenge.
Kung Food	Complete Rufus's 4th Hard Trial.
Legs of Legend	Beat Chun Li's 5th Hard challenge.
MESSATSU!!	Beat Akuma's 1st Hard challenge.
Red Cyclone	Beat Zangief's 5th Hard challenge.
Rice For The Win	Beat Sakura's 1st Hard challenge.
Righteous Avenger	Beat Guile's 1st Hard challenge.
Ruler Of Darkness	Beat M. Bison's 5th Hard challenge.
Samurai Fighter	Beat Ryu's 1st Hard challenge.
Seriously Emo	Beat Abel's 1st Hard challenge.
Spin It again	Beat Zangief's 1st Hard challenge.
Sumo Slammer	Beat E. Honda's 5th Hard challenge.
Viva Mexico	Beat El Fuerte's 5th Hard challenge.
Working up a Sweat	Complete Rufus's 1st Hard Trial.
You Are Beneath Me	Beat M. Bison's 1st Hard challenge.

STREET FIGHTER 4 (PlayStation 3)

CHARACTERS

UNLOCKABLE	HOW TO UNLOCK
Akuma	After unlocking Sakura, Dan, Cammy, Fei Long, Gen and Rose, fight him on Arcade mode. To do that, get at least 2 perfects and 2 Ultra Finishes.
Cammy	End the Arcade mode with Crimson Viper.

UNLOCKABLE	HOW TO UNLOCK
Dan	End the Arcade mode with Sakura.
Fei Long	End the Arcade mode with Abel.
Gen	End the Arcade mode with Chun-Li.
Gouken	After unlocking Akuma, Sakura, Dan, Cammy, Fei Long, Gen and Rose, fight him on Arcade mode. To do that, get at least 2 perfects and 3 Ultra Finishes.
Rose	End the Arcade mode with M. Bison.
Sakura	End the Arcade mode with Ryu.
Seth	End the game with all the other characters.

PERSONAL ACTIONS

UNLOCKABLE	HOW TO UNLOCK
Personal Action 10	Beat Time Attack Normal Level 20.
Personal Action 2	Beat Time Attack Normal Level 2.
Personal Action 3	Beat Survival Normal level 2
Personal Action 4	Beat Time Attack Normal level 7
Personal Action 5	Beat Survival Normal level 7
Personal Action 6	Beat Time Attack Normal level 12
Personal Action 7	Beat Survival Normal level 12
Personal Action 8	Beat Time Attack Normal level 17
Personal Action 9	Beat Survival Normal level 17

COLORS

To unlock every color in the game you have to play the Time Trial and Survival modes in order. Don't skip to the challenges where the colors are. Once completed you gain the colors for every fighter on the roster.

UNLOCKABLE	HOW TO UNLOCK
Color 10	Survival Normal 16
Color 3	Time Attack Normal 1
Color 4	Survival Normal 1
Color 5	Time Attack Normal 6
Color 6	Survival Normal 6
Color 7	Time Attack Normal 11
Color 8	Survival Normal 11
Color 9	Time Attack Normal 16

STREET FIGHTER EX3 (PlayStation 2)

UNLOCKABLE	OBJECTIVE
Bonus Characters	Beat the game on Normal difficulty without using a Continue to unlock one of the hidden characters. (See below for more info)
Evil Ryu	Beat Original mode eight times with Ryu and without continuing. Go to the Character Selection screen and highlight Ryu. Press ×, ■, or ●.
M. Bison II	Beat Original mode eight times with M. Bison and without continuing. Go to the Character Selection screen and highlight M. Bison. Press ×, ■, or ●.
Narrator Sakura	Beat Original mode eight times with Sakura and without continuing. Go to the Character Selection screen and highlight Sakura. Press SELECT.

IN ORDER TO UNLOCK ALL THE BONUS CHARACTERS, REPEAT THE METHOD DESCRIBED ABOVE NINE TIMES. HOWEVER, EACH TIME YOU BEAT THE GAME, YOU MUST USE A DIFFERENT REGULAR CHARACTER. THE ORDER OF BONUS CHARACTERS ARE: SAGAT, VEGA, GARUDA, SHADOW GEIST, KAIRI, PULLUM, AREA, DARUN, AND VULCANO.

STREETS OF RAGE (Wii)

UNLOCKABLES

UNLOCKABLE	HOW TO UNLOCK
Bad Ending	Choose to be Mr. X's righthand man the first time you meet him. Then complete the game.
Extra Continues	Press ←, ←, Ⓑ, Ⓑ, Ⓑ, Ⓒ, Ⓒ, Ⓒ, START at the title screen.
Final Boss Duel	When you get to the final boss in 2-player mode, have one player choose "yes" and the other choose "no." You duel against each other.
Level and Lives Select	Go to the main menu. Hold Ⓐ+Ⓑ+Ⓒ+↓ on controller 2 while selecting Options on controller 1 (best if done with two people). You can now select how many lives you start with and which stage to start on.

STREETS OF RAGE 2 (Wii)

UNLOCKABLES

UNLOCKABLE	HOW TO UNLOCK
Level and Lives Select	Go to the main menu. Hold Ⓐ+Ⓑ on controller 2 while selecting Options. Now select how many lives you start with (up to 9), choose your starting stage, and play at the Very Easy and Mania difficulty levels.
Same Character in 2 Player	At the title screen, hold →+Ⓑ on controller 1 and hold ←+Ⓐ on controller 2. Press ↓ on controller 2 with everything else still held down. Now both players can be the same person in 2 Player!

STREETS OF RAGE 3 (Wii)

UNLOCKABLES

UNLOCKABLE	HOW TO UNLOCK
Ending 1	Rescue the Chief in Stage 6 before his health runs out. Then, at the end of Stage 7, defeat Robot Y before the time limit runs out.
Ending 2	Rescue the Chief before his health runs out in Stage 6. Then, in Stage 7, defeat Robot Y but let the time limit run out.
Ending 3	Let the Chief's health run out in Stage 6. When you go to Stage 7, you will see that it is changed. Make it to the last boss and defeat him.
Ending 4	Set the difficulty to Easy and beat Robot X in Stage 5.
Extra Lives Select	Go to the Options screen and select the "Lives" option. Press and hold ↑+Ⓐ+Ⓑ+Ⓒ on controller 2, and press ← or → on controller 1 to select the number of lives you can start the game with. You can now select 9 lives, instead of the default max of 5.
Play as Ash	To select Ash, defeat him, then hold Ⓐ on controller 1. After losing all of your lives, continue, and you can choose Ash as your character.
Play as Roo	When you fight the clown and Roo, defeat the clown first and Roo should hop away off the screen. When you lose all your lives and continue, cycle through the characters and Roo is now available.
Play as Roo	At the title screen, hold ↑+Ⓑ, then press START. A kangaroo named Roo is now available at the Character Select screen.
Play as Shiva	After beating Shiva in the first stage when you get the last hit, hold Ⓑ+START. When the continue screen comes up, you can play as Shiva. (He is weaker than his *Streets of Rage 2* character).
Play as Super Axel	Press ↓ to select a player, then quickly hold Ⓐ and sweep the D-pad in a clockwise circle until Axel appears. Then press Ⓐ.
THIS CHEAT IS VERY HARD TO GET WORKING.	
Play as Super Skate	Pick Skate. As the first level starts, lose your first life having 0 points. You will now be Super Skate, with a much more powerful combo.

Play as the Same Character	Hold ✚+Ⓒ on controller 2 as you enter 2-player mode with controller 1.
Secret Items	In Stage 1, at the Warehouse area, go to the bottom-left region blocked by the crates in the background and press Ⓑ. You get 5,000 points and a 1-UP. Stage 7, (City Hall) also contains lots of hidden items. Search in areas blocked off by the background such as lampposts, flower pots, etc.
Secret Passageways	On Stage 5, in the first room with all the ninjas, there are three secret routes that you can access by killing all enemies here. These rooms have more items than the normal rooms. Route 1: Above the door where you follow your normal route, notice a white wall with cracks near the top. Punch it to access Secret Route 1. Route 2: Go to the bottom center of this room and punch a few times. You eventually bust a hole in the floor leading you to the basement of Stage 5 and also Secret Route 2. Route 3: Go to the top of the screen and go up to the red walls. A certain red wall has a few cracks in it. Punch it to access Secret Route 3. There are a lot of enemies here, so be careful.
Stage Select	Hold Ⓑ+✚, then press START. Stage Select appears on the Options screen.

SUPER C (Wii)

UNLOCKABLES

UNLOCKABLE	HOW TO UNLOCK
10 Lives (Player 1)	On the title screen, press ✚, ✚, ✚, ✚, Ⓐ, Ⓑ, then START
10 Lives (Player 2)	On the title screen, press ✚, ✚, ✚, ✚, Ⓐ, Ⓑ, SELECT, then START
Access Sound Test	On the title screen, hold down Ⓐ+Ⓑ then press START
Retain Old Score and # of Lives on New Game	On the title screen, after you've beaten the game, press Ⓐ, and then START
Retain Old Score on New Game	On the title screen, after you've beaten the game, press Ⓐ, Ⓑ, then START

SUPER CASTLEVANIA IV (Wii)

UNLOCKABLES

UNLOCKABLE	HOW TO UNLOCK
Higher Difficulty	Heart, Axe, Space, Water. Axe, Space, Space, Heart. Space, Axe, Space, Space. Space, Heart, Space, Space.

DIFFICULT LEVEL PASSWORDS

Use these passwords to get to stages on the Difficult setting. You need to use a blank name.

PASSWORD	EFFECT
Space, Axe, Space, Space. Water, Water, Space, Space. Space, Heart, Space, Axe. Water, Axe, Space, Space.	Difficult mode Stage 6 level 1
Space, Axe, Space, Heart. Water, Heart, Space, Space. Space, Space, Space, Water. Space, Axe, Space, Space.	Difficult mode Stage 7 level 1
Space, Axe, Space, Space. Water, Water, Space, Space. Space, Heart, Space, Water. Water, Water, Space, Space.	Difficult mode Stage 8 level 1

STAGE PASSWORDS

WHEN YOU COME TO "ENTER YOUR NAME," LEAVE THE SPACE BLANK OR THESE PASSWORDS WON'T WORK.

PASSWORD	EFFECT
Space, Space, Space, Space. Firebombs, Space, Space, Space. Space, Space, Space, Space. Firebombs, Space, Space, Space	Level 2
Sspace, Space, Space, Heart. Firebombs, Space, Space, Space.	Level 3

Space, Space, Space, Space. Heart, Space, Space, Space	
Space, Space, Space, Firebombs. Firebombs, Firebombs, Space, Space. Space, Firebombs, Space, Axe. Space, Space, Space, Space	Level 4
Space, Space, Space, Space. Firebombs, Space, Space, Space. Space, Space, Space, Axe. Firebombs, Axe, Space, Space	Level 5
Space, Space, Space, Space. Firebombs, Firebombs, Space, Space. Space, Firebombs, Space, Axe. Firebombs, Axe, Space, Space	Level 6
Space, Space, Space, Firebombs. Firebombs, Hart, Space, Space. Space, Heart, Space, Firebombs. Space, Heart, Space, Space	Level 7
Space, Space, Space, Space. Firebombs, Firebombs, Space, Space. Space, Firebombs, Space, Firebombs. Firebombs, Firebombs, Space, Space	Level 8
Space, Space, Space, Heart. Firebombs, Firebombs, Space, Space. Space, Firebombs, Space, Firebombs. Heart, Firebombs, Space, Space	Level 9
Space, Space, Space, Axe. Firebombs, Space, Space, Space. Space, Space, Space, Heart. Heart, Heart, Space, Space	Level B
Space, Space, Space, Firebombs. Firebombs, Firebombs, Space, Space. Space, Firebombs, Space, Space. Space, Heart, Axe, Space	Level B (Dracula)

UNLOCKABLES

UNLOCKABLE	HOW TO UNLOCK
Full Arsenal	In the last stage, before you climb the stairs to Dracula, jump down to the left. You land on an invisible platform. Move all the way left and you will get full health, 99 hearts, a cross, a fully upgraded whip, and a III stone.

HIDDEN ROUTES

There are three hidden branches from the main path.

UNLOCKABLE	HOW TO UNLOCK
Hidden Route 1	In stage 3-1, when you must descend a short vertical shaft, halfway down here is a wall of pillars to the left. Demolish these, and you find a small side room containing hearts, cash bags, and some Roast.
Hidden Route 2	The second secret, which is an actual hidden Block, is in stage 6-2. At the very beginning you pass a hallway with Axe Knights and falling chandeliers. The third archway has a chandelier but no guard. Hit the floor a couple of times and it'll crumble, revealing a stairwell into a secret area.
Hidden Route 3	The last one is in Block 9-2. You jump across a bed of spikes at the beginning. After this you see several whirlwind tunnels and some coffins. The last upper platform on the right has a coffin and a tunnel. Let the tunnel suck you in and you'll find a hidden area full of bonuses.

SUPER CONTRA (XBOX 360)

UNLOCKABLE	HOW TO UNLOCK
Unlimited Lives and Super Machine Gun	On the main menu, select Arcade Game, and then enter the following code: (using the D-Pad) ↑, ↑, ↓, ↓, ←, →, ←, →, Ⓑ, Ⓐ. If done correctly, the game will start up instead of backing out to the main menu. You will begin with 5 lives that never decrease when killed, and you will have a super machine gun weapon equipped at all times! Using this code disables all Achievements and you cannot upload scores to Xbox Live Leaderboards. The code remain active until you exit the game using the Exit Game option in the Pause menu.

SUPER GHOULS 'N GHOSTS (Wii)

UNLOCKABLES

UNLOCKABLE	HOW TO UNLOCK
Level Select	Highlight "Exit" on the Option screen with controller 1. Hold L + START on controller 2 and press START on controller 1.
Professional Mode	Beat the game on Normal mode.

SUPER MONKEY BALL: BANANA BLITZ (Wii)

UNLOCKABLES

UNLOCKABLE	HOW TO UNLOCK
Baby Robo	To unlock the minigame version of Baby for the main game, play each minigame at least once (the game displays a play count on each minigame). After playing each minigame once, play one more minigame of your choice so that the game saves your stats. Baby Robo is now available in the main game. To select Baby Robo, you have to highlight Baby on the Character Select screen and press 1.
Staff Credits Game	Beat the first World
World 9	Complete Worlds 1-8 without continuing
World 10	Complete World 9 without continuing

SUPER PUZZLE FIGHTER II TURBO HD REMIX (XBOX 360)

HIDDEN CHARACTERS

UNLOCKABLE	HOW TO UNLOCK
Akuma	Press ♀, while having Hsien-Ko highlighted on the Player Select screen
Anita	Press (LB) or (RB) on Donovan, then press Ⓐ
Bat	Press (LB) or (RB) on Morrigan then press Ⓐ
Dan Hibiki	Press ♀, while having Donovan highlighted on the Player Select screen
Devilot	Press ♀, while having Morrigan highlighted on the Player Select screen
Mei-Ling	Hold the (LB) or (RB) button on Hsien-Ko, then press Ⓐ

ALTERNATE FINISHING MOVES

UNLOCKABLE	HOW TO UNLOCK
Ken's Alternate Finishing Move	Hold (LB) or (RB) during selection of Ken
Ryu's Alternate Finishing Move	Hold (LB) or (RB) during selection of Ryu

SUPER STAR SOLDIER (Wii)

CHEAT MENU

Following code unlocks a Cheat menu where you can mess with all the options for the game such as level selection and enemy difficulty. Input at the title screen.

UNLOCKABLE	HOW TO UNLOCK
Unlock Cheat Menu	Press ←, ②, ↑, ②, →, ②, ↓,②, ←, ①, ↑, ①, →, ①, ↓, ①, ①+② x8, ①+SELECT x8

SUPER SWING GOLF (Wii)

UNLOCK CADDIES

You unlock caddies by defeating the Pangya Festa with certain characters (except for Pipin). You must purchase them from the shop first just like the players. Outfits for the caddies will be unlocked and available for purchase when you unlock the caddies as well.

UNLOCKABLE	HOW TO UNLOCK
Brie	Beat Arin's first Pangya Festa
Dolfini	Complete the first Pangya Storyline with Kooh
Lola	Complete the first Pangya Storyline with Uncle Bob

Pipin	Complete the Tutorial
Quma	Complete the first Pangya Storyline with Hana
Tiki	Complete the first Pangya Storyline with Max
TitanBoo	Beat Cecilia in Arin's first Pangya Festa

UNLOCKABLE CHARACTERS

To unlock a new character, beat Pangya Festa with another character. This means the first storyline of Pangya Festa, unless otherwise mentioned.

UNLOCKABLE	HOW TO UNLOCK
Arin	Beat Pangya Festa with Kooh
Cecilia	Beat Pangya Festa with Hana or Uncle Bob
Kaz	Beat Arin's final storyline (to access this storyline, beat the first storyline with everyone but Kaz, and wear Arin's Magic School Uniform)
Kooh	Beat Pangya Festa with Max
Max	Beat Pangya Festa with Cecilia
Uncle Bob	Beat Pangya Festa with Scout

SUPER THUNDER BLADE (Wii)

LEVEL SELECT

Press these controller actions at the title screen to begin at the desired level.

CODE	EFFECT
Press Ⓐ, ↑, ↓, ←, →, →, ←, ↓, ↑, START	Level 2
Press Ⓐ, Ⓐ, ↑, ↓, ←, →, →, ←, ↓, ↑, START	Level 3
Press Ⓐ, Ⓐ, Ⓐ, ↑, ↓, ←, →, →, ←, ↓, ↑, START	Level 4
Press Ⓐ, Ⓐ, Ⓐ, Ⓐ, ↑, ↓, ←, →, →, ←, ↓, ↑, START	Level 5

UNLOCKABLES

UNLOCKABLE	HOW TO UNLOCK
Avoid Enemy Fire	Begin the game with Hard difficulty. Stay in the upper right or left corners and fire your weapon continuously in levels 1 through 3.
Extra Lives	Enable the Level Select code and get a continue. Highlight "Option" and hold Ⓐ+Ⓑ+Ⓒ and press START. A picture of a panda appears on the "Player" selection to confirm the code.

SUPERMAN RETURNS (XBOX 360)

CHEAT CODES

Anytime during gameplay after the Gladiator Battle first set, pause the game. Enter the following buttons to unlock the cheats. A chime confirms that the code has been entered correctly.

UNLOCKABLE	HOW TO UNLOCK
Infinite Health (Metropolis)	Ⓨ, →, Ⓨ, →, ↑, ←, →, Ⓨ
Infinite Stamina	↑, ↑, ↓, ↓, ←, →, ←, →, Ⓨ, Ⓧ
Unlock All Costumes, Trophies, and Theater Items Unlock All Moves	←, ↑, →, ↓, Ⓨ, Ⓧ, Ⓨ, ↑, →, Ⓧ ←, Ⓨ, →, Ⓧ, ↓, Ⓨ, ↑, ↓, Ⓧ, Ⓨ, Ⓧ

UNLOCKABLES

UNLOCKABLE	HOW TO UNLOCK
Bizarro	↑,→,↓,→,↑,←,↓,→,↑ (Enter it when you load your game, at the menu that lets you choose Metropolis or Fortress of Solitude before you start the game you loaded.)
Golden Age Superman Suit	Save Metropolis from the tornadoes
Pod Suit	Beat Bizarro

SUPERMAN: THE MAN OF STEEL (XBOX)

Pause the game to enter these codes.

UNLOCKABLE	CODE
All Levels and Bonuses	RT, BLK, Y, BLK, LT, WHT
Unlimited Health	BLK, WHT, LT, Y, LT, WHT

SURF'S UP (XBOX 360)

PASSWORDS

PASSWORD	EFFECT
MYPRECIOUS	All Boards unlocked
GOINGDOWN	All Leaf Slide stages unlocked
WATCHAMOVIE	Unlocks all videos
TINYBUTSTRONG	Unlocks Arnold
THELEGEND	Unlocks Big Z
SURPRISEGUEST	Unlocks Elliot
SLOWANDSTEADY	Unlocks Geek
KOBAYASHI	Unlocks Kobayashi
IMTHEBEST	Unlocks Tank Evans

SURF'S UP (PlayStation 3)

PASSWORDS

PASSWORD	EFFECT
MYPRECIOUS	All Boards
FREEVISIT	All championship locations
GOINGDOWN	All leaf sliding locations
MULTIPASS	All multiplayer levels
NICEPLACE	Art gallery
ASTRAL	Astral board
TOPFASHION	Customizations for all characters
MONSOON	Monsoon board
IMTHEBEST	Plan as Tank Evans
TINYBUTSTRONG	Play as Arnold
SURPRISEGUEST	Play as Elliot
SLOWANDSTEADY	Play as Geek
KOBAYASHI	Play as Tatsuhi Kobayashi
THELEGEND	Play as Zeke Topanga
TINYSHOCKWAVE	Tine shockwave board
WATCHAMOVIE	Video Gallery

SURF'S UP (Wii)

PASSWORDS

PASSWORD	EFFECT
NICEPLACE	Unlocks all art galleries
MYPRECIOUS	Unlocks all boards
GOINGDOWN	Unlocks all leaf-sliding locations
MULTIPASS	Unlocks all multiplayer levels
FREEVISIT	Unlocks all the locales
WATCHAMOVIE	Unlocks all video Galleries
TINYBUTSTRONG	Unlocks Arnold
ASTRAL	Unlocks Astral's board
DONTFALL	Unlocks bonus missions

TOPFASHION	Unlocks character customization
SURPRISEGUEST	Unlocks Elliot
SLOWANDSTEADY	Unlocks Geek
MONSOON	Unlocks Monsoon Board
IMTHEBEST	Unlocks Tank Evans
KOBAYASHI	Unlocks Tatsuhi Kobayashi
TINYSHOCKWAVE	Unlocks Tiny Shockwave board
THELEGEND	Unlocks Zeke Topanga

UNLOCKABLES

UNLOCKABLE	HOW TO UNLOCK
Arnold	Obtain 30,000 points in Shiverpool 2
Big Z	Obtain 100,000 points in Legendary Wave
Elliot	Obtain 40,000 points in Pen Gu North 3
Geek	Obtain 60,000 points in Pen Gu South 4
Tank	Obtain 40,000 points in the Boneyards
Tatsuhi	Obtain 15,000 points in Pen Gu South 2

SWORD OF VERMILION (Wii)

UNLOCKABLES

UNLOCKABLE	HOW TO UNLOCK
Quick Cash	In Keltwick, when Bearwulf gives you the dungeon key to get to Malaga, sell it. It's worth 1,000 kims and Bearwulf has an unlimited number of them. Just go back, talk to him, and he'll say "Did you lose the key? I have another one." He'll give it to you, and you can repeat the process as much as you want.
Test Menu	Any time during the game, hold Ⓐ+Ⓑ+Ⓒ and press START on controller 2. A test menu appears with Input, Sound, and C.R.T. tests. And when you exit, it sends you back to the SEGA logo screen.

SYPHON FILTER: LOGAN'S SHADOW (PSP)

BONUS ABILITIES AND UPGRADES

Earn the Career Ratings to unlock these abilities and upgrades.

UNLOCKABLE	HOW TO UNLOCK
Dual Wield	Earn Combat Sharp Shooter Rating 3
Increased Health	Earn Survival Specialist Rating 2
Max Darts x 5 (MB150)	Earn Elite Weapons Expert 1
Max Darts x 8 (MB150)	Earn Elite Weapons Expert 2
Max Darts x 10 (MB150)	Earn Elite Weapons Expert 3

BONUS MISSIONS

UNLOCKABLE	HOW TO UNLOCK
Behind the Scenes Bonus Mission	Beat Story Mode on Normal Difficulty
Bonus Lian Mission	Complete all 5 training missions
Killing Time	Earn Combat Knife Specialist Rating 4
Left Behind	Earn Elite Weapons Expert Rating 4
Shadowed Bonus Mission	Beat Story Mode on Hard Difficulty

BONUS WEAPONS

UNLOCKABLE	HOW TO UNLOCK
C11	Earn Combat Knife Specialist 2
Calico HE	Earn Survival Specialist Rating 4
Chinese Type 56	Earn Combat Knife Specialist Rating 3
EPDD	Earn Stealth Combat Specialist Rating 4
FAMAS	Complete Training 2 in less than 3 minutes

UNLOCKABLE	HOW TO UNLOCK
Flashbang Grenade	Earn Combat Knife Specialist Rating 1
Jackhammer HE	Earn Tactical Combat Specialist Rating 4
Jerico-41	Earn Tactical Combat Specialist Rating 2
M4 Silenced	Earn Survival Specialist Rating 3
M67 Grenade	Earn Tactical Specialist Rating 3
M82 BFG	Earn Combat Sharp Shooter Rating 4
MDS A4 Silenced	Earn Stealth Combat Specialist Rating 2
Over Under	Earn Combat Sharp Shooter Rating 2
Sawed-Off Pistol	Earn Survival Specialist Rating 1
Silenced .44	Earn Stealth Combat Specialist Rating 3
SP - 57	Complete Training 1 in less than 1 minute and 30 seconds
SSP 90	Earn Combat Sharp Shooter Rating 1
TK-9 Silenced	Earn Stealth Combat Specialist Rating 1
UNP .45	Complete Training 3 without wasting a shoot
USAS - 12	Earn Tactical Combat Specialist Rating 1

TAO FENG: FIST OF THE LOTUS (XBOX)

UNLOCKABLE	HOW TO UNLOCK
Unlock Extra Stage	Clear advance training.
Unlock Zhao Yen	Beat Quest Mode with every member of the Black Mantis and Pale Lotus and beat Zhao Yen with both factions.

TATSUNOKO VS. CAPCOM: ULTIMATE ALL STARS (Wii)

UNLOCKABLES

UNLOCKABLE	HOW TO UNLOCK
Hold the partner button during the character introduction sequence prior to the start of a match to start the match with your second character.	
Frank West	Get three different Capcom characters' Arcade endings.
Joe the Condor	Get six different Tatsunoko characters' Arcade endings.
Tekkaman Blade	Get three different Tatsunoko characters' Arcade endings.
Yatterman-2	Get Frank West, Zero, Tekkaman Blade, and Joe the Condor's Arcade endings.
Zero	Get six different Capcom characters' Arcade endings.
Special Illustration #2	Beat Survival Mode and buy it from shop.
Fourth Color	Clear stage 8 (final boss) of Arcade Mode.
Third Color	Clear stage 4 (giant opponent) of Arcade Mode.
Opening Movie 2	Unlock Yatterman-2
Secret Movie	Beat the game with Frank West, Zero, Tekkaman Blade, Joe the Condor, and Yatterman-2.

TEENAGE MUTANT NINJA TURTLES (Wii)

UNLOCKABLES

UNLOCKABLE	HOW TO UNLOCK
Restore Power	Find a doorway that has a pizza slice or full pizza right at the beginning. Enter, grab the pizza, and exit. The pizza regenerates when you reenter. Use this to restore power to all your turtles.
Remove Crushers in Level 3	Hop in the Party Wagon. Whenever you see a pesky Crusher, press SELECT. You exit the car, and the Crusher vanishes.
Share Boomerangs	When you get the boomerangs, throw up to 3 of them in the air, then switch turtles, and have the new turtle catch them. The new turtle can use those boomerangs without having picked up a boomerang icon.

TEENAGE MUTANT NINJA TURTLES (PSP)

CODES

Enter this in the Mission Briefing screens.

CODE	EFFECT
→, ←, →, ←, ↓, ↑, ↓, ↑, ×	Unlocks a Fantasy Costume

TEENAGE MUTANT NINJA TURTLES 2: THE ARCADE GAME (Wii)

UNLOCKABLES

UNLOCKABLE	HOW TO UNLOCK
Extra Lives and Stage Select	At the title screen, press Ⓑ, Ⓐ, Ⓑ, Ⓐ, ↑, ↓, Ⓑ, Ⓐ, ←, →, Ⓑ, Ⓐ, START

NEW! A B C D E F G H I J K L M N O P Q R S T U V W X Y Z

UNLOCKABLE	HOW TO UNLOCK
Extra Lives Without Stage Select	On the title screen, press ↑, →, →, ↓, ↓, ↓, ←, ←, ←, ←, Ⓑ, Ⓐ, START
Stage Select	On the title screen, press ↓, ↓, ↓, ↓, ↓, →, →, →, →, →, →, →, Ⓑ, Ⓐ, START
Easier Battle with Shredder	During the final battle against Shredder, Shredder splits up into two forms. They're identical in appearance, but only one is real and the other is fake. However, both forms use the lightning attack that instantly kills you by turning you into a normal turtle. However, when either form is weakened to near death, his helmet flies off. As you're beating up on the two forms of Shredder, one of them loses his helmet very quickly. When this happens, leave him alone. This Shredder is the fake, and he cannot use the lightning attack without his helmet on. Only the real Shredder can use the attack, but because it's only him using it, you can avoid it and slowly beat him down with ease. For the rest of the fight, ignore the fake. If you kill him, the real Shredder releases another fake.

TEENAGE MUTANT NINJA TURTLES 3: MUTANT NIGHTMARE (XBOX)

PASSWORDS

PASSWORD	EFFECT
MSRLSMML	2x Enemy Attack
SLRMLSSM	2x Enemy Defense
DMLDMRLD	Endurance—No health pickups available on map
LDMSLRDD	Instant Death—Die in 1 hit
MDLDSSLR	Invincibility—Never die or even lose health!
RRDMLSDL	Max Ougi—Unlimited Ougi!
LLMSRDMS	Shuriken loser—Shurikens no longer available on maps
SLLMRSLD	Sushi Party—All Health pickups become Sushi!
LMDRRMSR	Unlimited shuriken—Unlimited shuriken

TEKKEN 4 (PlayStation 2)

UNLOCKABLE	OBJECTIVE
Fight as Eddy Gordo	Successfully complete the game in Story mode as Christie Monteiro. Highlight Christie and press ▲ at the Character Selection screen. Eddy Gordo plays exactly like Christie.
Fight as Ling Xiaoyu in School Uniform	Complete the game in Story mode as Ling Xiaoyu. Highlight Ling Xiaoyu and press ▲ at the Character Selection screen.
Fight as Miharu	Complete the game in Story mode as Ling Xiaoyu. Highlight Ling Xiaoyu and press ● at the Character Selection screen. Miharu looks like Ling in her schoolgirl outfit from Tekken 3 and Tekken Tag Tournament and plays just like her.
Fight as Panda	Highlight Kuma at the Character Selection screen, then press ▲ or ●.
Fight as Violet	Highlight Lee at the Character Selection screen, then press ●.
Unlocking All Characters	Complete the game with the indicated character to unlock the corresponding fighter.

TEKKEN 6 (XBOX 360)

UNLOCKABLES

UNLOCKABLE	HOW TO UNLOCK
Arena	Clear Southern Woodlands
Kigan Island stage	Go to Abyss Gate on Hard difficulty and defeat a man with straw hat and grab his loot. Then exit to world map.

UNLOCKABLE	HOW TO UNLOCK
Medium and Hard difficulty	Clear Azazel's Temple, Central Corridor.
Mishima Industries, Biotech Research Station Ruins stage	Go right at the first junction in Seahorse Grand Hotel, defeat the kangeroo and clear the stage.
Nightmare Train stage	Clear Azazel's Temple, Central Corridor.
Play as Anna in Arena	Defeat her in G Corporation, Millennium Tower.
Play as Armour King in Arena	Defeat him in Lost Cemetery.
Play as Asuka in Arena	Defeat her in Kazama-Style Traditional Martial Arts Dojo.
Play as Baek in Arena	Defeat him in West Coast Canal Industrial Complex.
Play as Bob in Arena	Defeat him in Central District, 11th Avenue.
Play as Bruce in Arena	Defeat him in G Security Service, Operations Headquarters.
Play as Bryan in Arena	Defeat him in Southern Woodlands.
Play as Christie in Arena	Defeat her in Seahorse Grand Hotel.
Play as Devil Jin	Defeat him in Nightmare Train.
Play as Dragunov in Arena	Defeat him in container Terminal 7.
Play as Eddy in Arena	Defeat him in Tekken Force 4th Special Forces Operation Group Compound.
Play as Feng in Arena	Defeat him in Deserted Temple.
Play as Ganryu in Arena	Defeat him in Aranami Stable.
Play as Hwoarang in Arena	Defeat him in Industrial Highway 357.
Play as in Heihachi Arena	Defeat him in Mshima Estate.
Play as Jack-6 in Arena	Defeat him in Container Terminal 3.
Play as Jin	Defeat him in Azazel's Temple, Central Corridor.
Play as Julia in Arena	Defeat all enemies in G Science and Technology, Research Building 3.
Play as Kazuya in Arena	Defeat him in G Corporation, Millennium Tower Heliport.
Play as King in Arena	Defeat him with Marduk in Mixed Martial Arts Gym "Wild Kingdom."
Play as Kuma or Panda in Arena	Defeat Kuma in North Nature Park.
Play as Law in Arena	Defeat him in West District, Chinatown.
Play as Lee in Arena	Defeat him in Violet Systems.
Play as Lei in Arena	Defeat all enemies in ICPO Branch Office.
Play as Leo in Arena	Defeat it in 16th Archaeological Expedition's Excavation Site.
Play as Lili in Arena	Defeat her in Queen's Harbour.
Play as Marduk in Arena	Defeat him with King in Mixed Martial Arts Gym "Wild Kingdom."
Play as Miguel in Arena	Defeat him in South Bay Warehouse Area.
Play as Mokujin	Defeat it in Subterranean Pavilion.
Play as Nina in Arena	Defeat her in Mishima Zaibatsu, Central Subway Line.
Play as Paul in Arena	Defeat him in West District, 13th Avenue.
Play as Raven in Arena	Defeat him in Secret Underground Passage.
Play as Roger Jr. in Arena	Defeat it in Mishima Industries, Biotech Research Station Ruins.
Play as Steve in Arena	Defeat him in Abyss Gate.
Play as Wang in Arena	Defeat him in Fujian Tulou.
Play as Xiaoyu in Arena	Defeat her in Mishima Polytechnic.

UNLOCKABLE	HOW TO UNLOCK
Play as Yoshimitsu	Defeat him in Kigan Island.
Play as Zafina	Defeat all enemies in Mystic's Village.
Subterranean Pavilion stage	Clear 16th Archaeological Expedition's Excavation Site on Hard difficulty.

WIN POSE

Just before the win sequence plays at the end of a match, hold left punch, right punch, left kick, or right kick to select your win pose. Some characters may have more win poses than others.

TEKKEN TAG TOURNAMENT (PlayStation 2)

To unlock the different stages, first highlight Practice mode at the Main menu, then enter the code listed.

UNLOCKABLE	OBJECTIVE
Eddy's Stage (Day)	Hold L2 and press R2 13 times.
Eddy's Stage (Sunset)	Hold L2 and press R2 ten times.
Heihachi's Stage	Hold L2 and press R2 12 times.
Hwoarang's Stage	Hold L2 and press R2,R2,R2,R2.
Jin's Stage (Day)	Hold L2 and press R2 17 times.
Jin's Stage (Night)	Hold L2 and press R2 eight times.
King's Stage	Hold L2 and press R2 11 times.
Law's Stage (New)	Hold L2 and press R2 once.
Law's Stage (Old)	Hold L2 and press R2 15 times.
Lei's Stage	Hold L2 and press R2,R2,R2,R2,R2.
Ling's Stage	Hold L2 and press R2,R2,R2.
Nina's Stage (Day)	Hold L2 and press R2 nine times.
Nina's Stage (Night)	Hold L2 and press R2 18 times.
Ogre's Stage	Hold L2 and press R2 six times.
Paul's Stage	Hold L2 and press R2 20 times.
School Stage (Day)	Hold L2 and press R2 16 times.
School Stage (Night)	Hold L2 and press R2 seven times.
Supercharging	During a match, press all buttons to charge up. Press ×+●+▲+■ if you kept the default buttons.
Unknown Stage	Hold L2 and press R2 14 times.
Yoshimitsu's Stage (Heavy Snow)	Hold L2 and press R2 19 times.
Yoshimitsu's Stage (Light Snow)	Hold L2 and press R2,R2.

WHEN UNLOCKING THE BONUS CHARACTERS, EXPECT THEM TO APPEAR IN THIS ORDER: KUNIMITSU, BRUCE IRVIN, JACK-2, LEE CHAOLAN, WANG JINREY, ROGER AND ALEX, KUMA AND PANDA, KAZUYA MISHIMA, OGRE, TRUE OGRE, PROTOTYPE JACK, MOKUJIN AND TETSUJIN, DEVIL AND ANGEL, THEN UNKNOWN.

TENCHU FATAL SHADOWS (PSP)

While the game is paused, enter code on the second controller.

UNLOCKABLE	CODE
View Score Status	■,■,⇩,⇩,⇧,⇧

TERMINATOR 3: THE REDEMPTION (XBOX)

UNLOCKABLE	CODE
All Upgrades	Highlight Credits and press B+Y+LT

TERMINATOR 3: THE REDEMPTION (PlayStation 2)

In the Main menu, choose "Credits." While watching the credits, enter the following:

UNLOCKABLE	CODE
All Levels	●+R2+▲
All Upgrades	●+▲+L1
Invincibility	●+R2+R1

TEST DRIVE (XBOX)

PASSWORDS

PASSWORD	EFFECT
Unlock 2 Jaguars and an Aston Martin Vanquish	Set a new record on the drag racing level in Story mode and enter SOUNDMAX
Unlock the G4TV Viper	Set a new record on any track and Enter KQXYKGVY as the name

THRILLVILLE (PSP)

CODES

Enter these while in a park. You hear a chime if it worked.

UNLOCKABLE	HOW TO UNLOCK
Add $50,000	■, ●, ▲, ■, ●, ▲, ×
Mission Complete	■, ●, ▲, ■, ●, ▲, ●
Unlock All Parks	■, ●, ▲, ■, ●, ▲, ■
Unlock All Rides in Park	■, ●, ▲, ■, ●, ▲, ▲

TIGER WOODS PGA TOUR '07 (XBOX 360)

CODES

From the main menu enter the codes to get the corresponding effects.

EFFECT	CODE
Big Head mode for crowds.	tengallonhat
Unlock all Nike items.	justdoit

TIGER WOODS PGA TOUR '07 (PlayStation 3)

UNLOCKABLE	HOW TO UNLOCK
EA Black Series Clubs	Complete the game 100% to get the EA Black Series Clubs

TIGER WOODS PGA TOUR '07 (Wii)

Enter these codes under passwords in the Options menu.

UNLOCKABLE	CODE
Acquire all Cobra gear	SnakeKing
Unlock all Adidas items	THREE STRIPES
Unlock all Bridgestone items	SHOJIRO
Unlock all Grafalloye items	JUST SHAFTS
Unlock all Level 3 EA Sports items	INTHEGAME
Unlock all Macgergor items	MACTEC
Unlock all Mizuno items	RIHACHINRZO
Unlock all Nike items	JUSTDOIT
Unlock all Oakley items	JANNARD
Unlock all PGA Tour items	LIGHTNING
Unlock all Ping items	SOLHEIM
Unlock all players in team play	GAMEFACE
Unlock all Taylormade items	MRADAMS

TIGER WOODS PGA TOUR '07 (XBOX)

PASSWORDS

PASSWORD	EFFECT
ELDRICK	Unlocks 20+ golfers and 30+ course memberships
THREE STRIPES	Unlocks the Adidas sponsorship
JUSTDOIT	Unlocks the Nike sponsorship (Does not unlock the Nike TW items, only the regular Nike items)

TIGER WOODS PGA TOUR '08 (XBOX 360)

PASSWORDS

PASSWORD	EFFECT
cream	Unlimited money
allstars	Unlock all golfers
playfifa08	Unlock Wayne Rooney
greensfees	Unlocks All Courses

TIGER WOODS PGA TOUR '08 (PlayStation 3)

PASSWORDS

Go to the Password sub-menu from the EA Sports Extras menu and enter the following passwords to get the corresponding effects. Passwords are not case sensitive.

PASSWORD	EFFECT
Cream	Infinite money
PlayFIFA08	Unlock Wayne Rooney
Greensfees	Unlock all course
AllStars	Unlock all golfers

TIGER WOODS PGA TOUR '08 (Wii)

PASSWORDS

PASSWORD	EFFECT
PROSHOP	All Clubs Unlocked
NOTJUSTTIRES	Unlock Bridgestone Items
THREESTRIPES	Unlock Buick Items
CLEVELAND	Unlock Cleveland Golf Items
SNAKEKING	Unlock Cobra Items
INTHEGAME	Unlock EA Items
JUSTSHAFTS	Unlock Grafalloy Items
JLINDEBERG	Unlock J.Lindeberg Items
RIHACHINRIZO	Unlock Mizuno Items
JUSTDOIT	Unlock Nike Items
GUYSAREGOOD	Unlock Precept Items

TIGER WOODS PGA TOUR 09 (PlayStation 2)

CODES

Go to Extras at the main menu, then Passwords, and enter the following codes.

EFFECT	CODE
1 Million Dollars	JACKPOT
All Clothing & Equipment Unlocked	SHOP2DROP
All Cover Stories Unlocked	HEADLINER
All PGA Tour Events Unlocked	BEATIT
Max Skill Points, All Clothing & Equipment Unlocked	IAMRUBBISH

TIGER WOODS PGA TOUR '10 (XBOX 360)

UNLOCKABLES

UNLOCKABLE	HOW TO UNLOCK
Bonus Challenge 1	Complete all Tournament Challenges.
Bonus Challenge 2	Complete Bonus Challenge 1.
Bonus Challenge 3	Complete Bonus Challenge 2.
Bonus Challenge 4	Complete Bonus Challenge 3.

TIGER WOODS PGA TOUR '10 (PlayStation 3)

UNLOCKABLES

UNLOCKABLE	HOW TO UNLOCK
Doral	Beat the first Tournament Challenge on this course or buy the course pass.
East Lake	Beat the first Tournament Challenge on this course or buy the course pass.
Harbor Town	Beat the first Tournament Challenge on this course or buy the course pass.
Hazeltine	Beat the first Tournament Challenge on this course or buy the course pass.
Oakmont	Beat the first Tournament Challenge on this course or buy the course pass.
Pebble Beach	Beat the first Tournament Challenge on this course or buy the course pass.
Pinehurst no.2	Beat the first Tournament Challenge on this course or buy the course pass.
Torrey Pines	Beat the first Tournament Challenge on this course or buy the course pass.
Tpc Boston	Beat the first Tournament Challenge on this course or buy the course pass.
Wentworth	Beat the first Tournament Challenge on this course or buy the course pass.

TIM BURTON'S THE NIGHTMARE BEFORE CHRISTMAS: OOGIE'S REVENGE (PlayStation 2)

Enter this code while playing.

UNLOCKABLE	CODE
Pumpkin Jack and Santa Jack costumes	⇩, ⇧, ⇨, ⇦, L3, R3

TIME CRISIS 2 (PlayStation 2)

UNLOCKABLE	OBJECTIVE
Auto Bullets	Clear the Story mode twice at any difficulty level to be able to fire 20 bullets in one trigger.
Auto Reload	Clear the Story mode at any difficulty level using Auto Bullets to earn unlimited firepower with your gun.
Increase Your Credits in Arcade Mode	Receive extra credits if you clear the Story mode at any difficulty level. (See below for more info)
Mirror Mode	To activate the Mirror mode, clear the Story mode without using the "Continue" function.
Music Player	To access the Music Player, clear the final mission of the "Crisis" Mission.
Shoot Away 2 Arrange Mode	To access Arrange mode, score very high points in the Arcade Original mode (Retro). Hit two clay pigeons with one bullet to double your points for that shot.
Shoot Away 2 Extra Mode	To access Extra mode, score good points in the Arcade Original mode (Retro).

UNLOCKABLE	OBJECTIVE
Stage Trial 2	To reach Stage Trial 2, clear Stage 1 of the Story mode at any difficulty level.
Stage Trial 3	To reach Stage Trial 3, clear Stage 2 of the Story mode at any difficulty level.
Wide Shots	Clear the Story mode at any difficulty level with the Auto Reload function to enable your firearm to shoot wide shots (shotgun type with nine bullets per reload).

FOR THE "INCREASE YOUR CREDITS IN ARCADE MODE" CODE, ONCE YOU'VE CLEARED THE MODE SEVERAL TIMES, YOU ARE EVENTUALLY ENTITLED TO "FREE PLAY" AND A MAXIMUM OF NINE LIVES THAT YOU CAN SET IN THE "GAME" OPTIONS.

TIMESPLITTERS 2 (XBOX)

Complete these levels in Story mode under the Medium difficulty setting to access the playable characters.

LEVEL REWARD	PLAYABLE CHARACTER
1853 Wild West	The Colonel
1895 Notre Dame Paris	Notre Dame
1920 Aztec Ruins	Stone Golem
1932 Chicago	Big Tony
1972 Atom Smasher	Khallos
1990 Oblask Dam Siberia	The Mutant TimeSplitter
2019 NeoTokyo	Sadako
2280 Return to Planet X	Ozor Mox
2315 Robot Factory	Machinist
2401 Space Station	Reaper Splitter See Tip

COMPLETE THE 2401 SPACE STATION LEVEL UNDER THE EASY DIFFICULTY SETTING TO UNLOCK THE ENDING SEQUENCE.

TIMESPLITTERS 2 (PlayStation 2)

Beat each level listed in Story mode under Medium difficulty to unlock its secret character. You'll be able to play these unlockable characters in Arcade mode.

LEVEL	PLAYABLE CHARACTER
1853 Wild West Level Reward	The Colonel
1895 Notre Dame Paris Level Reward	Notre Dame
1920 Aztec Ruins Level Reward	Stone Golem
1853 Wild West Level Reward	The Colonel
1895 Notre Dame Paris Level Reward	Notre Dame
1920 Aztec Ruins Level Reward	Stone Golem

BEAT THE 2401 SPACE STATION LEVEL ON "EASY" DIFFICULTY TO UNLOCK THE ENDING SEQUENCE.

TMNT (XBOX 360)

CODES

At the main menu screen, hold LB and enter the code, then release LB. You should hear a sound to confirm you entered the code right.

CODE	EFFECT
AABA	Unlocks challenge map 2
BYAX	Unlocks Don's big head goodie

TMNT (Wii)

UNLOCKABLES

At the main menu, hold Z on the Nunchuk and enter the following codes. Release Z after each code to hear a confirmation sound.

UNLOCKABLE	CODE
Unlock Don's Big Head Goodie	①, Ⓐ, Ⓒ, ②

Unlock Challenge Map 2	Ⓐ, Ⓐ, Ⓐ, ①, Ⓐ

TNA IMPACT! (XBOX 360)

ARENAS

UNLOCKABLE	HOW TO UNLOCK
Armoury Arena	Defeat James Storm in Story mode
England Arena	Accumulate 420,000 Style Points
Freedom Center Arena	Become the X Division Champion in Story mode
Japanese Arena	Defeat the Motor City Machine Guns in Story mode
Mexican Arena	Win the Mexican Gauntlet Match in Story mode
Vegas Arena	Defeat Kurt Angle in Story mode

UNLOCKABLES

UNLOCKABLE	HOW TO UNLOCK
Abyss	Win Abyss in Story mode Part 6
Benny the Clown (from Story mode, Chapter Two)	350,000 SP
Brother Ray	Beat Team 3D in Story mode
Don West	Earn 260,000 Style Points
Eric Young	Win your tag match in Story mode
Jay Lethal	Beat Jay Lethal in Story mode
Jeff Jarrett	Win Jarrett in Story mode Part 6
Senshi	Earn 200,000 Style Points
Sonjay Dutt	Beat Sonjay Dutt in Story mode
Suicide	Complete Story mode, and Suicide is unlocked after the credits are finished
Tomko	Beat Tomko and AJ Styles in Story mode

TNA IMPACT! (PlayStation 3)

UNLOCKABLES

UNLOCKABLE	HOW TO UNLOCK
Abyss	Defeat Abyss in Story mode Part 6.
Black Machismo	Defeat him in Story mode.
Brother Ray	Defeat TEAM 3D in Story mode.
Don West	Gain 250,000 style points.
Eric Young	During Story mode, you will eventually be paired up with Eric Young. After successfully winning your first tag team match, he will be unlocked.
Jay Lethal	Defeat Lethal in your TNA tryout gauntlet match in Story mode.
Jeff Jarrett	Defeat him in Story mode.
Kevin Nash	Defeat him during Story mode.
Moves for Your Created Superstar	Various moves are unlocked as your progress through Story mode.
Senshi	Gain 200,000 style points.
Suicide	Defeat Jeff Jarrett in Story mode.
Tomko	Win the tag team match.

TNA IMPACT! (PlayStation 2)

UNLOCKABLES

UNLOCKABLE	HOW TO UNLOCK
Abyss	Defeat Abyss in Story mode Part 6
AJ Styles X	Defeat AJ Styles in a singles match in Story mode
Brother Ray	Defeat Team 3D in a tag team match in Story mode
Chris Sabin X	Defeat Chris Sabin in a singles match in Story mode

UNLOCKABLE	HOW TO UNLOCK
Don West	Gain 250,000 Style points
Eric Young	Win the TNA Tag Team Titles in Story mode
Jay Lethal	Win the 3 man gauntlet match in Story mode
Jeff Jarrett	Defeat Jeff Jarett in Story mode
Senshi	Gain 200,000 Style points
Sonjay Dutt	Defeat Sonjay Dutt in a singles match in Story mode
Tomko	Defeat AJ Styles and Tomko in a tag team match in Story mode

TOEJAM AND EARL (Wii)

UNLOCKABLES

UNLOCKABLE	HOW TO UNLOCK
Free Presents	Sneak up on Santa Claus before he takes off and he gives you a few presents.
Level 0	On Level 1, on the bottom left side, a small hole leads to level 0, which has hula dancers in a tub and a lemonade man who gives you another life.
Present Island	At the top right of the map on level 1, there is a hidden island with a load of presents for the taking. You need rocket skates, an inner-tube, or icarus wings to get there.
Ultimate Cheat	Pause the game, then press the following button combinations: ✜↑+Ⓐ+Ⓑ+Ⓒ, ✜→+Ⓐ, ✜↓+Ⓑ, ✜←+🔍. You hear a sound if you entered the code correctly. Unpause the game, and you have all but one of the ship pieces collected. The last piece will always be located on the next level.

TOEJAM AND EARL IN PANIC ON FUNKOTRON (Wii)

PASSWORDS

PASSWORD	EFFECT
R-F411W9Q986	Level 3
PJ04EK-5WT82	Level 5
MW0WEE6JRVF7	Level 7
VANDNEHF9807L	Level 9
MWAAK!8MDT76	Level 11
F!!NEHNW0Q73	Level 15
TOEJAMTEARL!	View Credits

HIGH FUNK PASSWORDS

Enter these passwords at the password screen to go to your desired level with lots of Funk.

PASSWORD	EFFECT
RWJ21EW1R80X	Level 03 with 37 Funk
VJW6EK21-J07	Level 05 with 80 Funk
P0W09KAN-VQ	Level 07 with 95 Funk
VDJF7M2DyT6L	Level 09 with 99 Funk
VYJF73TH1PQQ	Level 11 with 99 Funk
DKYQHX4!EV!7	Level 13 with 89 Funk
J11L3R4C13H7	Level 15 with 49 Funk

TOM AND JERRY WAR OF THE WHISKERS (PlayStation 2)

To enter these codes, go into Options then open Cheats menu.

UNLOCKABLE	CODE
Auto Refill Health Bars	×, ●, ×, ▲, ▲, ■, ●, ▲
Infinite Ammo	●, ■, ●, ▲, ×, ■, ×, ×
Unlock All Character Costumes	●, ●, ×, ■, ●, ▲, ×, ●

TOM CLANCY'S ENDWAR (XBOX 360)

CODES

Under Community and Extras, press "Y" on Downloadable Content. Battalions can be used in Theater of War mode.

EFFECT	CODE
Unlock upgraded European Federation (EFEC) Battalion	EUCA20
Unlock upgraded Joint Strike Force (JSF) Battalion	JSFA35
Unlock upgraded Spetznaz (Russian) Battalion	SPZT17
Unlock upgraded Spetznaz (Russian) Battalion	SPZA39

TOM CLANCY'S ENDWAR (PlayStation 3)

CODES

Go to the Community & Extras screen on the Main Menu, highlight the VIP option and press the Triangle button to input the special codes.

EFFECT	CODE
European Enforcer Corps	EUCA20
Russian Spetsnaz Guard Brigade	SPZA39
U.S. Joint Strike Force	JSFA35
Unlocks the special Spetsnaz Battalion	SPZT17

TOM CLANCY'S ENDWAR (PSP)

MEDALS

UNLOCKABLE	HOW TO UNLOCK
Air Keeper	No air units lost.
Bombing Master	Destroy more than 3 enemy units with the bombers.
Demon of The Sea	Destroy more than 3 enemy units using the submarine.
Exceptional Marksman	Destroy more than 6 enemy units by using long-range units.
Gunship Falcon	Destroy more than 6 enemy units by using the helicopters.
Incredible Dogfighter	Destroy more than 3 enemy units with fighters or helicopters.
Land Keeper	No land units lost.
Marvelous Conquistador	Control all buildings.
Merciless Fighter	Destroy more than 10 enemy units by using close-combat units.
Preserver Of The Infantry	No Infantry lost in battle.
Ray of Light	Win within a certain number of cycles.
Sea Keeper	No Sea units lost.
Submarine Executioner	Destroy all submarine units on the map.

TOM CLANCY'S GHOST RECON (PlayStation 2)

Enter the codes at the Title screen:

UNLOCKABLE	CODE
All Missions	×, L2, ▲, R2, SELECT
All Special Features	L1, L2, R1, R2, ×, SELECT
Invincibility	Pause the game and press L1, R2, L2, R1, SELECT

TOM CLANCY'S GHOST RECON 2: SUMMIT STRIKE (XBOX)

Pause the game during gameplay, choose "In Game Options," then choose "Enter Cheats."

UNLOCKABLE	CODE
Complete Current Mission	B, B, X, Y
Refill Ammo	B, B, X, X
Superman (Player Invincibility)	B, B, X, A
Team Superman (Team Invincibility)	B, B, X, B

TOM CLANCY'S GHOST RECON: ADVANCED WARFIGHTER (XBOX 360)

When the game is paused, enter these codes while holding BACK, LT, RT.

UNLOCKABLE	CODE
Full Life	L3, L3, RB, X, RB, Y
Scott Mitchell Invincible	Y, Y, X, RB, X, L3
Team Invincible	X, X, Y, RB, Y, L3
Unlimited Ammo	RB, RB, L3, X, L3, Y

Enter this code on the Mission Select screen while holding BACK, LT, RT.

UNLOCKABLE	CODE
All Levels	Y, RB, Y, RB, X

TOM CLANCY'S GHOST RECON: ADVANCED WARFIGHTER 2 (XBOX 360)

Enter this password as a name.

UNLOCKABLE	CODE
FAMAS in Quick Missions Only (works in Australian version only)	GRAW2QUICKFAMAS

TOM CLANCY'S HAWX (XBOX 360)

CODES

Go to the hangar screen, then enter the codes to unlock the corresponding aircraft.

EFFECT	CODE
Unlocks A-12 Avenger II	Hold LT and enter X,LB,X,RB,Y,X
Unlocks F-18 HARV	Hold LT and enter LB,Y,LB,Y,LB,X
Unlocks FB-22	Hold LT and enter RB,X,RB,X,RB,Y

TOM CLANCY'S HAWX (PlayStation 3)

CODES

Go to the hangar screen, then enter the codes to unlock the corresponding aircraft.

EFFECT	CODE
Unlocks A-12 Avenger II	Hold L2 and press ■,L1,■,R1,▲,■
Unlocks F-18 HARV	Hold L2 and press L1,▲,L1,▲,L1,■
Unlocks FB-22	Hold L2 and press R1,■,R1,■,R1,▲

TOM CLANCY'S RAINBOW SIX 3 (PlayStation 2)

UNLOCKABLE	CODE
All Custom Mission maps	Press L1,R2,L2,R1,←,→,■,● at the Main menu.

TOM CLANCY'S RAINBOW SIX 3: BLACK ARROW (XBOX)

UNLOCKABLE	CODE
Guns fire lasers instead of bullets	Enter Up,Down,Up,Down,RT,RT
God Mode	Enter Up,Up,Down,Down,Left,Right,Left,Right,B,A during gameplay.

TOM CLANCY'S RAINBOW SIX 4 (XBOX)

This code only works in single player mode.

UNLOCKABLE	CODE
God mode	Press Up, Up, Down, Down, Left, Right, Left, Right, B, A

TOM CLANCY'S RAINBOW SIX VEGAS (XBOX 360)

The following are ranks and their corresponding unlockables.

RANK	UNLOCKABLES
01 Private 2nd Class	All Starting Equipment
02 Private 1st Class	Headgears 1: Tactical Helm, Balaclava

03 Specialist	Rainbow Weapons: MP7A1, SIG552, USP40
04 Corporal	Camo 1: Desert, Urban, Russian, Guerrilla, Fall, Desert 2
05 Sergeant	Tactical Armor: Raven Recon Armor, Vulture Combat Armor, Falcon Assault Armor
06 Staff Sergeant	Headgears 2: 3 Hole Balaclava, Baseball Cap, Breathing Mask
07 Sergeant First Class	Camo 2: Flecktarn, Orange, Swedish, War2k5, Alpen, White
08 Master Sergeant	Freedom Fighter weapons: AK47, Raging Bull, SV98
09 First Sergeant	Headgears 3: Bonnie Hat, Beret, Tinted Goggles
10 Sergeant Major	Black Market Armor: Typhoon Recon Armor, Cyclone Combat Armor, Hurricane Assault Armor
11 2nd Lieutenant	Camo 3: Pink, Blue, Woodland, Wasp, Sand, Crimson
12 1st Lieutenant	Headgears 4: Half-Face Mask, Reinforced Helm, Tactical Goggles
13 Captain	Merc Weapons: MG36, SPAS12, Deagle
14 Major	Military Armor: Vier Recon Armor, Diamondback Combat Armor, Anaconda Assault Armor
15 Lt. Colonel	Camo 4: Yellow Urban, Red Urban, Tiger, Rust, Urban 2, Grey
16 Colonel	Headgears 5: Ballistic Face Mask, Riot Helm, NVGs
17 Elite	Camo 5: Custom 1, Custom 2, Custom 3

TOM CLANCY'S RAINBOW SIX VEGAS 2 (XBOX 360)

CODES

During gameplay, pause the game, hold the right shoulder button, and enter the following codes.

UNLOCKABLE	HOW TO UNLOCK
GI John Doe Mode	L3, L3, A, R3, R3, B, L3, L3, X, R3, R3, Y
Super Ragdoll	A, A, B, B, X, X, Y, Y, A, B, X, Y
Third Person Mode	X, B, X, B, L3, L3, Y, A, Y, A, R3, R3

WEAPONS

When you are customizing your character, hold down the right bumper and insert the following code.

UNLOCKABLE	HOW TO UNLOCK
AR-21 Assault Rifle	↓, ↓, ↑, ↑, X, B, X, B, Y, ↑, ↑, Y

COMCAST MULTIPLAYER MAP

At the main menu, go to the Extras menu, select Comcast Gift, then enter the following password.

PASSWORD	EFFECT
Comcast faster	Comcast multiplayer map

ACHIEVEMENTS

UNLOCKABLE	HOW TO UNLOCK
Ace of Spades (15)	Perform five consecutive kills without dying in an adversarial match without respawns.
Bring It On! (10)	Complete a Terrorist Hunt mission at the hardest difficulty.
Cluster Bomb (10)	Kill three enemies at once using explosives with at least six players present.
Come Closer (20)	Kill 100 enemies using a shotgun with at least six players present.
Completed Convention Center (25)	Complete Convention Center in Story mode at any difficulty.
Completed Estate (25)	Complete Estate in Story mode at any difficulty.
Completed Nevada Desert (25)	Complete Nevada Desert in Story mode at any difficulty.

NEW! A B C D E F G H I J K L M N O P Q R S T U V W X Y Z

UNLOCKABLE	HOW TO UNLOCK
Completed Old Vegas (25)	Complete Old Vegas in Story mode at any difficulty.
Completed Pic des Pyrénées (25)	Complete Pic des Pyrénées in Story mode at any difficulty.
Completed Recreational Center (25)	Complete Recreational Center in Story mode at any difficulty.
Completed Theater (25)	Complete Theater in Story mode at any difficulty.
Covert Ops Specialist (10)	Extract the intel item 10 times with at least six players present.
Demo Expert (10)	Defuse 10 bombs in Attack & Defend with at least six players present.
Don't Mess With Me (45)	Kill 1,000 enemies in multiplayer adversarial with at least six players present.
Double or Nothin' (10)	Win two ranked matches in a row.
Elite (50)	Achieve the rank of Elite.
Extreme Hunter (50)	Complete all Terrorist Hunt missions on Realistic difficulty.
Eye of the Sniper (30)	Kill 500 enemies in multiplayer adversarial with at least six players present.
Freedom Shall Prevail (75)	Complete the Story mode on Realistic difficulty.
Gimme a High Five! (10)	Complete five scenes as Bishop's teammate, Knight, in co-op Story mode at any difficulty.
Gun Shark (25)	Kill 300 enemies in multiplayer adversarial with at least six players present.
Haute Couture (10)	Create your own custom camouflage.
Here's for a Wicked Five! (20)	Complete 10 scenes as Bishop's teammate, Knight, in co-op Story mode at any difficulty.
I Like the Sound It Makes (25)	Kill 150 terrorists with a Shotgun.
Kamikaze (10)	Plant and detonate 10 bombs in Attack & Defend with at least six players present.
Machine Gunner (20)	Kill 100 enemies using a Light Machine Gun with at least six players present.
My Hero! (10)	Rescue both Hostages 10 times in Attack & Defend with at least six players present.
My Name Is Sam (25)	Neutralize five terrorists in a row by performing headshots using a Sound Suppressor.
Natural Leader (15)	Lead your team to Victory 20 times in Team Leader with at least six players present.
Novice Hunter (5)	Complete your first Terrorist Hunt mission at any difficulty.
Officer (30)	Achieve the rank of Officer.
One Shot, One Kill (30)	Kill 100 enemies using a Sniper Rifle with at least six players present.
Pointman (10)	Kill 50 enemies in multiplayer adversarial with at least six players present.
Private First Class (10)	Achieve the rank of Private First Class.
Rappel King (20)	Kill 25 enemies while suspended from a rope.
Royal Flush (30)	Win 100 adversarial matches with at least six players present.
Short Controlled Bursts (15)	Kill 100 enemies using an Assault Rifle with at least six players present.
Sidearm Frenzy (25)	Kill 100 enemies using a Pistol with at least six players present.

Spray and Pray (15)	Kill 100 enemies using a Sub-Machine Gun with at least six players present.
That Wasn't So Hard (5)	Complete a scene as Bishop's teammate, Knight, in co-op Story mode at any difficulty.
The Ace Always Wins (5)	Win your first ranked match online.
The House Always Wins (15)	Host and win 10 matches with at least six players present.
Three of a Kind (15)	Win three consecutive ranked matches in a row.
Triggerman (20)	Kill 150 enemies in multiplayer adversarial with at least six players present.
True Identity (20)	Use the Xbox Live Vision to create a character with your appearance.
Veteran Hunter (20)	Complete five Terrorist Hunt missions at any difficulty.
Weapon Collector (30)	Unlock every weapon in the game.

TOM CLANCY'S RAINBOW SIX VEGAS 2 (PlayStation 3)

CODES

At the Title screen, hold R1 and press the following.

UNLOCKABLE	HOW TO UNLOCK
M468 Assault Rifle	↑,▲,↓,×,←,■,→,●,←,←,→,■
MTAR-21 Assault Rifle	↓,↓,↑,↑,■,●,■,●,▲,↑,↑,▲

SINGLE PLAYER CODES

During gameplay, pause the game, hold R1, and insert the following codes.

UNLOCKABLE	HOW TO UNLOCK
Red and Blue Tracers (also works online, host must enter code)	L3, L3,×, R3, R3,●, L3, L3,■, R3, R3,▲
Third-Person View	■,●,■,●, L3, L3,▲,×,▲,×, R3, R3
Super Ragdoll Mode	×,×,●,●,■,■,▲,▲,×,●,■,▲

COMCAST MULTIPLAYER MAP

At the game's main menu, go to the Extras menu, select Comcast Gift, then enter the following password.

PASSWORD	EFFECT
Comcast faster	Comcast multiplayer map

TOM CLANCY'S SPLINTER CELL: CHAOS THEORY (DS)

UNLOCKABLES

UNLOCKABLE	HOW TO UNLOCK
Argus Mercenary Costume	In Machi Akko, go to the bar and use the microphone. Look behind you for a keycard. Go back to the hallway with three doors, and use it on the closet.
Camouflage Sam Costume	In the Lighthouse level, snipe the man on the roof, but don't rappel down. On the high right corner is the costume.
Displace Mercenary Costume in Display Level	Go to floor three. Use the optic cable to see which room has the green package. Enter the room, and use keypad code 5800.
Displace Suit	Room next to the room where you have a last chance to save, code is 5800.
Masked Sam Costume	In the Penthouse level, go to Zherkezhi's apartment, and go to the first room on the top floor. Go down the long, dark hall and type 5698 in the pad.
National Guard Costume	In the Manhattan Streets level, go to the open area before the penthouse. Climb the pipe, jump left, and go down to the next platform, in the corner.

UNLOCKABLE	HOW TO UNLOCK
Shadownet Agent Costume	In Kokubo Sosho, go down the elevator, where lasers are at the bottom. Find a ladder to climb back up. The room will have lasers and the costume.
Short Sleeved Sam Costume in Bank Level	Go to the small vault left of the computer and use the lockpick.
Snow Guard Costume in Battery Level	Get the wrench, and go to the U-shaped room. Enter the keycard room, take out the guard, climb on the crate, and bash next crate.
Thermal Suit Costume in Hokkaido Level	Find the wrench, and find the man who is shooting on the roof, get to him and fall through the vent, exiting the room, and bash the door.
Full Equipment Mode (infinite ammo etc.)	Beat the game at least once.

TOM CLANCY'S SPLINTER CELL: DOUBLE AGENT (XBOX 360)

UNLOCKABLES

UNLOCKABLE	HOW TO UNLOCK
Spy—Second Skin	Achieve RECRUIT level (with a general average higher that 1%)
Spy—Third Skin	Achieve SPECIAL AGENT level (with a general average higher than 45%)
Uspilon Forces —Second Skin	Achieve FIELD AGENT level (with a general average higher than 20%)
Upsilon Forces Third Skin	Achieve COMMANDER level (with a general average higher than 95%)
Unlock All Multiplayer maps	Win 6 games as a Spy, 6 games as a UPSILON Force member, and play 25 games overall.
Electric Lock Pick	Complete the primary objectives in JBA HQ 1
EMP Device—Enhanced	Complete the primary objectives in JBA HQ 1
EMP Grenade	Complete the secondary objectives in the Iceland Assignment
EMP Grenade Attachment	Complete the secondary objectives in the Cozumel Assignment
Explosive Sticky Camera Attachment	Complete the secondary objectives in the Iceland Assignment
Frag Grenade Attachment	Complete the primary objectives in JBA HQ 3
Gas Grenade	Complete the primary objectives in JBA HQ 1
Gas Grenade Attachment	Complete the secondary objectives in the Cozumel Assignment
Hacking Device— Force Hack Upgrade	Complete the primary objectives in JBA HQ 2
Hacking Device— Software Upgrade	Complete the secondary objectives in the Shanghai Assignment
Night Vision—Enhanced	Complete the primary objectives in JBA HQ 3
Shotgun Shell Attachment	Complete the secondary objectives in the Okhotsk Assignment
Smoke Grenade - Attachment	Complete the secondary objectives in the Shanghai Assignment
Sonic Grenade Attachment	Complete the primary objectives in JBA HQ 2
Ultrasonic Emitter	Complete the secondary objectives in the Ellsworth Assignment
Wall Mine—Flash	Complete the secondary objectives in the Okhotsk Assignment
Wall Mine—Stun	Complete the secondary objectives in the Ellsworth Assignment

Ending A: Good	NSA trust above 33%, and you managed to save at least two of the three targets.
Ending B: Normal	NSA trust below 33%, but you managed to save the three targets. Or destroy two of the three targets, and NSA trust above 33%.
Ending C: Bad	Destroy/Kill all three targets. Or Destroy/Kill two of the targets, and NSA trust below 33%.

TOM CLANCY'S SPLINTER CELL: DOUBLE AGENT (Wii)

UNLOCKABLES

UNLOCKABLE	HOW TO UNLOCK
Elite Mode	Clear the Solo mode once
Elite Mode (Co-op)	Beat the game in Co-op mode to unlock Co-op Elite mode

TOM CLANCY'S SPLINTER CELL: ESSENTIALS (PSP)

BONUS MISSION CODES

Enter the following at the bonus mission screen (you have to enter the code each time you want to play the mission).

UNLOCKABLE	HOW TO UNLOCK
Unlock the Heroin Refinery Mission	Hold Select and press L+R three more times
Unlock the Paris-Nice Mission	Hold Select and press L+R 12 more times
Unlock the Television Free Indonesia Mission	Hold Select and press L+R three times

TOMB RAIDER LEGENDS (XBOX 360)

Enter these codes in game. Codes can not be used until they are unlocked.

UNLOCKABLE	CODE
Bulletproof	Hold LT press A, RT, Y, RT, X, LB
Draw enemies' health	Hold LT press X, B, A, LB, RT, Y
Excalibur	Hold LB press Y, A, B, RT, Y, LT
Infinite Assault Ammo	Hold LB press A, B, A, LT, X, Y
Infinite Grenade Launcher Ammo	Hold LB press LT, Y, RT, B, LT, X
Infinite Shotgun Ammo	Hold LB press RT, B, X, LT, X, A
Infinite SMG Ammo	Hold LB press B, Y, LT, RT, A, B
One Shot Kills	Hold LT press Y, A, Y, X, LB, B
Soul Reaver	Hold BLK press A, RT, B, RT, LT, X
Textureless Mode	Hold LT press BLK, A, B, A, Y, RT

TOMB RAIDER: LEGENDS (PSP)

CODES

Enter these codes while playing a level, but they only work once you have unlocked them.

CODE	EFFECT
Bulletproof	Hold L, then: ×, R, ▲, R, ■, R
Draw Enemy Health	Hold L, then: ■, ●, ×, R, R, ▲
Infinite Assault Rifle Ammo	Hold L, then: ×, ●, ×, R, ■, ▲
Infinite Grenade Launcher	Hold L, then: R, ▲, R, ●, R, ■
Infinite Shotgun Ammo	Hold L, then: R, ●, ■, R, ■, ×
Infinite SMG Ammo	Hold L, then: ●, ▲, R, R, ×, ●
One Shot Kill	Hold L, then: ▲, ×, ▲, ■, R, ●
Wield Excalibur	Hold L, then: ▲, ×, ●, R, ▲, R
Wield Soul Reaver	Hold L, then: ×, R, ●, R, R, ■

UNLOCKABLE CHEATS

These cheats are only unlocked when you clear the game or meet the following criteria.

UNLOCKABLE	HOW TO UNLOCK
Bulletproof Lara	Clear England under 27:00 in Time Trials
Infinite Grenade Launcher Ammo	Clear Kazakhstan under 27:10 in Time Trials
Infinite MG415 Ammo	Clear Peru under 21:30 in Time Trials
Infinite RC650 Ammo	Clear Japan under 12:15 in Time Trials
Infinite shotgun Ammo	Clear Ghana under 20:00 in Time Trials
One Hit Deaths	Clear Bolivia (stage 8) under 4:15 in Time Trials
Show Enemy Health	Clear Bolivia under 12:30 in Time Trials
Textureless Mode	Clear the game on any difficulty
Unlock Excalibur	Clear Nepal under 13:40 in Time Trials
Unlock the Soul Reaver	Clear the game and complete all time trials

UNLOCKABLES

UNLOCKABLE	HOW TO UNLOCK
Alister Fletcher	Collect 90% of all bronze rewards
Amanda Evert	Collect 70% of all bronze rewards
Anaya Imanu	Collect 30% of all bronze rewards
Biker, Brown Jacket Outfit	Complete Bolivia on the Medium setting in Treasure Hunt mode
Bolivia Redux—100% of all object models	Collect all silver rewards in Bolivia (level 8)
Bolivia	Collect all bronze rewards from Bolivia
Bolivia—100% of all object models	Collect all silver rewards in Bolivia
Bronze Gallery	In Tomb trials, finish all levels in Treasure Hunt mode on Easy difficulty
Croft Manor—100% of all object models	Collect all silver rewards in Croft Manor
England	Collect all bronze rewards from England
England—100% of all object models	Collect all silver rewards in England
Ghana	Collect all bronze rewards from Ghana
Ghana—100% of all object models	Collect all silver rewards in Ghana
Gold Gallery	In Tomb trials, finish all levels in Treasure Hunt mode on Hard difficulty
Increased Accuracy	50% of silver and bronze rewards
Increased Damage	75% of silver and bronze rewards
Increased Magazine Capacity	25% of silver and bronze rewards
James Rutland	Collect 50% of all bronze rewards
Japan	Collect all bronze rewards from Japan
Japan—100% of all object models	Collect all silver rewards in Japan
Kazakhstan	Collect all bronze rewards from Kazakhstan
Kazakhstan—100% of all object models	Collect all silver rewards in Kazakhstan
Lara Croft	Collect 10% of all bronze rewards
Legend, Camo Shorts	Beat Bolivia on the Hard setting in Treasure Hunter mode
Nepal	Collect all bronze rewards from Nepal
Nepal—100% of all object models	Collect all silver rewards in Nepal
Peru	Collect all bronze rewards from Peru
Peru—100% of all object models	Collect all silver rewards in Peru
Shogo Takamoto	Collect 60% of all bronze rewards
Silver Gallery	Complete Bolivia, Croft Manor, and Fiery Maze on the Easy setting in Treasure Hunt mode
Silver Gallery	In Tomb trials, finish all levels in Treasure Hunt mode on Medium difficulty
Special	Collect all bronze rewards from Croft Manor
Toru Nishimura	Collect 40% of all bronze rewards
Unknown Entity	Collect 100% of all bronze rewards

Winston Smith	Collect 80% of all bronze rewards
Zip	Collect 20% of all bronze rewards

TOMB RAIDER LEGENDS (XBOX)

Enter these codes in game. Codes can not be used until they are unlocked.

UNLOCKABLE	CODE
Bulletproof	Hold LT press A, RT, Y, RT, X, BLK
Draw enemies' health	Hold LT press X, B, A, BLK, RT, Y
Excalibur	Hold BLK press Y, A, B, RT, Y, LT
Infinite Assault Ammo	Hold BLK press A, B, A, LT, X, Y
Infinite Grenade Launcher Ammo	Hold BLK press LT, Y, RT, B, LT, X
Infinite Shotgun Ammo	Hold BLK press RT, B, X, LT, X, A
Infinite SMG Ammo	Hold BLK press B, Y, LT, RT, A, B
One Shot Kills	Hold LT press Y, A, Y, X, BLK, B
Soul Reaver	Hold BLK press A, RT, B, RT, LT, X
Textureless Mode	Hold LT press BLK, A, B, A, Y, RT

TOMB RAIDER LEGENDS (PlayStation 2)

Enter these codes in game. Codes can not be used until they are unlocked.

UNLOCKABLE	CODE
Bulletproof	Hold L1 press ×, R1, ▲, R1, ■, L2
Draws Enemies Health	Hold L1 press ■, ●, ×, L2, R1, ▲
Excalibur	Hold L2 press ▲, ×, ● R1, ▲, L1
Infinite Assault Ammo	Hold L2 press ×, ●, ×, L1, ■, ▲
Infinite Grenade Launcher Ammo	Hold L2 press L1, ▲, R1, ●, L1, ■
Infinite Shotgun Ammo	Hold L2 press R1, ●, ■, L1, ■, ×
Infinite SMG Ammo	Hold L2 press ●, ▲, L1, R1, ×, ●
One Shot Kill	Hold L1 press ▲, ×, ▲, ×, L2, ●
Textureless Mode	Hold L1 press L2, ×, ●, ×, ▲, R1
Wield Soul Reaver	Hold L2 press ×, R1, ●, R1, L1, ■

TOMB RAIDER: THE ANGEL OF DARKNESS (PlayStation 2)

UNLOCKABLE	CODE
Infinite Air	When Lara is swimming, save the game while underwater. When you load that save, the oxygen gauge will be restored to full.
Skip Level	Pause the game and press and hold L1+R2+↓+▲ then press ●,↑,■,▲,→,↓.

TOMB RAIDER: UNDERWORLD (XBOX 360)

UNLOCKABLES

UNLOCKABLE	HOW TO UNLOCK
Lara's bathing suit	Complete the game on any difficulty setting and this becomes unlocked in Treasure Hunt mode when you revisit the Mediterranean Sea Expedition.
Treasure Hunt mode	Complete the game on any difficulty to unlock Treasure Hunt mode, which allows you to revisit all levels to claim Treasures/Relics missed through storm.

TOMB RAIDER: UNDERWORLD (PlayStation 3)

UNLOCKABLES

All items can be found under the Extras section once the following conditions are met.

UNLOCKABLE	HOW TO UNLOCK
All environment concept art for Arctic Sea and Amelia concepts	Complete Arctic Sea Expedition.

UNLOCKABLE	HOW TO UNLOCK
All environment concept art for Coastal Thailand and Alister concepts	Complete Coastal Thailand Expedition.
All environment concept art for Croft Manor and Doppelganger concepts	Complete Croft Manor Expedition.
All environment concept art for Jan Mayen Island and Gear and Artifacts concepts	Complete Jan Mayen Island Expedition.
All environment concept art for Mediterranean Sea and Amanda concepts	Complete Mediterranean Sea Expedition.
All environment concept art for Mexico and All Men concepts	Complete Southern Mexico Expedition.
All environment concept art for Ship and Natla concepts	Complete Andaman Sea Expedition.
Creature concepts	Collect every single Treasure.
Game flow storyboards Survivalist difficulty level.	Complete the entire game on the Master
Lara concepts	Collect all six Relics.
Zip and Winston concepts	Complete Prologue.

TONY HAWK'S AMERICAN SK8LAND (DS)

UNLOCKABLES

UNLOCKABLE	HOW TO UNLOCK
Always Special	Beat Classic mode 9 times
Crate-a-Skater	Beat Classic mode once
First Person Camera	Beat Classic mode 6 times
Giant Mode	Beat Classic mode 4 times
Hoverboard	Beat Classic mode 11 times
Lip Balance	Beat Classic mode twice
Manual Balance	Beat Classic mode twice
Matrix Mode	Beat Classic mode 5 times
Nearly Always Ribbon	Beat Classic mode 12 times
Ninja Skater	Beat Classic mode with all characters (13 times)
Paper Tony	Beat Classic mode 10 times
Rail Balance	Beat Classic mode twice
Replay Cam	Beat Classic mode 7 times
Tiny Mode	Beat Classic mode 3 times
Turbo Mode	Beat Classic mode 8 times

TONY HAWK'S AMERICAN WASTELAND (XBOX 360)

In the Options menu, select the Cheats menu and enter these passwords. (Note: case sensitive)

UNLOCKABLE	PASSWORD
Matt Hoffman	the_condor
Perfect Grinds	grindXpert
Perfect Manuals	2wheels!

TONY HAWK'S AMERICAN WASTELAND (XBOX)

Enter this code at the Cheats menu. (Note: case sensitive)

UNLOCKABLE	CODE
Mat Hoffman	the_condor

TONY HAWK'S AMERICAN WASTELAND (PlayStation 2)

Enter this code in the Cheats menu. (Note: case sensitive)

UNLOCKABLE	CODE
Mat Hoffman	the_condor

TONY HAWK'S DOWNHILL JAM (Wii)

Enter these passwords in the Cheats menu.

UNLOCKABLE	PASSWORD
Always Special	PointHogger
Chipmunk Voices	HelloHelium
Demon Skater	EvilChimneySweep
Display Coordinates	DisplayCoordinates
Enables Manuals	IMISSMANUALS
Extreme Car Crashes	WatchForDoors
First Person Skater	FirstPersonJam
Free Boost	OotbaghForever
Giganto-Skater	IWannaBeTallTall
Invisible Skater	NowYouSeeMe
Large Birds	BirdBirdBirdBird
Mini Skater	DownTheRabbitHole
Perfect Manual	TightRopeWalker
Perfect Rail	LikeTiltingAPlate
Perfect Stats	IAmBob
Picasso Skater	FourLights
Power of the Fish!	TonyFishDownhillJam
Shadow Skater	ChimneySweep
Tiny People	ShrinkThePeople
Unlock All Boards and Outfits	RaidTheWoodshed
Unlock All Events	AdventuresOfKwang
Unlock All Movies	FreeBozzler
Unlock All Skaters	ImInterfacing

TONY HAWK'S PRO SKATER 2X (XBOX)

UNLOCKABLE	CODE
All Cheats	While playing, pause the game and hold the LT, then press START, A, WHT, ↑, →, ↓, A, Y, B, A, B, Y.

TONY HAWK'S PRO SKATER 3 (XBOX)

To enter these codes, select Cheats in the Options menu.

UNLOCKABLE	CODE
All Characters	teamfreak
All Decks	neverboard
All Movies	rollit
Complete game with selected Character	stiffcomp
Max Stats	juice4me

TONY HAWK'S PRO SKATER 3 (PlayStation 2)

From the Options menu, choose "Cheats" and enter the following codes. (Cheats can be activated in the Pause menu.)

UNLOCKABLE	CODE
All Characters	YOHOMIES
All FMV Movies	Peepshow

NEW! A B C D E F G H I J K L M N O P Q R S T U V W X Y Z

UNLOCKABLE	CODE
All Levels	ROADTRIP
Cheat Menu	backdoor
Lots of Stat Points	PUMPMEUP

TONY HAWK'S PRO SKATER 4 (XBOX)

To enter these codes, select Cheats in the Options menu.

UNLOCKABLE	CODE
Always Special	i'myellow
Daisy	(o)(o)
Everything	watch_me_xplode
Matrix Mode	fbiagent
Moon Gravity	moon$hot
Perfect Manuals	freewheelie
Perfect Rails	belikeeric
Perfect Skitch	bumperrub
Stats 13	4p0sers

TONY HAWK'S PRO SKATER 4 (PlayStation 2)

Go to the Options menu and choose "Cheats." Enter the following:

UNLOCKABLE	CODE
Cheat Mode	watch_me_xplode
Daisy	(o)(o)
Full Special Meter	doasuper
Hidden Skaters	homielist
Perfect Manual	mullenpower
Perfect Rail Balance	ssbsts
Matrix Mode	nospoon
Moon Gravity	superfly

At the Create a Skater screen, enter the following names to unlock hidden skaters:

#$%@!
Aaron Skillman
Adam Lippman
Andrew Skates
Andy Marchal
Angus
Atiba Jefferson
Ben Scott Pye
Big Tex
Brian Jennings
Captain Liberty
Chauwa Steel
Chris Peacock
ConMan
Danaconda
Dave Stohl
DDT
DeadEndRoad
Fakes the Clown
Fritz
Gary Jesdanun
Grjost
Henry Ji
Jason Uyeda
Jim Jagger
Joe Favazza
John Rosser
Jow
Kenzo
Kevin Mulhall
Kraken
Lindsey Hayes
Lisa G Davies
Little Man
Marilena Rixfor
Mat Hoffman
Matt Mcpherson
Maya's Daddy
Meek West
Mike Day

Mike Lashever	Stacey D
Mike Ward	Stacey Ytuarte
Mr. Brad	Stealing Is Bad
Nolan Nelson	Team Chicken
Parking Guy	Ted Barber
Peasus	Todd Wahoske
Pete Day	Top Bloke
Pooper	Wardcore
Rick Thorne	Zac ZiG Drake
Sik	

TONY HAWK'S PROJECT 8 (XBOX 360)

Enter these passwords in the Cheats menu.

UNLOCKABLE	PASSWORD
All decks unlocked and free except for inkblot deck and Gamestop deck	needaride
All specials in shop	yougotitall
Travis Barker	plus44
Grim Reaper (Freeskate)	enterandwin
Jason Lee	notmono
Anchor Man	newshound
Big Realtor	shescaresme
Christian Hosoi	hohohosoi
Colonel and Security Guard	militarymen
Inkblot Deck	birdhouse
Kevin Staab	mixitup
Nerd	wearelosers
Photographer Girl and Filmer	themedia
Zombie	suckstobedead
Dad and Skater Jam Kid	strangefellows

TONY HAWK'S PROJECT 8 (PlayStation 3)

In the Options menu, select Cheats to enter these passwords.

UNLOCKABLE	PASSWORD
Big Realtor	shescaresme
Christian Hosoi	hohohosoi
Colonel and Security Guard	militarymen
Dad and Skater Jam Kid	strangefellows
Full Air Stats	drinkup
Grim Reaper	enterandwin
Inkblot Deck	birdhouse
Jason Lee	notmono
Kevin Staab	mixitup
Mascot	manineedadate
Most Decks	needaride
Nerd	wearelosers
Photographer and Cameraman	themedia
Travis Barker	plus44
Unlock Specials in Skate Shop	yougotitall

TONY HAWK'S PROJECT 8 (XBOX)

In the Options menu, select Cheats to enter these passwords.

UNLOCKABLE	PASSWORD
Big Realtor	shescaresme
Christian Hosoi	hohohosoi
Colonel and Security Guard	militarymen
Dad and Skater Jam Kid	strangefellows
Full Air Stats	drinkup
Grim Reaper	enterandwin
Inkblot Deck	birdhouse
Jason Lee	notmono
Kevin Staab	mixitup
Mascot	manineedadate
Most Decks	needaride
Nerd	wearelosers
Photographer and Cameraman	themedia
Travis Barker	plus44
Unlock Specials in Skate Shop	yougotitall

TONY HAWK'S PROJECT 8 (PlayStation 2)

In the Options menu, select Cheats to enter these passwords.

UNLOCKABLE	PASSWORD
Big Realtor	shescaresme
Christian Hosoi	hohohosoi
Colonel and Security Guard	militarymen
Dad and Skater Jam Kid	strangefellows
Full Air Stats	drinkup
Grim Reaper	enterandwin
Inkblot Deck	birdhouse
Jason Lee	notmono
Kevin Staab	mixitup
Mascot	manineedadate
Most Decks	needaride
Nerd	wearelosers
Photographer and Cameraman	themedia
Travis Barker	plus44
Unlock Specials in Skate Shop	yougotitall

TONY HAWK'S PROVING GROUND (XBOX 360)

CHEATS Enter the codes in the Options menu of the main menu.

UNLOCKABLE	HOW TO UNLOCK
100% Branch Completion (NTT)	FOREVERNAILED
Invisible Man	THEMISSING
Mini Skater	TINYTATER
No Bails	ANDAINTFALLIN
No Board	MAGICMAN
Perfect Manual	STILLAINTFALLIN
Perfect Rail	AINTFALLIN
Super Check	BOOYAH
Unlimited Focus	MYOPIC

Unlimited Slash Grind	SUPERSLASHIN
Unlock Judy Nails	LOVEROCKNROLL

ITEMS

UNLOCKABLE	HOW TO UNLOCK
50 Extra Skill Points	NEEDSHELP
All CAS Items	GIVEMESTUFF
All Decks	LETSGOSKATE

SKATERS

UNLOCKABLE	HOW TO UNLOCK
All Fun Items	OVERTHETOP
All Game Movies	WATCHTHIS
All Lounge Bling Items	SWEETSTUFF
All Lounge Themes	LAIDBACKLOUNGE
All Rigger Pieces	IMGONNABUILD
All Special Tricks Available	LOTSOFTRICKS
All Video Editor Effects	TRIPPY
All Video Editor Overlays	PUTEMONTOP
Full Stats	BEEFEDUP

LEVELS

UNLOCKABLE	HOW TO UNLOCK
Unlock Air and Space Museum	THEINDOORPARK
Unlock FDR	THEPREZPARK
Unlock Lansdowne	THELOCALPARK
Boneman	CRAZYBONEMAN
Bosco	MOREMILK
Cam	NOTACAMERA
Cooper	THECOOP
Eddie X	SKETCHY
El Patinador	PILEDRIVER
Eric	FLYAWAY
Mad Dog	RABBIES
MCA	INTERGALACTIC
Mel	NOTADUDE
Rube	LOOKSSMELLY
Shayne	MOVERS
Spence	DAPPER
TV Producer	SHAKER

ACHIEVEMENTS

UNLOCKABLE	HOW TO UNLOCK
1,000 Online Games Played (20)	Accumulate 1,000 games played.
5 out of 5! Online Domination (20)	Win all five rounds in a match with at least four gamertags in the room.
Aggro Episode (10)	Mike V's Go Epic episode completed.
All Classic (10)	Complete all Classic goals at AM ranking or better.
All Film Goals (10)	Complete all Film goals at AM ranking or better.
All Gaps (50)	Find all the Gaps on the View Gaps list.
All Hawk-man (10)	Complete all Hawk-man goals at AM ranking or better.
All Line Goals (10)	Complete all Line goals at AM ranking or better.

UNLOCKABLE	HOW TO UNLOCK
All Photo Goals (10)	Complete all Photo goals at AM ranking or better.
All Pro (70)	Complete all goals at PRO ranking or better.
All Skater Items (20)	Purchase all Skater Gear including unlocked items.
All Skill Goals (10)	Complete all Skill Challenges at AM ranking or better.
All Skill Upgrades (10)	Upgrade all skater skills.
All Uber Goals (20)	Complete all Lifestyle Uber Goals.
AM All Goals (40)	Complete all goals at AM ranking or better.
Bowl Skating Episode (25)	Lance's Bowl Skating episode completed.
Build Your Team (10)	Achieved "Build Your Team" Game Milestone.
Cashtastic (40)	Find all cash spots.
Climbing Episode (15)	Bam's Climbing episode completed.
Complete All Hawk-man Goals Pro (15)	Complete all Hawk-man Goals at PRO ranking or better.
Deck Milestone (10)	Achieve "Get your own skate deck" Milestone.
High Score Video (10)	Make a video worth 20,000 points.
Join Team Milestone (30)	Achieved the "Join Team" Game Milestone.
Mod All Spots (35)	Modify all environment areas.
Mod the World (25)	Daewon and Rodney's Modify the World episode completed.
NTG Episode (15)	Bob's Nail the Grab episode completed.
NTM Episode (25)	Stevie's Nail the Manual episode completed.
NTT Episode (10)	Arto's Nail the Trick episode completed.
Pro All Classic (15)	Complete all Classic goals at PRO ranking or better.
Pro All Film Goals (15)	Complete all Film goals at PRO ranking or better.
Pro All Line Goals (15)	Complete all Line goals at PRO ranking or better.
Pro All Photo Goals (15)	Complete all Photo goals at PRO ranking or better.
Pro All Skill Goals (15)	Complete all Skill Challenges at PRO ranking or better.
Rigging Episode (10)	Jeff's Rigging episode completed.
Shoe Milestone (10)	Achieve "Get your own skate shoe" Game Milestone.
Sick All Classic (40)	Complete all Classic goals at SICK.
Sick All Film Goals (40)	Completed all Film Goals at SICK.
Sick All Hawk-man (40)	Complete all Hawk-man Goals at SICK.
Sick All Line Goals (40)	Complete all Line goals at SICK.
Sick All Photo Goals (40)	Complete all Photo goals at SICK.
Sick All Skill Goals (40)	Completed all Skill Challenges at SICK.
Skate Check Episode (15)	Dustin's Skate Checking episode completed.
Sponsored Milestone (15)	Achieve the "Sponsored" Game Milestone progress.
Team Built (20)	Achieved "Team Built" Game Milestone.
Thug Check Distance (5)	Knock Thug 150 feet.
Win $100,000 in Wagers Online (25)	Win enough wagers to accumulate $100,000 in winnings. Ranked matches only.

TONY HAWK'S PROVING GROUND (PlayStation 3)

CHEATS

Enter the codes in the options menu of the main menu

UNLOCKABLE	HOW TO UNLOCK
100% Branch Completion (NTT)	FOREVERNAILED
Invisible Man	THEMISSING
Mini Skater	TINYTATER

No Bails	ANDAINTFALLIN
No Board	MAGICMAN
Perfect Manual	STILLAINTFALLIN
Perfect Rail	AINTFALLIN
Super Check	BOOYAH
Unlimited Focus	MYOPIC
Unlimited Slash Grind	SUPERSLASHIN
Unlock Judy Nails	LOVEROCKNROLL

ITEMS

UNLOCKABLE	HOW TO UNLOCK
50 Extra Skill Points	NEEDSHELP
All CAS Items	GIVEMESTUFF
All Decks	LETSGOSKATE
All Fun Items	OVERTHETOP
All Game Movies	WATCHTHIS
All Lounge Bling Items	SWEETSTUFF
All Lounge Themes	LAIDBACKLOUNGE
All Rigger Pieces	IMGONNABUILD
All Special Tricks Available	LOTSOFTRICKS
All Video Editor Effects	TRIPPY
All Video Editor Overlays	PUTEMONTOP
Full Stats	BEEFEDUP

LEVELS

UNLOCKABLE	HOW TO UNLOCK
Unlock Air & Space Museum	THEINDOORPARK
Unlock FDR	THEPREZPARK
Unlock Lansdowne	THELOCALPARK

SKATERS

UNLOCKABLE	HOW TO UNLOCK
Boneman	CRAZYBONEMAN
Bosco	MOREMILK
Cam	NOTACAMERA
Cooper	THECOOP
Eddie X	SKETCHY
El Patinador	PILEDRIVER
Eric	FLYAWAY
Mad Dog	RABBIES
MCA	INTERGALACTIC
Mel	NOTADUDE
Rube	LOOKSSMELLY
Shayne	MOVERS
Spence	DAPPER
TV Producer	SHAKER

TONY HAWK'S PROVING GROUND (Wii)

ITEMS

UNLOCKABLE	HOW TO UNLOCK
50 Extra Skill Points	NEEDSHELP
All CAS Items	GIVEMESTUFF
All Decks	LETSGOSKATE

UNLOCKABLE	HOW TO UNLOCK
All Fun Items	OVERTHETOP
All Game Movies	WATCHTHIS
All Rigger Pieces	IMGONNABUILD
All Special Tricks Available	LOTSOFTRICKS
Full Stats	BEEFEDUP

LEVELS

UNLOCKABLE	HOW TO UNLOCK
Unlock Air and Space Museum	THEINDOORPARK
Unlock FDR	THEPREZPARK
Unlock Lansdowne	THELOCALPARK

SKATERS

UNLOCKABLE	HOW TO UNLOCK
Boneman	CRAZYBONEMAN
Bosco	MOREMILK
Cam	NOTACAMERA
Cooper	THECOOP
Eddie X	SKETCHY
El Patinador	PILEDRIVER
Eric	FLYAWAY
Mad Dog	RABBIES
MCA	INTERGALACTIC
Mel	NOTADUDE
Rube	LOOKSSMELLY
Shayne	MOVERS
Spence	DAPPER
TV Producer	SHAKER

TONY HAWK'S PROVING GROUND (DS)

CHEATS

Enter the codes in the Options menu of the main menu.

UNLOCKABLE	HOW TO UNLOCK
100% Branch Completion (NTT)	FOREVERNAILED
Invisible Man	THEMISSING
Mini Skater	TINYTATER
No Bails	ANDAINTFALLIN
No Board	MAGICMAN
Perfect Manual	STILLAINTFALLIN
Perfect Rail	AINTFALLIN
Super Check	BOOYAH
Unlimited Focus	MYOPIC
Unlimited Slash Grind	SUPERSLASHIN
Unlock Judy Nails	LOVEROCKNROLL

ITEMS

UNLOCKABLE	HOW TO UNLOCK
50 Extra Skill Points	NEEDSHELP
All CAS Items	GIVEMESTUFF
All Decks	LETSGOSKATE
All Fun Items	OVERTHETOP
All Game Movies	WATCHTHIS

All Lounge Bling Items	SWEETSTUFF
All Lounge Themes	LAIDBACKLOUNGE
All Rigger Pieces	IMGONNABUILD
All Special Tricks Available	LOTSOFTRICKS
All Video Editor Effects	TRIPPY
All Video Editor Overlays	PUTEMONTOP
Full Stats	BEEFEDUP

LEVELS

UNLOCKABLE	HOW TO UNLOCK
Unlock Air & Space Museum	THEINDOORPARK
Unlock FDR	THEPREZPARK
Unlock Lansdowne	THELOCALPARK

SKATERS

UNLOCKABLE	HOW TO UNLOCK
Boneman	CRAZYBONEMAN
Bosco	MOREMILK
Cam	NOTACAMERA
Cooper	THECOOP
Eddie X	SKETCHY
El Patinador	PILEDRIVER
Eric	FLYAWAY
Mad Dog	RABBIES
MCA	INTERGALACTIC
Mel	NOTADUDE
Rube	LOOKSSMELLY
Shayne	MOVERS
Spence	DAPPER
TV Producer	SHAKER

TONY HAWK'S PROVING GROUND (PlayStation 2)

CHEATS

Enter the codes in the Options menu of the main menu.

UNLOCKABLE	HOW TO UNLOCK
100% Branch Completion (NTT)	FOREVERNAILED
Invisible Man	THEMISSING
Mini Skater	TINYTATER
No Bails	ANDAINTFALLIN
No Board	MAGICMAN
Perfect Manual	STILLAINTFALLIN
Perfect Rail	AINTFALLIN
Super Check	BOOYAH
Unlimited Focus	MYOPIC
Unlimited Slash Grind	SUPERSLASHIN
Unlock Judy Nails	LOVEROCKNROLL

ITEMS

UNLOCKABLE	HOW TO UNLOCK
50 Extra Skill Points	NEEDSHELP
All CAS Items	GIVEMESTUFF
All Decks	LETSGOSKATE
All Fun Items	OVERTHETOP

UNLOCKABLE	HOW TO UNLOCK
All Game Movies	WATCHTHIS
All Lounge Bling Items	SWEETSTUFF
All Lounge Themes	LAIDBACKLOUNGE
All Rigger Pieces	IMGONNABUILD
All Special Tricks Available	LOTSOFTRICKS
All Video Editor Effects	TRIPPY
All Video Editor Overlays	PUTEMONTOP
Full Stats	BEEFEDUP

LEVELS

UNLOCKABLE	HOW TO UNLOCK
Unlock Air & Space Museum	THEINDOORPARK
Unlock FDR	THEPREZPARK
Unlock Lansdowne	THELOCALPARK

SKATERS

UNLOCKABLE	HOW TO UNLOCK
Boneman	CRAZYBONEMAN
Bosco	MOREMILK
Cam	NOTACAMERA
Cooper	THECOOP
Eddie X	SKETCHY
El Patinador	PILEDRIVER
Eric	FLYAWAY
Mad Dog	RABBIES
MCA	INTERGALACTIC
Mel	NOTADUDE
Rube	LOOKSSMELLY
Shayne	MOVERS
Spence	DAPPER
TV Producer	SHAKER

TONY HAWK'S UNDERGROUND (XBOX)

UNLOCKABLE	CODE
Moon Gravity	getitup
Perfect Manuals	keepitsteady
Perfect Rails	letitslide

TONY HAWK'S UNDERGROUND (PlayStation 2)

From the Options menu, choose "Cheat Codes" and enter the following:

UNLOCKABLE	CODE
All Thug Movies	digivid
Moon Gravity	getitup
Perfect Manual	keepitsteady
Perfect Rail	letitslide
Perfect Skitch	rearrider

From the Options menu, choose "Cheat Codes" and enter the following:

1337

Akira2s

Alan Flores

Alex Garcia

Andy Marchel

arrr

Bailey

Big Tex

Chauwa Steel

Chris Rausch

ChrisP

CodePirate

crom

Daddy Mac

Dan Nelson

Dave Stohl

DDT

From the Options menu, choose "Cheat Codes" and enter the following:

deadendroad

fatass

FROGHAM

GEIGER

Glycerin

GMIAB

Greenie

grjost

Guilt Ladle

Hammer

Henry Ji

Jason Uyeda

Jeremy Andersen

Joel Jewett

Johnny Ow

leedsleedsleeds

MARCOS XK8R

Mike Ward

moreuberthaned

M'YAK

Noly

NSJEFF

POOPER

sik®

Skillzombie

Stacey D

Steal2Liv

tao zheng

The Kraken

The Swink

THEDOC

Todd Wahoske

TOPBLOKE

TSUEnami! (

woodchuck
Y2KJ
Yawgurt
ZiG

TONY HAWK'S UNDERGROUND 2 (XBOX)

To enter these codes, select Cheats in the Options menu.

UNLOCKABLE	CODE
Paulie Ryan	4wheeler
Perfect Rails	straightedge

TONY HAWK'S UNDERGROUND 2 (PlayStation 2)

Go to Cheat Codes and enter the following:

UNLOCKABLE	CODE
All Levels	d3struct
All Movies	boxoffice
Always Special	likepaulie
Bonus Characters	costars
Infinite Rail	straightedge
Natas Kaupas	oldskool
Nigel Beaverhausen	sellout
Paulie	4-wheeler
Phil Margera	aprilsman

TONY HAWK'S UNDERGROUND 2 REMIX (PSP)

Go to Game Options, then Cheat Codes and enter the following codes.

UNLOCKABLE	CODE
Perfect Rail Balance	Tightrope
Unlock Tony Hawk from Tony Hawk Pro Skater 1	Birdman

TOUCH THE DEAD (DS)

CODES

Enter the following code at the main menu. A zombie will moan if you enter the code successfully and the Logo Screen will turn red. After that you will have access to all missions, all modes, and all bonuses. You will also be able to use the L and R shoulder buttons to switch to the next/previous camera.

EFFECT	CODE
Unlocks everything, allows camera switching	X, Y, →, ←, X

TOWER OF DRUAGA (Wii)

CODES

Enter this code at the title screen. If entered properly, the word "DRUAGA" will turn green. The game is now harder and the levels require different solutions.

CODE	EFFECT
↑, ↑, ↑, ↑, ↑, ↑, ←, ←, ←, ←, →, →, ↓	Another Druaga (Second Quest)

TRANSFORMERS: REVENGE OF THE FALLEN (XBOX 360)

CODES

Enter with the D-Pad in the "Cheat Codes" option in the Main menu. Note: These characters will only be playable in multiplayer.

EFFECT	CODE
Always in Overdrive Mode	LB, B, LB, A, X, R3
Extra Energon (ex: 4x from defeated enemies)	Y, X, B, R3, A, Y
Golden Megatron	↓, ↑, →, →, ←, ↑
Golden Optimus Prime	↑, ↓, ←, ←, →, ↓

Increased Enemy Accuracy	Y,Y,B,A,X,LB
Increased Enemy Damage	LB,Y,A,Y,R3,R3
Increased Enemy Health	B,X,LB,B,R3,Y
Increased Weapon Damage in Root Form	Y,Y,R3,A,LB,Y
Increased Weapon Damage in Vehicle Form	Y,B,RB,X,R3,L3
Invincibility	R3,A,X,L3,X,X
Lower Enemy Accuracy	X,L3,R3,L3,R3,RB
Melee Instant Kills	R3,A,LB,B,R3,LB
No Special Cool Down Time	R3,X,R3,R3,X,A
No Weapon Overheat	L3,X,A,L3,Y,LB
Play as Autobot Protectobot Scout MP in Autobot-based Single-player (only when mission begins, not in character select) Does not work in Deep 6.	R3,LB,LB,Y,X,A
Plays as Decepticon Seeker Warrior MP in Decepticon-based Single-player (only when mission begins, not in character select)	X,Y,X,LB,A,LB
Special Kills Only Mode (Cannot kill enemies except with special kills)	B,B,RB,B,A,L3
Unlimited Turbo	B,L3,X,R3,A,Y
Unlock all Cairo Missions and Zones	R3,Y,A,Y,L3,LB
Unlock All Deep Six Missions and Zones	X,RB,Y,B,A,LB
Unlock All East Coast Missions and Zones	R3,L3,RB,A,B,X
Unlock All Shanghai Missions and Zones	Y,L3,R3,LB,Y,A
Unlock All West Coast Missions and Zones	LB,RB,R3,Y,R3,B
Unlock and activate ALL Upgrades	LB,Y,LB B,X,X
Unlocks Generation 1 Starscream	B,A,B,RB,Y,RB

TRANSFORMERS: REVENGE OF THE FALLEN (PlayStation 3)

CODES

From the Main Menu go to Cheat Codes and enter the codes there.

EFFECT	CODE
Always in Overdrive Mode	L1,●,L1,×,■,R3
Extra Energon (ex: 4x from defeated enemies)	▲,■,●,R3,×,▲
G1 Colors Ironhide (single-player only)	L1,R1,R1,×,●,▲
G1 Starscream	●,×,●,R1,▲,R1
Gold Megatron	↓,↑,→,→,←,↑
Gold Optimus Prime	↑,↓,←,←,→,↓
Increased Enemy Accuracy	▲,▲,●,×,■,L1
Increased Enemy Damage	L1,▲,×,▲,R3,R3
Increased Enemy Health	●,■,L1,●,R3,▲
Increased Weapon Damage in Robot Form	▲,▲,R3,×,L1,▲
Increased Weapon Damage in Vehicle Form	▲,●,R1,■,R3,L3
Invincibility	R3,×,■,L3,■,■
Lower Enemy Accuracy	■,L3,R3,L3,R3,R1
Melee Instant Kills	R3,×,L1,●,B,L1
No Special Cooldown Time	R3,■,R3,R3,■,×
No Weapon Overheat	L3,■,×,L3,▲,L3
Play as Autobot Protectobot Scout MP in Autobot-based single-player (only when mission begins, not in character select) Does not work in Deep 6.	R3,L1,L1,▲,■,×

Plays as Decepticon Seeker Warrior MP in Decepticon-Based single-player (only when mission begins, not in character select)	■,▲,■,L1,×,L1
Special Kills Only Mode (Cannot kill enemies except with special kills)	●,●,R1,●,×,L3
Unlimited Turbo	●,L3,■,×,▲
Unlock all Cairo Missions and Zones	R3,▲,×,▲,L3,L1
Unlock All Deep Six Missions and Zones	■,R1,▲,●,×,L1
Unlock All East Coast Missions and Zones	R3,L3,R1,×,●,■
Unlock All Shanghai Missions and Zones	▲,L3,R3,L1,▲,×
Unlock All West Coast Missions and Zones	L1,R1,R3,▲,R3,●
Unlock and activate ALL Upgrades	L1,▲,L1,●,■,■

TRANSFORMERS: THE GAME (XBOX 360)

CODES

Enter codes at the "Campaign/Bonus Features" main menu. Enter codes for each character during one of their missions. This changes the character's appearance to their Generation 1 skin. Note: Using these cheats prevents you from achieving gamerscore!

CODE	EFFECT
↓,←,←,↓,→,→,↑	Generation 1 Skin Megatron
↑,→,←,↑,↓,↓,←	Generation 1 Skin Prime
←,↑,↓,↓,←,↑,→	Generation 1 Skin Jazz
↓,↓,↑,↑,→,→,→	Generation 1 Skin Optimus Prime
→,↓,←,←,↓,↑,↑	Generation 1 Skin Starscream
←,←,↑,←,→,↓,→	Infinite Health—Invincible
↑,↓,←,→,↑,↑,↓	No Ammo Reload
→,←,→,←,→,←,→	No Military or Police
↓,↑,←,→,→,→,↑,↓	Unlock All mission including 2 special mission
→,↑,↑,↓,→,←,←	Unlocks the two Cybertron missions.

UNLOCKABLES

UNLOCKABLE	HOW TO UNLOCK
G1 Megatron	Collect all the Transformer Shields in the Decepticons Story mode
G1 Optimus Prime (Cartoon Model)	Find all the Autobot faction symbols during the Autobot campaign.
G1 Robo-vision Optimus	Finish the Autobot campaign.
Jazz G1 Repaint	Complete all of the "challenge" sub-missions in both Autobot and Decepticon campaigns.
Starscream G1 repaint	Complete Decepticon Story mode.

TRANSFORMERS: THE GAME (Wii)

CODES

Enter the following codes at the Campaign/Bonus Features/Credits menu.

CODE	EFFECT
↓,↑,←,→,→,→,↑,↓	Unlock all missions
←,←,↑,←,→,↓,↓	Infinite health—invincible
→,←,→,←,→,←,↓	No vehicles running on the street and no tanks/cops attack
→,↑,↑,↓,→,←,←	Unlock Cybertron missions
↓,→,←,↑,↓,↓,←	Unlock G1 Optimus Prime
←,↑,↓,↓,←,↑,↓	Unlock Generation 1 Jazz Repaint

→, ↓, ←, ←, ↓, ↑, ↑	Unlock Generation 1 Starscream Repaint
↓, ↓, ↑, ↑, →, →, ↓	Unlock Robovision Optimus Prime
↓, ←, ←, ↓, →, →, ↑	Unlock G1 Megatron

UNLOCKABLES

UNLOCKABLE	HOW TO UNLOCK
G1 Jazz Repaint	Clear all sub-missions in Autobot and Decepticon Story modes
G1 Megatron	Collect all of the Decepticon icons on all of the maps
G1 Optimus Prime	Collect all of the Autobot Icons on all of the maps
G1 Starscream Repaint	Beat the Decepticon's Story mode
Robovision Optimus Prime	Beat the Autobot's Story mode

TRAUMA CENTER: SECOND OPINION (Wii)

UNLOCKABLE	HOW TO UNLOCK
X Missions for both doctors	Once unlocked, the first X mission will be available to both doctors. If you complete an X mission with one doctor, the next mission will be available to both doctors.
Episode 6	Complete all operations in episodes 1-5 and Z to unlock episode 6.

TRIGGERHEART EXELICA (XBOX 360)

GAMER PICTURES

Gamer Pictures can be unlocked by doing the following.

UNLOCKABLE	HOW TO UNLOCK
Crueltear	Begin the story as Crueltear.
Exelica	Begin the story as Exelica.

TRUE CRIME: NEW YORK CITY (XBOX)

While on the Compstat/Map, hold LT+RT and enter these codes.

UNLOCKABLE	CODE
A Million Dollars	X, X, Y, X, Y, X
Double Damage	A, A, X, A, A, A
Redman Gone Wild Mini Game	Y, A, A, X, A, X
Super Cop	Y, A, Y, A, Y, Y
Ultra Easy Mode	B, X, A, A, Y, B
Unlimited Ammo	B, X, A, X, X, Y
Unlimited Endurance	B, X, A, X, A, B

TRUE CRIME: NEW YORK CITY (PlayStation 2)

While on the Compstat/Map, hold L1+R1 and enter these codes.

UNLOCKABLE	CODE
A Million Dollars	■, ■, ▲, ■, ▲, ■
Double Damage	×, ×, ■, ×, ×, ×
Redman Gone Wild Mini-Game	▲, ×, ×, ●, ▲, ■
Super Cop	▲, ×, ▲, ×, ▲, ▲
Ultra Easy Mode	●, ■, ×, ×, ▲, ●
Unlimited Ammo	●, ■, ×, ■, ■, ▲
Unlimited Endurance	●, ■, ×, ■, ×, ●

TRUE CRIME: STREETS OF LA (XBOX)

Enter the following codes on the Map screen.

UNLOCKABLE	CODE
All Driving skills	←, →, ←, →, A
All Gunplay Skills	→, ←, →, ←, A
All Fighting Skills	↑, ↓, ↑, ↓, A

TRUE CRIME: STREETS OF LA (PlayStation 2)

Enter the following codes at the City Map screen:

UNLOCKABLE	CODE
All Driving Upgrades	←,→,←,→,×
All Fighting Moves	↑,↓,↑,↓,×
All Gun Upgrades	→,←,→,←,×
Bigger Vehicle	↓,↓,↓,×
Nick Kang's Location	×,●,■,▲
Smaller Vehicle	↑,↑,↑,×

Go to Create a License Plate and try the following codes:

UNLOCKABLE	CODE
Asian Worker	HARA
Bartender	HAWG
Bum	B00Z
Chief, The	B1G1
Commando	M1K3
Dirty Morales	BRUZ
Donkey	JASS
Gangsta	TFAN
George	FATT
Jimmy Fu	MRFU
Lola Gees	B00B
Pimp	PIMP
Policeman	FUZZ
Rose in Lingerie	HURT M3
Rosie	ROSA
Sewer Ghoul	J1MM
Street Punk	MNKY
SWAT Officer	5WAT
Tattoo Concubines	TATS
Triad Butcher	PHAM

TURNING POINT: FALL OF LIBERTY (XBOX 360)

ACHIEVEMENTS

UNLOCKABLE	HOW TO UNLOCK
Clingy (25)	Kill 15 enemies in a row by grappling them on any difficulty.
Combat Experience (10)	Kill 50 enemies in the campaign on any difficulty.
Combat Veteran (25)	Kill 250 enemies in the campaign on any difficulty.
Dead-eye (50)	Complete any mission with an accuracy of 80% or higher on Normal or higher difficulty.
Defender (20)	Help defend the barricade in New York on Normal or higher difficulty.
Dolly Madison Award (20)	Save the Constitution from being burned on Normal or higher difficulty.
Environmentalism (15)	Complete 40 environmental or grapple kills on any difficulty.
Exploding Monkey (20)	Kill at least four enemies with one explosion on any difficulty.
First Time for Everything (5)	Finish a multiplayer game.
Going Nuclear (30)	Rewire an Atom Bomb on Normal or Higher difficulty.
Gravity Is a Harsh Mistress (5)	Toss a paratrooper onto the streets below New York on any difficulty.

I Saved the General (20)	Rescue General Donnelly from the D.C. courthouse on Normal or higher difficulty.
Impeached (30)	Oust the false president from office on any difficulty.
Killer (20)	Get 100 ranked match kills in any mode.
Killer Instinct (30)	Get 500 ranked match kills in any mode.
Master Sniper (35)	Kill 10 enemies in a row with a headshot on any difficulty.
Maybe I Should Go Outside... (40)	Get 2,500 ranked match kills in any mode.
MVP (30)	Win an 8-player ranked or player match in Team Deathmatch mode with the highest score.
Need a Ride? (20)	Meet up with the rescue team in Washington, D.C. on Normal or higher difficulty.
Next Time Take the Stairs (5)	Fall to your death during a multiplayer game.
Oh, the Humanity! (30)	Destroy all the assault blimps at the Tower Bridge on any difficulty.
One in the Chamber (10)	Kill a player in a ranked match with the last bullet in a pistol clip.
One Man Army (45)	Kill 400 enemies in the campaign on any difficulty.
Presidential Citizens Medal (75)	Complete the campaign on Hard difficulty.
Presidential Medal for Merit (35)	Complete the campaign on Normal difficulty.
Presidential Medal of Freedom (100)	Complete the game on Insane Difficulty.
pwnt (15)	Finish an 8-player ranked or player match in Deathmatch mode with the highest number of kills.
Reservation for One (5)	Make your way down to Hotel Langteau on Normal or higher difficulty.
Run! (25)	Sprint for a total of 30 minutes throughout the campaign on any difficulty.
Save Yourself (25)	Escape from New York on any difficulty.
Sharpshooter (10)	Kill all the paratroopers as you make your way down the skyscraper on any difficulty.
Stayin' Alive (25)	Finish a ranked match in Deathmatch mode without dying.
Stowaway (30)	Sneak onto the zeppelin on Normal or higher difficulty.
Swirly Time! (5)	Drown a German in a toilet in the Tower of London on any difficulty.
Team Player (25)	Win 20 ranked matches in Team Deathmatch mode.
Turning Point (25)	Complete the campaign on any difficulty.
TV Repairs (5)	Smash an enemy's head through a TV in the White House on any difficulty.
Uberdork (25)	Win 5 ranked matches in Deathmatch mode.
World Tour (15)	Finish a multiplayer game on every map in every mode.

BONUS CODES

UNLOCKABLE	HOW TO UNLOCK
Double Health Regeneration Rate	Complete the game on any difficulty.
Infinite Ammo	Complete the game on any difficulty.
Infinite Grenades	Complete the game on any difficulty.

TUROK (XBOX 360)

ACHIEVEMENTS

UNLOCKABLE	HOW TO UNLOCK
5, 4, 3, 2, 1...BOOM! (15G)	Kill 3 soldiers with one Frag Grenade in the Story mode campaign.
Accuracy Award (20G)	Achieve an accuracy of 75 percent or greater with at least 20 shots fired in one ranked match.
All-Purpose Warrior (30G)	Win 10 public games of each team game option (Small Team, Large Team, Co-Op).
Angler Ribbon (20G)	Fishing anyone?
Arch-Nemesis (15G)	Kill the same player five times in a row without killing anyone else between during a public match.
Arsenal (20G)	Kill at least one enemy with every weapon in the game during public play.
Big Game Ribbon (20G)	You managed to survive Mama Scarface.
Boomstick (10G)	Destroy a dino with the stickygun during a public match.
Buddy Blowout (20G)	Play a full 8-on-8 private team game.
Co-Op 1 (30G)	Finish Co-op Map 1.
Co-Op 2 (30G)	Finish Co-op Map 2.
Co-Op 3 (30G)	Finish Co-op Map 3.
Crack Shot (15G)	Kill five opponents in a public game with headshots.
Dino Dominance (25G)	You skillfully knife-killed 50 creatures in the Story mode campaign.
Dino Hunter (15G)	Kill 20 dinos in one public game.
Exterminator (15G)	Kill 20 bugs in one public game.
Gamesman (15G)	Play a full round of each gametype in public or private matches.
Grab Bag (10G)	Kill at least one creature, one enemy, one teammate, and yourself in the same round of a public match. (Patched 1/08 to eliminate the teammate kill requirement.)
Great Round (15G)	Finish a public DM match with a Battle Rating of greater than 100.
Hometown Hero (25G)	Return five flags to your base in one public game.
Impaler Ribbon (10G)	Pin an enemy to the wall with an arrow in the Story mode campaign.
It's a Trap! (15G)	Get dinos to kill five soldiers by sticking them with the flare in the Story mode campaign.
Loud Love (15G)	Kill three soldiers with one ORO Copperhead Rocket Launcher shot in the Story mode campaign.
Man or Animal (30G)	Record 100 stealth kills of soldiers with the ORO P23 Combat Knife.
Massive Battle (10G)	Participate in a public 6-on-6 team game.
Medal of Citation (50G)	Achieve 100 player kills in ranked matches.
Multiplayer First-Class (35G)	Finish a ranked match with 100 percent accuracy and at least five kills.
Multiplayer Master-Class (40G)	Finish a ranked match with all headshots and at least five kills.
Pacifist (15G)	Play a public match with no shots fired or kills awarded, capturing the flag at least twice.
Pincushion (25G)	Pin 50 enemies with the bow in the Story mode campaign.
Practically Canadian (20G)	How aboot defending your flag, eh? And that's in ranked matches, sorry.
Primitive Weapons (15G)	Play a public match using only the bow or knife, earning at least 10 kills.

Resurrection (15G)	Finish a player match free-for-all game with at least 10 deaths and 10 kills.
Retribution (15G)	Knife-kill your rival in a public match.
Sell Your Shotguns (35G)	Just for fun, you completed "Mother Superior" without using the ORO Shotgun.
Sniper! (40G)	Head shot 10 enemies in a row during the Story mode campaign.
Thorn in Side (20G)	Kill the flag carrier five times in a ranked match.
Triple Kill (20G)	Kill three opponents within four seconds of each other in a ranked match.
Turok Campaign Ribbon (60G)	Complete the Story mode campaign on Inhuman difficulty.
Turok Defense Force (25G)	Successfully fight off 20 raptor mauls during the Story mode campaign.
Turok Service Ribbon (40G)	Complete the Story mode campaign and unlock Inhuman difficulty.
Unbreakable (30G)	Play through a ranked match without dying.

INHUMAN MODE

UNLOCKABLE	HOW TO UNLOCK
Inhuman Mode	Beat the game on Normal or Hard difficulty.

TUROK: EVOLUTION (XBOX)

Go to the Cheats menu and enter the following codes.

UNLOCKABLE	CODE
All Cheats	FMNFB
All Weapons	TEXAS
Big Head Mode	HEID
Demo Mode/Mini-Game	HUNTER
Invincible	EMERPUS
Invisible	SLLEWGH
Level Select	SELLOUT
Opens All Codes	FMNFB
Unlimited Ammo	MADMAN
Zoo Level	ZOO

TUROK: EVOLUTION (PlayStation 2)

Enter the following codes at the Cheat menu.

UNLOCKABLE	CODE
All Available Weapons	TEXAS
Big Head Mode	HEID
Demo Mode and Target Mini-Game	HUNTER
Invincibility	EMERPUS
Invisibility	SLLEWGH
Level Select	SELLOUT—after entering, load a saved game to unlock all levels.
Master Code	FMNFB
Unlimited Ammunition	MADMAN
Zoo Mode	ZOO—you can now kill any animal in the game with the war club as a weapon.

THERE ARE TWO PARTS TO THE "DEMO MODE AND TARGET MINI-GAME" CODE. BESIDES STARTING DEMO MODE, YOU CAN ALSO PLAY THE TARGET MINIGAME AT THE MAIN TITLE SCREEN. USE THE D-PAD TO MOVE THE POINTER AND FIRE TO SHOOT.

To access the following unlockables, pause gameplay, hold L1, then enter code. A message confirms correct code entry. Repeat the code to disable its effect.

UNLOCKABLE	CODE
Invincible NPCs	■,●,▲,×,■,●,▲,×
Unlimited Ammunition	←,●,→,■,↑,▲,↓,×
Unlimited Health	▲,■,▲,■,▲,●,▲,●
Unlimited Rage	←,↓,←,↓,→,↑,→,↑

TWISTED METAL: BLACK (PlayStation 2)

UNLOCKABLE	CODE
Change Camera	To change the camera angle, press and hold SELECT, then press ↓. To switch between horizontal and vertical, hold SELECT, then press ←.
Convert Weapons into Health	During the game, hold down all four shoulder buttons, then press ▲,×,■,●. Your weapons vanish and your health fills up a little.
Decipher Minion	To understand what Minion's numbered codes mean on the load screens (when playing as him), match the number with its corresponding letter. (A=1, B=2, and Z=26.)
Different Weapons Display	Press and hold SELECT, then press → during gameplay to change the weapons selection display.
Infinite Ammo	To have unlimited ammunition for your ride, press and hold the shoulder buttons, then press ↑,×,←,●.
Invincibility	During gameplay (this includes story mode), press and hold the shoulder buttons, then press →,←,↓,↑.
Mega Machine Guns	To enable the Mega Machine Guns feature, press and hold the shoulder buttons, then press ×,×,▲.
One Hit Kills	During gameplay, hold the shoulder buttons and quickly press ×,×,↑. At the top of the screen, a message confirms correct code entry.
Unlock God Mode	During gameplay, hold the shoulder buttons and rapidly press ↑,×,←,●. A message reading "God Mode On" appears at the top of the screen to confirm correct code entry.

TWISTED METAL HEAD ON (PSP)

Input these codes during gameplay.

UNLOCKABLE	CODE
Invulnerability	→, ←, ↓, ↑ and finally press L1 + R1
Infinite Weapons	▲, ▲, ↓, ↓, L1 + R1

TWO WORLDS (XBOX 360)

CODES

Note that Bonus codes do NOT stop you from getting achievements. But all other codes DO. To open the code menu hold down LB + RB and hit A. A small text box appears. Now hit X to open up the keyboard menu. Remember, only codes that start with "Bonuscode" will not affect your achievements. All codes other than the Bonuscodes require you to put in "twoworldscheats 1" first before entering the code. This permanently disables achievements for this character.

CODE	EFFECT
ec.dbg addskillpoints	Add skill points
AddGold XXXX	Adds gold, where XXXX is the amount of gold added
AddParamPoints	Adds Param Points, where X is the number of points added
AddSkillPoints X	Adds Skill Points, where X is the number of skill points added
AddExperiencePoints XXX	Adds XXX amounts of experience

Bonuscode 9728-1349-2105-2168	Armor of Darkness
BonusCode 9470-4690-1542-1152	Aziraal's Sword of Fire
Create Lockpick	Creates a lockpick
Create Personal_Teleport	Creates a Teleport Stone
Bonuscode 9470-6557-8820-9563	Great Shield of Yatolen
ec.dbg levelup	Level Up
ec.dbg skills	Makes all skills available
Create Teleport_Activator	Recover lost teleport activator
ResetFog	Reveal map
ec.dbg levels X	Sets you to level 'X'
Bonuscode 9144-3879-7593-9224	Spear of Destiny
Bonuscode 9447-1204-8639-0832	The Great Bow of Heaven's Fury
Jump2	Transports player to where mouse is pointing
PhysX.Door.RemoveAll 1	Walk through doors and walls

TY THE TASMANIAN TIGER (PlayStation 2)

UNLOCKABLE	CODE
Aquarang, Elemental Boomerangs, Dive, and Swim Abilities	Press L1, R1, L1, R1, ▲, ▲, ■, ■, ▲, ■ during gameplay.
Show Objects	Press L1, R1, L1, R1, ▲, ▲, ●, ■, ■, ●, R2, R2 during gameplay.
Technorangs	Press L1, R1, L1, R1, ▲, ▲, ▲, ■, ▲, ■ during gameplay.
Unlimited Health	Quickly press L1, R1, L1, R1, ▲, ▲, ▲, ▲, ●, ● when "Press Start" appears.
Unlock Gallery and Movies	Quickly press L1, R1, L1, R1, ▲, ▲, ×, ×, R2, ■, R2, ■ when "Press Start" appears.

TO UNLOCK AN ENDING BONUS, COMPLETE THE GAME WITH ALL COGS, EGGS, AND OPALS COLLECTED FOR A 100 PERCENT COMPLETION. THE ENDING BONUS INCLUDES A BONUS LEVEL, AN EXTRA FMV SEQUENCE AFTER THE ENDING CREDITS, AND THE "MOVIES" OPTION AT THE EXTRAS MENU.

AFTER YOU USE THE SHOW OBJECTS CODE, THE LOCATIONS OF HIDDEN OPALS, BILBIES, GOLDEN COGS, RAINBOW SCALES, AND THUNDER EGGS ARE SHOWN WITH COLORED LINES FROM THE SKY (OPALS AND RAINBOW SCALES WITH A GREEN LINE, GOLDEN COGS WITH A GOLD LINE, THUNDER EGGS WITH A PURPLE LINE, AND BILBIES WITH A WHITISH LINE).

TY THE TASMANIAN TIGER 2: BUSH RESCUE (XBox)

Enter these codes during gameplay.

UNLOCKABLE	CODE
100,000 Opals	START, START, Y, START, START, Y, B, A, B, A
All Bunnyip Licenses	START, START, Y, START, START, Y, X, B, X, A
All Level One Rangs	START, START, Y, START, START, Y, B, X, B, X
All Level Two Rangs	START, START, Y, START, START, Y, X, B, X, Y

UFC 2009 UNDISPUTED (XBOX 360)

UNLOCKABLE

UNLOCKABLE	HOW TO UNLOCK
Unlock Punkass	To unlock the TapOut crew member Punkass as a fighter, obtain a Sponsorship from TapOut during Career mode.
Unlock Mask	In Career mode, get 3 consecutive wins by tapout/submission. He will then be selectable in exhibition matches in the light heavyweight weight class.

UFC 2009 UNDISPUTED (PlayStation 3)

UNLOCKABLE

UNLOCKABLE	HOW TO UNLOCK
Unlock Punkass	To unlock the TapOut crew member Punkass as a fighter, obtain a Sponsorship from TapOut during Career mode.
Unlock Mask	In Career mode, get 3 consecutive wins by tapout/submission. He will then be selectable in exhibition matches in the light heavyweight weight class.

ULTIMATE MORTAL KOMBAT 3 (XBOX 360)

CODES

Enter codes at the VS screen.

CODE	EFFECT
Player 1: LPx9, BLx8, LKx7; Player 2: LPx6, BLx6, LKx6	"Hold Flippers During Casino Run" Message
Player 1: LPx7, BLx1, LKx1; Player 2: LPx3, BLx1, LKx3	"Rain Can Be Found in the Graveyard" Message
Player 1: LPx1, BLx2, LKx3; Player 2: LPx9, BLx2, LKx6	"There Is No Knowledge That Is Not Power" Message
Player 1: LKx4; Player 2: LPx4	"Whatcha Gun Do?" Message
Player 1: BLx2; Player 2: BLx2	Blocking Disabled
Player 1: LPx6, BLx8, LKx8; Player 2: LPx6, BLx8, LKx8	Dark Kombat
Player 1: LPx1, BLx2, LKx2; Player 2: LPx2, BLx2, LKx1	Display "Skunky !!" Message
Player 1: LPx4, BLx4, LKx8; Player 2: LPx8, BLx4, LKx4	Don't Jump at Me
Player 1: LPx2, BLx2, LKx7; Player 2: LPx2, BLx2, LKx7	Explosive Combat (2 on 2 only)
Player 1: LPx6, BLx8, LKx8; Player 2: LPx4, BLx2, LKx2	Fast Uppercut Recovery Enabled
Player 1: BLx9, BLx1; Player 2: LPx1, BLx9	Kombat Zone: Bell Tower
Player 1: LPx3, BLx3; Player 2: BLx3, LKx3	Kombat Zone: Jade's Desert
Player 1: LKx4; Player 2: BLx7	Kombat Zone: Kahn's Kave
Player 1: LPx8, BLx8; Player 2: LPx2, BLx2	Kombat Zone: Kahn's Tower
Player 1: LPx6; Player 2: BLx4	Kombat Zone: Kombat Temple
Player 1: BLx5; Player 2: BLx5	Kombat Zone: Noob Saibot Dorfen
Player 1: LKx2; Player 2: LKx3	Kombat Zone: River Kombat

Player 1: LPx3, BLx4, LKx3; Player 2: LPx3, BLx4, LKx3	Kombat Zone: Rooftop
Player 1: LPx9, BLx3, LKx3	Kombat Zone: Scislac Busorez
Player 1: LPx6, BLx6, LKx6; Player 2: LPx4, BLx4, LKx4	Kombat Zone: Scorpion's Lair
Player 1: LPx1, BLx2, LKx3; Player 2: LPx9, LKx1	Kombat Zone: Soul Chamber
Player 1: BLx7, LKx9; Player 2: BLx3, LKx5	Kombat Zone: Street
Player 1: LPx8, BLx8; Player 2: BLx8, LKx8	Kombat Zone: Subway
Player 1: BLx7, LKx7; Player 2: BLx2, LKx2	Kombat Zone: The Bridge
Player 1: LPx6, BLx6, LKx6; Player 2: LPx3, BLx3, LKx3	Kombat Zone: The Graveyard
Player 1: LPx8, BLx2; Player 2: BLx2, LKx8	Kombat Zone: The Pit 3
Player 1: LPx2, BLx8, LKx2; Player 2: LPx2, BLx8, LKx2	No Fear = EB Button, Skydive, Max Countdown
Player 1: LPx9, BLx8, LKx7; Player 2: LPx1, BLx2, LKx3	No Powerbars
Player 1: BLx3, LKx3	Player 1 Half Power
Player 1: LPx7, LKx7	Player 1 Quarter Power
Player 2: BLx3, LKx3	Player 2 Half Power
Player 2: LPx7, LKx7	Player 2 Quarter Power
Player 1: LPx4, BLx4, LKx4; Player 2: LPx4, BLx4, LKx4	RandPer Kombat (Method 1)
Player 1: LPx4, BLx6; Player 2: LPx4, BLx6	RandPer Kombat (Method 2)
Player 1: LPx9, BLx9, LKx9; Player 2: LPx9, BLx9, LKx9	Revision
Player 1: LPx5, BLx5; Player 2: LPx5, BLx5	See the Mortal Kombat LiveTour !!
Player 1: LPx3; Player 2: LPx3	Silent Kombat
Player 1: LPx1; Player 2: LPx1	Throwing Disabled
Player 1: LPx6, BLx4, LKx2; Player 2: LPx4, BLx6, LKx8	Two-Player Minigame of Galaga
Player 1: BLx4, LKx4; Player 2: LPx4, BLx4	Unikoriv Referri: Sans Power
Player 1: LPx4, BLx6, LKx6 Player 2: LPx4, BLx6, LKx6	Unlimited Run
Player 1: LPx9, BLx6, LKx9; Player 2: LPx1, BLx4, LKx1	Winner of this round battles Motaro
Player 1: BLx3, LKx3; Player 2: LPx5, BLx6, LKx4	Winner of this round battles Shao Kahn
Player 1: LPx2, LKx5; Player 2: LPx2, LKx5	Winner of this round battles Smoke
Player 1: LPx7, BLx6, LKx9; Player 2: LPx3, BLx4, LKx2	Winner of this round battles Noob Saibot

UNLOCK AND SAVE HIDDEN CHARACTERS

Choose Arcade mode, lose a match. Then let the timer run out. You have 10 seconds to enter the ultimate kombat code for the character, one at a time. After unlocking them in Arcade mode, get to the Character Select screen. Pause, then exit the game. You'll have them for the rest of that play session. Now, very important, when you start the game up the next time around, you need to first go to the Arcade mode. This loads the characters you unlocked. Just wait and get to the Character Select screen, then exit. Now you can play with the characters online. If you do not go to the Arcade mode first, you will erase the characters. Just load and exit, then play online.

ULTIMATE SPIDER-MAN (XBOX)

Enter these codes in the Controller Setup menu. A sound confirms a correct entry.

UNLOCKABLE	CODE
Unlock All Characters	→, ↓, →, ↓, ←, ↑, ←, →
Unlock All Comic Covers	←, ←, →, ←, ↑, ←, ←, ↓
Unlock All Concept Art	↓, ↓, ↓, ↑, ↓, ↑, ←, ←
Unlock All Landmarks	↑, →, ↓, ←, ↓, ↑, →, ←

ULTIMATE SPIDER-MAN (PlayStation 2)

Enter these codes in the Controller Setup screen.

UNLOCKABLE	CODE
All Characters	→, ↓, →, ↓, ←, ↑, ←, →
All Comic Covers	←, ←, →, ←, ↑, ←, ←, ↓
All Concept Art	↓, ↓, ↓, ↑, ↓, ↑, ←, ←
All Landmarks	↑, →, ↓, ←, ↓, ↑, →, ←

UNCHARTED: DRAKE'S FORTUNE (PlayStation 3)

DRAKE'S JERSEY

To unlock a baseball jersey for Drake, go to the Costume section of the game, and input the following code.

UNLOCKABLE	HOW TO UNLOCK
Baseball Jersey	←,→,↓,↑,▲,R1,L1,■

SECRET VIDEOS

To unlock secret videos in the Making a Cutscene section of the game, input the following codes.

UNLOCKABLE	HOW TO UNLOCK
Video for Grave Robbing	←,R2,→,↑,L2,▲,■,↓
Video for Time's Up	L1,→,■,↓,←,▲,R1,↑

CONCEPT ART

Go to the Rewards section of the game, and insert the following codes.

UNLOCKABLE	HOW TO UNLOCK
More Art	■,L1,→,←,↓,R2,▲,↑
Video	L2,→,↑,■,←,▲,R1,↓

UNCHARTED 2: AMONG THIEVES (PlayStation 3)

UNLOCKABLES

UNLOCKABLE	HOW TO UNLOCK
Crushing Difficulty	Beat the game on Hard difficulty to unlock.
Genghis Khan Villain Skin	Beat Crushing difficulty. Cost: 1,500,000
Marco Polo Hero Skin	Get the Platinum trophy. Cost: Free.

FREE IN-GAME MONEY

In Uncharted 2: Among Thieves, you'll have the option to hit the Square button when in the store to check for Uncharted: Drake's Fortune save data. If you have any save data you get cash! The cash can be used in both single-player, and multiplayer stores.

$20,000 In-Game Cash	Have a saved game of Uncharted: Drake's Fortune.
$80,000 In-Game Cash	Have a saved game of Uncharted: Drake's Fortune with the story completed at least once.

MULTIPLAYER BOOSTERS

Boosters give your character more tools to use in multiplayer. Unlock them by reaching certain levels (for the most part you unlock a booster every two levels), then purchase them from the multiplayer store. There are two different booster slots you can use.

UNLOCKABLE	HOW TO UNLOCK
Bandoleer (Booster Slot 2)	Reach Level 4; Costs $2,000
Break Up (Booster Slot 1)	Reach Level 10; Costs $11,250
Come Get Some (Booster Slot 2)	Reach Level 58; Costs $2,000,000
Deposit (Booster Slot 2)	Reach Level 40; Costs $98,250
Down the Irons (Booster Slot 1)	Reach Level 14; Costs $18,750
Evasion (Booster Slot 1)	Reach Level 50; Costs $210,000
Explosive Expert (Booster Slot 2)	Reach Level 20; Costs $32,250
Fleet Foot (Booster Slot 2)	Reach Level 16; Costs $23,250
From the Hip (Booster Slot 1)	Reach Level 6; Costs $5,000
Glass Jaw (Booster Slot 1)	Reach Level 56; Costs $1,500,000
Half Loaded (Booster Slot 2)	Reach Level 54; Costs $400,000
Hell Blazer (Booster Slot 1)	Reach Level 18; Costs $27,750
Invalid (Booster Slot 1)	Reach Level 52; Costs $350,000
Juggler (Booster Slot 1)	Reach Level 38; Costs $94,500
Keep Firing (Booster Slot 2)	Reach Level 12; Costs $14,250
Launch Man (Booster Slot 2)	Reach Level 28; Costs $58,500
Monkey Man (Booster Slot 2)	Reach Level 32; Costs $72,000
Point and Shoot (Booster Slot 1)	Reach Level 2; Costs $2,000
Rapid Hands (Booster Slot 1)	Reach Level 42; Costs $111,000
Revenge (Booster Slot 2)	Reach Level 48; Costs $134,250
Rocket Man (Booster Slot 2)	Reach Level 44; Costs $120,000
Scavenger (Booster Slot 2)	Reach Level 8; Costs $8,250
Scoped In (Booster Slot 2)	Reach Level 36; Costs $87,000
Situational Awareness (Booster Slot 1)	Reach Level 46; Costs $129,000
Sure Foot (Booster Slot 2)	Reach Level 26; Costs $52,500
Sure Shot (Booster Slot 1)	Reach Level 30; Costs $64,500
Treasure Bearer (Booster Slot 2)	Reach Level 24; Costs $43,500
Turtle (Booster Slot 1)	Reach Level 22; Costs $40,500
Veiled (Booster Slot 1)	Reach Level 51; Costs $300,000
Walk Softly (Booster Slot 1)	Reach Level 34; Costs $79,500

MULTIPLAYER SKINS

These skins that can be purchased in the multiplayer store after you reach certain levels.

UNLOCKABLE	HOW TO UNLOCK
Cameraman Jeff	Reach Level 30; Costs $100,000
Doughnut Drake	Reach Level 60; Costs $2,000,000
Genghis Khan Villain Skin	Beat Crushing Difficulty. Cost: 1,500,000
Harry Flynn	Reach Level 20; Costs $50,000
Heist Drake	Reach Level 10; Costs $20,000
Heist Flynn	Reach Level 20; Costs $50,000
Karl Schafer	Reach Level 50; Costs $1,000,000
Lieutenant Draza	Reach Level 50; Costs $1,000,000
Marco Polo Hero Skin	Get the Platinum trophy. Cost: Free.
Skelzor	Reach Level 60; Costs $2,000,000
Winter Chloe	Reach Level 20; Costs $50,000
Winter Drake	Reach Level 40; Costs $250,000
Winter Elena	Reach Level 30; Costs $100,000

UNLOCKABLE	HOW TO UNLOCK
Winter Flynn	Reach Level 30; Costs $100,000
Zoran Lazarevic	Reach Level 40; Costs $250,000
Zorskel	Reach Level 10; Costs $20,000

MULTIPLAYER TAUNTS

UNLOCKABLE	HOW TO UNLOCK
Flex Taunt	Reach Level 20; Costs $50,000
Flurry Taunt	Reach Level 30; Costs $100,000
Kiss Taunt	Reach Level 10; Costs $10,000
Pump Taunt	Reach Level 53; Costs $500,000
Yes Taunt	Reach Level 40; Costs $250,000

GLITCH

This glitch is to enable "tweaks" on difficulties that have not been completed. First, start a game on a difficulty you haven't finished and play through until you have a real gun. Next, go to in-game options and set the difficulty where you have unlocked the tweaks. Enable your tweaks, then select "Save and quit". Finally, go to main menu and set the difficulty back to the one you where you just got a real gun. Start the game on that difficulty and enjoy.

UNREAL CHAMPIONSHIP (XBOX)

UNLOCKABLE	CODE
Agility Power-up	When your adrenaline reaches 100 and starts to flash, quickly tap ↓, ↓, ↓, ↑.
Berserk Power-up	When your adrenaline reaches 100 and starts to flash, quickly tap ↑, ↑, ↑, ↑.
Invincibility Power-up	When your adrenaline reaches 100 and starts to flash, quickly tap →, →, ←, ←.
Regeneration Power-up	When your adrenaline reaches 100 and starts to flash, quickly tap ↓, ↓, ↓, ↓.
Wall Jump	If a wall exists to your right, jump up and to the right, and then jump off the wall to your left.

UNREAL CHAMPIONSHIP 2: THE LIANDRI CONFLICT (XBOX)

UNLOCKABLE	CODE
Cheat Menu	Pause, then hold down LT+RT and press WHT. Turn on any of the cheats you want.

UNREAL TOURNAMENT 3 (XBOX 360)

ACHIEVEMENTS

UNLOCKABLE	HOW TO UNLOCK
Ace (10)	Get the "Top Gun" award in 20 matches.
Armadillo (10)	Get the "Roadkill" award in 10 matches.
Around the World (20)	Win a multiplayer match on every map.
Bag of Bolts (30)	Complete Chapter 3 in Insane.
Being a Hero (10)	Return 100 Orbs in Warfare matches.
Big Game Hunter (10)	Get the "Big Game Hunter" award in 10 matches.
Brain Surgeon (10)	Get the "Head Hunter" award in 10 matches.
Connect the Dots (20)	Complete 100 Warfare matches played to at least 3 points.
Deathwish (10)	Get "Bullseye" (self-destruct to destroy an enemy) award in 20 matches.
Delivering the Hurt (10)	Have over 20 minutes of "UDamage Time."
Does Not Compute (30)	Complete Chapter 3.

Don't Taze Me Bro! (10)	Get the "Combo King" award in 10 matches.
Equal Opportunity Destroyer (20)	Win a Ranked match in every game type.
Fear the Reaper (60)	Defeat Akasha and complete the campaign in Insane.
Flag Waver (20)	Complete 100 CTF matches played to at least 3 captures.
Get a Life... (50)	Get 200 kills in multiplayer on 50 different days.
Goo God (10)	Get the "Biohazard" award in 10 matches.
Got Your back (20)	Complete 10 missions in co-op.
Hammerhead (10)	Get the "JackHammer" award in 10 matches.
Hat Trick (20)	Achieve a Hat Trick in 10 CTF or VCTF matches.
Have a Nice Day! (20)	Get the "Rocket Scientist" award in 10 matches and "Flak Master" award in 10 matches.
I Need Some Backup (10)	Complete 1 mission in co-op.
I See How It Is (10)	Complete an Instant Action match in every game mode.
I'm Not on a Holy War (60)	Defeat Akasha and complete the campaign.
Jack of All Trades (10)	Kill an enemy with every vehicle (except hoverboard).
Just Business (30)	Complete Chapter 2 in Insane.
Just Warming Up (10)	Finish playing a "Versus" Ranked match.
Killjoy (10)	End sprees in 20 matches.
Lets Get It On (20)	Complete a multiplayer match in every game type.
Like the Back of My Hand (40)	Collect every power-up on every map.
Lock and Load (10)	Complete Chapter 1.
Never Saw It Coming (10)	Have over 20 minutes of "Invisibility Time."
Not in Kansas Anymore (30)	Complete Chapter 4.
Off to a Good Start (10)	Get the "First Blood" award in 40 matches.
Open War (30)	Complete Chapter 4 in Insane.
Paint the Town Red (20) played to at least 20 kills.	Complete 100 Deathmatch or Duel matches
Pistolero (10)	Get the "Gun Slinger" award in 10 matches.
Ranked Champion (50)	Win 500 Ranked matches.
Seeing Red (10)	Have over 20 minutes of "Berserk Time."
Serial Killer (20)	Get the "Killing Spree" award in 20 matches.
Shard-o-matic (10)	Get the "Blue Streak" award in 10 matches.
Sir Slays a Lot (20)	Get the "Monster Kill" award in 20 matches.
Soldier's Blood (30)	Complete Chapter 2.
Spice of Life (20)	Play a match with every mutator, using only 1 per match.
Strongest Link (10)	Get the "Shaft Master" award in 10 matches.
Survival of the Fittest (10)	Have over 10 minutes of "Invulnerable Time."
Thanks to All the Little People (40)	Complete a campaign in co-op.
Thirty Minutes or Less (20)	Complete 100 VCTF matches played to at least 3 captures.
Untouchable (20)	Reach 20 kills against a god-like bot in instant action without dying.
Winning Is the Only Thing (10)	Finish with the highest points in a Ranked match.

UP (PlayStation 2)

CODES

EFFECT	CODE
Carl wears Muntz's aviator goggles.	AVIATORGOGGLES
Russell attracts all butterflies.	BUTTERFLY
To lift Russell end up in the air, Carl just needs to jump from the teeter totter.	CARLHEAVYWEIGHT
When he jumps, Carl creates multicolored balloons.	BALLOONPARTY

URBAN CHAOS RIOT RESPONSE (XBOX)

At the Main menu, enter ↑, ↑, ↓, ↓, Ⓨ, ↓, ↑, Ⓨ to open the Cheat menu. Then input these passwords.

UNLOCKABLE	PASSWORD
All Levels and Emergencies	KEYTOTHECITY
Assault Rifle Mk3 with Infinite Shells	ULTIMATEPOWER
Disco Mode	DANCINGFEET
Enhanced (Longest Ranged) Stun Gun Unlocked	FRYINGTIME
Headless Enemies	KEEPYOURHEAD
Mini-Gun Unlocked	MINIFUN
Pistol Mk4. Unlocked	ZEROTOLERANCE
Shot Sets Enemy on Fire	BURNINGBULLET
Squeaky Voices	WHATWASTHAT
Terror Difficulty Unlocked	BURNERSREVENGE

URBAN REIGN (PlayStation 2)

Enter these codes at the Title screen.

UNLOCKABLE	CODE
All characters	R1, R2, ×, ←, →, ■, ■, ■, ■, L1, ■, ▲, ●
All weapons	L1, R1, ×, ×, ▲, R1, R1, ▲, ■, ×, R1
Bonus weapon in multi-player mode	L2, L2, ×, ×, ▲, R1, R1, ■, R1
Two players in story and free modes	L1, R2, ●, ●, ▲, L2, R1, ●, ▲, ●

VALKYRIA CHRONICLES (PlayStation 3)

GAME COMPLETION BENEFITS

After you complete the game you are given the opportunity to save the game. This is the New Game + data, and when you load it, you're given a couple of benefits that are listed below:

UNLOCKABLE	HOW TO UNLOCK
Character Stats	You retain the EXP, Money, Weapons and Levels that you've gained on your previous excursions.
Hard Mode	You unlock Hard Mode which can be selected ONLY for Skirmishes.
Mission Replayability	You can now play all of the storyline missions as many times as you'd like. (You will need to go through chapter by chapter clearing the missions first).
Music Tab	You can now listen to the various musical pieces from the game.
Statistics Tab	You can now see the statistics of the missions. (The rank you gained for the particular mission, and the number of turns it took you to complete.)

HIDDEN RECRUITS

Unlock the following hidden characters for each class by doing specific in-game tasks.

UNLOCKABLE	HOW TO UNLOCK
Audrey (Lancer)	Earn 10 or more medals.
Emile (Sniper)	Unlock Oscar's hidden potential, the let him die in battle.
Knute (Engineer)	Enter the Command Room with 1,000,000 DCT.
Musaad (Scout)	Beat the game.

VALKYRIA CHRONICLES: BEHIND HER BLUE FLAME DLC (PlayStation 3)

UNLOCKABLES

UNLOCKABLE	HOW TO UNLOCK
Mission 2a	Finish the first mission without defeating the "Boss" tank in the southwest part of the map.
Mission 2b	Defeat the "Boss" tank in the southwest part of the map and finish the first mission.
Mission 3	To unlock the last mission you have to get an A rank in all the previous missions (the first, and both 2a and 2b).
Ruhm	Complete two missions (the first and either 2a or 2b) to unlock this weapon in the main game.

VAN HELSING (XBOX)

During gameplay, enter the following. Access the movies in the Gallery.

UNLOCKABLE	CODE
Bonus Movie 1	↑,↓,↑,↓,←,←,→,→,LT,L3,R3,RT
Bonus Movie 2	↑,→,↓,←,↑,←,↓,→,↑,RT,BLK,R3
Bonus Movie 3	LT,WHT,BLK,RT,BLK,WHT,LT,↑,↑,↓,↓,BACK
Bonus Movie 4	BACK,L3,R3,BACK,R3,L3,BACK,←,←,↑,→,→
Bonus Movie 5	WHT,BLK,LT,RT,BACK,BACK,LT,LT,BLK,BLK,L3,R3

UNLOCKABLE	CODE
Bonus Movie 6	BLK, RT, BLK, RT, LT, WHT, LT, WHT, ←, →, BACK, BACK
Bonus Movie 7	L3, ←, R3, RT, WHT, ↑, BLK, ↓, LT, ←, RT, →

VAN HELSING (PlayStation 2)

During gameplay, enter the following:

UNLOCKABLE	CODE
Bonus Movie 1	↑,↓,↑,↓,←,←,→,→,L1,L2,R3,R3
Bonus Movie 2	↑,→,↓,←,↑,←,↓,→,↑,R1,R2,R3
Bonus Movie 3	L1,L2,R2,R1,R2,L2,L1,↑,↑,↓,↓,SELECT
Bonus Movie 4	SELECT, L3, R3, SELECT, R1, L3, SELECT, ←,←,↑,→,→
Bonus Movie 5	L2,R2,L1,R1,SELECT,SELECT,L1,L1,R2,R2,L3,R3
Bonus Movie 6	R2,R1,R2,R1,L1,L2,L1,L2,←,→,SELECT,SELECT
Bonus Movie 7	L3,←,R3,→,L2,↑,R2,↓,L1,←,R1,→

VANDAL HEARTS: FLAMES OF JUDGMENT (XBOX 360)

UNLOCKABLES

Optional battle map stages. In case you miss any, all stages can be returned to once you reach Act 4. You can go back to get any of the optional maps up until you board the ship to the research facility.

UNLOCKABLE	HOW TO UNLOCK
Avery Fields	Examine the well at the top of the Church of Restoration on your second visit.
Foreign Quarter	Examine the barrel at the beginning of the Biruni University stage to your left.
Four Swordsman Spring	Examine the hollowed out tree at the dry riverbed.
Gillbari's Gardens	Examine the skeleton on the side of the central tree opposite from the chest in Timion Vale.
Halls of Atonement	Examine the king's throne in the Royal Courtyard.
Keliask's Tomb	Examine the glimmering tablet on the ground in the ancient ruins.
Ragnar's Gorge	Examine one of the crates during the mission in Tolby.
Trivishim's Corridor	Use the second mine cart in Dread to open up a cave entrance.

VANDAL HEARTS: FLAMES OF JUDGMENT (PlayStation 3)

UNLOCKABLES

Optional battle map stages. In case you miss any, all stages can be returned to once you reach Act 4. You can go back to get any of the optional maps up until you board the ship to the research facility.

UNLOCKABLE	HOW TO UNLOCK
Avery Fields	Examine the well at the top of the Church of Restoration on your second visit.
Foreign Quarter	Examine the barrel at the beginning of the Biruni University stage to your left.
Four Swordsman Spring	Examine the hollowed-out tree at the dry riverbed.
Gillbari's Gardens	Examine the skeleton on the side of the central tree opposite from the chest in Timion Vale.
Halls of Atonement	Examine the king's throne in the Royal Courtyard.
Keliask's Tomb	Examine the glimmering tablet on the ground in the ancient ruins.
Ragnar's Gorge	Examine one of the crates during the mission in Tolby.
Trivishim's Corridor	Use the second mine cart in Dread to open up a cave entrance.

VECTORMAN (Wii)

UNLOCKABLES

UNLOCKABLE	HOW TO UNLOCK
Blow Up SEGA Logo	At the SEGA screen, move Vectorman slightly to the right of the logo. Aim upward and shoot. There is a hidden TV monitor there. Once it is broken, grab and use an orb power-up. The SEGA logo goes dark and the background stops moving.
Debug Mode	On the Options screen press Ⓐ, Ⓑ, Ⓑ, Ⓐ, ↓, Ⓐ, Ⓑ, Ⓑ, Ⓐ. A menu then offers health, lives, level select, and weapon options.
Full Health	Pause the game and press Ⓐ, Ⓑ, →, Ⓐ, Ⓒ, Ⓐ, ↓, Ⓐ, Ⓑ, →, Ⓐ.
Invisibility and Invincibility	First grab a bomb morph, and detonate Vectorman. Pause the game while Vectorman is still exploding and enter CALLACAB (Ⓒ, Ⓐ, ←, ←, Ⓐ, Ⓒ, Ⓐ, Ⓑ). Unpause the game. Pause again and enter the CALLACAB code. Unpause it, and Vectorman is invisible and invincible. Reenter the CALLACAB code to turn it off. No bomb morph is needed to disable it.
Level Warp	When you turn on the game, you can move Vectorman around on the SEGA screen. Shoot the SEGA logo 24 times, jump and hit the SEGA logo with Vectorman's head 12 times, and the letters S, E, G, and A start falling. Catch 90 to 110 letters to start on Stage 5, catch more than 110 letters to start on Day 10.
Light Bulbs	During gameplay, pause and enter Ⓐ, Ⓑ, Ⓐ, Ⓒ, Ⓐ, Ⓑ and press pause. A group of lights should be around you. The four lights that surround Vectorman indicate the field of collision detection. The light at the bottom indicates the collision detection of Vectorman's jets.
Slow Motion	This code slows down the game whenever you're hit. While playing, pause and press ↓, →, Ⓐ, Ⓒ, ↑, ←, Ⓐ. Turn it off by entering the code again.
Stage Select	Ⓑ, Ⓐ, Ⓐ, Ⓑ, ↓, Ⓑ, Ⓐ, Ⓐ, Ⓑ
Taxi Mode	Pause and press Ⓒ, Ⓐ, ←, ←, Ⓐ, Ⓒ, Ⓐ, Ⓑ (Call a Cab). You turn into a small cursor/arrow and can travel anywhere in the level. Enemies can also be killed by coming in contact with them. Bosses cannot be killed this way. To return to normal, pause and enter the code again.

VIRTUA FIGHTER 2 (Wii)

UNLOCKABLES

UNLOCKABLE	HOW TO UNLOCK
Different Costumes	To play in a character's different costumes, Hold ↑ and then select your character with Ⓐ or ↓. Or hold ↓ and select your character with Ⓐ, ↓, or START.
Extra Character Selection Time	Press ↓, ↑, ↓, Ⓐ+← at the Character Selection Screen for 99 seconds of extra time.
Hidden Options	Enter the Options screen, highlight the "Exit" selection, and tap ← until the hidden options are displayed.
No Damage	Hold Ⓑ while highlighting player 1's life selection at the Options screen, until the message "No Damage" appears. Then press START.
Play as Dural	Highlight Akira using controller 1 or Jacky using controller 2. Then press ←, ↓. Repeat this a few times and Dural appears as a selectable character.

VIRTUA FIGHTER 4 (PlayStation 2)

UNLOCKABLE	OBJECTIVE
Alternate Costumes	Hold START at the Character Selection screen. Press × to select that character while holding START to wear the alternate costume.

UNLOCKABLE	OBJECTIVE
Alternate Main Menu Background	Enter the Game Option menu, and press R1 to cycle forward or L1 to cycle backward through the list of backgrounds for the Main menu.
Classic Victory Poses	Use a created fighter to reach the Second Kyu level. Hold Punch + Kick + Guard during the replay to do a classic victory pose from Virtua Fighter 1.
Dural's Stage in Versus Mode	Use a created fighter to reach the Emperor or High King rank and unlock the hangar stage in Versus mode.
Fight as Dural	Defeat Dural in Kumite mode to unlock her in Versus mode.
Training Stage 1 in Versus Mode	Use a created fighter to reach the First Dan rank and unlock the first training stage in Versus mode.
Training Stage 2 in Versus Mode	Use a created fighter to reach the Fifth Dan rank and unlock the second training stage in Versus mode.
Training Stage 3 in Versus Mode	Use a created fighter to reach the Champion rank and unlock the third training stage in Versus mode.
Training Trophy	Complete the trial events in Training mode with a created fighter. A small trophy icon is displayed over your character's health bar.
Virtua Fighter 1 Fighter Model	Use a character fighter to reach at least the First Dan rank. Select that fighter and hold Punch + Kick until the match begins.

VIRTUA FIGHTER 5 (PlayStation 3)

UNLOCKABLE	CODE
DOJO training stages	Complete the Time Attack mode
Costume C	Reach the rank of 1st Dan
Costume D	Complete the first orb disc

VIRTUA TENNIS 2009 (XBOX 360)

UNLOCKABLES

UNLOCKABLE	HOW TO UNLOCK
Tim Henman	Complete all Academy Challenges on Beginner and Advanced difficulty to unlock Tim Henman for play.
Boris Becker	Beat Singles Arcade Mode.
Stephan Edberg	Beat Doubles Arcade Mode.

VIRTUA TENNIS 2009 (Wii)

UNLOCKABLES

UNLOCKABLE	HOW TO UNLOCK
Tim Henman	Complete all Academy Challenges on Beginner and Advanced difficulty to unlock Tim Henman for play.
Boris Becker	Beat Singles Arcade Mode.
Stephan Edberg	Beat Doubles Arcade Mode.

COSTUMES

By clearing certain minigames in the World Tour, you can unlock costumes to buy. You can wear these to allow you to enter the fancy-dress-only tournament.

UNLOCKABLE	HOW TO UNLOCK
Bowling Clothes	Clear the Pin Crusher minigame on all levels.
Karate Clothes	Clear the Avalanche minigame on all levels.
-Skeleton Clothes	Clear the Block Buster minigame on all levels.
Superhero Costume	Clear the Shopping Dash minigame on all levels.
Zookeeper Clothes	Clear the Zoo Feeder minigame on all levels.

VIRTUA TENNIS 3 (XBOX 360)

Enter these codes at the main menu.

UNLOCKABLE	CODE
Unlock All Courts	↑, ↑, ↓, ↓, ←, →, ←, →
Unlock King & Duke	↑, ↑, ↓, ↓, ←, →, ←, →
Unlock All Gear	←, →, ↓, ←, →, ↓, ↑, ↓
Test End Sequence (win one match to win tournament)	↓, ←, ↓, →, ↓, ↑, ↓, ↓

VIRTUA TENNIS WORLD TOUR (PSP)

Enter these codes at the Main menu while holding R3.

UNLOCKABLE	CODE
All Racquets and Clothing A vailable in the Home Screen	→, ←, →, →, ↑, ↑, ↑
Begin World Tour mode with $1,000,000	↑, ↓, ←, ↓, ▲, ▲, ▲
Earn $2000 Every Week in World Tour mode	↑, ↓, →, ↓, ▲, ■, ▲
Unlock All Stadiums	↑, ↓, ←, →, ■, ■, ■
Unlock the players King & Queen	↑, ↓, ↑, ↓, ■, ▲, ■

VIVA PIÑATA (XBOX 360)

Enter these passwords as names for your garden.

UNLOCKABLE	PASSWORD
Five Extra Accessories at the Pet Shop	chewnicorn
Items for Your Piñatas to Wear	goobaa nlock
Items for Your Piñatas to Wear	Bullseye
YMCA Gear	Kittyfloss

WALL-E (XBOX 360)

CHEATS

Enter the following codes in the cheat section of the Bonus Features menu.

EFFECT	CODE
All Bonus Features Unlocked	WALL-E, Auto, EVE, ZPM
All Game Contents Unlocked	M-O, Auto, ZPM, EVE
Costumes	ZPM, WALL-E, M-O, Auto
Gives WALL-E Super Laser Blaster	WALL-E, Auto, EVE, Mo
Invincibility	WALL-E, M-O, Auto, M-O
Make Any Cube Any Time	Auto, M-O, Auto, M-O

ACHIEVEMENTS

UNLOCKABLE	HOW TO UNLOCK
500 Cubes (30)	Crush down 500 Cubes in the entire game.
All Concepts (30)	Get all Sketchbooks in the game.
All Echoes of EVE (30)	Find all EVE Radios.
All Echoes of WALL-E (30)	Find all WALL-E Radios.
Boosters Activity (10)	Complete the activity in the Directive level.
Crushing, Part 1 (25)	Crush down 100 Basic Cubes.
Crushing, Part 2 (25)	Crush down 100 Heavy Cubes.
Crushing, Part 3 (25)	Crush down 100 Charge Cubes.
EVE Suitcases (30)	Find all of EVE's costumes in the game.
I Am the Best! (60)	Beat the entire game.
Junk Buster Activity (10)	Complete the activity in the Directive level.
Knocking Over Humans (30)	It's possible that knocking over humans could be advantageous.
M-O Is Easily Distracted (15)	M-O will clean what is dropped on the floor in the Life on the Axiom level.
Making of the Game (5)	Watch the credits.
Panicking Protection Procedures (30)	Avoid taking damage from any humans in the Captain's Orders level.
Power to the Axiom (30)	Free all Reject Bots to enter a secret location in the Good Intentions level.
Power to the City (30)	Turn on all Power Pylons to enter a secret location in the Welcome to Earth level.
Ring Race Activity (10)	Complete the activity in the Time Together level.
Scan Racer Activity (10)	Complete the activity in the Directive level.
Short Storks (15)	Complete the Sandstorm level in 30 stork jumps or less.
Special Object, Part 1 (30)	Collect the Special Object in the Welcome to Earth level.
Special Object, Part 2 (30)	Collect the Special Object in the Directive level.
Special Object, Part 3 (30)	Collect the Special Object in the Sandstorm level.
Special Object, Part 4 (30)	Collect the Special Object in the Life on the Axiom level.
Special Object, Part 5 (30)	Collect the Special Object in the Good Intentions level.

Special Object, Part 6 (30)	Collect the Special Object in the Time Together level.
Special Object, Part 7 (30)	Collect the Special Object in the 100% Unsanitary level.
Special Object, Part 8 (30)	Collect the Special Object in the Captain's Orders level.
Special Object, Part 9 (30)	Collect the Special Object in the EVE Loves WALL-E level.
Super Quick Scanning (30)	Scan all WALL-E parts in less than 2 minutes in the EVE Loves WALL-E level.
Taking out the Trash Activity (10)	Complete the activity in the Time Together level.
The Cockroach (5)	Find the cockroach.
The Spoils of Steward (15)	Clear out the Stewards in the Good Intentions level.
Total Perseverance, Part 1 (15)	Beat the Welcome to Earth level without losing all health!
Total Perseverance, Part 2 (15)	Beat the Directive level without losing all health!
Total Perseverance, Part 3 (15)	Beat the Sandstorm level without losing all health!
Total Perseverance, Part 4 (15)	Beat the Life on the Axiom level without losing all health!
Total Perseverance, Part 5 (15)	Beat the Good Intentions level without losing all health!
Total Perseverance, Part 6 (15)	Beat the Time Together level without losing all health!
Total Perseverance, Part 7 (15)	Beat the 100% Unsanitary level without losing all health!
Total Perseverance, Part 8 (15)	Beat the Captain's Orders level without losing all health!
Tunnel Time Trials, Part 1 (15)	Complete all tunnels in the Directive level without running out of time.
Tunnel Time Trials, Part 2 (15)	Complete all tunnels in the Time Together level without running out of time.
WALL-E Away Activity (10)	Complete the activity in the Time Together level.
WALL-E Suitcases (30)	Find all of WALL-E's costumes in the game.

WALL-E (Wii)

CHEATS

In the password screen enter the codes for the following effects. ZPM = Zero Point Mover.

EFFECT	CODE
All Bonus Features Unlocked	WALL-E, Auto, EVE, ZPM
All Game Content Unlocked	M-O, Auto, ZPM, EVE
All Holiday Costumes Unlocked	Auto, Auto, ZPM, ZPM
All Multiplayer Costumes Unlocked	ZPM, WALL-E, M-O, Auto
All Multiplayer Maps Unlocked	EVE, M-O, WALL-E, Auto
All Single Player Levels Unlocked	Auto, ZPM, M-O, WALL-E
EVE Permanent Super Laser Upgrade	EVE, WALL-E, WALL-E, Auto
Infinite Health	WALL-E, M-O, Auto, M-O
WALL-E & EVE Laser Gun Any Time	ZPM, EVE, M-O, WALL-E
WALL-E & EVE Make Any Cube Any Time	M-O, ZPM, EVE, EVE
WALL-E Always Has Super Laser	WALL-E, Auto, EVE, M-O
WALL-E Makes Any Cube Any Time	Auto, M-O, Auto, M-O
WALL-E with Laser Gun Any Time	WALL-E, EVE, EVE, WALL-E

WALL-E (PSP)

CHEATS

Enter the following codes in the Cheats menu in the corresponding code slot.

EFFECT	CODE
Code 1: Kills or Stuns Everything within Range	BOTOFWAR
Code 2: Can Move Undetected by any Enemy	STEALTHARMOR

EFFECT	CODE
Code 3: Laser Switches Color Continuously	RAINBOWLASER
Code 4: Every Cube Is a Explosive Cube	EXPLOSIVEWORLD
Code 5: Lights Dark Areas	GLOWINTHEDARK
Code 6: Wears Ski Goggles	BOTOFMYSTERY
Code 7: WALL-E has Golden Tracks	GOLDENTRACKS

WALL-E (PlayStation 2)

ENTERABLE CHEATS

Enter the codes in the following order.

EFFECT	CODE
Code 1: Kills or Stuns Everything within Range	BOTOFWAR
Code 2: Can Move Undetected by any Enemy	STEALTHARMOR
Code 3: Laser Switches Color Continuously	RAINBOWLASER
Code 4: Every Cube Is an Explosive Cube	EXPLOSIVEWORLD
Code 5: Lights Dark Areas	GLOWINTHEDARK
Code 6: Wears Ski Goggles	BOTOFMYSTERY
Code 7: Wall-E has Golden Tracks	GOLDENTRACKS

WANTED: WEAPONS OF FATE (XBOX 360)

CODES

Enter these at the "Secret Codes" screen in the Main menu.

EFFECT	CODE
Unlocks Airplane Bodyguard	01010111
Unlocks Cinematic Mode	01110100
Unlocks Close Combat Mode	01100101
Unlocks Cross	01010100
Unlocks Health Improvement	01001100
Unlocks Infinite Adrenaline	01101101
Unlocks Infinite Ammo	01101111
Unlocks Janice	01000100
Unlocks One Shot One Kill	01110010
Unlocks Special Suit	01100001
Unlocks Super Weapons	01001111
Unlocks Wesley	01000011

WANTED: WEAPONS OF FATE (PlayStation 3)

CODES

Enter these at the "Secret Codes" screen in the "Main Menu."

EFFECT	CODE
Unlocks Airplane Bodyguard	01010111
Unlocks Cinematic Mode	01110100
Unlocks Close-Combat Mode	01100101
Unlocks Cross	01010100
Unlocks Health Improvement	01001100
Unlocks Infinite Adrenaline	01101101
Unlocks Infinite Ammo	01101111
Unlocks Janice	01000100
Unlocks One Shot One Kill	01110010
Unlocks Special Suit	01100001
Unlocks Super Weapons	01001111

Unlocks Wesley	01000011

WARHAWK (PlayStation 3)

TROPHIES

Complete each condition to get the allotted trophies. There are 36 Bronze, 13 Silver, 7 Gold, and 1 Platinum trophy (including the secret trophies).

UNLOCKABLE	HOW TO UNLOCK
Aerial Ballet (Silver)	While flying a jetpack, kill an enemy (who is also flying a jetpack) with any weapon other than the RocketLauncher.
Anti-Air Ninja (Bronze)	Shoot down a Warhawk with any infantry weapon other than a Rocket Launcher.
Are You Aim-Botting? (Silver)	Snipe an enemy who is flying a jetpack.
Bandit Award (Bronze)	Earn all in-game badges at Bandit level.
Bandwidth Donor (Gold)	Host a ranked dedicated server for four consecutive hours.
Behind Enemy Lines (Silver)	Drive an APC into the enemy's home base, then have at least one teammate spawn into that APC.
Chief Sergeant (Bronze)	Achieve a rank of Chief Sergeant.
Collector (Bronze)	Capture four cores at once in Collection mode.
Combat Driver (Bronze)	Complete Vehicle Combat Training.
Commander (Silver)	Achieve a rank of Commander.
Cowboy (Bronze)	Play a perfect Team Deathmatch (top player, no deaths).
Dead-Eye (Bronze)	Achieve a sniper kill from more than 2,500 feet away.
Decorated Soldier (Silver)	Earn any 15 in-game medals.
Dumbfire (Bronze)	Destroy an enemy aircraft with a dumbfired Swarm or Homing Missile.
Emergency Evasion (Bronze)	Break at least 6 simultaneous missile locks using Chaff.
Enlistee (Bronze)	Join a clan.
Executive Honor (Gold)	Earn all in-game medals.
Flying Fortress (Silver)	Awarded to the driver and all six passengers of a fully loaded Dropship.
General (Gold)	Achieve a rank of General.
Giant Killer (Silver)	Shoot down an enemy Dropship while using a Warhawk.
Ground Pounder (Bronze)	Complete Ground Combat Training.
Hat Trick (Bronze)	Get three flag captures in a single round of CTF.
How Did You Do That? (Bronze)	Destroy an enemy aircraft with a Cluster Bomb.
Invincible (Bronze)	While on foot, take at least 250 damage within 10 seconds without dying.
Irony (Bronze)	Kill an enemy with his own Proximity Mine.
Lone Wolf (Bronze)	Play a perfect Deathmatch (top player, no deaths).
Lt. Colonel (Silver)	Achieve a rank of Lt. Colonel.
Master Award (Silver)	Earn all in-game badges at Master level.
One in a Million (Bronze)	Shoot down an enemy aircraft using the tank's main cannon.
Overkill (Bronze)	Destroy an enemy aircraft with a volley of 8 Swarm Missiles.
Pilot's License (Bronze)	Complete Warhawk Combat Training.
Porcupine (Gold)	Destroy an enemy Warhawk with the APC's E-POD shield.

UNLOCKABLE	HOW TO UNLOCK
Recognition of Merit (Bronze)	Earn any five in-game medals.
Remote Pilot (Bronze)	Destroy an enemy aircraft with a TOW Missile.
Resourceful Driver (Bronze)	Achieve a road kill and a .50 cal kill using the same 4x4, without dismounting.
Rivalry (Bronze)	Win a clan match (red server) as either clan leader or a regular member.
Saboteur (Bronze)	Destroy an enemy vehicle with the Field Wrench.
Secret Anti-Camper (Bronze)	Kill an enemy in a Missile or Flak Turret after that enemy has achieved at least five kills in that type of turret.
Secret Canyon Run (Silver)	Using a Warhawk, shoot down an enemy Warhawk in the central gorge in Vaporfield Glacier.
Secret Daredevil (Bronze)	Get 100 feet off the ground in a ground vehicle. Does not count if the vehicle is being carried by a Dropship.
Secret Hit List (Bronze)	Kill every member of the opposing team at least once during a round.
Secret King of the Jungle Gym (Silver)	Retrieve the Proximity Mines from the top of the dome on the Omega Factory Rumble Dome layout.
Secret Minesweeper (Bronze)	Get killed by Proximity Mines five times in a single round.
Secret Reckless Pilot (Bronze)	Commit suicide in a Warhawk by running into your own Aerial Mine.
Secret Safety Violation (Silver)	Kill a distant enemy from on top of the salvage crane in Tau Crater.
Secret Vengeance (Bronze)	Kill an enemy within 60 seconds of that enemy killing you.
Secret What's That Green Line? (Bronze)	Get killed by a Binoculars strike while piloting an aircraft.
Shield Breaker (Silver)	Break an enemy E-POD shield using the Lightning Shell.
Surgical Strike (Gold)	Shoot down a Dropship with a Binoculars strike.
Survivalist (Bronze)	Survive for one minute as the hero in Hero mode.
Tail Shaker (Bronze)	Destroy an enemy aircraft with an Aerial Mine within 5 seconds of deploying it.
Taxi Driver (Bronze)	Help a teammate capture the flag (in CTF) or cogs (in Collection) by transporting him back to the base, using any vehicle.
That Was Some Bug (Gold)	Kill an enemy who is flying a jetpack by hitting him with any vehicle or aircraft.
Warhawk Award (Gold)	Earn all in-game badges at Warhawk level.
Warhawk Supreme Achievement (Platinum)	All your base trophies are belong to platinum.
Warlord (Bronze)	Create a clan and get nine other members to join. (Awarded at 10 members while you are the clan leader.)
World Victory (Bronze)	Control all capturable bases in a Zones match, and reduce the enemy's home base to level 1.

WATER WARFARE (Wii)

UNLOCKABLES

By clearing single player mission mode you can unlock new characters to play as.

UNLOCKABLE	HOW TO UNLOCK
Biker Ben	Beat Biker Ben on the Training Level 6.
Cavegirl Carmen	Beat Cavegirl Carmen on Mission 8 of the Nature Park.

Rabid Rabbit	Beat Rabid Rabbit on Mission 8 of the Playground.
Snorkel Jane	Beat Snorkel Jane on Mission 8 of the Beach.
Trooper Tim	Beat Trooper Tim on Mission 8 of the Plaza.

WAY OF THE SAMURAI (PlayStation 2)

UNLOCKABLE	CODE
Change Characters	In the New Game menu, press L1,R1,R1,L2,L2,L2,R2,R2,R2+■. To choose a character, press ← or →.
Full Health	Pause the game, hold L1+L2, and press ↓,↑,↓,↑,→,←,●.
Increase Sword Toughness +1	Pause the game, hold R1+R2, and press →,→,←,←,↓,↑,●.
Versus Mode	At the Title screen, hold L1+R1, and press ●+■.

WAY OF THE SAMURAI 2 (PlayStation 2)

UNLOCKABLE	CODE
All Characters	Select Character Customization, highlight name and press L1,R2,R1,L2,L1,R2,R1,L2,■
More Store Items	In the Main Map, press L1,R1,L1,R1,R2,R2,▲.

WET (XBOX 360)

UNLOCKABLE

Beat the game on any difficulty. After the credits roll Challenge Modes are unlocked.

UNLOCKABLE	HOW TO UNLOCK
Boneyard Challenges	Beat the game.
Points Count	Beat the game.

WHERE THE WILD THINGS ARE (XBOX 360)

UNLOCKABLES

These are unlockable cheats that can be activated once you have completed the requirements.

UNLOCKABLE	HOW TO UNLOCK
Infinite Health	Collect all skulls (60).
Kill enemies in one hit	Collect all turtles (60).
The Wild Things won't eat you	Collect all beehives (60).
Treasures show up when holding the back button	collect all geodes (60).
Your ship doesn't take damage	Collect all seeds (60).

WILD ARMS 5 (PlayStation 2)

COSTUMES

If you beat the game after collecting all of the Ex File Keys, you unlock the Nine Lives costume, which looks like the Knight Blazer from *Wild ARMs 2*. Once you have beaten the game with the keys you can use the costume by starting a new game over your old save file.

WINBACK COVERT OPERATIONS (PlayStation 2)

Enter these codes at the Start screen.

UNLOCKABLE	CODE
All Versus Characters	⇧, ⇩, ⇩, ⇨, ⇨, ⇨, ⇦, ⇦, ⇦, ⇦, then press ●+START
Max Power Mode	L1, R2, L2, R2, L2, ▲, ●, ▲, ●, then hold L1 and press START
Sudden Death Mode	L2, R2, L2, R2, ●, ▲, ●, ▲, then hold L1 and press START

A B C D E F G H I J K L M N O P Q R S T U V W X Y Z

NEW!

WIPEOUT FUSION (PlayStation 2)

Enter these codes in the Codes menu under Extras.

UNLOCKABLE	CODE
Animal Ships	▲, ●, ●, ▲, ×
Infinite Shield	▲, ▲, ■, ■, ■
Infinite Weapons	▲, ●, ×, ●, ■
Mini Ships	●, ■, ■, ×, ●
Retro Planes	×, ●, ▲, ■, ×
Super Fast ships	■, ×, ×, ×, ▲
Unlock all Features	×, ▲, ●, ▲, ●

WOLFENSTEIN (XBOX 360)

UNLOCKABLES

UNLOCKABLE	HOW TO UNLOCK
Cheats	Beat the game on any difficulty. Activating cheats will disable achievements.

WONDER BOY IN MONSTER WORLD (Wii)

UNLOCKABLES

UNLOCKABLE	HOW TO UNLOCK
Stay at the Inn for Free	Any Inn throughout the game will let you spend the night, even if you don't have enough gold. They just take whatever You have, even if you don't have any gold at all.

WORLD SERIES OF POKER: TOURNAMENT OF CHAMPIONS (Wii)

UNLOCKABLES

UNLOCKABLE	HOW TO UNLOCK
All Locations	Input ↑, ↑, ↓, ←, ↓ at the main menu

WORLD SOCCER WINNING ELEVEN 7 (PlayStation 2)

UNLOCKABLE	OBJECTIVE
Premier All Star Team	Win the LG Championship Cup.
World All Star Team	Win the Multi International Cup.

WORLD TOUR SOCCER (PlayStation 2)

At the Main menu, enter the following:

UNLOCKABLE	CODE
All Bonuses	L2, L2, L1, R1, ←, ↑, ←, ↓
Infinite TIF Tokens	↑, ↓, ↑, ↓, R1, R1, R2, R2, ↑, ↓, ↑, ↓
QA Liverpool, TIF OldBoys,	↓, →, L2, R1, ←, R1
TimeWarp Teams	R2, L2, R2, L2, ↑, L1

WRATH UNLEASHED (XBOX)

UNLOCKABLE	CODE
Big World Map Critters	←, X, ↑, Y, →, B, ↓, B
Extended Fighting	↓, ↓, ↑, ↓, ←, →, ↓, ↑, ↑, ↑, →, ←, X
Team Fighter Character Variation	LT, LT, ↓, ↓, BLK, WHT, BLK, WHT, RT, LT, BLK, RT, RT, RT, WHT
Versus Character Variations	LT, LT, ↓, ↓, BLK, WHT, BLK, WHT, RT, LT, BLK, RT, RT, WHT

WRATH UNLEASHED (PlayStation 2)

UNLOCKABLE	OBJECTIVE
Elephant Pool Arena	Win 20 Team Battles.
Metal Age Arena	Win 100 Arena Battles.

WRC: FIA WORLD RALLY CHAMPIONSHIP (PSP)

Enter these passwords as Profile names.

UNLOCKABLE	PASSWORD
Bird camera	dovecam
Enables Supercharger cheat	MAXPOWER
Extra avatars	UGLYMUGS
Ghost car	SPOOKY
Reverses controls	REVERSE
Time trial ghost cars	AITRIAL
Unlock everything	PADLOCK

WRECKING CREW (Wii)

UNLOCKABLES

UNLOCKABLE	HOW TO UNLOCK
Gold Hammer	In Phase 6, there are five bombs, 2 on the bottom, 2 in the middle of the level, and 1 on the top. Hit the 2 bombs on the bottom and then hit the middle left bomb. In a few seconds, a hammer appears. Hit it to obtain it. You now have the gold hammer. The music changes and you can hit enemies. You have the hammer until you die.

WWE CRUSH HOUR (PlayStation 2)

CODES

Special Meter Fills Quickly	Pause the game, hold L3, and press ▲,●,●,●,●.
Unlimited Turbo	Pause the game, hold L3, and press ×,R1,R2.
All Levels and Vehicles	From the main menu, press ■,L2,R2,●,■,L2,L2,L2.
Kevin Nash	From the character select screen, press L2,■,R2,●.

UNLOCKABLES

All Levels	Beat Season mode with any character to unlock all levels.
Bradshaw	Beat Season mode with Brock Lesnar.
Christian	Beat Season mode with Chris Jericho.
D-Von Dudley	Beat Season mode with Bubba Ray Dudley.
Hulk Hogan	Beat Season mode with The Rock.
Lita	Beat Season mode with Matt Hardy.
Ric Flair	Beat Season mode with The Big Show, Rob Van Dam and Triple H.
Stephanie McMahon	Beat Season mode with Kurt Angle.
Vince McMahon	Beat Season mode, facing Vince in the final battle.

WWE SMACKDOWN! VS. RAW 2008 (PlayStation 3)

ARENAS

To unlock arenas, get the following number of points in Hall of Fame mode.

UNLOCKABLE ARENAS	POINTS NEEDED
No Way Out	5 points
Vengeance	6 points
ECW One Night Stand	7 points
December to Dismember	8 points
New Year's Revolution	9 points

UNLOCKABLE ARENAS	POINTS NEEDED
Summerslam	10 points
Wrestlemania 23	12 points

OUTFITS AND COSTUMES

Enter the codes in the in-game Cheats menu to unlock the outfits.

UNLOCKABLE OUTFITS	CODES
DX Costumes	DXCostume69K2
Kelly Kelly's Alternate Outfit	KellyKG12R

WWE SMACKDOWN VS. RAW 2009 (XBOX 360)

CODES

Enter the following cheats under the Cheat Code menu in Options to instantly unlock the following features.

EFFECT	CODE
Chris Jericho classic attire	AltJerichoModelSvR09
Ric Flair	FlairWoooooooooooooo
Saturday Night's Main Event Arena	SatNightMainEventSvR
Unlock Curt Hawkins and Zack Ryder	Ryder&HawkinsTagTeam
Unlock Hornswoggle as a Manager	HornswoggleAsManager
Unlock Jillian	PlayAsJillianHallSvR
Unlock Layla	UnlockECWDivaLayla09
Unlock Mr. McMahon	VinceMcMahonNoChance
Unlock Snitsky	UnlockSnitskySvR2009
Unlock Tazz	UnlockECWTazzSvR2009
Unlock The Boogeyman	BoogeymanEatsWorms!!
Unlocks CM Punk's alternate costume	CMPunkAltCostumeSvR!
Unlocks Rey Mysterio's alternate costume	BooyakaBooyaka619Svr

UNLOCKABLES

UNLOCKABLE	HOW TO UNLOCK
Brothers of Destruction entrance	Complete Undertaker's Road to WrestleMania (RTW).
CAS Moveset 1	In Batista/Rey's RTWM, have Batista win the Rumble, Rey lose to Edge at NWO, and then have Rey lose the tag titles against Morrison and Miz.
CAS Moveset 2	In Batista/Rey's RTWM have Rey win the Rumble, Batista lose to Edge at NWO, and then have Batista lose the tag titles against Morrison and Miz.
Cena and Tony's Military Vehicle entrance	Complete Cena's Road to WrestleMania.
CM Punk's Attire B	Put Elijah Burke through a table in Road to WrestleMania Mode.
D-Generation X attires, entrance music, video and animations	Beat HHH's RTW.
Finlay's Zombie attire	Have Undertaker help Rey beat Finlay in his Road to WrestleMania.
Gauntlet Match	Finish John Cena's RTWM.
Hornswoggle (non-playable Manager)	Defeat Santino Marella in Undertaker's Road to WrestleMania, then defeat Finlay in a faster time.
Layla	Defeat Big Daddy V at the No Way Out PPV in under 2:30 minutes during CM Punk's Road to WrestleMania.
Masked Man	Complete Chris Jericho's Road to WrestleMania.

More moves for Create-A-Move Set Mode	Pin Edge in Triple H's first match in Road to WrestleMania.
Mr. McMahon	Finish Rey and Batista's RTWM.
Santino Marella's Zombie attire	Have Undertaker help Rey beat Santino in his Road to WrestleMania
Tazz	Finish CM Punk's RTWM.
The Boogeyman	Completed The Undertakers RTW Story.
Tony	Give both Umaga and Regal an 'FU' during Cena's RTWM Story line.
Tribute to the Troops Arena	Defeat MVP via submission in John Cena's RTWM.
WCW Heavyweight Belt and WCW Faction	Pin Finlay in Week 3 of Chris Jericho's Road to WrestleMania.
Zombie Santino Marella	Complete Undertakers Match of the Week (MOTW).

WWE SMACKDOWN VS. RAW 2009 (PlayStation 3)

CODES

Input the following cheats in the options menu.

EFFECT	CODE
Play as Boogeyman	BoogeymanEatsWorms!!
Play as Jillian Hall	PlayAsJillianHallSvR
Play as Layla	UnlockECWDivaLayla09
Play as Snitsky	UnlockSnitskySvR2009
Play as Tazz	UnlockECWTazzSvR2009
Play as Vince McMahon	VinceMcMahonNoChance
Unlock alternate attire for Chris Jericho	AltJerichoModelSvR09
Unlock alternate attire for CM Punk	CMPunkAltCostumeSvR!
Unlock Hornswoggle as a non-playable Manager	HornswoggleAsManager
Unlock Rey Mysterio alternative costume	BooyakaBooyaka619SvR
Unlock Ric Flair	FlairWoooooooooooooo
Unlock the Saturday Night Main Event Arena	SatNightMainEventSvR
Unlocks Curt Hawkins & Zack Ryder	Ryder&HawkinsTagTeam

UNLOCKABLES

UNLOCKABLE	HOW TO UNLOCK
Brothers of Destruction entrance	In Undertaker's RTW make Finley bleed on Week 8.
Evolution Theme Song, Entrance video, And Trio entrance	HHH RTW: Make sure Orton wins at No Way Out, And go on to beat him and Shawn at WrestleMania.
Gauntlet Match	During Cena's RTW defeat Mr. Kennedy in under 2:30 on Week 12.
Generic Code Animation for CAE	During Jericho's RTW, make Kennedy bleed on Week 12.
Hornswoggle as non-playable manager	On the second week of Undertaker's RTW, defeat Finley in less time than it took you to beat Santino.
Masked Man	Beat Road to WrestleMania with Chris Jericho.
Old Jericho Model	In Jericho's RTW, defeat Jeff Hardy without using a finisher on Week 6.
Santino Zombie	Play as The Undertaker, and help Rey Mysterio defeat Santino by Pinfall in Week 8.
Snitsky	In Cena's RTW, make MVP bleed on Week 11.
Special WrestleMania Jeep Entrance for CAE	Complete Cena's RTW.

UNLOCKABLE	HOW TO UNLOCK
The Boogeyman	Beat Road to WrestleMania with The Undertaker.
Tony	Unlock Tony by going through John Cenas Road to WrestleMania.
Unlock CAS moveset #3	Whilst doing HHH RTW near the start.
Unlock CM Punk alternate attire	Whilst doing CM Punk's RTW, in the second week, put Jeff Hardy through a table.
Unlock DX alternate attire	Whilst doing HHH RTW, in special ref match you play as referee, make sure Shawn Michael's is victorious and then go on to defeat him at WrestleMania.
Unlock DX Entrance	Whilst doing HHH RTW, Pedigree Randy Orton 3 times to unlock.
Unlock Jillian Hall	Whilst doing HHH RTW, win Tag Match in the third week of February.
Unlock Layla	Whilst doing CM Punk's RTW, Defeat Big Daddy V at No Way Out, in 2:30.
Unlock Locker Room	Whilst doing CM Punk's RTW, pin John Morrison in an triple threat in March to unlock a new Backstage Brawl.
Unlock Ric Flair	Whilst doing HHH RTW, in special ref match you play as referee, make sure Orton is victorious.
Unlock Tazz	Whilst doing CM Punk's RTW, complete CM Punk's Road to WrestleMania.
Unlock Tribute to the Troops Arena	Whilst doing John Cena's RTW, make MVP submit at the Tribute to the Troops arena.
Unlock Zack Ryder & Curt Hawkins	During the Mysterio/Batista RTW, spear Edge twice.
WCW Brand and Title Belt	Complete the challenge for Week 2, while on Chris Jericho's Road to WrestleMania story.
Zombie Finlay Model	Help Mysterio beat Zombie Finlay in Taker's RTW.

WWE SMACKDOWN VS. RAW 2009 (PlayStation 2)

CODES

Go to My WWE, at the options choose CHEAT CODES and input the following codes (case sensitive).

EFFECT	CODE
Alternative Chris Jericho	AltJerichoModelSvR09
CM Punk Scenario	CMPunkAltCostumeSvR!
Jillian Hall unlocked	PlayAsJillianHallSvR
Play as Layla ECW	UnlockECWDivaLayla09
Play as Ric Flair	FlairWoooooooooooooo
Unlock Boogeyman	BoogeymanEatsWorms!!
Unlock Saturday Night	SatNightMainEventSvR
Unlock Snitsky	UnlockSnitskySvR2009
Unlock Tazz	UnlockECWTazzSvR2009
Unlocks Hawkins & Ryder	Ryder&HawkinsTagTeam
Unlocks Hornswoggle as a non-playable Manager	HornswoggleAsManager
Unlocks Rey Mysterio's alternate costume	BooyakaBooyaka619SvR
Vincent McMahon unlocked	VinceMcMahonNoChance